Social Behavior as Resource Exchange

Social Behavior as Resource Exchange

Explorations into the Societal Structures of the Mind

Edited by

KJELL YNGVE TÖRNBLOM AND ALI KAZEMI

OXFORD
UNIVERSITY PRESS

Oxford University Press is a department of the University of Oxford. It furthers the University's objective of excellence in research, scholarship, and education by publishing worldwide. Oxford is a registered trade mark of Oxford University Press in the UK and certain other countries.

Published in the United States of America by Oxford University Press 198 Madison Avenue, New York, NY 10016, United States of America.

© Oxford University Press 2023

All rights reserved. No part of this publication may be reproduced, stored in a retrieval system, or transmitted, in any form or by any means, without the prior permission in writing of Oxford University Press, or as expressly permitted by law, by license, or under terms agreed with the appropriate reproduction rights organization. Inquiries concerning reproduction outside the scope of the above should be sent to the Rights Department, Oxford University Press, at the address above.

You must not circulate this work in any other form and you must impose this same condition on any acquirer.

Library of Congress Cataloging-in-Publication Data
Names: Törnblom, Kjell Yngve, editor. | Kazemi, Ali, editor. |
Foa, Uriel G., 1916-1990. Societal structures of the mind.
Title: Social behavior as resource exchange : explorations into the
Societal structures of the mind / [edited by] Kjell Yngve Törnblom and Ali Kazemi.
Description: New York, NY : Oxford University Press, [2023] |
Includes bibliographical references and index. |
Identifiers: LCCN 2022060610 (print) | LCCN 2022060611 (ebook) |
ISBN 9780190066994 (hardback) | ISBN 9780190067014 (epub) |
ISBN 9780190067021 (online)
Subjects: LCSH: Foa, Uriel G., 1916–1990. Societal structures of the mind. |
Interpersonal relations. | Social role. | Cognition.
Classification: LCC HM1106 .S6193 2023 (print) | LCC HM1106 (ebook) |
DDC 302—dc23/eng/20230207
LC record available at https://lccn.loc.gov/2022060610
LC ebook record available at https://lccn.loc.gov/2022060611

DOI: 10.1093/oso/9780190066994.001.0001

Printed by Integrated Books International, United States of America

Contents

Acknowledgments	vii
Contributors	ix
Introduction	xiii
Ali Kazemi and Kjell Yngve Törnblom	

PART I. ABRIDGEMENT OF URIEL G. FOA AND EDNA B. FOA (1974) *SOCIETAL STRUCTURES OF THE MIND*

Précis of the Chapters Included	3
1. Introduction: Man's Structuring of His Social World	7
2. The Development of Basic Social Concepts	29
3. From Developmental Sequence to Adult Structure	57
4. Prelude to Resource Exchange	79
5. Some Areas of Socio-Psychological Research in the Light of the Resource Exchange Paradigm	122
6. Epilogue: Man and His Society	170
Appendixes A–E	181
References	203

PART II. NEW THEORETICAL AND EMPIRICAL DEVELOPMENTS

Précis	227
7. Recent Theoretical Advances in Social Resource Theory	232
8. Resource Theory and Levels of Explanation: From Universal Structure to the Construal of Interpersonal Behavior	271

vi CONTENTS

9. Resources and Social Justice in Meso- and Macro-Level
   Environmental Conflict   294

10. Extending Social Resource Exchange to Events of
    Abundance and Sufficiency   323

11. When Your Heart Goes Bumpity Bump: Neurological
    Characteristics of Love   357

12. Evaluating Foa and Foa's Social Resource Theory:
    A Data-Analytic Perspective   376

PART III. HISTORICAL NOTES

How and Why This Volume Came Into Existence   419

What Is Included and Omitted from the Original Foa and
Foa Monograph?   424

Index   425

Acknowledgments

We are greatly indebted to Edna Foa, who made it possible for the editors to prepare this book by transferring full rights to her and Uriel Foa's original 1974 monograph, *Societal Structures of the Mind*, to Kjell Törnblom.

Many thanks are also extended to our invited chapter authors for their valuable contributions, prepared during a time of social hardships, mainly due to the COVID-19 pandemic. Without their scholarship, this book would not have been possible.

Thanks are also due to Faye Crosby, who provided valuable suggestions regarding the organization and contents of the book.

We are very grateful for the skillful and generous assistance by Sandro Bösch, Department of Environmental Systems Science, ETH Zürich, Switzerland, in preparing tables and figures as well as formatting of Word documents for Part I.

Four anonymous reviewers of our book proposal thoroughly scrutinized our ideas and provided valuable feedback and support. We sincerely appreciate their generous gifts of their time and energy; they are owed many thanks.

Our Oxford University Press Editor Katharine Pratt treated us with great understanding for how we were affected by the various bumps and grinds we encountered during the preparation of this book. She thereby created a stress-free working climate that greatly facilitated our work.

Finally, a *dedication* on behalf of co-editor Ali Kazemi. The completion of this book would have not been possible if three persons in different ways, without making any direct contributions to the contents of this book, dexterously and conscientiously had not done their jobs. Ali therefore expresses his indebtedness and most sincere gratitude to physicians Reza Khorshidi at Helsingborg Hospital, Tomasz Jakubczyk at Ryhov County Hospital, and, last but definitely not least, Henrik Wehtje at Karolinska University Hospital.

Contributors

John Adamopoulos, PhD, is Professor Emeritus of Psychology at Grand Valley State University in Allendale, Michigan, and a Research Associate at Aristotle University in Thessaloniki, Greece. He has also taught at the University of Illinois and Indiana University at South Bend. He studied with Harry Triandis at the University of Illinois, receiving his PhD in 1979. His research focuses on the emergence of interpersonal meaning systems across individuals, cultures, and historical periods, with a special emphasis on the structure of social behavior. In addition, he is interested in the cultural basis of intention formation and in the critical analysis of theoretical systems that connect culture and psychological processes. He was a member of the Executive Council of the International Association for Cross-Cultural Psychology for several years, editor of the *Cross-Cultural Psychology Bulletin* (1990–1994), and associate editor of the *Journal of Cross-Cultural Psychology* (1997–2001). He edited, with Yoshi Kashima, the volume *Social Psychology and Cultural Context* (Sage, 1999).

Jonas Bååth is a Postdoctoral Fellow in Sustainability at the Department of Service Management and Service Studies and a research affiliate at CIRCLE (Centre for Innovation Research), both at Lund University, Sweden. He holds a doctorate in sociology from Uppsala University, Sweden. His research resides within socioeconomic approaches to the societal provisioning of food, beverages, and intoxicants, focusing on markets. His research has appeared in outlets such as *Journal of Rural Studies*, *Current Sociology*, and *Socio-Economic Review*.

Stephanie Cacioppo is one of the world's leading authorities on the neuroscience of social connections. Her work on the neuroscience of romantic love and loneliness has been published in top peer-reviewed academic journals and covered by *The New York Times*, CNN, and *Women's Health*, among others. Named a "Rising Star" by the Association for Psychological Science, she is the director of the brain dynamics research laboratory and Assistant Professor of Psychiatry and Behavioral Neuroscience at the University of Chicago Pritzker School of Medicine.

Adel Daoud is an Associate Professor at the Institute for Analytical Sociology, Linköping University, Sweden, and Affiliated Associate Professor in Data Science and Artificial Intelligence for the Social Sciences, Department of Computer Science and Engineering, Chalmers University of Technology, Gothenburg, Sweden. Previously, he held positions at Harvard University, University of Cambridge, Max Planck Institute for the Studies of Societies, and the Alan Turing Institute. His theoretical work comprises scarcity, abundance, and sufficiency, and his empirical work

X CONTRIBUTORS

focuses on the impacts of economic, political, and natural shocks on global poverty. Methodologically, he implements novel methodologies in machine learning and causal inference to analyze the causes and consequences of poverty. He has published in journals such as *Proceedings of the National Academy of Sciences of the USA, World Development, Cambridge Journal of Economics, Food Policy, Epidemiology, International Journal of Epidemiology*, and *Ecological Economics*.

Edna B. Foa, PhD, is a Professor of Clinical Psychology in Psychiatry at the University of Pennsylvania and director of the Center for the Treatment and Study of Anxiety. She received her PhD in clinical psychology and personality from the University of Missouri, Columbia, in 1970. She devoted her academic career to study the psychopathology and treatment of anxiety disorders, primarily obsessive–compulsive disorder (OCD) and post-traumatic stress disorder, and is currently one of the world's leading experts in these areas. She was the chair of the DSM-IV Subcommittee for OCD. She has published several books and more than 350 articles and book chapters, and she has lectured extensively throughout the world. Her work has been recognized with numerous awards and honors, including the following: Distinguished Scientific Contributions to Clinical Psychology Award from the American Psychological Association, Lifetime Achievement Award presented by the International Society for Traumatic Stress Studies, 2009 Lifetime Achievement Award presented by the Association for Behavior and Cognitive Therapies, *TIME* 100 most influential people of the world, 2010 Lifetime Achievement in the Field of Trauma Psychology Award from the American Psychology Association, and Outstanding Career Achievement Award presented by the International OCD Foundation.

Uriel G. Foa (February 25, 1916–January 15, 1990), born in Italy, was a Professor and Professor Emeritus of Psychology, 1971–1990, at Temple University, Philadelphia. He received his PhD from the Hebrew University of Jerusalem, and prior to his tenure at Temple University, he taught at Bar Ilan University, Israel (1958–1965); the University of Illinois Urbana–Champaign (1965–1967); and the University of Missouri–Columbia (1967–1971). His many publications in professional journals and books covered a broad variety of topics in personality, social psychology, and methodology. The first paper of his resource theory of social exchange was published in *Science* in 1971. He continued to develop this theory and conducted studies to examine its empirical validity with his wife, Edna B. Foa. This work culminated in the book, *Societal Structures of the Mind*, which they coauthored and published in 1974. This book is one of the most frequently quoted books in social psychology. He founded the Israel Institute of Applied Social Research and was its executive director until 1965 when he moved to the United States. He received several awards for his work, and he was a fellow of the American Psychological Association, the American Association for the Advancement of Science, and the New York Academy of Science.

Elaine Hatfield is a Professor of Psychology at the University of Hawaii and past president of the Society for the Scientific Study of Sex. In 2012, the Association for

Psychological Science awarded her the William James Fellow Award. Her honors include distinguished scientist awards (for a lifetime of scientific achievement) from the University of Hawaii, the Society of Experimental Social Psychology, and the Society for the Scientific Study of Sex (SSSS); the Alfred Kinsey Award from the Midwest Region of SSSS; the Society for Personality and Social Psychology's Methodological Innovator Award; and the International Academy for Intercultural Research's Lifetime Achievement Award.

Ali Kazemi, PhD, is a Professor of Psychology at the Department of Social and Behavioural Studies, University West, Sweden, where he also serves as the director of the Research Center for Positive Organizational and Leadership Studies. He has previously been incumbent of professorships in social psychology and health psychology at other universities and research institutes in Sweden. He has published more than 100 articles, book chapters, technical reports, and books in various branches of psychology. He has together with Kjell Törnblom edited the *Handbook of Social Resource Theory* (Springer, 2012). He is also editor of two volumes in Swedish: *Wellbeing in the Workplace: Social Psychological Perspectives* (Studentlitteratur, 2009) and *Positive Organizational Studies* (Studentlitteratur, forthcoming). He is the co-author of *Management in Retailing* (in Swedish; Liber, 2013), nominated as the best HR book of 2013 in Sweden. He serves as ad hoc reviewer for several academic journals and he has since 2011 been co-editor-in-chief (with Kjell Yngve Törnblom) of *Social Justice Research* (Springer).

Susan Opotow, PhD, is a Professor of Sociology at John Jay College of Criminal Justice and Professor and Program Head of the PhD Program in Critical Social/ Personality Psychology at the Graduate Center. Both are campuses of the City University of New York. A social psychologist, she studies the psychology of justice and conflict, focusing on the dynamics of exclusionary and inclusionary change in society. A Fellow of the American Psychological Association (APA), she currently serves as Chair of the APA Board for Educational Affairs. Previously, she served as Chair of APA's Board for the Advancement of Psychology in the Public Interest, as Editor-in-Chief of Peace and Conflict: Journal of Peace Psychology, and as President of the Society for the Psychological Study of Social Issues. She publishes widely and has co-edited two books, Identity and the Natural Environment: The Psychological Significance of Nature (MIT Press, 2003, with S. Clayton) and New York After 9/111 (Fordham University Press, 2018, with Z. B. Shemtob). In 2021, she was honored with an American Psychological Association Presidential Citation for her commitment to using the lens of psychology to understand and foster social justice in society and for her teaching and service to the field.

Richard L. Rapson is a Professor of History at the University of Hawaii. He came to Hawaii in 1966 after teaching at Amherst College and at Stanford University. He has written more than a dozen books, most of which focus on the psychological side of American life, past and present. His books include *Amazed by Life: Confessions of a Non-Religious Believer* (Xlibris, 2004) and *Magical Thinking and the Decline of*

xii CONTRIBUTORS

America (Xlibris, 2007). He has collaborated with Elaine Hatfield on the book, *What's Next in Love and Sex: Psychological and Cultural Perspectives* (Oxford University Press, 2020).

Clara Sabbagh is a Sociologist of Education at the Department of Leadership and Policy in Education, University of Haifa, Israel. Her research interests include distributive justice, social justice, facet theory, cross-cultural research, nonformal education, education and family justice, social inequality, and youth. She has served as President of the International Society for Justice Research (2010–2012).

Manfred Schmitt is a retired Professor of Psychology who taught Personality and Psychological Assessment at the University of Koblenz–Landau, Germany, until 2019. His research interests include emotion dispositions, individual differences in justice sensitivity, personality and information processing, nonlinear person × situation – interactions, objective personality assessment, and the consistency and interaction of implicit and explicit dispositions. In addition, he has made contributions to the advancement of research methods and their application.

Kjell Yngve Törnblom obtained his PhD in social psychology from the University of Missouri–Columbia, where Uriel Foa was one of his teachers. They have since collaborated on several publications, including *Resource Theory: Explorations and Applications* (Emerald, 1992). He is Professor Emeritus in social psychology and is currently affiliated with the Transdisciplinarity Lab, Department of Environmental Systems Science, Swiss Federal Institute of Technology Zurich, Switzerland. He has published research on social justice, resource theory, conflict, intergroup relations, theory integration; co-edited three books; and was awarded a Distinguished Alumni Award by the University of Missouri. He has been co-editor-in-chief (with Ali Kazemi) of *Social Justice Research* since 2011 and is a member of the International Society for Justice Research Executive Board. He has served at universities in Sweden, the United States, Canada, and Switzerland.

Introduction

Ali Kazemi and Kjell Yngve Törnblom

Humans are social animals. Thus, we cannot survive in isolation. We satisfy our needs through seeking, maintaining, and engaging in relationships and interaction with other people. However, social interactions are complex.

One way to conceptualize interactions is to see them as exchanges. When two or more people interact, they can be thought of as exchanging resources. Indeed, starting in the 1950s, numerous social scientists conceptualized human interactions in just this way (Blau, 1964; Emerson, 1976; Gergen, 1969; Gouldner, 1960; Homans, 1958; Longabaugh, 1963; Thibaut & Kelley, 1959), and such conceptualizations have been popular to this day (e.g., Adams, 1965; Berger et al., 1972; Cook & Emerson, 1978; Cook & Hegtvedt, 1983).

A particular pair of investigators, Uriel and Edna Foa, brought their own unique contribution to the field of exchange theory. In their classic monograph, *Societal Structures of the Mind* (1974), the Foas made a fundamental observation: Not all resources are the same.

Prior to the work of the Foas, the heavy emphasis on economically oriented transactions and exchanges limited the scope of theoretical progress. Researchers looked at the *quantities* of resources being exchanged but gave scant attention to the *qualities* of the resources. Homans (1958), for example, analyzed how people's satisfaction in relationships would be a function of their cost–benefit analyses, which in turn were influenced by social comparisons—both those readily at hand and those imagined to be available elsewhere. However, Homans never paused to consider any aspects of the concept of resources.

The simple but profound principle at the center of Foas' social resource theory (SRT) is that scholars who wish to use exchange theory to understand the nature and consequences of social interactions must specify what it is that people give and receive in their interactions. Examples abound. Giving love to someone will not diminish your "supply" of love, but giving away money

Social Behavior as Resource Exchange. Kjell Yngve Törnblom and Ali Kazemi, Oxford University Press.
© Oxford University Press 2023. DOI: 10.1093/oso/9780190066994.001.0001

xiv INTRODUCTION

will leave you with less. Receiving affection from an unknown salesperson will mean something different than if it was provided by your sweetheart. Paying for a pound of potatoes with a compliment rather than money is inappropriate. Taking away a child's winter coat as a punishment for an insult is unacceptable. Clearly, different types of resources will be guided by different exchange rules.

SRT presents a description of the psychological mechanisms required for these exchanges and specifies their course of development, their qualities and dimensions, and the function they serve in interpersonal encounters. It relates individual structure to the structure of society and provides a basis for classifying differences among individuals and cultures.

To grant that scholars must look at the nature of the resources to be exchanged and not just at the quantities of some abstract concept called "resources" means that thoughtful scholars must have a way of describing or classifying the nature of resources. Humans give meanings to behaviors, and those with similar meaning might be categorized together and separated from behaviors with different meanings in any typology of resources. Can one imagine a typology of resources? Are there dimensions or vectors that can help in the task of creating such a typology?

Many readers may already be familiar with Foas' famous typology of resources. In many texts appears the figure showing the circular arrangement of the six major resource classes articulated in SRT: love, services, money, information, goods, and status. Some texts also explain how the arrangement takes into account how particularistic the resource is (with love being the most particularistic and money the least) and how concrete it is (with goods being the most concrete and with information and status being the least concrete) (Törnblom & Kazemi, 2012). But it is only in the Foas' 1974 monograph that the serious scholar can see the deductive and inductive processes by which the Foas came to create their typology. Alas, the monograph is out of print.

The present volume seeks to advance research on SRT in two ways. First, Part I presents an abridged version of the 1974 monograph. Careful reading of Part I shows the Foas' conviction that it is possible for the observant scholar to discern natural structures in people's thinking, even if people themselves are unable to articulate the structures. Part I contains the story behind the famous circle.

Page limits have constrained us. In ways described in Part III, we made some editorial decisions, leaving out parts of some chapters. Some chapters of the original monograph were excluded entirely.

Out of respect for history, our editing did not include the modernizing of the language of the original monograph. Contemporary readers may notice language that sometimes appears sexist, as in the use of "man" to mean "human being." Because we want to situate SRT theory within the development of social sciences in the 20th century, we leave intact the original language, changing only the occasional typographical errors. Part I includes an important addition that we have made. We introduce Part I with a précis of the chapters included in order to briefly highlight the main ideas.

Part II of this volume provides a testament to the fertility of SRT. Building on the foundation laid by the Foas, 11 scholars present research in six chapters that carries forward the work started approximately a half century ago. Törnblom and Kazemi (Chapter 7) offer an overview of some theoretical advances that have been proposed since the Foas' original 1974 monograph and discuss some issues for further improvements of SRT. Adamopoulos (Chapter 8) highlights three distinct levels of operation—that is, the universal structure, cultural patterns of interpersonal relations, and cognitive processes involved in the construal of unique interpersonal events. Opotow (Chapter 9) focuses on the applicability of the Foas' six resource classes at the meso- and macro-levels. Bååth and Daoud (Chapter 10) provide theoretical extensions of SRT via a synthesis of SRT and their theory of scarcity, abundance, and sufficiency. Hatfield, Rapson, and Cacioppo (Chapter 11) present the most recent research by neuroscientists on the neurological characteristics of the particular resource passionate love. Sabbagh and Schmitt (Chapter 12) discuss the use of smallest space analysis and factor analysis in addition to the potential use of other multivariate (untraditional) methods for exploring new research questions and hypotheses derived from SRT.

Our sincere hope is that this volume will spur new research. Just as the contributors to Part II have honed and modified prior conclusions, so may future work bring new refinements.

It is not difficult to generate interesting theoretical questions. How will attitudes toward the way a positive or negative resource is acquired (e.g., purchased or stolen) or produced (e.g., ecologically, locally, and ethically or not) affect exchanges? Do people use different procedures when transacting different types of resources? Are justice evaluations of/attitudes toward/ preferences for a particular resource affected by the manner in which it is provided, and how will these affect behavioral reciprocal responses? Will the valence of a resource affect the choice of exchange procedure? Do universalistic resources tend to be "compounded" in particularistic relationships (i.e., coupled with affection), while they are "cleaner" in universalistic relationships? What roles do institutional context and culture play for any of the behaviors done by individual actors as they exchange resources of different types? Evidently, questions abound.

Nor is it difficult to envision practical applications of SRT. Psychotherapeutic interventions with individuals may be facilitated by making use of the concepts in SRT. In educational settings, teachers might benefit by being alert to the ways that resources matter to their students. Similarly, organizations might achieve smooth functioning if they pause to consider the dimensions of their reward systems. Maintaining a balanced pattern of social exchange in organizations can lead not only to smoother functioning but also to the thriving or flourishing of its members, as supported by the burgeoning fields of positive psychology and positive organizational scholarship (Cameron & Spreitzer, 2012). At the societal level, the integrative and holistic approach of SRT emphasizes that effective solutions to pressing social issues, particularly those related to sustainable development, require the development of technologies for the production and allocation of not only economic resources but also socio-emotional resources. To achieve this, SRT reminds us that new forms of social organization are needed to provide a more balanced supply of resources to citizens. It is even possible to imagine that statesmen might harness the power of SRT to prevent the rise of authoritarian demigods. If so, it would indeed be true as Lewin (1952) proposed that "there is nothing more practical than a good theory" (p. 169), and SRT lives up to this motto with flying colors.

References

Adams, J. S. (1965). Inequity in social exchange. In L. Berkowitz (Ed.), *Advances in experimental social psychology* (pp. 267–299). Academic Press.

Berger, J., Zelditch, M., Jr., Anderson, B., & Cohen, B. P. (1972). Structural aspects of distributive justice: A status value formulation. In J. Berger, M. Zelditch, & B. Anderson (Eds.), *Sociological theories in progress* (*Vol. 2*, pp. 119–246). Houghton-Mifflin.

Blau, P. M. (1964). *Exchange and power in social life*. Wiley.

Cameron, K. S., & Spreitzer, G. M. (2012). *The Oxford handbook of positive organizational scholarship*. Oxford University Press.

Cook, K. S., & Emerson, R. M. (1978). Power, equity, and commitment in exchange networks. *American Sociological Review, 43*, 721–739.

Cook, K. S., & Hegtvedt, K. A. (1983). Distributive justice, equity, and equality. *Annual Review of Sociology, 9*, 217–241.

Emerson, R. M. (1976). Social exchange theory. *Annual Review of Sociology, 2*, 335–362.

Foa, U. G., & Foa, E. B. (1974). *Societal structures of the mind*. Charles C Thomas.

Gergen, K. J. (1969). *The psychology of behavior exchange*. Addison Wesley.

Gouldner, A. W. (1960). The norm of reciprocity: A preliminary statement. *American Sociological Review, 25*, 161–179.

Homans, G. C. (1958). Social behavior as exchange. *American Journal of Sociology, 63*, 597–606.

Lewin, K. (1952). *Field theory in social science: Selected theoretical papers by Kurt Lewin*. Tavistock.

Longabaugh, R. (1963). A category system for coding interpersonal behavior as social exchange. *Sociometry, 26*, 319–344.

Thibaut, J. W., & Kelley, H. H. (1959). *The social psychology of groups*. Wiley.

Törnblom, K., & Kazemi, A. (Eds.). (2012). *Handbook of social resource theory*. Springer.

PART I
ABRIDGEMENT OF
URIEL G. FOA AND EDNA B. FOA
(1974) *SOCIETAL STRUCTURES*
OF THE MIND

Précis of the Chapters Included

Taking the two terms of *cognition* (cf. the term mind in the title of the monograph)—defined as "an organized set of categories into which perceived events are classified according to the meaning assigned to them; events having an equivalent meaning are placed in the same class"—and *structure*—defined as "a configuration of variables or classes in a space of stated coordinates"—as the points of departure, Foa and Foa delineate the theoretical fundaments of social resource theory (SRT) in Chapter 1. Foa and Foa remind us that cognition is about meaning, and meaning is essential for a deeper understanding of interpersonal behavior as "the reaction to a given message depends on the meaning which is ascribed to it." And, following well-established Gestalt-theoretical principles, understanding the meaning of behavior is the most important reason for studying structures as "the whole is more than the sum of its parts." Only by investigating the whole are we able to specify the structure of the parts (i.e., the identification of parts as well as a specification of their relationship). The next two chapters deal with the development of the structures that are required for cognizing social events.

In Chapter 2, Foa and Foa define cognitive growth as a sequence of differentiations and generalizations (i.e., the process of discovering common attributes between previously discriminated stimuli), the latter following the former. They continue by stating that six basic dimensions underlay the development of the classes essential to the cognition of social events: (a) the mode containing the two elements of giving (acceptance) and taking away (rejection), (b) the actor who is doing the action (self and/or other), (c) the object or recipient of behavior (self and/or other), (d) interpersonal resources (a specification of what is given or taken away generates six classes of resources for classifying social events: love, services, goods, status, information, and money), (e) the level of an event (actual/what is actually done or ideal/what should be done), and (f) the viewpoint (person or other).

Having identified the component elements of cognitive classes and described the cognitive development of social interaction in Chapter 2, Foa and Foa consider the relationships among the cognitive classes in Chapter 3.

Social Behavior as Resource Exchange. Kjell Yngve Törnblom and Ali Kazemi, Oxford University Press.
© Oxford University Press 2023. DOI: 10.1093/oso/9780190066994.003.0001

4   PART I ABRIDGEMENT OF *SOCIETAL STRUCTURES OF THE MIND*

The six interpersonal resources of love, status, information, money, goods, and services are ordered along the two dimensions of particularism and concreteness. *Particularism* indicates the extent to which the value of a given resource is determined by the identity of the persons involved in the exchange. At one extreme of this dimension is love, the most particularistic resource, and at the other extreme is money, the least particularistic resource. *Concreteness* ranges from concrete to symbolic and suggests the form of expression characteristic of each resource class. Services and goods are the most concrete as they involve the exchange of overt activity or of a tangible product, whereas status and information, typically conveyed by verbal behaviors, are more symbolic. Love and money occupy an intermediate position as they are exchanged in both concrete and symbolic forms. Certain classes are nearer to each other, whereas certain others are more distant. The nearer two classes are, the more likely they are to be similar in meaning, to influence each other, and to occur jointly in interpersonal situations.

In Chapter 4 (Chapter 5 in the original), Foa and Foa examine the function of cognitive structures in the dynamics of interpersonal interaction. Social experiences are interpersonal encounters in which resources are given and taken away. Three factors that determine whether a given exchange will take place are identified: the motivational state of the potential exchangers, the institutional setting, and the properties of the resources to be exchanged. When the amount of a given resource possessed by a person at a given time falls below the optimal range, it is experienced as a need. Thus, exchanges are likely to be initiated when they are expected to reduce actual or potential needs and are compatible with the person's actual power (i.e., the needy person's supply of a resource that the person must provide in return for the needed resource). Power is defined as the amount of a given resource that is available to the individual for eventual giving. There are six classes of power, one for each resource class. Power cannot be exercised unless there is a corresponding need on the part of the receiver. Because exchanges take place so often, society has developed mechanisms, called institutions, for facilitating the encounter of individuals having reciprocal needs and powers. In addition to social institutions, the nature of the resources being exchanged may also impose restraints on the type of transaction. For example, money is an appropriate means of exchange in several social institutions, whereas there are fewer exchange possibilities for particularistic resources such as love and affection.

Chapter 5 (Chapter 7 in the original) focuses on a number of issues that have attracted considerable theoretical and empirical research attention in social psychology. They are reanalyzed in terms of the social resource exchange framework and include research on frustration–aggression (i.e., an event in which A deprives B of a certain resource and B in return deprives A by retaliating), interpersonal attraction (i.e., romantic attraction in that a person will find another person attractive to the extent that this person is seen as a potential partner for transaction of valuable resources), equity (i.e., when equity prevails individuals experience justice, and when equity does not prevail they attempt to restore equity by modifying the value of the resources involved, with symbolic resources being more amenable to perceptual modification than concrete resources), ingratiation (involving a situation in which a person is dependent on another for certain resources but cannot engage in an honest exchange), conformity (i.e., referring to a first step in an exchange in that the person changes belief/behavior to become more similar to another person/group), and Machiavellianism (referring to a personality trait typified by the manipulation and exploitation of others, and a tendency to view particularistic transactions as stepping stones to obtaining universalistic resources that persons high in Machiavellianism seem to value more).

Chapter 6 (Chapter 11 in the original) is an epilogue and includes a philosophical and sociological discussion of man as a structurer and of the dialectics of stability versus change in addition to an examination of the practical relevance and application of SRT to social problems. Foa and Foa suggest that identification of different types of resource deficits and their likely consequences for individuals and society is a fruitful approach to dealing with acute social problems. The authors conclude that the goal is to evolve toward forms of social organization which will offer a more balanced supply of resources and that the integrative approach advocated by SRT is conducive to realizing this goal.

1

Introduction: Man's Structuring of His Social World

Human beings, no matter what they are doing, seek companionship. At work, or while enjoying their leisure, the contact with other people is of primary importance. When this contact is denied, as in the case of a prisoner in solitary confinement, it is a dreadful punishment. Even activities which appear to rest on the skills of the individual may be influenced by the social situation. It has been reported, for instance, that children perform better in intelligence tests when their teachers expect them to be brighter (Rosenthal & Jacobson, 1968). Similarly, workers increase production after becoming the focus of attention (Roethlisberger et al., 1939).

Man, then, is indeed a social creature, devoting a great deal of time and passion to his dealings with his fellow man. The behavior which is displayed in these encounters varies from explicit transactions involving money, goods, services, and information, to a subtler exchange of words and gestures through which affection and appreciation are conveyed. The need for money, goods, services, or information, as well as the need for the less tangible resources of love and status, are seldom satisfied in isolation. We depend on one another for these resources which are necessary for our well-being, and therefore, we seek social situations in which to exchange them through interpersonal behavior.

Although these exchanges are a common occurrence, engaging in even the simplest of them demands complex skills of which we may be largely unaware. To carry out these transactions, then, behaviors must be given meaning and those with similar meaning must be classed together and separated from behaviors with different meanings. Thus, for example, one has to separate behavior of giving from behavior of taking away, behavior of self from behavior of other. Likewise, it is helpful to recognize that norms and actual behavior may differ, and that one view of a social event is not necessarily the universal view. These differentiations constitute the dimensions of our picture of the

---

Social Behavior as Resource Exchange. Kjell Yngve Törnblom and Ali Kazemi, Oxford University Press.
© Oxford University Press 2023. DOI: 10.1093/oso/9780190066994.003.0002

8 PART I ABRIDGEMENT OF *SOCIETAL STRUCTURES OF THE MIND*

social world, a picture which enables us to understand, predict, and to some extent control the exchange of resources.

Resource theory presents a description of the psychological mechanisms required for these exchanges, specifies their course of development, their parts and dimensions and the function they play in interpersonal encounters. It relates individual structure to the structure of society and provides a basis for classifying differences among individuals and cultures. In examining shared and dissimilar properties of economic and non-economic resources, it establishes a link between economics and other social sciences. Within this theory seemingly disparate notions, such as cognitive dissonance, interpersonal communication, social roles, cross-cultural training, leadership, need, power, alienation, and psychotherapy are integrated into a coherent whole.

A convenient point of departure for identifying the resource exchange apparatus of the adult is to consider how its basic dimensions become progressively differentiated early in life, when the child interacts mainly with its mother. Then, as the child begins to move beyond the exclusiveness of relationship with his mother, further differentiations are needed for him to be able to participate in the various roles of the family, relate to peers, as well as function in other social institutions, such as school and work. Different resources are, indeed, suitable to each one of these institutional settings, so that institutions provide both limitations and channels for resource exchange: paying for transportation is appropriate in a public vehicle, but not when a neighbor offers you a ride. Even if the neighbor needs money, the loss of status involved in a request for payment would probably keep him from making such a demand. Thus, an institutional setting may prevent a given transaction while facilitating another. An additional condition for an exchange to be satisfactory is that it should be consistent with the participants' previous experience of social events. A person who expects equitable compensation for a big effort will feel dissonance when receiving a small reward. To resolve this inconsistency, he may conclude that the effort he made was not that big and that, in fact, he rather enjoyed it. In this example the restructuring of the dissonant event reduces the feeling of loss, while, at the same time, safeguarding the cognitive organization of the individual. In other instances however, the need for a given resource may conflict with the need to preserve the structure: a person who expects failure may give up status rather than recognize success.

Institutional setting, need-states of the individual, as well as the properties of the resource involved, all affect the likelihood of an exchange occurring.

INTRODUCTION: MAN'S STRUCTURING OF HIS SOCIAL WORLD   9

Once an exchange has taken place it is pertinent to inquire how it influences the participants' satisfaction and willingness to enter further transactions. Experiments conducted by us indicate that the appropriateness of the resources exchanged constitutes a significant factor for satisfaction; people seem to have definite preferences about what should be exchanged with what. Serious difficulties in the transaction of resources are likely to arise when the participants do not share similar mechanisms for classifying interpersonal behavior and for assigning meaning to it. These cognitive differences appear indeed to hinder performance, interaction among members of different cultures, and relations with mentally disturbed individuals.

Clearly, identification of the latent cognitive structures underlying interpersonal behavior is a central concern for a theory of resource exchange. Yet the twin notions of "cognition" and "structure" have been subjected to so many different treatments and interpretations that it appears desirable to specify in this introductory chapter the position we take on these issues. We shall begin with a short overview. Cognition is an organized set of categories into which perceived events are classified according to the meaning assigned to them; events having an equivalent meaning are placed in the same class. Cognitive classes are organized into patterns which reflect their similarities and differences; these patterns or cognitive structures provide a representation of self and environment. The significance of studying cognition, for understanding interpersonal behavior, rests on the notion that the reaction to a given message depends on the meaning which is ascribed to it. Since a message has meaning for the sender as well as for the receiver, interpersonal communication is based on the match between their respective cognitions. Uniformity in categorizing social events is facilitated by a common culture. Culture thus constitutes a blueprint or template for the classification and organization of social events. This blueprint is acquired by the child in his cognitive development, through exposure to differential reinforcement contingencies. Such a set of contingencies defines a culture, while the reinforcement contingencies of a specific experimental setting may be seen as a mini-culture.

Cognition

Being the psychological mechanism by which meaning is assigned to the external and internal stimuli we experience, cognition indicates the relationship

10   PART I ABRIDGEMENT OF *SOCIETAL STRUCTURES OF THE MIND*

between events, i.e., how one event is "caused" by another. It is through the possession of such mechanism that we are capable of predicting and controlling our environment: the rat which experienced red light followed by shock will soon jump a shuttle box when the light appears; the child who was comforted with candy will soon cry when craving for it. It is indeed through cognition that past experience becomes a guide for operating in the present and for anticipating the future. By cognition we achieve a fairly sensible and ordered view of the world which surrounds us, of the web of interpersonal relations to which we belong and of our position in the community.

In order to accomplish these complex functions cognition must provide some representation of the environment somewhat analogous to a geographical map. Few modern psychologists would, however, consider cognition a passive mirror of reality in which events are merely recorded, a view, this latter, which had enjoyed some popularity in the past. Nevertheless, the debate over the nature of cognition has not disappeared from current thinking, even if it has lost some of its earlier vehemence (Sarbin et al., 1960, Ch. 2). Major conflicting views are represented by the proponents of materialism and by the idealistic school: for the former, cognition reflects external reality while for the latter reality is constructed by cognition. It is only recently that a third alternative, which came to be known as "structuralism," has emerged. This new development is described by Stent (1972) as follows: "Both materialism and idealism take it for granted that all the information gathered by our senses actually reaches our mind; materialism envisions that, thanks to this information, reality is mirrored in the mind; whereas idealism envisions that, thanks to this information, reality is constructed by the mind. Structuralism, on the other hand, has provided the insight that knowledge about the world enters the mind, not as raw data, but in already highly abstracted form, namely, as structures. In the preconscious process of converting the primary data of our experience, step by step, into structures, information is necessarily lost, because the creation of structures, or the recognition of patterns, is nothing else than the selective destruction of information. Thus, since the mind does not gain access to the full set of data about the world, it can neither mirror nor construct reality. Instead, for the mind, reality is a set of structural transforms of primary data taken from the world" (p. 92).

Selective destruction of information is a necessary operation in the process of categorizing events into classes by which we reduce the complexity of the environment as well as the need for incessant learning (Bruner et al., 1956, p. 12). Yet what constitutes important information may vary with the

INTRODUCTION: MAN'S STRUCTURING OF HIS SOCIAL WORLD   11

circumstances. The fact that my old friend Joe is wearing a new suit does not make him a different person to me, therefore I do not have to modify my behavior and expectations; his new suit is an irrelevant cue. This same information, the new elegant suit, may constitute quite an important cue for a person who, having never met Joe before, tries to classify him and behave for accordingly. Individuals may vary in the cues they select to destroy, and so that the same raw data, which originate in the environment, do not always lead to an identical cognitive representation. The simplification of an event by selective suppression is a necessary but not a sufficient condition for processing information. An additional requirement is the fit between cognition and the event.

Congruence Between Event and Cognition

When we see an unfamiliar dog we are immediately able to recognize it as a member of the class "dog," although this particular dog constitutes a totally new event for us. Once again, congruence between this event and the class "dog" is achieved by selective suppression of the cues which are specific to this particular dog. We attend only to cues which are common to all "dog" events, according to the previous experience as recorded in our cognition. Suppose now that this dog meows instead of barking; since this sound is not associated with the events of the "dog" class, we shall experience difficulty when attempting to categorize this strange creature. More generally, when the latent structure of an event is congruent with cognition so that it can be assigned to a certain class or cluster of classes then, and only then, the event becomes meaningful.

The concept of congruence between cognition and environment underlies, with varying degrees of explicitness, many theoretical notions in the psychological literature such as reality testing, confirmation of expectation, adaptation level and discrepancy. The idea that these notions involve a comparison between cognition and event was suggested more recently by Foa et al. (1971). Independently, Feather (1971) proposed a distinction between abstract and perceived structures; abstract cognitive structures, being relatively stable, "provide continuity and meaning under changing circumstances, but ... they are susceptible to change ... as new and discrepant information is received that cannot readily be interpreted in terms of existing abstract structures." "In contrast, the perceived structure refers to the way information provided

12 PART I ABRIDGEMENT OF *SOCIETAL STRUCTURES OF THE MIND*

by the immediate situation is organized. This type of structure, therefore, is dependent on the immediate situational context and does not have the stable transituational character of an abstract structure" (p. 356). Similarly it was suggested by Stent (1972) that stronger structures are formed from weaker ones through the selective destruction of information. A set of primary data acquires meaning only if its transformation makes its weaker structure congruent with the stronger structure pre-existing in cognition. Noting that some important scientific discoveries were ignored by contemporaries, Stent proposed that the structure of these new ideas was out of tune with the cognitive structure prevalent at such time among scientists.

The comparison between cognition and perceived event also constitutes an important aspect of Kelley's (1973) attribution theory, dealing with the manner in which people ascribe causes to behavior. Kelley proposed two kinds of attribution processes: one is based on pre-existing casual schemata, such as stereotypes, where a certain "effect" is associated in cognition with a certain "cause." The second process refers to the analysis of data from immediate experience. In giving an example of incongruence between the two processes Kelley quotes a study in which clinically naive undergraduate students were shown randomly paired protocols of projective tests and reports on patients' problems. The students found a relationship between the two sets of data. Since protocols and problems were paired at random the reported association must have originated from the cognition of the students. Kelley notes that the effect of the pre-existing cognitive state on the processing of new information also appears in the issues of primacy versus recency in attitude change, of proactive versus reactive inhibition and of assimilation versus accommodation.

In spite of its relevance to a great variety of phenomena, the comparison between cognition and event is not sufficient when social events are considered. A social event originates from people; therefore its structure should be compared not only with the receiver's cognition, but also with that of the sender. It is reasonable to expect that in most cases an event will be congruent with the cognition from which it ensued, it will in fact be modeled on it. Consequently, a social event will be incongruent for the receiver when his cognition differs from that of the sender. In social situations the critical matching is not between event and cognition, but between the cognitions of the participants; when they differ—as may be the case in mental disturbances or in heterocultural contacts—difficulties in understanding and predicting the behavior of the other person are likely to occur.

INTRODUCTION: MAN'S STRUCTURING OF HIS SOCIAL WORLD   13

For this reason, we shall not focus on the structure of the social event but rather concentrate throughout this book on the cognitions of the persons involved in it and on their cognitive matching.

Cognition and Awareness

Before concluding these introductory remarks on cognition its relationship to awareness should be briefly examined; often these two terms have been considered as synonyms. Baldwin (1969, pp. 336–337) suggests that learning without awareness is non-cognitive. This view is also pursued by Peterson (1968, p. 40), who offers the following syllogism: Earthworms learn, they do not cognize—therefore, learning does not require awareness; in the same volume he later notes (p. 75) that ". . . some actions occur under clear and definite cognitive control, while others reel off automatically beyond the reportable awareness of the agent." There is no question that some cognitive activities, such as relating one item to another, often are in the realm of awareness, and thus verbalizing them may facilitate learning (Dulany, 1962). However, other cognitive activities, such as classifying a stimulus according to its attributes, are more likely to be unconscious. Wickens (1970) reported results which suggest that the process of perceiving a word involves some kind of multiple classification, as the word is placed along a number of cognitive dimensions. In proposing that this process is unconscious he comments: " . . . I do not think that the identity of the many encoding attributes or dimensions enter very much into the individual's consciousness. Consequently, we are unaware intellectually of the richness of the encoding of a single word. If we were to consciously recognize this richness, then so much time would be required for the perceptual ingestion of a single word that we would find it next to impossible to listen to series of words and remember any but the first and last of them. We handle the intellectual and conceptual meaningful reactions to common words with the same kind of automatic skill as the veteran big league outfielder who turns his back to a hard-hit fly ball, runs at top speed, and then without stopping and almost without looking, raises his gloved hand at exactly the right instant and in exactly the right location to grasp the ball.

"The ball player's marvelous competence is the product of his years of experience in the bush leagues, in the training camp, and in the big league ball parks themselves. So, too, our automatic ability to transform the sounds or

14 PART I ABRIDGEMENT OF *SOCIETAL STRUCTURES OF THE MIND*

the sight of a word into many attributes is the product of the many, many experiences we have with words in this highly verbal world of ours. We are more complex and facile in our reactions that we witness ourselves as being, and in our dealing with words, much of an intellectual nature goes on about which we are cognitively blind, deaf, and therefore mute" (p. 1–2).

The Notion of Structure

The choice of a structuralist approach in considering the nature of cognition compelled us to introduce the term structure before discussing its meaning. Unlike cognition, structure is a notion which occurs not only in psychology but in other sciences as well. Physicists are concerned with the structure of the atom; i.e., with the interrelationship between its subparticles; biochemists investigate the structure of DNA and complex proteins, to locate the mutual position of their component elements. In their investigations of structures these scientists have a big advantage over their psychological colleagues: they use the familiar three-dimensional physical space for determining the place of their units. When Einstein treated time as a fourth dimension, his innovation was hailed as a major intellectual achievement. The challenge faced by the student of cognitive structure is even more radical: physical space is not suitable for ordering his elements, except as a vague and sometimes misleading analogy. Available methods for determining the spatial configuration of a set of psychological variables do not provide identification of the coordinates by which the space is defined, an essential requirement of a structural theory. Attempts in this direction are compounded by the difficulty we experience in conceptualizing spaces, other than the familiar physical one. Our strong dependence on the physical notion of space is clearly apparent in Kurt Lewin's writings: although his theoretical formulation refers to psychological spaces, his examples are mostly drawn from the physical one. This conceptual barrier is also reflected in the frequent use of the expression "psychological dimension" where the term "coordinate" would be appropriate. In the physical space the two notions happen to coincide, since the coordinates are independent of one another. Independence among the various coordinates is less likely to occur in psychological spaces; in this volume we shall indeed present several configurations with three coordinates, which can be adequately described on two dimensions. Bowing to the general custom we shall also use dimensions as synonymous with coordinate. We shall, however,

INTRODUCTION: MAN'S STRUCTURING OF HIS SOCIAL WORLD   15

avoid using the term dimension for indicating a variable. This distinction is made clear by defining structure as a *configuration of variables or classes in a space of stated coordinates*. It follows that coordinate and variable coincide only if the space is unidimensional. A virtue of such a configuration is that it indicates parsimoniously the dimensions on which variables are similar or different, as well as the relative similarity of each pair of variables in the given set.

Structure in the Science of Man

At a theoretical level, the study of structures or organized wholes has attracted the attention of psychologists in the past and increasingly so in more recent times. Freud's (1949) notions of Id, Ego and Superego, Lewin's (1936) topological spaces, and Piaget's (1952) schemata are all attempts to provide structural models. Closer to our topic of person cognition is Kelly's (1955) theory of personal constructs, the development of a structural model applied to clinical inference (Sarbin, et al., 1960), and Kelly's (1973) treatment of causal attribution. Persistent interest in this notion is evidenced by recent reviews of its application to child development (Emmerich, 1968) and to psychology in general. In disciplines related to psychology the notion of structure is prominent in the anthropological work of Levi-Strauss (1963) and Goodenough (1967), as well as in studies of linguistics (Chomsky, 1957; McNeil, 1966); and recurs often in sociological literature.

In spite of this theoretical interest, the notion of structure had only limited influence in empirical research. Many investigators ignore it altogether. Their work typically consists of investigating the relationship among a few variables; taking three or four variables at a time, it offers an almost endless variety of experimental designs. Consequently, this line of research generates a large amount of data, but also great difficulty in relating the results of various experiments and in attempting broader generalization. This difficulty may be partly due to the fact that in these studies each variable is considered in isolation, rather than in its relationship to a larger organized whole.

Other directions of research have either focused on a single dimension or subsumed the existence of multidimensional structures, without attempting to specify their dimensions.

GENERALIZATION. Most investigations of generalization in experimental psychology involve the notion of dimension but not of structure. The

16 PART I ABRIDGEMENT OF *SOCIETAL STRUCTURES OF THE MIND*

stimuli preferred in these investigations are those which can be ordered on a physical dimension (e.g., light, sound) thus avoiding the problem of spelling out psychological coordinates. This choice of stimuli limits the study of more complex phenomena. For example: displacement of aggression, when formalized as a generalization phenomenon (Berkowitz, 1965), would require specification of the psychological coordinates along which various persons are perceived as similar or different.

Stimuli possessing physical properties of order are found quite easily, while responses are unlikely to be so manifestly ordered; consequently stimulus generalization has been studied much more than response generalization. Ignoring the notion of structure, studies of generalization too often deal with unidimensional situations. A pigeon learns to peck a red circle for obtaining food and then it is tested on circles of various colors. Few studies were interested in forcing our pigeon to choose between a green circle and a red square.

COGNITIVE COMPLEXITY AND CONSTRUCT VALIDITY. A third group of studies is concerned with structure, but avoids spelling out its dimensions. Investigations of cognitive complexity belong to this group. Complex individuals are held to have a larger number of differentiated dimensions in their cognitive structure than "simpler" persons: a complex cognition presumedly including all the dimensions which exist in a simpler cognition plus some additional ones. If, however, one person is more complex than another person on one dimension and less complex than him on some other dimension, then it will be impossible to say which of the two is more complex without referring to specific dimensions. Some studies suggest indeed that complexity is not a unitary trait (Scott, 1963; Vannoy, 1965) and thus cannot be divorced from the quest for dimensions. In spite of these limitations, the notion of complexity has generated a considerable amount of research contributing to the understanding of the relationship between cognitive representation and external situation (e.g., Harvey et al., 1961; Schroder et al., 1967).

Another direction in the study of structure without searching for its dimensions is the construct validity procedure. It is used, particularly in the personality area, to validate new instruments for observation and consists essentially in correlating the score provided by the instrument with variables expected on intuitive grounds to be related to it, i.e., to be proximal to it in the unspecified structure.

The difficulties posed by the absence of dimensionally specific descriptions of structures are particularly evident in the investigation of

INTRODUCTION: MAN'S STRUCTURING OF HIS SOCIAL WORLD   17

dissonance: dissonance is said to occur when two elements of an event are incompatible (Berscheid & Walster, 1969, p. 131). It appears, however, that for dissonance to occur, the incompatible elements should be cognitively close. Indeed, one way to resolve dissonance is to increase the cognitive distance between the contrasting items. In other words: dissonance implies a discrepancy between the structure of the event and cognitive structure (Feather, 1971). In absence of a specific structural description, the intuition of the investigator remains the only source for deciding whether the elements of the event are incompatible with cognition. This problem, which is not specific to dissonance but applies to consistency models in general, is clearly stated by Pepitone (1966, p. 262): "The wholly unrestricted generality of the dissonance model with respect to the nature and size of the elements of inconsistency can and does create problems on the experimental plane. Without rules or guidelines as to what the elements of dissonance should be, the investigator can only select them on a purely intuitive basis. If he does not know the class of cognitions from which the dissonant ones are derived, he cannot count elements, and this is crucial for obtaining a measure of the strength of dissonance."

Partial or total disregard for the identification of cognitive structures has thus limited the usefulness of investigation in several areas of psychology. Conversely, the study of structures is likely to open new lines of research.

Why Structures Should Be Studied

The dictum "the whole is more than the sum of its parts," has a rather long history in psychology: its influence is apparent in the Gestalt school, in the ideographic approach to personality (Allport, 1937) and, more recently, in humanistic psychology (Buhler, 1971).

In studying the "whole," we obtain information about each of its parts as well as about their relationship, i.e., their pattern of organization. Thus only by investigating the whole are we able to specify the structure of the parts. It follows that the study of the "whole" requires the identification of its parts as well as a specification of their relationship.

The terms "part" and "whole" are relative to the level of analysis (Koestler, 1968, pp. 47–49). The part of a molar system becomes the whole of a molecular one. The cell is a part for the student of tissues; but a Whole for the microbiologist; "avoidance" is a distinct "part," in the behavior of an

18   PART I ABRIDGEMENT OF *SOCIETAL STRUCTURES OF THE MIND*

experimental animal, but also a complex neuromuscular pattern in its own right. The nature of the relationship among different levels of observation provides still another reason for investigating structures before attempting to relate variables from different levels. In contrast to this suggestion, a considerable amount of current research in psychology attempts to relate isolated variables from one domain to variables in another domain: psychophysiological variables to behavioral ones, cognitive variables to environmental ones and the like. This line of research tacitly assumes one-to-one correspondence between the variables of one domain and the variables of the other one: for each variable in one system there should be one and only one corresponding variable in the other system. The evidence available seems to militate against this assumption.

In language, for example, different words may have the same meaning and conversely, words often have more than one meaning, so that one-to-one mapping of words and meaning is not always possible. This ambiguity of meaning is usually resolved when the word is seen in the context of an organized whole, a sentence.

A similar situation occurs in the coding of genetic information: each instruction is represented by a specific sequence of three bases, selected from the four found in the DNA structure. The information is provided by the sequence and not by each base taken in isolation, so that the mere frequency distribution of the four bases bears no relationship to the meaning of the instructions. In the era before the identification of DNA as the genetic material, biologists assumed that the heritable differences between organisms must be determined by protein structures, because proteins were the only molecules known to be capable both of sufficient variety of form and specificity of function, as exemplified by enzymes. The structure of DNA, containing as it does only four different kinds of bases, did not seem to offer sufficient potential for either structural variation or specificity. In fact, it was at one time believed that DNA consisted of a mixture of small molecules, containing one of each of the four bases in random sequence, the so-called "statistical tetranucleotide." The discovery in the 1940's that DNA molecules are very much longer than this, and that the genetic material is indeed DNA, was followed by the finding that the frequency distribution of the four bases varies widely among the DNA of different organisms (Strickberger, 1968, pp. 48–59). The elucidation of the structure of DNA by Watson and Crick stimulated speculation in the 1950's on the nature of the genetic code, including the following proposal, which subsequently proved to be correct. By

INTRODUCTION: MAN'S STRUCTURING OF HIS SOCIAL WORLD   19

taking the four bases three at a time, 4^3 or 64 different kinds of instructions can be encoded into a linear DNA molecule, and this is more than sufficient to specify a linear sequence of the 20 different kinds of amino acid on which protein structure, and hence enzyme specificity, depend.[1]

This example is particularly instructive because it shows how an unwarranted one-to-one assumption (one base for each instruction) can lead the investigator astray. Again the riddle is solved when the component elements are considered in their structural relationship rather than in isolation. It is not by chance that the breaking of the genetic code followed the discovery of the structure. It could not possibly have preceded it, since the information is carried by the structure.

In an area of more direct interest to the psychologist, the relationship between behavior and brain functioning, the one-to-one assumption is denied in some recent work of Luria (1966). His research on disturbances of higher mental functions in the presence of local brain lesions indicates that more than one brain activity is involved in any given behavior and conversely a given activity participates in several behaviors. For example, a complex activity such as handwriting may be impaired in a manner which is distinctively associated with the location of the brain lesion. Such components as spelling, distortion of the letters, and directionality (i.e., writing on a line from left to right) will be variously affected depending on the localization of the cerebral lesions. Moreover, when a handwriting component such as directionality is impaired, we may also expect to find this component impaired in other domains of behavior. Social direction (e.g., differentiation between what one does to self and what one does to other) is one example of a behavior which may be defective due to disturbances in the directionality component. More recently Luria and his associates went even further by suggesting, on the basis of clinical observations, that the same behavioral system may be related to different cortical structures at different stages of its ontogenetic development ". . . a psychological operation changes not only its structure, but also its cerebral organization in the course of its functional development" (Luria et al., 1970). A complex brain–task relationship is also evident in sensory functions. Employing a visual discrimination task, Iversen (1969) found that monkeys with a posterior intratemporal lesion show impairment of pattern discrimination but perform as well as normal monkeys, in color discrimination. These

[1] John A. Grunau: Personal communication, 1971.

results suggest that more than one brain function is involved in visual discrimination.

Common observation suggests that the assumption of one-to-one mapping is not supported any better in the area of social cognition: behaviors which are quite different in their intrinsic characteristics may have similar meaning and, thus, are cognited into the same class: smiling, waving the hand, saying "hello" or "hi," are all forms of greeting. Conversely, behaviors which are motorically similar may have a different meaning: raising a clenched list and raising an open hand will probably go into different cognitive classes, as do kissing and biting which are two forms of oral activity. From these considerations emerges what could well be the most important reason for studying structures: understanding the meaning of behavior.

The Study of Meaning

In an interpersonal situation we exchange messages: many of them are verbal, others, no less important, are not: facial expression, gestures, body posture, eye contact and even the distance maintained with the other person (Duncan, 1969; Hall, 1963), are all interpersonal messages. In either case the significance of the message comes from the *meaning* that the sender and/or the recipient attach to it. The same meaning may be conveyed in quite different ways. If we want to warmly greet the other, we can do it by smiling, raising and waving an arm, or saying "hi." These various messages are largely equivalent in their meaning, all belonging to the same class.

As Bruner, Goodnow and Austin (1956, p. 1) have already noted, one cannot interact with the environment unless he categorizes events. Any perception of events involves the process of categorization, including the scientific conceptualization which always involves the cognitive activity of the scientist, in classifying the subject matter of his investigation. In cognitive studies, however, the subject matter is cognition; thus the task of the investigator of cognition is to cognite about the hidden cognitive structure of his subject. It involves building up hypotheses about the manner in which events are grouped into classes and investigating the order and relations among these classes.

The study of cognition is essentially the study of meaning. Why are we interested in the meaning of behavior? After all, there are other, more

INTRODUCTION: MAN'S STRUCTURING OF HIS SOCIAL WORLD   21

explicit, criteria for grouping behaviors, such as the type of organs involved (e.g., verbal vs. nonverbal; Buss, 1961, p. 4). Our choice is determined by the assumption that it is the meaning attributed to a certain interpersonal message or stimulus, which determines the subsequent response, and is therefore crucial for prediction of outcome. In the Far East, for example, a pat on the back is considered as an insult, whereas in Western cultures it will be interpreted as a sign of friendship. Naturally, we will expect different responses to this stimulus depending on the cultural background of the person.

Moreover, the meaning ascribed to the stimulus appears to influence not only the overt response, but also brain activity. John et al. (1969) trained cats to obtain food when presented with a flicker light of a certain frequency, and to avoid shock when exposed to a different frequency. Subsequently, the cats were presented with a flicker frequency midway between the earliest two. All through the trials, electrical activity in the brain of the animals was recorded by electrodes implanted in the visual cortex or in the lateral geniculate bodies. The shape of the brain wave, following the ambiguous flicker of intermediate frequency, was affected by the meaning attributed to the signal: when this flicker elicited the food response, the wave recorded was similar to the one which was present for the flicker associated with food; likewise, when the avoidance response followed the ambiguous stimulus, the wave shape resembled the one previously produced by the shock avoidance signal. Apparently, the same stimulus activated different neuronal activities depending on the meaning attributed to it by the animal. The alternative interpretation, that differential brain activity is related to the forthcoming response rather than to the meaning of the stimulus, is rejected by other studies showing similar results in absence of overt response. Cohn (1971) recorded brain activity in human subjects merely exposed to verbal and non-verbal auditory stimuli. The verbal material evoked activity mainly in the left hemisphere, while the activity for the meaningless noise was always in the right one. The two sets of stimuli differed in meaning, although both belonged to the same physical class of sounds.

From these experiments we learn that: (a) different stimuli may have the same meaning; (b) the same stimulus may have different meanings; (c) response depends on the meaning ascribed to the stimulus. We have also noted that knowledge of meaning requires identification of cognitive structures; thus the notion of structure enables us to relate the stimulus to the response.

Identification of Structures and Factor Analysis

So far the most sustained attack on the identification of structures has been made through factor analysis. There is no essential difference between the notions of factor and dimension, so that factor analysis constitutes a type of dimensional analysis.

Opinions differ as to the value of this approach for the identification of dimensions. On one hand, it is difficult to dismiss such work as the one done by Cattell (1966) and Cattell and Warburton (1967) which sign produced a sophisticated picture of personality structure. On the other hand, one cannot easily disregard data showing that factorial findings, quite acceptable by current standards, can be obtained from random data (Humphreys et al., 1969). In spite of these disturbing results, factor analysis continues to be widely used, possibly because it is so easily employed: the data are fed into the computer with the analytic program and outcome the factorial results. No matter what the data are, some results will be obtained. Consequently there has been an increasing tendency to use factor analysis blindly, i.e., without any theoretical guidance as to which variables should or should not be included in the analysis, and without a hypothesis regarding the structure of the variables. The fact that factor analysis was originally devised as a method for testing structural hypotheses has been often forgotten in current practice. Yet any analytic method can, at best, only reveal the order which is already implicit in the input. An analytic procedure can be compared to a cooking stove: the best stove will not make a good soup out of the wrong ingredients. Even more serious is the suspicion that the factor analytic space rests on metric assumptions which are unsuitable to psychological spaces, and therefore the factors obtained may not necessarily indicate primary dimensions of psychological organization.

In evaluating the factor analytical approach, we should note that even in areas like intelligence, where it has been used most consistently and rigorously, factor analysis failed to yield an acceptable structural pattern. When Guilford (1967) proposed a structural theory of intelligence, he had to follow an intuitive procedure of interpretation and classification of the many factors available in order to develop his dimensional model. A sharper departure from factor analysis is represented by Osgood (1970) who, also using an intuitive approach has identified ten semantic features for classifying interpersonal verbs and generating structural hypotheses.

INTRODUCTION: MAN'S STRUCTURING OF HIS SOCIAL WORLD   23

Blind reliance on factor analysis in the absence of specific hypotheses has delayed the identification of psychological structures. Another obstacle has been posed by the long-accepted dichotomy between structure and dynamics.

Structure and Function

Traditionally, in psychology, "structure" and "function" are considered as separate if not contrasting notions. A structure is characterized by endurance, permanence and stability, while functions are activities or processes, which change in response to environmental stimuli (English & English, 1958). As late as 1968, the *Annual Review of Psychology* maintained this dichotomy by devoting separate chapters to studies on personality structure and to the work on personality functioning. The fact that this practice has been criticized (Wiggins, 1968) and dropped may indicate that the structure–function dichotomy is becoming less rigid (View, 1969).

The separation between the structure and its function originates in a mechanistic view of the organism. In studying a car engine, it is expedient to become familiar with its parts and their relationship before learning about the functioning of the engine. Separation is justified here because the structure of the engine determines its function, while the only influence functioning has on the structure is that of causing a relatively slow wearing. Non-reciprocal relation between structure and function exists also in conventional computer programs, where the program determines the output but is not modified by it. This is not true of more recent and sophisticated programs devised in studies of artificial intelligence (Slagle, 1971, esp. pp. 130–133). Here the outcome can modify the program thus enabling the computer to capitalize on previous experience instead of proceeding blindly according to the rules set out at the beginning.[2]

Once we accept the view that structure and function are interrelated, not only a major conceptual obstacle in the study of structural dynamics is removed, but also its direction becomes clear. We suggest that the study of dynamics should concentrate on investigating and spelling out the types of changes which occur in structures as well as the conditions under which they occur. With amazing foresight Lewin (1936, p. 155) described three kinds

---

[2] Paul K. Blackwell: Personal communication, 1971.

24 PART I ABRIDGEMENT OF *SOCIETAL STRUCTURES OF THE MIND*

of structural changes: *differentiation*, or categorizing events, which were previously included in the same class, into different classes; *integration* (the opposite of differentiation), when items, previously classified in different categories, are reunited into the same class; *restructuring*, a change in the relative position of classes. Lewin also suggested some of the conditions in which these changes may occur.

The Lewinian notion of structural change is prominent in modern views of cognitive development (Baldwin, 1969; Emmerich, 1968; Kohlberg, 1969a). In general, psychological development may be perceived as a process of interaction between cognitive representation and behavioral experiences, a process which does not necessarily terminate in adulthood. Commenting on the fruitfulness of this approach for generating research, Emmerich et al. (1971) single out the following problems: "(a) How changes in social inputs influence the individual's normative structurings, (b) how changes in normative structures influence the individual's social behavior, and (c) how changes in social behavior feedback to influence normative structures" (p. 348).

Structuring and Interpersonal Communication

Behavior must be assigned to a cognitive class to acquire meaning; thus interpersonal communication requires categorization of the interaction. Two cognitions are involved in the transmission of a message—that of the sender and that of the receiver; a successful communication requires a match between these two cognitions. When will a message be received as intended? First, the receiver should have the class appropriate for the message; and second, the sender and the receiver should both recognize the message as belonging to the same class. When these conditions are missing, communication will be impaired. There are several ways for reducing misunderstanding. A common one is redundant communication, where several messages from the same class are sent in succession. Often we combine verbal and nonverbal messages to enhance our intention: when we want to convey friendship, we may follow the message "I like to be with you" with a smile or a warm look. In addition there are messages which intend to clarify the meaning of previous ones, such as "I was really joking," "I did not mean to insult you," etc. The most powerful factor for reducing misunderstanding is, however, a shared culture.

The Cultural Blueprint for Meaning

Culture provides a template or model for the cognitive structure of its members, so that persons belonging to the same culture tend to have similar structures and are able to communicate more effectively. The same idea is conveyed by Bruner et al. (1956, p. 10), "The categories in terms of which man sorts out and responds to the world around him reflect deeply the culture into which he is born." Culture also determines which message goes into which class—it determines the meaning of messages. In consequence, we can compare different cultures in terms of how different their blueprints are. Certain characteristics of cognition may well be common to different cultures and perhaps to all human beings, as well as to certain higher animals, enabling us to communicate with people from other cultures and even with animals, such as dogs. These pancultural aspects of cognition are probably present from birth, while the culture-specific ones are learned in childhood by interacting with other individuals, especially parents, who are carriers of the cultural blueprint. Thus, while cognitive structures are acquired through early interpersonal experiences, once developed they become determinants of later experiences by affecting their meaning.

Reinforcement Contingencies and Culture

Reinforcement contingencies provide a mechanism for learning the cultural model, quite similar to the one used in laboratory experiments: "correct" responses are rewarded, while "wrong" ones are punished; usually communication failure results in an inappropriate response followed by punishment. Suppose, for example, that a person behaves in the same way in two different situations when his culture dictates that behavior A is appropriate for the first situation and behavior B for the second one. The culture demands that in each situation the behavior should come from different classes, while our person uses the same class in both cases. He might be taught to discriminate between the situations in the way a white rat learns that when green light is on, pressing left bar releases food, pressing right bar produces shock; when red light is on, pressing left bar produces shock, pressing right bar releases food.

This simple experimental paradigm demonstrates the fact that reinforcement contingencies in a learning experiment constitute a pattern

26   PART I ABRIDGEMENT OF *SOCIETAL STRUCTURES OF THE MIND*

of interrelated events which is comparable to the cultural blueprint from which the child learns to structure his cognition. Solomon et al. (1968) noted the fruitfulness of laboratory learning situations that can be extrapolated to conditions of socialization and provided a good example of them. In an experiment they did, dogs were punished for eating "forbidden" and highly preferred food; some of the animals received immediate punishment as soon as they touched the taboo meat, while for others punishment was delayed so that they had a chance to eat some of the forbidden food. Compared to quickly-punished dogs, those in the delayed punishment group were less resistant to temptation, appeared more frightened during and after violation of the taboo, and their attraction for the permitted food was lower. These findings may be applicable to socialization of the child, and they illustrate the usefulness of regarding reinforcement contingencies as artificial mini-cultures. As such, they serve the same purpose a culture does, in developing and modifying the structural arrangements of experimental work, it will be necessary, however, to devise contingencies that replicate specific cultural patterns. Interest in conceptualizing reinforcement contingencies as an organized pattern has already been evidenced by some modern learning theorists (see e.g., Jenkins, 1971). Even more significant is the fact that a model of a non-culture (i.e., a random or disorganized schedule where no contingencies exist) has been proposed as a control procedure in classical conditioning (Rescorla, 1967). According to our reasoning, a random schedule will result in structural disorganization of the subject. Indeed, this procedure produces powerful negative effects, such as stomach ulcers, loss of weight, defecation, absence of response. These destructive effects, while impairing the effectiveness of the random schedule as a control procedure (Seligman, 1969), emphasize the interplay between organization of the environment and organization of the organism.

Individual Deviance from Culture

Learning of the cultural model is unlikely to be perfect: some deviations will occur, thus generating individual differences in structure, which in most cases, will be only minor. The cognitive organization acquired by the child may, however, differ considerably from the cultural blueprint when the parents themselves deviate, when the child is unable to receive or process the information communicated to him, or through some subtle interaction of both. Whatever the cause, a severe deviation from the typical structure of society will produce difficulties in interpersonal communication, since it will result in attributing uncommon meaning to messages. Suppose, for example, that a cognitive deviation consists of mixing up feelings and behaviors pertaining to self with those directed toward other (as it happens to schizophrenics), instead of sorting them into separate classes. Then the message "I am tired," will be decoded as "We are tired." If the deviant recipient is not tired and in fact intends to read a book, interpretation of the message as "We should sleep rather than read" will result in distress.

Various types of disturbances in interpersonal communication may be characterized by specific deviance patterns in the structural arrangement of classes. Treatment would then be specific to each pattern of deviance and would consist of an attempt to modify the structure in the direction consistent with the culture, through the use of suitable reinforcement contingencies. Experimental work on learning, focusing on the cognitive effects of various reinforcement contingencies, would offer a rich source of information for solving therapeutic problems of structural change; this research would indeed provide the mini-culture therapeutically indicated for specific structural deviances.

Toward an Integrated Psychological Theory

The considerations developed in this introduction to the subject matter of our book propose an important conclusion: The cognitive structure of social events, used as a central concept, leads to convergence and integration for different areas of psychology, which have tended to grow increasingly apart. In this framework, development becomes the process through which the structure of society is acquired by the individual member; abnormal psychology becomes concerned with the patterns of structural deviance; experimental psychology investigates the effects of environmental structures on the organization of the individual and thus provides techniques for structural change which can be applied to psychotherapy. At the same time, cross-cultural comparison of various structures may indicate what aspects of the structure are basic and invariant and what the differentiating aspects are. Thus, while deviance patterns of individuals may provide a taxonomy of psychopathology,

28 PART I ABRIDGEMENT OF *SOCIETAL STRUCTURES OF THE MIND*

cross-cultural comparison leads to a classification of cultures on the basis of their different structural characteristics. Through the following chapters of this volume we shall consider the interdependence among these various aspects of the social environment. We begin by describing the development of its cognitive representation.

2

The Development of Basic Social Concepts

Overview

Much of the work on child development and on the socialization process deals mainly with *how* the child acquires social behavior (e.g., Aronfreed, 1969; Bandura, 1969; Gewirtz, 1969). A typical procedure in this line of research consists of choosing a given behavioral class, such as aggression or self-criticism, and investigating the mechanisms (imitation, reinforcement) by which this behavior is acquired, as well as the conditions facilitating or hindering its acquisition. The cognitive organization (along psychological dimensions) of the behaviors learned is at most noted as an open problem. Thus, Gewirtz (1969, p. 74) refers to "dimensional learning" and Aronfreed, more explicitly, states that "It is the cognitive structures which are transmitted in the verbal communication of socializing agents, rather than the cues which are immediately inherent in overt behavior. . . . These concepts and standards can be used to make complex discriminations within and among large classes of behavior, along cognitive dimensions which represent the properties of the behavior . . ." (1969, p. 183).

The present chapter specifies those concepts which are transmitted through socialization. It describes *what* classes of social behaviors are acquired by the child as well as their organization along psychological dimensions. Occasionally we may offer hypotheses as to the conditions which facilitate or inhibit the acquisition of a structure, but most of our attention will be devoted to a description of the basic social concepts which constitute the course of development of social cognitive structures. We shall first examine some general notions pertaining to cognitive development. The processes of differentiation and generalization will be discussed in their relationship to cognitive growth, and the notion of boundary will be elaborated. Then, we shall proceed with specifying the differentiations which underlie elementary forms of social behavior, namely, differentiation between acceptance and rejection, between self and other and among resources exchanged in interpersonal transactions. The differentiation between actual and ideal

Social Behavior as Resource Exchange. Kjell Yngve Törnblom and Ali Kazemi, Oxford University Press.
© Oxford University Press 2023. DOI: 10.1093/oso/9780190066994.003.0003

30 PART I ABRIDGEMENT OF *SOCIETAL STRUCTURES OF THE MIND*

level, i.e., what is perceived as done and what ought to be done, will complete this review of the basic notions in social interaction. The last portion of the chapter takes up the problem of the developmental sequence among these differentiations, in the process of cognitive development.

Some Remarks on Cognitive Development

In the previous chapter an intuitive notion was given about some properties of a cognitive structure. The classes are ordered so that those containing similar messages are nearer to each other, while messages in the same class are equivalent in meaning. Whether any two messages are similar enough to enter the same class or different enough to go into separate classes is learned by interacting with members of a particular culture. When, for example, expressions of affect (love) and expressions of esteem (status) occur in separate occasions, or lead to different outcomes, two classes are needed for handling communications of love and of status in an efficient manner. Conversely when these behaviors have a high frequency of joint occurrence and/or lead to similar outcomes, they will be considered as equivalent. Consequently, contrary to a fairly common assumption (e.g., Capehart et al., 1969), equivalence in meaning does not necessarily reflect similarity of physical properties but rather depends on similarity of consequences.

At the beginning of his social life an infant will have very few categories, his classes of interpersonal behavior will be largely *undifferentiated*. He will not, for example, interact with a stranger differently than with one of the parents. But slowly, through successive steps of differentiation among social events, the structure will grow, and new classes will become available for sorting incoming and outgoing messages. Later on, a reverse process takes place: the child may behave in a similar way toward two persons to whom he previously behaved differently. Therefore, social development is conceived as a process of differentiation and generalization of social events. This view is similar to Piaget's conceptualization of cognitive development: "accommodation" is essentially a process of differentiation, while "generalizing assimilation" corresponds to generalization; the latter should not be confused with "recognitory assimilation," the assigning of a new stimulus to a pre-existing class, an operation which does not modify the cognitive structure. By contrast, cognitive structure does change in generalization: the emergence of a new dimension, on which previously differentiated classes have the same value, makes them more similar to one another. Closer to the viewpoint proposed here are Harvey, Hunt and Schroder who state that "learning occurs through a process of differentiation and integration, during which time the person breaks down the environment into parts relevant to his current conceptual structure . . ." (1961, p. 4).

Differentiation and Generalization

If generalization consists of discovering some common attributes between previously discriminated stimuli, then it should occur after differentiation between these stimuli has been established. Furthermore generalization is obtained when a successive differentiation, along a new dimension, takes place; the previously differentiated classes are then found to be similar on the newly established dimension. It is precisely this added dimension which allows generalization to occur. This relationship between differentiation and generalization may be clarified by the following example. The child first learns to interact differently with father and mother; later on he realizes that these two interactions have some common elements which differentiate them from interactions with siblings. Thus father–mother generalization, expressed by the term "parent," is based on the new differentiation between parents and siblings. To discover that two classes of social events have common features it is first necessary to recognize them as different and then to contrast them with a third class without the features. In a similar vein Harvey et al. (1961, p. 88) suggest that any developmental stage is characterized by a new differentiation, which in turn requires a transitional stage of integrating the previous differentiation. Conceptualizing generalization as integration avoids confusing it with the undifferentiated state which precedes differentiation. This point is well made by Brown (1958) who states: "The child who spontaneously hits on the category four-legged animals will be required to give it up in favor of dogs, cats, horses, cows, and the like. When the names of numerous subordinates have been mastered, he may be given the name quadruped for the superordinate. This abstraction is not the same as its primitive forerunner. The schoolboy who learns the word quadruped has abstracted from differentiated and named subordinates. The child he was abstracted through a failure to differentiate. Abstraction after differentiation may be the mature process; and abstraction from a failure to differentiate the primitive.

32   PART I ABRIDGEMENT OF *SOCIETAL STRUCTURES OF THE MIND*

Needless to say, the abstractions occurring on the two levels need not be co-incident, as they are in our quadruped example."

The literature on learning often treats non-discrimination and generalization as equivalent phenomena since behavior resulting from generalization may appear to be non-discriminative. Recent studies, however, suggest that non-discrimination yields flat gradients whereas generalization results in steep ones. Furthermore it seems that a generalization gradient cannot be established unless there is previous discrimination among the generalized stimuli. Peterson (1962) reared ducklings in a monochromatic light from the moment of hatching and trained them to peck at a key that was also transilluminated by the same light. In a later generalization test these ducklings were exposed to other wavelengths of which they had no previous experience. No generalization gradient was established for this group. Similar results were obtained by Ganz and Riesen (1962) showing that macaque monkeys reared in darkness later yielded a flat generalization gradient of wavelength. The gradient becomes, however, steeper through repetitions of the same generalization test. Jenkins and Harrison (1960) have further shown that exposure to a range of stimuli is not sufficient for obtaining generalization gradients and that an actual differential training should take place beforehand. Since, however, Jenkins and Harrison tested tone-frequency generalization while the other studies tested wavelength generalization it could be that, for a given species, discrimination between certain stimuli may be obtained by sheer exposure, while for certain other stimuli an actual differential training is necessary in order to establish discrimination. All these studies, however, indicate that discrimination should occur before generalization can take place.

Differentiation and Cognitive Growth

We have proposed that cognitive development results from the twin processes of differentiation and generalization. Since generalization has been interpreted as an eventual by-product of a successive differentiation, the growth of social competence can be conceptualized as a sequence of differentiations, which increases the number of cognitive classes available for categorizing social events and provides a behavioral repertoire appropriate to each class. This view has been repeatedly advanced in the past: Levin (1936, p. 155) stated that ". . . the development of the life space from infancy

THE DEVELOPMENT OF BASIC SOCIAL CONCEPTS 33

to adulthood can be characterized to a large extent as a process of differentiation"; Brown (1958) said that "cognitive development is increasing differentiation"; and Parsons (1955) conceptualized socialization as a series of differentiations.

Cognitive growth begins when the first differentiation partitions the undifferentiated class of "all social events" into two compartments. The next differentiation subdivides the previous partition and results in four classes of events. Parsons (1955, pp. 395–399) has noted the similarity between this pattern of cognitive development and the early embryological stages; both develop by binary divisions: like cognitive classes, a cell divides into two, then each is again divided into two, and so on. Perhaps this parallelism between tissue growth and psychological growth is just a matter of curiosity. On the other hand, as Piaget (1952) has suggested, psychological functions may be modeled on pre-existing biological functions. Accepting the notion that nature is parsimonious, we expect a basic mechanism such as the binary division to serve more than one system. Such parallelism in functions cannot be proved or disproved; however, it is an assumption which is supported by some observations. It has been found (Cone, 1968) that some cancer cells are undifferentiated: a stimulus applied to one cell diffuses to the others as well; this does not happen in normal tissues. Similarly we have found (see p. 353) that under-differentiation among certain cognitive classes is found in schizophrenics. Thus, in both cases under-differentiation is associated with a pathological state.

In psychological structures, partitions are not tight, so that what happens in one class influences the state of neighboring compartments, although it may not affect the state of remote classes. Thus instead of defining a given social event as belonging to one, and only one class, it would be more appropriate to say that it belongs *mainly* to a given compartment but to a lesser degree it also belongs to proximal compartments. When somebody, for example, runs a personal errand for us we classify his behavior as "giving services," but also as a sign of friendship ("giving love"). These interrelationships of neighboring classes are reflected in language as well. Verbs pertaining to social interaction can be categorized into more than one behavioral class; "advising" definitely belongs to the class of "giving information," but it also may convey some loss of status for the advisee. In general we would expect to find many words expressing meaning which pertain to two *neighboring* classes and few words which will cover two *remote* classes. Thus, semantic analysis provides a way for investigating the relative proximity of classes. A promising beginning in

34 PART I ABRIDGEMENT OF *SOCIETAL STRUCTURES OF THE MIND*

this direction has already been made. Osgood (1970) has proposed a scheme of *semantic features* for analyzing the language of interpersonal behavior. Wickens (1970) analyzed a series of experiments on short-term words recall; the results support the view that "... when a person hears or sees a word, the process of perceiving this word consists of encoding it within a number of different aspects, attributes, or conceptual psychological dimensions." He also noted that: "The results of the experiments indicate that different dimensions vary in their effectiveness for proactive inhibition release. In general, semantic dimensions (taxonomic categories or semantic differential) are highly effective, whereas physical characteristics such as word length or figure-ground colors of the slide presentation are relatively ineffective in releasing proactive inhibition."

Another approach to the study of mutual influences among classes consists of applying a stimulus to a given class and then observing the extent to which other classes are affected by it; obviously proximal classes should show a stronger effect than those which are remote from the stimulated class. Such gradient of effect has been repeatedly reported, sometimes under the different labels of *irradiation, diffusion,* and *response generalization* (Rosnow, 1968).

Boundaries

Since differentiation does not result in complete independence among differentiated events, the partitions between classes can be perceived as boundaries which are more or less permeable. Again, comparison of cognitive classes to cell tissues seems appropriate. The conceptualization of psychological structures as having permeable boundaries among their elements is well rooted in psychology though not always explicitly. The idea that psychological events (such as memories and emotions) may move from the unconscious to the conscious has been advanced by Freud, Jung and many others; it implies a permeable boundary between awareness and non-awareness. Lewin's notion of the nature of psychological boundaries is more explicit; for him the barrier (defined as a boundary which offers resistance to psychological locomotion) is like a more or less permeable membrane (1936, pp. 124–125).

In discussing various types of boundaries Ruesch (1956, p. 341) notes: "Many terms in psychiatric practice essentially refer to boundaries. The

THE DEVELOPMENT OF BASIC SOCIAL CONCEPTS   35

term dependent, which is used psychiatrically in many different ways, refers to people who eliminate certain boundaries. If you have two people who are mutually interdependent, both have formed a symbiotic system in which they function as a unit. Consider the case of compulsive people who stick to rules and rituals and do things just so. They seem to classify, order and divide, and they see boundaries where others do not see them. Informal people, in contrast, by mutual consent omit formalities and temporarily discard existing boundaries." Later, in the same paper (p. 343), he states: "Perceptual boundaries exist where the stimulation changes. If there is continuous stimulation, there is no boundary. If it stops, or becomes more intensive, or decreases, or changes in nature, there we detect a boundary . . . whenever there is a change of discontinuity, the chances of finding boundaries increase."

It is easy to conceptualize the notion of boundary in physical terms. When one steps out of the door, he has just crossed the boundary between the house and the back yard. Similarly the boundary between two cells is marked by a visible membrane. But what is a cognitive boundary? Events are categorized into classes according to specific criteria which consist of dividing a given dimension or coordinate into parts. This division is the product of differentiation. We shall call the cognitive dimension along which a differentiation occurs *facet*, and the notions differentiated *facet elements*. The conceptual difference between two elements is a *cognitive boundary*. A class of events is defined by a combination of elements from different facets. Thus any two classes may have one or more boundaries, depending on the number of elements in which they differ. The differentiation between domestic and wild animals provides a boundary between the class of cats and the class of jaguars, although both are feline; dogs and cats are both domestic but only the latter is a feline. The weaker the differentiation between the facet elements the more permeable the boundary is. Empirically a weak boundary will result in: (a) high relationship between events belonging to the two classes, which differ in the elements of a given dimension; (b) when one such class is manipulated, the other class will also be affected. For most purposes cats and dogs are considered more similar than cats and jaguars, so that the boundary between canine and feline is more permeable than the one between wild and domestic. On the other hand a jaguar and a cat are more similar than a bird and a cat, the last pair having more than one boundary between them. Thus the relationship between two classes is dependent on the number of boundaries between them as well as on their permeability.

36 PART I ABRIDGEMENT OF *SOCIETAL STRUCTURES OF THE MIND*

In conclusion, social growth is a process by which more and more classes are added to the cognitive structure of an individual by a sequence of differentiations along given dimensions or facets. Often, but not always, each successive differentiation occurs along a new dimension, thus resulting in the subdivision of the classes which previously existed according to the dimension newly introduced. Hence the facets of differentiation are not specific to one or few classes but cut across all the classes of a given domain. Consequently a few facets are sufficient to produce a large number of classes, an arrangement which is most economical. For example: six facets, with two elements each, will bound or define 64 classes. The number of classes is simply obtained by multiplying across all facets the number of elements of each facet. Thus the many classes used for categorizing social events can be described by a relatively small number of facets, differentiated into their elements. To these differentiations we now turn.

Dimensions of Social Interaction

In the remaining part of this chapter we shall be concerned mainly with describing the dimensions or facets which, by being differentiated, lead to a classification of social events. Because of the strong relationship between the developmental sequence of these dimensions and the structural properties of social cognition, a systematic discussion of the sequence will be given in the next chapter, which deals with cognitive structures. However, since each successive differentiation rests on previous ones, a presentation of the dimensions cannot be entirely divorced from their sequence. We shall thus begin with the earliest development.

The Foundation: Acceptance and Rejection

Observation of a newborn infant suggests that he possesses at least one differentiation, so that from the first minute of his life he can classify events into the two classes of comfort and distress; a stimulus may be pleasant or unpleasant. Accordingly he has two gross types of behaviors: he can either take the nipple (*accepting*) when it adds to his comfort or he may refuse (*rejecting*) it when it disturbs his pleasant sensation; he will swallow the milk or he may throw it up. This inborn differentiation is purely physiological. However, it constitutes the basis for cognitive differentiation. In the first months of life the infant is mainly enlarging these two classes of acceptance and rejection or "pleasure and pain" (Freud, 1965, p. 58), by including in each class more and more stimuli. Now it is not only the milk and warmth of the mother's body which makes him feel pleased but also certain colors and certain objects (toys); unfamiliar objects or noises are incorporated into the unpleasant class.

It is convenient to have a term for each dimension and we shall indicate this first one as differentiation of *mode* or *direction*. The labels of acceptance and rejection are suitable for naming the two poles of this dimension at the early stages of cognitive development: they provide a link to physiological mechanism and implicitly convey the notion that affect is a prominent resource in early transactions with mother. Acceptance of a child is expressed by *giving* him affection and care; rejection is deprivation of both or *taking away*. Later, when resources other than love and care become differentiated, it will be more appropriate to denote the elements of the mode by giving and taking away, rather than by acceptance and rejection.

Self–Other Differentiations

Self and not-self are standard terms in immunology (Burnet, 1969) by which the organism's rejection of foreign cells and acceptance of its own is indicated. Thus, like acceptance and rejection, the cognitive distinction between self and not-self may have a physiological forerunner. Unlike the former, however, it is not manifested behaviorally in the first few months of life and consequently the idea that the newborn infant does not differentiate between self and other is widely accepted. Baldwin (1894) described this state by the term "adualism" where no consciousness of the self exists; Freud talked about a state of "primary narcissism," which was later elaborated by Freud (1965) as lack of differentiation between self and other. There is considerable agreement that the differentiation between self and non-self is the basis for social growth. When such differentiation is achieved the child is able to observe an action and say whether it was emitted by him or by somebody else and whether it was directed toward him or toward the other. Moreover, the child may realize that his interpretation of a certain event may not correspond to the other's interpretation. These examples suggest that the distinction between self and other occurs on more than one dimension. It might refer to the person doing the action, to the target of it and to the viewpoint taken.

38 PART I ABRIDGEMENT OF *SOCIETAL STRUCTURES OF THE MIND*

The first two differentiations between self and other are primed by sensoric and motoric perceptions. When the child is fed he gets sensoric feedback coming from tasting the food. Later, when he becomes able to grasp the food with his hands and put it into his mouth, the previous sensoric feedback is combined with the motoric feedback of him putting the food in his mouth. Now the child starts to differentiate between self and non-self as actors. When mother is the actor only sensoric feedback is experienced; when he himself is the actor both motoric and sensoric stimuli are present. The child comes to differentiate self from non-self as actors on the basis of the fact that sometimes sensory and motor feedback are correlated (when self is actor) and sometimes they are not (when other is actor). Behavior toward self thus precedes differentiation between actors. However, when a preference for one of the two behaviors (feeding himself or being fed) is manifested and extended to other behaviors of the same type, we are justified to state that differentiation has been established.

Observations made on an eight-month-old baby girl revealed that acquisition of the skill to feed herself was almost immediately followed by refusal to take food from others. Thus, acceptance was linked to the behavior emitted by self, and rejection to the behavior of other. We interpret this pattern as a device for strengthening the newly acquired differentiation between actors by pairing it to the pre-existing differentiation between acceptance and rejection. For this particular linkage to occur, the motoric feedback should be pleasant for the baby. Imagine how difficult it would be for the baby to acquire new behaviors if self as an actor was linked to rejection. The idea that being an actor is a source of pleasure has already been advanced by Piaget (1952) in the concept of "circular response." Piaget conceives of a sort of sensuous satisfaction in the exercise of schemas, especially those that are not yet fully adapted to the circumstances (Baldwin, 1967, p. 197). As Kohlberg (1969a, p. 450) aptly notes: "At this point, the desire for mastery is reflected in the need to do things oneself. Atypical incident is a two-year-old's frustration at putting on his coat, followed by a temper tantrum if his mother tries to help him. The temper tantrum indicates that the child clearly differentiates what he can cause from what others can do, and as a result only what he can do leads to a sense of mastery."

The differentiation between actors provides the baby with a perception of himself as an actor. At this stage the baby mostly does things for himself, i.e., he is the object of his own behavior. Sometime later a new kind of behavior appears: he begins to put food in the mouth of the other. This new behavior signals the occurrence of yet another differentiation: this time between self and other as *objects* or *targets* of behavior. Once again, the same behavior (feeding by self) leads to different sensations. When the baby feeds himself, he gets both kinesthetic and gustatory feedback whereas feeding the mother results in kinesthetic feedback only. Often, we observe that a baby alternates between feeding himself and feeding the other "one spoon to Jimmy and one spoon to mommy"; this behavior may be interpreted as an exercise in the newly acquired differentiation between objects—feeding *himself* and feeding the *other*.

Initially, both differentiation of actors and objects are linked to acceptance and rejection: there is an acceptance of the other as an object when the self is an actor and rejection of the other as an actor when the self is an object. When the two differentiations are established their linkage to acceptance and rejection is loosened, and the whole range of combinations of the three differentiations, resulting in eight classes, becomes available for sorting interpersonal events. Figure 2.1 represents the eight classes in a schematic way. This scheme is merely a way to summarize the differentiations discussed so far and should not be interpreted as reflecting the structural relationship among classes. The reasons for this note of caution will become apparent in the next chapter.

Some of the classes are self-explanatory; observation of giving things to the other or taking away things from him are very common. Even the behaviors of giving to self may be intuitively understood, but when does the self take away from self? Concepts such as self-rejection or self-criticism represent examples of this class; the child takes away love from himself when he addresses himself by saying: "Johnny is a bad boy," "Johnny is mean."

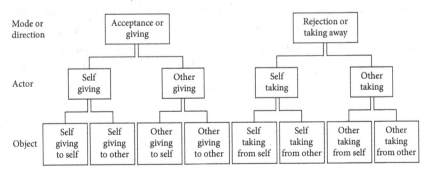

Figure 2.1 A schematic representation of eight classes of social events resulting from three successive differentiations.

40 PART I ABRIDGEMENT OF *SOCIETAL STRUCTURES OF THE MIND*

Behavior toward oneself, such as talking when alone, is not uncommon among young children, but tends to disappear with age, probably because it violates cultural norms. Even in the absence of overt behavior one does continue to relate to self.

The emergence of the differentiations between actors and between objects has the important effect of enabling the child to relate his own behavior to the behavior directed by other toward him and to develop contingent expectations regarding the probability that a given proaction will be followed by a given reaction. Establishment of the proaction–reaction sequence, in turn, provides the ground for two further developments: the notion of norm or ideal and the notion of reciprocal roles, roles of self toward other and of other toward self. Both these notions will be considered later.

The proaction–reaction sequence also provides a basis for imitative behavior. Moreover, the cognitive classes acquired offer a classification of the various types of imitation:

1. The child does to himself what mother does to him—feeds himself.
2. The child does to mother what mother does to him—tries to help her dress up, combs her hair.
3. The child does to mother what mother does to herself—puts jewelry on her.
4. The child does to himself what mother does to herself—puts make-up on his face.

The last class has been often termed as "taking the role of the other" (O'Toole & Dubin, 1968) rather than imitation proper.

Imitation is extended also to interaction with other people and to objects such as dolls, thus providing the beginning of role differentiation. The examples of imitative behavior illustrate the fact that we can hardly talk about any behavior without specifying its content. To specify what is given or taken away, we shall turn to discuss a further series of differentiations which results in formation of resource classes.

Interpersonal Resources

In the previous section we discussed the development of two aspects of an action: *who* is doing the action and towards *whom* it is directed. Earlier we

THE DEVELOPMENT OF BASIC SOCIAL CONCEPTS   41

proposed that an action results in a gain (giving) or in a loss (taking away) for the object. Thus, social action has been conceptualized as a behavior through which the actor increases or decreases the amount of *something* possessed by the object, by giving to or taking it away from him; in short, interpersonal behavior is a channel for resource transmission. Accordingly, a resource is any commodity—material or symbolic—which is transmitted through interpersonal behavior. In a similar vein, Levinger (1959, p. 84) defines a resource as "any property of an individual which he makes available to persons in his environment as a means for their positive or negative need-satisfaction."

The messages exchanged between adults present a great variety and several classes are needed to classify them adequately. There are messages dealing with love or affect such as "your company is very pleasant," or "you are charming." There are messages of status, like "well done," "I am honored by your presence here." Other messages deal with information which does not refer to either love or status: "It is five o'clock," "The door is on the left side," "Two and two make four." Goods, material things of any sort, and money are also resources exchanged in interpersonal situations. Finally, one may give services, increasing the recipient's physical comfort, by running an errand for him, doing something to his body (cutting his hair), or to his belongings (cleaning his clothes). Altogether we have listed six classes of resources: *love, status, information, money, goods* and *services*. The usefulness of this classification and its fitness to people's perception of social behavior will be discussed later. For the time being let us accept it provisionally and turn to the development of these classes in childhood.

The resources received by an infant at the beginning of his life constitute an undifferentiated bundle of love and service: the flowing milk, the warmth and softness of the mother's body and her care for him are all presented simultaneously. The differentiation between love and services becomes possible after the child has acquired some psychomotoric skills, sufficient for serving himself, like feeding himself, washing hands, etc. At this time mother can give him love without services, by requesting him to serve himself and at the same time encouraging him to do so. "The child then is to her no longer alone the object of her care, but also the object of her *love* . . ." (Parsons, 1955, p. 70). Thus differentiation between love and services is again built on the previous differentiation between self and other as *actors*; mother gives love (to the child), the child gives services (to himself), so that love is linked to the "other as an actor" and services is linked to "self as an actor." In both cases the child is the object of the action. Again, when the boundary between love and

42   PART I ABRIDGEMENT OF *SOCIETAL STRUCTURES OF THE MIND*

services is established all possible combinations of self and other as actors and as objects with respect to these two resources occur. The child provides services not only for himself but also for other persons, and "he not only is loved, but he actively loves" (Parsons, 1955, p. 43).

A situation in which love and services were provided by different actors from the onset was experimentally devised by Harlow (1958): infant monkeys were placed with two mother surrogates, a cloth surrogate—warm and soft (giving love) and a wire surrogate—hard and cold. Only one of the two mothers lactated; thus in the group where the wire mother provided milk (service) the two resources of love and service were given by different mothers. The monkeys developed affection (giving love) for the soft mother, independently of whether she lactated or not. These results show that attachment or giving love to the other is related to receiving love and not to receiving services. However, three of the four monkeys nursed by the cloth mother preferred to spend most of the time being close to the surrogate rather than to a gauze-covered heating pad that was on the floor of the cages (Harlow & Zimmerman, 1959). It seems that it is precisely the initial non-differentiation between services and love which is responsible for the amazing attachment to the mother.

Subsequently to the differentiation between love and services, goods are differentiated from services and status from love. Consumption goods, like food, are hard to differentiate from service because they appear simultaneously with service and are used only once. It is only when the child realizes that some objects disappear (the notion of "all gone") while others can be used again and again that the differentiation between services and goods becomes feasible. The differentiation of esteem or status from love requires some acquisition of language since most behaviors which pertain to status ("gee you did it") are verbal. In many cultures distinction between status and love overlaps with differentiation between mother and father as social objects, which we shall encounter later: love is often given mainly by mother and status by father (Parsons, 1955, p. 45; Zelditch, 1955). It is interesting to note that evolvement of status from love is also evident in some species; submissive gestures of dogs contain certain friendly elements which arise directly from the relation of the young animal to its mother, and the submissive behavior of baboons evolved from the female invitation to mate (Lorenz, 1966, pp. 135–136).

In the last stage of resource differentiation, money is differentiated from goods and information from status. For a two-year-old child money is perceived as a shiny object or a piece of paper. It gets its distinctive meaning when the child realizes that money may be exchanged for goods. Rarely is a child able to get goods immediately after receiving money, so that the perception of money as a resource requires the ability to delay rewards and anticipate an event which will take place in the future. The close relationship between differentiation of money from goods and ability to delay rewards is supported by experiments in behavior modification. Children have been trained to regard tokens as reinforcers (a type of money) by pairing them with appreciable goods, like M & M candies (Hamblin et al., 1969). The notion that money is exchangeable for most other resources and thus has a generalized and intrinsic value comes only later.

Parents usually expect their two-year-old child to repeat the information they give him (e.g., parents point at an object, call it by name and ask the child to repeat it). A successful repetition is usually followed by praise. Thus information is almost always paired with status, and consequently these two classes are hardly distinguishable. When the child broadens his social world and enters a peer group, he discovers criteria for status, other than information, such as physical strength. This new situation facilitates the differentiation of information from status.

A schematic representation of the differentiation of resource classes is given in Figure 2.2. In this figure a newly differentiated class is indicated by a double frame (highlighted in gray).

We have already noted that differentiation does not result in complete independence; since boundaries among classes are permeable, some

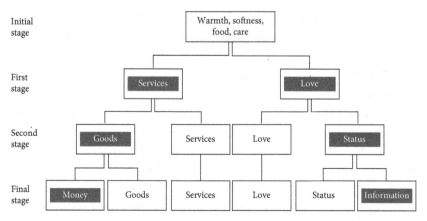

Figure 2.2 The differentiation of resource classes.

44   PART I ABRIDGEMENT OF *SOCIETAL STRUCTURES OF THE MIND*

relationship still exists. Children insist on receiving services from others long after being able to serve themselves, since being served is interpreted as being loved. Similarly an adult may prefer a restaurant where "service is good" (i.e., where love and concern is given in addition to service). The original non-differentiation of love and service is maintained to a large extent in sex, although some sexual relations are mainly viewed as an exchange of services while in some others, the exchange of love dominates. These examples suggest that service and love are not fully differentiated. The same is true for the second class which is differentiated from love, namely status. Messages such as "I am very proud of you" contain both love and status elements; more often than not, we tend to respect the people we do love. The close relationship between status and love is reflected in the fact that they often are combined in psychological studies under the variable "attraction," or "liking." However, some investigators like Jones, Bell and Aronson (1972) noted that the notion of "attraction" contains two distinct classes: social attractiveness which is equivalent to love, and competence which we call status.

The relationship between status and information is reflected in the common expectation that high status individuals are perceived as a more reliable source of information and advice than low status ones. Some evidence to this effect is provided by the finding that children tend to imitate more high-status adults (Baldwin, 1967, p. 431). The same phenomenon seems to take place among monkeys (Hall, 1963), and in experiments on conformity where statements attributed to prestigious individuals were more likely to be accepted (Asch, 1948; Lewis, 1941; Sherif, 1935b). Informal observation suggests that wise men are honored and the humble are assumed to be ignorant.

The less differentiated the resources the more likely they are to be conveyed together in the same behavior: rare is an expression of love which does not include some connotation of status or services, while a gift—the simultaneous giving of love and goods—is a less common occurrence, often reserved for special occasions.

The degree of permeability of any given boundary between two resources depends on the developmental sequence. Resources which are proximal in this sequence are more related, more likely to occur jointly, and will tend to be perceived as more similar than remote ones; love and status, for example, have more in common than love and money. This partial differentiation leads to an order among resource classes whereas complete differentiation would have resulted in independence among the classes and the structure of

THE DEVELOPMENT OF BASIC SOCIAL CONCEPTS   45

resources which will be presented and discussed in the next chapter would not have been developed.

Giving and Taking Away Resources

In discussing the development of resource classes we mainly referred to examples of behaviors in which resources are given by an act or to an object. We shall recall however that even when resources are still undifferentiated the infant already possesses the differentiation between acceptance and rejection; thus a resource can be taken away, as well as given. *Giving* is then defined as *increasing* the amount of resources available to the object; conversely, *taking away* is a *decrease* in the amount of resources available for the object. Thus, giving love expresses acceptance, friendship, and liking; taking away love means rejection, expressing disliking or hate. Giving status means expressing esteem and respect while taking away status is done by indicating disesteem by belittling or by giving a low rating. Cheating, misleading and deceiving are examples of taking away information: the deceived is left with less information than he had beforehand, while when being given information the amount of knowledge one possesses is increased. Taking away and giving goods or money are self-evident notions. For services, taking away means damaging the body (e.g., spanking) or the belongings of the object, while giving services would increase the object's physical comfort, or save him expenditure of energy, such as running an errand for him.

For taking away, as for giving, the boundaries between resources proximal in the developmental sequence are more permeable than those between remote resources. Thus the probability of taking away, simultaneously, two proximal resources is higher than a joint occurrence of taking away two remote resources. One may hit physically the hated person; the word "insult" conveys the taking away of both love and status; the confidence man is likely to take away both information and money. On the other hand, the thief is unlikely to express hate for his victim and physical assault does not go well together with cheating. Having differentiated between giving and taking away between self and other as objects and actors and among resource classes, the child is equipped with the necessary tools for classifying social actions. These differentiations yield a $2 \times 2 \times 2 = 8$ type of behaviors for each resource, or a total of $8 \times 6 = 48$ classes of interpersonal behavior. The ability to classify actions does not terminate social development, neither does it provide

46 PART I ABRIDGEMENT OF *SOCIETAL STRUCTURES OF THE MIND*

sufficient equipment for becoming a member of a given society. One should be able to tell whether a given action is appropriate and one should also realize that different people may hold different opinions about a given action. To the development of these notions we now turn.

Norms and Viewpoints

In the previous section we covered all the concepts necessary for classifying actions emitted in a given dyad, such as child–mother. Having acquired the differentiation between modes, actors, objects, and resources the child is able to attribute a meaning to what is actually done by himself and by his mother. He is also able to relate his behavior to the behavior of his mother. But any given dyadic relationship, or a role, includes more than the emission of actions. There are also expectations and wishes which characterize this relationship. They may be presented in terms of "What does mother want me to do?" "What do I want mother to do?" and then "What should I do?" and "What should mother do?" These questions provide a hint to an additional differentiation between self and other.

While the previous differentiations of actors and objects were based originally on sensoric–motoric feedback, the new differentiations depend on social feedback, i.e., on the reaction of the parent to the behavior of the child. It is precisely the previous development of the notions of actor and object, which has provided the cognitive tools necessary for relating the behavior of self to the behavior of other. In fairly normal conditions the reaction of the adult will tend to be contingent upon the proaction of the child. Certain proactions of the child will be followed by love giving behavior of the parent while certain other proactions will usually be followed by taking away behavior. If there is a certain consistency in the reaction of the adult, the child will come to expect this reaction. An attentive observer will notice that one-year-old or slightly older children often probe the proaction–reaction relationship by looking for the expected reactions as soon as they have initiated the proaction. Many little children's games, like peek-a-boo or superimposing hand, have the same goal: exercising the proaction–reaction sequence. To the grown-up these games may look somewhat boring, because of their utter predictability. For the young child their outcome is still uncertain and each confirmation becomes a source of delight.

THE DEVELOPMENT OF BASIC SOCIAL CONCEPTS   47

Predictability of the reaction means essentially that proaction is classified according to the reaction which follows it. Two important classes are: behaviors which are followed by mother's acceptance and those which are followed by rejection. This is the beginning of the notion of normative or *ideal behavior*. The occurrence of this development requires a certain consistency in the reactions to the child's behavior. When the reaction of the grown-up depends on his mood or on his relations to a third individual rather than on the actual behavior of the child, the child is not provided with an opportunity for differentiating between what ought to be done and what ought not to be done; proaction and reaction will tend to statistical independence, creating a random environment similar to the control condition in Rescorla's (1967) experimental design. But consistency alone is not a sufficient condition for differentiation to occur. When every action of the child is followed by punishment consistency is very high, but contingency is missing, and all the behaviors will be classified into one class of "ought not to be done." Perhaps the catatonic is the perfect example of such one-sided classification of behaviors. Through the process of consistent and contingent reaction, ideal or normative behavior becomes differentiated from actual behavior so that what ought to be done (in order to receive a reaction of giving) may or may not be identical with what is actually done. When such differentiation is possessed by the child, he is able to perceive himself tearing a book and at the same time classifying this behavior as "should not be done." On the basis of the two classes, *ideal* and *actual*, which emerge from the differentiation between levels of perception, we can define the concepts of expectation and aspiration. Both these notions are merely a projection of the actual and ideal levels into the future. Expectation refers to future actual behavior while aspiration is the future ideal behavior.

Again, this new differentiation between actual and ideal is linked to a previous differentiation—between self and other as actors. The ideal behavior is linked to the other as an actor, since it emerges from the mother's contingent behavior, while the actual is linked to the behaviors of the self; and again when differentiation between actual and ideal becomes more established it separates from the previous one and all four combinations take place. There is the actual behavior of self and the actual behavior of the other, i.e., what mother does and what I do. There is also the ideal behavior of the self and the ideal behavior of the other, i.e., what mother should do and what I should do.

An additional level of perception is the *desire* or the *wish*. Very early in his life the child becomes familiar with the experience that what *actually*

48   PART I ABRIDGEMENT OF *SOCIETAL STRUCTURES OF THE MIND*

happens does not always correspond to what he *desires*. For an infant, however, what he wishes is pleasurable and accepted; what he does not wish is painful and rejected. Hence the experience of a discrepancy between actual and wished for overlaps with the differentiation between acceptance and rejection. Moreover the discrepancy between actual and desired usually occurs when the other is the actor and the self is the object, since the infant is likely to do what he wishes, while mother may not always do what he wants. It is only with the onset of the ideal level that the child begins to do something against his own wishes. The child wants to wet his pants but his mother wants him to sit on the pot. In order to get mother's approval the child will sit on the pot, and now he is doing something that he does not wish to do. When this happens the early identity between wish and pleasure becomes untenable and the wish level emerges in its own right, as distinct from the actual and ideal ones.

When mother imposes her wishes on the child, the child realizes that what he wishes does not always correspond to what mother desires and a new differentiation begins to develop: the differentiation between *the viewpoint of the self and the viewpoint of the other*. When this differentiation is established, the child becomes able to realize that other individuals may differ from him in the way they see a given actual behavior, or in what they believe to be an appropriate behavior, i.e., the ideal level. This differentiation enables the child to develop and construct an internal model of the other individual. Any event has two perspectives now, and thus is classified twice; from his own point of view and from the other's point of view.

Differentiation between actual and ideal levels permits the evaluation of what is being done by comparing it to what ought to be done, and thus provides the individual with internal standards of behavior. It would hardly be possible to exaggerate the pervasive importance of moral judgment for the functioning of the individual and of human society as well. It is therefore not surprising that this topic has attracted the attention of theoreticians and investigators and has resulted in a very large body of literature. Some recent and comprehensive treatments have been provided by Aronfreed (1968) and Kohlberg (1969b).

The acquisition of the viewpoint of the other has often been considered as the hallmark of mature social communication, enabling a person to take into account the other's perceptions, feelings and needs. Asch (1958) stated that "the study of person cognition is, in good part, the study of the ways in which we observe and take into account perceptions, intentions, thoughts, and passions of others." In Heider's discussion on perception and communication (1958) differentiation between viewpoints is perceived as the core of the difference between persons and non-persons interaction, since it is only on the basis of this differentiation that we become aware of the fact that as much as we perceive, we are also the objects of the other's perception.

Investigating the development of the ability to take the viewpoint of the other, Miller et al. (1970) found an increase from the first to the fifth grade, leveling off afterward. While relatively little research was devoted to the development of the differentiation between viewpoints, there have been many studies of "assumed similarity" in which the perception of the subjects was compared with the perception they attribute to the other. The results (Byrne, 1969, pp. 42–44) suggest that differentiation between viewpoint is rather weak so that the perception ascribed to the other is more likely to be similar to the perception held by the self, than to this perception as reported by the other (i.e., real similarity).

With the differentiation between viewpoints we have concluded the review on the development of basic concepts of interpersonal communication in a child. Starting from the differentiation between modes, giving and taking away, we have discussed differentiation by actor and object, then differentiation of resources into six classes and, finally, the differentiations by level and viewpoint. In three of these differentiations, by actor, object and viewpoint, the differentiated classes have been indicated by the same terms of "self" and "other." In everyday language the structure of the sentence or the situation usually clarifies who is self and who is other in each one of these differentiations. If one says for example: "He thinks he was nice to me," it is clear that the actor is the other, the object is the self and the viewpoint is the other's. However when these terms are considered in isolation there may be some ambiguity as to who is called self and who is called other. Viewpoint of the "other," for example, may mean either the viewpoint of the actor or the viewpoint of the person observing the action, when observer and actor are not the same individual. To avoid confusion let us agree on the following convention. With regard to the actor the term "self" indicates that the action is done by the individual observing the action, the observer, while the term "other" pertains to the non-observer. When a subject reports about his own behavior, he is the observer and the actor and therefore his report pertains to behavior of the "self." For example when mothers are interviewed with respect to their children's behavior, the mother is the observer and she reports

50 PART I ABRIDGEMENT OF *SOCIETAL STRUCTURES OF THE MIND*

on the other's (her child's) behavior, so that the actor is the "other." When she reports on her behavior she refers to behavior of "self."

As to the differentiation by object, the term "self" pertains to behaviors of the actor which are directed towards himself while the term "other" denotes behaviors of the actor towards the non-actor. In both the following statements the object is the self: "My son usually considers himself as an excellent student" (my son gives status to himself); "I consider myself a competent mother" (I give status to myself). For the differentiation by viewpoint the terms "self" and "other" are denoted with respect to the actor. When the actor's point of view is reported we refer to it as the self's point of view while the term "other" refers to the non-actor's perception. Thus "Ron thinks he is doing fine at school" and "I think I did a good job" both pertain to the self's point of view. "Dan thinks his father would not like his new painting" and "I think my husband would approve of my approach" are both reports about the other's point of view.

In summary, the term "self" is equivalent to the observer, for differentiation by actor; it denotes the actor in object and viewpoint differentiations, while the term "other" will be equivalent to non-observer and to non-actor, respectively.

Environmental Conditions and the Development of Boundaries

So far we have described the essential dimensions required for the emergence of a mature person who is capable of communicating efficiently with his social environment. Although it is not in the scope of this book to describe the mechanisms by which these differentiations are acquired, we do have some thoughts in this line which we would like to share with the reader before leaving the topic of development.

As we have already stated, differentiation among conceptual elements (e.g., self and other) never results in complete independence. It follows that the child should learn an *appropriate degree* of differentiation rather than a complete one.

For any differentiation to occur, the child should be exposed to a great number of events belonging to the different classes. First, he learns to discriminate between specific instances of the classes, so that when the events are slightly changed discriminative behavior disappears. It is only after being

THE DEVELOPMENT OF BASIC SOCIAL CONCEPTS 51

exposed again and again to different instances of the same classes, that the child's discrimination becomes associated with the relevant elements which differentiate between the two classes. For example, the child is praised when sharing a cookie with another child and punished when taking it from him; then praise is contingent upon giving a toy, a kiss, etc., and punishment comes after hitting or taking a toy from the other. Gradually the elements of "taking away" and "giving" any resource become relevant. At the same time the child is being hugged strongly when getting love from parents, the hugging may sometimes be an unpleasant experience and the kisses may be pleasant—he learns that as much as "giving" and "taking away" behaviors results in differential reaction, they still sometimes appear simultaneously so that differentiation is not complete.

In this acquisition of boundaries with an appropriate degree of permeability, there is an interplay between the mechanisms of learning: imitation and differential reinforcement. The child imitates the differentiating behaviors of the adult by perceiving the appropriate situational cues which are associated with different behaviors. At the same time the child's own behavior is followed by differential rewards and punishment, a contingency which also facilitates differentiation. Parents will, for example, punish the child for taking away behaviors and will reward him for giving behaviors. In this manner they provide models of giving (reward) and taking away (punishment) behaviors, while, at the same time, exposing the child to differential reinforcements of these behaviors when emitted by him.

The relationship among behavioral classes, or the appropriate degree of differentiation, is learned by imitation and reinforcement. The child observes that certain classes of behaviors are emitted simultaneously or successively by the model while the joint occurrence of certain other classes is rare. Likewise, certain behaviors emitted by himself result in similar responses while certain others produce differential responses. Reinforcements as well as punishments are mostly administered by parents on an intermittent schedule. More than this, the same behaviors may sometimes be punished and sometimes rewarded, although some behaviors would be reinforced most of the time and some others would mostly result in punishment. These "errors" in the schedule leave some relationship between differentiated classes while at the same time serve to stabilize the degree of differentiation, in its reflection on the frequency of emitting differential behaviors in different situations (Aronfreed, 1968, p. 23).

52 PART I ABRIDGEMENT OF *SOCIETAL STRUCTURES OF THE MIND*

The two learning models, imitation and reinforcement, may lead to oppo-site predictions about change in the child's behavior. Consider, for example, a child who has been punished for beating his younger brother (taking away services). The imitation model predicts an increase in taking away behavior of the child, who will imitate the aggressive punitive parent. The reinforce-ment model, on the other hand, predicts a decrease of the punished behavior. A solution to this dilemma may be provided by the findings of Sears et al. (1957, Ch. 7). Their results suggest that if the child takes away a service (e.g., beating) and he is punished by his parents by taking away the same resource from him (physical punishment) the imitation model will prevail and the child will show high frequency of taking away services. If, on the other hand, punishment consists of taking away from the child a *different* resource, such as status ("you are a bad boy") then the reinforcement model will operate, with consequent low frequency of the punished behavior. This interpreta-tion of Sears' findings suggests that imitation is more resource-specific than reinforcement. Both mechanisms, however, require that the differentiation to be learned by the child pre-exists in the adult. If, in the behavior of the parents, giving and taking away are not well differentiated, it will be difficult for the child to acquire such a differentiation, since both imitation and dif-ferential reinforcement will produce poor differentiation. Evidence on this point is provided by McDavid and Schroder (1957). These authors subjected delinquent and non-delinquent adolescents to a test of interpreting interper-sonal events in terms of success and failure or positive and negative. They found that normal boys differentiate well between positive and negative events, while delinquent boys did not differentiate at all. The author explains this difference in differentiation as a result of inconsistency of discipline. Other dimensions are similarly affected by parent–child interaction: when the behavior of the parents is determined by their own needs, rather than by those of the child, differentiation between self and other as objects may be impaired; likewise a child receiving money or goods where love and status would be appropriate, and vice versa, may experience difficulties in differentiating among resources.

Frustration and Delay of Reinforcement

We have suggested that several differentiations are linked, at their onset, to the basic differentiation between giving and taking away. In particular, we

THE DEVELOPMENT OF BASIC SOCIAL CONCEPTS   53

have said that self as an actor toward self is linked to giving or acceptance (a pleasurable sensation) while other as an actor toward self is rejected. The differentiation between ideal and actual is related to giving behavior of the other toward self and non-ideal consists of all behaviors which are followed by taking away reactions by the other toward self (i.e., punishment administered by the parents). At this point the ideal of the other and the ideal of the self are not differentiated. It is only when the child realizes that the viewpoint of the other may be different from his that the other may be perceived as having a different ideal.

Viewpoint is a most abstract notion which cannot be differentiated either by imitation or by differential reinforcement. If the parent reinforces behavior which is appropriate from his point of view this is perceived by the child as an ideal behavior, but not as a difference in opinion. It is only in situations of conflict between the parents and himself that the child may realize different viewpoints. When the child asks for candy just before mealtime and the mother refuses, the child is exposed to different opinions about having candy. If he does not get the candy he is frustrated, if he gets it there is no confrontation with a different viewpoint. Thus, through repeated instances of frustration and conflicts with other people, the differentiation between viewpoints is acquired. Moreover, the schedule of differential reinforcement and punishments exposes the child to many frustrations so that other differentiations involve frustration as well. We may conclude then, that exposure to frustration is a necessary condition for differentiation to develop and strengthen. A child who is never exposed to refusal will not develop differentiation between actual and ideal and between his viewpoint and the other's viewpoint. Children at the age of one to three years old are said to be negativistic. They reject almost any request coming from other persons. One has the impression that they are "seeking" disapproval from the parents; they do things that they know would result in negative response. This negativistic behavior may be interpreted as an exercise for establishing the differentiation of the self-viewpoint from that of the other. In Piaget's terminology, a new schema is developed and there is an intrinsic motivation to exercise it until it is established. Indeed, past the third year negativistic behavior decreases and the child does not deliberately confront himself with frustrating situations. Still many situations embed frustrating elements for children as well as for adults. Any situation in which reinforcement is delayed is frustrating (Bandura & Walters, 1963). We do see, however, an increased ability in children to accept a delay of reinforcement without too much distress. For this to

54 PART I ABRIDGEMENT OF *SOCIETAL STRUCTURES OF THE MIND*

happen the child should have accumulated the resources of love and status, so that he may constitute an independent source of resources for himself. He should be able to give love and status to himself, as intermediate reinforcement, while working toward a delayed reward. The separation of the ideal behavior from the other's reaction (i.e., internalizing it) is a necessary condition for such self-reinforcement, and thus is a prerequisite for long-term delay of reward.

Summary

Cognitive growth consists of a sequence of differentiations and generalizations, the latter being a by-product of the former. Generalization, which follows differentiation, is altogether different from the initial state of non-differentiation. Basic cognitive elements for interpersonal relations are acquired mainly through a process of binary division. These elements, however, are never fully differentiated, so that some relationship between them remains. Consequently the boundaries among cognitive classes are permeable. The closer two classes are in the developmental sequence the more permeable will be the boundary between them.

Six basic dimensions or facets, each differentiated into elements, underlay the development of the classes essential to the cognition of social events. The first dimension, the *mode* or *direction*, appears differentiated from the beginning of the infant's life; it contains the two elements of *giving* (acceptance) and *taking away* (rejection). Consequently the newborn infant is capable of sorting events into two classes: events which are pleasurable are categorized into the class of giving while painful events are classified as taking away. The existence of cognitive classes in the infant is inferred from the fact that certain events are followed by the same or similar responses while certain others are met with different reactions.

The second dimension, the actor (who is doing the action), is differentiated into the elements of *self* and *other*. Its acquisition is based on the motoric feedback that the infant gets when he is the doer of the action, and which is missing when the other is the actor. Within a short period of time a third differentiation occurs resulting in acquisition of the notion *object* or recipient of behavior; again the elements are *self* and *other*. This dimension is based on sensoric feedback. When the infant is feeding himself, he can taste the food; when he feeds his mother, the motoric feedback still exists, but no gustatory

THE DEVELOPMENT OF BASIC SOCIAL CONCEPTS 55

sensation follows. These two differentiations between self and other as actors and objects are exercised and sharpened by attaching their elements to the previously established elements of acceptance and rejection. Self as an actor and other as an object are accepted; while other being the actor and self being its object are rejected. This attachment results in the "negativistic" period, evident in children aged one to three years.

On the basis of the differentiation between self and other as actor, a new dimension starts its development when the child is required to do things, i.e., to serve himself, and at the same time these actions are reinforced by the mother's love. Thus *interpersonal resources* start to be formed into distinct classes with the differentiation between *love* and *services*. Next, *goods* are differentiated from services and *status* from love. Later, *information* and *money* become distinct classes. Altogether six classes of resources become available for classifying social events.

The four dimensions of mode, actor, object and resources result in $2 \times 2 \times 2 \times 6 = 48$ classes of social actions in a dyad. But any given social interaction consists of more than emission of actions. There are wishes, expectations and norms of each person. To account for these aspects two additional dimensions are developed: the *level* of an event may be either *actual* (what is actually done) or *ideal* (what should be done). For the infant, the wished and ideal are equivalent. They become differentiated when the child is required to do things (to be the actor) against his wishes.

The last dimension, the *viewpoint*, results from yet another differentiation between *self* and *other*; the child learns that an event may be perceived differently by him and by the other; having candy before a meal may be a desirable event for him but not for his mother. These two last dimensions increase the number of social cognitive classes to 192, each defined by one element from each dimension.

None of the notions proposed here to account for the cognitive development of social interaction is novel. They are all current in psychological literature and have been the object of many studies. Yet there is some virtue in bringing them together in a systematic manner and in showing that a large number of classes can be accounted for by the combination of a few basic notions. Laying bare the component elements of cognitive classes does more than just provide more parsimonious definition; it also reveals their similarities and differences. Consider, for example, the notion of self-esteem, central to the brilliant study of Coopersmith (1967), who investigated both its social consequences and its socialization antecedents. For the reader of this chapter it will be clear that self-esteem is a complex notion involving an actor, a mode (giving), a resource (status) and an object (self). Translating self-esteem into "the actor gives status to self" may appear as merely pedantic, but immediately it invites hypotheses regarding the relationship between this cognitive class and similar ones, differing from it in actor, mode, resource or object, such as getting status from other or taking away status from self. Such relationships among cognitive classes are considered in the next chapter.

3

From Developmental Sequence to Adult Structure

Overview

Having defined "structure" as "a configuration of classes in a space of stated coordinates" (Chapter 1), we have, in Chapter 2, proceeded to spell out basic cognitive classes of social events by identifying the coordinates along which they become differentiated. We have thus considered two of the notions appearing in the definition of structure—classes and coordinates. In the present chapter we turn to examine the third notion: the configuration of classes. In this configuration certain classes are nearer to each other while certain others are more distant. We are already familiar with a psychological interpretation of distance: the nearer two classes are, the more likely they are to be similar in meaning, to influence each other, and to occur jointly in interpersonal situations.

We propose that the spatial arrangement of the classes originates from the sequence in which various differentiations develop in the child. In this chapter we shall derive structural hypotheses from the development sequence and then examine pertinent results. The instruments and the procedures by which these data were collected are described in Appendix A. The reader who is interested in methodology may wish to consult this appendix before proceeding with the findings.

The sequence of differentiations has been mentioned in the previous chapter only to the extent that this was necessary in describing the various dimensions. However, in view of its importance in determining the adult's structure, it becomes appropriate to begin this chapter with a more systematic treatment of the developmental sequence.

Social Behavior as Resource Exchange. Kjell Yngve Törnblom and Ali Kazemi, Oxford University Press.
© Oxford University Press 2023. DOI: 10.1093/oso/9780190066994.003.0004

Differentiation Sequences

It was already noted that for some differentiation to develop, certain others should have already been established, so that the latter should occur at an earlier age than the former. It seems improbable that all social dimensions develop in a single sequence, one after the other. Most likely, some differentiations occur almost simultaneously and fairly independently of one another. Therefore we shall first consider some partial sequences and then discuss the relationship among them. For purposes of convenience and clarity we treat each differentiation as an all-or-none phenomenon, as if it were established at a given point in the developmental sequence. Obviously, this presentation grossly simplifies the developmental process. It is more accurate to conceive each differentiation as a process in time, consisting of a gradual and slow buildup of a boundary between classes, through the repeated occurrence of events which reinforce the boundary, until it becomes well established and its permeability stabilizes. Thus the statement that differentiation B follows differentiation A should be understood to mean that the onset of B follows the onset of A; it is quite likely, however, that the beginning of B will occur *before* the stabilization of A.

Let us first examine and describe separately two partial sequences of differentiations, and then link them into a more complete picture. The first sequence includes the differentiations by mode, object, and resources (love and status). The second involves the differentiation by actor, level, and viewpoint. We shall refer to the first sequence as a *behavioral* one; the second will be called a *perceptual* sequence.

The Behavioral Sequence

The initial differentiation in this sequence results in the two classes of giving and taking away, which first appear in the primitive form of accepting and rejecting at a physiological level. Observation on neonates suggests that positive responses or approach behavior is present from the first minute after birth while withdrawal or rejection develops later. Schaller and Emlen (1962, cited by Salzen, 1970) have found that avoidance responses are absent at first in precocial birds and appear by about ten hours after birth. They also find that for an altricial species, all objects were accepted and given positive rather than negative response until several days after birth. The observation that approach precedes avoidance response is also evident in imprinting (Lorenz, 1935) when precocial birds follow any object present immediately after emerging from the egg. As to the human neonate, the Darwinian reflex appears shortly after birth and when it disappears, intentional grasping starts to develop with a chronological overlapping of the two (Halverson, 1936). Little is known about early avoidance behavior. On a rational level, one should approach objects in order to survive and only later reject those things which interfere with survival. Thus the neonate approaches the nipple and swallows the milk; it is only when he is satiated that he drops the nipple or gets rid of an excess amount of milk.

The elementary classification of events in terms of pleasant–unpleasant (acceptance and rejection) is necessary before the notions of actor and object become relevant and then meaningful. At the same time the development of the notion to whom (self or other) an action is directed precedes the differentiation of the resources involved. While differentiation by object can develop in the dyadic interaction of infant–mother, the latter differentiation between status and love requires the additional infant–father role. It is only with the ability to differentiate between same-sexed and different-sexed roles that the differentiation between love and status can be developed.

In view of these considerations it is suggested that in the behavioral sequence differentiation between giving and taking will occur first, followed by differentiation between self and other as objects, while status and affect are the last to be differentiated. The three stages of this proposed sequence are represented, schematically, in Figure 3.1. In this figure each successive binary division is built on the previous one. The inner circle represents the first differentiation between giving and taking away. At the next stage (second circle from the center of the figure) the differentiation between self and other as objects is superimposed on the previous one. Thus, while in the first stage only the two simple classes of giving and taking away are available, at the completion of the second stage the repertoire of behavioral classes is doubled to four: giving to and taking from other, giving to and taking from self. At this second stage the differentiation of resources has probably yet to begin so that the four behavioral classes involve a single undifferentiated resource. When the first differentiation between resources occurs, the number of behavioral classes is doubled again to eight. The differentiation between status and love is represented in the third circle of Figure 3.1. The eight classes of behavior resulting from the three stages are given in the outer circle of the figure.

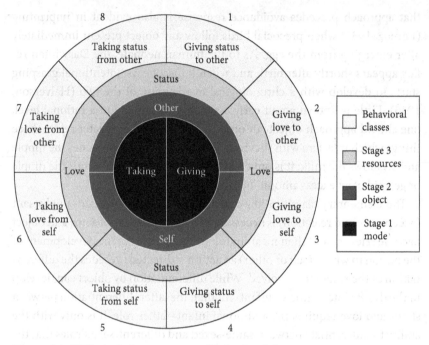

Figure 3.1 Differentiation sequence of behavioral classes.

The reader will probably wonder why we have chosen love and status as an example for resource differentiation, even though the distinction of services from love was said to appear earlier. The only reason for this choice was the fact that the relationship between status and love had been studied intensively by the first author before the classification of resources was developed. Consequently the order among the behavioral classes, represented in the outer circle of Figure 3.1, was empirically studied mainly with respect to love and status. Its extension to other resources will be discussed later.

Let us now turn to the next partial sequence, the perceptual one.

The Perceptual Sequence

The perceptual sequence consists of differentiations by actors, levels and viewpoints. As suggested earlier the differentiation between self and non-self, as actors, begins when the child acquires the ability to perform actions that had been previously performed by the mother. He then realizes that his behavior and his mother's behavior are not one and the same thing. Actors differentiation provides the child with his first two roles: his role toward his mother and the role of the mother toward him. The differentiation between actual and ideal level could not be easily made before actors are differentiated. Ideal behavior, in its elementary form, is that behavior of the child which is followed by acceptance behavior of the adult. It requires an ability to distinguish between the two actors, the child and the adult. The realization that "what mother wants me to do" may be different from "what I want to do," provides the beginning of the third differentiation between the viewpoint of the actor and the viewpoint of the other. If indeed, differentiation by level requires prior differentiation by actor and contains the beginning of differentiation by viewpoints, the following sequence of development will be sustained: Non-self as actor is differentiated from self, then ideal behavior is differentiated from actual behavior and, finally, the viewpoint of the other becomes differentiated from the point of view of the self. Initially, the child perceives himself as the actor of everything being done, so that self, as actor, and his viewpoint are primary elements of the perceptual dimensions; so is the actual level which precedes the ideal one.

These elements, however, become meaningful only after they become differentiated from the other, secondary elements. As Piaget (1954, p. 237) has noted "Precisely because he feels omnipotent, the child cannot yet contrast his own self with the external world."

The three stages of the perceptual sequence are represented in Figure 3.2. The inner circle indicates differentiation by actor, between self and other or, more precisely, between the actions of the observer and those of the non-observer. Moving away from the center, the next circle shows how the differentiation by actor subdivides according to the level—actual and ideal, so that four perceptual categories are now available: the actual and ideal behavior of self as well as the actual and ideal behavior of the other. The third circle indicates the further subdivision by viewpoint: the point of view of the person doing the action, the actor, becomes discriminated from the viewpoint of the other, the non-actor. The outer circle represents the eight perceptual classes, resulting from the three-stage-process of successive binary divisions.

The concept of observer is not included in this developmental scheme. A child learns to differentiate between actors, objects, modes, etc., only after *becoming* an observer. But no differentiation between observers occurs at any stage of development. What in common parlance is often described

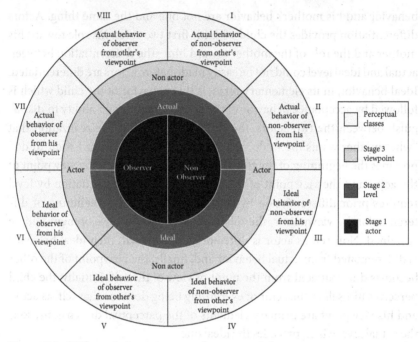

Figure 3.2 Differentiation sequence of perceptual classes.
Observer as actor = the action is emitted by the person who reports it.
Non-observer as actor = the action is emitted by the "other," not by the person reporting it.
Viewpoint of actor = the viewpoint of the person emitting the action.
Viewpoint of non-actor = the viewpoint of the "other," the person who did not emit the action.

as differentiation between observers is in fact differentiation between points of view of the same observer. The realization that so many classes of observations are all possessed by one observer provides a common denominator to the various differentiations. Accordingly, we can perceive the notion "observer" as the source of a certain degree of unity and integration maintained by the individual with respect to the enormous variety of social events that are perceived by him.

Each behavioral class results from the combination of mode and object with one of the resource classes. A perceptual class, on the other hand, is the combination of actor, level and viewpoint. This division of the various interpersonal dimensions into behavioral and perceptual sequence is useful for analytic purposes; it should not, however, obscure the fact that they are both parts of the same interpersonal structure. Each cognition of a social event results from the combination of a given behavior, a given resource and

FROM DEVELOPMENTAL SEQUENCE TO ADULT STRUCTURE   63

Table 3.1 Developmental Sequence of Differentiations in the
Interpersonal Domain

Behavioral Dimensions	Resources	Perceptual Dimensions
Mode (giving vs. taking)	Love Services	Actor (observer vs. non-observer)
Object (self vs. other)	Status	Level (actual vs. ideal)
	Information Goods Money	Viewpoint (actor vs. non-actor)

a given perception. In view of this unity it appears justified to consider the differentiation sequence as a whole. This is done in Table 3.1. Differentiations are listed according to their approximate time of occurrence, those at the top appearing earlier than those at the bottom of the table.

The Behavioral Structure

Let us begin with a very simple structure, which is obtained by combining the *mode* of an action (i.e., the direction) and its *object* in a dyadic interaction for a given constant *resource*. The mode has two elements—giving and taking away; the elements of the object are self and other. Thus four behavioral classes are obtained by all the possible combinations of the four elements: giving to other, giving to self, taking away from self and taking away from other, *one* given resource (love, status, etc.). Each one of the four classes has one element in common with two of the other classes, and no element in common with the fourth class. For example, "giving to self" has the *mode* in common with "giving to other" while sharing the *object* with "taking away from self." Between "giving to self" and "taking away from other" neither mode nor object are shared. By keeping the resource constant and varying only mode and object we are, in effect, considering the first two stages of the sequence depicted in Figure 3.1 and ignoring the third stage of differentiation between the resources of love and status.

Neighboring classes may either share the object or differ in the mode, or they may share the mode and differ in the object. Thus, the similarity between two given classes may be due either to the mode or to the object. When the object changes and the mode is shared, the relationship between two

64 PART I ABRIDGEMENT OF *SOCIETAL STRUCTURES OF THE MIND*

classes indicates how much similarity is perceived, by a given observer, between behavior toward self and the behavior toward the other. A high positive relationship (measured by correlation coefficient) will indicate weak differentiation between self and other as objects; low correlation will be taken as indicator for strong differentiation.

SELF AND OTHER. The idea that in interpersonal situations one relates to himself as well as to other persons is reflected in the literature by concepts such as self-acceptance (giving love to self), self-hatred (taking away love from self), and self-esteem (giving status to self). Considerable attention has been devoted to the relationship between attitudes toward self and toward other. There seems to be an agreement among clinicians that a person who accepts himself will also accept others (Fromm, 1939; Homey, 1939; Rogers, 1951). Adler (1926) adds that those who feel inferior depreciate others. Indeed, Berger (1952), Crandall and Bellugi (1954), Omwake (1954), and Stock (1949) all report a positive relationship between self-acceptance and acceptance of others; Henry (1956) found a positive correlation between tendencies toward blaming one's self and blaming others. Similar results are reported by Wylie (1961, pp. 235–240), in a review of twenty-one studies on the relationship between acceptance of self and of other. It is, however, unfortunate that no data were provided in these studies for the relationship between acceptance and rejection, as well as for love and status. Another interesting point which deserves attention is whether the size of the correlation tends to change systematically in accordance with different "others." In the studies reported by Wylie, subjects were asked to rate a wide range of "others"—from parents to strangers. Since, however, they used different instruments, such comparison is not possible. We would hypothesize that the more intimate the relationship the weaker the differentiation between self and other; therefore the higher the intimacy with the other, the higher will be the correlation between the relation toward him and toward self.

GIVING AND TAKING. When the object of an action is kept constant while the mode changes, the correlation between the two classes will indicate the amount of differentiation between "giving" and "taking away." Low differentiation results in ambivalence, defined in Webster's Dictionary as "simultaneous attraction toward and repulsion from an object, person or action." In the case of complete lack of ambivalence, the relationship between loving and hating the same person (or self) would be perfect and negative. To avoid negative correlations which are inconvenient to analyze we can simply correlate the degree of *presence* of love with the degree of *absence* of hate. Then a complete absence of ambivalence will be indicated by a positive correlation of 1, and a negative coefficient will indicate that the more we love a person the more we hate him.

Although the notion "ambivalence" recurs in theories of personality and psychopathology, we do not know of empirical studies on it. On the contrary, research tools such as personality inventories and questionnaires were constructed with the implicit assumption of non-ambivalence. Acceptance and rejection are usually used as two poles of the same dimension. Thus, when the subject is asked to indicate how much he likes a person, on a scale which ranges from dislike to like, by definition the more he likes the less he dislikes. It is only when two separate scales are provided that the relationship between liking and disliking can be studied.

The intercorrelations of the four basic behavioral classes provide us with the possibility to investigate the amount of differentiation between objects as well as between modes. To complete the analysis we should also consider the relationship between the classes which do not share any elements, i.e., between giving to other and taking away from self, as well as between giving to self and taking away from other.

We have predicted that classes sharing one element, which thus are neighbors in the circular order, will be correlated more than classes which have no element in common. This prediction is supported by the intercorrelations among the four behavioral classes for love as well as for status, which were obtained from different samples. (See Appendix A for a description of instrument and procedure.)

In Table 3.2 examples from three different cultures, Missouri, Israel, and Senegal, are given. As indicated in the left column, the samples differ with respect to the roles, level (idea actual), and viewpoint (actor, non-actor). In spite of these differences, the hypothesis that classes which share the same element correlate higher than classes differing in all elements, is confirmed in all samples. Consequently, we may conclude that the structure of behavioral classes is constant across cultures, roles, levels and viewpoint.

In each row the highest correlations are situated on either side of the main diagonal, while the coefficient which is most removed from the diagonal is usually the lowest in the row. There is one deviation from this pattern in the first example, and a couple of them in the third one. These examples were chosen because they provide good illustrations of the predicted structural pattern. Nevertheless, the total frequency of deviation in all data available so

66 PART I ABRIDGEMENT OF *SOCIETAL STRUCTURES OF THE MIND*

Table 3.2 Examples of Intercorrelation Among Types of Behavior for Love and for Status in Different Roles and Cultures (Samples of Normal Subjects)

Population of Subjects and Role	Sample Size	Mode	Object		Resource							
					Love				Status			
					1	2	3	4	1	2	3	4
Columbia, Mo. High school male pupils. Role of father to son. Actual level, viewpoint of subject.	46	Giving to	Other	1	—				—			
		Giving to (Not)	Self	2	.66	—			.12	—		
		Taking from (Not)	Self	3	.13	.27	—		.02	.05	—	
		Taking from	Other	4	.39	.31	.53	—	.46	.02	.37	—
Jerusalem, Israel Married females. Role of wife to husband. Ideal level, viewpoint of other.	633	Giving to	Other	1	—				—			
		Giving to (Not)	Self	2	.23	—			.19	—		
		Taking from (Not)	Self	3	.01	.08	—		.03	.15	—	
		Taking from	Other	4	.20	.00	.14	—	.30	.01	.25	—
Dakar, Senegal females. Role of father to daughter. Ideal level, viewpoint of subject.	50	Giving to	Other	1	—				—			
		Giving to (Not)	Self	2	.43	—			.10	—		
		Taking from (Not)	Self	3	.29	.40	—		−.17	.01	—	
		Taking from	Other	4	.40	.67	.37	—	−.07	.00	.22	—

far remains well below chance level: the hypothesis is confirmed in 529 out of 640 intercorrelations.

Relationship Between Giving to and Taking Away from Self and Other

Earlier we suggested that it would be interesting to investigate separately the relationship between acceptance of self and of other and between rejection of self and of other. Re-examination of Table 3.2 does not indicate any differences. Out of six possible comparisons, three coefficients are higher for "giving," and three are higher for "taking away."

Another interesting question is whether people are more ambivalent toward others or toward themselves. Again we can answer this question by re-examining the six patterns of intercorrelations in Table 3.2. The

FROM DEVELOPMENTAL SEQUENCE TO ADULT STRUCTURE 67

intercorrelation between variables 1 and 4 represents the amount of ambivalence toward others, and the intercorrelation between variables 2 and 3 indicates ambivalence toward the self. We shall remember that the higher the coefficient the lower the ambivalence. In the Missouri and Israeli samples all correlations between giving to, and taking away from self are lower than the corresponding ones pertaining to attitudes toward other. There is more ambivalence toward self than toward other in these two samples, although there is a considerable amount of ambivalence directed toward significant others (the correlations are far from approaching 1). In the Senegal sample a similar amount of ambivalence is directed toward self as toward others.

Relationships Between Love and Status

In the literature concerning the relationship between self and other, status and love are often treated as equivalent notions. Measures of regard, esteem, liking, evaluation and rating, are all considered to tap the notion of "acceptance." Since we consider status (esteem, regard) and love (acceptance, liking) as two different interpersonal resources, we shall examine the similarity and difference between behavioral classes involving each one of them.

The data of Table 3.2 suggest that the structure of behavioral classes remains essentially the same for status as for love. There are, however, certain fairly systematic differences between the correlations for love and those for status, which are implicitly suggested by the development sequence depicted in Figure 3.1. In this figure behavior toward self and behavior toward other are proximal for love but more apart for status. If we interpret proximity as indicating less differentiation or stronger relationship, it follows that the correlation between self and other should be higher for love than for status. A quick glance at Table 3.2 shows that this is usually the case. There is, however, one exception in the Israeli data where the correlation between taking away from self and from other is higher for status than for love. In the set of data available, 55 out of 80 possible comparisons confirmed the hypothesis that differentiation between self and other as object is higher for behaviors involving status than for those involving transmission of love. The probability of getting this result by chance is .0014 as computed by Sign Test.

The sequence of development depicted in Figure 3.1 also suggests that the correlation between giving and taking away will be higher for status than for love, since giving and taking away status are neighbors in the figure, while

68 PART I ABRIDGEMENT OF *SOCIETAL STRUCTURES OF THE MIND*

giving and taking away love are removed from one another. Higher correlation indicates less ambivalence, so that ambivalence would be more profound for love than for status. Indeed, the term ambivalence, in psychological literature mainly refers to expressions of love and hate. There is no support for this hypothesis in the examples given in Table 3.2. Other data of this type show a slight tendency in the predicted direction, but not strong enough to be significant.

We have repeatedly suggested that the structure of the adult reflects the pattern of development in childhood. Thus, a developmental explanation should be provided for the noted difference between the behaviors of love and status. Status, as a distinct resource class, became differentiated from love, and therefore emerged later in the developmental sequence. The boundaries between love and status appear after the differentiations between giving and taking away, as well as between self and other as objects, have begun to be firmly established. Therefore these differentiations are stronger for status than for love. Apparently, each resource picks up the degree of differentiation between behavioral classes which exist when this resource becomes an autonomous class. If this is the case, one can expect that resources like information, goods and money, which occur after status, will exhibit even a stronger differentiation among behaviors. Support for this prediction is found in a study done by Meir Teichman. The subjects were 30 advanced undergraduate and graduate students from the University of Missouri, who were participating in a group task required by their coursework. They were asked to state their expectations regarding the behavior of two co-workers, the one they preferred most and the one they preferred least as a partner. Six classes of behavior were studied: Giving and taking away love, status, and information (see Appendix E). The correlations between giving and taking away of each resource are presented in Table 3.3.

For both the most and the least preferred co-worker the correlation is lowest for love, increases for status and is highest for information. Remembering that giving has been correlated with not-taking so that the higher the correlation the less the ambivalence, these results indicate that the strongest ambivalence is found in love, followed in decreasing order by status and then by information. There is more ambivalence (lower correlation) in the expectations toward the most preferred co-worker than toward the least preferred one; this difference, given in the right-most column of Table 3.3, is largest for love, declines for status and closely approaches zero for information. The stronger ambivalence toward the most preferred co-worker

FROM DEVELOPMENTAL SEQUENCE TO ADULT STRUCTURE 69

Table 3.3 Correlation Between Giving and Taking for Various Resources in the Expected Behavior of Most and Least Preferred Co-Worker

Resource	Most Preferred Co-Worker	Least Preferred Co-Worker	Difference (Least Less Most)
Love	−.13	.21	.34
Status	.11	.36	.25
Information	.39	.40	.01

supports the previously suggested hypothesis, that the more intimate the relationship to other the stronger will be the ambivalence.

Love and Status Behaviors Combined

We expect those behavioral classes which are nearer to each other to be more related than classes farther apart. Let us now see whether this hypothesis is supported by data.

Table 3.4 contains two examples out of the many available matrices of correlations for the eight behavioral classes of love and status. These two examples are again chosen from different cultures and roles. The order resulting from the developmental sequence is well reflected in both matrices. Behavioral classes which are close in the order correlate higher than remote classes. The coefficients are high near the main diagonal; they decrease and then increase again. Let us examine the first row of the left matrix (Israeli subjects): the coefficients decrease as one moves from the first column to the right, reach the lowest point in column 5, then increase again gradually. Thus class 1 correlates most with its two neighbors, classes 2 and 8. In the second row, the highest correlations are again situated next to the diagonal cell, and again the pattern of gradual decreasing and increasing is sustained. The same is true for all other rows, as well as for the second matrix (Missouri subjects) on the right side of the table. There are four deviations from the predicted order of size of correlations in the Israeli sample and six in the Missouri sample. These two examples differ not only with respect to the culture but also in sex and age of subjects, as well as in the role and in the viewpoint. Apparently, these differences do not change the cognitive structure of behaviors involving love and status. Later we shall examine some aspects of

Table 3.4 Examples of Intercorrelation Among Behaviors of Love and Status

					Population, Sample and Role															
	Mode	Object	Resource		633 Married Males, Jerusalem, Israel. Role of Husband to Wife. Actual Level Viewpoint of Other.								47 High School Female Pupils. Role of Daughter to Father. Actual Level, Viewpoint of Subject.							
					1	2	3	4	5	6	7	8	1	2	3	4	5	6	7	8
	Giving	Other	Status	1	—								—							
	Giving	Other	Love	2	.76	—							.71	—						
	Giving	Self	Love	3	.44	.40	—						.64	.71	—					
	Giving	Self	Status	4	.34	.27	.59	—					.48	.39	.50	—				
(Not)	Taking	Self	Status	5	.11	.07	.14	.19	—				.16	.15	.30	.16	—			
(Not)	Taking	Self	Love	6	.17	.17	.20	.13	.45	—			.02	.00	.11	.15	.67	—		
(Not)	Taking	Other	Love	7	.41	.34	.11	.00	.31	.34	—		.23	.10	.14	.00	.28	.42	—	
(Not)	Taking	Other	Status	8	.51	.38	.19	,01	.29	.34	.65	—	.37	.15	.25	.02	.37	.46	.66	—

FROM DEVELOPMENTAL SEQUENCE TO ADULT STRUCTURE   71

the structure which are influenced by these factors; the order of the classes, however, remains constant for all the normal subjects that were investigated. It follows the pattern emerging from the developmental sequence of differentiation illustrated in Figure 3.1.

Some Metatheoretical Considerations

This point in our exposition appears appropriate for a brief methodological aside. The reader who is not interested may skip this section without loss of continuity.

We have predicted the relationship among the four behavioral classes (for a given resource) from their similarity in the facet elements defining these classes. Thus classes having the same mode or the same object were predicted as more related than classes having neither in common. In doing so we have applied the *principle of contiguity* (Foa, 1958a, 1965) which states that variables more similar in their conceptual elements will be more related empirically. This principle does not assume that all the coordinates will have a similar degree of differentiation. If the differentiation among elements of facet A, for example, is much stronger than for the elements of facets B and C, then variables differing in the elements of A but alike in B and C will correlate less than variables alike in A but differing in both B and C. Therefore, a structure predicted from the principle of contiguity is assumed to have as many dimensions as the number of facets which define the variables. In our case this principle was adequate for proposing a circular, i.e., a *two*-dimensional structure for the four behavioral classes defined by the elements of *two* facets.

When, however, behaviors of love and of status were considered together, three facets (mode, object and resource) were involved in the definition of the eight classes. The contiguity principle would have then suggested a three-dimensional structure. Yet in Figure 3.1 the eight variables are ordered in the two-dimensional space of a circle rather than in a cubical one. A three-facet structure yields a situation in which any given variable shares two elements with three other classes, while in a circular order each variable has only two neighboring classes. Thus some criterion is required for deciding which of the *three* classes will be neighbors and which will not; according to the contiguity principle, they all would be neighbors. Such a criterion is provided by the notion of *semantic principle components* (Foa, 1961, 1965) which brings into the picture the notion of a hierarchical relationship among the facets.

72 PART I ABRIDGEMENT OF *SOCIETAL STRUCTURES OF THE MIND*

SEMANTIC PRINCIPAL COMPONENTS. Let us consider a set of eight variables defined by three facets, each facet having two elements. One element of Facet A will be indicated by a1, and the other element by a2; in the same way we can indicate the elements of Facets B and C, and denote the variables as follows:

1. a1b1c1
2. a1b1c2
3. a1b2c2
4. a1b2c1
5. a2b2c1
6. a2b2c2
7. a2b1c2
8. a2b1c1

There are several different ways to order these variables in a circle. The problem is how to predict a particular order. Let us suppose, for the sake of argument, that we predict the above order. In this order, Facet A behaves as the first semantic principal component; it changes value only once. Facet B behaves as the second component; it changes value twice. Facet C behaves as the fourth component; it changes value four times.

Reversing the argument, one can now say that knowledge of the facet components tells a good deal about the order of the variables, but not everything. An alternative order, which preserves the components, may indeed be obtained by interchanging, in the above order, Variable 1 with Variable 2, Variable 3 with Variable 4, and so on, as follows:

2.   a1b1c2
1.   a1b1c1
4.   a1b2c1
3.   a1b2c2
6.   a2b2c2
5.   a2b2c1
8.   a2b1c1
7.   a2b1c2

To determine a unique order it is also necessary to identify the first variable of the order. If the first variable is a1b1c1, then the alternative order given above is ruled out. Identification of the first variable is also required for differentiating between the first and the second components. Since the proposed order is circular, one could otherwise start, for example from the third variable; then Facet A would behave as the second component and Facet B as the first one.

The first variable cannot be identified simply by indicating the subscripts of its facet elements. If these subscripts are assigned arbitrarily, any one of the variables can be indicated by a1b1c1 or by any other combination of subscripts we wish. It is therefore necessary to assign subscripts to the elements of the facets in a meaningful manner.

In conclusion: to predict a unique two-dimensional order, for the eight variables defined by three dichotomous facets, it is necessary and sufficient to identify the principal component of each facet and the first variable in the order. The position of each facet in the differentiation sequence suggests the principal component appropriate for it: the component shall be higher for later developing facets. In this way the first criterion for a single order is satisfied. The second criterion, determination of the first variable in the order, can be satisfied by the following steps: (a) In each facet the two elements are ordered from the more to the less interpersonal, or according to some other suitable notion of order; (b) subscript 1 is consistently assigned to the element of each facet coming first in the order; (c) the variable defined by a1b1c1 will then be considered the first one (Foa, 1965).

THE NOTION OF ORDER. Both the principle of contiguity and the semantic principal components provide rules for predicting the configuration of variables in a psychological space, in which more related variables will be found nearer to each other than less related ones. Familiarity with the physical space may lead us to make assumptions which are not appropriate to a psychological space. The configuration of variables in the latter space does not necessarily reflect the absolute strength of the relationship between any two variables, but only its relative value in respect to other relationships. In consequence the ordering of the variables in the configuration is not necessarily a linear function of the strength of their relationships; for the order to be meaningful a monotonic function is sufficient. Thus, for example, variable 1 will be more related to its neighbor variable 2 (which is only one step removed from variable 1) than to variable 3 which is two steps removed; likewise variable 1 will be more related to 3 than to 4. The decrease in relationship when moving from 2 to 3 does not, however, have to be the same as the decrease occurring when moving from 3 to 4.

74 PART I ABRIDGEMENT OF *SOCIETAL STRUCTURES OF THE MIND*

An intuitive way to grasp these limitations in the notion of order, as used here, is to imagine that a structure of classes, such as the one shown in Figure 3.1, is not represented on paper but on rubber which can be stretched in different directions. Pulling it will make distances between certain variables larger while shortening the distance between other variables. But no matter how much and in which direction we pull, the order among the variables will not change: variable 2 will still be between 1 and 3, variable 4 between 3 and 5 and so on.

Interpersonal Resources

In addition to love and status, the development of four other classes of resources, information, money, goods, and services, has been discussed in Chapter 2. Status and service are differentiated from love. The notion of goods is an offshoot of services; money, in turn, derives from goods and information from status. Implicit in this differentiation sequence is the notion that resource classes which are derived from one another will have more permeable boundaries, will be perceived as more similar, and will be more likely to occur jointly. Thus, once more, developmental assumptions generate structural hypotheses: resources consecutive in the differentiation sequence will also be nearer in the structure of resource classes and, as we shall see later, share similar exchange properties. Services and status, for example, will be more similar or related to love than money, and services and money will be more related to goods than status. If resources may be ordered with respect to their relative similarity, one should be able to specify the nature of these similarities and differences. What makes love similar to status and services, and different from money? This question points to the need for specifying the coordinates on which resources may be ordered, independently of their differentiation sequence and of the empirical relationship among them.

Two attributes on which the six resource classes can be compared are particularism and concreteness. The coordinate of *particularism* derives from the writings of Parsons (1951) and Longabaugh (1966) and is similar to Blau's (1967) notion of intrinsic and extrinsic rewards. This attribute indicates the extent to which the value of a given resource is influenced by the particular persons involved in exchanging it and by their relationship. Changing the bank teller will not make much of a difference for the client wishing to cash a check. A change of doctor or lawyer is less likely to be accepted with indifference. One is even more particularistic with regard to a friend, a spouse, or a mother. Indeed, Harlow and Suomi (1970) showed that when the facial features of a surrogate mother are altered, the baby monkey reacts with fear, refusing to accept the change. In some animal species certain communications are more target specific than others. Mating calls are more particularistic than status signals and the latter are less general than distress or alarm signals (Johnsgard, 1967, pp. 71–72).

In operant terminology this coordinate may be thought of as the extent to which variables associated with the agent of reinforcement are important discriminative stimuli affecting the salience of the reinforcer. At one extreme of this coordinate is love, the most particularistic resource. Money, the least particularistic resource, is situated at the other extreme. It matters a great deal from whom we receive love as its reinforcing effectiveness is closely tied to the person–stimulus. Money, however, is most likely of all resources to retain the same value and meaning regardless of the relation between, or characteristics of, reinforcing agent and recipient. Services and status are less particularistic than love, but more particularistic than goods and information.

The attribute of *concreteness* ranges from concrete to symbolic and suggests the form or type of expression characteristic of the various resources. Some behaviors, like giving an object or performing an activity upon the body or the belongings of another individual, are quite concrete. Some other forms of expression, such as language, posture of the body, a smile, a gesture, or facial expression, are more symbolic. Services and goods involve the exchange of some overtly tangible activity or product and are classed as concrete. Status and information, on the other hand, are typically conveyed by verbal or paralinguistic behaviors which are more symbolic. Love and money are exchanged in both concrete and symbolic forms, and thus occupy an intermediate position on this coordinate.

The plotting of each resource class according to its degree of particularism and concreteness, produces the structure of resources presented in Figure 3.3.

This order is identical with the one suggested in the previous chapter, although this time it has been derived independently of developmental considerations. Therefore, the two coordinates, particularism and concreteness, may suggest the cognitive criteria along which the differentiation of resources develops. For example, both status and services are differentiated from love and are less particularistic than this class. Services, however, are more concrete and status is less concrete than love. Thus while the general

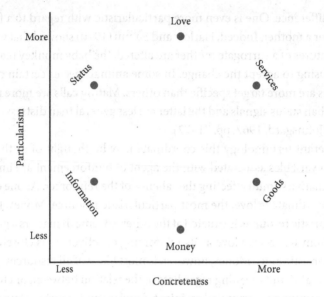

Figure 3.3 The cognitive structure of resource classes.
(Copyright 1971 by the American Association for the Advancement of Science.)

path of differentiation is from more to less particularism, in each stage, another boundary is superimposed on the previous differentiation—the boundary between more and less concreteness.

In the structural model presented in Figure 3.3, resource classes are shown as discrete and neatly separated one from the other. It would be more accurate, but also more confusing, to present each resource class by a segment which merges gradually into its neighboring classes on both sides. We should remember that the resource classes are categories of the *meaning* assigned to actions and not a classification of actions. Consequently, each class covers a wide range of actions all conveying the same resource. For example, one can convey his liking for the other by verbal means, by a smile, a kiss, etc. Thus, for any given resource, there are some forms of expression which are closer to one neighbor while other expressions will be closer to the other neighboring resource. A verbal expression of love such as "I like you very much" is symbolic and thus is more similar to status than to services. Conversely, fondling and kissing are concrete ways of expressing affection, and are closer to services than to status. Services to the body are proximal to love, while services to one's belongings are nearer to goods. Likewise, consumption goods are closer to services than durable goods. A credit card can be considered a kind

FROM DEVELOPMENTAL SEQUENCE TO ADULT STRUCTURE   77

of money, but it is more particularistic than currency; not every merchant will honor a credit card, and the card is not issued to everybody. This form of payment is also more symbolic than currency; although nothing concrete is given in a credit card payment, currency actually changes hands. Thus a credit card will be nearer to information than currency. In fact, the card provides information on the solvency of its holder.

In general it appears that for each resource class some specific forms are more similar to one neighbor while other forms are nearer to the second neighbor. These similarities are responsible for the permeability of the boundaries among resource classes, and for the structural relationship among them. However, one might question the usefulness or the accuracy of the proposed classification if boundaries are so permeable. The answer is an empirical one: as long as events of the same class tend to be more similar than to events of different classes, it will still be possible to obtain empirical evidence for the order.

Summary

The elements underlying classes of social events are differentiated in parallel partial sequences, rather than in a single sequence. Within each sequence, for some differentiations to develop, other dimensions should have already been established.

The *behavioral* sequence starts with differentiation between giving and taking away in the primitive form of acceptance and rejection. This elementary classification of events in terms of pleasant and unpleasant is necessary for the notion of object to become relevant and meaningful. Thus the second stage in the behavioral sequence consists of differentiation between self and other as *objects* of an action. This differentiation is developed in the two-role-system of infant–mother interaction. When the child interacts differentially with the two parents, then "status" starts to emerge as a distinct resource class, different from "love." Thus, the third stage in the behavioral sequence consists of differentiation between the *resources* of love and status.

Another partial sequence is the *perceptual* one. It starts with the differentiation of self and other as *actors*. This first stage is based on motoric feedback while the basis of the behavioral sequence was sensoric feedback (pain, pleasure). The second stage of the perceptual sequence consists of differentiation between actual and ideal *level*. It could not emerge before the actors are

78 PART I ABRIDGEMENT OF *SOCIETAL STRUCTURES OF THE MIND*

differentiated, since ideal behavior in its elementary form is the behavior of the child (self) which is followed by acceptance behavior of the adult (other). The third perceptual stage emerges with the differentiation between the *viewpoint* of the actor and that of the non-actor. This dimension is based on the previous differentiation by levels; it starts with the realization that "what mother wants me to do" may differ from "what I want to do," which is a differentiation between two ideals.

The developmental sequence determines the cognitive structure of the adult, so that the relationships among classes of social events could be predicted by developmental considerations. The relative distance between any pair of classes in a given structure was tested by correlating their frequency of occurrence in a given dyadic interaction. The higher the coefficient of correlation the less differentiated the two classes are; therefore, the smaller the cognitive distance between them.

The six interpersonal resources of love, status, information, money, goods, and services are ordered on two coordinates: *particularism* and *concreteness*. Particularism indicates the extent to which the value of a given resource is influenced by the particular persons involved in its exchange. At one extreme of this coordinate is love, the most particularistic resource; it matters a great deal *from whom* we receive love. Money is the least particularistic resource, since most likely of all resources, it retains the same value regardless of the relationship between the giver and the receiver. Services and status are less particularistic than love, but more particularistic than goods and information.

The coordinate of concreteness ranges from concrete to symbolic and suggests the form of expression characteristic of each resource class. Services and goods involve the exchange of overt activity or of product and therefore are the most concrete. Conversely, status and information are typically conveyed by verbal behaviors which are more symbolic. Love and money are exchanged in both concrete and symbolic forms and thus occupy an intermediate position on this coordinate. The plotting of each resource class according to its degree of particularism and concreteness, results in a circular structure. Data on perceived similarity among the six resources, as well as on preferences for each one, support the theoretical model.

The structures examined in this chapter refer to the cognitive recording of behavior within *one* given role-pair.

4

Prelude to Resource Exchange

Overview

After having described the growth and organization of the basic cognitive elements in social behavior, we now turn to explore the function of these cognitive structures in the dynamics of interpersonal interaction. Social experiences are interpersonal encounters in which resources are given and/or taken away. Whether or not an exchange will take place depends on conditions which will be explored in this chapter. In essence, there are two sets of conditions which we shall consider: One pertains to the motivational state of the potential exchangers, their need to receive and capacity to give; the other set refers to the appropriateness of the environment for an exchange of a particular type.

We shall begin by proposing that for each resource class there is an optimal range; when the amount of a given resource possessed by the individual is within this range, he feels comfortable and is not motivated to induce a change. When the amount falls below the lower bound of the range, the situation will be subjectively perceived as a need for this particular resource and the person will be motivated to increase the amount in his possession. Contrariwise, when the amount exceeds the upper limit of the optimal range, one will be motivated to "get rid" of some of the resource, through suitable exchange behaviors. By accumulating an amount beyond his need, the individual acquires power in this specific resource class.

These definitions of need and power suggest that an optimal condition for exchange exists whenever a person who needs resource A and has power in resource B meets a person needful of B and powerful in A. Yet, the intrapersonal state of the exchangers constitutes only part of the requirements for an exchange to take place. The institution within which the exchange occurs and the role of each participant are important factors for enhancing or abating it. We have already noted briefly that exchanges appropriate to one institution may not be permissible in another one. In this chapter we shall expand on the function of institutions in channeling and limiting exchanges.

Social Behavior as Resource Exchange. Kjell Yngve Törnblom and Ali Kazemi, Oxford University Press.
© Oxford University Press 2023. DOI: 10.1093/oso/9780190066994.003.0005

Another significant element of the exchange situation is the particular resources involved, since resources differ in their exchange and environmental properties. If two persons who need money, exchange dollar bills with one another, neither of them will benefit much. On the other hand, an exchange of love increases the amount of it possessed by both participants. The reason is that in love, unlike money, giving to the other is positively related to giving to self; consequently, one cannot reduce his amount of love by giving it to other, as he could do with money, since by giving love to the other he also increases the amount possessed by him. This positive relationship is also reflected in negative exchange: when one takes away love from the other he simultaneously takes away from himself. Lovers' quarrels may have this homeostatic function: keeping the amount of love below the upper limit of the optimal range. Resources also differ in the environmental conditions in which they can be best exchanged: lovers will seek solitude, shoppers a crowded marketplace. Thus both exchange and environmental characteristics of resources will influence the feasibility of a particular transaction. These properties will be discussed in the last part of this chapter and their eventual significance for problems of modern society, particularly urban society, will be explored.

In summary, the present chapter examines factors influencing the occurrence of an exchange: the motivational state of the participants in terms of optimal range, need and power; the facilitation and limitations imposed by social institutions; the consequences of resource properties. The latter factor includes both individual and social aspects and thus provides a link between the motivational state of the person and the environmental conditions.

Motivational State of the Individual

The term motivation usually refers to internal states of the individual which spur the emission of a certain behavior. When discussing social motivation, we aim at answering such questions as: What drives a person to interact with others? What determines the type of this action, its direction and vigorousness?

We shall focus here on two basic mechanisms which motivate social behavior. The first is the strive to maintain the amount of each resource within an optimal range, and the second is the strive to maintain the cognitive structures.

The Optimal Range[1]

In physiology the concept of homeostasis or normal range of the organism's parameters was proposed by Cannon (1939). He saw it as the tendency for an organism as a whole to maintain constancy, or to attempt to restore equilibrium if constancy is disturbed. Need was defined, in turn, as a condition arising from the lack of something essential to the organism and motivation as a state existing from a desire to maintain equilibrium or homeostasis. When the homeostatic balance of a particular factor is disrupted, an aversive and motivating state develops. It seems likely also that a need may be present at times other than during disequilibrium and that the unbalanced state does not directly produce motivation but instead gives rise to a need, an intervening process which, once established, in turn produces the motivation by which energy is expended and the system moves once again to equilibrium. That is, disequilibrium produces a need within the system; as the system becomes aware of the need through action of the homeostats, motivation arises and instigates action. Shortly after equilibrium is restored, the need disappears, motivation is removed and activity ceases. From the early ideas of Cannon, a large body of research has developed. For example, McClelland (1955) has suggested that an individual's personality characteristics are determined in large part by the efficiency of *his homeostatic system*. And Tomkins (1962), who notes that the homeostatic system is silent and unconscious in its operation, adds (Tomkins, 1965) that if a drive state (a state that is instigated by homeostatic imbalance) is not reduced within the tolerance limits of the organism, the drive becomes stronger. Other researchers (Benzinger, 1961; Pribram, 1960) delving into the physiological aspects have provided evidence that the regulatory mechanisms necessary for maintaining physiological balance or homeostasis are located in the hypothalamus.

From Tomkins' (1965) notion of "tolerance limits," it follows that either too much or too little of a particular necessary factor may destroy homeostasis and consequently motivate the organism to act in order to restore the system's balance. For example, too little water will lead to dehydration and—death—just as too much water within a system will produce bloating and death. Homeostasis is that tolerable range of deviation (for any factor) within which behavior remains unmotivated for that particular actor.

---

[1] We are indebted to Roger D. Pigg for his contribution to this section.

82   PART I ABRIDGEMENT OF *SOCIETAL STRUCTURES OF THE MIND*

Before a homeostatic model may apply to any dimension, whether physiological or psychological, certain necessary conditions must be met. The dimension or factor being considered must exist on a continuum where the possibility exists for the system to have either a zero amount of it, some greater amount, perhaps infinite, or any amount in between. There must be the possibility of variation as to the amount of the factor "held" by the system in question. And there must exist some upper and lower "tolerance limits" upon the continuum such that no need will be experienced by the system when the amount held by it falls within these limits. Beyond these tolerance limits, however, needs arise and motivated behavior will result.

The notion of optimal level is found in several theoretical models of motivation. The classical drive reduction paradigm (e.g., Hull, 1943) mainly emphasizes this internal state which occurs when the amount of resource possessed by an organism is *below* a certain limit. Lack of food induces unpleasant physiological stimulation; the organism's activity is then directed toward reducing such stimulation. Yet, under the notion of avoiding pain or discomfort one can easily include the state of having "too much." Hunger and oversatiation both produce unpleasant physiological cues, and as such both can be accounted for in the drive-reduction paradigm. More explicit in postulating an optimal range is Berlyne (1960) who suggested that the organism strives toward maintaining an optimal level of arousal; any state below or above this level activates a search for a change so that there are stimulus-seeking behaviors as much as stimulus-reducing ones. One may argue that a state of too-little arousal produces cues of discomfort and therefore behaviors directed toward increased arousal are again drive reducing. It seems that the argument between these two formulations (Lana, 1960, 1962) boils down to the question of what the optimal range arousal is. While the drive reduction theory assumes lack of internal stimulation as the optimal level, Berlyne suggests a higher and wider range.

By applying the homeostatic model to resources, the nature of the discomfort that is aroused in the organism and drives him toward a search for change is specified. The amount of resources one possesses at any given time can be described on a continuum. Let us consider "love" as an example. The system may potentially "hold" no love at all, or some amount which may vary from time to time. There are obviously times when love is actively sought by a system; at other times even when available, the opportunity to receive love is ignored and even rejected. Gewirtz and Baer (1958) found that children previously deprived of companionship learned faster than non-deprived ones a discriminative task which was reinforced by social approval. The slowest learning occurred in those who were previously satiated with social interaction. Reformulating these results, the isolated children possessed an amount of love and status below the optimal range; for them the learning task provided an opportunity to acquire these resources in exchange for the correct response. On the other hand, the potential exchange did not prove attractive to those who already possessed a sufficient amount of the resources offered.

In general, it appears reasonable to assume that for every resource there is a lower limit below which motivational arousal will occur. The upper limit, however, varies for the different resources and consequently the optimal range also differs from one resource to another: it will be smallest for love and practically infinite for money. The optimal range of the remaining resources will follow the structural order. The closer they are to love the narrower will be their optimal range, while resources closer to money will have a wider range.

When the optimal range is narrow, the balance is upset frequently and requires constant restoration by increasing or decreasing the amount held by the system. We feel miserable being far away from those who love us, but when close to them, we sometimes want to be alone. Similarly, it is pleasurable to dine in a good restaurant where service is prompt; yet, in those exclusive restaurants with several waiters in constant attendance, one may wish they would disappear. It is only with regard to those resources that can be stored outside the system (mainly money, but also goods and information) that we can own large quantities without being disturbed.

Obviously, there are individual differences in the optimal range. It seems that at least for the more particularistic resources, the range will be narrower for those who received little of them in early childhood. A person who has not received enough love will probably feel unbalance when suddenly confronted with the necessity to absorb large quantities of it. He may react to this disturbance of his homeostasis with hostility, in order to get rid of the overdose of love smothering him.

Below the Optimal Range: Need

Need is defined as a state of deficiency in a given resource; it occurs when the individual possesses an amount below the lower bound of the optimal range. It follows that there are six classes of need, one for each resource class.

84 PART I ABRIDGEMENT OF *SOCIETAL STRUCTURES OF THE MIND*

Several of the needs recurring in the literature on motivation refer to a specific resource or to a combination of two neighboring resources; some examples are given in Table 4.1. Other needs found in the literature cover a wider range of resources. The need for affiliation (Schachter, 1959), for example, appears to include all the resources which are exchanged in face-to-face contact: love, status, information, and services; the desire to be with another person represents an expectation to receive some resource rather than being an end in itself. Such expectation for resources is also embedded in the similar notions of "social instinct" (Young, 1936) and gregariousness (Cattell, 1950; McDougall, 1932; Tolman, 1951). Still other needs focus on additional aspects of resource acquisition; the need for security (Stagner & Karwoski, 1952) indicates a desire to assure *future* supplies of unspecified resources; one may need security for love, status, money etc. The need for independence (Rotter, 1954, p. 132) represents a wish to have many alternative sources, thus avoiding reliance on any specific individual for obtaining resources; the need for dependence, in turn, implies a tendency to maintain supplies only from specific others. Once more these needs may apply to any of the six resource classes: one may have many sources of money but few persons from whom to receive love. Indeed, the more particularistic the resource, the less one is likely to be independent in it; since for particularistic resources, the giver is relevant, it becomes more difficult to secure alternative sources of supply. Quite often a person is independent and secure with regard to one resource while manifesting dependency and insecurity in another.

Table 4.1 Some Needs Referring to One Resource or Two Neighboring Ones

Resource	Need	Reference
Love	Love	(Tolman, 1951)
	Affection	(Schutz, 1958)
Love and Status	Approval	(Crowne & Marlowe, 1964)
Status	Achievement	(McClelland et al., 1953)
	Recognition	(Murray, 1938)
Status and Information	Competence	(White, 1959)
Information	Curiosity	(Berlyne, 1960; Harlow, 1953)
	Exploration	(Stagner & Karwosky, 1952)
Goods and Money	Acquisition	(Cattell, 1950; McDougall, 1932; Murray, 1938; Stagner & Karwosky 1952)
Services and Love	Succorance	(Murray, 1938)
	Comfort	(McDougall, 1932)

Thus it is necessary to specify the resource as well as the patterns of behaviors connected with it. Moreover, we sometimes accept a loss in one resource in order to secure a supply of another, which is needed more. Staub and Sherk (1970) provided children with their favorite candies; they could eat and share them with another child while listening to a recorded story. High need approval children ate less and gave less to the other. Presumably they expected that such a restrained behavior would be approved by the experimenter; approval was more valuable to them than eating their favorite candy.

All the needs discussed here, although different with respect to resources, share a common characteristic: they all refer to a situation where the object is "self," the behavior "giving," and the actor is mainly "other." A resource is sought after by the individual in order to reduce a present or future deficit, and to maintain the amount held by his system within the optimal range. However, the term "need" has also been used to indicate situations where the potential object is the "other" and behavior is either giving or taking. The mother "needs" to give love and care to her infant; the aggressive individual "needs" to express hostility, i.e., to take away love from the other. What deficits are behind such needs? Let us consider first the need to give to the other by analyzing the outcomes of these "needed" behaviors. The most obvious explanation for the urge to give evolves from the notion of optimal range: when the amount of a given resource exceeds the upper limit, one would be motivated to "get rid" of it by giving to the other. In spite of its simplicity, this explanation is ruled out by theoretical considerations, which are, however, different for particularistic and non-particularistic resources. When one dispenses money, he indeed becomes poorer. But we did propose that no upper limit exists for money, hence there should be reasons other than discomfort for such behavior. As to love, excessive amount does indeed cause discomfort, but giving love to other increases rather than decreases the amount possessed by the self, and therefore is not a successful way to restore balance. It seems more plausible to perceive "generosity" (giving to other) as a device for obtaining access to needed resources. It is quite uncommon for a person to give away money indiscriminately. Benefactors are usually quite choosy: they will give for a "worthy" cause which will bring them honor or self-respect. Often the donation is part of an exchange situation: beggars are likely to reciprocate the alms with a blessing for the giver. The benevolent mother is likely to be praised by her family and friends besides increasing her self-acceptance. In general, three exchange paradigms, which are *not* mutually exclusive, provide access to needed resources through benefiting others: (1) A gives to B and is reciprocated by him with a needed resource. (2) A gives to B and is reciprocated by giving to himself. (3) A gives to B and is reciprocated by a third person, C. Thus giving behavior, even when it appears unconditional, provides access to some needed resource so that one's own balance is restored. But what is achieved by taking away behaviors? How is balance restored by aggression? The effect of taking away from the other is reversed in comparison to giving. Taking non-particularistic resources may increase the amount held by the taker and thus serve to satisfy his deficit. Yet sometimes the aggressor purposely destroys the other's possessions, without any obvious gain to himself. Common observation indicates that some satisfaction is derived from such destruction. By reducing the amount in possession of the victim, the aggressor decreases the difference between himself and the victim. If a poor, desperate person sets afire the house of the well-to-do, he indeed does not become richer absolutely, but will be less poor in comparison to the other. We shall consider this relative increase resulting from social comparison later in this chapter.

While taking away non-particularistic resources serves to increase the amount possessed, taking away love from the other has the effect of decreasing the amount in one's possession, thus reestablishing equilibrium when the amount previously held exceeded the upper limit. In summary, taking away from the other non-particularistic resources reestablishes a balance by increasing the absolute or relative amount held by the self; taking away particularistic resources reduces the amount possessed by the taker and thus reestablishes the balance when this amount was excessive.

The foregoing discussion of the effects of taking away focused on dyadic relationship. As in giving behavior, often a third party joins the exchange and rewards the taker for his aggressive behavior with a needed resource. When taking away behavior is directed toward an outgroup, often the group reacts by rewarding the aggressor; taking from the "foe" of the group results in receiving from the group members. The hero who killed many enemies is hailed; he receives status from his comrades.

ACTUAL AND POTENTIAL NEEDS. We have already briefly noted that the optimal range may be altered by cognitive operations. Reducing the amount of resources possessed by the other eliminates the discrepancy between one's own possession and the other's belonging. Thus, although the *potential* need is still high, the *actual* need has been decreased. The distinction between actual and potential need is even clearer on a physiological level: a person who has been starving for a long time needs a great amount of nourishment. Yet he will not be able to digest large quantities at once; in fact he may become seriously ill if he does. Potentially his need for food is high, but his actual need is rather limited. Likewise, a person who has received little love, particularly in early childhood, may have a strong potential need, but little ability to actually absorb it.

The potential need can be reduced only by receiving the appropriate resource. An actual need, on the other hand, can be modified by cognitive manipulations. One way of changing an actual need is by social comparison (Festinger, 1954), which, as we have seen, may influence the *lower* bound of the optimal range for non-particularistic resources. TV advertisements obviously serve to raise the lower bound by exposing the individual to "all the people" who own luxurious goods, have better education and earn more money; sibling rivalry has the same effect of increasing demand with regard to particularistic resources. The influence of social comparison on the upper limit is more obscure: Will one be able to receive more love if he is among people who are much beloved?

Similar questions can be raised with regard to expectation; the latter differs from social comparison in that there the need is modified by past experience of the subject, while in the latter the modification results from past experience of others. It is well known that failure to receive an expected resource produces discomfort as it is receiving an unexpected one. We do not know, however, whether these effects are due to changes in the optimal range or result from the motivation to maintain the structure, which shall be considered later in this chapter.

We have attempted to show that many of the psychological needs and motivational states proposed in the literature can be seen in function of the six resource classes. As the structure of these classes has already been established, hypotheses about the relationship among needs and their interchangeability can be suggested: needs pertaining to proximal classes will be more related than needs which refer to distal resources. A person exposed to loss of love will also feel, to a lesser degree, a need for status. The positive correlation of .55 between need for approval and the TAT measure of need for affiliation (Crowne & Marlowe, 1964, p. 163) could be predicted, for example, on the grounds that the two needs share common resources.

The dilemma between too many and too few motives is well described by Madsen (1961, p. 313): "According to the usual scientific principle of economy it is *practical to presuppose as few motives as possible.* One must therefore avoid using a list of motives which is so long that the notion of motive does not

88 PART I ABRIDGEMENT OF *SOCIETAL STRUCTURES OF THE MIND*

explain anything. If the list becomes too long the result is that the explanations employing these motives as their basis do not really explain anything.... But it would also be a mistake to try to explain everything from a single or a few motives. The explanations would then either be too vague and imprecise, or they would become too artificial and *speculative* because so many hypotheses would have to be assumed that simplicity would be lost." We believe that parsimony can be achieved not only by limiting the number of needs, but also by determining the structural relationship among them.

Within the Optimal Range: Power

As noted by Cartwright (1959b, pp. 1–2) the study of power has been neglected by social psychologists. Yet, this notion generated theoretical interest, which is reflected in the many definitions proposed in the literature (Cartwright, 1959a, pp. 185–187). Common to several of these definitions is the idea that power implies control over others, or as proposed by Blau (1967, p. 117), the ability to influence the behavior of others. These definitions seem inadequate as they focus on the effect of power rather than on what constitutes power; to define power as the ability to induce behavioral changes is like defining rain as the ability to make wet. Certainly such a definition is not helpful in predicting its occurrence or classifying its various types. More enlightening are Thibaut and Kelley (1959, p. 101), who define power as the amount of reward and punishment one can administer to the other. This definition implies two types of power: the power to give a certain resource and the power to take it away. So rephrased, Thibaut and Kelley's definition invites a further classification of power according to the resources involved in the punishment and the reward. Indeed, as Cartwright and Zander (1968, Ch. 17) have noted, a close relationship between the notion of power and resources has been frequently implied in the literature. Such relationship is reflected, to a certain degree, in the classification of power proposed by French and Raven (1959). Two out of the five powers suggested by these authors, reward and coercive power, correspond to Thibaut and Kelley's definition. French and Raven, however, proposed three additional classes: legitimate, referent and expert power. Legitimate power stems from the values held by the person that the other has the right to influence him. This notion clearly introduces the self as a source of reward and punishment: compliance to a legitimate power results in self-esteem or as stated by Berkowitz (1969a, p. 73) "the individual following the powerful person obtains the satisfaction of doing what is 'right' and he avoids the guilt often arising from norm-deviating actions." The last two bases of power refer to specific resources. In "referent power" the resources of love and status are implicit. The powerful person, by being highly attractive and his opinions and actions appealing, serves as a model for the other. French and Raven held that imitation does not have to be followed by the external reward, but rather the act of imitation is rewarding in itself, or, as we would say, it provides the imitator with a reason to give love and status to himself. It is likely that the model himself is perceived as possessing a considerable amount of those resources. Power as possession of a specific resource becomes explicit in the last type, expert power, which is also labeled "informational power" (Deutsch & Gerard, 1955). It indicates knowledge or information in a specific area, *possessed* by the holder of power and *needed* by the other individual. This formulation provides an exchange paradigm which can be extended to other resources as well.

We shall thus define power as *the amount of a given resource that is available to an individual for eventual giving*. This definition suggests six basic classes of power, one for each class of resources. Possession of power is not necessarily reflected in influencing other's behaviors or opinions as often suggested. More generally, the powerful person is in a position to enter an exchange in which he offers some resource and, in turn, expects to be reciprocated.

By defining power in terms of resource possession, some hypotheses about the relationship among the different types of power can be developed. The structure of resources suggests that proximal types will be more related than distal ones. A person powerful in money may easily possess valuable goods, but not always status and certainly can be quite "poor" in love. The specificity of power with respect to resources has been obscured by the fact that a person having great power in a particular resource may acquire other resources through exchange (Benoit, 1944): an individual possessing a large amount of money may acquire status by donations to appropriate institutions such as educational, medical, religious, etc. This possibility of exchanging one class of power with another is limited. One cannot buy genuine love with money, at most he buys personal services; likewise the "nouveau riche" is often rejected by those circles he most wishes to join, although they may possess less money than he. In many instances, the "self-made man" achieves the desirable status only through his offspring whom he helps to possess information, a proximal resource to status. Again, the limitations in exchanging one type of power with another may be predicted from the structure of resources.

90   PART I ABRIDGEMENT OF *SOCIETAL STRUCTURES OF THE MIND*

ACTUAL AND POTENTIAL POWER. As Cartwright and Zander (1968, pp. 216–217) have pointed out, power cannot be exercised unless there is a corresponding need on the part of the receiver. A person may have great potential power and little actual power when there is scarce demand for the resource he possesses in abundance. No matter how much love one can give, he may not attract the girl who has an already highly satisfactory relationship with another person. Likewise, the expert in aeronautics has little actual power when the airplane industry is in crisis. Thus the distinction between actual and potential, already applied to needs, holds for power as well. Potential power is an attribute of a single agent, whereas actual power is "a relationship between two agents" (Cartwright, 1959a, p. 213), the one who can give and the other who needs the specific resource.

The reciprocal relationship between need and power is well illustrated by Levinger's experiment (1959) dealing with the resource of information. Sixty-four subjects were requested to work with a partner (the experimenter's confederate) in solving some town-planning problems. In one group the confederate presented himself as ignorant and as lacking self-confidence. In the other group he introduced himself as having considerable expertise and as a self-assured person. Each group was further exposed to differential treatment: in half of the cases the confederate most often accepted the proposals of the subject, while rejecting the ideas of the other in the remaining cases. Subjects felt more powerful when they believed they had more information than their partner, i.e., when the other needed their information. Levinger also found that this effect of the initial presentation decreased over the 24 trials, depending on the reaction of the confederate to the subject's proposals: when acceptance was prevalent, the feeling of power increased. In rejection there was some decrease, particularly for those who were previously led to believe they were superior. Since most of these changes occurred in the first half of the trials, it seems that interaction tends to stabilize on a definite power relationship. Subjects who felt more powerful were more likely to be assertive, to attempt influencing the other and to reject his attempts to influence.

SYMMETRY OF POWER. This experiment illustrates a situation where only one resource is involved so that the power relationship is likely to be asymmetric: one of the participants possesses this resource in an amount larger than the one possessed by the other. In most interactions, several resources are exchanged; then, A may be more powerful in one resource and B in another, so that symmetry does occur, and both partners may gain the

PRELUDE TO RESOURCE EXCHANGE 91

needed resource. Obviously, the notion of symmetry (Cartwright, 1959a, pp. 197–198) refers to actual power; in a satisfactory exchange situation, each participant is powerful in the specific resource the other needs.

THREAT. When symmetry is absent the power of the other is more likely to be perceived as a threat: when the other possesses a resource we need, and we do not have any resource that he needs, he gains control without us being able to limit it by withholding what we own. Consequently, individuals or groups possessing a large amount of resources are often perceived as threatening; contemporary examples are the big corporation, the big union, the big government.

Cohen (1959) investigated two conditions which may influence the perception of threat: ambiguity of the situation and self-esteem. In the ambiguous situation, the subject was presented with vague and contradictory cues as to what was expected of him, a manipulation interpreted by us as reduction in the information available to the subjects. This information was necessary for performing adequately on the assigned task and thus obtaining status from the powerful person, the "supervisor." It was found that subjects who received ambiguous information perceived the powerful person as more threatening than those exposed to structured and clear tasks. Low self-esteem subjects perceived more threat in the structured situation than did high self-esteem ones. However, in the ambiguous situation, the degree of self-esteem did not influence the perceived amount of threat. It seems that the amount of need for status is a relevant factor only when there is an access to this resource, i.e., when the type of information available is sufficient for successful performance. On the other hand, when there is no way to reduce the need, the situation is equally threatening for both high- and low-need persons. The interpretation of threat as absence of symmetry in the power relationship suggests that the feeling of being threatened will decrease when several opportunities for exchange are opened for the powerless person. Evidence on this prediction was provided by Stotland (1959). Subjects under "threat" who were permitted to meet another subject in a similar condition, were better able to stand up against the threatening figure and particularly so when they developed an "interest" in the other subject, i.e., when they had meaningful exchanges with him. As Stotland (1959, p. 67) perceptively noted, "By establishing a positive relationship with one person, the subject was protected from having to establish a similar relationship with another, less satisfactory person." Stotland's experiment presented exchanges among three persons. The asymmetry between the powerful and the powerless

92 PART I ABRIDGEMENT OF *SOCIETAL STRUCTURES OF THE MIND*

persons decreased when the latter, through symmetrical relations with a third party, increased the amount of resources available to him. This relationship among several exchanges of one individual introduces the problem of transitivity.

TRANSITIVITY OF POWER. In analyzing the various properties of power, Cartwright (1959a, pp. 198–199) asks: "If A has power over B and B has power over C, does it necessarily follow that A has power over C?" Although stated in terms of actual power, this problem of transitivity pertains as well to potential power: If A has *more* power than B and B has more power than C, does it follow that A has more power than C? Cartwright's examples suggest that power may be transitive when the various power relationships are within the same institution; when different institutions are involved, power is intransitive. But we already know that resources tend to differ in various institutions, so that the property of transitivity can be stated, more precisely, as follows: Both potential and actual power are transitive within each resource class even across different roles and institutions. When different classes are involved, the power relationship is intransitive, particularly when the resources involved are distal. The boss is powerful over his employee as a source of money; if, in turn, this employee retains power over his wife, *only* through the provision of material resources, then the boss is more powerful than the employee's wife in *this* resource. When, however, the husband's power is rooted in his ability to give love, his boss will have no power over the worker's wife.

ACCUMULATION OF POWER. One could argue that the power possessed by an individual will increase in proportion to the amount of a given resource he receives. This way of achieving power seems to fit those resources which can be stored outside the individual, mainly money and goods; with regard to other resources, some qualifications are needed. We have already stated that there is an upper limit to the optimal range of resources which are stored within the organism. Any amount that exceeds this limit results in satiation (Gewirtz & Baer, 1958). The upper limit, in turn, depends on previous experience in receiving and possessing resources. When little was received in the past, satiation will occur after absorbing a small amount; consequently, a rapid increase in power is not feasible. The finding (Eldred et al., 1964) that schizophrenics appear unsuccessful in obtaining resources from other persons, even after making allowances for their resource bankruptcy, is significant in this respect. A person possessing little power seems to be less able to increase it, not only because he has little to offer in exchange, but also because he is less able to receive what is given to him for the little he has to offer. Paradoxically, such inability to receive limits also the power of the giver. This may explain the feeling of helplessness sometimes experienced when interacting with an emotionally disturbed individual.

The Power of the Powerless

We have defined power as possession of resources. Certainly without "owning" the resource, it cannot be dispensed to others; likewise, a threat to withhold it is meaningless unless the resource is available for dispensation. Yet, one can threaten to take away or actually create a loss without previous possession of it. One can deceive the other without having the right information, as well as stealing without having money. With regard to particularistic resources, especially love and status, such power is limited. To be insulted by a low-status person is less damaging than being degraded by a high-status individual. However, the amount of money owned by the thief does not affect the amount of loss he may inflict on his victim. This may be the reason why social and legal sanctions are imposed on acts of taking away less particularistic resources. Taking away is likely to be followed by retaliation: the victim, on being deprived, acts to inflict a loss on the taker. If, however, the taker possesses very little resources, the possibility of retaliation is reduced. Thus, the state of having little confers to the "desperate" a sort of quasi-power, the power of the powerless.

A different kind of quasi-power, possessed by the weak individual is noted by Parsons (1955, pp. 46–47): The child, although being dependent on his parents, may be able to influence their behavior; often children gain control over their parents, not by taking away from them, but rather by creating a loss to themselves. Refusal to eat or hitting the head on the floor constitute examples of such behaviors. This quasi-power depends, however, on the love of the parents for their child. Those parents who are indifferent toward their child would probably not be influenced by the latter inflicting loss on himself. Only the mother who is powerful in love may feel incompetent when confronted with the self-depriving behavior of the child. This behavior would not be equally effective with strangers and, in fact, children usually reserve it for their parents. Grown-ups may also resort to this technique, as in hunger strikes. But again, they are unlikely to succeed unless the party they attempt to control has some positive attitude toward them, either directly

94 PART I ABRIDGEMENT OF *SOCIETAL STRUCTURES OF THE MIND*

or through a third party: the jailer may be indifferent to the prisoners' refusal to eat but would lose status by ignoring public opinion sympathetic to them. In summary, there are three techniques for controlling the behavior of the other: (a) threat to deny him a resource he needs and cannot obtain elsewhere; (b) threat to take away from him a resource he possesses; and (c) taking away from self.

By examining the notions of need and power, we have dealt with one motivational mechanism: the strive for maintaining an optimal amount of resources by giving what we have and receiving what we need. We now turn to consider a second motivational mechanism.

Preservation of Structure from Dissonant Events

In the introductory chapter we have noted the significance of cognitive structures as a frame for ordering perceived events, without which one would be overwhelmed and confused by the richness of environmental stimuli. If cognitive structures are essential to our well-being, we need means for protecting them from events which challenge their validity.

The need for maintaining cognitive structures has been acknowledged by many scholars under various labels, such as "drive for understanding" and "drive for meaning." In reviewing the area of cognitive consistency, Berkowitz lucidly states that " 'understanding' entails knowledge of the relations among stimuli, or possession of a 'coding system' which enables the person to predict what leads to what, or what goes with what" (1969a, p. 88). The drive for understanding is then an attempt to maintain cognitive patterns of relationships. A threat to the structure occurs when one is confronted with an event which contains dissonant components. Indeed, the notion of dissonance and cognate concepts, such as imbalance and incongruity (Zajonc, 1960) are usually taken to indicate the coexistence of incompatible elements.

The threat to the structure posed by incongruent elements is not explicit in the original formulation of dissonance. Festinger (1957, p. 13) proposed that two elements are dissonant when "the obverse of one element would follow from the other." To borrow one of Festinger's examples, the element "I smoke cigarettes" is incongruent with the element "cigarette smoking produces cancer." To reduce the discomfort created by dissonance, some behavioral and/or cognitive change will take place (Festinger, 1957, p. 3).

In spite of the varied and exciting research generated by dissonance theory, even benign critics have recognized its lack of precision (Aronson, 1969; Zajonc, 1968). The main criticism has turned on the following points:

1. No clear-cut rule is provided by dissonance theory for determining when two elements of a situation are psychologically inconsistent. Aronson (1969, p. 7) asks, for example, whether dissonance would occur after learning that my favorite novelist beats his wife.
2. Even in the simplest situation, more than two elements are likely to be involved; whether or not two of them are dissonant may depend on a third one (Aronson, 1969, pp. 24–26). Smoking and danger of cancer will be dissonant only if one wants to avoid the possibility of getting cancer.
3. There are various ways in which dissonance may be resolved: one can either stop smoking or disbelieve the information that smoking produces cancer. Yet no specific criteria for predicting which alternative will be chosen in a given situation are offered by the theory.
4. Some results predicted by dissonance theory appear to contradict the ones derived from reinforcement theory. According to dissonance theory, a person advocating a view he opposes will tend to accept it more after receiving a smaller compensation. Conversely, reinforcement theory would predict that the larger the compensation, the greater will be the change in attitude. Some experiments have supported the first prediction, while others have corroborated the second one. The critical question is, then: What are the conditions leading to each of the two outcomes?

A more precise definition of dissonance may contribute to the solution of these problems.

DISSONANCE REDEFINED. We proposed earlier that an event reaches cognition as a structure, displaying a relationship pattern among its component elements. This pattern may or may not be homologous to the appropriate cognitive structure; a consonant event is readily absorbed into cognition; indeed, it provides additional confirmation to the validity of the cognitive structure. On the other hand, an event which does not fit cognition constitutes a threat to its structure. It seems, then, that dissonance involves a comparison between two structures, the structure of the event and the cognitive structure onto which it is mapped. Dissonance is thus defined as the

96   PART I ABRIDGEMENT OF *SOCIETAL STRUCTURES OF THE MIND*

condition in which these two structures do not match. A similar conceptualization has been independently developed by Feather (1971).

Consider, for example, events which involve receiving love and losing status, or vice versa. Such events will produce dissonance, since love and status are positively related in the cognitive structure. A negative relationship between love and status was indeed produced by Sampson and Insko (1964), who manipulated the subject's liking for another person, as well as the degree to which he disagreed with him on judging the movement of light in an autokinetic situation. The results are summarized by Berkowitz (1969a, p. 94): "Relatively great cognitive imbalance existed in this study when (1) the subject liked the other person and initially held a dissimilar opinion, or (2) there was a dislike for the other person but the subject's initial judgment was similar to his. This imbalance caused a greater tendency for the subject to alter his judgments of the light movement (toward increased balancing), and also to feel anxious while making these judgments, than did the more balanced conditions."

Other dissonance experiments involve a manipulation of the exchange paradigm. In cognition, giving a resource is positively related to receiving one; consequently, a situation where the subject experiences a loss which is not compensated by an acquisition will be perceived as dissonant. In a classic experiment, Festinger and Carlsmith (1959) found that subjects who were paid little for expressing an opinion they did not share tended later to accept it more than those who were paid a larger amount of money. By being hypocrites, subjects lost status or self-esteem; this loss was compensated when a large sum was received in exchange. On the other hand, when only one dollar was paid, imbalance was restored by reduction of the status loss; this was obtained by agreeing with the opinion they had previously stated. It should be noted that a status–money exchange is not common and consequently, the cognitive relationship underlying the assumed dissonance might not be particularly strong: indeed, later replication did not support the original outcome (Sampson, 1971, pp. 113–114). Perhaps more clear-cut results would have been obtained by using exchanges which were more firmly established in the learning history of the subjects.

A formalization of the dissonance situation and its resolution is presented in Figure 4.1. This figure depicts the positive relationship between two classes (e.g., amount of resource taken and amount of resource received) embodied in the experience of past events represented in cognition. In the deviant event the relationship is negative (high giving is associated with low receiving). Dissonance is then reduced by decreasing the value of one element

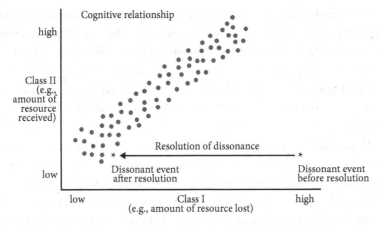

Figure 4.1 Schematic representation of the cognitive relationship between classes and of the dissonant event.

(the resource given), thus bringing the event into line with cognition. In other experiments (e.g., Aronson & Mills, 1959) resolution was obtained by an increase in value of the resource received: harsher initiation made the group discussion more attractive. Here the dissonant event is resolved by transferring it to the upper right corner of Figure 4.1. This figure shows, indeed, that even in relatively simple situations there are at least two ways to increase the fit between event and cognition. Sampson and Insko's subjects could have changed their liking for the other (love), rather than their judgment of the light movement (status). Subjects paid one dollar would have convinced themselves that they had received a large amount of money, rather than modifying their attitude (status). Finally, in the Aronson and Mills experiment, participants could have considered the initiation "ritual" milder than it was (services), rather than finding the group topic interesting (information). In all three experiments dissonance was resolved by modifying the perceived value of symbolic resources—status or information—rather than of love, money, or services, which are more concrete. Perhaps the more symbolic the resource is, the less it may be resistant to a perceptual change of its value. Further support for this hypothesis will provide a basis for predicting the way in which dissonance is reduced.

The reanalysis of these experiments suggests that, once the cognitive structure is known, it becomes possible to predict whether a given event will create dissonance. Many dissonance investigations capitalized upon the invariance of the structure: the experimenter relied implicitly and intuitively on his own

98   PART I ABRIDGEMENT OF *SOCIETAL STRUCTURES OF THE MIND*

cognition in deciding whether an event would or would not be dissonant. This method was successful when the experimenter's structure resembled that of his subjects—a common occurrence when both parties were normal individuals from a common culture; it tended, however, to exclude from experimentation cases in which the event was not perceived as dissonant by the experimenter but would create dissonance in individuals who, for one reason or another, possessed a different structure.

DISSONANCE VS. REINFORCEMENT. Quite often the prediction of reinforcement theory is contradicted by the outcomes in dissonance experiments. Indeed, it was found that agreement or liking are higher when the reward is smaller or punishment stronger. Aronson (1969, pp. 20–24) has provided a brilliant review of those investigations where dissonance prediction was supported under certain conditions while reinforcement prediction appeared to prevail under different ones.

1. Subjects who had performed a dull task were requested to describe it as interesting; later they expressed their opinion of the task. When the positive description was given face-to-face, thus committing the subject, a smaller reward resulted in a more favorable opinion of the task (dissonance effect). When the description took the form of an anonymous essay, the contrary was found: higher reward resulted in a more positive opinion (reinforcement effect) (Carlsmith et al., 1966).

2. Subjects were requested to write an essay favoring close paternalistic supervision of students by college authorities. Later on they expressed their opinion on the topic. Subjects left free to choose whether or not to write the essay expressed more favorable opinions the smaller the reward (dissonance); those who were not left with such a choice expressed a more favorable opinion when the reward was higher (reinforcement) (Linder et al., 1967).

3. Subjects were asked to record a short statement which they did not believe, ostensibly to be played to a large student audience; later they gave their opinion regarding the statement. When the recording was on videotape, along with personal details of the subject, those who received a smaller reward became more favorable (dissonance). When the recording was on audio and anonymous, those who received a larger reward expressed a more favorable opinion (reinforcement) (Helmreich & Collins, 1968).

PRELUDE TO RESOURCE EXCHANGE   99

4. Freedman's (1963) subjects were asked to evaluate a dull task they had previously performed; some subjects were told that the data would be of no value, since they were too late to be used by the experimenter; other subjects were informed that the data would be of great value. When this information regarding the value of the data had been given *before* the task was performed, subjects in the no-value condition enjoyed it more than those in the high-value condition (dissonance); however, when the same information was given *after* task completion, the results were reversed (reinforcement).

5. Gerard and Mathewson (1966) exposed subjects to strong or mild electric shock before admitting them to an ostensible group discussion, which was, in fact, pre-taped. Those told that receiving shock was a requirement for joining the group rated the taped discussion as more attractive when shock was higher (dissonance); subjects who simply received shock before listening to the tape, but not as a condition for participation, found the discussion somewhat more enjoyable when shock was milder (reinforcement).

Clearly, as suggested by Aronson (1969, p. 24) the variable responsible for the reversal of results is the degree to which the subject had previously committed himself, by public endorsement of the view, by freely choosing to perform a task or to join a group. The question is, then, how does commitment operate as contingent variable?

Commitment appears to have two effects:

1. It produces a loss of status for the subject who endorsed a view he opposes, a dull task, or a boring discussion.
2. It changes the connotation of the attitude or evaluation expressed by the subject in the final stage of the experiment. In the absence of commitment, attitude change or positive evaluation gives status to the experimenter who presented the view or the task. On the other hand, for committed subjects the same behavior avoids a further loss of status for himself, which would occur if he disagreed with the position previously taken.

With these two effects in mind, let us examine differences in the exchange situation for committed and uncommitted subjects. The loss of status incurred by the committed subject is counterbalanced when compensation is large: he lost status but gained a rather substantial amount (in money or in the status derived from doing something of high value). However, when compensation is small and incommensurate to the loss, support of the previous position reduces the perceived amount lost. For the uncommitted subject, the exchange situation is simpler: the amount of status he gives the experimenter, by agreeing with him, is commensurate to the amount of whatever resource he received: he agrees more when the experimenter was generous in his reward, or as in the Gerard and Mathewson's investigation (1966), moderate in the punishment he inflicted.

There is no real contradiction between the two sets of results and no need for two different theories. Resource theory provided an explanation for both sets. In cognition, loss and gain are positively related; therefore, an event displaying a different relationship will create dissonance. Such discrepancy may be experienced by committed, as well as by uncommitted subjects: receiving a small compensation for a large loss is not more dissonant than gaining a large compensation for a minimal loss. The committed subject reduces dissonance by limiting his loss, while in the absence of commitment the reduction of dissonance is obtained by giving status to the experimenter.

INDUCING DISSONANCE BY COGNITIVE CHANGE. Most dissonance investigations consist essentially of comparing subjects confronted with a dissonant event with others experiencing a non-dissonant situation. In devising these two types of event, the experimenter relies intuitively on his own cognition; the cognitive structure of the subjects does not appear in the experimental design, although it is tacitly assumed to resemble that of the experimenter; hence, the manipulation of the event constitutes the independent variable. In a radical departure from this traditional design, Bramel (1962) kept the event constant while manipulating differentially the cognition of his subjects. By increasing self-esteem in half of the subjects and decreasing it in the other half, he modified the relationship between actual and ideal self. Subjects were then exposed to a situation indicating that they had homosexual tendencies. A bogus machine, to which they were hooked, showed "physiological arousal" when they observed pictures of nude males. The machine was, of course, controlled by the experimenter and not by the reactions of the subject. Bramel correctly predicted that those with increased self-esteem will experience more dissonance. Indeed, high self-esteem denotes a strong positive relationship between actual and ideal self—the notion of actual self covaries with desirable traits; by contrast, actual self is associated with an undesirable characteristic in the event "I have homosexual tendencies." Hence, such events are particularly dissonant when self-esteem is greater.

Bramel's experiment shows that the same event—evidence of homosexual tendencies—may be more or less dissonant, depending on the cognitive structure of the subject. Thus, a prediction of dissonance should consider both the event and the cognition of its observer. As Aronson (1969, p. 28) notes, being untruthful is not dissonant for a psychopathic liar; but then, wouldn't he experience dissonance when telling the truth? Limiting the investigation of dissonance to cognitions which are widely shared and thus more readily predictable by the experimenter has obscured the relationship between dissonance and some other areas of psychological study.

DISSONANCE AND PSYCHOPATHOLOGY. Consider a person with extremely low self-esteem; for him, the event of succeeding in a task would create dissonance: he would either tend to downgrade his success or he will ascribe it to some factor unrelated to his abilities. Situations of this type have not been recognized as cases of dissonance, although they are well-known to students of psychopathology. For a long time it has been noted that some individuals court failure, become upset when things go too well, refuse love and are embarrassed by praise. For them, receiving status and/or love are dissonant events, threatening their cognitive structure; they will seek interpersonal relations in which they can be consonantly deprived of resources. This type of behavior has been widely discussed in the literature. Mechanisms for the maintenance of a congruent self-image to avoid tension have been investigated by Secord and Backman (1961, 1965); Leary (1957) has propounded the notion that interpersonal behavior is also an invitation to the "appropriate" reaction from the other; thus, for example, hostility wards off the threatening possibility of receiving love. Jackson (1957) has shown how disturbed individuals may have a stabilizing effect in disturbed family systems, in which somebody else gets worse when the "patient" gets better.

The basic unity of these phenomena has been often obscured because of the different terminology used by various authors. Carson (1969) has provided an integrated treatment of this area, summarized in his view of psychotherapy; "... the strategic task of the psychotherapist is to change his client's self-in-relation-to-world image. . . . An image is changed through the provision of experience that is both new and assimilable in terms of existing, accessible cognitive categories. Cognitive categories, especially perhaps those relating to self, cannot be bludgeoned into change; they tend to repel experiences that do not 'fit them'" (p. 275).

102   PART I ABRIDGEMENT OF *SOCIETAL STRUCTURES OF THE MIND*

For disturbed individuals, the need for resources and the motivation to preserve the structure are often in conflict as resource-providing events may be incongruent with their cognition. This conflict between resource accumulation and structure preservation has originated rival hypotheses regarding the effect of criticism and praise on their recipient, summarized by Jones (1973). The consistency hypothesis suggests that ". . . for individuals with high evaluations of themselves or some aspect of self, positive evaluations from others are consistent, whereas for individuals with low self-evaluations, positive evaluations are inconsistent and negative evaluations are consistent. Therefore, the prediction from the self-consistency theories is that high self-evaluators will react more favorably to approval than to disapproval and that low self-evaluators will react more favorably to disapproval than to approval" (p. 186). By contrast, the self-esteem hypothesis proposes that ". . . low self-esteem individuals are predicted to respond more favorably to positive evaluations from others and more unfavorably to negative evaluations from others as compared to high self-esteem individuals. This prediction . . . follows from the assumption that low self-esteem people have greater needs for esteem enhancement and are therefore more satisfied by the approval of others and more frustrated by the disapproval of others than are high self-esteem people" (p. 187). It is not by chance that the two hypotheses differ mainly with regard to low self-esteem subjects. Those are the people who find themselves in a conflict: if they absorb criticism and ignore praise, their need for status becomes greater with every encounter; if they accept praise and reject criticism, they experience inconsistency between their cognitive structure and the external event. Jones (1973), in reviewing relevant evidence, reported more support for the self-esteem hypothesis. This finding, however, may be due to a characteristic of the subjects in the investigations he considered. The analysis presented here suggests that the lower self-esteem is the more dissonance is experienced by the individual when praised. Therefore, a person possessing very low self-esteem will tend to reject praise in favor of maintaining the structure. Such extreme individuals are rare in the college population from which subjects in psychological research are usually obtained. Among them one is more likely to find persons of moderately low self-esteem who fulfill their need for status, since the threat to their structure is not very great. Stronger support for the consistency hypotheses is likely to be found in a clinical setting, where cases of extremely low self-esteem are more common.

Conceptualizing dissonance as a contrast between past experience of the organism (as represented in the cognitive structure) and current experience reveals its relationship to other notions which have been considered unrelated to it.

EXTENDING THE NOTION OF DISSONANCE. A threat to the preservation of structure may come not only from an event with a different structure, but also from a series of unstructured events. Such random environment, in which the conditioned and unconditioned stimuli would be statistically independent (i.e., the probability of their joint occurrence is equal to the product of their marginal probabilities) was proposed by Rescorla (1967) as a control for classical conditioning experiments. This suggestion was criticized (Seligman, 1969) on the ground that a random environment produced disruptive side effects. These effects may be due to the threat posed to the cognitive structure by random events. It is interesting to note that any learning experiment involving a change in reinforcement schedule produces some dissonance: after the organism had learned to associate response A with reward and response B with punishment, it is presented with a contrasting situation. Since the learning period is usually short, the schedule is unlikely to become firmly established in cognition and the dissonant effects are weak. Even "superstitious behavior" (Skinner, 1953, pp. 84–87) when contrasted by future events may create dissonance. A pigeon fed small amounts at frequent intervals may acquire the habit of repeating whatever it was doing when food was first administered, although food release was regulated by the clock independently of the pigeon's behavior. When, in future trials, the coincidence between emission of behavior and provision of food disappear, dissonance may occur.

So far we have considered dissonant events characterized by elements which deviate from the relationship among their respective cognitive classes. Incongruence may also occur when a person is presented with an event which belongs to class A according to one cue, but should be classified into class B according to another cue. For example, a person having a beard but wearing a female dress represents an incongruent event; the dress suggests that this person should be classified as "female," yet the beard provides a cue for the "male" class. A similar situation arises when the experience of one sense is not supported by other senses. Seeing a person but being unable to feel him when touched is a strange experience; such apparition is likely to be labeled ghost. But again, incongruence will be experienced only when sight and touch are cognitively related; one does not feel uncomfortable because he can see but not touch the images appearing on a TV screen.

104 PART I ABRIDGEMENT OF *SOCIETAL STRUCTURES OF THE MIND*

DISSONANCE AND VISUAL ILLUSIONS. Our re-definition of dissonance also suggests the interpretation of perceptual constancy and spatial illusions as special cases of dissonance reduction. It is well known that an object moving away from the observer is not perceived as shrinking in size, although its image on the retina becomes smaller as the distance increases; likewise a coin tilted at 45 degrees is perceived as round rather than elliptical in spite of the fact that the shape seen by the observer is elliptical. Perceptual constancy thus consists in modifying perception to fit the relevant cognitive image, a process which also occurs in dissonance reduction.

Spatial illusions, systematically misjudging the size, shape, or other properties of objects under certain conditions, have often been considered a class of phenomena distinct from perceptual constancy; Day (1972) has, however, proposed that illusions occur when stimuli that normally preserve constancy are present while the image of the object does not change. Clearly events presenting this combination are dissonant, as they deviate from the common experience recorded in cognition; dissonance reduction produces the illusion: the perceived size of the object is modified as it should be when constancy stimuli are present.

DISSONANCE AND COGNITIVE GROWTH. Classes are positively related in cognition when their elements tended to occur jointly in the events previously experienced by the organism; thus the structure reflects past experience. A dissonant event contradicts the wisdom accumulated in the cognition, or it disconfirms a hypothesis held by the observer. Being an isolated instance, its perception is modified to fit cognition. If the same deviant event continues to occur, one would expect a permanent modification of the structure, as it happens during cognitive development. Both dissonance and cognitive development are characterized by a discrepancy between events and cognition. In dissonance, however, the deviant event is an isolated case and the solution involves perceptual modification to fit the structure. In development, on the other hand, dissonant events tend to be repetitive and eventually result in a modification of the cognitive structure.

Structure-Related Properties of Resources

On various occasions we have noted that resource classes differ systematically on some characteristics; for example, we have proposed that the relationship between self and other is stronger for love than for status, and mutual exclusion between giving and taking is least pronounced in love, increases for status, and more so for information. Another characteristic was suggested earlier in this chapter; the optimal range is smallest for love and increases gradually as one moves toward money in the structure of resource classes.

A more comprehensive review of resource properties will be given here. The characteristics we shall consider seem to be related to the cognitive structure of resource classes, so that the values proximal resources assume on any of them will be more similar than the values of remote resources. The value taken by each resource on any property may depend on the cognitive and environmental conditions existing at the time this particular class became differentiated. We shall discuss this point after considering the various properties. Finally, we shall examine the consequences of these differential characteristics for resource exchange.

In view of their effects on transactions, it seems appropriate to consider resource properties before we turn to interpersonal dynamics in the next chapter. Some of these properties pertain to environmental conditions (or institutional settings) facilitating or hindering the exchange: a small group, for example, is more suitable for exchanges of love; a large group facilitates the exchange of money. Some other properties bear upon the effects of resource exchange on the motivational state of the individual: giving to self and to other, for example, are related positively for love and negatively for money; consequently, when one gives love he becomes richer, while after giving money he is poorer. This property reflects a cognitive state (self and other are less differentiated for love than for money), which, in turn, determines differential rules of exchange for the various resources. As noted earlier, reduction in the amount of love one possesses requires *taking it away* from the other, while a decrease in one's bank account would be accomplished by *giving* some money to the other.

There are probably properties which have not yet been identified. Of those we know, love and money differ most; this suggests that the particularistic dimension may be the more relevant one, as love and money are at its opposite poles. By stating the values that love and money assume on each characteristic, we shall provide also an approximate idea about the values of other resources. Services and status will be more similar to love, while information and goods will assume values proximal to money. Let us start with those properties which bear on rules of exchange.

106 PART I ABRIDGEMENT OF *SOCIETAL STRUCTURES OF THE MIND*

Properties Affecting the Motivational State

We have identified six properties which influence the balance of resources after the exchange had taken place.

RELATIONSHIP BETWEEN SELF AND OTHER. It is proposed that the relationship between the amount of resource given to the other and the amount left to self is positive for love, decreases and becomes negative as one moves along the structure toward money. We have already seen that the relationship between giving to self and to other (as well as between taking away from self and from other) tends to be weaker for status than for love, although both are positive. The more we give love or status to the other, the more is left for ourselves. Giving information to another does not appear to reduce or increase the amount possessed by the giver. It can be argued, however, that sharing may reduce the value of the information if the situation is competitive (e.g., industrial or military secrets). On the other hand, transmission of information may also result in some increase of information available to self, as for instance when repressed information is brought to the surface during a psychotherapeutic session. Likewise, misleading another person (i.e., taking away information from him) does not change the amount of information possessed by the deceiver, except for the eventual knowledge that the victim has been hooked. On the whole, it seems that the amount of information left to the giver is independent of the amount he had given, so that information is characterized neither by positive nor by negative relationship between self and other. Strong negative relationship is characteristic of money and goods, where giving to other definitely reduces the amount left for self. Services may show a more moderate but still negative relationship: performing a service for another person usually results in physical discomfort for the performer, as it involves expenditure of energy. In general, the relationship between giving to other and to self appears to change gradually for the various resources, along their position in the structure: love has the most positive relationship; status is less positive; information, independent; money and goods most negative. Service is again less negative.

THE RELATIONSHIP BETWEEN MODES. A positive relationship between giving and taking, denoted by the term "ambivalence," usually refers to love exchange. It is inconceivable to describe money transactions as ambivalent. Indeed the relationship between giving and taking is most positive for love. One can love and hate the same person simultaneously. We have already seen data suggesting that in love there is a considerable amount of ambivalence, even among normal individuals. We also noted some ambivalence for status, although lower than for love. Ambivalence in status is well exemplified by expressions such as "to pay respect grudgingly." Still less ambivalence has been found in information; yet some erroneous, misleading or ambiguous item may be included in a given transmission of information. Likewise, an information mainly erroneous may contain some correct items. Sometimes one tells "half the truth." Money suggests absence of ambivalence; giving money appears to exclude taking it away. Even counterfeit money is just not given, but neither is it taken away. Ranking of resources by decreasing degree of ambivalence has so far followed the structural order. If this rule is also valid for the remaining resources, ambivalence will now increase as we are approaching the most particularistic resource, love, from the other side of the circle. For goods, the extent to which giving and taking occur jointly may be slightly higher than for money: defective goods may actually cause damage. The "ambivalence" of services may be higher than for goods. It happens that some damage is done in the performance of a service: the barber may cut the client's skin, the physician may cause some damage to the patient's body in the course of treatment, the mover may damage the furniture, and the housewife may burn the roast. These considerations suggest that the joint occurrence of giving and taking away will follow the circular structure of resources, being highest for love and lowest for money.

The preceding analysis of the relationship among behaviors proposes that different resources do not obey the same rules. The change from one resource to another appears, however, to be gradual and to follow the order. At one extreme there is money, where giving to self excludes giving to other and taking away excludes giving. For money, therefore, each transaction can be described by a single value: if A gives five dollars to B, A has five dollars less and B five dollars more. As any accountant knows, the amount credited to an account should be the same as the amount debited to another account. At the other extreme there is love: our accountant would probably tend his resignation if requested to keep books on love exchanges. Here, giving to the other often increases the amount left for self and giving does not necessarily rule out a certain amount of taking away. It should be noted, however, that the same types of behavior occur for money as for other resources. It is only the *relationship* among these behaviors that varies for different resources. Attempts to extend the rules of money transactions to other resources have caused some difficulties in applying the notion of exchange to other forms of interpersonal communication, since the fact that one can give without

108 PART I ABRIDGEMENT OF *SOCIETAL STRUCTURES OF THE MIND*

reducing the amount in his possession has been considered contradictory to the very notion of exchange (Cartwright & Zander, 1968, p. 233).

Building on the notion that information, unlike goods, can be transmitted without loss to the giver, Rosen (1966) predicted that the monetary price demanded for information would be lower than for goods. To test this hypothesis, Rosen gave his subjects control over a box which contained three pieces of a jigsaw puzzle needed by another person in order to complete his picture and win points. Some subjects were given a key for the lock; others were told the combination for opening it. Both groups of subjects were asked to set a price for giving the key or the combination to the other person. The price demanded for the key was, on average, higher than for the combination. This differential property of goods and information was neutralized in other experimental groups by stipulating that: (a) the key would be used and then returned; and (b) the information on the combination would not be given to a third individual. In these conditions, the prices for key and combination tended to equalize, particularly when the other person was expected to comply with these limitations.

VERBALIZATION OF NEED. We propose that the easiest need to express is that for money and the one most difficult to communicate is the need for love. Statements such as "I demand an increase in salary" or "I have to raise the price" are quite commonly heard, particularly in times of inflation. A straightforward bidding for love is relatively rare, even among intimates. This difference may be related to the degree to which verbal communication is suitable for the various resource classes. Language appears quite appropriate for money dealings; love, on the other hand, is more easily expressed by paralinguistic communication: touching, expressions of the face, eye's contact, body posture, or physical proximity. We often say that we have no words to express our feelings. Indeed it takes a poet to accomplish this feat; for common mortals, a misty look is more handy.

This property affects the resources exchanged and their substitution. In expressing a need, or in bidding for a resource, there will be a tendency to "skid" toward less particularistic ones. A child in need of love may ask for a toy, some candy, or will complain of pain. A lovelorn adult may settle for professional success, for information and perhaps even for money. On the other hand, a person who needs money is unlikely to ask for sympathy. Thus, substitution of one resource for another is not a two-way street; a less particularistic resource is more likely to be substituted for a more particularistic one than the other way around.

PRELUDE TO RESOURCE EXCHANGE   109

EXCHANGE OF SAME RESOURCE. A lonely individual, needing love, will wish to meet another lonely person, so that they would be able to exchange love. But meeting another pauper will not help the person who is short of money. Thus, the more particularistic a resource, the higher the probability that it will be exchanged with the same resource, while non-particularistic resources will tend to be exchanged with different ones.

In a study of exchange preferences, it was found that the preference for exchanging love with love was maximal, 32 percent (because of the way the questionnaire was constructed, no preference could be higher than 33 percent in this study). Following the structure of resources, the preference for same-resource exchanges decreased gradually: status 27 percent; information 25 percent; money 22 percent and goods 18 percent; then the figure went up again for services, 25 percent. Although these data are restricted to exchanges in a specific social institution—friendship—they support the notion that exchanges within the same resource are more likely for particularistic than for non-particularistic ones.

RANGE OF EXCHANGE.[2] This property refers to the number of resources with which a given one may be exchanged. It is related to the self-exchange property but does not necessarily follow from it: a given resource, although not often exchanged with itself, may be transacted only for a specific other resource. We propose that the more particularistic a resource is, the narrower is the range of resources with which it can be exchanged. Few resources can be exchanged with love, but several can be obtained for money; in consequence, money appears as an appropriate means of exchange in several social institutions, while love is suitable only in a few. In other words, there are more possibilities of exchange for non-particularistic resources; many things can be obtained with money, but few in exchange for love.

RELATIONSHIP BETWEEN INTERPERSONAL SETTING AND EXCHANGE. Transmission of money does not require a face-to-face interaction; it can be sent conveniently through a third person. Moreover, money may be kept for future exchange. Exchange of love, on the other hand, can hardly be separated from the interpersonal situation, and love cannot be kept for a long time in the absence of actual exchange, or transmitted by an intermediary without incurring loss. This property is closely related to the *locus* of storage of the resource. Love is stored (but not for long) in the "heart"; money is kept at the bank or under the mattress. Some other resources can

---

[2] This property was proposed by Meir Teichman.

be stored either inside or outside the individual. Information, for example, can be memorized or recorded in writing, tape, punch cards, etc. Food can be stored in the refrigerator or inside the body as fat.

The relationship between the interpersonal setting and the resource exchanged influences the outcome of the exchange and, in turn, is influenced by the environment or, more precisely, by the level of technology. In cultures which do not possess a written language, information must be memorized, i.e., stored inside. Where food cannot be kept long enough to assure a steady supply, being fat is considered an advantage, while being overweight constitutes a problem when freezing and canning are within easy reach. Thus, in a sense, this property mediates between the motivational states of the individual and his environment. Let us turn now to some of the properties which are more clearly influenced by environmental conditions.

Properties Affected by Environment

These properties indicate characteristics of the environment or institutional setting which will enhance or inhibit the exchange of a given resource.

TIME FOR PROCESSING INPUT. Giving and receiving love cannot be done in a hurry; it requires time and even some leisure. Money, to the contrary, can change hands very rapidly. In an environment providing an overload of stimuli, those resources which require a longer processing time are more likely to receive low priority. Such selection will thus favor the less particularistic resources.

An experiment done by Meir Teichman showed that subjects allotted 15 minutes for affective exchanges were significantly less satisfied than comparable subjects who had 25 minutes available for the interaction. The number and content of love messages received by the subject was the same in both conditions so that subjects who interacted longer did receive the same amount of affection as those in the other group; for the former participants the remaining time was filled by neutral messages. By contrast, increasing the time available did not alter satisfaction when the resource exchanged was money. These results support the notion that time available is a significant factor in love exchanges but not in monetary transactions.

DELAY OF REWARD. Love is a relatively long-term investment, with rewards being reaped only after several encounters; a friendship needs to be "cultivated" and a girl needs to be courted. Therefore exchanges of love require the possibility of repeated encounters and trust, i.e., high expectation that the transaction will be completed. On the other hand, an exchange of money with goods can be consummated in a single encounter and, at least in cash payments, does not require trust in the buyer. In an environment where most encounters are with strangers and are non-repetitive, the less particularistic the resource, the more likely it is to be an object of exchange.

OPTIMUM GROUP SIZE. It has been noted that in animal species living in groups, such as monkeys and apes, there is an optimum group size (Carpenter, 1942). When the group becomes too large, behavior which disrupts its normal functioning appears to increase (Calhoun, 1962). The work of Bailey (1966) suggests that such negative effects are obtained even when the increase in group size does not result in higher density; in Bailey's experiment, density was kept constant by increasing the space available to the animals in proportion to their augment in number. The sheer effect of group size, as distinct from crowding, may be explained by limitations in the cognitive capacity of the animals to handle an overly large number of mates.

As for human beings, it appears that the more particularistic a resource is, the heavier are its demands on cognitive representation for the following reasons:

1. The very notion of particularism implies that the uniqueness of the exchange partner as an individual is important; hence there is a desire to obtain a large amount of information about him and to provide him with information about us. Indeed, the significance of self-disclosure, particularly in relationship with intimates, was stressed by Jourard (1964). One of the first things lovers do is to exchange intimate information; and Mowrer (1964) has held that avoidance of self-disclosure is a major source of alienation from the group. Perhaps not by chance, the verb "to know" is used in biblical Hebrew to indicate sexual intercourse, a highly particularistic form of behavior.
2. The more particularistic a resource, the less it is amenable to external conservation and therefore it depends more on internal, cognitive storage: the very idea of a lover taking notes on the self-disclosure of his beloved sounds ridiculous.

Since the amount which can be stored within the system is limited, small group settings should be more suitable for particularistic exchanges than large groups. Evidence for this prediction is reported in the literature. Zimet

112   PART I ABRIDGEMENT OF *SOCIETAL STRUCTURES OF THE MIND*

and Schneider (1969) observed discussion groups who met over a period of three or four years. Group composition remained the same over the total period, but the actual number of participants varied between two and five at different meetings because of absences. The frequency of direct personal expressions referring to a group member decreased as the group size increased; communication—apparently—became less particularistic when more people were present.

Nye et al. (1970) investigated the relationship between family size and interpersonal exchanges among its members. Instead of direct observation, as in the Zimet and Schneider study, they relied on self-reports of family members, obtained partly by mail and partly by direct interviewing. A large sample from the state of Washington participated in this study. Among the variables investigated, the following are relevant to our topic:

1. Adolescents' perception of their parents' affect toward them.
2. Adolescent's affect toward their parents.
3. Mutual affect of spouses as perceived by the wife.
4. Mutual affect of spouses as perceived by adolescent children.

In all four variables, the same general trend appeared: there was a slight increase of reported affection as the number of children in the family rose from one to two; affective exchanges decreased steadily as the number of children became larger. Hutt and Hutt (1970, pp. 151–152) found that normal children reduced their social contacts as the size of the group increased; results for brain-damaged and autist children were, however, open to various interpretations, although the frequency of their contacts was below normal in every group size. In summarizing results of studies on group size and particularistic exchanges, Goldstein et al. (1966, pp. 340–341) noted the following effects of larger groups: (1) "sense of belonging" decreased (Miller, 1950); (2) affectional ties among members decreased (Coyle, 1930; Kinney, 1953); and (3) the tendency to form subgroups and cliques increased (Hare, 1962).

Latane and Darley (1969) conducted a series of experiments to identify variables influencing the willingness to help or to safeguard the well-being of another individual in an emergency situation. In our classification, helping belongs to the class of services, a neighbor of love. Latane and Darley varied the number of persons present in the emergency situation; they consistently found that the probability of helping behavior decreased when the number of bystanders increased.

All these investigations indicate that exchanges of particularistic resources are more likely to occur in a small group than in a large one. By contrast, economic transactions appear to be facilitated by larger groups: access to a wide market is considered advantageous by businessmen; shoppers will tend to prefer a store where sales are brisk; and one will prefer a stock or commodity exchange where many people convene. We can thus expect that in an environment of large size groups, non-particularistic resources will be exchanged more than particularistic ones.

Properties and Cognitive Development

We have considered certain characteristics of resources bearing on the outcome of the exchange and on the environmental conditions suitable for its occurrence. We have also proposed that these characteristics are related to the position of the resource class in the structure and, especially, to its particularistic dimension; partial evidence has been presented supporting the relationship between properties and structure. It should be remembered that their structure has been derived from a sequence of differentiation among resource classes. If resource properties also originate in the development sequence, then this sequence will provide the link between the properties and the structure. It is indeed proposed that the value assumed by a resource class on each property reflects the cognitive and environmental conditions which had existed when the class became differentiated.

Love develops early, before the differentiations between giving and taking, as well as between self and other have become firmly established; its development precedes the acquisition of language, as well. Therefore, in love, there is ambivalence between giving and taking, a high positive relationship between self and other, less amenability to verbal expression, and less opportunity for exchanging it with a wide range of other resources. Money, on the other hand, acquires its meaning much later after one has acquired some mastery of language, has learned that giving is not taking and other is not self, and has already differentiated a full range of resource classes. Furthermore, love begins to be exchanged in the small and relatively stable family group, while money, even at an early age, is mostly used for exchanges outside the family. In summary: (1) Resources are best

114 PART I ABRIDGEMENT OF *SOCIETAL STRUCTURES OF THE MIND*

exchanged in environmental conditions that resemble those under which they had been developed in the past. (2) They reflect the cognitive state which existed at the time of their differentiation. (3) The closer two resource classes are, the more similar are the values they assume on each one of the properties.

Some Important Implications of Properties

It is perhaps too early to judge the impact that the identification of resource properties will have on the understanding and control of human affairs; neither is it possible to discuss all social phenomena which are related to them. At this stage we can only attempt to outline some of the consequences that look particularly important.

Differential Laws of Exchange

We have seen that in exchanges of love, unlike economic transactions, someone's profit does not have to be another's loss. Consider for example sexual relationships, an interpersonal exchange at the borderline between love and services; it would be rather difficult to specify costs and rewards in such a situation. Thus the rules of economic exchange apply to only one subset of resources, while other resources follow different rules. Consequently, attempts to interpret non-economic exchanges in terms of profit and loss would meet with considerable difficulties.

The difference between love and money exchanges has always been realized intuitively: accountants were never renowned for their expressions of love, nor poets for their ability to keep books. Yet the fact that in love, two and two do not make four but rather, five or six, and the non-verbal forms of expressing it have lent a phantomatic quality to this resource class; serious, hard-minded people like economists, engineers or social planners are not supposed to be concerned with exchanges of love. With the realization that the exchanges of more particularistic resources are just as lawful as economic transactions, although their laws may differ, the resistance to consider their importance and significance to human welfare may decrease, leading us to a fuller and more integrated view of the role played by the various resources in individual and societal functioning.

Effects of Urban Environment

The environmental properties of resources, i.e., time for processing input, delay of reward and optimum group size, combine to hinder the exchanges of some resources from urban society. Very succinctly, an environment in which there is strong competition among inputs, encounters are brief and non-repetitive, and where every person engages in numerous contacts, constitutes an obstacle to the exchange of particularistic resources, while facilitating non-particularistic transactions. When these conditions appear concurrently, their effects will be cumulative. Often, in a large crowd there are many more competing stimuli than in a small group and less opportunity for repeated encounters. Yet there are situations where the group is small but unlikely to meet again: it is improbable that patients in the doctor's waiting room, visitors to an art gallery, or buyers in a fashionable boutique will maintain personal contacts. These examples suggest that the size and stability of a group can vary in different social institutions: although a family may be similar in size to a group of friends, the former is more stable; groups at work are likely to be larger and less stable, and in commercial setting one can usually find large crowds and non-recurrent encounters.

The conditions within a particular institution, in turn, are influenced by the wider social setting. In a small town, for example, one is likely to meet frequently the same group of people at the corner drugstore; in a large metropolis these encounters are most often non-recurrent. In general, in the urban environment, the conditions are less conducive to particularistic exchanges, beyond any specific institutional setting. Milgram (1970) has proposed that reducing the time allocated to each input is an adaptive response to the overload of interpersonal stimuli which characterizes an urban center; if processing a love stimulus requires longer time, it follows that in the city these stimuli will be filtered out more than stimuli pertaining to less particularistic resources. It is hardly necessary to point out the existence of large crowds in the city and to the non-repetitiveness of many encounters.

The selective influence of the urban setting in resource exchanges contributes to the understanding of some of the less savory aspects of city life. We shall briefly consider three of them: crime, alienation and drugs.

CRIME. It is unnecessary to note that crime is on the increase, particularly in densely settled areas. Some interesting aspects of it are revealed in an experiment reported by Zimbardo (1970). A car with license plate removed and hood open was left in the Bronx near the New York University campus. Another car in the same condition was left for an identical time in Palo Alto, near the Stanford University campus. All the movable parts were stolen from the New York car within the first day. Nothing was removed from the Palo Alto car during the whole period. In New York the pilferage occurred in broad daylight when other people were present and was done also by middle-class-looking white adults. In a small community these same individuals would probably behave as pillars of law and order, but there, antisocial or asocial behavior would entail loss of status long before any eventual legal punishment. The relative scarcity of particularistic exchanges in the city deprives society of powerful informal instruments of social control, particularly the giving and taking of status. The law enforcement system is built on the assumption that for most people the threat of status deprivation by other and by self, which are positively related, is a sufficient deterrent against the violation of social norms. Even the arm of the law becomes less effective when particularistic means of social control fail. When one does not care about the opinion held by his neighbors about him, sitting in jail becomes merely a temporary loss of freedom and not a permanent loss of face. Moreover, the judicial procedure becomes inefficient and cumbersome when attempting to take care of all those cases that previously had been handled by non-formal means.

ALIENATION. We have already learned that the relationship between self and other is positive and highest for love. Thus, it is through love exchanges that we relate to other persons. Scarcity of particularistic transactions is subjectively experienced as loneliness and estrangement. In consequence, alienation will be more frequent among the large city crowds than in rural areas.

Alienation has often been interpreted to mean self-estrangement, a notion which was criticized for its apparent lack of rigor: how can one be alienated from himself? The puzzle is solved when we reflect that only in the particularistic resources giving to other also implies giving to self, so that the self is *both* actor and object, rather than being either actor or object. Thus a worker that does his job only to get his wages is more likely to be alienated than a worker who takes pride in what he does, i.e., who gives himself status in addition to receiving money from the employer. Seeman (1959) came close to this interpretation when stating that ". . . what has been called self-estrangement refers essentially to the inability of the individual to find self-rewarding . . . activities that engage him" (p. 790).

DRUGS. It seems that in modern society the use of drugs has increased with scarcity of particularistic resources. When something is scarce, there are two alternative solutions: increasing its supply or reducing the need. This is not a world-shaking thought, yet it suggests that certain drugs may facilitate particularistic exchanges in unfavorable environmental conditions, while certain others may reduce the discomfort caused by the shortage of particularistic resources. Investigating the effects of marihuana, Halpern (1968, pp. 381–382) administered several psychological tests to 45 subjects, when they were under the influence of marihuana and when free from its influence. In comparing results from the Thematic Apperception Test in the two conditions, she reported a reduction in needs in the drugged condition, with the exception of the need for dominance, which increased. All the needs analyzed were in the service-love-status range and thus quite particularistic. While these results may suggest that the need for particularistic resources is reduced under the influence of marihuana, more recent work on marihuana[3] (Hollister, 1971; Weil et al., 1968) did not provide data which are directly related to the hypothesis proposed here.

Reports on the effects of LSD seem to suggest that this drug may facilitate exchanges rather than reduce the need. Mogar and Savage (1964) reported that after a single strong controlled experience with LSD, a subject "values human brotherhood more... tends to be less distrustful and guarded with others, warmer and more spontaneous in expressing emotions..." (Mogar, 1966, p. 102). According to some investigators (Harman et al., 1969, p. 457; Stafford & Golightly, 1967, pp. 61–93), subjects who were administered LSD reported improved ability to relate interpersonally. In a study of drug use in nonliterate societies (Blum, 1969, pp. 150–151), it was found that hallucinogen drugs, similar to LSD, were used in a group situation almost as often as in private; marihuana and opium, on the other hand, were taken mainly in private. Although these results are based on a small number of cultures, they again tend to suggest that while certain drugs increased interpersonal sensitivity, other drugs reduce the need for friendship. There is little in the literature which bears on these hypotheses: in spite of the widely accepted assumption that drugs constitute a response to emotional problems, studies of drugs often deal with their effect on other variables, such as intellectual abilities and task performance.

---

[3] We are grateful to David Davis for bringing these works to our attention.

City Life: Selection and Training

The growth of large metropolitan areas with their high population density, the increased institutional specialization, and the opportunities for physical and social mobility, is a rather novel feature of human society. It has greatly facilitated economic exchanges, while hindering particularistic transactions. The parallel with the physical environment is striking: in both cases technology has created new problems in the process of solving old ones. The private car is a great means of transportation; it also pollutes the air. D.D.T. has increased food production; it also poisons the environment. Modern society, and particularly urban society, has provided new opportunities for trade and work; it also reduces the exchange of particularistic resources. As suggested here, certain negative features of modern society may be due to this reduction.

We know next to nothing about the minimum level of these resources necessary for proper functioning of the individual, although there is solid evidence on the negative effects of resource deprivation at an early age. There are probably considerable individual differences in the tolerance of deprivation. Those having a lower minimum level, the "cold," "distant," "manipulative" individuals, may adjust more to the conditions of city life. They may constitute the "urban type," better fitted to operate in the urban environment.

THE APPEARANCE OF NEW INSTITUTIONS. For those who cannot endure the lack of particularism, new institutional forms are created for the exchange of particularistic resources in spite of unfavorable environmental conditions. What is common to these institutions is that their norms call for the exchange of love and sometimes also sex, which is on the borderline between love and services. These norms endorse spontaneity, expression of feelings, touching and other forms of nonverbal behavior. The various institutions differ mainly in the size and the stability of the group; the innovative aspect of these attempts consists of introducing love exchange in conditions which are usually considered to be unfavorable to it, such as extended and/or temporary groups. Size is relatively large, but there is considerable stability in communes and in group sex. Youth festivals of the Woodstock type are characterized by large and temporary groups. Temporary, but smaller in size, are groups having the purpose of training a person in particularistic exchanges, with the expectation that he will be able to perform these transactions in other situations as well. These groups go under different names such as sensitivity training, encounter, marathons; some stress touching, body movements and other forms of nonverbal communication; some demand nudity of the participants. They all constitute recognition of the fact that in the environment provided by modern society, particularistic exchanges are hindered, and thus special training and opportunities are necessary in order to surmount these obstacles. When successful, these types of training may reduce the negative aspects of city life which have been previously briefly noted.

Summary

Social experiences are interpersonal encounters in which resources are given or taken away. Whether or not a particular exchange will take place depends on three sets of conditions: the motivational state of the potential exchangers, the appropriateness of the environment and the properties of the resources to be exchanged.

The individual tends to steer his interpersonal contacts to maintain an optimal amount of resources. Possessing too little as well as too much is experienced as discomfort, which the organism wishes to eliminate. For each resource there is a lower limit, below which a motivational arousal occurs; the upper limit, however, varies for the different resources. Consequently, the optimal range differs from one resource to another. It will be smallest for love and practically infinite for money. The optimal range of the remaining resources will follow the structural order. The closer they are to love, the narrower will be their optimal range; resources closer to money will have a wider range.

When the amount of a given resource possessed by the organism at a given time falls below the optimal range, it is experienced as a need. It follows that there are six classes of needs, one for each resource.

Most of the needs refer to situations where the object is the "self" and the behavior "giving." A resource is sought after by the individual in order to reduce a present or future deficit and to bring the amount held by his system within the optimal range. Even the need to "give" may be perceived as means for increasing the amount possessed by the giver. Particularistic resources are accumulated by the giver through the positive relationship between self and other; when one expresses love toward the other, he simultaneously accepts himself. When one dispenses non-particularistic resources, he expects to be reciprocated. But what about the need to destroy or to take away? Again, for particularistic resources, there are positive relationships between self and

120 PART I ABRIDGEMENT OF *SOCIETAL STRUCTURES OF THE MIND*

other; while rejecting the other, one also rejects himself to a certain degree. Thus the urge to express hostility may reflect a state of satiation. When the amount of love possessed by an individual exceeds the upper limit, he cannot get rid of it by giving some to the other, as giving love will further increase the amount possessed by him. By expressing hate, he also rejects himself, thus decreasing the amount of love within the optimal range. For non-particularistic resources, taking them away from the other re-establishes a balance by increasing the actual or perceived amount held by the self.

While need is a deficit in a particular resource, power may be defined as the amount of a given resource that is available to the individual for eventual giving. Again, there are six classes of power, one for each class of resources. A powerful person is in a position to enter an exchange in which he offers some resource and in turn expects to be reciprocated. Yet, power cannot be exercised unless there is a corresponding need on the part of the receiver. A person may have great potential power and little actual power when there is scarce demand for the resource he possesses in abundance.

The power to give requires possession of a certain amount which is beyond the lower limit of the optimal range. Yet even the poorest person may create a great loss. With regard to particularistic resources, such power of the powerless is limited. To be insulted by a low status person is less damaging than being degraded by a high status one. However, the amount of non-particularistic resources that can be taken away is independent of the amount possessed by the taker; therefore, formal punishment is exercised to protect the owner, where expressions of hostility are handled by non-formal means.

Beside the striving to maintain an optimal amount of each resource, the individual's behavior and perception is directed toward protecting his cognitive structure. An event containing relationships among elements which differ from the relationship among the relevant cognitive classes will create dissonance. The perception of such an event will be distorted so that it will fit the structure. However, when a dissonant event occurs frequently, the structure would have to be altered.

For an exchange to take place, a person needing a given resource and powerful in another should meet an individual who is in a complementary motivational state. Since exchanges take place so often, society has developed mechanisms for facilitating the encounter of individuals having reciprocal needs and powers. These mechanisms are called social institutions. They provide a suitable setting for the exchange and determine what resources each party should give and what should be received in return. Each institution specializes in certain resources, which tend to be proximal in the structure of resources; it follows that each institution focuses on a particular segment of the structure. Indeed, there are no institutions where money is exchanged with love or status with goods. While institutions facilitate the exchange process, they also constitute limitations and barriers. One should address himself to the appropriate institution for a given exchange. Yet he may not have access to it, and he may have to invest more to get the same amount of resource in an inappropriate institution.

Besides the motivational state of the potential exchanger and their access to the appropriate institutions, the completion of an exchange and its consequences are influenced by the properties of the particular resources exchanged. Some of these properties affect the motivational state of the participants after the exchange had taken place; other properties dictate the differential environmental conditions for each resource, within the appropriate institutions. In general, these properties are related to the cognitive structure, so that proximal resources are more similar with respect to the values they assume on each property than do remote ones. Moreover, the value assumed by a resource class on each property reflects the cognitive and environmental conditions which had existed when the classes became differentiated. Indeed, resources are best exchanged in environmental conditions that resemble those under which they had developed. Since the cognitive structure is a developmental product, the sequence of development constitutes a link between the structure and the properties of resources.

The environmental properties of resources combine to reduce particularistic exchanges in modern society. An environment in which a person is exposed to a large amount of stimuli and many contacts is not suitable for exchange of love. Many encounters are not repeated, and groups, although sometimes small, are often unstable in urban environments. Moreover, the highly specialized institutions of modern society do not provide a frame for exchanges of love as an addition to other exchanges. Consequently, people in such environment suffer from alienation and love deprivation. Criminal behavior increases as the criminals are not afraid to lose status and love from their neighbors; the latter do not provide these resources even when one behaves properly. Usage of drugs increases to overcome the feeling of alienation, either by reducing the need for human companionship, or by facilitating these exchanges in spite of unfavorable environmental conditions. Still another consequence of particularistic poverty is the development of group encounters; those are new institutions with the sole function of exchanging love.

5

Some Areas of Socio-Psychological Research in the Light of the Resource Exchange Paradigm

Overview

The theoretical concepts developed in the previous chapters constitute a framework for describing and understanding interpersonal behavior. As such, they should bear relevance to practical and theoretical notions which have been widely discussed in the literature of social psychology and personality. In the present chapter, we shall attempt to demonstrate what additional insight could be gained by applying the resource exchange paradigm to issues such as the frustration–aggression hypothesis, complementarity of needs, interpersonal attraction, conformity, distributive justice (and cognate notions of reciprocity and legitimacy of exchange), and various strategies for obtaining resources, such as Machiavellianism and ingratiation. We shall start with the frustration–aggression hypothesis, which clearly belongs to exchanges of taking away, and proceed through the other topics which pertain to exchanges of giving.

Frustration–Aggression as Exchange of Taking

Taking away (negative) behavior has rarely been considered from an exchange viewpoint, although some authors (e.g., Berscheid et al., 1968) came close to this formulation. More often, a theoretical framework for the study of negative behavior has been provided by the frustration–aggression hypothesis. Since it was first proposed some thirty years ago (Dollard et al., 1939), the hypothesis that frustration instigates aggression has generated an impressive amount of empirical work, leading, in turn, to a reexamination of its theoretical foundations (e.g., Berkowitz, 1962,

Social Behavior as Resource Exchange. Kjell Yngve Törnblom and Ali Kazemi, Oxford University Press.
© Oxford University Press 2023. DOI: 10.1093/oso/9780190066994.003.0006

SOME AREAS OF SOCIO-PSYCHOLOGICAL RESEARCH   123

1965, 1969b; Buss, 1961; Yates, 1962). By conceptualizing the frustration–aggression sequence as a type of exchange, we incorporate an enormous amount of research into the resource exchange framework and, hopefully, throw some new light on the rich data this research provided. To begin, let us examine similarities and differences between the frustration–aggression and the exchange formulations.

The Notion of Frustration

Two types of definition have been proposed for frustration. One type is exemplified by the classic definition of Dollard, et al. (1939), "an interference with the occurrence of an instigated goal response at its proper time in the behavior sequence" (p. 7). For these authors, as well as for Berkowitz (1965, p. 308) thwarting of a goal-oriented response is a central element of the frustrating event. While sharing the same view about frustration, Buss (1961) considered the delivery of noxious stimuli as an additional antecedent of aggression. Later, Buss (1966) suggested that attack is a more potent antecedent than thwarting; furthermore, he specified that only interference of a response "that has in the past led to a reinforcer" would create frustration. With this qualification of thwarting, Buss approaches the second type of definition, which centers on the *worsening of the reinforcement situation*. Representative of this approach are Bandura and Walters (1963, pp. 115–116), who define frustration as "delay of reinforcement."

The discrepancy between these two types of definitions is not as big as it seems: as noted by Buss, thwarting results in frustration only when the interfered activity is actually or potentially rewarding. Interference with the interminable chattering of a boring visitor will hardly lead to frustration. Thus, both types of definition suggest that a frustrating event consists of depriving the object-person of an expected resource. Indeed, in experimental manipulations, both actual and potential taking away of resources has been employed to create a state of frustration.

RESOURCES IN FRUSTRATION–AGGRESSION STUDIES. There is hardly a resource class which was not used in frustration–aggression studies. Yet, the fact that no explicit taxonomy of resource was available to the investigators had some undesirable consequences: (1) Resources belonging to two or more classes were often used jointly to create frustration, thus

124 PART I ABRIDGEMENT OF *SOCIETAL STRUCTURES OF THE MIND*

barring the study of their differential effects. (2) Some resource classes, such as services (e.g., electric shocks) and status, were exhaustively studied while other resources were neglected.

Mosher, Mortimer and Grebel (1968), for example, combined goods and status in creating frustration by making the loss of goods contingent upon losing a game. Geen and Berkowitz (1966) combined services and status by having their confederate express evaluation of the subject's performance through the administration of electric shock. The only study which employed deceiving as a source of frustration had it combined with loss of money (Conn & Crowne, 1964). The combination of resources is especially noticeable in the notion of "derogation," which includes loss of both love and status.

Since the resource involved in frustration or aggression was not considered a theoretically important variable, investigators preferred those resources which could easily be manipulated in an experimental setting. Thus, several manipulations were developed to induce loss of status. A common form is *ego threat*, which consists of creating a threat of failure or negative evaluation of the subject's performance. In some experiments, the subject is not allowed to finish an important task, or his performance is hindered, resulting in negative evaluation (Buss, 1963). In other experiments, competition is used to produce a threat of failure (Epstein & Taylor, 1967; Mosher & Proenza, 1968). In all these manipulations, a potential (future) loss of status is created. An actual loss of status is obtained by insult and failure, when the subject's performance or abilities are negatively evaluated (Feshbach, 1955; Geen & Berkowitz, 1966). Many studies had combined a potential loss of status with an actual one (e.g., the "insult-failure" technique proposed by Worchel, 1957, 1958, 1961). A second class of resources often used is services, mainly in the form of administering electric shock. A large number of studies utilized shock to measure aggression (Berkowitz et al., 1969; Buss, 1961, 1963; Mallick & McCandless, 1966; Walters & Thomas, 1963). Epstein and Taylor (1967), as well as Taylor (1967), manipulated a potential and an actual loss of services as a source of frustration by informing subjects of the intensity of shock their opponents intended to administer them, as well as by actually administering shock.

In conclusion, the resources most frequently used in frustration–aggression studies were services, love and status, while information, money and goods have been rather neglected.

DEPRIVATION, NEED AND REACTION. This brief review of theoretical viewpoints and experimental practice suggests that both actual and potential deprivation of specific resources may lead to frustration. Some results (Geen & Berkowitz, 1967; Geen, 1968; Mallick & McCandless, 1966) support Buss' suggestion (1966) that actual deprivation produces more powerful effects than does potential deprivation, as measured by the strength of reaction. Yet the effects of both actual attack and interference are in the same direction, both are likely to induce frustration.

A substantial amount of research was directed towards exploring the conditions under which actual or potential deprivation will result in frustration. If frustration is defined as deprivation, obviously there is no place for such investigation. Yet current conceptualizations of frustration cover not only the taking away behavior of the frustrator but also, with various degrees of explicitness, the internal state or drive situation of the victim (see, e.g., Dollard et al., 1939, p. 11). Thus the issue can be stated in terms of the conditions under which deprivation will result in a state of internal imbalance. Such imbalance will depend not only on the act of deprivation, but also on the previous state of the victim in terms of resource accumulation: an individual who had plenty of a given resource will be less affected by the deprivation than he who had little of it. Support for this suggestion is provided by Rosenbaum and deCharms (1960) who exposed high and low self-esteem subjects to insult. Some subjects were then given an opportunity to retaliate either directly or vicariously. The residual aggression of each subject was finally measured. High self-esteem subjects were not irritated by the insult as much as the low self-esteem ones. Moreover, their residual aggression after retaliation did not decrease as much as for low self-esteem subjects.

This experiment illustrates the general problem of how to measure the degree of frustration (in terms of internal imbalance). Usually the intensity of the following aggression is taken to measure the degree of frustration. It is reasonable to assume that when frustration is low, retaliation will be milder. However, the reverse may not be true: aggression may be inhibited and its expression mild in spite of a high level of internal imbalance. It has been found, for example, that anticipation of punishment reduces the expression of aggression (Berkowitz, 1962, pp. 75–79); there is no reason to assume that such anticipation reduces the level of imbalance. In some situations, however, a decrease in expressed aggression may well reflect a reduction in drive level. Kregarman and Worchel (1961), for example, found that subjects who expected interference in task completion were less aggressive than those who expected to complete their task. Apparently, the first group expected the task to be less rewarding and thus the interference created a lower level of imbalance. Some conditions may influence both the drive level and the degree of inhibition to aggress. It has been repeatedly reported that less aggression is expressed when the frustrating action is non-arbitrary (Allison & Hunt, 1959; Cohen, 1955; Pastore, 1952). Later results indicated that this reduction of aggression is partly due to inhibition, possibly because aggressive reaction to legitimate deprivation would result in social disapproval, i.e., loss of status. Rothaus and Worchel (1960) repeated the Pastore study but asked subjects to indicate the reaction of another imaginary person, in addition to their own. The result that in the non-arbitrary conditions more hostility was attributed to the other person than to the self, was taken to indicate inhibition of aggressive tendencies. While these results were based on questionnaire responses, subsequent experimental findings essentially supported them (Burnstein & Worchel, 1962).

There is an additional aspect differentiating between arbitrary and non-arbitrary frustrations which has not been noted by previous investigators, probably because of the scarce attention paid to the resources *involved*: an arbitrary deprivation produces the loss of more resources, often love and/or status, in addition to those lost in a comparable but non-arbitrary situation. If the bus failed to stop because it was on its way to the garage, one was deprived of a service; if, however, the driver did not care to stop to pick him up, a person lost not only service, but also status. This difference is bound to reflect on the resulting state of need since a broader range of resources is involved when deprivation is arbitrary. Hence, arbitrariness appears to affect not only the inhibition of aggressive response, but also the need state.

In summary, the notion of frustration, as treated in current theory and practice, embraces two elements: one is a taking away behavior which deprives the object-person of some resources; the other is the state of need created in the object-person who has been so deprived. In an individual who possesses a large amount of a given resource, deprivation of moderate strength may not create a need, and therefore no retaliation is required. But even when deprivation does reduce the residual amount below minimum, the deprived individual may not attempt to reestablish it by retaliatory action. Such aggressive reactions tend to be inhibited when it is likely to result in a further loss of resources.

The Notion of Aggression

We have already noted that several studies operationalized aggression by employing loss of resources. Proposed definitions of this notion, although differing in details, show considerable congruence with the operations employed. For Dollard, et al. (1939, p. 9), aggression is a sequence of behavior "the goal-response to which is the injury of the person toward whom it is directed." Buss (1961, p. 1) defines aggression as a response that delivers noxious stimuli to another organism. Walters (1964) adds that aggression is usually characterized by responses of high magnitude. There is substantial agreement among the various definitions that aggressive behavior is injurious to the recipient. The injury may be directed towards the belongings of the recipient, or towards his person. In the latter case, it can take physical and symbolic forms, or it may worsen the individual's information state, when deception or misleading is employed. Each of these various types of injury damages the recipient in a particular resource. It appears, therefore, that aggression is *a behavior which deprives the recipient of one or more resources*. Once again, deprivation may pertain to an *actual* loss of a resource already possessed by the victim, or it may consist of depriving him of a resource he expects to obtain in the future.

It has been suggested that mere deprivation is not sufficient to characterize aggression (e.g., Bandura & Walters, 1959; Sears et al., 1957). An *intention* to harm is an essential element of its definition; another qualification which has been widely accepted (e.g., Walters, 1964) is the *absence of social approval*. Thus, the motorist who unintentionally hurts a person in a traffic accident, and the judge who legitimately imposes a fine on the defendant, would not be considered aggressive, although both events result in loss of resources. These qualifications may be important, yet we believe it is preferable to consider them as conditions impinging on the *perception* of aggression, rather than as elements of its definition. At least we should recognize that frustrative behavior and aggression are both forms of taking away resources, although they may have additional characteristics which differentiate them from other forms of taking.

Experiments in social exchange often include taking away behaviors which are basically similar to those employed in frustration–aggression studies (e.g., Blumstein & Weinstein, 1969; Leventhal & Bergman, 1969; Pepitone et al., 1970; Weinstein et al., 1968). Yet the use of a different terminology hindered an exploration of the relationship between the investigations

128   PART I ABRIDGEMENT OF *SOCIETAL STRUCTURES OF THE MIND*

of equity in social exchanges and studies on antecedents of aggression. By pointing to the similarities between these two theoretical approaches, studies in one tradition may be used to develop the other.

Classification

In recognizing frustration and aggression as forms of taking away behaviors, we are immediately provided with a classification of their types according to the resources involved. Moreover, we are able to re-analyze various phenomena in this area, as well as forming and testing new hypotheses, by considering the structure of resources which has already been established.

Previous attempts at classification are not altogether remote from the present one. Rosenzweig (1944) realized that frustration involves unsatisfied needs but faced difficulties in using needs as a criterion for classifying frustration: "It is not possible," he states, "in the present state of psychology to provide an adequate classification of needs perhaps because the criteria for such a classification have not yet been discovered . . ." (p. 38). The beginning of a classification based on needs or resources has been provided by Maslow (1941). For him, need deprivation will be followed by frustration only when it involves a threat to personality. In essence, Maslow suggests that frustration should involve a perceived loss of love or status. A child deprived of an ice cream cone is not frustrated unless he perceived this act as denial of love by his mother. According to Maslow, no frustration will occur when deprivation of ice cream is perceived as intended to avoid a stomach ache.

Buss' (1961) classification of aggression, although stated in instrumental terms, bears relevance to various resources; indeed the specific behaviors involved in deprivation may differ for different resources. Buss differentiates between two major types of aggression according to the body's organs involved: physical and verbal aggression. The former is an assault against an organism by means of the attacker's teeth, limbs or by weapons; the latter is delivered by speech. In both types, noxious stimuli are delivered: in physical aggression, they consist of pain and injury, while noxious stimuli delivered by verbal aggression are rejection and threat. Rejection includes negative affective reaction as well as criticism and derogation. Buss is aware of the shortcomings stemming from the use of the organ system as a criterion for classification: rejection, for example, may be conveyed by nonverbal as well as by verbal means. Nevertheless, in most cases, insult and emotional rejection are likely to be verbal.

While Buss (1963) did use his classification to investigate the reactive effects of different types of frustration, most other investigators paid little attention to the resources involved in their experiments; moreover, some (e.g., Berkowitz, 1962, p. 49) argued against any differentiation in terms other than intensity. Consequently, the vast majority of the studies on frustration–aggression do not bear upon the findings reported: preference to react with a resource similar to the one involved in the proaction, and higher intensity of reaction, as well as of residual aggression (particularly in the resource of proaction), found when proaction and reaction differ in their resources. Some studies which are relevant to these issues, although somewhat indirectly, will be considered next.

Resource Reciprocity

Graham et al. (1951) presented subjects, through a questionnaire, with a variety of frustrating situations, differing in intensity. They found that each intensity of frustration tended to elicit aggression of a similar intensity. Since, in this study, different intensities were represented by different resources (physical aggression, i.e., services, represented the highest intensity), the results indicate a preference for retaliation in kind.

Relevant to the hypothesis that aggressive reaction is more intense when retaliation is not appropriate, is Buss' study (1963) which was already mentioned. Three different procedures to induce frustration were used, one for each group of subjects: two procedures involved status (task failure and thwarting the obtaining of a good grade) and one involved money. All three experimental groups were only slightly higher than controls in the intensity of the shock they delivered to the frustrator. These results appear to contradict Donnenwerth's findings (1971): since shock (services) is rather distal in the structure from both resources of frustration (status and money), one would have expected a higher intensity of reaction. Moreover, in another study, when subjects were told that by administering shock to the other, they would increase their chance of succeeding in their task (gaining status), they gave more shocks than controls (Buss, 1966).

Experiments in which residual aggression is measured usually support Donnenwerth's finding that residual aggression is lower when proaction and reaction involve similar resources. Baker and Schaie (1969) created frustration by interfering with the subject's task, thus depriving him of the resource (probably status) expected from successful completion. Each subject was then provided with an opportunity to aggress: some could take status, some employed services and still others took away information. Blood pressure after aggression was lowest for those who aggressed by taking away status, the resource which was also involved in their frustration. Geen and Berkowitz (1966) frustrated subjects by shock (service) and communication of failure (status). Subjects were then enabled to reciprocate in kind, and finally expressed their liking (love) for the frustrator by filling a questionnaire. Frustrated subjects were more aggressive than controls, but no differences were found in the amount of disliking expressed. It seems that retaliation in kind was effective in reducing residual aggression. In another experiment (Mallick & McCandless, 1966), subjects were deprived of status and money; after an intervening activity, which varied for each group, they were given an opportunity to retaliate against the frustrator by depriving him of services (shock) and love. The least aggressive were those for whom the intervening activity consisted of talking about the frustrator with the experimenter who depicted him as penniless, sleepy, and upset, suggesting that he would have behaved better had the subject shared with him some of the money he had received. The two other activities consisted of target shooting and of an irrelevant social talk with the experimenter. The intervening activity which succeeded in lowering aggression is, admittedly, a complex one; in our interpretation it involves lowering the status of the frustrator. Since status was one of the resources involved in frustration, the effectiveness of the intervening activity in reducing aggression may be due to this common resource.

The Object and the Actor in the Frustration–Aggression Sequence

We have been concerned so far with the relationship between resource of frustration and that of subsequent aggression. In particular, we suggested that the preference for a certain type of aggression is determined by the type of frustration previously experienced, and that the amount of residual hostility is affected by the structural relationship between the two resources. The resource employed, however, is only one element of a social event; other essential elements are the person emitting the response (the actor) and the

SOME AREAS OF SOCIO-PSYCHOLOGICAL RESEARCH   131

one towards whom it is emitted (the object). The classical exchange paradigm of frustration–aggression involves two individuals, A and B, and two stages—frustration and aggression. In the first stage, the frustrator, A, is the actor, while the victim, B, is the object or the recipient of A's aggression. The roles are reversed in the aggression stage: the previous object (B) becomes the actor of aggression, while the previous actor (A) becomes the object. As in any dyadic exchange, here too, the two participants alternate in being actors and recipients of the action.

. Yet, isolated dyads are found mainly in the laboratory; in everyday life, the relationship between two individuals often affects a third person. An individual who was refused recognition by his boss may berate his subordinate; an older child may protect his younger brother by aggressing against the latter's frustrator. In the first example, B was frustrated by A, but the object of retaliation is not the previous frustrator; this phenomenon of directing retaliation towards a third individual is denoted as displacement. The second example is a case of vicarious aggression, when B is frustrated by A, and C, a third individual, retaliates against A; here the actor of retaliation is not the previous victim.

We shall discuss these three paradigms—direct retaliation, displacement, and vicarious aggression—with respect to the two issues considered before: the effects on residual aggression and preferences, this time not among resources, but among various available "third persons." The differential effects of resources have been usually considered as generalization of the aggressive response; the choice and effects of the participants is known as *stimulus* generalization. While this terminology is not particularly suitable to the present theoretical approach, it is desirable to recognize the relationship of topics discussed here with the research and theoretical approaches advanced by other authors.

DIRECT RETALIATION. The effectiveness of direct retaliation in restoring internal balance is often estimated from the amount of residual aggression left after retaliation had taken place. The findings usually suggest that direct retaliation results in a decrease of subsequent aggression. Berkowitz and Holmes (1960) found that college girls who were frustrated by a confederate, as well as by a peer, expressed more favorable judgments on their peer's fairness after administering shock to him. Pepitone and Reichling (1955) found that those who expressed the strongest hostility tended to give the most favorable ratings later on. Berkowitz (1966) reported that subjects who expected to retaliate and were permitted to do so were less aggressive

132 PART I ABRIDGEMENT OF *SOCIETAL STRUCTURES OF THE MIND*

than those who were not permitted to retaliate. We have noted earlier that Rosenbaum and deCharms (1960) found a decrease in hostility after communicating with the frustrator as compared to non-communication groups, but only for low self-esteem subjects. For high self-esteem subjects, who had more status to begin with, deprivation was probably not strong enough to reduce the level below the optimal range, so that they did not feel imbalance. Hokanson (1961) frustrated subjects by insult, permitted them to aggress physically and then measured residual hostility in love and status. He found that the more the subjects aggressed physically, the less hostile they were afterwards. Reduction in aggression expressed in attitude scale was found by Worchel (1957), whose subjects were insulted and then given an opportunity to criticize the frustrator in his absence. Lower residual hostility following aggression is also reported by Berkowitz et al. (1962) and Thibaut and Coules (1952).

In these studies, at least two out of the three resources involved were identical or close in the structure. Rosenbaum and deCharms (1960) used status and love for the frustration, retaliation and residual aggression stages. Worchel (1957) used status for all three stages. Berkowitz et al. (1962), used status and services both for frustration and retaliation while measuring the residual aggression for love, a neighbor of both status and services in the proposed structure.

DISPLACEMENT. Three types of displacement, i.e., change of object, have been discussed in the literature: displacement towards a third individual, towards self and towards an inanimate object. Let us consider each briefly.

Displacement towards a third person. Laboratory and field studies have indicated that displacement of aggression to a third individual or group occurs when either of the following conditions exists: (a) the original object is not within reach, or (b) the original object is perceived as powerful in that he can deprive the subject of important resources if retaliated against.

Who is likely to become a target of displaced aggression? Berkowitz (1962, p. 139) aptly noted that the choice of displaced object is influenced by the conditions which had led to displacement. When the original target is not available, aggression will be directed toward a target most similar to the original one. The choice of object under such conditions is parallel to the choice of substitute resource; in both, preference is based on the similarity between the new event and the original but unavailable one. However, when aggression against the primary target is inhibited by fear of retaliation, the choice of a substitute target will be governed by two conflicting tendencies: the

SOME AREAS OF SOCIO-PSYCHOLOGICAL RESEARCH   133

tendency to choose a target similar to the original one, and the tendency to reduce the chances of a punitive reaction by choosing a target less powerful than the original one. The resultant, suggests Berkowitz, will be to choose an individual with an intermediate similarity. It should be noted that the conflict between the two tendencies refers only to the power dimension and not to other dimensions of similarity. Thus, when the primary target is too powerful to be attacked, the displaced target will be less powerful than the original, but similar to him in other aspects.

At this point it is appropriate to recall the dimensions of role differentiation, sex, power and resources, which may prove to be relevant criteria for object similarity. It was suggested earlier that the target of displacement will differ from the original one on the power dimension. If, however, the six types of power are considered, one for each resource class, we may be able to make more precise predictions: We suggest that the target of displacement will be less powerful than the original one with respect to that specific resource which the actor fears to lose. For example, if one is inhibited to aggress against an individual powerful in love, he will displace aggression to a person less powerful in this resource; the displaced target, however, may not be less powerful than the original one in other resources, to which no fear of loss is attached.

Roles are also characterized by specific resources, so that not every resource may be employed in a given role. From previous work on resource substitution, we know that people prefer to retaliate with the resource previously involved in their frustration. Since not every resource may be employed in a given role, the preference for a specific reaction constitutes a restriction on displacement. The substitute target will be chosen from a role similar to that of the original target, so that it will be appropriate to employ the resource previously used by the frustrator. This hypothesis is reflected in notions such as "father figure." A child may tend to displace aggression from an authoritarian father to the teacher—in both, status is a prominent resource, but the father is more powerful in it.

Another dimension of roles to be considered is sex. We have suggested that the earlier the differentiation, the less permeable are its boundaries. Sex is the first role dimension to be differentiated; therefore, diffusion of aggression across sexes is least likely. Resources are differentiated last and their boundaries more permeable, thus they are more likely to be substituted one for another. Differentiation by power, which occupies an intermediate position with regard to developmental sequence, will also occupy an intermediate

134 PART I ABRIDGEMENT OF *SOCIETAL STRUCTURES OF THE MIND*

position with respect to generalization facilitation. There is little in the literature which is relevant to these hypotheses, but they are definitely testable.

Some indication that instigation to aggression—as distinct from its actual expression—may be reduced by aggressing against a third individual, is provided by the work of Gambaro and Rabin (1969). Their subjects were insulted and then permitted to shock the experimenter, who was not the previous frustrator. Diastolic blood pressure decreased after aggression in low-guilt subjects, but no change was found in high-guilt subjects. These results may indicate that displacement does not affect instigation to aggression in high-guilt individuals; a feasible alternative explanation, however, is that aggression against an innocent target has increased their guilt and subsequently emotional arousal remained high, although instigation to aggression may have been reduced.

Work on displacement of aggression involved the three most particularistic resources: services (Hovland & Sears, 1940; Janis, 1951; Miller, 1948, 1959; Miller & Bugelsky, 1948); love (Pepitone & Reichling, 1955); and status (Burnstein & Worchel, 1962; Gambaro & Rabin, 1969; Mosher & Proenza, 1968; Thibaut & Coules, 1952). We were unable to find evidence of displacement for the remaining three resource classes: goods, money and information. Since, as already noted, investigators of aggression, in general, employed particularistic resources more than non-particularistic ones, this preference may be reflected in displacement studies as well. An alternative explanation to be considered is that displacement occurs mainly for particularistic resources. This explanation, however, contradicts the notion of particularism, which means that the particular partner with whom the exchange takes place is an important determinant. If particularism is a relevant dimension in displacement, a change of target is more likely to occur when the exchange involves non-particularistic rather than particularistic resources.

SELF-AGGRESSION. There is evidence indicating that frustrated subjects may direct aggression toward themselves. Burnstein and Worchel (1962) found that frustrated subjects evaluated themselves more negatively than non-frustrated ones, especially when frustration was non-arbitrary. A somewhat related finding is reported by Rothaus and Worchel (1960) who showed that frustrated subjects with high self-ideal discrepancy reported significantly higher self-hostility than those with low self-ideal discrepancy: for the former groups of subjects, self-hostility was indeed consonant, while being dissonant for the latter group.

SOME AREAS OF SOCIO-PSYCHOLOGICAL RESEARCH   135

Opinions differ as to the conditions inducing self-aggression. Dollard et al. (1939) believe that it occurs when there are barriers to expressing aggression toward the other, while Berkowitz (1962) states that self-aggression results from perceiving the self as the source of frustration. A third alternative is suggested here: self-aggression is the product of response generalization or spread of effect from the other to the self, and stems from perceived proximity between self and other. This proximity, in turn, depends partly on the resource involved in aggression and its position in the structure: it will be highly positive for love, and will decrease and become negative as one moves around the circle from love to money. For the latter resource, the relationship will be high and negative.

The theoretical considerations discussed above suggest that displacement to self will occur when the frustration involves particularistic resources and when the aggression expressed is particularistic. One would not tend to inflict loss of money on himself while intending the other to lose it, whereas he may direct resentment and disrespect towards himself and even damage his own body (e.g., commit suicide).

SYMBOLIC DISPLACEMENT. A change of object occurs also in symbolic displacement, where the object of aggression is inanimate, such as dolls, shooting at a target, T.A.T. stories, etc. (Bandura, 1965; Feshbach, 1956; Hokanson & Burgess, 1962; Mallick & McCandless, 1966). In the literature, fantasy aggression (Feshbach, 1955) is often considered a form of symbolic displacement. While both phenomena have in common the characteristic of not requiring an actual interpersonal situation (in neither case aggression is communicated to a human being), displacement to another object does not necessarily happen in fantasy aggression. The object can be, and is likely to be, the frustrator himself.

In most of the studies dealing with the effect of displacement on aggression, retaliation was directed toward an inanimate object while residual aggression was observed with respect to the original frustrator. No difference in residual aggression was reported by Mallick and McCandless (1966) in three experiments where money was taken away from subjects, who then either shot a target with figures of boys and girls or did not aggress. All frustrated groups were more hostile than the non-frustrated ones, no matter whether they displaced aggression or did not aggress at all. Likewise, Feshbach (1956) did not find change in classroom aggressive behavior before and after letting the children aggress in play sessions. In several experiments, T.A.T. cards were used for expression of aggression. Feshbach (1955) found a decrease in

136 PART I ABRIDGEMENT OF *SOCIETAL STRUCTURES OF THE MIND*

hostility toward the frustrator following T.A.T. stories. Hornberger (1959) attempted to replicate the Feshbach experiment but failed to get differences among the various groups except an *increase* of hostility for the group who hammered nails.

Vicarious Aggression: Generalization of Actor

Displacement has been defined as a change in object while the actor is the previously frustrated individual. Vicarious aggression, on the other hand, occurs when the actor of the aggression is a third person but the victim is the original frustrator (DeCharms & Wilkins, 1963; Rosenbaum & deCharms, 1960). While some investigators used the term "vicarious" to convey change of both actor and object (Bandura, 1965; Feshbach, 1955), there is an agreement that this term involves a change of *actor*. In most of the studies on the effect of vicarious experience on subsequent behavior, a movie is shown to the subject. In those movies, the aggressor and his victim are usually different individuals from those involved in the previous frustration (Berkowitz, 1965; Berkowitz & Geen, 1966; Feshbach, 1955; Geen & Berkowitz, 1966). Sometimes when the object is inanimate, only the actor may differ (Bandura, 1962). Very often the resource in the movie is the same as in the aggressive act, mainly services (e.g., Berkowitz & Geen, 1966; Geen & Berkowitz, 1966), but sometimes the resource also changes, being service in the movie and love and status in the measurement of aggression (Feshbach, 1956).

There are not many studies on residual aggression where only the actor changed. Rosenbaum and deCharms (1960) let the subject hear, but not see, a vicarious aggressor berating their frustrator. They found a decrease in residual hostility for low self-esteem subjects, but no change for high self-esteem ones. Indirect support for a cathartic effect of vicarious aggression is suggested by Baker and Schaie (1969), who found no difference in systolic blood pressure and other physiological indications of arousal, between those who aggressed directly and those who did it vicariously. On the other hand, DeCharms and Wilkins (1963) reported an increase in aggression following vicarious retaliation. The subjects who witnessed another person aggressing toward their frustrator were the most aggressive. Similar results were obtained by Pirojnikoff (1958) in a study combining direct with vicarious aggression, but probably with a prevalence of the latter. This investigator allowed insulted subjects to complain and insult the experimenter in a group

SOME AREAS OF SOCIO-PSYCHOLOGICAL RESEARCH   137

discussion. He found that subjects performed worse on tasks after this group interaction had taken place than before, possibly as a result of increased anger. Since in group discussion, each participant spends more time in listening to the attacks of others (vicarious) than in talking (direct aggression), the increased anger may be seen mainly as an effect of vicarious retaliation.

Most studies on the effects of watching an aggressive movie showed an increase in subsequent aggression (Albert, 1957; Berkowitz, 1966; Hartman, 1969; Lovaas, 1961). Similarly, watching an aggressive game such as football also results in increased hostility, while no such increase is evident after observing a gymnastic meet (Goldstein & Arms, 1971). Although Feshbach (1955, 1961) did find a decrease in aggression following a violent movie, there is considerable agreement that exposure to violent behavior increases subsequent aggression. The previous review on displacement indicates that a mere change of object does not increase residual aggression, therefore it seems justified to ascribe the increment of aggression following a movie to change of actor.

It seems reasonable that similarity between the original and the vicarious actor is a relevant variable in predicting the magnitude of subsequent aggression. The more similar the actors are, the more increment in aggression will occur. Moreover, the role dimensions discussed in reference to third person displacement may prove relevant as well, to similarity among actors. There appears to be no work which bears upon similarity between actors, but there is evidence that increased aggression in the frustrated individual is a function of similarity between the object of vicarious aggression and the original frustrator, who is the object of retaliation.

For theoretical and practical purposes, it seems important to study systematically the differential effects of direct retaliation, displacement and vicarious aggression. The available data tend to suggest that direct retaliation yields a decrease in residual aggression, displacement does not affect it, and vicarious aggression results in an increase of subsequent aggression. This suggestion, however, is only tentative, since the data came from many studies differing in methodology as well as in types of frustration and aggression. Keeping all relevant variables constant while changing only the *paradigms* would yield a purer test of their differential effects on residual aggression. It seems that programs for controlling aggression of individuals as well as groups may benefit from such research.

Up to now we have examined the consequences of changing resources, objects, and actors in aggressive interaction. To complete the discussion, we

138   PART I ABRIDGEMENT OF *SOCIETAL STRUCTURES OF THE MIND*

shall turn to the remaining behavioral dimension—the mode or direction of the action.

Change of Mode: Restitution

The aggressive sequences considered so far were characterized by a change of object and/or actor from proaction to reaction. In direct retaliation the two participants just alternate positions: the previous actor becomes an object, while the former object becomes the actor. In displacement and vicarious aggression a third individual becomes, respectively, object or actor. All three paradigms were perceived as ways for restoring the victim's internal balance, which had been disrupted by the frustrative act. If indeed frustration does impair the internal balance of resources by being an act of deprivation, then an obvious means by which it can be reestablished, and residual aggression reduced, is *restoration*. In this paradigm neither the actor nor the object changes, only the mode alters: the same actor who had emitted the frustrative act now provides the victim with one or more resources.

Surprisingly, the restoration paradigm has barely been explored. The scarce research that has been done on it is mostly within the framework of dissonance and exchange studies rather than in reference to aggression: "the possibility for compensation is eliminated from experimental designs so consistently that experimenters sometimes forget that this reaction to harming a victim exists," noted Berscheid and Walster (1967).

The first question to be asked is whether, indeed, restoration reduces the instigation to aggression after frustration has taken place. Worchel (1961) clearly showed that hostility induced by taking away status is subsequently reduced by status restoration. Even more cogent evidence for the effect of restitution is implicit in the results of an experiment on attraction by Aronson and Linder (1965). In their investigation subjects in one group received only positive evaluations; in a second group evaluation was always negative; evaluation changed from positive to negative in a third group and from negative to positive in fourth one. Subjects in this last group were thus deprived of status in the early stage of the experiment and then obtained restitution. These subjects liked the person who evaluated them much more than subjects who were deprived but did not experience restitution; in fact liking for the evaluator was highest in this group. This cathartic effect of restoration cannot be easily explained by interpreting frustration to thwarting. Restoration does not undo thwarting as would resumption of the interrupted activity; it does, however, counteract the resource deprivation experienced in frustration, thus reducing or eliminating the need to reestablish balance by retaliation. The conceptualization of frustration–aggression sequence as an exchange which is directed toward maintaining an internal balance provides, therefore, a straightforward explanation for the effects of restoration. This explanation is further supported by some experimental work. Walster et al. (1966) found that subjects who had expressed unjustified hostility towards an individual, later on expressed more liking than did controls; those who had expressed unjustified liking, subsequently tended to give less favorable ratings than did controls. One might say that the amount of liking expressed in the second evaluation was guided by the perception of what constitutes a proper balance.

Why do people tend to restore what they have taken away? Carlsmith and Gross (1969) suggested that guilt rather than sympathy was the critical variable. Those subjects who had shocked the confederate were later significantly more likely to comply with his request to run an errand for him (i.e., make some telephone calls), than did those subjects who only witnessed the confederate being shocked by a third person. The authors reasoned that hurting another individual results in guilt feelings which are then decreased by helping him. In our terminology, the actor of aggression takes away love from himself (feels unworthy) and consequently, his internal balance is disrupted; the act of restitution, while restoring the victim's internal balance, also restores the actor's own balance—he is again a worthy person. Another reason for restitution is probably the fear of retaliation; by restoring the victim's internal balance, one assures that his own balance will not be disrupted by a retaliatory act.

Another question to be asked is what constitutes a proper restitution? We know that the probability of emitting a restorative act increases as one can give back exactly what he had taken away (Berscheid & Walster, 1967); indeed, both deprivation and restitution usually involve the same resource class in studies of restoration. What happens when the resource of deprivation differs from that of restoration? It seems reasonable to suggest that the more the two resources are removed in the structure, the higher will be the amount of restitution needed for reestablishing the victim's internal balance. Thus, if deprivation involves love, and restitution is done by giving money, a larger amount of the latter resource is needed for reestablishing balance than if love was restored. Moreover, the victim may never feel that the harm was undone when restitution involved an improper resource: The German government

140 PART I ABRIDGEMENT OF *SOCIETAL STRUCTURES OF THE MIND*

spent enormous sums of money to compensate those who had suffered under the Nazis, yet it is doubtful that this restitution allayed hostile feeling.

In everyday life, restoration is often offered by a third individual rather than by the previous frustrator. A child may be rejected by his peers and then comforted by his parents. Would such restoration, by a third individual, be effective in reestablishing the disrupted balance? The theoretical considerations on displacement and vicarious aggression may apply also here. The more similarity there is between the original frustrator and the actor of restoration, the less residual aggression will be left. Again, similarity may involve the role dimensions of sex, power and resources. The boy who was rejected by his male peers will feel less frustrated if restoration is carried on by his father than if it is done by his mother; the former is more similar to peers, having the same sex and in using the same resource (status). This hypothesis, like some other questions we have previously raised in discussing restitution, must await further research.

Investigation of the cathartic effects of restitution is important not only because of its significance in clarifying the conceptualization of frustration, but also in view of its practical relevance: restitution has the obvious advantage over counter-aggression (direct, displaced or vicarious) that it may reduce residual hostility while avoiding further taking away behavior.

With these considerations on restitution, our review of the frustration–aggression sequence comes to an end. Two main points emerge from our reanalysis of the research literature on this problem: (1) The frustration–aggression sequence is an exchange of taking away which may differ from other such exchanges by some specific conditions. (2) The previously developed notions of interpersonal exchange provide a framework suitable for classifying earlier investigations in this area and for suggesting new, more specific hypotheses.

In the studies discussed so far in this chapter, behaviors of taking were prominent; giving appeared only in the proaction of the restitution paradigm. We now turn our attention to investigations dealing with problems in exchanges of giving.

Needs of Exchange Partners: Similar or Dissimilar?

A good deal of controversy has developed around the issue of what need combination is most suitable to exchange partners. In particular, it was debated whether similarity of needs leads to more stable relations than does dissimilarity. Winch (1958) proposed that a person will tend to choose a spouse whose needs are different than his own rather than one having similar needs. Later, when faced with seemingly contradictory results, Winch (1967) introduced the congruence between role demands and needs as an additional element in predicting the stability of exchange relationship. The more congruence there is between role demands and the participants' needs, the more stable will be the relationship. Instability will occur, for example, when a dominant person occupies a role which is culturally defined as submissive (e.g., employee), or vice versa, when a dominant role (e.g., boss) is occupied by a submissive person. Having noted earlier that institutional norms may conflict with individual needs, we find ourselves in full agreement with Winch's statement. However, this amplification has little to do with the original problem, as it does not predict if and when stability is associated with similarity of needs between exchange partners.

In a later study, Centers and Granville (1971) reported disconfirmation of Winch's hypothesis, but aptly noted that "applying the principle to those need variables where it was seen as logically and theoretically appropriate resulted in a distinctly more supportive picture for it." A more specific prediction of when complementarity will or will not provide better conditions for partnership is provided by two of the resource properties: the relationship between self and other as objects, and the exchange in kind. It will be recalled that the more a resource is particularistic, the stronger the relationship between giving (or taking from) to self and to other and the higher the likelihood for exchange in kind. Love is most often exchanged with love and by giving love to the other one also gives love to himself; thus in an exchange of love one gains not only what he receives, but also by giving to himself. In consequence, when two persons need love they can hardly do any better than exchanging love with one another; here similarity of needs contributes to the stability of the relationship. The contrary happens for money; if two persons need money, they are unlikely to enter into a transaction: money is rarely exchanged with money; furthermore, the amount of it given to the other is lost to self. Therefore, if one is in need of money, he will probably refer to somebody willing to buy his services, his goods or his information; here dissimilarity of needs is advantageous.

In general, it is proposed that dissimilarity of needs will become more desirable the less particularistic the resources needed are. Yet, it has been suggested (see, e.g., Carson, 1969, p. 153) that in a resource as close to love

142 PART I ABRIDGEMENT OF *SOCIETAL STRUCTURES OF THE MIND*

as status, complementarity will result in a better outcome than similarity: a dominant individual will be more satisfied with a submissive partner. The simplicity of this formulation is convincing, but deceptive. Being dominant means giving status to self and taking it from the other. Contrariwise, the submissive person gives status to the other and takes it from himself. If, indeed, such need combination is frequent, we would expect a negative correlation between giving status to self and to other. Yet, we have seen that empirical data point in the opposite direction; giving status to self and to other are positively related, at least in the family roles of normal individuals.

It follows that mutual exchanges of status are more common than the situations where one always takes while the other always gives. Furthermore, the failure to take into account all the exchanges which take place between two individuals may hinder our understanding of this problem.

Usually, complementarity implies that while one partner has the need to receive a certain resource, the other has the need to give it. If we limit our observation to one resource, we may conclude that this is a general pattern of exchange for a given pair of persons. But when all resources are observed, we probably will find that while one is willing to give one resource, he expects the other to reciprocate with another resource. For example, when one partner is dominant with respect to status, the other may dominate in information. Consequently, the total exchange pattern will tend to approach balance rather than being a flow of resources only in one direction. Whether the resources exchanged are identical or different will depend, at least in part, on their location in the structure: the more particularistic they are, the more they will be exchanged in kind.

If need combination determines the stability of an exchange, it can be suggested that partners who are matched in their respective needs will find one another attractive. This leads us to the more general topic of interpersonal attraction.

Interpersonal Attraction

The attraction one individual feels for another, and particularly romantic attraction, has always been a focus of interest and speculation, and a recurring theme in the literature. However, it became subjected to scientific investigation only in the last two decades. The research work on attraction has mainly concentrated on conditions which enhance attraction and on

SOME AREAS OF SOCIO-PSYCHOLOGICAL RESEARCH   143

personality variables of the attractive person. In discussing this area of research we shall be mainly concerned with the additional insight which may be contributed by the resource exchange paradigm, rather than attempting an exhaustive review of the literature. The reader interested in a comprehensive survey may wish to consult Marlowe and Gergen (1969, pp. 621–637) or the work of Berscheid and Walster (1969). These latter authors organized their presentation of attraction around the proposition that we are attracted by those who can provide rewards for us, a position rather close to the one advanced here.

We have repeatedly suggested that social interaction constitutes an opportunity for resource exchange; in keeping with this approach, we propose that a person will be found attractive to the extent that he is considered as a potential partner for the transaction of resources. Attractiveness, so defined, rests essentially on two factors: (a) the extent to which the other is a potential provider of resources we need, and (b) the extent to which we are in a position to satisfy some of his needs. The second factor plays a larger role as a determinant of attraction when the probability of an actual interaction with the other is perceived to be high. One may be attracted to a movie star or to a charismatic statesman even when he has nothing to offer; since the likelihood of actual interaction with such a figure is very low, one can be attracted without worrying about his part in the exchange. Such "abstract" attraction is mainly influenced by the resources the figure possesses.

When an actual exchange appears within the realm of possibilities, one estimates the probability of its success. We all know that in order to have a satisfactory relationship, some balance of giving and receiving should be maintained. Consequently, we take in account what the other can offer to us as well as what we can offer to him in return. A superior individual is not an ideal partner for exchange; while he has a great deal to offer, there is not much that he needs. When, however, this individual shows some weakness, he becomes potentially a better exchange partner, as the possibility of benefiting him, if only through sympathy, is brightened. This is precisely what Aronson et al. (1966) demonstrated. Their subjects listened to a tape of a stimulus person answering a quiz. Half of them were exposed to the performance of a superior person, while for the other half, the individual on tape showed only average ability; each group was further subdivided into two conditions: half of the subjects heard the stimulus person spilling a cup of coffee on his suit and making apologetic remarks; this episode was omitted in the performance heard by the other subjects.

144   PART I ABRIDGEMENT OF *SOCIETAL STRUCTURES OF THE MIND*

The superior person who spilled the coffee was liked more than one without pratfall; the contrary was found for the average person: he was liked less when spilling the coffee. The experiment was replicated by Helmreich et al. (1970) with one addition which proved important: subjects were classified into low, average and high self-esteem, prior to being randomly assigned to the four experimental conditions. The previous findings were supported only by the subjects of average self-esteem; they indeed liked the less-than-perfect superior most. However, high and low self-esteem subjects expressed more liking for the "perfect superior." How can these results be interpreted? We suggest that the amount of liking experienced by subjects with moderate degree of self-esteem was influenced by the two factors —their own potential to give as well as the other's potential. However, for low and high self-esteem, attractiveness was determined mainly by what the other person had to offer and, therefore, they liked more the perfect superior. The effect of the second factor—what they could offer to the other was weakened in these subjects, although for different reasons. High self-esteem subjects, having high regards for themselves, could hardly doubt their capacity to give, thus they become more tuned to the resources the other could bring to the exchange. Low self-esteem subjects, on the other hand, view themselves as having little to offer even to the less-than-perfect superior; both superiors were not perceived as serious potential partners for exchange, and therefore the question of what the subjects could offer had little relevance.

If this explanation is valid, we should expect people with low self-esteem to be attracted by highly endowed individuals. Yet, the contrary was reported in the following experiments. Kiesler and Baral (1970) manipulated the self-esteem of male subjects by telling them that they had done well or poorly on a bogus test predicting "success in life." During a following "break," the subject was introduced to a female confederate who was made up to be very attractive or unattractive. Subjects who believed they succeeded in the test directed more attention to the girl when she was beautiful, while those who "failed" were more attentive to her when she was sloppy. In a similar experiment (Sigall & Aronson, 1969), it was found that male subjects who had been positively evaluated by a female clinical psychologist liked her more when she was pretty than when she was ugly. Following negative evaluation, however, the ugly psychologist was liked slightly more than the beautiful one. The psychologist was again a confederate of the experimenter and, as in the previous experiment, her change in appearance was obtained by appropriate make-up and dressing.

Apparently in these two experiments, attractiveness was influenced not only by what the target person had to give, but also by what the subject could offer in exchange. How to account for the discrepancy between this finding and the ones obtained by Aronson (1970) and his associates? Some explanations can be suggested:

1. In the last two studies, self-esteem was manipulated by the single event of confronting the subject with information about his success or failure; it is possible that this manipulation was not strong enough to push self-esteem to extreme high or low values and the subjects remained within the mean range where consideration of their own ability to give is an effective determinant of attraction.
2. The latter experiments were more realistic, as the stimulus was a real person, rather than on tape; moreover, attraction was measured *after* an interaction had actually occurred, rather than in respect to a hypothetical future interaction as done in the previous investigation. This difference may have enhanced the relevance of what one himself has to offer.
3. In the latter experiments, subjects were males, and the stimulus person was a female, whereas in the other study both the subjects and the stimulus person were males. In a relationship between males, non-particularistic resources may be more prevalent, while a heterosexual relationship is dominated by exchange of love. Since love requires need-similarity (see p. 239), one is inclined to be attracted by a partner who is similar to him in the need to be loved; similarity, on the other hand, becomes less appropriate when the resources are less particularistic.

In general, it is suggested here that people are attracted by those who are potential partners for exchange of the *particular* resource they need. It follows that attraction is not a unitary concept; those who need money will be attracted to the rich, while those who seek status would be attracted by "important" persons. A long time ago, Moreno (1934) insisted that a sociometric investigation should refer to a specific situation since a person chosen as a partner for a given purpose will not necessarily be preferred in a different situation; indeed, the resources involved in the two situations may be different. An attractive business partner does not *ipso facto* constitute an attractive love partner. Studies supporting this view have been reviewed by Marlowe and Gergen (1969, p. 633). The structure of resources suggests, however, that a

146 PART I ABRIDGEMENT OF *SOCIETAL STRUCTURES OF THE MIND*

person will be similarly attractive for resources proximal in the order: an important individual may be a potential source not only of status, but also of information. In Teichman's study of expectations in a task group, we would predict that members will be attracted to the person who is expected to give more information, as the task consisted of preparing a joint paper. It was indeed found that the most and least attractive partners differed most in the amount of information expected from them; the difference for status was lower than that of information, but higher than the difference for love, which is more remote from information than status in the structure of resources.

In conclusion: we are attracted by people whom we consider to be potential partners for exchange because they are perceived as able to give some resource we need and appear to need some resource we possess. Thus, attraction is resource-specific, yet it generalizes to resources proximal in the order. Attraction is essentially a condition which precedes the exchange, although it may be influenced by past experiences of exchange situations with the same or different partners. We now turn to discuss studies which attempt to predict the outcome of the exchange.

Fairness in Exchange

The intuitive notion that an exchange of resources may be more or less equitable appears often and prominently in the discussion of human affairs. One may hear the argument that it is unfair to pay migrant agricultural workers subsistence wages for their labor, or that depriving a child of his preferred toy because he had disrespected his parents constitutes excessive punishment. Thus, the notion of fairness is applied to exchanges of giving as in the migrant workers' example, as well as to exchanges of taking away, as in the case of the rebellious child. This notion is also used when resources are apportioned among individuals or groups by a third party: it is unjust for a mother to allocate unequal amounts of love to her children; it is unfair to pay different wages to people doing the same job or to punish one person more severely than another for the same violation.

There have been many attempts to spell out, in more precise terms, the intuitive notion of fairness. Social philosophers and reformers, concerned mainly with the distribution of wealth, have proposed rules such as: the same to everybody; a guaranteed minimum income to everybody; to each one according to his needs, his efforts, or abilities. Industrial psychologists dealing with job evaluation have struggled with the problems of determining fair wages for jobs differing in skills, danger, effort, or unpleasantness. They too were concerned with economic resources.

Attempts to incorporate particularistic resources within the notion of equity were pursued by a relatively small group of social psychologists. Two issues are prominent in their work: (a) definition of a fair or just exchange; and (b) predicting the consequences of an unjust exchange.

Theoretical Formulations

RECIPROCITY. Gouldner (1960) postulated a norm of reciprocity which he considered to be universal and applicable to every human society, although varying in its specific manifestation by time and place; the norm consists essentially in the obligation we have to help those who had helped us and not to injure them. The amount reciprocated would be commensurate to the amount and value of the reward previously received.

DISTRIBUTIVE JUSTICE. A formulation which takes into account reciprocal rewards as well as reciprocal costs was proposed by Homans (1961, p. 75). Distributive justice occurs when the ratio of profit to investment is the same for each participant. Profit, in turn, is defined as the difference between reward and cost. According to this formulation, just exchange will occur when, for example, A's reward is valued 14, his cost 6 and his investment 20, while the respective values for B are 10, 8 and 5. Then A's profit is $14 - 6 = 8$ and B's profit is $10 - 8 = 2$. The ratio between profit and investment is the same for both participants, being 2/5 in each case. It appears realistic to assume, as this example does, that the reward of each participant will be higher than the cost incurred by the other; if indeed, each participant gives what he has in relative abundance and receives what is scarce to him, then the marginal utility of the receiver is higher than the one of the giver. Indeed, we tend to value more what is scarce than what we have in abundance.

Of particular interest to us is Homans suggestion that a person who cannot repay in kind might reestablish justice by giving status to the other, e.g., by expressing gratitude, esteem or indebtedness. Here is the beginning of a differentiation among various resources with the consequent notion that when appropriate resource is not available, another can be substituted for it. Testing this proposition, Blumstein and Weinstein (1969) found that indeed, subjects who received more than their fair share from their partner expressed more esteem

148 PART I ABRIDGEMENT OF *SOCIETAL STRUCTURES OF THE MIND*

for him. Another study (Weinstein et al., 1969) showed, however, that status is not the sole substitute resource: when the other person was a friend, subjects who previously benefited beyond fairness gave him status by openly expressing gratitude, by thanking him for his superior performance and by inviting him to assume leadership in a second joint task; when, however, the partner was a stranger to the subject, he preferred to reestablish reciprocity by giving services.

For distributive justice to be established, the previous recipient should reciprocate appropriately. A proper reciprocation may be defined in terms of the relationship between the amount of the resource one has received and the amount he can give. When more than one resource is involved, proper reciprocation may also be defined in terms of the appropriateness of a given resource as an exchange for that which was previously received; for example, there is considerable agreement that money is not an appropriate resource for love. What happens when a recipient finds himself unable to reciprocate appropriately? In the exchange paradigm of aggression–restoration, Berscheid et al. (1968) reported that when the proper channels for restoration are not open to the harm-doer, he usually justifies his act by derogating his victim. Generalizing these results to the present paradigm of positive reciprocation, one would predict that the recipient of resources, who is not in a position to reciprocate appropriately (in terms of the amount and/or the class of resource available to him), he will feel scarce attraction for the giver. This prediction was indeed confirmed in an experiment done by Gergen and his associates (Gergen, 1969, pp. 77–80). Players who were made to lose in a game, received an unexpected amount of chips from an anonymous source. Attached to the chips was a note prepared in three different ways: one version stated that the subjects could keep the chips without incurring any obligation; another version requested them to return the same amount of chips; the third one demanded payment of interest and some other unspecified favors. The highest attraction for the unknown giver was expressed by those requested to return the same amount of chips. These findings had an international flavor in more than one sense. First, they were replicated in three different countries (United States, Japan, and Sweden). Secondly, as noted by Gergen, they have broad implications for foreign aid. In this practical situation, the negative effect of inappropriate exchange is likely to be stronger than in the experiment just described since the donor is not anonymous and there are actual contacts between the receivers and the givers, who usually send technicians, experts, and missions. When an "undeveloped" country gets aid, it is usually expected that they will reciprocate with status. From

Teichman's and Donnenwerth's experiments, we would predict that if reciprocation involves a resource which is remote in the structure from the one previously given, the amount of the latter will be larger than when the resource reciprocated with is closer to the one given. Status is more remote from goods and money than from information. Consequently, it is less suitable for reciprocation when the aid consists of goods and money than when it provides training and instruction. Indeed, countries providing economic aid appear to be more disliked than countries providing training. It has been noted (Laufer, 1967, esp. p. 207) that Israel's modest program of foreign aid has been particularly attractive to recipients. Perhaps this success is related to the fact that the program, very much like the U.S. Peace Corps, provides information rather than goods and money. Furthermore, when the giver is a small country which sorely needs support, there are more opportunities for the recipient to reciprocate than when the giver is a superpower.

EQUITY. The formulation suggested by Adams (1965) appears rather close to the one proposed by Homans, although the terminology is different: instead of distributive justice, the term "equity" is used; input takes the place of investment; positive outcome replaces reward, and negative outcome might be somewhat similar to cost. Equity is then defined as a situation where the ratio of outcome to input is constant for various individuals or groups; in this formula the term "outcome" is presumably used to indicate the difference between positive and negative outcomes, thus perhaps corresponding to Homans' "profit." Adams' major contribution is a systematic treatment of the ways for reducing inequity and relating some of them to dissonance reduction; we have already noted that several dissonance experiments involve exchange situations in which the perceived inequity is reduced by modifying the value of the resources involved; for example, a subject who was paid little for presenting a view he opposes will reduce his "input" by accepting the view as his own.

PAY-OFF MATRIX. The conception of equity emerging from the social exchange theory of Thibaut and Kelley (1959) is more flexible than the ones examined so far. Like other students of social exchange, they assume that each participant in the transaction receives rewards and incurs costs; both reward and cost depend not only on the course of action chosen by the individual but also on the behavior of the other partner. This notion finds expression in the pay-off matrix, which is simply a tabular arrangement where rows indicate the various alternatives open to one participant and columns represent the options available to the other partner. Each cell, at the intersection of a given row with a given column, contains two entries which are the outcomes for each of the two

150 PART I ABRIDGEMENT OF *SOCIETAL STRUCTURES OF THE MIND*

participants when one of them chooses the alternative indicated by the row and the other chooses the option shown in the column. Thus, certain combinations of proaction and reaction may result in a loss for both participants, others may result in a gain for one of them or for both. The tendency of each participant to choose alternatives which maximize his gains is moderated by the fact that the outcome depends also on what the other is going to do, as well as by the possibility that the other may leave the exchange, finding it unattractive. The decision to terminate the exchange or to continue it depends on the reward obtained as well as on the availability of alternative exchanges for satisfying the same needs; for example, a worker may not be happy with his job, but he is unlikely to leave it unless he found another, more attractive place.

These constraints in the choice of alternative actions result in a process of accommodation between the exchange partners, which does not rest on a rigid definition of fairness, but rather on what they both find agreeable and profitable. It should be noted, however, that even in more formal definitions of equity, considerable flexibility is provided by recognition that the value of rewards, costs and investment depends in part on the subjective evaluations of the individuals concerned. Indeed, it was shown by Pruitt (1968) that the amount of money a subject reciprocated to the confederate depended not only on the amount given to him by the confederate, but also on the quantity of resource the confederate was thought to possess; since the marginal utility of money decreases for successive increments, the same amount had more value when given by a poor confederate than when allocated by a rich one. The same effect has been found for particularistic resources. In a series of studies Aronson and his associates (Aronson, 1970, pp. 150–159) have shown that when a confederate first expressed dislike towards the subject and then evaluated him positively, he was liked more than the one who was positive all the way.

The various theoretical formulations of exchange, although differing in details and, even more so, in terminology, have a common core in the notion that the amount given or taken by an individual is positively related to the amount which was previously given to or taken from him. There is indeed considerable empirical evidence in favor of this proposition.

Evidence for the Tendency Toward Equity

In view of the noted similarity among the major theoretical formulations, it seems unnecessary to present separately the empirical work of the various

SOME AREAS OF SOCIO-PSYCHOLOGICAL RESEARCH   151

schools; instead we shall follow the example set by Adams (1965) who, in reviewing the reduction of inequity, quotes works of Homans and of Thibaut as well as those closer to his own formulation. It is, however, desirable to discuss separately those studies in which equity is maintained by the subject as opposed to investigations in which the subject acts to reduce a pre-existing inequity. Let us begin with the maintenance of equity.

Pruitt (1968), in the experiment already mentioned, found that the amount of money the subject provided to the confederate was positively related to the amount the latter had previously made available to him. Investigating exchange of particularistic resources, Jones (1966) arranged groups of four subjects, continually exchanging evaluations of one another's artistic opinions. He found that subjects tended to reciprocate the evaluations they had received. It has also been shown that a person who received help is more likely than the one who was refused assistance to offer help to his benefactor (Goranson & Berkowitz, 1966) as well as to a third individual (Berkowitz & Daniels, 1964). In these studies, the same resource is involved in each stage of the exchange; keeping the resource constant while varying its amounts enhances the manifestation of reciprocity, since a change of resource modifies the effects of its amount. The effect of introducing an additional resource, although not explicitly, is well exemplified in a study by Leventhal and Bergman (1969). About 37 percent of the subjects who were grossly under-rewarded money-wise as well as derogated by the confederate, when having the opportunity to modify their share, chose to decrease it rather than increase equity. The evidence presented by the investigators suggests that this behavior served to *increase* the status of the subjects; thus, having to decide between establishing equity in status or in money, they chose the former. Indeed, only 22 percent of those who were deprived of money but not of status chose to decrease their share.

In this last experiment, the subject's reaction to inequity was studied. In several other investigations of this type, it was generally found that when subjects had been over- or under-rewarded, their behavior in a subsequent interaction tended to compensate for the "error," and was directed toward reestablishment of justice (Blurnstein & Weinstein; 1969; Leventhal et al., 1969; Pepitone, 1971; Walster et al., 1966). It was predicted that this tendency to restore equity will be stronger for the victims who were under-rewarded than for those who received above their fair share. While this prediction was confirmed for preschool children (Leventhal & Anderson, 1970), adults' behavior did not support it (Leventhal & Lane, 1970). In spite of the scarce empirical support, there is theoretical justification to expect that victims will attempt to redress injustice more than beneficiaries. When the subject is a victim, he faces both a dissonant situation due to a discrepancy between his efforts and his reward (Alexander & Simpson, 1964; Aronson, 1961), and a loss of resources; perceptual modification of the event takes care of dissonance, but not of the resource loss. On the other hand, when it is the other who received too little, it is possible to reduce dissonance by underestimating his contribution, without experiencing any actual loss. Of course, one could also reduce dissonance by allocating more to the other, but then at the cost of depriving himself. Consequently, perceptual modification appears more likely to occur with respect to the other than in regard to the self. Some support for this proposition is provided by Leventhal and Michaels (1969).

Other studies dealing with the reduction of inequity were reviewed by Adams (1965) who classified them according to the method by which inequity was reduced. Some of these studies show that workers paid above or below what they considered a fair wage tended to modify the amount and/ or quality of their performance to make it commensurate with their wage. Adams devotes considerable attention to the problem of which method for inequity reduction will be preferred in a given situation. We have already proposed that perceptual modification is more likely to be chosen for the behavior of the other than for the behavior of self; this proposition is shared by Adams, although on a somewhat different theoretical ground.

Earlier we have proposed that symbolic resources may be more amenable to perceptual modification than concrete ones: it might be easier to modify perception regarding the amount of information and status received or given, than to do so for goods and services. In summary, there is considerable evidence that individuals tend to behave in a manner consistent with maintaining or restoring a ratio between what they receive and what they give, but the order of preferences among various ways of restoring equity is only partially understood.

Resources and Equity

How different is this line of research from the theoretical and experimental work on resource exchange? There are at least two points which deserve to be noted: one is the notion of cost, the other is the specification of the resources involved in the exchange.

SOME AREAS OF SOCIO-PSYCHOLOGICAL RESEARCH   153

Most formulations of exchange theory, borrowing from economics, assume that a partner in an exchange must incur certain costs in order to obtain rewards, so that in every exchange there are losses as well as gains. This is perfectly plain in economic exchanges: one has to give money to obtain goods and thus, after the exchange had terminated, he will have more goods but less money; likewise, one has to work and expend efforts to obtain money; thus his profit, as Homans suggested, is the difference between the value of what he received and the value of what he gave. In the arithmetic of economic exchanges, costs are a value to be subtracted, a value with a negative sign; indeed, in these exchanges there is a negative relationship between what remains to self and what is given to other. This relationship, however, becomes less negative and then positive as one moves, in the structure of resources, toward the particularistic ones; hence the cost becomes smaller and then positive and turns into a reward. The property of resources regarding the relationship between self and other can be reformulated as follows: the more particularistic the resource, the less negative the cost of giving it. To illustrate this point, let us consider two lovers, or perhaps a married couple, having sexual relations: each is giving a great deal of pleasure to the other, but where is the "cost"? Giving pleasure to the other *adds* to rather than *subtracts* from one's own enjoyment; the cost is positive. Although this may be most evident in love making, the same considerations apply to other particularistic exchanges as well. One might experience a certain difficulty to associate the term "cost" with a positive value; words are tyrannical and rarely neutral; the term cost has intuitively a strong negative connotation. Yet it is not uncommon for a person, thanked for a favor done, to answer "Nothing at all," meaning "My cost was zero"; in French more than in English, one may also answer "It was my pleasure" which we interpret to indicate that he did it for love, so that his cost was positive as he derived pleasure from doing the favor.

These considerations lead us to the second point of our discussion— the relevance of the resources involved in the exchange. In the theoretical formulations just examined and in the related empirical work, the resources exchanged do not play an explicit role; they are all covered by the notion of amount of (positive or negative) reinforcement. We have seen, however, that quantity and quality interact: in Teichman's experiment the same amount of resource reciprocated had different effects on satisfaction depending on its appropriateness to the proaction. Donnenwerth's investigation further showed that a larger amount of an inappropriate resource was reciprocated. These and other studies reviewed show that resources are not equivalent;

154   PART I ABRIDGEMENT OF *SOCIETAL STRUCTURES OF THE MIND*

therefore it is not sufficient to state "how much," one should specify "how much of what."

It may be suggested that the more appropriate the resource is the smaller the amount of it required in order to establish equity and satisfaction. Appropriateness, in turn, depends on the need of the recipient and on the institutional setting; in our imperfect world these two do not always go together: one may need a given resource, which is not suitable for exchange in a particular institution. In such conflictual situations, giving precedence to individual needs over institutional requirements is likely to backfire, according to some experimental results. In a study by Schopler and Thompson (1968) female subjects who had received a small gift (a flower) from the confederate were later more responsive to his request of testing the handwashing of a blouse, than were those who received no flower. These results were, however, obtained only when the situation was described as informal, and were reversed in formal situation: here, those who received no favor were more willing to help than those who got a flower, possibly because the small gift was inappropriate in this setting.

Such interaction between the situation and personal needs was also reported by Brehm and Cole (1966) in an entirely different setting. Subjects were assigned to a task of rating a confederate. Half of them were told that the task was highly important; for the remaining subjects, the task was presented as of low importance. Within each condition, half the subjects received a soft drink by the confederate who bought himself a Coke from a vending machine and "thoughtfully" brought one back for the subject as well. The other half did not receive a drink. Later on, the confederate was requested to stack sheets of paper for the experimenter. When the rating was presented as unimportant, most subjects who had received the drink reciprocated by helping the confederate; they did not offer help when the task was important. Willingness to help was about the same in the two conditions of importance, for subjects who did not receive the drink. Givers of favor were not rated differently, on the average, than those who did not offer the drink. Unwillingness to help drink-providers when the rating was seen as important may be due to their favor being considered inappropriate to such a situation—sort of "bribe."

These two studies suggest that the initiation of an exchange which is institutionally inappropriate may well leave the proactor disappointed. Chances of success in obtaining the resource desired, in spite of it being contrary to institutional norms, will be presumably better when the proactor pretends to

SOME AREAS OF SOCIO-PSYCHOLOGICAL RESEARCH   155

propose a different, institutionally appropriate, exchange, without revealing his real purpose. To these manipulatory techniques we now turn.

Manipulative Techniques

When a person finds himself in a situation which does not permit an exchange of the very resource he needs, he may still attempt to achieve it within the same setting through manipulative techniques. There are several such non-conventional exchanges, of which two—ingratiation and Machiavellianism—have been studied intensively, although with different research strategies. Ingratiation experiments typically consist of placing the subject in a situation where he is dependent on the other for certain resources but cannot obtain them by proposing a straightforward exchange; his behavior in this situation is then observed. Studies of Machiavellianism on the other hand, focus on differences regarding the exchange behavior of individuals who had been previously rated high or low on a scale of Machiavellianism. Although this difference in research strategy does not facilitate a comparison between ingratiators and Machiavellians, they appear to have at least one element in common: concealing from the other what resource they strive to obtain from him.

Ingratiation

A most comprehensive and penetrating study of ingratiation has been provided by Jones (1964), who devoted considerable attention to the tactics and goals of the ingratiator. We shall refer to his work with only minimal changes in terminology; tactics denote the behavior of the ingratiator toward the other while goals are the behaviors that the ingratiator attempts to elicit in the other. Some of the tactics described by Jones pertain to the self-presentation of the ingratiator, or behavior toward self; Jones aptly notes that presentation of self may include various combinations of self-enhancement (giving status to self) and self-effacement (taking status from self) depending on the circumstances. We have noted earlier in discussing interpersonal attraction that giving status to self signals to the other that the ingratiator is a valuable exchange partner as he possesses large amounts of a valuable resource. On the other hand, taking away status from self is

156 PART I ABRIDGEMENT OF *SOCIETAL STRUCTURES OF THE MIND*

functionally equivalent to spilling coffee on the suit, in Aronson's experiment: it signals that although our person has much to give there is something he needs as well. Other tactics, also described by Jones, consist of providing the other with status, goods, and services, and perhaps some other resources which may be needed by him. Ostensibly the other will be expected to reciprocate this giving with love. We have indeed seen that in the institution of friendship, it is appropriate to reciprocate with love most of the resources received. Once a relation of friendship has been established, an attempt to achieve the hidden goals becomes feasible. Experimental results previously mentioned have indicated that the initiator of an illicit exchange runs the risk of being disliked by the other. Building a strong friendship first may offset this expected reduction in liking, making safer for the ingratiator to bid for his goals.

The goals of ingratiation considered by Jones are essentially of two types: (a) receiving from the other specific resources which are controlled by him and cannot be easily obtained elsewhere; (b) preventing the other from taking away the resources which are more valuable to the ingratiator than those he is willing to give. The resources which constitute the ingratiator's goal are unlikely to be the ones which characterize the friendship institution, i.e., love and, to a lesser extent, status, and services. If, indeed, these resources constitute his goal, there would be no need for ingratiation and for deception; in friendship it is well within the norms to expect particularistic resources. Therefore it is more likely that the ingratiator is after less particularistic resources, the very ones which are not usually exchanged among friends. Likewise when the ingratiator offers friendship to avoid a loss, it seems that the resources he is attempting to preserve are the less particularistic ones.

Another variation of ingratiation occurs when the goal is to receive status or avoid losing it in reference to a third individual or group. One may, for example, cultivate the friendship of a high-status person in order to receive status (and possibly other resources as well) from his peers by virtue of his highly placed relationship. Conversely, one may attempt to ingratiate an individual who can damage the ingratiator's standing in the community by revealing some unsavory details of his life and activities (e.g., that he is an ex-convict). Here again, resources less particularistic than status, such as the salary obtained from a job, may be protected by ingratiation. When the ingratiator protects himself by giving money rather than love, blackmail is the appropriate term for his behavior.

In the experiments described by Jones (1964) the subject is often asked to strive for a resource (a job, a travel fellowship) which is controlled by the other and which may be obtained by winning the other's approval (Jones, p. 158). In discussing the behaviors used by subjects to obtain this approval, Jones (p. 193) notes that the strategy for obtaining love will differ from the one used for status. When attempting to obtain a positive rating for task performance, the subject will tend to describe himself as "competent and respectworthy" rather than "friendly and affable." The latter presentation is more likely when "the goal is to be judged a congenial or compatible partner." Love and status do not, however, constitute goals but rather mediate toward the achievement of other, less personalistic resources. Another interesting finding is that low status subjects are more likely to use self-enhancement, to agree with the other on important items, and perhaps also to use other-enhancement as a technique of ingratiation. High status subjects, on the other hand, are more likely to present themselves as modest, to agree on non-important items and to avoid other-enhancement. Thus each type of ingratiator tends to stress the condition for exchange which is less evident on him: the low status ingratiator implies possession of resources; the high status one indicates his willingness to receive. These general trends are modified, Jones shows, by the need to maintain credibility.

Conformity

One of the tactics used by ingratiators is conformity, where they change their beliefs and behavior in order to become more similar to another person or group. In ingratiation, conformity will succeed only to the extent that the ingratiator is able to conceal his ulterior goal (Jones & Gerard, 1967, p. 586). Conformity also occurs outside the ingratiation situation, when there is no concealed purpose and as such, it has been widely studied (see Kiesler & Kiesler, 1969 for a review), particularly in the context of group pressure and attitude change. The terms compliance persuasion, influence, diffusion of innovation, which have been used in this line of investigation, have a good deal in common with the notion of conformity, although they differ in details and in emphasis. The basic unity of these phenomena in social influence has been put in evidence by Nord (1969) who suggests that individuals conform in order to obtain approval, love and status in our terminology. Seen in this light, conformity becomes a proaction in an exchange of resources: in

158 PART I ABRIDGEMENT OF *SOCIETAL STRUCTURES OF THE MIND*

accepting the values or behavior of the other (or of the group) the conformer implies high regard for him and expects to receive love and status in return, in the guise of approval. It has been found, indeed, that people tend to like those who are similar to them; by conforming one becomes more similar to the other, therefore increasing his chances of being liked.

The tendency to conform was demonstrated in the pioneer work of Sherif (1935a), Asch (1951), and Festinger et al. (1950, Chapters 5 and 6). Once this fact was established, subsequent research was directed at clarifying who is more likely to conform, and under which conditions conformity is more likely to occur. Some of the findings obtained fit remarkably the exchange interpretation of conformity.

If conforming is a bid for status and love, it can be expected that persons who have a stronger need for these resources will be more likely to conform. Yet the act of conforming implies giving these very resources to the other, thus it requires a previous possession of them by the conformer. In consequence, people who are more likely to conform will possess a moderate amount of status and love: they should have enough to make the initial investment, but not so much to disregard the opportunity to receive more of these resources. Individuals who are very rich or very poor in love and status will be less likely to conform, although for different reasons: the former do not need to receive, while the latter do not possess enough to make the initial investment, particularly if it requires a large amount, as for example when there was a previous public commitment to a different position (Lana, 1969). Furthermore, as noted earlier, the expectation of receiving status will be dissonant to persons who feel they do not deserve it. Therefore they will be more reluctant to invest toward a goal which will create a dissonant situation. These considerations suggest that when there are few "poor" individuals in the population studied, or when the amount required for investment is moderate, the relationship between conformity and the amount possessed will be negative: the more a person possesses love and status the less is the probability that he will conform. Conversely, a positive relationship is expected when the initial investment is high and/or when there are many resource-poor persons in the population. Finally, when the population includes both very "rich" and very "poor" persons and the initial investment is moderate, the relationship between the amount possessed and conformity will be curvilinear, with those possessing moderate amounts conforming most. This analysis of conformity as a proaction of an exchange may provide an explanation for the contrasting results reported in the literature regarding the

SOME AREAS OF SOCIO-PSYCHOLOGICAL RESEARCH   159

relationship between influenceability and self-esteem (i.e., the amount of status possessed by the person). Indeed, McGuire (1969a, pp. 250–251), in summarizing research in this area, notes that while many studies reported a negative relationship between self-esteem and influenceability, many others provided evidence for a positive or curvilinear relationship. A curvilinear relationship has also been reported between conformity and affiliation need: subjects with a moderate need conform more than those at the extremes (Byrne, 1962; Hardy, 1957). This need covers a range of resources, including the one involved in self-esteem, status; this common resource may explain the similarity of findings.

McGuire's attempt to account for this complex relationship between self-esteem and conformity is far less parsimonious than ours as it postulates five genotypical principles as well as differential interactions between personality and situational variables (McGuire, 1969a, pp. 243–247). In any event, neither his reasoning nor ours explains the strong negative relationship between conformity and non-manipulated self-esteem found in a population of hospitalized mental patients (Janis & Rife, 1959). Presumably self-esteem is low in such a population, so that we would have expected to find in them a positive, rather than a negative relationship between this variable and conformity. Our second proposition, that powerful persons who possess a large amount of status are less likely to conform, is reflected in Hollander's notion of idiosyncrasy credit (1958); indeed, the degree of deviation from norms permitted to an individual by the group before sanctions are applied, constitutes an indication for the amount of status and love he possesses.

There is a certain similarity in the relationship of self-esteem to conformity, just considered, and to attraction, which was examined earlier in this chapter: in both cases high and low self-esteem subjects are alike while differing from subjects of moderate self-esteem. This parallelism is not pure coincidence: both attraction and conformity involve consideration of what one needs to receive and of what he can give in the exchange, but attraction refers to expectations regarding a future exchange, while conformity is a first step in an exchange that has already begun; both involve love and status although love may be a more prominent resource in attraction while status is more prominent in conformity. The closeness of the two notions of attraction and conformity was noted by Festinger (1953) when he suggested that full acceptance of conformity, as distinct from mere compliance, occurs only when the conformer is attracted by the person to whom he conforms. Yet, experiments on dissonance suggest that compliance will

160 PART I ABRIDGEMENT OF *SOCIETAL STRUCTURES OF THE MIND*

increase attractiveness when non-particularistic reciprocation is scarce or absent: girls who complied with the demands of severe initiation found the bogus and boring sex discussion group most attractive. Research dealing more directly with the relationship between conformity and attraction was, however, mainly concerned with the effects of the latter on the former. It appears that one is more likely to conform to a group which he considers attractive (Marlowe & Gergen, 1969, pp. 615–616); in other words, the first actual step in an exchange (conforming) is more likely to be taken when an exchange seems to be feasible (attraction). Indeed, group variables which have been found to increase conformity are permanence of the group, the extent of interaction within it, and the existence of an achievable common goal (Tajfel, 1969, p. 336); all these factors appear to enhance the possibility of resource exchange within the group (Blake & Mouton, 1961).

After this digression on conformity, which may or may not be a manipulative tactic (depending on the resource expected to be gained), we return to the main topic with a discussion of Machiavellianism.

Machiavellianism

Since Machiavelli wrote "Il Principe," a book of cynical advice to the ruler, the name of this Florentine writer has become synonymous with manipulative behavior. In the last years there has been a surge of interest in the scientific study of this interpersonal behavior.

As noted earlier, studies of Machiavellianism have followed a paradigm quite different from those of ingratiation. Jones' work has been mainly concerned with studying the differential behavior patterns of subjects more or less dependent on the approval of the other. Research on Machiavellianism, on the other hand, has particularly focused on the identification of situational characteristics for which individuals scoring high on a Machiavellianism scale outperform low scorers (Christie & Geis, 1970). The Machiavellian was found to win more often when there is face to face interaction, when he can devise his response rather than having to choose it among predetermined alternatives, and when the situation has emotion-arousal connotations (which he usually disregards).

High Machiavellians are characterized as being less persuasible, less affected by social pressure or by inconsistencies in their attitudes or behavior, less likely to be emotionally involved, while more attentive to the informative

SOME AREAS OF SOCIO-PSYCHOLOGICAL RESEARCH   161

aspects of the situation. "In general, high Machiavellians appear to have as little defensive investment in their own beliefs as they have in others or in interpersonal relations" (Christie & Geis, 1970, p. 313). Thus, individuals who score high in Machiavellianism seem to be less in need to receive love (and perhaps also status) than individuals who score lower in Machiavellianism. Consequently, particularistic transactions do not constitute for them a goal in itself, but merely stepping stones to the acquisition of less particularistic resources which they value more. Their typical way to handle a competitive situation will be to maximize their share of non-particularistic resources while letting the other have the particularistic ones he cherishes. "The best way to handle people is to tell them what they want to hear" (i.e., to give them love and status), runs an item of the Machiavellianism scale (Christie, 1970). As for the Machiavellian himself, "it hurts more to lose money than to lose a friend" (scale version for children, Christie & Geis, 1970, p. 327).

This interpretation of Machiavellianism in terms of resource preference for dispensation and achievement explains why Machiavellians do better in situations which permit the transaction of particularistic resources in addition to the non-particularistic ones (chips, money) explicitly played for. In a face-to-face interaction and in a less structured situation, Machiavellians can give particularistic resources or "irrelevant affects" (Christie & Geis, 1970, p. 288) in exchange for the non-particularistic ones. These affects are irrelevant to individuals high in Machiavellianism, but quite valuable to individuals low in Machiavellianism.

There is also some evidence, albeit not conclusive, suggesting that the superiority of the Machiavellian approach is stronger when the experimental situation is more realistic. Indeed, only in a realistic situation are there non-particularistic resources to be gained, while lack of realism does not preclude, and may even enhance, the exchange of particularistic resources; when the chips are "worthless" they provide status for the winner, but no money. A person who values money but does not care for status is unlikely to take a great interest in such a game.

Machiavellians agree less with others and are less self-consistent. Agreeing with the other is a tactic for receiving love and status; it has been shown indeed (see, e.g., Byrne et al., 1970) that one is more likely to feel esteem for a person who holds attitudes similar to his own. Maintenance of self-consistency is also related to self-esteem. Since the Machiavellian is after less particularistic resources, he does not indulge in behaviors which will provide him with status (such as agreeing or being consistent), yet,

162 PART I ABRIDGEMENT OF *SOCIETAL STRUCTURES OF THE MIND*

he can be persuaded by "more factual" information which relates to resources he values. Agreement to the viewpoint of the other is, thus, likely to occur in the Machiavellian when winning his approval is necessary for obtaining resources controlled by him. This situation is often found in Jones' experiments on ingratiation and explains the apparent discrepancy between the high persuasibility of the ingratiator and the weak effect of social pressure on the Machiavellian. In those situations where approval results in obtaining only status, Machiavellians will not be persuasible; when, however, the other's approval mediates access to less particularistic resources, they will yield to social pressure. Indeed, when nothing but status was to be gained by winning the other's approval, Machiavellians were found to engage less in ingratiation than did subjects low on Machiavellianism (Jones et al., 1962).

If Machiavellians are usually rich in love and status, being charming individuals who are not particularly concerned with obtaining status or being approved by others, and willing to trade these resources for less particularistic ones, it can be expected that they will score low on approval need (Crowne & Marlowe, 1960), while being high on the need for non-particularistic resources. Non-Machiavellians, on the other hand, may or may not be high on need approval. Some support for this hypothesis is found in work done by Donnenwerth, who administered both the Crowne and Marlowe approval scale and the Mach IV scale to 140 female subjects. Both score distributions were then dichotomized at about the respective means for national norms, i.e., score 15 for the approval scale (Crowne & Marlowe, 1964, p. 211) and score 88 for Mach IV (Christie & Geis, 1970, p. 79). Subjects low in Machiavellianism are divided almost evenly with regard to their need for approval, 59 percent showing a low need and 41 percent a high need score. On the other hand, the large majority of Machiavellians (82%) are low in need approval.

Persons with a high Machiavellianism score are found more often among young people, among those raised in a large city and among those belonging to a less traditional culture (Christie & Geis, 1970, pp. 315–321). Modern society, and particularly its urban subculture, appears to favor non-particularistic exchanges over particularistic ones. It seems therefore, that Machiavellians are particularly adjusted to the exchange conditions of modern urban culture, having low need for particularistic resources and high need for non-particularistic ones. At the same time, they thrive on the need of others for particularistic resources in a culture scarce of them.

SOME AREAS OF SOCIO-PSYCHOLOGICAL RESEARCH   163

There are no legitimate institutional avenues for exchanging money with love and only a few for trading it with status, such as maecenatism (support of the arts and sciences) and philanthropy (support of the needy), where status is given to the donor by a third party rather than by the recipients of financial support. In the absence of an institutional setting where he can give love and status and receive money, the manipulator will have to dissimulate his real exchange intentions and to begin by offering what the other needs.

A more extreme variety of the Machiavellian pattern is the confidence plot, where the victim entrusts his material resources (usually money) for an empty promise such as high returns. As implied by the name, the plot may succeed only after the trust of the intended victim has been secured. As trust is a characteristic of particularistic resources, here again, the victim is given love and status and finally deprived of money or goods. Other illicit exchange patterns may be found in practice, although they have not attracted the same amount of investigation as ingratiation and Machiavellianism. We have already mentioned, *in passim*, blackmail, where the victim is offered a choice between losing particularistic resources (status and sometimes also love) or losing money to the blackmailer.

In a study, Staub and Sherk (1970) reported that children high in need for approval were likely to renounce a less particularistic resource (candy), presumably in a bid for approval. Similar results were obtained by Blumstein and Weinstein (1969). By manipulating both the share of a stooge in a joint task and his claim to a share of the reward, these authors created conditions in which the confederate's claim was above, below or commensurate to his actual contribution to the task. Dependent variables were the subject's claim on a second interaction with the same stooge and his evaluation of the confederate. Subjects high in need for approval were reluctant to claim a major share for themselves, even when previously victimized, possibly to avoid disapproval. Machiavellians, on the other hand, tended to claim more when the stooge's demands were modest. The different behavior of these two types of subjects illustrates once more the influence of the individual's needs: each person strives for the resource he values most.

Another illicit pattern of exchange is illustrated by the behavior of impostors, who are individuals posing as being richer in money, more learned or skilled than they really are in order to offer these imaginary resources in exchange for actual status. Their tragedy is that when they are discovered, they are likely to experience an almost total loss of status, the resource which they strived so hard to obtain.

164 PART I ABRIDGEMENT OF *SOCIETAL STRUCTURES OF THE MIND*

The patterns described in this section have two characteristics in common: (a) they do not conform to exchanges which are typical of any social institution; and (b) they meet the need for specific resources in the individual who initiated them. In other words, these exchanges are unorthodox and usually illicit patterns of achieving need satisfaction.

Licit but Roundabout Patterns

Other behavioral patterns for obtaining a resource which is not directly available through appropriate institutional exchange do not involve deception but may look peculiar to the outsider. We have already noted the case of a person going to the doctor in order to receive sympathy and affection rather than medical services (Shuval, 1970). Other examples of the longer and devious routes taken to achieve a needed resource are found among American blacks. Let us consider the following behavior patterns which have been ascribed to some of them: (a) preference for conspicuous consumption items like flashy cars and clothes, rather than purchasing more "solid" items; (b) demanding integrated facilities where there is separation and separate ones where there is integration; (c) enrolling in black studies programs which do not provide training for specific future jobs. There seems to be little in common among these behaviors except that none of them appears oriented toward long-range goals. A meaningful picture emerges, however, when they are seen as different paths of achieving status, the resource of which black people have been most deprived. Conspicuous consumption goods are exchangeable with status. Refusal of social contact, by insisting on separate facilities, means taking away status from the rejected ones, and thus the real issue is not integration versus separation but who is taking away status from whom. The information gained in black studies may not be useful on the job, but it is a means to a needed increase in self pride.

The comparison of these latter patterns with Machiavellianism provides an interesting contrast. The manipulator uses particularistic resources to gain non-particularistic ones. In the other examples of exchange, the reverse often occurs: particularistic resources are sought through the mediation of less particularistic ones. A person high in particularistic needs and low in non-particularistic ones is, indeed, the ideal partner for a sucker.

With an attempt to integrate several aspects of interpersonal relations within the framework of resource exchange, we have concluded the second part of this volume, dealing with the dynamics of interpersonal behavior. A basic requirement of efficient communication is that a message will have the same meaning for the receiver as for the sender; if one communicates love to the other, the latter should perceive that he received love and react accordingly. Sharing meanings of behavior requires a similarity between the cognitive structures of the participants; in the study of resource exchange, we have assumed the existence of such structural similarity.

Summary

Interpersonal behavior has been conceptualized in this book as a mechanism enabling individuals to maintain their optimal level of resources. If indeed any social interaction consists of an exchange of resources, then the notion of exchange should provide a framework for interpreting many socio-psychological phenomena. Thus in the present chapter, some of the issues in social psychology which generated theoretical and empirical work have been reanalyzed in terms of the resource exchange paradigm. We have discussed the frustration–aggression sequence, complementarity of needs for exchange partners, interpersonal attraction, equity or justice in resource transactions, ingratiation, conformity, and Machiavellianism.

The frustration–aggression sequence is a negative exchange where person A (the frustrator) causes a deficiency in person B (the victim) and is "reciprocated" with the latter attempting to deprive him of one or more resources. By considering definitions of frustration as well as the actual manipulations used in studies of frustration–aggression, it becomes clear that actual or potential (future) deprivation of resources is a necessary component of the frustrating event; a second component is the need state of the object-person. When deprivation results in producing a need, the victim will tend to reestablish balance by retaliation. It follows that an individual possessing a large amount of the resource of which he was deprived will be less likely than a "poor" person to experience a deficit, and therefore, to be aggressively aroused.

Often the degree of frustration has been inferred from the intensity of the following aggression; it is indeed reasonable to assume that when frustration is low, retaliation will be milder, but the reverse is not necessarily true; aggression may be inhibited and its expression mild in spite of a high level of internal arousal. Thus, the intensity of retaliation is a function of two

166 PART I ABRIDGEMENT OF *SOCIETAL STRUCTURES OF THE MIND*

factors—the drive level and the degree of inhibition to aggress. In general, retaliation serves to reestablish the optimal level. However, when a victim foresees a high probability that retaliation will bring a further loss of resources, he will refrain from retaliation.

Examination of the notion of aggression has led us to define it as a behavior which deprives the recipient of one or more resources. Thus, frustration and aggression are both events in which resources are taken away although they may differ as to the conditions producing them and the way they are perceived by the participants of the interaction.

By considering the frustration–aggression sequence as a case of negative resource exchange, we are immediately provided with a classification of both frustration and aggression in terms of the six resource classes. Then, we can explore the relationship between the class of frustration and that of aggression and study its effects on the restoration of internal balance, as measured by residual hostility. It is suggested that the preference for a certain class of aggression is determined by the class of frustration previously experienced, and that the amount of residual aggression is affected by the structural relationship between the two resources. There is a preference to retaliate in kind or with a resource similar to the one involved in the frustrating event. When preferred retaliation is feasible, residual aggression is lower than when a remote resource is employed.

Other factors which influence restoration of the internal balance are the actor and the object in the frustration–aggression sequence. Three paradigms of exchange have been studied with different degrees of intensity: (1) direct retaliation, where the previous actor (the frustrator) becomes the object of retaliation and the previous object (the victim) becomes the actor of retaliation; (2) displacement, where the object of retaliation is not the previous frustrator but a third individual although retaliation is carried out by the previous victim; (3) vicarious aggression, in which the object of retaliation is the original frustrator but retaliation is carried out by a third individual rather than by the previous victim. The available data tend to suggest that direct retaliation yields a decrease in residual aggression, displacement does not affect it, and vicarious aggression results in an increase of subsequent aggression. This suggestion, however, is only tentative since the data originated in many studies differing in methodology as well as in the resources of frustration and aggression.

Direct, displaced and vicarious retaliation have been investigated for their possible effectiveness in restoring the victim's internal balance, which had been disrupted by the frustrative act. If indeed frustration impairs the

SOME AREAS OF SOCIO-PSYCHOLOGICAL RESEARCH 167

internal balance of resources by being an act of deprivation, then a straightforward means by which it can be reestablished is restoration. In this paradigm, neither the actor nor the object changes, only the mode alters: the same actor who had emitted the frustrative act now provides the victim with one or more resources. The few data available on restoration point to its effectiveness in reducing residual aggression. Unless frustration is viewed as deprivation, this cathartic effect of restoration cannot be explained. Further research is needed in this area as to the differential effect of restoration and retaliation on residual hostility. Beside the theoretical interest, the study of restitution has practical relevance: restoration has the obvious advantage over counter-aggression that it may reduce residual hostility with positive rather than negative activities.

Turning to positive exchanges, the first issue examined was what need combination provides for a successful exchange partnership. While some data indicate that similarity of needs leads to more stable relations, other studies indicate the reverse. The dilemma can be solved by considering two exchange properties of resources: the relationship between self and other and the exchange in kind. The more particularistic a resource is, the stronger the relationship between giving it to self and to other and the higher the likelihood for an exchange in kind. Consequently, similarity of needs is advantageous for particularistic resources, while complementarity is desirable for non-particularistic ones.

If need combination determines the stability of a given relationship, it can be suggested that "matched" partners will find one another attractive. Attractiveness, then, is a perceived potential for a successful exchange. Thus defined, attraction rests on two factors: (a) the extent to which the other is a potential provider of resources we need, and (b) the extent to which we are in a position to satisfy some of his needs. When an actual exchange is considered, one estimates the probability of its success. We all know that a satisfactory relationship requires some balance of giving and receiving. A superior individual as well as an inferior one are not ideal partners for exchange. While the first has a lot to offer, there is not much he needs; the reverse is true for the inferior individual. It is further suggested that persons are attracted to those who are potential partners for exchange of the particular resource they need. Thus, attraction is resource-specific, yet it may generalize to resources proximal in the structure. Attraction is essentially a condition which precedes the exchange, it is an estimate of the feasibility of a particular exchange.

168 PART I ABRIDGEMENT OF *SOCIETAL STRUCTURES OF THE MIND*

This definition of attraction suggests that people have fairly clear ideas about what constitutes a successful transaction. There have been various attempts to spell out this intuitive notion of fair exchange, among them is Homans' formulation of distributive justice, Adams' notion of equity and Thibaut and Kelly's pay-off matrix. Common to these formulations is the idea that every social transaction involves certain rewards and certain costs. This is perfectly true for economic transactions concerning money and goods, as in these exchanges there is a negative relationship between what remains to self and what is given to other. This relation, however, becomes positive for the particularistic resources, hence the "costs" become positive; in an exchange of love, each participant gives pleasure to the other, but where is the "cost"? Giving pleasure to the other adds to one's own enjoyment, rather than subtracting from it. Another important variable in determining equity is the relationship between the resources exchanged. When the same resource is involved in proaction and reaction, the amount given and received determines the equity. But when two different resources are exchanged, the appropriateness of the exchange determines the amount necessary for establishing equity. The more appropriate the resource received is, the smaller the amount of it required for establishing equity. Appropriateness, in turn, depends on the need of the recipient and on the institutional setting.

What happens when a person finds himself in a situation which does not permit an exchange of the very resource he needs? This person may resort to a non-conventional exchange in which he gives a resource appropriate to the institution but aims at obtaining a non-appropriate one; he may, e.g., pretend to be friendly with a rich person with the hope of gaining financial help. Two such exchange strategies—ingratiation and Machiavellianism— have been studied intensively; both have the common element of the initiator concealing from the other what resource he strives to obtain from him. Most often the ingratiator is willing to exchange particularistic resources for non-particularistic ones. One of the tactics used by ingratiators is conformity, acceptance of the beliefs and behaviors of the other. Conformity is also used by non-ingratiators, but with the distinct difference that they are aiming at receiving, in exchange for giving status, particularistic resources, while the ingratiator reaches for non-particularistic ones.

The preference for non-particularistic resources over particularistic ones appears to characterize individuals who score high in Machiavellianism. Indeed, they were found to engage less in ingratiation when the situation offers only a gain of status. The modern urban environment is rich in

SOME AREAS OF SOCIO-PSYCHOLOGICAL RESEARCH   169

non-particularistic resources and poor in the particularistic ones. It seems, therefore, that Machiavellians are particularly adjusted to the exchange conditions of this subculture.

Another behavioral pattern is the use of non-particularistic resources for obtaining particularistic ones. The preference of some American blacks for conspicuous consumption items like flashy cars and clothes may be a path of achieving status, the resource of which black people have been most deprived. Sometimes the motivation behind charity is the same: giving money to gain status. In general, people prefer to give what they have in abundance and to receive what is scarce to them. It is only when the situation does not permit such exchange that one may resort to manipulative techniques, to satisfy one's needs in spite of institutional barriers.

This reinterpretation of some of the main topics of concern to socio-psychological research in terms of resource exchange is a main conclusion of this chapter.

6

Epilogue: Man and His Society

Overview

The reader who has accompanied us through this book may wonder whether the knowledge he has acquired here may contribute to a better understanding of human behavior and to the solution of the many problems existing in the relationship of man to man. This final chapter constitutes an attempt to answer these questions by clarifying the relevance of resource theory to current problems in our society.

We have conceptualized two types of man's needs, the need for resource accumulation and the need for confirmation of structure; the former is satisfied through interpersonal exchanges while the latter safeguards man's ability to enter these exchanges. Social organization, in turn, has been perceived as the mechanism for regulating the satisfaction of these needs. In any given society certain needs are better satisfied than certain others so that social problems arising out of unfulfilled needs differ from one society to another. An attempt to solve such problems should begin with the development of tools for measuring the performance of society and locating areas of shortage in need satisfaction. By overcoming methodological difficulties which still exist in the development of social indicators we shall be able to gain a clearer understanding of the proposed relationship between unsatisfied needs and social pathology. This line of investigation will spur the search for new forms of social organization providing optimal need satisfaction for the largest possible number of individuals.

Man the Structurer

Man classifies stimuli and organizes their classes; in this process the environment acquires meaning for him and the experiences of the past enable him to understand the present and to predict the future. We have examined the development and organization of cognitive structures pertaining to the

EPILOGUE: MAN AND HIS SOCIETY   171

social environment, noting the manner in which they differ from one society to another, their deviance in mental patients and the role they play in interpersonal communication. In this cognitive network the structure of resource classes deserves a special place; in a sense other structures are ancillary to it—tools in establishing the web of interpersonal relations through which resources are obtained and supplied, thus providing for the mutual satisfaction of needs among exchange partners. Indeed, role differentiation as well as the learning of social norms and viewpoint of the others, enable the individual to engage in those interpersonal transactions which will provide the resources he needs.

Seeking Resources

Psychological theorists have long recognized that interpersonal behavior is resource seeking. In the past, however, each scholar has stressed a particular class of resources while de-emphasizing the others. Love is preeminent in the Freudian conception of human motivation; Adler has seen interpersonal relations as a struggle for the acquisition of status; Karl Marx has taught us that man seeks economic resources—money and goods. More recently the conception of man as a processor of information has raised interest in psychology. Thus, there is hardly a resource class which has not served as the pivot of a theory on human behavior.

It has also been argued that man has a dual nature—rational and irrational: Economic man is rational, his goals are recognizable and his behavior predictable; Man the lover and the hater is irrational, a mystery to himself. The structure of resources goes beyond this dualistic conception: it suggests that motivational states are ordered and interrelated; moreover, their rules of exchange vary gradually with the position of the resource in the structure. Thus love is not less rational than money, it just follows a different logic, better known to poets than to accountants. The logic of other resource classes is more similar to money or to love, depending on whether they are nearer to the latter or to the former in the structure of resources.

If resource classes are ordered and if the rules of exchange depend on their position in the structure, then little justification is left for partial theories like economics which deal only with certain types of exchanges. The growing realization, particularly among economists, that economic and psychological problems interact and cannot be solved in isolation, requires integration at

172 PART I ABRIDGEMENT OF *SOCIETAL STRUCTURES OF THE MIND*

the theoretical level; perhaps the structure of resources will provide a point of departure toward this goal.

The Dialectics of Stability vs. Change

The structuring activity of man bears important consequences in determining the relationships between stability and change in viewing his environment. We have noted that events, not less than cognitions, contain structures in which the relationship among their component element is reflected; the structure of social events such as interpersonal messages, usually reflects the cognitive structure of their originator. Indeed, the cognitive development of the child results from perceiving sequences of events which have a fairly constant relationship among their component elements. Once the developing cognition, which reflects the structural constancy of past events, becomes established the problem of its fitness to successive events arises: if the world changes the pre-existing cognition will no longer represent it adequately. But how do we know that the environment has changed? Obviously, a single dissonant event will not be sufficient evidence of change; the perception of such an event is usually modified to fit the observer's cognition. Cognitive structures are indeed resistant to change, and perceptual modification satisfies the need for cognitive stability. Thus cognition acts as a stabilizer of our view of the world. If, however, later events continue to show the same deviant pattern, then it will become increasingly difficult to brush them off through perceptual modification.

The necessity for cognitive changes does not always stem from changes in the environment; the environment may remain constant, yet the individual may expand his field of experience by bringing into his observation phenomena which were previously excluded. In this case cognitive modification will usually consist of a further differentiation leading to the creation of new conceptual classes. The most common instance of this type of change is provided by the cognitive growth of the child. Artistic creation and scientific discovery also seem to result from such cognitive changes which provide a broader understanding of the environment, but do not necessarily imply that the environment has actually changed. On the contrary, scientific research assumes that no change will occur in the structure of the subject matter being investigated; "God is crafty but not mean" said Einstein when expressing the belief that the order of the physical universe remains invariant. A similar view regarding the stability of the social environment is suggested here: we have seen, indeed, that the structure of basic interpersonal cognitions is invariant across cultures. Yet, this consistency does not rule out changes in degree of differentiation or the appearance of new dimensions. In fact the occurrence of such cognitive changes may solve conflicts among various needs. One type of conflict appears when the structure interferes with the acquisition of resources. For the individual who has been constantly exposed to failure, success is experienced as a dissonant event, threatening the stability of his cognition. Stability can be maintained by perceiving the event as a failure or by decreasing the value of success—in both cases the individual would fail to benefit from the resource with which he was provided. More generally, mental patients often experience difficulty in interpersonal communication because of cognitive deviance, with consequent reduction in their ability to obtain resources through social exchange. Psychotherapy, then, becomes a procedure by which the individual's conflict between the need for cognitive stability and the need for resources is solved. This conflict appears at the societal level as well, albeit in a different form: when a given society or certain segments of it are deficient in some resources, pressure will generate to change the social fabric toward the satisfaction of these needs. For example, a strive toward economic resources may result in redistribution of income through taxation, nationalization of means of production and economic development. These changes, in turn, lead to the transformation of traditional societies into modern ones. But modern society, while providing more economic resources, also results in environmental changes which create dissonance and strain the ability of cognition to reflect accurately outside events. Thus, the conflict between maintaining stability and increasing provisions of resources occurs both at the individual and the societal levels and is prominent in modern culture.

The Dilemma of Traditional vs. Modern Society

Another conflict which exists at the individual and the societal levels involves the various resources; it stems from their differential environmental requirements. We have noted that resources differ with respect to the type of environment in which they can be best exchanged: particularistic resources require prolonged and repeated encounters in small group; the less particularistic resources are more efficiently exchanged in large groups and their

174   PART I ABRIDGEMENT OF *SOCIETAL STRUCTURES OF THE MIND*

exchange does not require long time nor repeated encounters. It so happens that conditions favoring particularistic exchanges are often found in traditional societies, while the environment provided by modern mass society is favorable to economic transactions. Furthermore, at least in some traditional societies the various institutions are less differentiated with respect to the resource classes appropriate for exchange. In these societies the range of resources transacted in a social institution is wider than in modern culture where more institutions are found, each specializing in the exchange of a few resources. The modern person will not seek emotional support from his boss, as will the member of a traditional culture; he will rather approach an intimate friend, a member of his family or perhaps a psychiatrist. Both institutional specialization and the conditions of the urban environment have concurred in making modern society richer in economic resources but poorer in particularistic ones. Those members of modern society who have not shared the general increase in wealth are in the worst situation of all, having lost emotionally without gaining economically. Thus, while developing nations struggle to achieve economic growth and disregard the particularistic losses involved, technologically advanced countries discover that a high standard of living is not a sure recipe for happiness.

The reactions to love poverty in modern society have resulted in efforts to increase particularistic exchanges which have taken mainly two directions: attempts for love exchanges in spite of unfavorable environmental conditions (e.g. youth festivals, blind dates, group sex) and creation of new institutions specializing in emotional exchanges (e.g. sensitivity groups, marathons, encounters). The hope is often voiced that once individuals learn to increase particularistic exchanges in these specialized institutions, they will eventually transfer the newly acquired skills to other institutions as well, thus reducing the trend toward resource specialization of the latter. Much of the work on community mental health is essentially based on similar principles.

More subtle is the solution adopted by various protest groups advocating drastic changes in modern society; their ideology varies from being religious to being political and their methods range from gentle persuasion to violence. Yet all these groups have a significant element in common: they offer a suitable setting for satisfying the particularistic needs of their members. Emotional fulfillment, in a society where love is scarce, provides the most immediate dividend for the dissident; it gives him the feeling that he has found an answer to the ills which beset the society he opposes. But this may be a satisfactory solution for certain individuals; it does not provide a pattern extendible to society at large.

In the search for solutions of more general applicability there has been an increasing interest in the development of social indicators, i.e. indices designed to measure the quality of life much as economic indicators represent the state of the economy.

Social Indicators

The growing attention paid to measuring quality of life stems from at least two factors. One factor involves the realization that a high level of economic production and consumption is not sufficient for securing human welfare; gross national happiness includes variables which are not covered by the gross national product. A second factor reflects the recognition that there is a close interplay between economic and social elements in society and therefore they should be considered jointly in attempts to solve societal problems.

The Economic Cost of Non-Economic Poverty

There is no point in dwelling on the economic cost of social problems such as crime and welfare which have reached staggering proportions in some countries; they are already well recognized. If, however, these problems result from deficiency in non-economic resources, then an indirect link would have been established between the shortage of non-economic resources and the expenditure of economic ones. Moreover, this link also manifests itself in the many instances where an unsatisfied non-economic need creates a demand for economic resources: workers striking for higher wages are not always short of money; they may also, as many studies have shown, be deprived of information or status; patients going to a physician may seek sympathy and support rather than treatment; a person feeling rejected and unloved may console himself by buying something he does not actually need; "The most powerful, the loudest and the most persistent command in our society is the command to buy" (Reich, 1971, p. 179).

One may wonder why people needing non-economic resources will not seek them rather than settle for economic ones which leave the original need largely unsatisfied. As stated earlier, economic resources are more readily

176   PART I ABRIDGEMENT OF *SOCIETAL STRUCTURES OF THE MIND*

available in modern society; not only are they relatively abundant, but there are many specialized institutions for their provision, and they are considerably more accessible than the few social institutions which provide non-economic resources. Furthermore, there is more awareness of economic needs, and it is easier to verbalize them than the non-economic ones. All these considerations lead to the proposition that non-economic shortages result in economic costs, as well as in plain human suffering.

The Non-Economic Cost of Economic Development

The other side of the coin is the influence of the economic resources on the non-economic ones. We have noted that environmental conditions which facilitate economic growth seem to hinder non-economic exchanges (the large metropolis is a typical example of this type of environment). Consequently some actions which reduce economic costs may increase non-economic deficits and in the long run the ultimate economic cost may be greater than the original saving. A larger school, hospital, industrial plant, or a taller housing development often results in lower cost per unit than a smaller project. In this large-scale environment, however, the exchange of particularistic resources becomes more difficult. The resulting shortage of these resources is reflected in turn in economic costs, as we have seen previously.

These reciprocal effects among various resources suggest the necessity of a social accounting system in which the costs and rewards of any given option will be considered in terms which are not merely economic. The first problem in developing appropriate indicators is to decide what items they should include or how to define "quality of life." A detailed list of all the events and conditions which make life pleasant, and worthy would be unmanageably long; on the other hand the global notion of "quality of life," being so vague and general, is not amendable to measurement. We have to settle somewhere in the middle with a classification which is detailed enough to pinpoint essential differences, and at the same time simple and parsimonious.

An answer to the question of which items contribute to the "quality of life" has been provided by the identification of resource classes and by the discovery of their relationship. All six classes of resources contribute to the "quality of life," so that when any of them falls below a minimum level, "quality of life" is impaired. Still, resources close in the order can compensate for one another; a person poor in love may still be reasonably happy if he acquires

EPILOGUE: MAN AND HIS SOCIETY 177

status or is pampered with personal services. On the other hand, a resource remote from the needed one does not constitute an efficient substitute.

Some Methodological Problems

Can we measure how much love one has deposited with his wife or how much status is credited to him by his boss in the same way we count the money deposited at the bank? Obviously, the research work described in this volume could not have been done in the absence of techniques for observation and for measurement. Yet the instruments used, given in the appendix, constitute only a beginning and in many aspects they are too crude and cumbersome. The goal of producing observation instruments, which are both simple to use and fairly precise, requires the solution of several methodological problems.

1. At the most, we can find out that A has more love than B and B has more than C; but, at the present state of knowledge, we cannot speak in absolute terms. Our measurement regarding quantities of money is more precise: the person who possesses ten dollars not only has more money than the one having five dollars, but he owns twice as much as the second person.
2. People are more aware of the need for certain resources than for some others: individuals know if they need money and usually have no difficulty in expressing such need verbally; the person who needs love or status is often unaware of it, he may just feel a vague discontent which cannot be easily translated into words: the language of love is mostly non-verbal—it consists of facial and bodily expressions which we have barely begun to understand.
3. Acknowledging the existence of particularistic needs may be hindered by cultural norms, thus preventing people from expressing them even when they are aware of their need. The last two differential characteristics of resources may also explain why people needing particularistic resources demand non-particularistic ones.

Lack of awareness and obstacles to verbalization, as well as the inability to measure precise amounts, constitute serious problems in the quantification of non-economic needs, but not insolvable ones. Partial contributions to their solutions are already available from socio-psychological research in other areas

178 PART I ABRIDGEMENT OF *SOCIETAL STRUCTURES OF THE MIND*

as for example, forced-choice techniques which overcome effects of social desirability. For other aspects of these problems, further research is needed to develop instruments which are reasonably reliable and suitable for mass use.

The Use of Social Indicators

Social indicators will enable us to assess the amount of resources possessed not only by society as a whole, but also by specific groups, strata and classes. The next step will be to investigate the relationship between the need state of various segments of society and social pathology. Working on the general proposition that resource deficiency results in inadequate social performance, it is possible to formulate more specific research questions: Is deficiency in love a factor in drug addiction? Do status-deprived people commit more crimes? Are they more likely to rely on welfare rather than being self-supporting? What is the effect of the welfare system on their status need? If welfare increases this need, then the system perpetuates the dependency of welfare clients on public money rather than leading them toward self-sufficiency. Are some antisocial acts such as political assassination committed as an attempt to gain status? This interpretation is supported by the fact that at least in the United States, these assassins often share a long history of past failures which presumably results in an extreme need for status.

We often hear that black Americans have fewer economic opportunities than whites; where do blacks stand in other resource needs? How do these other needs affect their wellbeing and performance? Furthermore, are patterns of economic consumption related to non-economic needs? People striving for status may, for example, choose goods according to their status value rather than their functionality.

This line of research will provide us with a more precise and detailed knowledge about the resource needs existing in various segments of society, as well as of their effects on social performance.

Toward New Social Forms

Identifying resource deficits and realizing their consequences will have a profound influence on our way of thinking about social problems. It may then strike us as a paradox that in our society a person in economic strictures can apply for relief, while the individual who needs love or status is often left to his own devices unless he first becomes an alcoholic or a drug addict. Providing first-aid for particularistic needs on a large scale may be helpful to some extent, yet it will not obviate the necessity of re-examining the structure of society in an attempt to find out ways of modifying it to optimize the satisfaction of all resource needs. This is not an easy task in view of the contradictory environmental requirements of particularistic and economic exchange: We have seen that particularistic resources require a small, stable, unhurried social environment, while economic resources demand mass production and mass consumption. Is it possible to devise social forms in which all types of exchange would thrive?

A modest step in this direction is provided by attempts to organize industrial production around groups of workers who assume autonomous responsibility for a limited sequence of the production process. In this way the group, rather than the individual worker, becomes a unit in the production line; at the same time the group provides a suitable environment for satisfying the particularistic needs of its members. A critical problem in these experiments is whether the autonomy delegated to the group is large enough to sustain its functioning, but not too large as to make production uneconomical. This type of two-tier organization could be extended to other institutions as well: residential planning, for example, could be organized around small groups of families choosing to live in proximity to one another. A main disadvantage of this solution lies in the fact that the individual is still required to have multiple membership in a variety of institutions conflicting not only for his time, as in present modern society, but for his emotional attention as well. This disadvantage may be overcome by extending the two-tier notion to society as a whole: individuals will be members of fairly permanent small social groups providing particularistic resources; these groups, in turn, will constitute the units of larger social systems which will be concerned mainly with economic exchanges.

Evolution toward forms of social organization which will offer a more balanced supply of resources is not merely a matter of developing technologies for the production and distribution of particularistic resources to complement the technics we already possess for economic production and distribution. An integrated approach to the complex socio-economic problems of modern society can hardly succeed in the absence of a unified science of man, integrating emotional, social and economic aspects of his resource seeking behavior. With this book we hope to have provided a small beginning toward such a goal.

Appendixes A–E

Appendix A
The Role Behavior Test

This instrument is designed to elicit the picture a person has of his exchanges of love and status with another person in a specific role relationship. The example given here refers to the wife–husband role-pair. To adapt the instrument to other roles it is merely necessary to change appropriately the role names appearing in the test.

The instrument consists of a series of statements describing the behavior of the wife (or husband) in giving (or taking away) love (or status) to (from) self and husband (wife). Three statements are provided for each variable. Each statement is followed by four questions dealing respectively with actual and ideal behavior from the viewpoint of subject and from the viewpoint of the other person in the role pair. The two latter questions were omitted in more recent versions of the instrument, which thus did not provide information on the viewpoint ascribed to the other. The same questions follow each statement; therefore, in the example provided they appear only after the first statement, to save space. Statements pertaining to the same variable (e.g., the wife giving love to the husband) do not follow one another in the text but are randomized to minimize sequential effects.

Wife–Husband Relationship

The purpose of this questionnaire is to help you to form as faithful and sharp a picture as possible of the relationship between you and your husband.

This is not a test. There are no right or wrong answers. Just answer the way you feel. This questionnaire will be kept in strict confidence.

On the following pages, you will find a number of brief statements describing behavior between husband and wife. Each statement is followed by some questions. For each question, quickly choose the answer which best reflects your situation. Please answer each question but give only one answer to each question; then go on immediately to the next statement.

(1) Pat shows her husband she loves him and cares for him; she tries to please him and do the things he likes.
   A. Do you act this way when you are with your husband?
      0 almost never
      1 seldom
      2 sometimes
      3 often
      4 almost always
   B. When she's with her husband, do you think a wife should act the way the wife in the story does?
      0 definitely not
      1 perhaps not

182   APPENDIX A

    2 perhaps yes
    3 yes
    4 absolutely yes

C. Would your husband say that you act this way with him?
    0 almost never
    1 seldom
    2 sometimes
    3 often
    4 almost always

D. Would your husband say that a wife should act as the wife in the story does?
    0 definitely not
    1 perhaps not
    2 perhaps yes
    3 yes
    4 absolutely yes

(2) Sue gives respect to her husband; she shows him she admires whatever he does.

(3) When she is with her husband, Sandy treats herself with dignity; she shows she respects herself by the way she talks and acts.

(4) When she is with her husband, Carol is a gloomy person who acts unhappy with herself.

(5) Dotty does not give love to her husband; she ignores his feelings and shows him she does not like him.

(6) Bobbie treats her husband with disrespect; she does not look up to him, and she downgrades whatever he does.

(7) When she is with her husband, Kate shows disrespect for herself and acts as if she thinks she is useless.

(8) Janet proves her love for her husband by helping him and sharing things with him.

(9) Ann shows she is proud of what her husband can do; she tells him he is worth a lot and that he can do things very well.

(10) When she is with her husband, Mary shows a lot of respect toward herself; she makes known her self-respect by what she says and does.

(11) Polly acts spitefully toward herself in front of her husband and does not try to please herself.

(12) Marie downgrades herself when she is with her husband; she does not show respect for herself and acts as if she cannot do anything right.

(13) Rose does not have pride in herself; she belittles herself in front of her husband and criticizes her abilities.

(14) Peggy does not show respect for her husband; she criticizes him and tells him he is useless.

(15) Barbara shows her husband she does not like him; she does things he dislikes, and she will not try to please him.

(16) When she is with her husband, Betty is a cheerful wife who acts pleased with herself.

(17) May belittles her husband when she talks to him; she looks down on his abilities and tells him he does not do things right.

(18) Margie acts as if everything her husband does is very important; she praises whatever he does.

APPENDIX A   183

(19) Jean is a happy person when she is with her husband; she acts like a wife who knows she is a nice, likable person.

(20) June gives her husband a lot of love; she shows trust in him and is very affectionate with him.

(21) Betsy acts spiteful toward her husband; she lets him know she dislikes him and cannot stand him.

(22) When she is with her husband, Terry acts displeased with herself and does not seem happy with herself.

(23) When she is with her husband, Sarah praises herself for her ability; she acts like a wife who does things very well.

(24) When she is with her husband, Terry acts contented with herself and seems to be satisfied with herself.

Now we turn to some statements about the behavior of a husband when he is with his wife:

(25) Dick shows his wife he likes her and cares for her; he tries to please her and do the things she likes.
   A. Does your husband act this way when he is with you?
      0 almost never
      1 seldom
      2 sometimes
      3 often
      4 almost always
   B. When he is with his wife, do you think a husband should act the way the husband in the story does?
      0 definitely not
      1 perhaps not
      2 perhaps yes
      3 yes
      4 absolutely yes
   C. Would your husband say that he acts this way with you?
      0 almost never
      1 seldom
      2 sometimes
      3 often
      4 almost always
   D. Would your husband say that a husband should act as the husband in the story does?
      0 definitely not
      1 perhaps not
      2 perhaps yes
      3 yes
      4 absolutely yes

(26) When he is with his wife, Bob shows disrespect for himself and acts like he thinks he is useless.

(27) James treats his wife with disrespect; he does not look up to her, and he downgrades whatever she does.

(28) Al proves his love for his wife by sharing things with her and helping her.

184 APPENDIX A

(29) When he is with his wife, Jack is a gloomy husband who acts unhappy with himself.
(30) William downgrades himself when he is with his wife; he does not show respect for himself and acts like he cannot do anything right.
(31) Mike acts spitefully toward himself in front of his wife, and does not try to please himself.
(32) Edward does not have pride in himself; he belittles himself in front of his wife and criticizes his abilities.
(33) Larry shows his wife he does not like her; he does things she dislikes, and he will not try to please her.
(34) David gives his wife a lot of love; he shows trust in her and is very affectionate with her.
(35) When he is with his wife, Peter acts displeased with himself and does not seem happy with himself.
(36) Gary does not show respect for his wife; he criticizes her and tells her she is useless.
(37) Robert acts as if everything his wife does is very important; he praises whatever she does.
(38) Richard belittles his wife when he talks to her; he looks down on her abilities and tells her she does not do things right.
(39) Joe is a happy husband when he is with his wife; he acts like a husband who knows he is a nice, likable husband.
(40) Dan acts spiteful toward his wife; he lets her know he dislikes her and cannot stand her.
(41) Chuck shows he is proud of what his wife can do; he tells her she is worth a lot and that she can do things very well.
(42) John gives respect to his wife; he shows her he admires whatever she does.
(43) Fred does not give love to his wife; he ignores her feelings and shows her he does not like her.
(44) When he is with his wife, Bill acts contented with himself and seems to be satisfied with himself.
(45) When he is with his wife, Paul praises himself for his abilities; he acts like a husband who thinks he does things very well.
(46) When he is with his wife, Tom is a cheerful husband who acts pleased with himself.
(47) When he is with his wife, Harry shows a lot of respect toward himself; he makes known his self-respect by what he says and does.
(48) When he is with his wife, Jim treats himself with dignity; he shows he respects himself by the way he talks and acts.

ADMINISTRATION. Although the instrument is suitable for self-administration, it also can be administered by a skilled interviewer who read the statements and questions to the subject and records the answers on an answer sheet.

SCORING. The score on any given variable is simply the sum of the weights of the answer to a particular question (A, B, C, or D) for the three statements pertaining to the given variable. The lowest score is thus 0 (zero) indicating low frequency (or desirability) of the behavior described in the statements; the highest possible score is 12. The grouping of the statements according to the variable to which they belong is shown in Table 6.

APPENDIX A   185

Table 6 Statements of Test Classified According to Their Variable

Variable	Statement Number	
	Behavior of Wife	Behavior of Husband
Giving status to other	2, 9, 18	37, 41, 42
Giving love to other	1, 8, 20	25, 28, 34
Giving love to self	16, 19, 24	39, 44, 46
Giving status to self	3, 10, 23	45, 47, 48
Taking status from self	7, 12, 13	26, 30, 32
Taking love from self	4, 11, 22	29, 31, 35
Taking love from other	5, 15, 21	33, 40, 43
Taking status from other	6, 14, 17	27, 36, 38

Appendix B
Statements Describing Behaviors of Giving for Various Resource Classes

For each one of the six resource classes three statements are provided indicating the giving of the resource to the other.

Love: I feel affection for you; I care about you; I enjoy being with you.

Status: You are a very important person; You do things very well; I admire and respect you.

Information: Here is the information; Here is my opinion; Here is my advice.

Money: Here is your pay; Here is a check for you; Here is some money for you.

Goods: Here is some merchandise for you; Here is a new product you may try; Here is a package for you.

Services: I repaired it for you; I ran that errand for you; I will do that for you.

Appendix C
Social Interaction Inventory for Exchanges of Giving

This inventory is designed to record preferences for receiving a certain resource in return for the resource given by the subject to the other. The resource assumedly given by the subject is described at the top of each list. The resources which can be received in return are presented in pairs; all the possible 15 pairs are given, so that each resource class appears five times, but each time is described by a different statement. The 15 pairs are in random order which varies for different resources given, i.e., for the resource described at the top of the list. The order of presentation of the resource given varies randomly across subjects.

The preference score for each resource desired in return for any given one is the number of times a given resource is chosen over the other ones paired with it. The lowest score is therefore 0 (zero) when the resource is never chosen and the highest score is 5, which is obtained when the resource is chosen every time it appears. Since 15 choices are made in each list the sum of the scores for any such list is always 15. This artificial interdependence of the score may be undesirable for certain analytic purposes (e.g., in computing correlation coefficients among preferences). This artifact was avoided in an alternative form of the inventory; in it every statement describing a resource which could be received in return was rated on a five-point scale from "highly desirable" to "not at all desirable;" in this rating three statements for each resource were presented. Thus, each score ranged, in this case, from 0 (zero) to 12.

Social Interaction Inventory (Giving)

Please carefully read the following instructions:

In this questionnaire you are given six hypothetical situations in which you do something for another person. Each of the six situations is presented at the top of a separate page. Listed below each situation are pairs of possible things which the person could do for you in return. From each of the fifteen pairs you are to choose either A or B as the alternative which you would prefer most. Indicate your preference by placing an X in the slot provided to the left of each item. Be sure to choose *only* one item from *each* pair.

Be certain that you are indicating your preference with respect to the particular situation which is given at the top of the page on which you are working. Refer to the situation as often as necessary to keep it strong and clear in your mind. There are no right or wrong answers, we are interested only in your preferences. Even if neither of the two alternatives seems appealing, or if both seem equally appealing, you are still to choose one alternative from each pair. Please work carefully and at your own speed. There is no time limitation.

EXAMPLE:
You let a person use your car. In return you would prefer that:

_____ A. The person thanks you for being so generous and considerate.
_X_ B. The person buys you a gift.

If you feel that in this situation you would prefer that the person buy you a gift, you would place an (X) next to that alternative, as shown in the example above.

188 APPENDIX C

You are helping a person by providing certain services. In return you would prefer that:

_____ A. The person provides you with the opportunity to acquire some new information.
_____ B. The person says that he is very fond of you.

_____ A. The person tells you that he respects you.
_____ B. The person provides you with some desirable wares.

_____ A. The person gives you the feeling that you are very likable.
_____ B. A money order is made out to you by the person.

_____ A. The person does something for you.
_____ B. You are given new information.

_____ A. You receive some object you like from the person.
_____ B. You are made to feel that the person enjoys your company.

_____ A. You receive a check from the person.
_____ B. The person runs an errand for you.

_____ A. The person tells you something that you didn't know beforehand.
_____ B. The person praises you.

_____ A. The person repairs something for you.
_____ B. You receive affection from the person.

_____ A. The person makes you familiar with new facts.
_____ B. The person gives you a certain product.

_____ A. The person tells you that he has confidence in your abilities.
_____ B. The person gives you money.

_____ A. The person gives you some merchandise.
_____ B. The person makes himself available to do some work for you.

_____ A. The person indicates that he wants to be your friend.
_____ B. The person expresses his esteem for you.

_____ A. You receive cash from the person.
_____ B. The person gives you the benefit of his familiarity with a certain subject.

_____ A. The person gives you prestige.
_____ B. The person provides you with some service.

_____ A. You receive a payment from the person.
_____ B. You receive some goods from the person.

You convey to a person that you enjoy being with them and feel affection for them. In return you would prefer that:

_____ A. The person gives you a certain product.
_____ B. The person does something for you.

_____ A. The person gives you the feeling that you are very likable.
_____ B. The person expresses his esteem for you.

_____ A. You receive cash from the person.
_____ B. The person gives you the benefit of his familiarity with a certain subject.

____ A. You are told that the person has confidence in your abilities.
____ B. The person makes himself available to do some work for you.

____ A. You receive payment from the person.
____ B. The person provides you with some desirable wares.

____ A. The person makes you familiar with new facts.
____ B. The person indicates that he wants to be your friend.

____ A. The person praises you.
____ B. You receive some object you like from the person.

____ A. You are made to feel that the person enjoys your company.
____ B. You receive a check from the person.

____ A. The person runs an errand for you.
____ B. The person tells you something that you did not know beforehand.

____ A. The person gives you some merchandise.
____ B. You receive affection from the person.

____ A. The person gives you money.
____ B. The person provides you with some service.

____ A. The person provides you with the opportunity to acquire some new information.
____ B. The person gives you respect.

____ A. The person repairs something for you.
____ B. The person says that he is fond of you.

____ A. The person gives you new information.
____ B. You receive some goods from the person.

____ A. The person gives you prestige.
____ B. A money order is made out to you by the person.

You provide a person with some money to meet a temporary need. In return you would prefer that:

____ A. The person makes himself available to do some work for you.
____ B. The person indicates that he wants to be your friend.

____ A. The person gives you the benefit of his familiarity with a certain subject.
____ B. You receive some goods from the person.

____ A. The person praises you.
____ B. A money order is made out to you by the person.

____ A. The person provides you with some desirable wares.
____ B. The person runs an errand for you.

____ A. You receive affection from the person.
____ B. The person expresses his esteem for you.

____ A. You receive cash from the person.
____ B. The person makes you familiar with new facts.

____ A. The person gives you prestige.
____ B. The person does something for you.

190 APPENDIX C

_____ A. The person gives you money.
_____ B. The person gives you some merchandise.

_____ A. The person gives you new information.
_____ B. The person says he is fond of you.

_____ A. You are told that the person has confidence in your abilities.
_____ B. You receive some object you like from the person.

_____ A. You are made to feel that the person enjoys your company
_____ B. You receive a check from the person.

_____ A. The person repairs something for you.
_____ B. The person tells you something that you didn't know beforehand.

_____ A. The person gives you a certain product.
_____ B. The person gives you the feeling that you are very likable.

_____ A. You receive a payment from the person.
_____ B. The person provides you with some service.

_____ A. The person provides you with the opportunity to acquire some new information.
_____ B. The person gives you respect.

You give a person certain objects that you possess. In return you would prefer that:

_____ A. The person gives you some merchandise.
_____ B. The person says that he is fond of you.

_____ A. You receive cash from the person.
_____ B. The person does something for you.

_____ A. The person makes you familiar with new facts.
_____ B. The person gives you prestige.

_____ A. The person repairs something for you.
_____ B. You receive affection from the person.

_____ A. The person gives you some new information.
_____ B. The person gives you a certain product.

_____ A. The person gives you respect.
_____ B. You receive a check from the person.

_____ A. You receive some object you like from the person.
_____ B. The person runs an errand for you.

_____ A. The person gives you the feeling that you are very likable.
_____ B. The person expresses his esteem for you.

_____ A. A money order is made out to you by the person.
_____ B. The person gives you the benefit of his familiarity with a certain subject.

_____ A. The person praises you.
_____ B. The person makes himself available to do some work for you.

_____ A. The person gives you money.
_____ B. You receive some goods from the person.

_____ A. The person provides you with the opportunity to acquire some new information.
_____ B. You are made to feel that the person enjoys your company.

_____ A. You are told that the person has confidence in your abilities.
_____ B. The person provides you with some desirable wares.

_____ A. The person indicates that he wants to be your friend.
_____ B. You receive a payment from the person.

_____ A. The person provides you with some service.
_____ B. The person tells you something that you didn't know beforehand.

You convey to a person your respect and esteem for his talents. In return you would prefer that:

_____ A. The person gives you prestige.
_____ B. The person provides you with some desirable wares.

_____ A. You are made to feel that the person enjoys your company.
_____ B. A money order is made out to you by the person.

_____ A. The person does something for you.
_____ B. The person tells you something you didn't know beforehand.

_____ A. You receive some object you like from the person.
_____ B. The person says that he is fond of you.

_____ A. The person gives you money.
_____ B. The person makes himself available to do some work for you.

_____ A. The person provides you with the opportunity to acquire some new information.
_____ B. The person expresses his esteem for you.

_____ A. The person runs an errand for you.
_____ B. The person gives you the feeling that you are very likable.

_____ A. The person gives you the benefit of his familiarity with a certain subject.
_____ B. The person gives you some merchandise.

_____ A. The person praises you.
_____ B. You receive a check from the person.

_____ A. The person gives you a certain product.
_____ B. The person provides you with some service.

_____ A. You receive affection from the person.
_____ B. You are told that the person has confidence in your abilities.

_____ A. You receive some cash from the person.
_____ B. The person makes you familiar with new facts.

_____ A. The person gives you respect.
_____ B. The person repairs something for you.

_____ A. You receive payment from the person.
_____ B. You receive some goods from the person.

_____ A. The person gives you new information.
_____ B. The person indicates that he wants to be your friend.

192   APPENDIX C

You provide certain information to a person. In return you would prefer that:

_____ A. The person gives you prestige.
_____ B. The person makes himself available to do some work for you.

_____ A. You receive cash from the person.
_____ B. You receive some goods from the person.

_____ A. The person gives you new information.
_____ B. The person gives you affection.

_____ A. You are told that the person has confidence in your abilities.
_____ B. The person provides you with some desirable wares.

_____ A. The person indicates that he wants to be your friend.
_____ B. A money order is made out to you by the person.

_____ A. The person provides you with some service.
_____ B. The person tells you something that you did not know beforehand.

_____ A. The person gives you a certain product.
_____ B. The person says that he is fond of you.

_____ A. You receive a check from the person.
_____ B. The person runs an errand for you.

_____ A. The person makes you familiar with new facts.
_____ B. The person gives you respect.

_____ A. The person repairs something for you.
_____ B. You are made to feel that the person enjoys your company.

_____ A. The person provides you with the opportunity to acquire some new information.
_____ B. The person gives you some merchandise.

_____ A. The person expresses his esteem for you.
_____ B. You receive a payment from the person.

_____ A. You receive some object you like from the person.
_____ B. The person does something for you.

_____ A. The person gives you the feeling that you are very likable.
_____ B. The person praises you.

_____ A. The person gives you money.
_____ B. The person gives you the benefit of his familiarity with a certain subject.

Appendix D
Social Interaction Inventory for Exchanges of Taking

This inventory is identical in format with the one described in Appendix C, except that it deals with exchanges of taking, rather than with giving. It thus records preferences for depriving the other of a given resource in retaliation for each resource of aggression used by the other.

Social Interaction Inventory

(Taking)

Please carefully read the following instructions:

In this questionnaire you are given six hypothetical situations in which another person expresses some form of interpersonal hostility toward you. Each of the six situations is presented at the top of a separate page. Listed below each situation are pairs of alternative ways in which you might respond to the person who misbehaved toward you. From each of the fifteen pairs you are to choose either A or B as the alternative which you would prefer most. You are to indicate your preferred response by placing an X in the appropriate slot to the left of each item. Be sure to choose only one item from each pair of alternatives.

Be certain that you are indicating your preference with respect to the particular situation which is indicated at the top of the page on which you are working. Feel free to refer to the situation as often as necessary to keep it strong and clear in your mind. There are no right or wrong answers, assume that all alternatives are equally permissible and legitimate. We are interested only in your *preferred* responses. Even if neither of the two alternatives seems appealing, or if both seem equally appealing, you are still to choose one alternative from each pair. Please work carefully and at your own speed.

EXAMPLE:

A person who could provide you with much needed transportation refuses to do so. Your most preferred response would be to:

  _X_ A. Avoid further association with the person and be unfriendly toward him.

  ____ B. Refuse him assistance when he requested a favor of you.

If you feel that in this situation you would be most likely to behave unfriendly and avoid further association with the person, you would place an (X) next to alternative A.

A person degrades or belittles you. He lets you understand that you are worthless and that you don't do things well. Your most preferred response would be that:

_____

  ____ A. You convey to the person that you have a low regard for him.

  ____ B. You help yourself to some of the other person's belongings.

  ____ A. You let the person feel that you dislike him.

  ____ B. You refuse to give money to the person when expected.

194   APPENDIX D

_____ A. You will be physically hostile to the other person.
_____ B. You tell the person things that will lead him to the wrong decision.

_____ A. You would confiscate goods belonging to the other person.
_____ B. You make the person realize that you would rather avoid his company.

_____ A. You help yourself to money belonging to the person.
_____ B. You cause inconvenience to the person or damage his belongings.

_____ A. You provide the person with knowledge that leads him to wrong conclusions.
_____ B. You belittle the person.

_____ A. You disturb the person's comfort through some disservice on your part.
_____ B. You convey to the person that you are displeased with him.

_____ A. You deliberately give the person wrong instructions.
_____ B. You take possession of goods belonging to the other person.

_____ A. You convey to the person that you hold him in low esteem.
_____ B. You withhold money that should be given to the person.

_____ A. You seize objects belonging to the other person.
_____ B. You physically harm the person.

_____ A. You convey to the person that you do not want to associate with him.
_____ B. You let the person feel that you don't respect his abilities.

_____ A. You make the person lose some money.
_____ B. You provide the person with bad advice.

_____ A. You make unflattering remarks to the person.
_____ B. You withhold aid causing hardship to the person.

_____ A. You manage to gain possession of some money belonging to the person.
_____ B. You would assume ownership of things that belong to the other person.

_____ A. You deceive the person regarding information he requests from you.
_____ B. You convey to the person that you resent him.

A person confiscates goods or objects which belong to you. Your most preferred response would be that:

_____

_____ A. You would assume ownership of things that belong to the other person.
_____ B. You convey to the person that you are displeased with him.

_____ A. You refuse to give money to the person when expected.
_____ B. You withhold aid causing hardship to the person.

_____ A. You deceive the person regarding information he requests from you.
_____ B. You convey to the person that you have a low regard for him.

_____ A. You disturb the person's comfort through some disservice on your part.
_____ B. You make the person realize that you would rather avoid his company.

_____ A. You deliberately give the person wrong instructions.
_____ B. You would confiscate goods belonging to the other person.

_____ A. You make unflattering remarks to the person.
_____ B. You withhold money that should be given to the person.

APPENDIX D 195

_____ A. You help yourself to some of the other person's belongings.
_____ B. You cause inconvenience to the person or damage his belongings.

_____ A. You convey to the person that you do not want to associate with him.
_____ B. You convey to the person that you hold him in low esteem.

_____ A. You manage to gain possession of some money belonging to the person.
_____ B. You tell the person things that will lead him to the wrong decision.

_____ A. You belittle the person.
_____ B. You physically harm the person.

_____ A. You make the person lose some money.
_____ B. You seize objects belonging to the other person.

_____ A. You provide the person with bad advice.
_____ B. You convey to the person that you resent him.

_____ A. You let the person feel that you don't respect his abilities.
_____ B. You take possession of goods belonging to the other person.

_____ A. You let the person feel that you dislike him.
_____ B. You help yourself to money belonging to the person.

_____ A. You will be physically hostile to the other person.
_____ B. You provide the person with knowledge that leads him to wrong conclusions.

A person cheats you by taking or withholding money which belongs to you. Your most preferred response would be that:

_____ A. You disturb the person's comfort through some disservice on your part.
_____ B. You convey to the person that you do not want to associate with him.

_____ A. You deliberately give the person wrong instructions.
_____ B. You help yourself to some of the other person's belongings.

_____ A. You convey to the person that you have a low regard for him.
_____ B. You manage to gain possession of some money belonging to the person.

_____ A. You seize objects belonging to the other person.
_____ B. You physically harm the person.

_____ A. You convey to the person that you resent him.
_____ B. You belittle the person.

_____ A. You make the person lose some money.
_____ B. You tell the person things that will lead him to the wrong decision.

_____ A. You let the person feel that you don't respect his abilities.
_____ B. You will be physically hostile to the other person.

_____ A. You refuse to give money to the person when expected.
_____ B. You take possession of goods belonging to the other person.

_____ A. You deceive the person regarding information he requests from you.
_____ B. You make the person realize that you would rather avoid his company.

_____ A. You convey to the person that you hold him in low esteem.
_____ B. You would confiscate goods belonging to the other person.

196 APPENDIX D

_____ A. You let the person feel that you dislike him.
_____ B. You withhold money that should be given to the person.

_____ A. You cause inconvenience to the person or damage his belongings.
_____ B. You provide the person with knowledge that leads him to wrong conclusions.

_____ A. You would assume ownership of things that belong to the other person.
_____ B. You convey to the person that you are displeased with him.

_____ A. You help yourself to money belonging to the person.
_____ B. You withhold aid causing hardship to the person.

_____ A. You provide the person with bad advice.
_____ B. You make unflattering remarks to the person.

A person conveys to you that he dislikes you. He is unfriendly and avoids your company. Your most preferred response would be that:

_____ A. You would confiscate goods belonging to the other person.
_____ B. You withhold aid causing hardship to the person.

_____ A. You let the person feel that you dislike him.
_____ B. You make unflattering remarks to the person.

_____ A. You manage to gain possession of some money belonging to the person.
_____ B. You deliberately give the person wrong instructions.

_____ A. You convey to the person that you have a low regard for him.
_____ B. You will be physically hostile to the other person.

_____ A. You help yourself to money belonging to the person.
_____ B. You help yourself to some of the other person's belongings.

_____ A. You tell the person things that will lead him to the wrong decision.
_____ B. You convey to the person that you resent him.

_____ A. You convey to the person that you hold him in low esteem.
_____ B. You would assume ownership of things that belong to the other person.

_____ A. You convey to the person that you do not want to associate with him.
_____ B. You withhold money that should be given to the person.

_____ A. You cause inconvenience to the person or damage his belongings.
_____ B. You provide the person with knowledge that leads him to wrong conclusions.

_____ A. You seize objects belonging to the other person.
_____ B. You make the person realize that you would rather avoid his company.

_____ A. You make the person lose some money.
_____ B. You disturb the person's comfort through some disservice on your part.

_____ A. You deceive the person regarding information he requests from you.
_____ B. You let the person feel that you don't respect his abilities.

_____ A. You physically harm the person.
_____ B. You convey to the person that you are displeased with him.

_____ A. You provide the person with bad advice.
_____ B. You take possession of goods belonging to the other person.

_____ A. You belittle the person.
_____ B. You refuse to give money to the person when expected.

A person gives you false or distorted information. His deceit leads you to make bad decisions in matters which are important to you. Your most preferred response would be that:

_____ A. You convey to the person that you hold him in low esteem.
_____ B. You disturb the person's comfort through some disservice on your part.

_____ A. You help yourself to money belonging to the person.
_____ B. You would assume ownership of things that belong to the other person.

_____ A. You tell the person things that will lead him to the wrong decision.
_____ B. You convey to the person that you are displeased with him.

_____ A. You belittle the person.
_____ B. You take possession of goods belonging to the other person.

_____ A. You convey to the person that you resent him.
_____ B. You manage to gain possession of some money belonging to the person.

_____ A. You will be physically hostile to the other person.
_____ B. You provide the person with bad advice.

_____ A. You would confiscate goods belonging to the other person.
_____ B. You make the person realize that you would rather avoid his company.

_____ A. You refuse to give money to the person when expected.
_____ B. You physically harm the person.

_____ A. You deceive the person regarding information he requests from you.
_____ B. You convey to the person that you have a low regard for him.

_____ A. You cause inconvenience to the person or damage his belongings.
_____ B. You convey to the person that you do not want to associate with him.

_____ A. You deliberately give the person wrong instructions.
_____ B. You seize objects belonging to the other person.

_____ A. You let the person feel that you don't respect his abilities.
_____ B. You withhold money that should be given to the person.

_____ A. You help yourself to some of the other person's belongings.
_____ B. You withhold aid causing hardship to the person.

_____ A. You let the person feel that you dislike him.
_____ B. You make unflattering remarks to the person.

_____ A. You make the person lose some money.
_____ B. You provide the person with knowledge that leads him to wrong conclusions.

A person injures you or gives you bad services. His behavior results in inconvenience or damage to you or your belongings. Your most preferred response would be that:

_____ A. You deliberately give the person wrong instructions.
_____ B. You convey to the person that you do not want to associate with him.

198 APPENDIX D

_____ A. You make unflattering remarks to the person.
_____ B. You help yourself to some of the other person's belongings.

_____ A. You let the person feel that you dislike him.
_____ B. You manage to gain possession of some money belonging to the person.

_____ A. You disturb the person's comfort through some disservice on your part.
_____ B. You deceive the person regarding information he requests from you.

_____ A. You would confiscate goods belonging to the other person.
_____ B. You convey to the person that you resent him.

_____ A. You make the person lose some money.
_____ B. You cause inconvenience to the person or damage his belongings.

_____ A. You tell the person things that will lead him to the wrong decision.
_____ B. You let the person feel that you don't respect his abilities.

_____ A. You will be physically hostile to the other person.
_____ B. You convey to the person that you are displeased with him.

_____ A. You provide the person with knowledge that leads him to wrong conclusions.
_____ B. You take possession of goods belonging to the other person.

_____ A. You belittle the person.
_____ B. You withhold money that should be given to the person.

_____ A. You would assume ownership of things that belong to the other person.
_____ B. You withhold aid causing hardship to the person.

_____ A. You make the person realize that you would rather avoid his company.
_____ B. You convey to the person that you have a low regard for him.

_____ A. You help yourself to money belonging to the person.
_____ B. You provide the person with bad advice.

_____ A. You convey to the person that you hold him in low esteem.
_____ B. You physically harm the person.

_____ A. You refuse to give money to the person when expected.
_____ B. You seize objects belonging to the other person.

Appendix E
Group Interaction Inventory

This inventory records the expectations of a task-team member regarding the behavior of the most and least preferred teammate in giving to the subject or depriving him of the three resources of love, status, and information. Each type of behavior (giving or taking one of the three resources) is represented in the test by four statements. Each is rated on a five-point scale ranging from 0 (zero) for "almost never" to 4 for "almost always." These ratings are then added up for the four statements pertaining to any given type of behavior yielding a score between 0 (zero)—when expectation is lowest—and 16 for the highest expectation.

Group Interaction Inventory

Please carefully read the following instructions:

Our group is divided into eight teams, and each team has to fulfill a given task, previously agreed upon by the team.

You have interacted previously with your fellow team members and have some impressions of them. You may prefer some of the team members more than some others.

In this questionnaire you are asked to rate your expectations of the most and least preferred team members. Indicate your choice by placing an X in one of the slots. Be sure to choose only one response for each item.

PLEASE, DO NOT WRITE THE NAMES OF THESE GROUP MEMBERS.

How much of the following behavior would you *expect* from the person you *preferred most* of your team?

	Almost never	Seldom	Sometimes	Often	Almost always
1. Would make you familiar with new facts.					
2. Would tell you things that would lead you to the wrong decision.					
3. Would call you and give you relevant reference for your paper.					
4. Would express esteem for you.					
5. Would convey to you that he dislikes you.					
6. Would make you realize that he would rather avoid your company.					

200 APPENDIX E

	Almost never	Seldom	Sometimes	Often	Almost always
7. Receiving affection from the person.					
8. Would give you prestige.					
9. Would give you the feeling that you are very likable.					
10. Would give you false information.					
11. Would praise you.					
12. Would convey to you that he is fond of you.					
13. Would deceive you regarding information you request from him.					
14. Would let you understand that you do not do things well.					
15. Would convey to you that he resents you.					
16. Would let you feel he does not respect your abilities.					
17. Would make unflattering remarks.					
18. Would indicate that he wants to be your friend.					
19. Would convey to you that he has low regard for you.					
20. Would be unfriendly toward you.					
21. Would give you respect.					
22. Would give you new information.					
23. Would deliberately give you wrong instructions.					
24. Would tell you something that you did not know beforehand.					

How much of the followng behavior would you *expect* from the *least preferred* person of your team?

	Almost never	Seldom	Sometimes	Often	Almost always
1. Would make you familiar with new facts.					
2. Would tell you things that would lead you to the wrong decision.					

	Almost never	Seldom	Sometimes	Often	Almost always
3. Would call you and give you relevant reference for your paper.					
4. Would express esteem for you.					
5. Would convey to you that he dislikes you.					
6. Would make you realize that he would rather avoid your company.					
7. Receiving affection from the person.					
8. Would give you prestige.					
9. Would give you the feeling that you are very likable.					
10. Would give you false information.					
11. Would praise you.					
12. Would convey to you that he is fond of you.					
13. Would deceive you regarding information you request from him.					
14. Would let you understand that you do not do things well.					
15. Would convey to you that he resents you.					
16. Would let you feel he does not respect your abilities.					
17. Would make unflattering remarks.					
18. Would indicate that he wants to be your friend.					
19. Would convey to you that he has low regard for you.					
20. Would be unfriendly toward you.					
21. Would give you respect.					
22. Would give you new information.					
23. Would deliberately give you wrong instructions.					
24. Would tell you something that you did not know beforehand.					

References

Adams, H. B. (1964). Mental illness or interpersonal behavior? *American Psychologist, 19,* 191–197.

Adams, J. S. (1965). Inequity in social exchange. In L. Berkowitz (Ed.), *Advances in experimental social psychology* (vol. 2, pp. 267–299). Academic Press.

Adler, A. (1926). *The neurotic constitution.* Dodd, Mead & Co.

Albert, R. S. (1957). The role of mass media and the effects of aggressive film content upon children's aggressive responses and identification choices. *Genetic Psychological Monographs, 55,* 271–285.

Alexander, C.N., & Simpson, R.L. (1964). Balance theory and distributive justice. *Social Inquiry, 34,* 183–184.

Allison, J., & Hunt, D. E. (1959). Social desirability and the expression of aggression under varying conditions of frustration. *Journal of Consulting and Clinical Psychology, 23,* 528–532.

Allport, B. W. (1937). *Personality: a psychological interpretation.* Holt.

Andrew, R. J. (1965). The origins of facial expressions. *Scientific American, 213,* 88–94.

Andry, R. (1960). *Delinquency and parental pathology.* Methuen.

Arieti, S. (1959). Schizophrenia: The manifest symptomatology, psychodynamics and formal mechanism. In S. Arieti (Ed.), *American handbook of psychiatry* (vol. I, pp. 455–485). Basic Books.

Aronfreed, J. (1968). *Conduct and conscience.* Academic Press.

Aronfreed, J. (1969). The concept of internalization. In D. A. Goslin (Ed.), *Handbook of socialization theory and research* (pp. 263–323). Rand McNally.

Aronson, E. (1961). The effects of effort on the attractiveness of rewarded and unrewarded stimuli. *Journal of Abnormal and Social Psychology, 63,* 375–380.

Aronson, E. (1969). The theory of cognitive dissonance: current perspective. In L. Berkowitz (Ed.), *Advances in experimental social psychology* (vol. 4, pp. 1–34). Academic Press.

Aronson, E. (1970). Some antecedents of interpersonal attraction. In Arnold W.J. & Levine D. (Eds.), *Nebraska symposium on motivation* (pp. 143–177). University of Nebraska Press.

Aronson, E., & Linder, D. (1965). Gain and loss of esteem as determinants of interpersonal attractiveness. *Journal of Experimental Social Psychology, 1,* 156–171.

Aronson, E., & Mills, J. (1959). The effect of severity of initiation on liking for a group. *Journal of Abnormal and Social Psychology, 59,* 177–181.

Aronson, E., Willerman, B., & Floyd, J. (1966). The effect of a pratfall on increasing interpersonal attractiveness. *Psychonomic Science, 4,* 227–228.

Asch, S. E. (1948). The doctrine of suggestion, prestige, and imitation in social psychology. *Psychological Review, 55,* 250–276.

Asch, S. E. (1951). Effects of group pressure upon the modification and distortion of judgment. In H. Guetzow (Ed.), *Groups, leadership and men.* (pp. 177–190) Carnegie Press.

204 REFERENCES

Asch, S. E. (1958). The metaphor: A psychological inquiry. In R. Tagiuri & L. Petrullo (Eds.), *Person perception and interpersonal behavior* (pp. 86–94). Stanford University Press.

Atkinson, J. W., Clark, R. A., & Lowell, E. L. (1953). *The achievement motive*. Appleton-Century-Croft.

Ayer, J. G. (1968a) *Effects of success and failure of interpersonal and task performance upon leader perception and behavior*. Unpublished M.A. thesis, University of Illinois.

Ayer, J. G. (1968b). *Semantic-game study: Progress report*. Unpublished manuscript.

Bailey, E. D. (1966). Social interaction as a population-regulating mechanism in mice. *Canadian Journal of Zoology, 44*, 1007–1012.

Baker, J. W., & Schaie, K. W. (1969). Effects of aggressing "alone" or "with another" on physiological and psychological arousal. *Journal of Personality and Social Psychology, 12*, 80–86.

Baldwin, A. L. (1967). *Theories of child development*. Wiley.

Baldwin, A. L. (1969). A cognitive theory of socialization. In D. A. Goslin (Ed.), *Handbook of socialization theory and research* (pp. 339–345). Rand McNally.

Baldwin, J. M. (1894). *Mental development in the child and the race*. Macmillan.

Bales, R. F., & Strodtbeck, F. L. (1951). Phases in group problem-solving. *Journal of Abnormal and Social Psychology, 46*, 485–495.

Bandura, A. (1962) Social learning through imitation. In M. R. Jones (Ed.), *Nebraska symposium on motivation* (pp. 211–274). University of Nebraska Press.

Bandura, A. (1965). Vicarious processes: A case of no-trial learning. In Berkowitz, L. (Ed.), *Advances in experimental social psychology* (vol. 2, pp. 1–55). Academic Press.

Bandura, A. (1969). Social learning theory of identificatory processes. In D. A. Goslin (Ed.), *Handbook of socialization theory and research*. Rand McNally.

Bandura, A., Ross, D., & Ross, S. A. (1963). A comparative test of the status envy, social power, and secondary reinforcement theories of identification learning. *Journal of Abnormal and Social Psychology, 67*, 527–534,.

Bandura, A., & Walters, R. (1958). Dependency conflicts in aggressive delinquents. *Journal of Social Issues, 14*, 52–65.

Bandura, A., & Walters, R. (1959). *Adolescent aggression*. Ronald Press.

Bandura, A., & Walters, R. (1963). *Social learning and personality development*. Holt, Rinehart & Winston.

Bannister, D., & Fransella, F. (1966). A grid test of schizophrenic thought disorder. *British Journal of Social and Clinical Psychology, 5*, 95–102.

Bannister, D., Fransella, F, & Agnew, J. (1971). Characteristics and validity of the grid test of thought disorder. *British Journal of Social and Clinical Psychology, 10*, 144–151.

Barker, R. G., & Wright, H. F. (1955). *Midwest and its children*. Row, Peterson.

Barron, M. L. (1954). *The juvenile in delinquent society*. Alfred A. Knopf.

Barron, N. M. (1967). *The effect of leadership style and leader behavior on group creativity under stress*. Unpublished Master thesis. Department of Psychology, University of Illinois.

Barry, H., Bacon, M. K., & Child, I. L. (1957). A cross-cultural survey of some sex differences in socialization. *Journal of Abnormal and Social Psychology, 55*, 327–332.

Bateson, G., Jackson, D. D., Haley, J., & Weakland, J. H. (1956). Toward a theory of schizophrenia. *Behavioral Sciences, 1*, 251–264.

Benoit-Smullyan, E. (1944). Status, status types, and status interrelations. *American Sociological Review, 9*, 151–161.

REFERENCES 205

Benzinger, T. H. (1961). The human thermostat. *Scientific American, 204*, 134–147.

Berger, E. M. (1952). The relation between expressed acceptance of self and expressed acceptance of others. *Journal of Abnormal and Social Psychology, 47*, 778–782.

Berkowitz, L. (1962). *Aggression: a social psychological analysis*. McGraw-Hill.

Berkowitz, L. (1965). The concept of aggression drive: Some additional considerations. In L. Berkowitz (Ed.), *Advances in experimental social psychology* (vol. 2, pp. 301–329). Academic Press,.

Berkowitz, L. (1962). *Aggression: a social psychological analysis*. McGraw-Hill,.

Berkowitz, L. (1966). On not being able to aggress. *British Journal of Clinical Psychology, 5*, 130–139.

Berkowitz, L. (1969a). The frustration–aggression hypothesis revisited. In L. Berkowitz (Ed.), *Roots of aggression*. Atherton.

Berkowitz, L., & Daniels, L. (1964). Affecting the salience of the social responsibility norm. *Journal of Abnormal and Social Psychology, 28*, 275–281.

Berkowitz, L., & Geen, R. G. (1966). Film violence and the cue properties of available targets. *Journal of Personality and Social Psychology, 3*, 525–530.

Berkowitz, L., Green, J. A., & Macaulay, J. R. (1962). Hostility catharsis as the reduction of emotional tension. *Psychiatry, 25*, 23–31.

Berkowitz, L., & Holmes, D. S. (1960). A further investigation of hostility to disliked· objects. *Journal of Personality, 28*, 427–442.

Berkowitz, L., Lepinski, J. P., & Angulo, E. J. (1969). Awareness of own anger level and subsequent aggression. *Journal of Personality and Social Psychology, 11*, 293–300.

Berlyne, D. E. (1960). *Conflict, arousal and curiosity*. McGraw Hill.

Berlyne, D. E. (1965). *Structure and direction in thinking*. Wiley.

Berscheid, E., Boye, D., & Walster, E. (1968). Retaliation as a means of restoring equity. *Journal of Personality and Social Psychology, 10*, 370–376.

Berscheid, E., & Walster, E. (1967). When does a harm-doer compensate a victim? *Journal of Personality and Social Psychology, 6*, 435–441.

Berscheid, E., & Walster, E. (1969). *Interpersonal attraction*. Addison-Wesley.

Bettelheim, B. (1959). Joey: A "mechanical boy." *Scientific American, 200*, 116–127.

Biddle, B. J., & Thomas, E. J. (1966). *Role theory: concepts and research*. Wiley.

Biller, H. B., & Weiss, S. D. (1970). The father–daughter relationship and the personality development of the female. *Journal of Genetic Psychology, 116*, 79–93.

Blake, R. R., & Mouton, J. S. (1961). Conformity, resistance, and conversion. In I. A. Berg & B. M. Bass (Eds.), *Conformity and deviation* (pp. 1–37). Harper and Brothers.

Blau, P. M. (1967). *Exchange and power in social life*. Wiley.

Bleuler, E. (1950). *Dementia praecox; or the group of schizophrenias*. International University Press. (Translated from the German edition, 1911)

Blum, R. H. (1969). A cross–cultural study. In R. H. Blum (Eds.), *Society and drugs* (pp. 277–292). Jossey-Bass.

Blumstein, P. W., & Weinstein, E. A. (1969). The redress of distributive injustice. *American Journal of Sociology, 74*, 408–418.

Bolles, R. C. (1970). Species-specific defense reactions and avoidance learning. *Psychological Review, 77*, 32–48.

Bramel, D. (1962). A dissonance theory approach to defensive projection. *Journal of Abnormal and Social Psychology, 64*, 121–129.

Brehm, J. W., & Cole, A. H. (1966). Effect of a favor which reduces freedom. *Journal of Personality and Social Psychology, 3*, 420–426.

206 REFERENCES

Bresnahan, J. L., & Blum, W. L. (1971). Chaotic reinforcement: A socioeconomic leveler. *Developmental Psychology, 4*, 89–92.

Breznitz, S., & Kugelmass, S. (1967). Intentionality in moral judgment: Developmental stages. *Child Development, 38*, 469–479.

Brim, O. G. (1958). Family structure and sex role learning by children: A further analysis of Helen Koch's data. *Sociometry, 21*, 1–16.

Brislin, R. W. (1970). *The content and evaluation of cross-cultural training programs.* Institute for Defense Analyses.

Bronowski, J. (1961). *Science and human values.* Hutchinson,.

Brown, D. G. (1958). Sex-role development in a changing culture. *Psychological Bulletin, 54*, 232–242.

Brown, R. W. (1956). Language and categories. In J. S. Bruner, J. J. Goodnow, & G.A. Austin (Eds.), *A study of thinking.* Wiley.

Brown, R. W. (1958). How shall a thing be called? *Psychological Bulletin, 65*, 14–21.

Bruner, J. S., Goodnow, J. J., & Austin, G. A. (1956). *A study of thinking.* Wiley.

Buhler, C. (1971). Basic theoretical concepts of humanistic psychology. *American Psychologist, 26*, 378–386.

Burnet, F. M. (1969). *Self and not-self.* Cambridge University Press,.

Burnstein, E., & Worchel, P. (1962). Arbitrariness of frustration and its consequences for aggression in a social situation. *Journal of Personality, 30*, 528–540.

Buss, A. H. (1961). *The psychology of aggression.* Wiley.

Buss, A. H. (1963). Physical aggression in relation to different frustrations. *Journal of Abnormal and Social Psychology, 67*, 1–7.

Buss, A. H. (1966). Instrumentality of aggression, feedback and frustration, as determinant of physical aggression. *Journal of Personality and Social Psychology, 3*, 153–162.

Butler, J., & Haigh, G. (1954). Changes in the relationship between self-concepts and ideal concepts consequent upon client-centered counseling. In C. R. Rogers & R. Dymond (Eds.), *Psychotherapy and personality changes* (pp. 55–75). University of Chicago Press.

Byrne, D. (1962). Response to attitude similarity–dissimilarity as a function of affiliation. *Journal of Personality, 30*, 164–177.

Byrne, D. (1969). Attitudes and attraction. In L. Berkowitz (Ed.), *Advances in experimental social psychology* (vol. 4, pp. 35–89). Academic Press.

Byrne, D., Ervin, C.R., & Lamberth, J. (1970). Continuity between the experimental study of attraction and real-life computer dating. *Journal of Personality and Social Psychology, 16*, 157–165.

Calhoun, J. B. (1962). Population density and social pathology. *Scientific American, 206*, 139–146.

Cannon, W. B. (1939). *The wisdom of the body* (Rev.). New York, Norton.

Capehart, J., Tempone, V. J., & Hebert, J. (1969). A theory of stimulus equivalence. *Psychological Review, 76*, 405–418.

Carlsmith, J. M., Collins, B. E., & Helmreich, R. L. (1966). Studies in forced compliance: I. The effect of pressure for compliance on attitude change produced by face-to-face role playing and anonymous essay writing. *Journal of Personality and Social Psychology, 4*, 1–3.

Carlsmith, J. M., & Gross, A. E. (1969). Some effects of guilt on compliance. *Journal of Personality and Social Psychology, 11*, 232–239.

Carpenter CR. (1942). Societies of monkeys and apes. *Biological Symposia, 8*, 177–204.

REFERENCES 207

Carr, J. E. (1970). Differentiation similarity of patient and therapist and the outcome of psychotherapy. *Journal of Abnormal and Social Psychology*, *76*, 361–369.

Carson, R. C. (1969). *Interaction concepts of personality*. Aldine.

Carson, R. C., & Heine, R. W. (1962). Similarity and success in therapeutic dyads. *Journal of Consulting and Clinical Psychology*, *26*, 38–43.

Cartwright, D. (1959a) A field theoretical conception of power. In D. Cartwright (Ed.), *Studies in social power* (pp. 183–220). University of Michigan.

Cartwright, D. (1959b). Power: A neglected variable in social psychology. In D. Cartwright (Ed.), *Studies in social power* (pp. 1–14). University of Michigan.

Cartwright, D., & Zander, A. (1968). Power and influence in groups: Introduction. *Group dynamics: Research and theory*, *3*, 215–235.

Cattell, R. B. (1950). *Personality: a systematic theoretical and factual study*. McGraw-Hill.

Cattell, R. B. (1966). Personality structure: The larger dimensions. In B. Semeonoff (Ed.), *Personality assessment*. Penguin.

Cattell, R. B., & Warburton, F. W. (1967). *Objective personality and motivation tests: A theoretical introduction and practical compendium*. University of Illinois Press.

Centers, R., & Granville, A. C. (1971). Reciprocal need gratification in intersexual attraction: A test of the hypotheses of Schutz and Winch. *Journal of Personality*, *39*, 26–43.

Chemers, M. M., Lekhyananda, D., Fiedler, F. E., & Stolurow, L. M. (1966). Some effects of cultural training on leadership in heterocultural task group. *International Journal of Psychology*, *1*, 301–314.

Chemers, M. M., & Skrzypek, G. J. (1972). An experimental test of the contingency model of leadership effectiveness. *Journal of Personality and Social Psychology*, *24*, 172–177.

Chomsky, N. (1957). *Syntactic structures*. The Hague.

Chomsky, N. (1962). Explanatory models in linguistics. In E. Nagel, P. Suppes, & A. Tarsky (Eds.) *Logic, methodology and philosophy of science* (pp. 528–550). Stanford University Press.

Chomsky, N. (1963). *Linguistic structure and cognitive processes*. Paper read at Western Psychology Association meeting, Santa Monica.

Christie, R. (1970). The Machiavellis among us. *Psychology Today*, *4*, 82–86.

Christie, R., & Geis, F. L. (1970). *Studies in Machiavellianism*. Academic Press.

Cohen, A. R. (1955). Social norms, arbitrariness of frustration, and status of the agent of frustration in the frustration–aggression hypothesis. *Journal of Abnormal and Social Psychology*, *51*, 222–226.

Cohen, A. R. (1959). Situational structure, self-esteem and threat-oriented reactions to power. In D. Cartwright (Ed.), *Studies in social power* (pp. 35–52). Oxford, England: University of Michigan.

Cohn, R. (1971). Differential cerebral processing of noise and verbal stimuli. *Science*, *172*, 599–601.

Cole, M., & Bruner, J. S. (1971). Cultural differences and inferences about psychological processes. *American Psychologist*, *26*, 867–876.

Cone, C. D. (1968). Observations of self-induced mitosis and autosynchrony in sarcoma cell networks. *Cancer Research*, *28*, 2155–2161.

Conn, L. K., & Crowne, D. P. (1964). Instigation to aggression, emotional arousal and defensive emulation. *Journal of Personality*, *32*, 163–179.

Cooley, C. H. (1902). *Human nature and the social order*. Scribner.

Cooley, W. W., & Lohnes, P. R. (1962). *Multivariate procedures for the behavioral sciences*. Wiley.

208 REFERENCES

Coopersmith, S. (1967). *The antecedents of self-esteem*. W.H. Freeman.

Cowie, J., Cowie, C., & Slater, E. (1968). *Delinquency in girls*. Heinemann.

Coyle, G. L. (1930). *Social process in organized groups*. R.R. Smith.

Crandall, V. J., & Bellugi, U. (1954). Some relationships of interpersonal and intrapersonal conceptualizations to personal-social adjustment. *Journal of Personality, 23*, 224–232.

Cronbach, L. J. (1957). The two disciplines of scientific psychology. *American Psychologist, 12*, 671–684,.

Crowne, D. P., & Marlowe, D. A. (1960). A new scale of social desirability independent of psychopathology. *Journal of Consulting and Clinical Psychology, 24*, 349–354.

Crowne, D. P., & Marlowe, D. A. (1964). *The approval motive*. Wiley.

Day, R. H. (1972). Visual spatial illusions: A general explanation. *Science, 175*, 1335–1340.

DeCharms, R., & Wilkins, E. J. (1963). Some effects of verbal expression of hostility. *Journal of Abnormal and Social Psychology, 66*, 462–470.

Deese, J. (1969). Behavior and fact. *American Psychologist, 24*, 515–522.

Deitz, G. E. (1969). A comparison of delinquents with non-delinquents on self-concept, self-acceptance and parental identification. *Journal of Genetic Psychology, 1*, 285–295.

Deutsch, M., & Gerard, H. B. (1955). A study of normative and informational social influences upon individual judgement. *Journal of Abnormal and Social Psychology, 51*, 629–636. Quoted by French and Raven, 1959.

Devereux, E. C., Bronfenbrenner, U., & Rodgers, R. R. (1969). Childrearing in England and the United States: A cross-national comparison. *Journal of* Marriage and Family, *31*, 257–270.

Dinwiddie, F. M. (1955). *An application of the principle of response generalization to the prediction of displacement of aggressive responses*. Catholic University of America Press.

Dollard, J., Doob, L., Miller, N., Mowrer, O., & Sears, R. (1939). *Frustration and aggression*. Yale University Press.

Donnenwerth, G. V. (1971). *Effect of resources on retaliation to loss*. Unpublished doctoral dissertation. University of Missouri.

Donnenwerth, G. V., Teichman, M., & Foa, U. G. (1973). Cognitive differentiation of self and parents in delinquent and non-delinquent girls. *British Journal of Clinical Psychology, 12*, 144–152.

Dulany, D. E. (1962). The place of hypotheses and intentions: An analysis of verbal control in verbal conditioning. *Journal of Personality, 30*, 102–129.

Duncan, S.D., Jr. (1969). Nonverbal communication. *Psychological Bulletin, 72*, 118–137.

Egeth, H., Marcus, N., & Bevan, W. (1972). Target-set and response-set interaction: Implications for models of human information processing. *Science, 176*, 1447–1448.

Ekman, P. (1969). Pan cultural elements in facial display of emotion. *Science, 164*, 86–88.

Ekman, P. (1971). Universals and cultural differences in facial expressions of emotion. *Nebraska Symposium on Motivation, 19*, 207–283.

Eldred, S. H., Bell, N. W., Sherman, L. J., & Longabaugh, R. H. (1964). Classification and analysis of interaction patterns on a ward for chronic schizophrenics. *Disord Communication, 42*, 381–386.

Emmerich, W. (1959). Young children's discriminations of parent and child roles. *Child Development, 30*, 403–419.

Emmerich, W. (1961). Family role concepts of children ages six to ten. *Child Development, 32*, 609–624.

REFERENCES 209

Emmerich, W. (1968). Personality development and concepts of structure. *Child Development, 39*, 671–690.

Emmerich, W., Goldman, K.S., & Shore, R. E. (1971). Differentiation and development of social norms. *Journal of Personality and Social Psychology, 18*, 323–353.

English, H. B., & English, A. C. (1958). *A comprehensive dictionary of psychological and psychoanalytical terms.* Longmans, Green, and Co.

Epstein, S., & Taylor, S. P. (1967). Instigation to aggression as a function of degree of defeat and perceived aggressive intent of the opponent. *Journal of Personality, 35*, 265–289.

Feather, N. T. (1971). Organization and discrepancy in cognitive structures. *Psychological Review, 78*, 355–379.

Federn, P. (1952). *Ego psychology and the psychoses.* Basic Books.

Feshbach, S. (1955). The drive-reducing function of fantasy behavior. *Journal of Abnormal and Social Psychology, 50*, 3–11.

Feshbach, S. (1956). The catharsis hypothesis and some consequences of interaction with aggressive and neutral play objects. *Journal of Personality, 24*, 449-462.

Feshbach, S. (1961). The stimulating versus cathartic effects of a vicarious aggressive activity. *Journal of Abnormal and Social Psychology, 63*, 381–385.

Festinger, L. (1953). An analysis of compliant behavior. In M. Sherif & M. O. Wilson (Eds.), *Group relations at the crossroads* (pp. 232–256). Harper.

Festinger, L. (1954). A theory of social comparison processes. *Human Relations, 7*, 117–140.

Festinger, L. (1957). *A theory of cognitive dissonance.* Row, Peterson.

Festinger, L., & Carlsmith, J. M. (1959). Cognitive consequences of forced compliance. *Journal of Abnormal and Social Psychology, 58*, 203–210.

Festinger, L., Schachter, S., & Back, K. (1950). *Social pressures in informal groups: a study of human factors in housing.* Harper.

Fiedler, F. E. (1964). A contingency model of leadership effectiveness. In L. Berkowitz (Ed.), *Advances in experimental social psychology* (vol. I, 149–190). Academic Press.

Fiedler, F. E. (1966). The effect of leadership and cultural heterogeneity on group performance: A test of the contingency model. *Journal of Experimental Social Psychology, 2*, 237–264.

Fiedler, F. E. (1967). *A theory of leadership effectiveness.* McGraw-Hill.

Fiedler, F. E. (1973). Personality and situational determinants of leader behavior. In E. A. Fleishman and J. G. Hunt (Eds.), *Current developments in the study of leadership* (pp. 41–60). Carbondale, IL: Southern Illinois University Press.

Fiedler, F. E. (1971). *On the death and transfiguration of leadership training.* Paper read at the American Psychological Association meeting, September.

Fiedler, F. E., Meuwese, W., & Oonk, S. (1961). An exploratory study of group creativity in laboratory tasks. *Acta Psychologica, 18*, 100–119.

Mitchell, T. R., & Triandis, H. C. (1971). The culture assimilator: An approach to cross-cultural training. *Journal of Applied Psychology, 55*, 95–102.

Flanagan, T. C. (1949). Techniques for developing critical requirements from critical incidents. *American Psychologist, 4*, 236.

Foa, E. B. (1970). *Schizophrenics and neurotics: some differences in their interpersonal cognitive organization.* Unpublished master's thesis, University of Illinois.

Foa, E. B. (1973). *The use of cognitive structures in behavior therapy.* Unpublished manuscript.

210 REFERENCES

Foa, E. B., Turner, J.L., & Foa, U. G. (1972). Response generalization in aggression. *Human Relations, 25*, 337–350.

Foa, U. G. (1958a). The contiguity principle in the structure of interpersonal relations. *Human Relations, 11*, 229–238,

Foa, U. G. (1958b). Empathy or behavioral transparency? *Journal of Abnormal and Social Psychology, 56*, 62–66.

Foa, U. G. (1960). Some correlates of the empathy of the workers with the foreman. *Journal of Applied Psychology, 44*, 6–10.

Foa, U. G. (1961). Convergences in the analysis of the structure in interpersonal behavior. *Psychological Review, 68*, 341–352.

Foa, U. G. (1963). A facet approach to the prediction of communalities. *Behavioural Sciences, 8*, 220–226.

Foa, U. G. (1954). Workers satisfaction in four disciplinary climates. In M.W. Riley (Ed.), *Sociological research* (pp. 436–439). Harcourt, Brace and World.

Foa, U. G. (1964). Cross-cultural similarity and difference in interpersonal behavior. *Journal of Abnormal and Social Psychology, 68*, 517–522.

Foa, U. G. (1965). New developments in facet design and analysis. *Psychological Review, 72*, 262–274.

Foa, U. G. (1966). Perception of behavior in reciprocal roles: The ringex model. *Psychological Monographs: General and Applied, 80*, 1.

Foa, U. G., & Chemers, M. M. (1967). The significance of role behavior differentiation for cross-cultural interaction training. *International Journal of Psychology, 2*, 45–48.

Foa, U. G., & Donnenwerth, G. V. (1971) Love poverty in modern culture and sensitivity training. *Social Inquiry, 41*, 149–159.

Foa, U. G., Mitchell, T. R., & Fiedler, F. E. (1971). Differentiation matching. *Behavioural Sciences, 16*, 130–142.

Foa, U. G., Mitchell, T. R., & Lekhyananda, D. (1969). Cultural differences in reaction to failure. *International Journal of Psychology, 4*, 21–25.

Foa, U. G., Triandis, H. C., & Katz, E. W. (1966). Cross-cultural invariance in the differentiation and organization of family roles. *Journal of Personality and Social Psychology, 4*, 316–327.

Frankl, V. E. (1962). *Man's search for meaning.* Beacon Press.

Freedman, J. L. (1963). Attitudinal effects of inadequate justification. *Journal of Personality, 31*, 371–385.

French, J. R. P., & Raven, B. (1959). The bases of social power. In D. Cartwright (Ed.), *Studies in social power* (pp. 150–167). University of Michigan.

Freud, A. (1965). *Normality and pathology in childhood.* International University Press.

Freud, S. (1949). *An outline of psychoanalysis.* Norton.

Fromm, E. (1939). Selfishness and self-love. *Psychiatry, 2*, 507–523.

Gambaro, S., & Rabin, A. I. (1969). Diastolic blood pressure responses following direct and displaced aggression after anger arousal in high- and low-guilt subjects. *Journal of Personality and Social Psychology, 2*, 87–94.

Ganz, L., & Riesen, A. H. (1962). Stimulus generalization to hue in the dark-reared macaque. *Journal of Comparative and Physiological Psychology, 55*, 92–99.

Geen, R. G. (1968). Effects of frustration, attack, and prior training in aggressiveness upon aggressive behavior. *Journal of Personality and Social Psychology, 9*, 316–321.

Geen, R. G., & Berkowitz, L. (1966). Name-mediated aggressive cue properties. *Journal of Personality, 34*, 456–465.

REFERENCES 211

Geen, R. G., & Berkowitz, L. (1967). Some conditions facilitating the occurrence of aggression after the observation of violence. *Journal of Personality, 35*, 666–676.

Gerard, H. B., & Mathewson, G. C. (1966). The effects of severity of initiation on liking for a group: A replication. *Journal of Experimental Social Psychology, 2*, 278–287.

Gergen, K. J. (1969). *The psychology of behavior exchange.* Addison Wesley.

Gewirtz, J. L. (1969). Mechanisms of social learning: Some roles of stimulation and behavior in early human development. In D. A. Goslin (Ed.), *Handbook of socialization theory and research* (pp. 57–72). Rand McNally.

Gewirtz, J. L. & Baer, D. M. (1958). Deprivation and satiation of social reinforcers as drive conditions. *Journal of Abnormal and Social Psychology, 57*, 165–172.

Goldstein, A. P., Heller, K., & Sechrest, L. B. (1966). *Psychotherapy and the psychology of behavior change.* Wiley.

Goldstein, J. H., & Arms, R. L. (1971). Effects of observing athletic contests on hostility. *Sociometry, 34*, 83–90.

Goodenough, E. W. (1957). Interest in persons as an aspect of sex difference in the early years. *Genetic Psychology Monographs, 55*, 287–323.

Goodenough, E. W. (1967). Componential analysis. *Science, 156*, 1203–1209.

Goodenough, E. W. (1969). Frontiers of cultural anthropology: Social organization. *Proceedings of the American Philosophical Society, 113*, 329–335.

Goranson, R. E., & Berkowitz, L. (1966). Reciprocity ana responsibility reactions to prior help. *Journal of Personality and Social Psychology, 3*, 227–232.

Gouldner, A. W. (1960). The norm of reciprocity: A preliminary statement. *American Sociological Review, 25*, 161–179. Reprinted in Hollander, E. P., & Hunt, R. G. (Eds.). (1967). *Current perspectives in social psychology* (2nd ed.). Oxford University Press.

Graham, F. K., Charwat, W. A., Honig, A. S., & Weitz, P. C. (1951). Aggression as a function of the attack and the attacker, *Journal of Abnormal and Social Psychology, 46*, 512–520.

Guilford, J. P. (1967). *The nature of human intelligence.* McGraw-Hill.

Hall, E. T. (1963). *The silent language.* Fawcett.

Hall, K. R. (1963). Observational learning in monkeys and apes. *British Journal of Psychology, 54*, 201–226.

Halverson, H. M. (1936). Complications of the early grasping reactions. *Psychological Monographs, 47*, 47–63.

Halwes, T., & Jenkins, J. J. (1971). Problem of serial order in behavior is not resolved by context-sensitive associative memory models. *Psychological Review, 78*, 122–129.

Hamblin, R. M., Buckholdt, D., Bushell, D., Ellis, D., & Ferritor, D. (1969). Changing the game from "get the teacher" to "learn." *Transaction, 6*, 20–31.

Hamlin, R. M., & Lorr, M. (1971). Differentiation of normals, neurotics, paranoids and non-paranoids. *Journal of Abnormal and Social Psychology, 77*, 90–96.

Handfinger, B. M. (1973). *Effect of previous deprivation on reaction time for helping behavior.* Paper presented at E.P.A. annual meeting.

Hardy, K. R. (1957). Determinants of conformity and attitude change. *Journal of Abnormal and Social Psychology, 54*, 289–294.

Hare, A. P. (1962). *Handbook of small group research.* Free Press of Glencoe.

Harlow, H. F. (1953). Mice, monkeys, men and motives. *Psychological Review, 60*, 23–32.

Harlow, H. F. (1958). The nature of love. *American Psychologist, 13*, 673–685.

Harlow, H. F., & Suomi, S. J. (1970). Nature of love–simplified. *American Psychologist, 25*, 161–168.

212 REFERENCES

Harlow, H. F., & Zimmerman, R. R. (1959). Affectional responses in the infant monkey. *Science, 130,* 421–432.

Harman, W. W., McKim, R. H., Mogar, R. E., Fadiman, J., & Stolaroff, M. J. (1966). Psychedelic agents in creative problem-solving: a pilot study. *Psychological Reports, 19,* 211–227.

Harrow, M., Fox, D. A., & Detre, T. (1969). Self-concept of the married psychiatric patient and his mate's perception of him. *Journal of Consulting and Clinical Psychology, 33,* 235–239.

Harrow, M., Markhus, K. L., Stillman, R., & Hallowell, C. B. (1968). Changes in adolescents' self-concept and their parents' perception during psychiatric hospitalization. *Journal of Nervous and Mental Disease, 147,* 252–259.

Hartman, D. P. (1969). Influence of symbolically modeled instrumental aggression and pain cues on aggressive behavior. *Journal of Personality and Social Psychology,* 280–288.

Harvey, O. J., Hunt, D. E., & Schroder, H. M. (1961). *Conceptual systems and personality organization.* Wiley.

Hatherington, E. M. (1966). Effects of paternal absence on sex-typed behaviors in Negro and White, preadolescent males. *Journal of Personality and Social Psychology, 4,* 87–91.

Heider, F. (1958). Consciousness, the perceptual world, and communications with others. In R. Tagiuri & L. Petrullo (Eds.), *Person perception and interpersonal behavior* (pp. 27–32). Stanford University Press.

Helmreich, R., Aronson, E., & LeFan, J. (1970). To err is humanizing—sometimes: Effects of self-esteem, competence and a pratfall on interpersonal attraction. *Journal of Personality and Social Psychology, 16,* 259–264.

Helmreich, R., & Collins, B. E. (1968). Studies in forced compliance: IV. Commitment and magnitude of inducement to comply as determinants of opinion change. *Journal of Personality and Social Psychology, 10,* 75–81.

Henry, A. F. (1956). Family role structure and self blame. *Social Forces, 35,* 35–38.

Higgins, J. (1968). Inconsistent socialization. *Psychological Reports, 23,* 303–336.

Hillson, J. S., & Worchel, P. (1957). Self-concept and defensive behavior in the maladjusted. *Journal of Consulting Psychology, 21,* 83–88.

Hokanson, J. E. (1961). The effects of frustration and anxiety on overt aggression. *Journal of Abnormal and Social Psychology, 62,* 346–351.

Hokanson, J. E., & Burgess, M. (1962). The effects of three types of aggression on vascular processes. *Journal of Abnormal and Social Psychology, 64,* 446–449.

Hollander, E. P. (1958). Conformity, status and idiosyncrasy credit. *Psychological Review, 65,* 117–127.

Hollister, L. E. (1971). Marihuana in man: Three years later. *Science, 72,* 21–29.

Homans, G. C. (1961). *Social behavior: its elementary forms.* Brace & World.

Hornberger, R. H. (1959). *The differential reduction of aggressive responses as a function of interpolated activities.* Paper presented at meeting of American Psychological Association (Quoted by Berkowitz, 1962, p. 219)

Hovland, C., & Sears, R. (1940). Minor studies in aggression: VI. Correlation of lynchings with economic indices. *Journal of Psychology, 9,* 301–310.

Hsu, F. L. K. (1961). Kinship and ways of life: An exploration. In F. L. K. Hsu (Ed.), *Psychological anthropology: approaches to culture and personality* (pp. 400–456). Illinois: Dorsey Press.

Hull, C. L. (1943). *Principles of behavior.* Appleton-Century-Croft.

REFERENCES 213

Humphreys, L. D., Ilgen, D., McGrath, D., & Montanelli, R. (1969). Capitalization on chance in rotation of factors. *Educational and Psychological Measurement, 29*, 259–271.

Hunt, J. (1961). *McV.: Intelligence and experience.* Ronald Press.

Hutt, S. J., & Hutt, C. (1970). *Direct observation and measurement of behavior.* Charles C Thomas.

Iversen, S. D. (1969). *The contribution of the ventral temporal lobe to visual analysis in the monkey.* Paper delivered at the XIX International Congress of Psychology, London, August.

Jackson, D. D. (1957). The question of family homeostasis. *Psychiatric Quarterly, 31*, 79–90.

Jackson, D. D. (1969) (Ed.) *Human communication* (vols. 1 & 2). Science and Behavior Books.

Jakobovitz, L. A. (1966). Comparative psycholinguistics in the study of cultures. *International Journal of Psychology, 1*, 15–37.

Janis, I. L. (1951). *Air war and emotional stress: Psychological studies of bombing and civilian defense.* McGraw-Hill.

Janis, I. L., & Rife, D. (1959). Persuasibility and emotional disorders. In C. I. Hovland & I. L. Janis (Eds.), *Personality and persuasibility* (pp. 121–137). Yale University Press.

Jenkins, H. M. (1971). Sequential organization in schedules of reinforcement. In W. N. Schoenfeld & J. Farmer (Eds.), *Theory of reinforcement schedules* (pp. 63–109). Appleton-Century-Croft.

Jenkins, H. M., & Harrison, R. H. (1960). Effects of discrimination training on auditory generalization. *Journal of Experimental Psychology, 59*, 246–253.

Jessor, R., & Richardson, S. (1968). Psychosocial deprivation and personality development. In *Perspectives on human deprivation: Biological, psychological and sociological.* U.S. Department of Mental Health, Education and Welfare.

John, E. R., Shimokochi, M., & Bartlett, F. (1969). Neural readout from memory during generalization. *Science, 164*, 1519–1521.

Johnsgard, P. A. (1967). *Animal behavior.* Brown.

Johnson, M. M. (1963). Sex role learning in the nuclear family. *Child Development, 34*, 319–333.

Jones, E. E. (1964). *Ingratiation: A social psychological analysis.* Appleton-Century-Croft.

Jones, E. E., Bell, L., & Aronson, E. (1972). The reciprocation of attraction from similar and dissimilar others: A study in person perception and evaluation. In C. C. McClintock (Ed.), *Experimental social psychology* (pp. 142–179). Holt, Rinehart & Winston.

Jones, E. E., & Gerard, H.B. (1967). *Foundations of social psychology.* Wiley.

Jones, E. E., Gergen, & Davis, K. E. (1962). Some determinants of reactions to being approved or disapproved as a person. *Psychological Monographs, 76*, 1–17.

Jones, S. C. (1966). Some determinants of interpersonal evaluating behavior. *Journal of Personality and Social Psychology, 3*, 397–403.

Jones, S. C. (1973). Self and interpersonal evaluation: Esteem theories versus contingency theories. *Psychological Bulletin, 79*, 185–199.

Jordan, J. E. (1971). Attitude-behavior research on physical-mental-social disability and racial-ethnic differences. *Psychological Aspects of Disability, 18*, 5–26.

Jourard, S. M. (1964). *The transparent self.* Van Nostrand.

Katz, E., Blau, P. M., Brown, M. L., & Strodtbeck, F. L. (1967). Leadership stability and social change. *Sociometry, 20*, 36–50.

214 REFERENCES

Katz, E. W. (1964). *A study of verbal and non-verbal behaviors associated with social roles.* Technical Report No. 20, November, University of Illinois, Department of Psychology and Institute of Communication Research, Contract NR 177-472, Nonr-1834 (36), Advanced Research Projects Agency.

Kelley, H. H. (1973). The process of causal attribution. *American Psychologist, 28,* 107–128.

Kelly, G. A. (1955). *Psychology of personal constructs.* Norton.

Kiesler, C. A., & Kiesler, S. B. (1969). *Conformity.* Addison-Wesley.

Kiesler, S. B. (1966). The effect of perceived role requirements on reactions to favor-doing. *Journal of Experimental Social Psychology, 2,* 198–210.

Kiesler, S. B., & Baral, R. L. (1970). The search for a romantic partner: The effects of self-esteem and physical attractiveness on romantic behavior. In K. J. Gergen & D. Marlowe (Eds.), *Personality and social behavior* (pp. 155–165). Addison-Wesley.

Killian, L. M. (1952). The significance of multiple group membership in disaster. *American Journal of Sociology, 57,* 309–314.

Kimble, G. A. (1971). The facts and a set of pressures. *Contemporary Psychology, 16,* 59–63.

Kinney, E. E. (1953). A study of peer group social acceptability at the fifth grade level in a public school. Journal *of* Educational *Research, 47,* 57–64.

Koch, S. (1969). Psychology cannot be a coherent science. *Psychology Today, 14,* 64–68.

Koestler, A. (1964). *The act of creation.* Macmillan.

Koestler, A. (1968). *The ghost in the machine.* Macmillan.

Kohlberg, L. (1969a). Stages and sequence: The cognitive–developmental approach to socialization. In D. A. Goslin (Ed.), *Handbook of socialization theory and research.* Rand McNally.

Kohlberg, L. (1969b). *Stages in the development of moral thought and action.* Holt, Rhinehart and Winston.

Kregarman, J. J., & Worchel, P. (1961). Arbitrariness of frustration and aggression. *Journal of Abnormal and Social Psychology, 63,* 183–187.

Lana, R. E. (1960). Manipulation-exploration drives and the drive-reduction hypothesis. *Journal of General Psychology, 63,* 3–27.

Lana, R. E. (1962). Exploratory phenomena and the drive-reduction hypothesis. *Journal of General Psychology, 67,* 101–104.

Lana, R. E. (1969). Pretest sensitization. In R. Rosenthal & R. L. Rosnow (Eds.), *Artifacts in behavioral research.* Academic Press.

Landfield, A. W., & Nawas, M. M. (1964). Psychotherapeutic improvement as a function of communication and adoption of therapist's values. *Journal of Counseling Psychology, 11,* 336–341.

Larson, L. L., & Rowland, K. M. (1972a). *Leadership style and cognition complexity.* College of Commerce and Business Administration, University of Illinois.

Larson, L. L., & Rowland, K. M. (1972b). *Leadership style, stress and behavior in task performance.* College of Commerce and Business Administration, University of Illinois.

Latane, B., & Darley, J. M. (1969). Bystander "apathy." *American Scientist, 57,* 244–268.

Laufer, L. (1967). *Israel and the developing countries: New approaches to cooperation.* Twentieth Century Fund.

Leary, T. (1957). *Interpersonal diagnosis of personality.* Ronald Press.

Leavitt, H. J. (1951). Some effects of certain communication patterns on group performance. *The Journal of Abnormal and Social Psychology, 46,* 38–50.

Leventhal, G. S. (1970). Influence of brothers and sisters on sex-role behavior. *Journal of Personality and Social Psychology, 16,* 452–465.

Leventhal, G. S., Allen, J., & Kemelgor, B. (1969). Reducing inequity by reallocating rewards. *Psychonomic Science, 14,* 295–296.

Leventhal, G. S., & Anderson, D. (1970). Self-interest and the maintenance of equity. *Journal of Personality and Social Psychology, 15,* 57–62.

Leventhal, G. S., & Bergman, J. T. (1969). Self-depriving behavior as a response to unprofitable inequity. *Journal of Experimental Social Psychology, 5,* 153–171.

Leventhal, G. S., & Lane, D. W. (1970). Sex, age, and equity behavior. *Journal of Personality and Social Psychology, 15,* 312–316.

Leventhal, G. S., & Michaels, J.W. (1969). Extending the equity model: Perception of inputs and allocation of reward as a function of duration and quantity of performance. *Journal of Personality and Social Psychology, 12,* 303–309.

Levine, M. (1971). Hypothesis theory and nonlearning despite ideal S-R reinforcement contingencies. *Psychological Review, 78,* 130–140.

Levine, S. (1969). Psychotherapy as socialization. *International Journal of Psychiatry, 8,* 645–655.

Levinger, G. (1959). The development of perceptions and behavior in newly formed social power relationships. In D. Cartwright (Ed.), *Studies in social power* (pp. 83–98). University of Michigan.

Levi-Strauss, C. L. (1963). *Structural anthropology.* Basic Books.

Levi-Strauss, C. L. (1966). *The savage mind.* University of Chicago Press.

Lewin, K. (1936). *Principles of topological psychology.* McGraw-Hill.

Lewis, H. B. (1941). Studies in the principles of judgments and attitudes: IV. The operation of prestige suggestion. *Journal of Social Psychology, 14,* 229–256.

Lewis, O. (1966). The culture of poverty. *Scientific American, 215,* 19–25.

Linder, D. E., Cooper, J., & Jones, E. E. (1967). Decision freedom as a determinant of the role of incentive magnitude in attitude change. *Journal of Personality and Social Psychology, 6,* 245–254.

Longabaugh, R. (1963). A category system for coding interpersonal behavior as social exchange. *Sociometry, 26,* 319–344.

Longabaugh, R. (1966). The structure of interpersonal behavior. *Sociometry, 29,* 441–460.

Longabaugh, R. (1971). *Sources of interactional uncertainty and their relationship to pre-morbid schizoid prognosis of schizophrenics: An exploratory study.* Unpublished manuscript.

Longabaugh, R., Eldred, S. H., Bell, N. W., & Sherman, L. P. (1966). The interactional world of the chronic schizophrenic patient. *Psychiatry, 29,* 78–99.

Longabaugh, R. H., & Whiting, J. W. (1963). A transcultural test of the Leary grid. *American Psychologist, 18,* 347.

Lorenz, K. (1966). *On aggression.* Brace and World.

Lovaas, O. I. (1961). Effect of exposure to symbolic aggression on aggressive behavior. *Child Development, 32,* 37–44.

Luria, A. R. (1966). *Higher cortical functions in man.* Basic Books.

Luria, A. R., Simernitskaya, E. G., & Tubylevich, B. (1970). The structure of psychological processes in relation to cerebral organization. *Neuropsychologia, 8,* 13–19.

Lynn, D. B. (1969). *Parental and sex role identification.* McCutchan Publishing Corp.

Lynn, D. B., & Sawrey, W. L. (1959). The effects of father-absence on Norwegian boys and girls. *Journal of Abnormal and Social Psychology, 59,* 258–262.

MacKay, D. M. (1963). Psychophysics of perceived intensity: A theoretical basis for Fechner's and Stevens' laws. *Science, 139,* 1213–1216.

216 REFERENCES

Madoff, J. M. (1959). The attitudes of mothers of juvenile delinquents toward child rearing. *Journal of Consulting Psychology, 23*, 518–520.

Madsen, K. B. (1961). *Theories of motivation.* Allen.

Mallick, S. K., & McCandless, B. R. (1966). A study of catharsis of aggression. *Journal of Personality and Social Psychology, 4*, 591–596.

Maltzman, I., Langdon, B., & Feeney, D. (1970). Semantic generalization without prior conditioning. *Journal of Experimental Psychology, 83*, 73–75.

Mandler, G. (1962). From association to structure. *Psychological Review, 69*, 415–427.

Marlowe, D., & Gergen, K. J. (1969). Personality and social interaction. In B. Lindzey & E. Aronson (Eds.), *The handbook of social psychology* (vol. 3, pp. 590–665) Addison-Wesley.

Maslow, A. H. (1941). Deprivation, threat and frustration. *Psychological Review, 48*, 364–366.

Mason, W. A. (1968). Early social deprivation in nonhuman primates: Implications for human behavior. In D. C. Glass (Ed.), *Environmental influences* (pp. 70–100). The Rockefeller University Press and Russell Sage Foundation.

Masserman, H. (1970). Is uncertainty a key to neurotigenesis? *Psychosomatics, 11*, 391–402.

McClelland, D. C. (1955). *Studies in motivation.* Appleton-Century-Croft.

McDavid, J., & Schroder, H. M. (1957). The interpretation of approval and disapproval by delinquent and non-delinquent adolescents. *Journal of Personality, 25*, 539–549.

McDougall, W. (1932). *The energies of men: a study of the fundamentals of dynamic psychology.* Methuen.

McGuire, W. J. (1969a). The nature of attitude and attitude change. In G. Lindzey & E. Aronson (Eds.), *The handbook of social psychology* (vol. 3, 2nd ed.). Addison-Wesley.

McGuire, W. J. (1969b). Suspiciousness of experimenter's intent. In R. Rosenthal, & R. L. Rosnow (Eds.), *Artifact in behavioral research.* Academic Press.

McNeill, D. (1966). Developmental psycholinguistics. In F. Smith, & G. A. Miller (Eds.), *The genesis of language* (pp. 15–84). Cambridge: M.I.T. Press.

Mead, G. H. (1964). *On social psychology.* Edited and with an introduction by A. Strauss. University of Chicago Press.

Merton, R. K. (1967). *On theoretical sociology.* Free Press.

Michaelsen, L. K. (1971). *Leader orientation, leader behavior, group effectiveness, and situational favorability: An extension of the contingency model.* Technical report, Institute for Social Research, University of Michigan, Ann Arbor, Michigan, September.

Milgram, S. (1970). The experience of living in cities. *Science, 167*, 1461–1468.

Miller, G.A., Galanter, E., & Pribram, K. H. (1960). *Plans and the structure of behavior.* Holt.

Miller, H., & Bieri, J. (1963). An informational analysis of clinical judgment. *Journal of Abnormal and Social Psychology, 67*, 317–325.

Miller, N. E. (1948). Theory and experiment relating psychoanalytic displacement to stimulus–response generalization. *Journal of Abnormal and Social Psychology, 43*, 155–178.

Miller, N. E. (1950). *Effects of group size on group process and member satisfaction.* University of Michigan.

Miller, N. E. (1959). Liberalization of basic S–R concepts: Extensions to conflict behavior, motivation and social learning. In S. Koch (Ed.), *Psychology: A study of a science* (vol. 2, pp. 196–292). McGraw-Hill.

REFERENCES 217

Miller, N. E., & Bugelski, R. (1948). Minor studies of aggression: The influence of frustrations imposed by the in-group on attitudes expressed toward out-groups. *Journal of Psychology, 25*, 437–442.

Miller, P. H., Kessel, F. S., & Flavell, J. (1970). Thinking about people thinking about people thinking about: A study of social cognitive development. *Child Development, 41*, 613–623.

Mirsky, A. (1968). Communication of affects in monkeys. In D. C. Glass (Ed.), *Environmental influences* (pp. 129–137). The Rockefeller University Press and Russell Sage Foundation.

Mitchell, T. R. (1970). Leader complexity and leadership style. *Journal of Personality and Social Psychology, 16*, 166–174.

Mitchell, T. R., & Foa, U.G. (1969). Diffusion of the effect of cultural training of the leader in the structure of heterocultural task groups. *Australian Journal of Psychology, 21*, 31–43.

Mogar, R. E. (1966). Psychedelic research in the context of contemporary psychology. *Psychedelic Review, 8*, 96–104.

Mogar, R. E., & Savage, C. (1964). Personality changes associated with psychedelic (LSD) therapy. *Psychotherapy, 1*, 154–162.

Money, J. (1961). Sex hormones and other variables in human eroticism. In W. C. Young (Ed.), *Sex and internal secretions* (pp. 1383–1400). Baltimore: Williams and Wilkins.

Moreno, J. L. (1934). *Who shall survive?: A new approach to the problem of human interrelations.* Nervous and Mental Disease Publishing Co.

Morin, R. E., Hoving, K. L., & Konick, D. S. (1970). Are these two stimuli from the same set? Response times of children and adults with familiar and arbitrary sets. *Journal of Experimental Child Psychology, 10*, 308–318.

Mosher, L. R. (1969). Schizophrenic communication and family therapy. *Family Processes, 8*, 43–63.

Mosher, D. L., Mortimer, R., & Grebel, M. (1968). Verbal aggressive behavior in delinquent boys. *Journal of Abnormal and Social Psychology, 73*, 454.

Mosher, D. L., & Proenza, L. M. (1968). Intensity of attack, displacement and verbal aggression. *Psychonomic Science, 12*, 359–360.

Mowrer, O. H. (1964). Freudianism, behavior therapy and "self-disclosure." *Behaviour Research and Therapy, 1*, 321–337.

Muller, H. P. (1970). Relationship between time-span of discretion, "leadership behavior," and Fiedler's LPC score. *Journal of Applied Psychology, 54*, 140–144.

Murdock, G. P. (1957). World ethnographic sample. *American Anthropologist, 59*, 664–687.

Murray, H. A. (1938). *Explorations in personality 2.* Oxford University Press.

Mussen, P., & Rutherford, E. (1963). Parent–child relations and parental personality in relation to young children's sex role preferences. *Child Development, 34*, 589–607.

Nord, W. R. (1969). Social exchange theory: An integrative approach to social conformity. *Psychological Bulletin, 71*, 174–208.

Nye, F. I., Carlson, J., & Garrett, G. (1970). Family size, interaction, affect and stress. *Journal of Marriage and Family, 32*, 216–226.

Omwake, K. (1954). The relationship between acceptance of self and acceptance of others shown by three personality inventories. *Journal of Consulting Psychology, 18*, 443–446.

Osgood, C. E. (1964). Semantic differential technique in the comparative study of cultures. *American Anthropologist, 66*, 171–200.

218 REFERENCES

Osgood, C. E. (1970). Speculations on the structure of interpersonal intensions. *Behavioral Sciences, 15*, 237–254.

O'Toole, R., & Dubin, R. (1968). Baby feeding and body sway: An experiment in George Herbert Mead's "Taking the role of the other." *Journal of Personality and Social Psychology, 10*, 59–65.

Parsons, T. (1951). *The social system.* Free Press.

Parsons, T. (1955). Family structure and the socialization of the child. In T. Parsons & R. F. Bales (Eds.), *Family, socialization and interaction process* (pp. 35–131). Glencoe, IL: Free Press.

Parsons, T. (1955). A note on some biological analogies. Appendix A in T. Parsons & R. F. Bales (Eds.), *Family, socialization and interaction process* (pp. 395–399). Glencoe, IL: Free Press.

Pastore, N. (1952). The role of arbitrariness in the frustration–aggression hypothesis. *Journal of Abnormal and Social Psychology, 47*, 728–731.

Pepitone, A. (1966). Some conceptual and empirical problems of consistency models. In S. Feldman (Ed.), *Cognitive consistency: motivational antecedents and behavioral consequences* (pp. 257–297). Academic Press.

Pepitone, A. (1971). The role of justice in interdependent decision making. *Journal of Experimental Social Psychology, 7*, 144–156.

Pepitone, A., Maderna, A., Caporicci, E., Tiberi, E., Iacono, G., DiMaio, G., Perfetto, M., Asprea, A., Villone, G., Fua, G., & Tonucci, F. (1970). Justice in choice behavior: A cross-cultural analysis. *International Journal of Psychology, 5*, 1–10.

Pepitone, A., & Reichling, G. (1955). Group cohesiveness and the expression of hostility. *Human Relations, 8*, 327–337.

Peterson, D. R. (1968). *The clinical study of social behavior.* Appleton-Century-Croft.

Peterson, N. (1962). Effect of monochromatic rearing on the control of responding by wavelength. *Science, 136*, 774–775.

Piaget, J. (1952). *The origins of intelligence in children.* International Universities Press.

Piaget, J. (1954). *The construction of reality in the child.* Basic Books.

Pirojnikoff, L. A. (1958). *Catharsis and the role of perceptual change in the reduction of hostility.* Unpublished dissertation.

Premack, D. (1965). Reinforcement theory. In *Nebraska symposium on motivation* (Vol. 13, pp. 123–180).

Pribram, K. H. (1960). A review of theory in physiological psychology. *Annual Review of Psychology, 11*, 1–40.

Pruitt, D. G. (1968). Reciprocity and credit building in a laboratory dyad. *Journal of Personality and Social Psychology, 8*, 143–147.

Reich, C.A. (1971). *The greening of America.* Bantam Books.

Rescorla, R. A. (1967). Pavlovian conditioning and its proper control procedures. *Psychological Review, 74*, 71–80.

Rice, R. W., & Chemers, M. M. (1973). Predicting leadership emergence using Fiedler's contingency model of leadership effectiveness. *Journal of Applied Psychology, 57*, 281–287.

Rodgers, D. A., & Ziegler, F. J. (1967). Cognitive process and conversion reactions. *Journal of Nervous and Mental Disease, 144*, 155–170.

Roethlisberger, F. J., Dickson, W. J., & Wright, H. A. (1939). *Management and the worker: An account of a research program conducted by the Western Electric Co.* Science Editions.

Rogers, C. R. (1951). *Client-centered therapy.* Houghton Mifflin.

REFERENCES 219

Rosen, B. C., & D'Andrade, R. (1959). The psychosocial origins of achievement motivation. *Sociometry, 22*, 185–218.

Rosen, S. (1966). The comparative roles of informational and material commodities in interpersonal transactions. *Journal of Social Psychology, 2*, 211–226.

Rosenbaum, M. E., & deCharms, R. (1960). Direct and vicarious reduction of hostility. *Journal of Abnormal and Social Psychology, 60*, 105–111,.

Rosenthal, R., & Jacobson, L. (1968). *Pygmalion in the classroom: Teacher's expectation and pupils' intellectual development.* Holt, Rinehart & Winston.

Rosenzweig, S. (1944). An outline of frustration theory. In J. McV. Hunt (Ed.), *Personality and the behavior disorders* (pp. 379–388). Ronald Press.

Rosnow, R. L. (1968). A spread of effect in attitude formation. In A. C. Greenwald, T. C. Brock, & T. M. Ostrom (Eds.), *Psychological foundations of attitudes* (pp. 89–107). Academic Press.

Rothaus, P., & Worchel, P. (1960). The inhibition of aggression under nonarbitrary frustration. *Journal of Personality, 28*, 108–117.

Rothbart, M. K., & Maccoby, E. E. (1966). Parents' differential reactions to sons and daughters. *Journal of Personality and Social Psychology, 4*, 237–243.

Rotter, J. B. (1954). *Social learning and clinical psychology.* Prentice-Hall.

Ruesch, J. (1957). *Disturbed communication.* Norton.

Ruesch, J. (1961). *Therapeutic communication.* Norton.

Salzen, E. A. (1970). Imprinting and environmental learning. In L. R. Aronson, E. Tobach, D. S. Lehrman, & J. S. Rosenblatt (Eds.), *Development and evolution of behavior* (pp. 158–178). W.H. Freeman.

Sampson, E. E. (1971). *Social psychology and contemporary society.* Wiley.

Sampson, E. E., & Insko, C. A. (1964). Cognitive consistency and performance in the autokinetic situation. *Journal of Abnormal and Social Psychology, 68*, 184–192.

Santrock, J. W. (1970). Paternal absence, sex typing, and identification. *Developmental Psychology, 2*, 264–272.

Sarbin, T. R., Taft, R., & Bailey, D. E. (1960). *Clinical inference and cognitive theory.* Holt, Rinehart & Winston.

Sawyer, J., & Levine, R. A. (1966). Cultural dimensions: A factor analysis of the world ethnographic sample. *American Anthropologist, 68*, 708–731.

Schachter, S. (1959). *The psychology of affiliation.* Stanford University Press.

Schaller, G. B., & Emlen, J. T. (1962). The ontogeny of avoidance behavior in some precocial birds. *Animal Behavior, 10*, 370–381.

Stent, G. S. (1972). Prematurity and uniqueness in scientific discovery. *Scientific American, 227*, 84–93.

Schopler, J., & Thompson, V. D. (1968). Role of attribution processes in mediating amount of reciprocity for a favor. *Journal of Personality and Social Psychology, 10*, 243–250.

Schroder, H. M., Driver, M. J., & Streufert, S. (1967). *Human information processing.* Holt, Rinehart & Winston.

Schutz, W. C. (1958). *FIRO: A three-dimensional theory of interpersonal behavior.* Holt, Rinehart & Winston.

Scott, W. A. (1962). Cognitive complexity and cognitive flexibility. *Sociometry, 25*, 405–414.

Scott, W. A. (1963). Cognitive complexity and cognitive balance. *Sociometry, 26*, 66–74.

220 REFERENCES

Sears, P. S. (1951). Doll-play aggression in normal young children: Influences of sex, age, sibling status, father's absence. *Psychological Monographs: General and Applied*, *65*, 1–42.

Sears, R. R., Maccoby, E. E., & Levin, H. (1957). *Patterns of child rearing*. Harper & Row.

Sears, R. R., Pintler, M. H., & Sears, P. S. (1946). Effect of father separation on preschool children's doll play aggression. *Child Development*, *17*, 219–243.

Secord, P. F., & Backman, C. W. (1961). Personality theory and the problem of stability and change in individual behavior: An interpersonal approach. *Psychological Review*, *68*, 21–32.

Secord, P. F., & Backman, C. W. (1965). An interpersonal approach to personality. In B. A. Maher (Ed.), *Progress in experimental personality research* (vol. 2, pp. 91–125). Academic Press.

Seeman, M. (1959). On the meaning of alienation. *American Sociological Review*, *24*, 783–791.

Seligman, M. E. P. (1969). Control group and conditioning: A comment on operationism. *Psychological Review*, *76*, 484–491.

Sherif, M. (1935a). An experimental study of stereotypes. *Journal of Abnormal and Social Psychology*, *29*, 371–375.

Sherif, M. (1935b). A study of some social factors in perception. *Archives of Psychology (Columbia University)*, *187*, 60.

Shima, H. (1968). The relationship between the leader's modes of interpersonal cognition and the performance of the group. *Japanese Psychological Research*, *10*, 13–30.

Shuval, J. T. (1970). *Social functions of medical practice: Doctor–patient relationship in Israel*. Jossey-Bass.

Siegel, S. (1956). *Nonparametric statistics for the behavioral sciences*. McGraw-Hill.

Sigall, H., & Aronson, E. (1969). Liking for an evaluator as a function of her physical attractiveness and nature of the evaluation. *Journal of Experimental Social Psychology*, *5*, 93–100.

Skinner, B. F. (1953). *Science and human behavior*. Macmillan.

Slagle, J. R. (1971). *Artificial Intelligence: The heuristic programming approach*. McGraw-Hill.

Solomon, R. L., Turner, L. H., & Lessac, M. S. (1968). Some effects of delay of punishment on resistance to temptation in dogs. *Journal of Personality and Social Psychology*, *8* (3, Pt.1), 233–238.

Stafford, P. G., & Golightly, B. M. (1967). *LSD: The problem solving psychedelic*. Award Books.

Stagner, R., & Karwoski, T. F. (1952). *Psychology*. McGraw-Hill.

Staub, E., & Sherk, L. (1970). Need for approval, children's sharing behavior, and reciprocity in sharing. *Child Development*, *41*, 243–252.

Stock, D. (1949). An investigation into the intercorrelations between the self concept and feelings directed toward other persons and groups. *Journal of Consulting Psychology*, *13*, 176–180.

Stolurow, L. M. (1965). Idiographic programming. *NSPI Journal*, *4*, 10–12.

Stotland, E. (1959). Peer groups and reaction to power figures. In D. Cartwright (Ed.), *Studies in social power* (pp. 53–68). University of Michigan.

Strickberger, M. W. (1968). *Genetics*. Macmillan.

Sullivan, H. S. (1956). *Clinical studies in psychiatry*. Norton.

REFERENCES 221

Sutton-Smith, B., & Rosenberg, B. G. (1965). Age changes in the effects of ordinal position on sex-role identification. *Journal of Genetic Psychology, 107,* 61–73.

Tajfel, H. (1969). Social and cultural factors in perception. In G. Lindzey & E. Aronson (Eds.), *The handbook of social psychology* (2nd ed., vol. 3, pp. 315–394) Addison-Wesley.

Tanaka, Y. (1967). Cross-cultural comparability of the affective meaning systems. *Journal of Social Issues, 23,* 27–46.

Tasch, R. J. (1952). The role of the father in the family. *Journal of Experimental Education, 20,* 319–361.

Tasch, R. J. (1955). Interpersonal perceptions of fathers and mothers. *Journal of Genetic Psychology, 87,* 59–65.

Taylor, S. P. (1967). Aggressive behavior and physiological arousal as a function of provocation and the tendency to inhibit aggression. *Journal of Personality, 35,* 297–310.

Teichman, M. (1971a). Antithetical apperception of family members by neurotics. *Journal of Individual Psychology, 27,* 73–75.

Teichman, M. (1971b). Ego defense, self–concept and image of self ascribed to parents by delinquent boys. *Perceptual and Motor Skills, 32,* 819–823.

Teichman, M. (1971c). *Satisfaction from interpersonal relations following resource exchange.* Unpublished doctoral dissertation, University of Missouri, Columbia, Missouri,

Teichman, Y., Bazzoui, W., & Foa, U. G. Changes in self-perception following short-term psychiatric hospitalization. *Journal of Psychiatric Research, 10,* 231–238.

Thibaut, J. W., & Coules, J. (1952). The role of communication in the reduction of interpersonal hostility. *Journal of Abnormal and Social Psychology, 47,* 770–777.

Thibaut, J. W., & Kelley, H. H. (1959). *The social psychology of groups.* Wiley.

Tomkins, S. S. (1962). *Affect, imagery, consciousness: Vol. 1. The positive affects.* Springer.

Tomkins, S. S. (1965). Affect and the psychology of knowledge. In S. S. Tomkins & C. E. Izard (Eds.), *Affect, cognition, and personality: Empirical studies* (pp. 72–97). Springer.

Triandis, H. C. (1959). Cognitive similarity and interpersonal communication in industry. *J Appl Psychol, 43,* 321–326.

Triandis, H. C. (1960a). Cognitive similarity and communication in a dyad. *Human Relations, 13,* 175–183.

Triandis, H. C. (1960b). Some determinants of interpersonal communication. *Human Relations, 13,* 279–287.

Triandis, H. C. (1964). Exploratory factor analyses of the behavioral components of social attitudes. *Journal of Abnormal and Social Psychology, 68,* 420–430.

Triandis, H. C. (1967). Interpersonal relations in international organizations. *Journal of Organizational Behavior and Human Performance, 2,* 26–55.

Triandis, H. C. (1971). *Attitude and attitude change.* Wiley.

Triandis, H. C. (1972). *A broad theoretical framework on which we may be able to build.* Unpublished manuscript.

Triandis, H. C., & Vassiliou, V. (1972). A comparative analysis of subjective cultures. In H. C. Triandis, V. Vassiliou, G. Vassiliou, Y. Tanaka, & A. V. Shanmugam (Eds.), *The analysis of subjective culture* (pp. 299–335). Wiley-Interscience.

Triandis, H. C, Vassiliou, V., & Nassiakou, M. (1968). Three cross-cultural studies of subjective culture. *Journal of Personality and Social Psychology Monographs, 8* (4, pt. 2), 1–42.

222 REFERENCES

Tuckman, B. W. (1964). Personality structure, group composition, and group functioning. *Sociometry, 27,* 469–487.

Tuckman, B. W. (1967). Group composition and group performance of structured and unstructured tasks. *Journal of Experimental Social Psychology, 3,* 25–40.

Turner, J. L. (1971). *For love or money: Pattern of resource commutation in social interchange.* Unpublished master's thesis, University of Missouri–Columbia.

Turner, J. L., Foa, E. B., & Foa, U. G. (1971). Interpersonal reinforcers: Classification, inter-relationship, and some differential properties. *Journal of Personality and Social Psychology, 19,* 168–180.

Uzgiris, I. C., & Hunt, J. McV. (1972). *Toward ordinal scales of psychological development in infancy.* Unpublished manuscript.

Vannoy, J. S. (1965). Generality of cognitive complexity–simplicity as a personality construct. *Journal of Personality and Social Psychology, 2,* 285–296.

Varble, D. L., & Landfield, A. W. (1969). Validity of the self-ideal discrepancy as a criterion measure for success in psychotherapy—A replication. *Journal of Counseling Psychology, 16,* 150–156.

Vieru, T. (1969). Quelques considerations sur la notion de "structure" dans la psychotherapie. *Annales Médico-Psychologiques, 2,* 487–492.

Wallace, A. F. C. (1961). The psychic unity of human groups. In B. Kaplan (Ed.), *Studying personality cross-culturally* (pp. 129–163). Harper and Row.

Walster, E., Walster, B., Abrahams, D., & Brown, Z. (1966). The effect on liking of underrating or overrating another. *Journal of Experimental Social Psychology, 2,* 70–84.

Walters, R. H. (1964). On the high magnitude theory of aggression. *Child Development, 35,* 303–304.

Walters, R. H., & Thomas, E. L. (1963). Enhancement of punitiveness by visual and audio-visual displays. *Canadian Journal of Psychology, 17,* 244–255.

Wechsler, H., & Pugh, T. F. (1967). Fit of individual and community characteristics and rates of psychiatric hospitalization. *American Journal of Sociology, 73,* 331–338.

Weil, A. T., Zinberg, N. E., & Nelsen, J. M. (1968). Clinical and psychological effects of marihuana in man. *Science, 162,* 1234–1242.

Weinstein, E. A., Beckhouse, L. S., Blumstein, P. W., & Stein, R. B. (1968). Interpersonal strategies under conditions of gain and loss. *Journal of Personality, 36,* 616–634.

Weinstein, E. A.,DeVaughan, W. L., & Wiley, M. G. (1969). Obligation and the flow of deference in exchange. *Sociometry, 32,* 1–12.

White, R. (1959). Motivation reconsidered: the concept of competence. *Psychological Review, 66,* 297–333.

Whiting, J. W. M. (1964). Effects of climate on certain cultural practices. In W. H. Goodenough (Ed.), *Explorations in cultural anthropology* (pp. 511–544). McGraw-Hill.

Whiting, J. W. M., & Child, I. L. (1953). *Child training and personality.* Yale University Press.

Wickens, D. D. (1970). Encoding categories of words: An empirical approach to meaning. *Psychological Review, 77,* 1–15.

Wiggins, J. S. (1968). Personality structure. *Annual Review of Psychology, 19,* 293–350.

Winch, R. F. (1958). *Mate selection.* Harper.

Winch, R. F. (1967). Another look at the theory of complementary needs in mate-selection. *Journal of Marriage and Family, 29,* 756–762.

Wohlford, P., Santrock, J.W., Berger, S. E., & Liberman, D. (1971). Older brothers' influence on sex-typed, aggressive, and dependent behavior in father-absent children. *Developmental* Psychology, *4,* 124–134.

REFERENCES 223

Wolpe, J. (1958). *Psychotherapy by reciprocal inhibition*. Stanford University Press.

Wolpe, J. (1969). *The practice of behavior therapy*. Pergamon.

Worchel, P. (1957). Catharsis and the relief of hostility. *Journal of Abnormal and Social Psychology*, 55, 238–243.

Worchel, P. (1958). Personality factors in the readiness to express aggression. *Journal of Clinical Psychology*, 14, 355–359.

Worchel, P. (1961). Status restoration and the reduction of hostility. *Journal of Abnormal and Social Psychology*, 63, 443–445.

Worchel, S., & Mitchell, T. R. (1970). *An evaluation of the effectiveness of the culture assimilator in Thailand and Greece*. Technical Report 70-13, Department of Psychology, University of Washington, Seattle.

Wylie, R. C. (1961). *The self concept*. University of Nebraska Press.

Wynne, L. C., & Singer, M. T. (1963). Thought disorders and family relations of schizophrenics: II. A classification of forms of thinking. *Archives of General Psychiatry*, 9, 199–206.

Yates, A. J. (1962). *Frustration and conflict*. Wiley.

Young, P. T. (1936). *Motivation of behavior*. Wiley.

Zajonc, R. B. (1960). The concepts of balance, congruity and dissonance. *Public Opinion Quarterly*, 24, 280–296.

Zelditch, M., Jr. (1955). Role differentiation in the nuclear family: A comparative study. In T. Parsons & R. F. Bales (Eds.), *Family socialization and interaction process* (pp. 307–351). Free Press.

Zimbardo, P. G. (1969). The human choice: Individuation, reason, and order versus deindividuation, impulse, and chaos. *Nebraska Symposium on Motivation*, 17, 237–307.

Zimet, C. N., & Schneider, C. (1969). Effects of group size on interaction in small groups. *Journal of Social Psychology*, 77, 177–187.

PART II
NEW THEORETICAL AND EMPIRICAL DEVELOPMENTS

Précis

In Chapter 7, Kjell Törnblom and Ali Kazemi provide an overview of the central definitions and terminological distinctions within Foas' theoretical framework as well as related but slightly different definitions and terms that appear in the works of other scholars. They examine the adequacy of the Foas' resource typology and raise the question of whether dimensions suggested by other theorists might be theoretically fruitful alternatives or complements to concreteness/particularism. Because the Foas did not discuss the possibility that within-class differences may sometimes be larger than between-class differences, a categorization of those subclasses seems necessary for further theoretical development and interpretation of the results from empirical research. Next, Törnblom and Kazemi examine the validity of some of the 15 new exchange rules that the Foas had formulated, as it seemed somewhat unclear how they were derived. Additional issues concern the production and acquisition of resources, how the way a resource is produced or acquired may affect our attitudes toward the resource, and the ways in which this knowledge might affect exchange. Some resources can be produced and acquired in ways in which other resources cannot and may in different ways affect the process of resource exchange. The chapter is completed by short descriptions of some additional resource-related theories or models as well as various attempts at integration between social resource theory (SRT) and other theoretical frameworks. The principal aim of this chapter is to highlight some issues that we think deserve attention for future theoretical and empirical developments of SRT.

SRT has made important contributions to our understanding of the structure of interpersonal behavior and the process of resource exchange in social interaction since the seminal work by Foa and Foa was published in 1974. Its influence has extended to a variety of areas, from the study of social development to social cognition, organizational psychology, and cross-cultural psychology. An implicit theme underlying the original theory was that its basic constructs may be applied to different levels of conceptualizing social exchange—from the cognition of interpersonal events to the universal

Social Behavior as Resource Exchange. Kjell Yngve Törnblom and Ali Kazemi, Oxford University Press.
© Oxford University Press 2023. DOI: 10.1093/oso/9780190066994.003.0008

228 PART II NEW THEORETICAL AND EMPIRICAL DEVELOPMENTS

constructs of social behavior. In Chapter 8, John Adamopoulos attempts to formalize this multilevel perspective of the early work on SRT by delineating its implications for three distinct levels of operation. These levels differ in abstractness and include (abstract to specific) (a) the universal structure— the fundamental dimensions—of social behavior, (b) cultural patterns of interpersonal relations, and (c) cognitive processes involved in the construal of unique interpersonal events. The chapter includes examples of research influenced by SRT at each level. The most significant contribution of the original theory is arguably at the universal level, which focuses on the culture-common features of interpersonal relations, with an emphasis on the structure of the resources involved in social exchange. The cultural level has inspired work on the emergence of various types of cultural patterns of social relations and is conceptually connected to the study of individualism–collectivism and the relationship between economic resource availability and cultural values. Finally, at the interpersonal event level, the theory can contribute to the exploration of the perception of specific interpersonal interactions and can inform current theories of event cognition.

Whereas the Foas' main focus is on the analysis of social resource exchange on the micro level, Susan Opotow takes a broader view. In Chapter 9, she considers meso- and macro-level resource issues in environmental conflict as well as their just resolution. Her interesting analyses examine whether the Foas' six resource classes and the two dimensions they identify, concreteness and particularism, apply and contribute to our understanding of meso- and macro-level processes. Her chapter examines how resources and social justice connect when the Foas' resource exchange framework is applied to environmental issues. Thus, with the constructs, resource, conflict, and justice, in mind, and drawing on her extensive work on inclusionary and exclusionary exchange, Opotow considers the relevance of the Foas' six resource classes for environmental resources based on five studies that involved various kinds of environmental resource conflicts. Examining resources in these studies, Opotow concludes, first, because of the complexity of environmental resources, the six resource classes identified by the Foas in their research at the interpersonal level are applicable but are different than resources at meso- and macro-levels. Second, Opotow views the particularism and concreteness dimensions as somewhat relevant because environmental resources vary on these two dimensions. However, she observes that the Foas' resources are narrower than environmental resources, which are inevitably quite complex. She notes that pairing the Foas' adjacent resource classes yields three kinds of resource contexts—physical (e.g., goods and services), societal (e.g., information and money), and individual/psychological (e.g., status and caring)—and these three environmental contexts work well as a typology of environmental resources. Turning to the relationship between social justice and environmental resources, Opotow observes that exclusionary policies that curtail access to resources for individuals, groups, or regions do so by legitimizing unjust, even cruel treatment of those positioned as outside the scope of justice and therefore as nonmembers of one's moral community. Inclusionary policies, in contrast, promote cooperation, resource sharing, and social justice. Opotow illustrates how positive and negative valences of the Foas' six resource classes are consistent with inclusionary and exclusionary orientations and actions. She concludes her chapter illustrating the linkage among the physical, societal, and individual/psychological resources by focusing on a prominent and increasingly urgent worldwide societal and environmental issue—that is, housing precarity and climate change.

Scarcity is a condition in which human requirements for a resource exceed the availability of that resource. Because many theories, including SRT, stipulate that scarcity universally exists, they assume that scarcity motivates individuals to exchange resources to satisfy their needs and requirements. However, especially in modern societies, scarcity is neither universal nor is it necessarily problematic. Individuals can create scarcity or abolish it, thereby creating events of abundance or sufficiency. The dynamics of scarcity, abundance, and sufficiency calls for further theorizing on how these three events affect exchange behavior. In Chapter 10, Jonas Bååth and Adel Daoud first discuss the assumption of scarcity in SRT and its consequences. Second, they introduce the theory of scarcity, abundance and sufficiency (SAS) and discuss how it allows for a richer theory about human behavior. Third, through two concrete cases—the protestant ethic and food systems—the authors demonstrate the merits of their synthesis of SRT and SAS for understanding exchange behavior. By synthesizing SRT and SAS, this chapter contributes to SRT scholarship by (a) extending its theoretical foundation to include abundance and sufficiency and (b) clarifying the fundamental motivational mechanisms of all three SAS resource states for exchange behavior via mathematical formalization.

In Chapter 11, Elaine Hatfield, Richard L. Rapson, and Stephanie Cacioppo review the classic formulation of SRT. They then recount what is known about one of mankind's most discussed resources—passionate love. They present the most recent research by neuroscientists on the neurological

230   PART II NEW THEORETICAL AND EMPIRICAL DEVELOPMENTS

characteristics of this resource. They review data on the advantages and disadvantages, in this age of COVID-19, of computer matching for dates and mates. They discuss how social exchange and market conditions operate in the pairing up of couples who are similar/dissimilar in social desirability, leading to the consequences of equitable as opposed to inequitable exchanges. Fifty years ago, when social scientists began to focus attention on love, they encountered great resistance to research on the topic. They were criticized for studying the trivial, being nonscientific, etc. Since then, scholars in many countries have realized the significance of love in our lives and began to conduct research on this universal phenomenon. The authors review the work of Andreas Bartels, Samir Zeiki, and Helen Fisher, who study the joys and the dark side of love.

Their chapter reminds us about the necessity/desirability of recognizing (and categorizing) subtypes of the Foas' six resource classes. In this vein, Binning and Huo (2012) distinguished among four types of status. Furthermore, the close relationship between status and love raises interesting questions in relation to the neuroscience context. Are differentiations of subtypes of the other resource classes also significant from a neuroscientific perspective? Hatfield, Rapson, and Cacioppo suggest that maternal and paternal love are different (and can perhaps be viewed as subtypes of love). Thus, not only are different "substantive" kinds/subtypes of love different (romantic, compassionate, companionate, etc.) but also so are different "kinds" as distinguished by the sentient person, the person who "harbors" or feels love, a crisscross combination that results in several types. Hatfield, Rapson, and Cacioppo conclude their chapter by proposing some important questions worth exploring in future research.

Finally, in Chapter 12, Sabbagh and Schmitt provide an overview of the traditional research methods (e.g., design and types of data analyses) applied to examine and validate Foas' SRT. In this regard, they elaborate on a comparative perspective of the strengths and shortcomings of two main traditional methods: smallest space analysis (SSA), the original multidimensional scaling method from which SRT stemmed, and factor analysis (FA). They further focus on SRT in a classroom setting as an applied illustration in which they formally test and validate SRT using SSA and FA. Finally, they discuss the potential use of other multivariate (untraditional) methods for exploring new research questions and hypotheses derived from SRT, hence expanding its scope and providing further possible validation of the theory.

References

Binning, K. R., & Huo, Y. J. (2012). Understanding status as a social resource. In K. Y. Törnblom & A. Kazemi (Eds.), *Handbook of social resource theory: Theoretical extensions, empirical insights, and social applications* (pp. 133–147). Springer.

7

Recent Theoretical Advances in Social Resource Theory

Kjell Yngve Törnblom and Ali Kazemi

Introduction

Social resource theory (SRT) addresses a core focus of psychology and social psychology, namely the study of human relationships (at interpersonal, intergroup, societal, as well as cultural levels).[1] Like theories of social exchange, which provide the major foundation of SRT, it is a theory about processes involving the initiation, maintenance, and termination of different kinds of social relationships. SRT addresses several issues: the cognitive organization of interpersonal resources, the cognitive mechanisms that underlie resource exchange, their development in childhood, cross-cultural differences, and the pathology of exchange. What people in their daily lives provide and receive, withhold and are deprived of, with regard to positive and negative resources of various kinds [e.g., love, hostility, money, respect, humiliation, information, lies, services, material goods, and jobs] have important consequences for their health, happiness, status, and motivation.

Social Resources: Definitions and Terminological Distinctions

A "*social resource*" refers to "any commodity—material or symbolic—which is transmitted through interpersonal behavior" (Foa & Foa, 1974,

---

[1] This chapter is an abridged and revised version of Törnblom, K., & Kazemi, A. (2012). Some conceptual and theoretical issues in resource theory of social exchange. In K. Törnblom & A. Kazemi (Eds.), *Handbook of social resource theory: Theoretical extensions, empirical insights, and social applications* (pp. 33–64). Springer. Permission granted by the publisher (CCC License #5266071033543).

Social Behavior as Resource Exchange. Kjell Yngve Törnblom and Ali Kazemi, Oxford University Press.
© Oxford University Press 2023. DOI: 10.1093/oso/9780190066994.003.0009

RECENT THEORETICAL ADVANCES IN SOCIAL RESOURCE THEORY   233

p. 36), "anything that can be transmitted from one person to another" (Foa & Foa, 1976, p. 101), "anything transacted in an interpersonal situation" or "any item, concrete or symbolic, which can become the object of exchange among people" (Foa & Foa, 1980, p. 78). A *"social resource class,"* on the other hand, is a category of "the meaning assigned to actions and not a classification of actions" (Foa & Foa, 1974, p. 82). Thus, the social resource class designated as "love," for example, encompasses a wide range of actions (e.g., kissing, hugging, verbal affective statements, gestures), all of which may *mean* the same, thus conveying a message of love. Conversely, a particular action may have several different meanings. A kiss may be provided as a sign of love or as a sign marking a death sentence. Thus, by viewing resource classes in terms of the meanings assigned to actions (or stimuli) we easily realize that "(a) different stimuli may have the same meaning; (b) the same stimulus may have different meanings; (c) response depends on the meaning ascribed to the stimulus" (Foa & Foa, 1974, p. 16–17). It is common knowledge, by now, that assignment of meaning is affected by the social and cultural context, the interpersonal relationship, the content of the interaction, the actors' values and attitudes, their emotional state, intentions and goals, the valence of the transacted resource, etc.

Most interpersonal and intergroup behavior include and may be interpreted and partly understood in terms of the particular material and non-material, particularistic and universalistic classes of social resources that Foa (1971) and Foa and Foa (1974, 1980) distinguished and systematically related to one another. Indeed, social resources have assumed a central place in many scholars' research. However, several of them have provided definitions of resource that are slightly different than Foas' (see Box 7.1). Most definitions seem to encompass Foas' resources but are more general than Foas' definition of resource. They have also suggested different *designations* (names) for the same type of resource; for instance, Caplan's (1974) *social support* corresponds to Foas' *status*. And Sabbagh and Malka (2012) concluded that the five types of resources used in a study by Randall and Mueller (1995) were identical or very similar to those in Foas' typology, but that they used other terms (e.g., opportunity for self-actualization rather than information, and opportunity for altruism rather than services). Finally, the same resource type is sometimes assigned to different categories; for instance, knowledge/information is an *energy resource* for Doane et al. (2012) and a *social resource* for Foa.

Box 7.1 Definitions of Resource

Foa and Foa's Definitions

"Any commodity—material or symbolic—which is transmitted through interpersonal behavior" (Foa & Foa, 1974, p. 36)

"Anything that can be transmitted from one person to another" (Foa & Foa, 1976, p. 101)

"Anything transacted in an interpersonal situation" (Foa & Foa, 1980, p. 78)

"Any item, concrete or symbolic, which can become the object of exchange among people" (Foa & Foa, 1980, p. 78)

Examples of Definitions Suggested by Other Theorists

"An ability, possession, or other attribute of an actor giving him the capacity to reward (or punish) another specified actor" (Emerson, 1976, p. 347)

"Those objects, personal characteristics, conditions, or energies that are valued by the individual or that serve as a means for attainment of these objects, personal characteristics, conditions, or energies" (Hobfoll, 1989, p. 516)

"Those entities that either are centrally valued in their own right (e.g., self-esteem, close attachments, health, and inner peace) or act as a means to obtain centrally valued ends (e.g., money, social support, and credit)" (Hobfoll, 2002, p. 307)

"Those objects, personal characteristics, conditions, or energies that are valued in their own right or are valued because they act as conduits to the achievement or protection of valued resources" (Diener & Fujita, 1995, p. 927)

"Any property of an individual which he makes available to persons in his environment as a means for their positive or negative need-satisfaction" (Levinger, 1959, p. 84)

"Any positively perceived physical, economic or social consequence" (Miller & Steinberg, 1975, p. 65)

"Possessions or behavioral capabilities that are valued by other actors" (i.e., they are resources in the context of that possessor's relations with other actors) (Molm, 2006, p. 26)

"Commodity is defined to mean anything which has usefulness to the possessor and which can be conveyed from person to person" (Brock, 1968, p. 246)

"Anything that functions to sustain persons and a system of interaction whether or not they are valued, scarce, consumable, possessable, negotiable, leverageable, tangible, or even cognizable" (Freese & Burke 1994, p. 9)

It is not unusual that the inadequately designated and rather unspecific term "resource" is used by researchers, leaving it up to the reader to figure out what kinds of resources are at stake (i.e., under what category they may be subsumed), how the results of different empirical studies may be compared, and to what extent different resource models and theories may be integrated. Thus, attempts to relate existing research to Foas' framework are well advised to make sure they are on the same page, not only concerning how resource is defined but also with regard to what category or class of resource that is investigated.

There are other ways of partitioning and designating resources (see Box 7.2). Nuckolls et al. (1972) and Harber et al. (2008) dealt with psychosocial resources (e.g., interpersonal assets such as social networks and support; intra-personal attributes like self-worth, personal control and optimism; belief systems that are conducive to a sense of meaning, order and fairness; and transitory affective states such as positive mood and feelings of wellbeing; see also Kazemi (2017) for social resources in occupational wellbeing). Caplan (1974) included both psychological and social resources in his research ("sense of mastery" and "social support," respectively); Gerson (1976) proposed a definition of "quality of life" in terms of a minimum of four "resource classes and constraints": money, time, skill and sentiment. Hobfoll

---

Box 7.2 Different Types of Resource Designations

- *social* resources (Foa, 1971)
- *psychosocial* resources (Nuckolls et al., 1972; Harber et al., 2008)
- *psychological* and *social* resources (Caplan, 1974)
- *quality of life* resources (Gerson, 1976)
- *status, material, social,* and *personal* resources (Hobfoll, 2002)
- *object, condition, personal,* and *energy* resources (Doane et al., Chapter 19 in Törnblom & Kazemi, 2012)
- *economic* and *social* resources. Social resources (rewards) are of two kinds: *process social resources* and *content social resources* (Buss, 1983)
- *personal* and *social* resources. Social resources are of two kinds: *network resources* and *contact resources* (Lin, 2001)
- *personal, interpersonal* and *structural* resources (Stets & Cast, 2007)
- *valued* resources (Stets & Cast, 2007)

236 PART II NEW THEORETICAL AND EMPIRICAL DEVELOPMENTS

(2002) mentions status, material, social, and personal resources, and he also makes a distinction among "object resources (those tangible resources necessary for survival or culturally highly valued; e.g., car, house), condition resources (those that directly or indirectly support survival; e.g., employment, marriage), personal resources (traits or skills central to survival or resilience; e.g., key skills and personal traits such as self-efficacy and self-esteem), and energy resources (those which can be used in exchange for other resources; e.g., credit, knowledge, money)" (see Doane et al., 2012, p. 302). Buss (1983) made a distinction between economic and social resources (or rewards, to use his term). Social resources are of two kinds: process resources (presence of others, attention from others, reciprocity, initiation—and their negative counterparts isolation, shunning, boredom, no interaction) and content resources (deference, praise, sympathy, affection—and their negative counterparts disrespect, criticism, contempt, hostility). Lin (2001) groups resources into two major types, personal and social. Personal resources are those that belong to an individual (including "such ascribed and achieved characteristics as gender, race, age, religion, education, occupation, and income as well as familial resources"). Social resources are of two kinds: network resources ("resources embedded in one's ongoing social networks and ties") and contact resources ("resources associated specifically with a tie or ties accessed and mobilized in a particular action"). Stets and Cast (2007) distinguished between personal, interpersonal and structural resources. Personal resources are those motivational processes within the self that lead one to act in ways that are efficacious and that either maintain or enhance the self (Gecas, 1991); interpersonal resources are those processes that validate and support the self, the other, and the interaction; structural resources are those conditions that afford individuals greater influence and power in society. They also discussed what they termed "valued resources," i.e., "those material and non-material processes that are important, given the culture, in maintaining and improving social actors' existence, for example, wealth, status, power, and esteem" (Stets & Cast, 2007).

For the sake of conceptual clarity, consider the following distinctions (see Box 7.3): *Resource designation* (e.g., social as in SRT, psychosocial, material, condition, energy), *Resource classification criterion* or dimension (e.g., particularistic vs. universalistic and abstract vs. concrete as in SRT, managerial vs. non-managerial, personality-based vs. social, dividable, fungible, valence, internal–external), *Resource class* (e.g., love–information–goods–status–money–services as in SRT, self-efficacy, self-esteem, optimism, resilience),

Box 7.3 Terminological Distinctions

Resource designation (e.g., social as in SRT, psychosocial, material, condition, energy)

Resource classification criterion or *dimension* (e.g., particularistic vs. universalistic and abstract vs. concrete; personality-based vs. social, dividable, fungible, internal-external)

Resource class (e.g., love–information–goods–status–money–services as in SRT, self-efficacy, self-esteem, optimism, resilience)

Empirical/concrete instance, or *resource subtype*, of each particular resource class (e.g., knife, plate, hat, book, boat, and wallet are all instances of the resource class *goods*)

Resource subclass (i.e., categorizations of the subtypes of each particular resource class)

Resource subclass (i.e., categorizations of the concrete instances of each particular resource class), and *Empirical/concrete instance*, or *resource subtype*, of each particular resource class (e.g., knife, plate, hat, computer, book, boat, and wallet are all instances of the resource class *goods*).

Further, and depending on the definition of terms, levels may "overlap." "Social," for example, may simultaneously signify a designation and a classification criterion: Resources *designated* as "social" (within SRT) may encompass both "personality-based" and "social" resource *categories*. For instance, although "*love*" is an example of what within SRT is *designated* as a "social" resource, it may also be further *categorized* as a personality-based (as opposed to a *social*) type of social resource.

Resource Configurations

Partly due to the different properties of different types of social resources, the possession or lack of these may have different consequences, affecting people's life conditions and life courses differently. To merely state that resource loss increases our vulnerability to negative stress or diminishes our quality of life does not make us much wiser. Predictions of more specific consequences from resource deprivation require specific information

238   PART II NEW THEORETICAL AND EMPIRICAL DEVELOPMENTS

about which particular resource(s) is (are) missing (objectively and/or subjectively). For example, would not being deprived of love and affection result in a different type of emotional and social predicament than would a loss of money? Would a rich but lonely person be happier than a poor but well-loved person? And which one of the following two persons "quality of life" is highest (all other conditions equal): (a) John has plenty of money, owns a luxurious home, has many business acquaintances, regrets missing out on higher education, but is not well respected in his neighborhood, while (b) Eric's financial situation is rather poor, he rents a small run-down apartment, enjoys several deep friendships, has an MA degree, and is well respected in his neighborhood? Although the latter question is considerably more complicated than the first two, the information provided by its analysis is likely to be more specific and useful. Thus, a full understanding of, say, an elderly or underprivileged person's life situation requires (among other things) a description and analysis in terms of the whole spectrum of social resources (not just money or services, which is commonly the case). More detailed information, making explicit the patterns or configurations of resource possession and resource loss, would facilitate the planning of adequate social welfare programs focusing on health, quality of life, etc. (see Kazemi & Kajonius, 2021 for a categorization of care behaviors based on SRT and how different care resources relate to satisfaction with care).

Some relatively common issues that arise in the context of empirical and theoretical research based on Foa and Foa's theory concern the adequacy of their classification system or resource typology,[2] to what extent it satisfies the four criteria of (i) parsimony, (ii) testable hypotheses generation, (iii) mutual exclusiveness, and (iv) exhaustiveness (which is partly dependent on the appropriateness of the dimensions along which the six resource classes are differentiated). We discuss these criteria in the following section. Another issue that will be discussed later in this chapter concerns the problem of how to conceptualize and categorize into *subclasses* the myriad of concrete instances that may represent each resource class.

---

[2] We use the terms typology and classification system interchangeably in this chapter. However, see Doty and Glick (1994) for distinctions among the terms classification system, typology, and taxonomy, the frequent confusion among which "has helped to conceal important differences among these tools" (p. 232). They also argue that typologies meet the criteria of a theory.

Foa and Foa's Social Resource Typology

Based on the realization that different types of resources appear to follow different rules of exchange (particularly when comparing economic to noneconomic or social resources), Foas' ambition was to develop a conceptual framework, a resource classification system, that would allow the construction of a more adequate social exchange theory than existing ones based on economic models. (See Sabbagh & Levy's 2012 vivid historical account of the development of Foas' framework.) The validity and usefulness of this new exchange theory is primarily contingent on the adequacy of the typology of resources on the basis of which new insights about interpersonal exchange were generated.

We examine below some important aspects of Foas' resource typology, viz., the extent to which it is exhaustive, whether or not its resource categories are mutually exclusive, whether other dimensions than those on which the classification is based (i.e., particularism and abstractness) might be more fruitful, how the huge variety of possible concrete instances representing each of the six resource classes might be accounted for and accommodated in the typology as well as categorized into subclasses. One may also ask whether the new exchange rules and the circular order among the six resource classes might be affected by the particular concrete instances chosen to represent each resource class.

Does Foa and Foa's Resource Typology Satisfy the Four Criteria?

By assuming that the same exchange rules can be applied to all exchanges, most hitherto existing models of social exchange did not need to pay particular attention to what is exchanged. The qualitative differences among different resources (objects of exchange) were frequently overlooked—only their quantity was deemed theoretically important. Foa recognized the significance of conceptualizing and differentiating among qualitatively different resource transactions and saw the need for a systematic theory that extended beyond the purely economic domain. To enable predictions about "which resources share more similar rules and to anticipate conditions under which certain resources will be valued and exchanged and what exchanges will not take place," he based his classification "on those resource attributes

240 PART II NEW THEORETICAL AND EMPIRICAL DEVELOPMENTS

which account for behavioral variance so that similarity of attributes correspond to similarity of behavior" (Foa, 1971, p. 346). Because interpersonal
behavior varies from concrete (e.g., providing food) to abstract (e.g., saying
"I love you"), and because the value of different resources varies with the significance of the providing person, it was possible to plot six different types of
resources in a circular order on the two coordinates of concreteness and particularism.[3] Foa offered three predictions based on the structural ordering
of the six resource classes: ". . . resources proximal in the order will (i) be
perceived as more similar, (ii) be more substitutable for one another, and (iii)
elicit similar resources in social exchange" (Foa, 1971, p.347).

A well-constructed and useful typology (taxonomy, classification system)
should satisfy at least four criteria:[4] (i) *parsimony*, (ii) generation of *testable
hypotheses*, (iii) mutual *exclusiveness*, and (iv) *exhaustiveness*. To what extent does Foas' typology meet these criteria? Well aware that there are several
ways in which resources may be classified, Foa and Foa (1976) justified their
typology on the bases of its *parsimony* in providing explanations of interpersonal behavior and its *ability to generate testable hypotheses*.

(i) *Parsimony*, in the context of theory evaluation, refers to explanation and prediction of events via the smallest number of terms and
propositions. In Foa and Foa's case, parsimony was accomplished by
using only two dimensions (one ranging from concrete to abstract and
the other from particularistic to universalistic) along which the six resources were classified. The resulting circular arrangement of resources
provided a framework for understanding interpersonal relationships,
their initiation, maintenance, and termination. As already mentioned,

---

[3] "Concreteness ranges from concrete to symbolic [abstract] and suggests the form of expression
characteristic of each resource class" (Foa & Foa, 1974, p. 91). "Particularism indicates the extent to
which the value of a given resource is influenced by the particular persons involved in its exchange"
(Foa & Foa, 1974, p. 91).

[4] Markovsky (1996) proposed that theory evaluation should be based on eight criteria: absence of
contradictions, absence of ambivalence, communicability, generality, abstractness, precision, parsimony, and conditionalization. As opposed to Doty and Glick (1994), for example, who argue that
typologies meet the criteria of a theory, Markovsky (2011, p. 647) requires stricter conditions on
which to base the definition of theory: "a set of general, parsimonious, logically related statements
containing clearly defined terms, formulated to explain accurately and precisely the broadest possible range of phenomena in the natural world." A formalization and analysis of Foa and Foa's resource theory (see Markovsky & Kazemi, 2012) revealed several shortcomings that make it difficult
to let it pass as a full-fledged theory (rather than a framework, typology, model, and the like). It is
likely that the same conclusion may be reached re: the other so-called resource theories mentioned
here, some of which stop short of elaborations beyond the level of a limited number of (often inadequately connected) propositions.

this framework allowed SRT to focalize several specific issues, notably the cognitive organization of interpersonal resources, the cognitive mechanisms that underlie resource exchange, their development in childhood, cross-cultural differences, and the pathology of exchange.

(ii) *Generation of testable hypotheses.* The typology should facilitate the generation of theory that includes *testable hypotheses.* The richness of propositions and hypotheses generated by SRT is impressive. This is evident in the Foa and Foa's research as well as in the work of numerous other scholars, several of whom are represented in this volume. A description of this research would require more space than available for this chapter. Overviews are provided in several of the Foas' publications (e.g., Foa & Foa, 1974, 1976, 1980). More recent theoretical and empirical developments of SRT are featured in a volume edited by Foa et al. (1993) as well as in the present volume. Also, a complete bibliography of Uriel Foa's publications is published in the 1993 volume.

(iii) *Mutual exclusiveness.* Does Foa and Foa's resource classification meet the criterion of mutual exclusiveness? The categories of a classification system are mutually exclusive if no concrete instance can be classified in terms of more than one resource category. However, if a box of chocolate presented as a gift may be sorted into more than one resource class, i.e., goods and love, or if a particular behavior, say, sexual intercourse, may simultaneously convey different meanings (e.g., be interpreted as a manifestation of love, the provision/reception of a service and, perhaps, the conferring/granting of status), then resources are not mutually exclusive.

The potential problem posed by the myriad of concrete instances of each resource class for the structural order among the six classes had already been recognized by the Foas:

> In general it appears that *for each resource class some specific forms are more similar to one neighbor while other forms are nearer to the second neighbor [italics added].* These similarities are responsible for the permeability of the boundaries among resource classes, and for the structural relationship among them. *However, one might question the usefulness or the accuracy of the proposed classification if the boundaries are so permeable [italics added].* The answer is an empirical one: as long as events of the same class tend to be more similar one to the other, than

242 PART II NEW THEORETICAL AND EMPIRICAL DEVELOPMENTS

to events of different classes, it will still be possible to obtain empirical evidence for the order. (1974, p. 83)

The extent to which Foas' resource classification meets the criterion of mutual exclusiveness has been assessed by a number of empirical research studies. In some of those studies subjects sorted items describing various acts involving resource transactions into six piles representing the six resource classes (e.g., Foa et al., 1982; Foa et al., 1987; Turner et al., 1971). Items representing giving and taking for the six resource types that have been included in instruments used in various studies can be found in Appendices C-E in Part I of this book.

(iv) *Exhaustiveness.* It is difficult to judge the extent to which exhaustiveness (completeness) has been reached. A typology is maximally exhaustive if its constituent categories can account for all possible empirical instances. Thus, in Foas' case, all empirical instances of social resources should be classifiable in terms of their typology's six resource classes. It seems that Foa and Foa were unclear about how they arrived at the six resource classes. Although they offer a convincing account within a coherent framework of how these classes are sequentially differentiated as the child develops and learns to distinguish between self and others, and between giving/receiving and taking away, it seems possible to think of additional resources that are missing or not classifiable in Foas' system.

Blau (1964), for example, discusses six types of resources (rewards): compliance (power), respect, personal attraction, social acceptance, social approval, and instrumental services. Compliance, respect, acceptance, approval, and attraction are all different types of status (as defined by Foa and Foa), and the remaining resource, service, is included in Foas' typology as well. Gerson (1976) suggested that *time* is one of four important classes of resources (the others are money, skill, and sentiment) in the analysis of quality of life, and for Heirich (1964) time is a resource in its own right with various social meanings and significant implications for the study of social change.

When students are asked to come up with additional resources they, too, frequently mention time. It is certainly possible to receive or devote/give time to a person. However, Foa and Foa (1976) maintain that time is a *prerequisite* for resource transaction (but not a resource, per se); resources vary in the amount of time required for their provision or deprivation. For instance, less time is required to hand over money to a person as compared to repairing her car.

However, even though time may be conceived as a prerequisite, in that different resources require different amounts of time for their transaction, it seems possible to think of time as a resource in its own right. For example, a superordinate may grant a subordinate extra time to complete a task, or a parent may allow a child to stay up a bit later than usual. These two examples do not necessarily have to be interpreted as events where the provision of time represents or is equivalent with status (i.e., esteem, respect, and the like, or their negative counterparts) or love. The notion of an individual "time budget" certainly appears to allow a view of time as a bona fide resource. It is at least theoretically possible to provide time and status simultaneously as well as independently, un-confounded of one another. Time is, in the view of Heirich (1964), valuable in its own right as a resource (as indicated by the sayings "Time is money," time can be spent, used well or wasted, and we can "buy time"). Thus, time is a fixed-sum scarce resource that cannot be regained once spent. Further, time is differently valued cross-culturally: "the value of time as a resource varies according to the relative emphasis placed on Being and Becoming" (Heirich, 1964, p. 387). Regardless of how time is evaluated, "it will be allocated for a variety of purposes" (Heirich, 1964, p. 387) and, if *less* time is spent on an activity, "other activities will have *gained* in relative importance" (p. 387). Time can be transmitted from one person to another, and it can become an object of exchange. Thus, it seems that time qualifies as a resource according to Foa and Foa's definition and should therefore perhaps be considered a seventh resource along with the original six in the typology.

Interestingly, and recalling that a social resource class is a category of the *meaning* assigned to actions, the meaning of giving/receiving/stealing/loosing time may vary. In Heirich's (1964, p. 387) words, "specific moments of time acquire a social meaning of their own" (e.g., time *sequence* may indicate priority—"homework before computer games"—as well as social distance—"important persons always arrive later than others" or "rank and file soldiers eat when their officers are done"). Finally, time may be interpreted on the basis of its quantity, quality, duration, speed, intensity, etc.

Buss (1983) discussed a different kind of social resource that he termed *process rewards*. These "occur naturally as people interact, and such rewards are simply part of the process of such interaction" (p. 556), "these rewards are an intrinsic part of social contact" (p. 554). There are four types of process rewards (and each one can be negatively valent as well): presence of others (isolation), attention from others (shunning), responsivity (boredom), and initiation (no interaction)—as listed in the order of increasing activity on the

244 PART II NEW THEORETICAL AND EMPIRICAL DEVELOPMENTS

part of the provider. The reinforcing part of each resource is in the middle, as too little or too much of any one of the four may be aversive (but not always). These rewards don't seem to be covered by Foas' typology, unless they are intentionally provided to meet the needs or desires of the recipient, in which case they would be classified as instances of status.

But can (and, if so, how can) *clean water*, *clean air*, and *energy*, for example, be classified in Foas' system? They are increasingly scarce items that are likely to become (or already are, at least to some extent) expropriated and used as objects of selective distribution and exchange. Water (like food) would most likely be classified as goods by Foa and Foa, while an individual's energy reserves might presumably be conceived as a function of the nature, quality, and quantity of the various resources the person possesses. The classification of some other types of energy resources (e.g., electric, nuclear, water, wind) appears to be more problematic. Additional examples of resources that can be transacted and that appear to be missing in Foas' typology are social influence (e.g., authority and power) and sex. However, social influence may (like a person's energy level) best be understood as a function of the amount and type of resources a person possesses,[5] resources that may be used strategically to attain more of the same resource or other types of resources which, in turn, may further increase his/her influence (see Lenski, 1966, for a similar standpoint). Social influence (e.g., power) may also be conceived in terms of resource liquidity or exchangeability. Money can be exchanged for a greater number of different kinds of resources as compared to love or information. Thus, a rich person has more exchange options, and thereby more influence, in social exchanges than does somebody who can only offer love. For Foa and Foa, *sex* is a concrete physical form of love (proximal to service in the resource circle) as compared to affection and "romantic love" which represent the abstract form of love (more proximal to status than to service).

As a resource class refers to the *meaning* assigned to an act (behavioral, verbal, written, mimicked, etc.), what might be viewed as another type of "higher-order" resource are items (acts, resources) that may be understood as combinations or composites of two or more resource classes. A "groupie" may understand the act of a passionate kiss from an idolized rock star as expressing his love to her as well as a status conferring act (i.e., the

---

[5] Foa and Foa (1974) defined power as "the amount of a given resource that is available to an individual for eventual giving" (p. 135), thus generating six types of power, one for each resource class.

well-known phenomenon of "status by association"). Similarly, a bouquet of flowers may by its recipient be valued both as good and as a symbol of love.

If two (or more) different resources may be provided via the same act (what might be called a "composite-" or "higher-order" resource), the mutual exclusiveness of Foas' resource typology would have to be questioned. In addition, the problem of dealing with a huge number of composite types would arise. Even if additional terms designating those new resource types would be coined, a practically limitless proliferation of instances of resource combinations would open up, setting the stage for ambiguities and arbitrariness similar to what happened in the days, now long past, when an endless number of instincts were named, robbing the concept of theoretical and practical value. We may also recall some typologies of emotion, consisting of primary emotions combining to produce higher-level complex secondary and tertiary emotions (e.g., MacDougall, 1908).

Are Other/Additional Dimensions than Particularism and Concreteness Desirable?

A cautionary note regarding the concreteness–symbolism dimension seems in order. There is a potential terminological confusion among the concepts of "symbolic," "abstract," and "intangible" as they are used in various writings. The words symbolic and abstract may have more than one meaning, and it seems that Foas' choice of "symbolic" rather than "abstract" may create some confusion. (1) According to Foa and Foa (1974, p. 81, 1976, p. 102, 1980, p. 79) status and information are *symbolic* resources, while love and money can be both symbolic and concrete. In the case of love, saying "I love you" is symbolic, while sex is concrete behavior; in the case of money, stock is symbolic, but coins are concrete. Goods and services are concrete—thus nonsymbolic—resources. However, it seems to us that all six resources may have symbolic value; the provision of each may, for example, symbolize (convey to the recipient) the provider's affection. (2) Similarly, status and information are *abstract* resources, while love and money can be both abstract and concrete. In the case of love, saying "I love you" is abstract, while sex is concrete behavior; in the case of money, stock is abstract, but coins are concrete. Goods and services are concrete resources. Thus, while all six resources may be *symbolic*, only status and information as well as some forms of love and money are *abstract*.

246 PART II NEW THEORETICAL AND EMPIRICAL DEVELOPMENTS

Could it be that Foa and Foa used the term symbolic rather than abstract by mistake? Would Foas' intentions, then, be better represented by an abstract–concrete rather than a symbolic–concrete dimension? Unfortunately, however, the term abstract may create more confusion than clarity (which might be the reason that Foa avoided that term) due to its various meanings, e.g., having conceptual rather than concrete existence, ideal, theoretical, transcendent, and indemonstrable (*The Merriam-Webster Thesaurus*, 1989). Symbolic, on the other hand, is a less ambiguous term meaning "representative of" or "representing," as when a book provided as a gift is meant to symbolize or represent love and affection for the recipient (although, as noted, that term is unable to distinguish among the six resources, as all of them may be symbolic). Perhaps Foas' intentions are better represented by an *intangible-tangible* rather than an abstract–concrete dimension? (3) Status and information are *intangible* resources, whereas love and money can be both *tangible* and *intangible* resources. Goods and services are *tangible* resources.

Do the two dimensions (particularism and concreteness) exclude the recognition and inclusion of hitherto neglected resources; would alternative dimensions facilitate the discovery of additional resource types or yield significant theoretical insights? Foa and Foa were well aware that there are many other possible ways in which resources may be classified. And other theorists, as well, have discussed this issue and proposed alternative and/or additional dimensions. Stangl (1989), for example, found in his study with Austrian participants that Foas' two-dimensional structure as verified in American studies must be complemented by an *evaluative* dimension. In a similar vein, Sabbagh and Levy (2012) state that resource exchange is not only governed by the two dimensions proposed by Foa and Foa. They mention "capacity for convertibility" as another organizing dimension suggesting that resources can be ordered from the easily converted resources (e.g., money)—being located in the more peripheral bands of a concentric resource circle—to the least convertible resource (i.e., love) located in the inner bands of the circle. Blalock (1991, p. 28–41) identified a number of resource properties that he thought should be taken into account when formulating a theory of allocation processes. Some of these appear to allow alternative arrangements regarding how resources are related to one another: divisibility, re-tractability, generalized value, depletion and replenishment, the degree to which they are subject to devaluation, the degree to which recipients share future power with allocators, and valence. In their comprehensive paper on nature of status and how it compares with six cognate concepts, Bothner et al. (2010) argue that status and quality (i.e., the skills an employee brings to a job) differ in their *stickiness*, i.e., the speed by which they fluctuate. Unlike quality, status sticks longer to a person as it is a function of opinions and affiliations, both of which evolve slowly. It seems that stickiness is a dimension on which the remaining five Foa resources may be characterized as well, i.e., love, information, services, goods, and money.

The ideal, addressed elegantly by Foa and Foa for the classification of the six resource classes, is to find dimensions along which all subtypes (i.e., all items representing all resource classes) may be sorted. If that turns out to be unlikely or outright impossible, it is desirable to find dimensions on which to base a classification of the items *within each* separate resource class, even though those classifications will be unique for each class.

May Each of the Foas' Six Resource Classes be Subdivided into Subclasses?

Whether or not categorizations of resource subtypes into resource subclasses are theoretically interesting or fruitful, it is evident that each one of the Foas' six (main) resource classes can be operationalized in several ways (i.e., exemplified by a large number of concrete instances, resource subtypes). The literature is rich with examples of different kinds of resources, each of which would fit into one of Foas' six resource classes. To be theoretically manageable this large variety of concrete instances of each resource should preferably be sorted into subclasses on the basis of some meaningful criteria.

The variety of empirical research studies using resources as independent or dependent variables reveal various ways in which the Foas' resource classes have been operationalized (see Foa & Foa, 1974; Foa et al., 1993, for overviews of the first two decades of this line of research effort; regarding more recent research see, for example, Chiaburu et al., 2012; Dorsch & Brooks, 2012; Sabbagh & Malka, 2012). This research hints at the fact that (a) each resource class encompasses a nearly endless number of different items, i.e., concrete instances (operationalizations into acts, facial expressions, verbal statements, utterances, etc.). In addition, (b) one particular item may have a *meaning* that is classifiable in terms of several resource classes (e.g., a pat on a person's back may be interpreted as a sign of friendship, hostility, encouragement, giving status, or a piece of information). Thus, for example, just like the resource class of goods encompasses a huge number of items, so may the

248 PART II NEW THEORETICAL AND EMPIRICAL DEVELOPMENTS

concrete item bouquet of flowers be not merely a good but also a sign of love or status—or even convey some information.

It appears likely that *intra-class differences* (i.e., differences between the various items of a particular resource class) may be as large, or larger, than *inter-class differences*. A bicycle and a bouquet of flowers (i.e., two instances of the same resource class goods), for example, seem more dissimilar than sexual intercourse and a massage (i.e., two instances of *different* resource classes—love and services, respectively). As Foas' framework includes no provisions for the possibility that within-resource-class differences between specific resource items might be larger than between-resource-class differences, it would be useful to find criteria on the basis of which intra- or within-category resource classifications may be constructed. This, in turn, would most likely yield more precise predictions.

Hatfield, Rapson and Cacioppo's chapter on love (in this book) and Binning and Huo's (2012) discussion of status alert us about the desirability of recognizing (and categorizing) subtypes of Foas' six resource classes. Hatfield et al. distinguish between maternal and paternal love. Thus, not only are different "substantive" kinds/subtypes of love different (e.g., romantic, compassionate, companionate, etc.), but so are different "kinds" as distinguished on the basis of the sentient person, the person who "harbors" or feels love. Combining these two different distinctions/classifications generates several additional (sub)types of love. Furthermore, the close relationship between status and love raises interesting questions in relation to the neuroscience context. Are differentiations of subtypes of the other resource classes also significant from a neuroscientific perspective?

Binning and Huo (2012) recognized that status is a multifaceted social resource, assuming multiple forms, and not easily quantified. Further, it varies along the particularistic–universalistic and symbolic–concrete dimensions, thus generating a testable theoretical framework featuring four status subtypes: symbolic/universalistic, symbolic/particularistic, concrete/universalistic, and concrete/particularistic. The authors distinguish among different status transactions and provide novel predictions regarding transaction violations and how exchange of status may affect social relations.

The interested reader can further consult Törnblom and Nilsson (1993) who—based on the notions of source (i.e., identity of resource provider) and resource profile (i.e., resources that are typically provided by a certain source or exchanged in a certain type of relationship)—proposed that by simultaneously considering the resource of exchange and the nature of the relationship

RECENT THEORETICAL ADVANCES IN SOCIAL RESOURCE THEORY 249

between the exchanging parties one could determine the congruence between the two as matching or mismatching which potentially could generate resource subtypes. For a similar reasoning the reader may consult Kayser et al. (1984) as well as Mitchell et al. (2012) for their discussions on the relational–attribute and relationship–context paradigms.

Foas' New Exchange Rules Revisited

A large number of new exchange rules emerged from Foas' work. They concern variables or properties with regard to which resource classes differ systematically, such that some resources will be more similar to each other than to others. We have included a number of occasional comments and additions related to the meaning and plausibility of some statements by the Foas. As the Foas often restricted their illustrations of the new rules to the resources of love and money, we need to ask whether reference to all six resource types will modify some of the rules. In the following we make an attempt for the first time to fill in the gaps. However, the extent to which the considerable variety of different concrete items that represent each one of the six resource classes might modify these rules cannot be systematically examined here.

i) *The relationship between giving resources to other and to self* changes with the positions of the resources in the circular structure. The relationship is positive for love and becomes increasingly negative the closer the resource is to money. One's supply of love does not decrease when giving it to other, but "For resources closer to money, the amount lost by the giver tends to approach the amount gained by the receiver" (Foa & Foa, 1980, p. 93). Information is described as independent, i.e., giving it to another results in no loss or gain for the provider (Foa & Foa, 1976, p. 107). For example, a teacher sharing her knowledge with students does not lose or gain information. However, whereas the amount of some types of information (e.g., secrets) does not decrease when providing it to another, its *value* to the provider might very well be lost.

Service, a particularistic resource in Foas' framework, seems to represent a special case. When we provide services to others, what happens to our own amount of service possession? Törnblom and Kazemi (2007) argued that service does not exist before it is provided. Service is produced in the same act by which it is provided. The

250 PART II NEW THEORETICAL AND EMPIRICAL DEVELOPMENTS

provider does not possess the resource service before it is produced. Moreover, the provider does not retain service for himself subsequent to the act of giving service to others.

ii) *The relationship between giving and taking away* is most positive for love (a condition called "ambivalence"). It is possible to simultaneously love and hate. And we can give and take away status in the same act. However, this is not the case for money—"the joint occurrence of giving and taking away will follow the circular structure of resources, being highest for love and lowest for money" (Foa & Foa, 1976, 108)—giving money excludes taking it away, and vice versa. Likewise, services, information and goods cannot be provided and taken away in the same act.

iii) *Verbalization of need for resources* seems to vary in difficulty with the extent to which verbal communication is suitable for each resource class. Foa and Foa (1976, p. 109) suggest that it is less difficult to express one's need for money than one's need for affection. However, ease of verbalization might be mostly determined by the social context and interpersonal relationship, for instance, rather than by some assumed inherent characteristic of the resource, per se. It is not difficult to think of situations when one would be more ashamed of asking for money as compared to affection or kindness.

iv) *Exchangeability.* The statements in (a)–(d) have been corroborated by empirical research.

    (a) "The nearer two resources are (in the structure), the more likely they are to be exchanged with one another" (Foa & Foa, 1980, p. 93).

    (b) Reciprocating the receipt of a given resource with an identical or similar resource is more likely for particularistic than for universalistic resources (Foa & Foa, 1974, p. 109). Providing money in return for money makes little sense, while affection is likely to be more welcome than $10 in return for love.

    (c) "The nearer to love a resource is, the more likely it is to be exchanged with same resource" (Foa & Foa, 1980, p. 93).

    (d) "When a resource is not available for exchange, it is more likely to be substituted by a less particularistic than by a more particularistic one" (Foa & Foa, 1980, p. 94). For love, this is of course inevitable, as a more particularistic resource does not exist in Foas' typology. However, what if status was received but is not available for exchange? Following this rule the recipient should reciprocate with information, goods, or money (all three being less particularistic). However, would not a kind word of affection (love) be a more likely response to praise (status), in which case the opposite rule is valid? Similarly, wouldn't praise or friendly words of gratitude in return for a rendered (and particularly unsolicited) service be equally (or sometimes more) likely than monetary payment, particularly if the servicing person is a friend or lover?

v) *Range of exchange.* Universalistic resources (money, in particular) can be exchanged for a wider range of resource types as compared to particularistic resources. "The nearer to love a resource is, the narrower the range of resources with which it is likely to be exchanged" (Foa & Foa, 1980, p. 93).

vi) *Resource optimality.* "The optimal range (neither too little nor too much) of a resource is most narrow for love, and increases progressively for resources closer to money" (Foa & Foa, 1980, p. 94). Thus, the optimal range for goods (which is proximal to money) should be wider than that for love. However, a person will only have usage or room for a very limited number of dinner tables, while she might welcome unlimited love from her lover and/or signs of affection from as many friends and acquaintances as possible. Also, the value of each increment of $10 for a love-starved millionaire is trivial, while each hint of affection from the opposite sex may be of substantial value. Thus, the declining marginal utility (or level of satiation) for a resource will vary according to its scarcity, the amount possessed, its value, its significance, etc. Of course, the lack of a common scale according to which different types of resources may be evaluated presents a veritable obstacle to comparable assessments of optimality. And even if a standardized scale were available, the notion of optimality yields limited information. Imagine a 100-point scale along which the amounts of two different types of resources may be validly measured, and that 10 represents the least tolerable amount for resource A and 60 for resource B. Also imagine that too much of A lies at 45 and too much of B at 95. Thus, the ranges for A and B are equally wide, 35 for both. However, 35 as a measure of the range width or optimality (designated as narrow, wide, or whatever) provides a limited amount of theoretically interesting information, in comparison to information of the points of lowest and

252 PART II NEW THEORETICAL AND EMPIRICAL DEVELOPMENTS

highest acceptance or tolerability regarding one's possession of a resource. Also, the intervals (ranges) for different resources may extend differently—in both directions for some, upwards for some, and downwards for others. In addition, it is important to distinguish between *amount* and *value*; a large amount may not necessarily be highly valued, while a small amount may be worth a great deal. As we shall see in point 7, substituting amount for value yields opposite rules/propositions.

vii) *Resource amount.*

(a) "The larger the amount of a resource possessed by a person, the more likely it is to be given to others" (Foa & Foa, 1980, p. 93). The conditions under and extent to which this claim might be valid would surely be interesting to study! However, (a) the greater the *value* of a resource possessed by a person, the *less* likely it is to be given to others, and (b) the smaller the value of a resource, the more likely it is to be given to others—regardless of its amount.

(b) "The smaller the amount of a resource possessed by a person, the more he is likely to take it away from others" (Foa & Foa, 1980, p. 93). Again, the conditions under which and the extent to which this claim might be valid would be interesting to study! However, taking from other is probably unlikely when the value of the small amount is considerable.

(c) "Taking away any resource (other than love) produces a loss of love" (Foa & Foa, 1980, p. 94). Surely, it would be difficult to like a person who takes my money or disrespects me, for example, as he is likely to be perceived as unfriendly with negative intentions.

(d) "In the absence of exchange, the decrease in amount of love possessed decreases [*it seems likely that the authors intended to say "increases"— our comment*], and is greater for resources closer to love" (Foa & Foa, 1980, p. 94). However, in the absence of love exchange, both the amount of love (see point 10 below) and its *value* and/or intensity may very well increase.

viii) "The *simultaneous transmission* of love and another resource increases the value of this other resource, or facilitates its transmission" (Foa & Foa, 1980, p. 94). Is it the value of the resource, per se, or the "extra" resource of love that provides a feeling of increased value of the act?

ix) *Physical proximity and exchange.* As opposed to love, "transmission of money does not require face-to-face interaction" (Foa & Foa, 1976,

p. 109). Is it not equally possible for love to be conveyed from a great distance via a love letter, telephone call, internet contact, or even via another person?

x) *Storage*. ". . . love cannot be kept for a long time in the absence of actual exchange" (Foa & Foa, 1976, p. 109). However, we have all heard of the proverbial spinster who never again entered into another love relationship after being abandoned by the man she never ceased to love and want. It is also quite possible to keep loving someone even after a person's death. These statements refer to love conceived as an emotion. However, if love is understood as an act or behavior by which love is provided (e.g., sexual behavior), then the Foas' new rule doesn't make sense or is irrelevant, and different propositions are in order. In addition, some resources (i.e., love in its concrete forms and services) do not exist before they are produced, thus cannot be possessed nor stored. Not until I make love, engage in physical sexual intercourse, does that form of love exist, and not until I perform a service (e.g., repair your car) does the service exist. Thus, there is nothing that can be possessed and/or stored (except as images of future acts, prepotent stimuli, or intentions).

xi) *Locus of storage*. "Love is stored . . . in the 'heart'; money is kept at the bank or under the mattress" (Foa & Foa, 1976, p. 109). Some resources can be stored both inside and outside the person, e.g., information and food. "The more particularistic a resource the less it is amenable to external conservation . . . it depends more on internal cognitive storage" (Foa & Foa, 1976, p. 111). However, a medal (and other material symbols of status, i.e., instances of a particularistic resource class) can be externally stored indefinitely.

xii) *Interpersonal relationship and exchange*. Interpersonal relationships may exhibit typical resource profiles. Love in its various forms is typical for close particularistic relationships, while money, goods, services, and information are dominant in business and other universalistic relationships. The match between type of resource and interpersonal relationship is probably less specific for particularistic relationships, particularly long-term ones. A wider range of resources are provided and exchanged within those, as compared to more formal relationships. Not only is the nature of exchange affected by the type of relationship between the partners: "Other conditions being equal, the probability of occurrence of a given exchange is

254   PART II NEW THEORETICAL AND EMPIRICAL DEVELOPMENTS

contingent upon the institutional setting in which it may take place" (Foa & Foa, 1980, p. 94).

xiii) *Time for processing input.* Giving, receiving, and taking away love takes more time than that for money (Foa & Foa, 1976, p. 110). However, this "rule" is probably more typical for the development of love and affection, as one's affection for a person may certainly be conveyed instantly. And the transaction of money in its various forms may require an extended period of time, particularly if it has to be transferred long distances.

xiv) *Delay of reward.* Love is less likely to be exchanged in non-repetitive encounters with strangers than what is the case with universalistic re- sources (Foa & Foa, 1976, p. 110).

xv) *Optimum group size.* "The probability of love exchange is higher in small groups. The opposite is true for money" (Foa & Foa, 1980, p. 94). However, some religious groups, for instance, often stage mass sermons/meetings during which love is shared among the congregational members and between them and the preacher. Further, in which sense is it typical for money to be exchanged in large groups?

In sum, it seems obvious that some of the above "new exchange rules" war- rant closer scrutinization and reformulation and, above all, need to be empir- ically tested. In addition, most of the new exchange rules are restricted to the provision and exchange of positive resources. This may require reformulations of some of the rules as well as formulation of additional rules to accommo- date negative resource exchange. Of course, this should not in any way detract from the theoretical value of the many insights generated by SRT.

Additional Issues

Mode: Giving and Taking

Foa and Foa (1974) distinguished between two basic modes (i.e., allocation directions)—giving and taking away. They defined *giving* as "*increasing* the amount of resources available to the object" (p. 40) and *taking away* as "a *de- crease* in the amount of resources available for the object" (p. 40). As Stangl (1989) points out, *receiving* and *losing* are the counterpart modes from the perspectives of the person to whom something is given and from whom a resource is taken, respectively.

Foas' mode of "giving" (i.e., the act of increasing the available amount of resources) encompasses but does not identify or discriminate among the various possible ways of, or motives behind, increasing a person's amount of resources. A person may, for example, give freely and spontaneously, give in return for a resource received, give as a response to a request, give as a response to a need, or as a response to being coerced to give. And she may give disrespectfully, give with great hesitation, give strategically to create indebtedness, or create status superiority, etc. The "kind" of giving that takes place will certainly matter in a variety of ways for both the provider and the recipient with regard to its perceived purpose and, subsequently, its consequences for the relationship and the possible ensuing interaction between the provider and the recipient.

It seems that *mode* is insufficiently developed in most theories involving social resource exchange. There are additional notions than giving, taking away, and denying that describe the way in which resources are distributed and exchanged and that are likely to yield different kinds of psychological and behavioral implications. For example, a conceptual framework proposed by Törnblom (1988) for positive and negative outcome allocation differentiated among three modes: *delivering*, *withdrawing*, and *withholding*. The latter mode, *withholding* (akin to *denying*), refers to a situation in which (an expected) resource is not forthcoming—i.e., there is neither an increase nor a decrease in the amount of the resources possessed by the potential recipient. Thus, an existing (positive or negative) situation is maintained. The first two modes correspond to giving and taking away or denying, respectively.

A second component in Törnblom's framework is *resource valence* which, when combined with mode generates several alternative outcomes of positive or negative valence. For example, a positive outcome (i.e., the result of an allocation) may be accomplished in three ways: by presenting a positive resource (e.g., praise), by withdrawing and by withholding a negative resource (e.g., a reprimand).

Obviously, the notions of giving and taking away are far too general to be of much predictive value as each encompasses a wide range of different ways in which giving and taking may be executed. In addition, various meanings may be assigned to each type of outcome created by giving or taking: a positive outcome may be interpreted as a reward, a gain, profit, benefit, etc.,

256 PART II NEW THEORETICAL AND EMPIRICAL DEVELOPMENTS

while a negative outcome may be understood as a punishment, a burden, a loss, cost, a retribution, etc. (Törnblom, 1988). These (and other) ways of interpreting and labeling the outcome will result in different behavioral, cognitive, and emotional reactions (see Törnblom & Ahlin, 1998; Gamliel & Peer, 2006, for empirical implications of Törnblom's framework).

Production Versus Acquisition

In the study of language, especially the emergence of language, researchers typically focus on the three processes of language production, comprehension, and language acquisition (e.g., Hammarberg, 2001; MacDonald, 1999). MacDonald notes that the prevailing isolationist strategy within each area hampers a needed cross-fertilization of interrelated findings, as ". . . the puzzling results in one field appear to have solutions in another" (1999, p. 177). And if "The intricate relationships between these puzzles hold important implications for the nature of the human language faculties . . ." (1999, p. 177), might it also be likely that some hitherto unattended relationships between the nature and dynamics of the two processes of production and acquisition of social resources have hitherto neglected implications for resource transactions, social exchange, people's distributive and procedural fairness conceptions, attitudes and emotions, product positioning, and other phenomena and issues?

Would, for example, the nature and amount of social influence (power and authority) accruing the owner of resources differ due to whether, when, why, and how resources were *produced* or manufactured by their owner or *acquired* by the owner from somebody else (e.g., via inheritance, theft, or purchase)? The manner in which they were produced or acquired and, if acquired from somebody else, what the identity of that person is, for instance, are often likely to make a big difference. Some types of resources may certainly be produced and acquired in a multitude of ways, while the production and acquisition of others are more restricted. Further, some resources can be produced and acquired in ways in which other resources cannot. For example, information containing industrial secrets may be acquired through espionage, while affection or services cannot. An example of possible relationships between production and acquisition is that the socially accepted manner of acquisition of a social resource is frequently affected by how the particular resource was produced. It is against the law to acquire illegally manufactured alcohol ("moonshine," "white lightnin"), while the acquisition of the same kind of product brewed in a legitimate state-controlled facility is permitted.

The distinction between production and acquisition brings our thoughts to research on public good social dilemmas concerning how members of a collective create or maintain a common resource through individual contributions (i.e., social resource production) from which all can benefit. Certainly, collectively owned resources (called public goods within this research tradition) may be produced and acquired in a variety of ways. Once public goods are produced, the question of their distribution and acquisition arises. The ways in which a particular type of resource was produced do very likely have a bearing on the manner in which they are shared and acquired among eligible recipients. An adequate analysis of the relationship between the *origin* of a resource and, say, its allocation (in terms of its fairness, for instance) may require information about the way in which the recourse was produced as well as acquired (see Törnblom & Kazemi, 2007, for more details).

Also, the kind of resource that results from production activity or acquisition needs to be specified, lest we are content with speaking about production and acquisition in a vacuum. Analyzing resource production and acquisition without specifying what is produced or acquired makes no more sense than analyzing resource allocation without specifying what is allocated. Several studies indicate that resource type may moderate distributive justice judgments (e.g., Törnblom & Foa, 1983). Further, Törnblom and Kazemi (2007) suggested that resource type may moderate the relevance of manner of production as well, such that manner of resource production is more relevant for universalistic than for particularistic resources (p. 42, Proposition 1). As we also know that resource valence may affect justice conceptions (e.g., Törnblom & Jonsson, 1985, 1987), theoretical statements need to focus on the production, acquisition, and distribution of negatively valent resources as well (e.g., hate, misinformation, disservice, insult), in addition to positive ones.

Mode of production and resource type may also affect procedural (justice) aspects of resource allocations. Indeed, the process by which resources are allocated seems even more likely than the resource distribution to be affected by several of the factors that are associated with resource production. Resources produced collectively may result in endorsement and application of the representativeness rule as the most just procedural principle.

258   PART II NEW THEORETICAL AND EMPIRICAL DEVELOPMENTS

Further, if unethical and unjust procedures were used in the production of resources, restoration of justice may very well take place via just allocation procedures that meet the criteria of ethicality, consistency, representativeness, etc. (Leventhal, 1980).

Finally, as will be discussed below, *production and distribution may coincide* for some resources, as in the case of physical lovemaking which does not exist before it takes place. And as the distribution of a service or lovemaking is accomplished via a process or procedure, we realize that it is equally true that *production and procedure may coincide* as well. However, this is not true for other, particularly universalistic, resources.

Do We Usually Know How Resources Are Produced and Acquired?

In order for mode of production to have an impact on acquisition, for example, availability and salience of information about the process of production is crucial. However, availability and salience are not to be taken for granted. Perhaps most of the time people are ignorant about, or at least temporarily don't think about, how the various resources they encounter and acquire in their daily lives are produced, manufactured, acquired, or made available. As Olsen (1978) noted, production is usually hidden. Such lack of information works in the favor of manufacturers and merchants when goods and food have been produced by methods that people would object to had they been informed. As suggested above, knowledge and awareness about the origin of a resource often influences people's attitudes and evaluations of it and may, at least partly, determine their use of it, their willingness to purchase it or flaunt it as a status symbol. Our resource possessions often hint at the nature of our tastes, morality, fashion awareness, identities, financial status, etc. Thus, some people would not consider wearing a fur coat made from an endangered species, from animals who are kept as pets, or from animals who are mistreated or imposed great pain when extracting their fur. Less dramatical examples of how knowledge about a resource's manner of production may influence our cognitive conceptions and behaviors easily come to mind. People increasingly prefer ecologically and biodynamically produced food, while questioning and avoiding genetically modified staples and food stuff whose production has involved pesticides, chemical fertilizers and hormones.

If ignorance or unawareness about manner of production is common (but nevertheless relevant and important), may some kind of heuristic operate in situations where knowledge is lacking? Research has shown that heuristics may be activated to allow the fairness and favorability of an outcome to be inferred from knowledge about the procedure, or to allow the fairness of a procedure about which information is lacking to be inferred from the fairness or favorability of the outcome (Lind et al., 1993; Törnblom & Vermunt, 1999). Particularistic resources are more likely to be relatively unambiguous with regard to the purpose of their provision. For example, receiving a hug signals that the provider wants to convey affection for you. However, receiving a universalistic resource—say a book or a piece of information—is not equally unambiguous. The book gift might be the provider's way of saying that s/he likes you, but the gift might also have been given for other reasons. Of interest for our purpose here is that using heuristics may be more prevalent in the case of universalistic than particularistic resources as the significance of the former is more ambiguous with regard to the purpose of their provision.

Research on issues like the ones mentioned above should be guided by questions like the following: For what resource and under what conditions does what category of people have access to what type of information about its production, and under what conditions do people care about and are affected by how what types of resources are produced and acquired? Further, and more generally, how might the manner in which a specific resource was produced affect the ordering, proximity, and exchangeability with other resources, and how might it affect people's cognitive, emotional, and behavioral reactions to the resource, to exchanges with it, and to gains and losses of the resource? If, for instance, people's emotional reactions to the manner in which a resource is produced influences their evaluation of the resource (see Törnblom & Kazemi, 2007:42, Assumption 1), how would people's reactions to the gain or loss of a liked and disliked resource be affected?

There are certain possible, but so far seemingly unrecognized, "resource transformations" that might occur due to certain linkages among the production, acquisition, possession, and provision of social resources, linkages that may characterize and affect exchange transactions. These insights reveal relationships among resource classes that have implications beyond the common focus on resource exchangeability. (See Törnblom & Kazemi, 2012, for details.)

Resource production and its distribution may coincide; it usually doesn't enter our mind that production and distribution often happen in one and the same process, they are the same, one phenomenon designated by two terms. For example, when a service is provided it is simultaneously materialized, i.e., the service does not exist before it is provided; it cannot be produced before it is provided (Kazemi & Elfstrand Corlin, 2021). The massage I give does not exist before I give it. We can, perhaps, claim that a service may exist in a pre-potent form as information or knowledge concerning how to perform the service. However, a service does not exist, has not been produced (and cannot be possessed) before it is provided. Only a "pre-potent service resource" in the form of information is available. Thus, *production is sometimes identical with distribution*; the two may constitute one process, rather than two separate processes. This seems equally true for status and is partly true for love in its physical forms. However, money, goods, and information resources must be produced before they can be allocated.

Other Resource-Related "Theories"

It should be noted that there are related bodies of literature in two areas that we will not discuss here. Social network theories focus on ties and relations among people and have recently started to explore the significance of resources. The other area is represented by a number of capital theories emanating from Marx's (1849) economic theory of capital and expanded into additional forms of capital, viz, human, social, and cultural. Social capital theory is a very diverse area with ongoing attempts to strengthen conceptualization, integrate theories, and analyze dimensions and types. For example, some research has focused on how capital resources contribute to creating different consumer lifestyles (e.g., Allen, 2002; Holt, 1998) and reinforce firm performance (e.g., Luo et al., 2004). Much of the current popularity of the capital area emanates from the writings of Bourdieu (1986), Coleman (1988), and Putnam (1993). Examples of other theorists who have contributed to the area are Inkeles (2008), Lin (2001), and Turner (1999). Among the dimensions of social capital is "network resources" which hints at a direct connection between social capital and social resource theories. Also, different types of cultural capital (embodied, objectified, and institutionalized—see Bourdieau, 1986, p. 47) and human capital (i.e., skills, training, and experience acquired on the job that increase an employee's value in the marketplace) are resources of various forms that provide direct links between theories and research on different types of capital and social resources.

Additional theoretical frameworks have been proposed and labeled as resource *theories*, many (if not all) of which might more appropriately be identified as models, typologies, or propositions rather than genuine theories (e.g., Baumeister and Vohs', 2004, interesting "Female Resource Theory"). Furthermore, several of them are limited in their scope, in that they are constructed with specific contexts or focus in mind—like marketing, stress management, health, and consumer behavior. Dorsch et al. (2017) distinguished among and reviewed the following five types of resource theories, in addition to the Foas' SRT (see also Gorgievski et al., 2011), and their implications for consumer behavior: *Key resource and multiple component resource theories* which focus on stress coping resources (e.g., Hobfoll, 2002; Thoits, 1994); *Resource-Based Theory of the Firm* (RBT) that identifies firm resource properties conducive to sustained competitive advantage (e.g., Barney, 1991; Hunt & Morgan, 1995); *Conservation of Resources Theory* (COR) describing how people acquire, protect and maintain their resources to enhance well-being (e.g., Hobfoll, 1989; Halbesleben et al., 2014); *Theory of Selective Optimization with Compensation* (SOC) attending to the relationship between age-related changes and resource management strategies (e.g.,Baltes, 1987; Hobfoll, 2002); and *Resource Exchange Theories* referring to theoretical frameworks for understanding social and economic resource transactions (e.g., Blau, 1964; Emerson, 1976; Foa, 1971; Homans, 1961; Thibaut & Kelly, 1959).

Hobfoll (2002, pp. 308–314) provided an excellent review and analysis of various kinds of resource models, theories, and empirical research studies in the areas of health and well-being (with particular emphasis on stress and coping). He distinguished among "key resource theories," "multiple-component resource theories," "integrated resource models," and "life span resource models." These theories and models feature different resource classifications (designations) than the one proposed by Foa. Thus, all researchers are not (only) concerned with what is designated as *social* resources, as previously defined.

Some Attempts at Integration Between SRT and Other Frameworks (Models, Theories)

The following is by no means intended to discuss an exhaustive list of integration attempts between SRT and other models and theories. Our aim

262 PART II NEW THEORETICAL AND EMPIRICAL DEVELOPMENTS

is to briefly illustrate how SRT has been drawn upon to expand some other theories and enrich our understanding of some basic mechanisms governing human cognition and behavior. The examples are presented in chronological order.

The first example is Stangl (1993) who explored relations between individual preferences for resources and personality traits. He found four types of persons: (A) persons characterized by a high preference for love but low for money, (B) those with low preference for love but high for goods and money, (C) persons with high preference for status but low for information, and (D) those with low preference for status but high preferences for goods and money. These different types could be characterized with respect to their self-rated personality profiles. Exemplified here only in terms of the connection between resource preference pattern and a couple of the associated positive types of personality characteristics, A was found to be interpersonally oriented and spontaneous; B was deliberative and purposeful; C was interpersonally oriented and self-assured; and D could be characterized as task-oriented and self-controlled.

A second example concerns how SRT has enriched social justice theory (see, for example, Törnblom and Kazemi (2007) on mode of production discussed in an earlier section of the present chapter). Equity, multiple distributive, and procedural justice theories share a focus on discrepancies between ideal and actual circumstances and psychological and behavioral reactions to these discrepancies. Noting each framework's limited ability to match specific discrepancies and appropriate reactions, Törnblom and Vermunt (2007) offered a number of predictions based upon congruence between reactions and violated procedural rules and type of inequity, as assessed on the basis of their respective resource isomorphism. Kazemi et al. (2012) tested a derived hypothesis that in a situation of procedural injustice, restoration of justice will be attempted via behaviors that are isomorphic with the resource with which the violated procedural rule is isomorphic. In support of this, the results showed that when the procedural rule of voice was violated, restoration of justice was attempted via status isomorphic behaviors.

A third interesting integration attempt between SRT and social comparison theory, worthy of notice, was made by Kazemi and Törnblom (2010). Festinger's (1954) social comparison theory posits that people acquire self-evaluative information by comparing one's own opinions and abilities to those of others. Other theorists suggested additional comparison objects, e.g., emotions (Schachter, 1959). Masters and Keil (1987) noted that theory and research on comparisons was limited to a relatively small range of comparison objects. Thus, conclusions from studies about comparison processes were tempered by an awareness of how the objects of comparison may limit generalizations. The appearance of social resource theory (Foa, 1971; Foa & Foa, 1974) provided a classification of the various types of comparison objects (i.e., social resources), greatly expanding the *variety of objects* in terms of which comparisons may take place. Drawing on insights from SRT, with a focus on its resource categorization along the particularism–concreteness dimensions and the rules that govern exchanges of these resources, Kazemi and Törnblom (2010) modified some basic propositions of social comparison theory and reformulated them into a new set of propositions. They proposed, for example, that "the tendency to compare oneself with some other specific person decreases with decreasing particularism of the resource that is the object of comparison," and that "Given a range of possible persons for comparison, the more particularistic the resource of comparison, the more likely someone part of one's close relationships will be chosen for comparison."

A fourth integration attempt is Gifford and Cave (2012) who argued that both the type of resource and the person with whom exchanges are carried out account for the motivation to exchange resources. They found the Foas' categorization of resources to be insufficient if the goal is to generate a full account of social interaction. The authors suggested that SRT should be complemented by their *Interpersonal Evaluation Theory*, IET, which is concerned with the match between person and resource and features a categorization of the types of persons who exchange the resources. Thus, while SRT features a classification of six resource classes, IET provides a complementary categorization of eight different types of persons who are seen as potential suppliers of these resources. These types are arranged in a circumplex model along the two dimensions of "communion" and "agency": Boss, Challenger, Enemy, Student, Employee, Ally, Friend, and Teacher. (See also Törnblom & Nilsson, 1993 regarding the match between the resource and its source (the provider) in terms of the particularism–universalism continuum and Kayser et al., 1984 regarding interaction between relationship type and resource class.)

A final example of attempts at integration is Bååth and Daoud's theorizing (in this book) about how the states of scarcity, abundance, and sufficiency may affect exchange behavior. They argue that it is commonly assumed that scarcity is universally existing and motivates individuals to exchange

264 PART II NEW THEORETICAL AND EMPIRICAL DEVELOPMENTS

resources to satisfy their needs. However, especially in modern societies, scarcity is neither universal nor is it necessarily problematic. Individuals can create scarcity or abolish it, thereby creating conditions of abundance or sufficiency. Acknowledging this, they present their *Theory of Scarcity, Abundance and Sufficiency* (SAS) and discuss how this framework allows for a richer theory about human behavior and demonstrate the merits of the synthesis of SRT and SAS for a deeper understanding of exchange behavior. By synthesizing SRT and SAS, Bååth and Daoud contribute to SRT scholarship by offering a modified definition of exchange rules and extending SRT's theoretical foundation to include positive as well as negative abundance and sufficiency.

Summary and Conclusions

Interpersonal and intergroup behavior may be interpreted and partly understood in terms of transactions involving the particular material/non-material and particularistic/universalistic classes of social resources that Foa and Foa distinguished and systematically related to one another. Indeed, social resources have assumed a central place in numerous scholars' research. In this chapter we provided an overview of the central definitions and terminological distinctions within Foas' theoretical framework as well as related but slightly different definitions and terms that appear in the works of other scholars. Most definitions of resource are more general but seem to encompass Foas' resources. Conceptual confusion is frequently occurring due to differing *designations* (names) for the same type of resource.

As different types of social resources have different properties, the possession or loss of a particular resource may have different consequences for peoples' life conditions than the possession or loss of another resource. To merely state, for example, that resource loss increases our vulnerability to negative stress or diminishes our quality of life does not make us much wiser. Predictions of more specific consequences from resource deprivation require specific information about exactly which particular resources are missing (objectively and/or subjectively). As a full understanding requires a description and analysis in terms of the whole configuration of lacking social resources (not just money, love, or services which is commonly the case), SRT greatly facilitates making explicit the configurations of resource possession and resource loss, and may thereby contribute to the planning of social welfare programs focusing on health, quality of life, etc.

We next raised the question of to what extent Foas' resource typology meets the criteria of parsimony, generation of testable hypotheses, mutual exclusiveness, and exhaustiveness. The adequacy of a typology is contingent on the extent to which these criteria are fulfilled. The first three criteria appeared to be largely satisfied, while exhaustiveness may require further elaborations of SRT. We also raised the question of whether dimensions suggested by other theorists might be theoretically fruitful (as alternatives or complements to concreteness/particularism).

Given the huge variety of concrete items that may exemplify each one of Foas' six resource classes, a categorization of those into subclasses seems necessary for further theoretical development and interpretation of the results from empirical research. It seems that the Foas did not discuss the possibility that within-class differences may sometimes be larger than between-class differences.

Next, we listed 15 new exchange rules that the Foas had formulated. We discussed the validity of some of these, as it seemed somewhat unclear how they were derived.

SRT features a distinction between two basic behavioral modes (i.e., allocation directions)—giving and taking away. The predictive value of this distinction can be improved by specifying the wide range of different ways in which giving and taking may be interpreted and enacted. A third mode not discussed by Foas is withholding, i.e., an act resulting in neither an increase nor decrease of the amount of a resource. However, even when status quo is maintained, withholding might be as frustrating as a withdrawal (taking away).

Additional issues that we discussed in this chapter concerned the production and acquisition of resources, how the way a resource is produced or acquired may affect our attitude toward the resource, and the ways in which this knowledge might affect exchange behavior. Some types of resources may certainly be produced and acquired in a multitude of ways, while the production and acquisition of others are more restricted. Further, some resources can be produced and acquired in ways in which other resources cannot and thus affect the process of resource exchange in specific ways. The linkages between production and acquisition may provide new insights concerning relationships among resource classes that have implications beyond the usual foci of exchange theories.

266 PART II NEW THEORETICAL AND EMPIRICAL DEVELOPMENTS

Finally, we closed the chapter with short descriptions of some additional resource-related theories or models as well as various attempts at integration between SRT and other theoretical frameworks.

In sum, the principal aim of this chapter was to provide a brief overview of recent advances and highlight some issues that we think deserve attention for future theoretical and empirical developments of SRT.

References

Allen, D. E. (2002). Toward a theory of consumer choice as sociohistorically shaped practical experience: The fits-like-a-glove (FLAG) framework. *Journal of Consumer Research, 28,* 515–533.

Baltes, P. B. (1987). Theoretical propositions of life-span development psychology: On the dynamics between growth and decline. *Developmental Psychology, 23,* 611–626.

Barney, J. (1991). Firm resources and sustained competitive advantage. *Journal of Management, 17,* 99–120.

Baumeister, R. F., & Vohs, K. D. (2004). Sexual economics: Sex as a female resource for social exchange in heterosexual interactions. *Personality and Social Psychology Review, 8,* 339–363.

Binning, K. R., & Huo, Y. J. (2012). Understanding status as a social resource. In K. Y. Törnblom & A. Kazemi (Eds.), *Handbook of social resource theory: Theoretical extensions, empirical insights,* and social applications (pp. 133–147). Springer.

Blalock, H. M., Jr. (1991). *Understanding social inequality. Modeling allocation processes.* Sage Publications, Inc.

Blau, P. (1964). *Exchange and power in social life.* John Wiley.

Bothner, M. S., Godart, F. C., & Lee, W. (2010). *What is social status? Comparisons and contrasts with cognate concepts.* Working paper, European School of Management and Technology, Berlin, Germany.

Bourdieu, P. (1986). The forms of capital. In J. G. Richardson (Ed.), *Handbook of theory and research for the sociology of education* (pp. 241–58). Greenwood Press.

Brock, T. C. (1968). Implications of commodity theory for value change. In A. G. Greenwald, T. C. Brock, & T. M. Ostrom (Eds.), *Psychological foundations of attitudes* (pp. 243–275). Academic Press.

Buss, A. H. (1983). Social rewards and personality. *Journal of Personality and Social Psychology, 44,* 553–563.

Caplan, G. (1974). *Support systems and community mental health.* Behavioral Publications.

Chiaburu, D. S., Byrne, Z. S., & Weidert, J. (2012). Resources and transactions in the organization's underworld: Exchange content and consequences. In K. Y. Törnblom & A. Kazemi (Eds.), *Handbook of social resource theory: Theoretical extensions, empirical insights, and social applications.* Springer.

Coleman, J. S. (1988). Social capital in the creation of human capital. *American Journal of Sociology, 94,* 95–120.

Diener, E., & Fujita, F. (1995). Resources, personal strivings, and subjective well-being: A nomothetic and idiographic approach. *Journal of Personality and Social Psychology, 68,* 926–935.

Doane, L. S., Schumm, J. A., & Hobfill, S. E. (2012). The positive, sustaining, and protective power of resources: Insights from conservation of resources theory. In K. Y. Törnblom & A. Kazemi (Eds.), *Handbook of social resource theory. Theoretical extensions, empirical insights, and social applications* (pp. 301–310). Springer.

Dorsch, M. J., & Brooks, C. L. (2012). Initiating customer loyalty to a retailer: A resource theory perspective. In K. Y. Törnblom & A. Kazemi (Eds.), *Handbook of social resource theory: Theoretical extensions, empirical insights, and social applications* (pp. 311–331). Springer.

Dorsch, M. J., Törnblom, K. Y., & Kazemi, A. (2017). A review of resource theories and their implications for understanding consumer behavior. *Journal of the Association for Consumer Research, 2*, 5–25.

Doty, D. H., & Glick, W. H. (1994). Typologies as a unique form of theory building: Toward improved understanding and modeling. *Academy of Management Review, 19*, 230–251.

Emerson, R. (1976). Social exchange theory. In A. Inkeles, J. Coleman, & N. Smelser (Eds.), *Annual review of sociology* (Vol. 2, pp. 335–362). Annual Reviews.

Festinger, L. (1954). A theory of social comparison processes. *Human Relations, 7*, 117–140.

Foa, U. G. (1971). Interpersonal and economic resources. *Science, 171*, 345–351.

Foa, U. G., & Foa, E. B. (1974). *Societal structures of the mind*. Charles C. Thomas.

Foa, E. B., & Foa, U. G. (1976). Resource theory of social exchange. In J. W. Thibaut, J. T. Spence, & R. C. Carson (Eds.), *Contemporary topics in social psychology* (pp. 99–131). General Learning Press.

Foa, E. B., & Foa, U. G. (1980). Resource theory: Interpersonal behavior as exchange. In K. J. Gergen, M. S. Greenberg, & R. H. Willis (Eds.), *Social exchange: Advances in theory and research* (pp. 77–94). Plenum.

Foa, U. G., Foa, E. B., & Schwarz, L. M. (1982). Generalization of anxiety along the structure of interpersonal resources. *Journal of Social and Biological Structures, 5*, 189–198.

Foa, U. G., Converse, J., Jr., Törnblom, K. Y., & Foa, E. B. (Eds.). (1993). *Resource theory: Explorations and applications*. Academic Press.

Foa, U. G., Salcedo, L. N., Törnblom, K. Y., Garner, M., Glaubman, H., & Teichman, M. (1987). Interrelation of social resources: Evidence of pancultural invariance. *Journal of Cross-Cultural Psychology, 18*, 221–233.

Freese, L., & Burke, P. J. (1994). Persons, identities, and social interaction. *Advances in Group Processes, 11*, 1–24.

Gamliel, E., & Peer, E. (2006). Positive versus negative framing affects justice judgments. *Social Justice Research, 19*, 307–322.

Gecas, V. (1991). The self-concept as a basis for a theory of motivation. In J. A. Howard & -P. L. Callero (Eds.), *The self-society dynamic* (pp. 171–187). Cambridge University Press.

Gerson, E. M. (1976). On "quality of life." *American Sociological Review, 41*, 793–806.

Gifford, R. G., & Cave, M. (2012). The complementary natures of resource theory and interpersonal evaluation theory. In K. Y. Törnblom & A. Kazemi (Eds.), *Handbook of social resource theory: Theoretical extensions, empirical insights, and social applications* (pp. 223–236). Springer.

Gorgievski, M. J., Halbesleben, J. R. B., & Bakker, A. B. (2011). Introduction: Expanding the boundaries of psychological resource theories. *Journal of Occupational and Organizational Psychology, 84*, 1–7.

Halbesleben, J. R. B., Neveu, J.-P., Paustian-Underdahl, S. C., & Westman, M. (2014). Getting to the "COR": Understanding the role of resources in conservation of resources theory. *Journal of Management, 40*, 1334–1364.

Hammarberg, B. (2001). Roles of L1 and L2 in L3 production and acquisition. In J. Cenoz, B. Hufeisen, & U. Jessner (Eds.), *Cross-linguistic influence in third language acquisition: Psycholinguistic perspectives* (pp. 21–41). Multilingual Matters.

Harber, K. D., Einev-Cohen, M., & Lang, F. (2008). They heard a cry: Psychosocial resources moderate perception of others' distress. *European Journal of Social Psychology, 38,* 296–314.

Heirich, M. (1964). The use of time in the study of social change. *American Sociological Review, 29,* 386–397.

Hobfoll, S. E. (1989). Conservation of resources: A new attempt at conceptualizing stress. *American Psychologist, 44,* 513–524.

Hobfoll, S. E. (2002). Social and psychological resources and adaptation. *Review of General Psychology, 6,* 307–324.

Holt, D. B. (1998). Does cultural capital structure American consumption? *Journal of Consumer Research, 25,* 1–25.

Homans, G. C. (1961). *Social behavior: Its elemental forms.* Harcourt, Brace & World.

Hunt, S. D., & Morgan, R. M. (1995). The comparative advantage theory of competition. *Journal of Marketing, 59,* 1–15.

Inkeles, A. (2000). Measuring social capital and its consequences. *Policy Sciences, 33,* 245–268.

Kayser, E., Schwinger, T., & Cohen, R. L. (1984). Laypersons' conceptions of social relationships: A test of contract theory. *Journal of Social and Personal Relationships, 1,* 433–458.

Kazemi, A. (2017). Conceptualizing and measuring occupational social well-being: A validation study. *International Journal of Organizational Analysis, 25*(1), 45–61.

Kazemi, A., & Elfstrand Corlin, T. (2021). Linking supportive leadership to satisfaction with care: Proposing and testing a service–profit chain inspired model in the context of elderly care. *Journal of Health Organization and Management, 35*(4), 492–510.

Kazemi, A., Gholamzadehmir, M., & Törnblom, K. (2012). Predicting reactions to procedural injustice via insights from resource theory. In K. Törnblom & A. Kazemi (Eds.), *Handbook of social resource theory: Theoretical extensions, empirical insights, and social applications* (pp. 373–381). Springer.

Kazemi, A., & Kajonius, P. (2021). Understanding client satisfaction in elderly care: New insights from social resource theory. *European Journal of Ageing, 18,* 417–425.

Kazemi, A., & Törnblom, K. Y. (2010). *Revisiting social comparison theory from the perspective of resource theory.* Paper presented at the XVII World Congress of Sociology, Gothenburg, Sweden.

Lenski, G. (1966). Power and privilege. A theory of social stratification. McGraw-Hill, Inc.

Leventhal, G. S. (1980). What should be done with equity theory? New approaches to the study of fairness in social relationships. In K. Gergen, M. Greenberg, & R. Willis (Eds.), *Social exchanges: Advances in theory and research* (pp. 27–55). Plenum.

Levinger, G. (1959). The development of perceptions and behavior in newly formed social power relationships. In D. Cartwright (Ed.), *Studies in social power* (pp. 83–98). University of Michigan.

Lin, N. (2001). *Social capital: A theory of social structure and action.* Cambridge University Press.

Lind, E. A., Kulik, C. T., Ambrose, M., & de Vera Park, M. V. (1993). Individual and corporate dispute resolution: Using procedural fairness as a decision heuristic. *Administrative Science Quarterly, 38,* 224–251.

Luo, X., Griffith, D. A., Liu, S. S., & Shi, Y. Z. (2004). The effects of customer relationships and social capital on firm performance: A Chinese business illustration. *Journal of International Marketing, 12*, 25–45.

MacDonald, M. C. (1999). Distributional information in language comprehension, production, and acquisition: Three puzzles and a moral. In B. MacWhinney (Ed.), *The emergence of language* (pp. 177–196). Erlbaum.

Markovsky, B. (1996). Theory, science, and "micro–macro" bridges in structural social psychology. *Current Research in Social Psychology, 4*, 30–42.

Markovsky, B. (2011). Theory. In G. S. Ritzer (Ed.), *The Blackwell concise encyclopedia of sociology* (pp. 646–647). Blackwell.

Markovsky, B., & Kazemi, A. (2012). Formalizing Foa's social resource theory of exchange. In K. Y. Törnblom & A. Kazemi (Eds.), *Handbook of social resource theory: Theoretical extensions, empirical insights, and social applications* (pp. 81–98). Springer.

Masters, J. C., & Keil, L. J. (1987). Generic comparison processes in human judgment and behavior. In J. C. Masters & W. P. Smith (Eds.), *Social comparison, social justice, and relative deprivation: Theoretical. empirical, and policy perspectives* (pp. 11–54). Erlbaum.

McDougall, W. (1908). *An introduction to social psychology*. Methuen & Co.

Miller, G. R., & Steinberg, M. (1975). *Between people: A new analysis of interpersonal communication*. Science Research Associates.

Mitchell, M. S., Cropanzano, R. S., & Quisenberry, D. M. (2012). Social exchange theory, exchange resources, and interpersonal relationships: A modest resolution of theoretical difficulties. In K. Y. Törnblom & A. Kazemi (Eds.), *Handbook of social resource theory. Theoretical extensions, empirical insights, and social applications* (pp. 99–118). Springer.

Molm, L. D. (2006). The social exchange framework. In P. J. Burke (Ed.), *Contemporary social psychological theories* (pp. 24–45). Stanford University Press.

Nuckolls, K. G., Cassel, J., & Kaplan, B. H. (1972). Psychosocial assets, life crisis, and the prognosis of pregnancy. *American Journal of Epidemiology, 95*, 431–441.

Olsen, M. E. (1978). *The process of social organization: Power in social systems* (2nd edition). Holt, Rinehart & Winston.

Putnam, R. D. (1993). The prosperous community: Social capital and public life. *The American Prospect, 4*, 13.

Randall, C. S., & Mueller, C. W. (1995). Extensions of justice theory: Justice evaluations and employees' reactions in a natural setting. *Social Psychology Quarterly, 58*, 178–194.

Sabbagh, C., & Levy, S. (2012). Toward an expansion of resource exchange theory: A facet approach. In K. Y. Törnblom & A. Kazemi (Eds.), *Handbook of social resource theory: Theoretical extensions, empirical insights, and social applications* (pp. 67–80). Springer.

Sabbagh, C., & Malka, H. (2012). Evaluating the distribution of various resources in educational settings: The views of Jewish and Arab teachers in Israel. In K. Y. Törnblom & A. Kazemi (Eds.), *Handbook of social resource theory: Theoretical extensions, empirical insights, and social applications* (pp. 407–422). Springer.

Schachter, S. (1959). *The psychology of affiliation*. Stanford University Press.

Stangl, W. (1993). Personality and the structure of resource preferences. *Journal of Economic Psychology, 14*, 1–15.

Stangl, W. (1989). The structure of resource preferences. *Arch. Psychological, 141*, 139–154.

Stets, J. E., & Cast, A. D. (2007). Resources and identity verification from an identity theory perspective. *Sociological Perspectives, 50*, 517–543.

270   PART II NEW THEORETICAL AND EMPIRICAL DEVELOPMENTS

The Merriam-Webster Thesaurus. (1989). Merriam-Webster.

Thibaut, J. W., & Kelly, H. H. (1959). *The social psychology of groups.* Wiley.

Thoits, P. A. (1994). Stressors and problem solving: The individual as psychological activist. *Journal of Health and Social Behavior, 35,* 143–160.

Törnblom, K.Y. (1988). Positive and negative allocations: A typology and a model for conflicting justice principles. In E. Lawler & B. Markovsky (Eds.), *Advances in group processes* (Vol. 5, pp. 141–168). JAI Press.

Törnblom, K. Y., & Ahlin, E. (1998). Mode of accomplishing positive and negative outcomes: Its effects on fairness evaluations. *Social Justice Research, 11,* 423–442.

Törnblom, K. Y., & Foa, U. G. (1983). Choice of a distribution principle: Crosscultural evidence on the effects of resources. *Acta Sociologica, 26,* 161–173.

Törnblom, K. Y., & Jonsson, D. R. (1985). Subrules of the equality and contribution principles: Their perceived fairness in distribution and retribution. *Social Psychology Quarterly, 48,* 249–261.

Törnblom, K. Y., & Jonsson, D. R. (1987). Distribution vs. retribution: The perceived justice of the contribution and equality principles for cooperative and competitive relationships. *Acta Sociologica, 30,* 25–52.

Törnblom, K. Y., & Kazemi, A. (2007). Toward a resource production theory of distributive justice. In K. Y. Törnblom & R. Vermunt (Eds.), *Distributive and procedural justice: Research and social applications* (pp. 39–66). Ashgate Publishing Company.

Törnblom, K., & Kazemi, A. (Eds.) (2012). *Handbook of social resource theory.* Springer.

Törnblom, K. Y., & Nilsson, B. O. (1993). The effect of matching resources to source on their perceived importance and sufficiency. In U. G. Foa, J. Converse, Jr., K. Y. Törnblom & E. B. Foa (Eds.), *Resource theory: Explorations and applications* (pp. 197–218). Academic Press.

Törnblom, K. Y., & Vermunt, R. (1999). An integrative perspective on social justice: Distributive and procedural fairness evaluations of positive and negative outcome allocations. *Social Justice Research, 12,* 39–64.

Törnblom, K. Y., & Vermunt, R. (2007). Towards an integration of distributive justice, procedural justice, and social resource theories. *Social Justice Research, 20,* 312–335.

Turner, J. H. (1999). The formation of social capital. In I. Serageldin (Ed.), *Social capital: A multifaceted perspective* (pp. 94–147). World Bank.

Turner, J. L., Foa, E. B., & Foa, U. G. (1971). Interpersonal reinforcers: Classification, interrelationship and some differential properties. *Journal of Personality and Social Psychology, 19,* 168–180.

8

Resource Theory and Levels of Explanation: From Universal Structure to the Construal of Interpersonal Behavior

John Adamopoulos

There is little doubt that the pioneering work on resource theory by Foa and Foa (1974) has had a significant and enduring impact on the development of social exchange theories and their many applications in the social and behavioral sciences (e.g., Foa et al., 1993; Törnblom & Kazemi, 2012). The work also influenced thinking in the related areas of interpersonal behavior (e.g., Adamopoulos, 1984; Triandis, 1977), social cognition (e.g., Adamopoulos, 2012; Haslam & Fiske, 1992), social relationships (Haslam, 1995), and, more broadly, in psychological work exploring the genesis of social meaning (Adamopoulos, 1999). A less recognized but significant achievement of resource theory—which was originally framed primarily in structural terms—is that it has contributed, albeit rather subtly, to a growing awareness that there is an intimate connection between structure and process (e.g., Radvansky & Zacks, 2014; see also Foa & Foa, 1974, p. 18) and that content-based and context-dependent processes must be an essential component of any exploration of human cognition. For example, a basic requirement of theories of bounded rationality in the study of human decision-making is the specification of the environment in which a system functions (e.g., Lieder & Griffiths, 2020). Resource theory provides a rich framework for the development of models of the social environment in which meaning is generated and social interaction takes place (e.g., Adamopoulos, 2012).

Recent years have seen an increased concern in psychology and related disciplines with the challenges associated with the exploration of topics that can be identified on multiple levels of complexity and generality. For example, Adamopoulos (2008) has examined a potential isomorphism between the structure of individualism and collectivism at the cultural level and that of

Social Behavior as Resource Exchange. Kjell Yngve Törnblom and Ali Kazemi, Oxford University Press.
© Oxford University Press 2023. DOI: 10.1093/oso/9780190066994.003.0010

272   PART II NEW THEORETICAL AND EMPIRICAL DEVELOPMENTS

idiocentrism and allocentrism at the individual level (e.g., Triandis, 1995). Caporael (2007) has described the theoretical advantages of a multilevel selection theory in applying evolutionary principles to understanding social behavior at the individual and cultural levels. Finally, as a third example among many, Voelklein and Howarth (2005) have discussed the controversies associated with understanding social representations as a collective experience as opposed to a cognitive process to be understood strictly at the individual level.

Similarly, one can easily argue that the phenomena encompassed by resource theory may exist on multiple levels of abstractness and generality. Foa and Foa (1974) seem to accept this idea implicitly by occasionally applying the same constructs to culturally invariant structures and to cognitions of specific social events. For example, they state, "Resource theory . . . relates individual structure to the structure of society and provides the basis of classifying differences among individuals and cultures" (p. 4). Therefore, it is essential to explore the actual range of the original theory and trace its implications for different levels. In other words, how are we to understand this theory, and particularly its central component, the basic resource model? At what level of generality does this theory offer the best insights? How can it be extended to other levels?

In this chapter, I discuss the advantages associated with viewing the original formulation of resource theory from a multilevel perspective. I then present a framework that examines different levels of the theory and the phenomena associated with them, and I conclude with some basic examples of theoretical work at each level. At the core of this discussion, underlying all suggestions for the conceptualization and extension of resource theory, lies the fundamental proposal that the theory offers the opportunity to circumscribe the context in which human cognition and behavior occur and to appreciate the importance of integrating structure and content-dependent process as we try to understand how human beings make meaning.

Levels of Explanation in Resource Theory

As noted previously, the original formulation of resource theory (Foa & Foa, 1974) spans, ambitiously, a number of levels in which it is applied, although not always in a systematic manner. For example, there are clear references to the description of processes at the cultural level: "Culture provides a template or model for the cognitive structure of its members, so that persons belonging to the same culture tend to have similar structures" (p. 19). At the same time, concern with the "dynamics of interpersonal interaction" and with motivational states clearly indicates a strong interest in capturing cognitive processing at the individual event level (p. 125).

Psychologists have long emphasized the distinction between formal and actual, real-world theories of human cognition and behavior, traditionally framed in terms of the contrast between *normative* and *descriptive* models (e.g., Komorita, 1976; Wright & Drinkwater, 1997). This parallels in some ways the search to understand the theoretical status of resource theory: Is it a formal/normative model, a theory of a culture-level interpersonal system, or an event-level model of cognitive processes in social exchange? Perhaps a more inclusive and informative approach to answering this question is to frame it in the context of hierarchy theory, which can accommodate multiple levels of explanation and can offer a more comprehensive point of view in explaining related phenomena (e.g., Adamopoulos, 2008; Ahl & Allen, 1996; Simon, 1973). Different levels of explanation permit the search for the fine details of a system with global implications about human behavior. From such a perspective, then, and considering the questions raised explicitly or implicitly about the nature of social experience and cognition by Foa and Foa (1974), it is reasonable to propose that resource theory—at least as originally formulated—can best be described as a three-level hierarchy that captures connections between a universal model of social exchange, the cultural contexts that generate the environments in which exchanges occur, and the individual cognitions that are involved in interpersonal interactions. The main features of such a hierarchy are shown in Figure 8.1.

Even a cursory review of the early work that led to the formulation of the basic tenets of resource theory as presented in Foa and Foa (1974) suggests a top-down approach to exploring the hierarchy presented in Figure 8.1, from the most abstract level of more-or-less idealized cognitive structures to the perception of specific interpersonal interactions. Specifically, the emphasis in the early work was on the delineation of formal, universal, perhaps even normative structures that capture the basic elements of social exchange (*universal level*). Structural variations at the *cultural level* may reflect differential resource availability and affordances across very different cultures. Finally, at the level of individual cognitive events (*interpersonal events level*), situational constraints, or, perhaps, the "institutional setting" according to Foa and Foa (1974, p. 150), may influence the dynamics of the exchange between specific individuals and, consequently, the understanding of the particular interaction. The next several sections of this chapter describe in more detail each level outlined in Figure 8.1, beginning with the universal level. Note

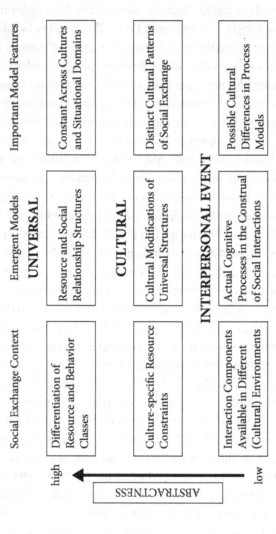

Figure 8.1 Levels of explanation in social resource theory (and its possible extensions).

that at each level, the theoretical models that emerge, and their most important attributes or features, must be understood within the context of the environment, sociocultural constraints, or psychological processes associated with social interaction.[1]

Finally, some major advantages of this scheme are that it points to possible extensions and amplifications of resource theory, facilitates connections with related areas of research, and focuses attention on theoretical issues that must be further elaborated and clarified. Examples of such possibilities are explored in subsequent sections of this chapter.

The Universal Level

The roots of resource theory are steeped in the strong "universalist" tradition in the 20th-century history of cross-cultural psychology that came of age primarily in the 1960s and 1970s (Adamopoulos & Lonner, 2001; Lonner & Adamopoulos, 1997). The fundamental assumption in this tradition is that while psychologists seek to uncover shared commonalities in human experience, they must not underestimate the significant influence of cultural contexts in shaping it. Cross-cultural research thus becomes an essential tool for separating the culture-specific from the culture-general and for understanding cultural variations in the manifestation of basic psychological processes and structures (Adamopoulos & Lonner, 1994). Work by U. Foa, in collaboration with other pioneers in cross-cultural psychology at the time, placed a great deal of emphasis on establishing the universality (cross-cultural invariance) of fundamental social structures, including interpersonal behavior, social relationships, and social resources (e.g., Foa, 1963, 1964; Foa et al., 1966).

The universal level reflects the core and most substantial contribution of resource theory, not only in its original formulation by Foa and Foa (1974)

---

[1] A vaguely analogous scheme to the three-level framework discussed here is the proposal for the organization of information processing systems by Griffiths et al. (2015). The "computational" level is associated with formal models offering optimal solutions in specific domains (e.g., rational models of decision-making) and would correspond to the "universal" level proposed in the present analysis. The "rational process models" level may include idealized as well as more realistic models subject to the resource constraints present in the specific domain. This corresponds to the "cultural" level in the present scheme because it reflects resource conditions and constraints within specific cultural contexts. Finally, the "algorithmic" level taps the specific cognitive processes involved in information processing, and it corresponds to the "interpersonal event" level, which includes models of actual cognitive processes involved in interpersonal interaction.

276 PART II NEW THEORETICAL AND EMPIRICAL DEVELOPMENTS

but also in many subsequent elaborations (cf. Törnblom & Kazemi, 2012). The concept of "differentiation" is central to this work because it is used to explore the structure of social exchange by partitioning the major components (resources, behaviors, roles, etc.) into their constituent classes, thus leading to a better understanding of the role of cognitive complexity in understanding interpersonal relationships. Foa (1961, 1963, 1965) accomplished this through the systematic and elaborate utilization of facet theory, which resulted in the description of generic or formal structures with no action-, person-, or culture-specific features. The implicit, but testable, assumption in such models is that they are expected to be culturally invariant. As mentioned previously, a significant amount of such testing took place over a span of more than 30 years, beginning with the early 1960s. A general conclusion reached on the basis of this research was that the theoretical structures generated by resource theory are sufficiently stable and cross-culturally invariant (e.g., Foa et al., 1987). Most current work on resource theory also appears to be at the universal level, involving refinements of the formal structure and tests of the stability of the resource circumplex either in different institutional settings or in distinct populations (cf. Törnblom & Kazemi, 2012).

It is important to recognize the inherent limitations of the formal, universal structural model in explaining actual behavior in specific social situations. In fact, Foa et al. (1993) described such limitations as a "weakness" of the theory. However, the multilevel scheme outlined in this chapter argues quite clearly against considering this a problem of the theory. Rather, the scheme invites us to consider theoretical extensions of the model at a different level of explanation in order to deal with specific interpersonal events—an issue that is considered in more detail later in this chapter.

The Cultural Level

Integrating Resource Theory with Cultural Types

Foa and Foa (1974) recognized the important role that culture plays in determining the perception of social events. As discussed previously, they saw culture as a "template" for the classification of social exchanges and recognized that "uniformity in categorizing social events is facilitated by a common culture" (p. 5). Unfortunately, there were no well-developed cultural theories in psychology at the time, and therefore it was not easy to connect the formal universal structure to specific cultural conditions. However, by the late 1980s, psychological theorizing about context-dependent human thought, emotions, and behavior was supported by substantive theories of culture (e.g., individualism/collectivism [Triandis, 1995, 2001] and independence/ interdependence [Markus & Kitayama, 1991]). It thus became possible to place universal models such as resource theory within specific cultural contexts, as in individualistic and collectivist cultures.

I have proposed elsewhere a direct connection between social resource theory and cultural theories in psychology (Adamopoulos, 1999, 2012). In particular, the basic types of individualism and collectivism (Triandis, 1995, 2001) and their many variants can be defined in terms of the exchange of particular classes of resources that are frequently found in different cultural contexts. In other words, the influence of culture in social exchange goes far beyond providing the "blueprint or template for the classification and organization of social events" (Foa & Foa, 1974, p. 5). It can facilitate the formation of distinct patterns of social interaction by constraining the kinds of resources that are available to a group of people throughout their lives and thus lead to the emergence of significant modifications of the universal structure proposed by resource theory. Examples of the outcomes of such processes are discussed below.

Some possible associations between resources and types of individualism/collectivism appear in Figure 8.2 and have been discussed in detail by Adamopoulos (1999). In general, in individualistic cultures, there is an emphasis on independent self-construal (Markus & Kitayama, 1991), attitude-based decisions about behavior, and concern with the fulfillment of individual needs and wishes. In other words, in individualistic cultures, the definition of the self is based primarily on a sense of the uniqueness of individuals and on personality dispositions and behavioral attributes that differentiate them from others. In addition, behavioral intentions are often based on individual preferences and opinions rather than on societal expectations and demands.

By contrast, in collectivist cultures, conceptions of the self are more interdependent, behavior is frequently more normative, and there is a greater concern with communal relationships. Thus, in collectivist cultures, individuals may "share" significant aspects of their sense of self with members of their ingroup, and they often base their behavioral decisions on social norms rather than on their specific needs and desires (cf. Triandis, 1995, 2001). Triandis (2001) has further refined the two cultural types by proposing that both can

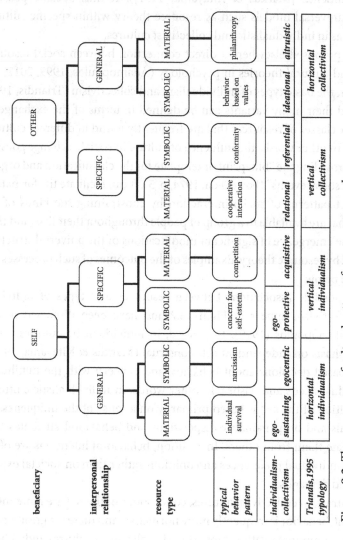

Figure 8.2 The emergence of cultural patterns from resource exchange. Adapted from Adamopoulos (2012).

be either vertical or horizontal. Vertical individualism is characterized by an emphasis on the uniqueness and primacy or significance of the individual, whereas horizontal individualism involves the uniqueness of the individual among similarly distinct and equal others. Vertical collectivism involves the primacy of the group and high-status people over individual needs, and horizontal collectivism emphasizes the equality of all individuals within a group.

Social exchange involves the giving or denying of resources that aims to benefit either the self or another person or group (*self* vs. *other*). This fundamental assumption can lead to further refinements of the constructs of individualism and collectivism. For example, interactions with others primarily aimed at securing material resources for the individual may result in the emergence of *ego-sustaining individualism* (in the sense of individual sustenance and survival), whereas emphasis on symbolic interactions (involving abstract resources) may result in patterns characterized as *egocentric individualism* and may involve status promotion or *ego-protective individualism* (in the sense of protection of self-worth) with an emphasis on the maintenance of self-esteem. Finally, *acquisitive individualism* involves competitive exchanges with others who may be interested in the same resources as the individual.

As the focus of social exchange changes toward consideration of the group interests, collectivist patterns tend to emerge. Concern with providing material resources to others in general may lead to an emphasis on philanthropic and altruistic behavior (*altruistic collectivism*) and can be accompanied by a concern with values-based conduct (*ideational collectivism*). Systematic interactions with particular groups or individuals may lead to an emphasis on cooperative behavior (*relational collectivism*) or acceptance of another person's or group's authority (*referential collectivism*). Generally, it is expected that these exchange patterns will be found across cultures, but the preponderance of specific patterns in a given culture will be influenced by the resources that are available in it.

An important caveat. The labels used in the structure outlined in Figure 8.2 are, to some extent at least, dependent on differing definitions of theoretical constructs in the social and behavioral sciences. For example, it is well known that across cultures, cooperative and helping behavior is more frequently directed toward in-group rather than out-group members (e.g., Triandis, 1994). At the same time, the term "altruism" is understood in social psychology in particular—as opposed to evolutionary biology—as involving prosocial behavior without any consideration of specific circumstances and

280 PART II NEW THEORETICAL AND EMPIRICAL DEVELOPMENTS

expectations of reciprocation. Thus, the term "altruistic collectivism" is used in Figure 8.2 to refer to giving resources to generalized others regardless of the particular relationship among exchange participants.

Finally, it must be made clear that the descriptions of cultural patterns in Figure 8.2 are idealized forms of the most likely exchange patterns that emerge from specific types of interactions. As the structural model implies, these patterns are related to each other in different degrees based on the number of shared attributes and reflected in their distance from each other. Thus, for example, ego-protective and acquisitive individualism share several exchange characteristics and are highly correlated. However, the primarily symbolic nature of the former contributes to individual sense of self (e.g., status), whereas the material nature of the latter contributes to a tendency to compete with others for resources.

Ultimately, the predictions of outcomes emerging from the processes outlined in the model in Figure 8.2 can be empirically tested against alternative patterns of emergence under similar constraining conditions (i.e., exchange characteristics). Some supportive evidence for the present model has appeared elsewhere (e.g., Adamopoulos, 1984). In addition, predictions are in line with findings about cultural syndromes such as individualism and collectivism or related patterns described by other theorists (e.g., Fiske, 1991, 1992; Schwartz, 1992; Triandis, 1995).

Environmental Constraints, Resources, and Culture

Foa (1993) advocated in favor of utilizing resource theory to address significant societal problems associated with modern conditions. It was an inspired statement that captured the need for social interventions to be more sensitive to nuanced psychological issues. For example, resource theory implies that economic programs in a society do not involve exclusively exchanges of money but also may involve interpersonal resources (e.g., caring for others), and interventions should incorporate this knowledge in planning and implementation.

Recent work in understanding how environmental and resource conditions affect psychological well-being can point to additional questions that resource theory may address fruitfully. Van de Vliert (2013a) has explored in some detail the relationship between climato-economic habitats and human needs—particularly freedom—at the national level. By considering

RESOURCE THEORY AND LEVELS OF EXPLANATION 281

combinations of economic resources (rich/poor) and climatic conditions (cold, temperate, and hot) that lead to climatic demands (demanding or undemanding), Van de Vliert described different human habitats with varying implications for the satisfaction of human needs, the experience of stress in everyday life, and the desire for various freedoms (e.g., freedom of expression and freedom from discrimination). These habitats were classified into three categories: threatening, challenging, and comforting.

In this impressive and expansive work, Van de Vliert (2013a) found strong indications of the threat freedom faces in the presence of environmental and economic challenges throughout the world—particularly in poor nations with demanding climates. On the other hand, demanding climates may be associated with high levels of experienced freedom in rich populations. Nations with temperate climates tend to be in an intermediate position regardless of economic conditions. This points to the complex dynamics of environmental conditions, resources, and human experiences to which Foa (1993) alluded in his brief proposal. As is suggested at the *cultural level* of Figure 8.1, consideration of the specific resource constraints found in particular cultures may significantly influence patterns of social exchange and, consequently, the emergence of culture-specific models of interpersonal structure.

It is possible to establish direct connections between climato-economic habitats and culture types. For example, there is a tendency for poor countries with cold climates to have low scores on individualism and for rich countries with temperate or cold climates to have higher individualism scores (Adamopoulos, 2013b). Based on considerations stemming from the cultural level of Figure 8.1, it follows that there may very well be connections among resource theory, cultural theories such as individualism–collectivism, and the work on habitats just described. For example, constraints such as the climate that make certain resources (un)available in a culture and thus require family members to become interdependent or spend more time together may lead to the emergence of collectivism as the predominant cultural system. This in turn may affect exchange relationships among individual members of the culture (e.g., lead to different amounts of prosocial behavior toward in-group and out-group members).

Some of these connections have been described elsewhere (Adamopoulos, 2013a). Poor societies with demanding climates, for example, may have high levels of interdependence and, hence, allow a great deal of normative behavior control that can lead to low perceived freedom. In harsh climates with high

282 PART II NEW THEORETICAL AND EMPIRICAL DEVELOPMENTS

levels of economic resources, however, people may believe that they worked very hard for their wealth and thus value freedom highly. This reasoning offers an alternative way to explain the findings of the climato-economic model (Van de Vliert, 2013a) that focuses on the need to consider the full resource model (Foa & Foa, 1974), rather than just money, in addressing the connection between climate, resources, and human behavior. Indeed, Van de Vliert (2013b) acknowledged that such a resource-inclusive approach may contribute to a greater understanding of this complex relationship.

Just as resource theory can enrich work on the relationship between the ecology and human experience, the latter can benefit resource theory by specifying much more precisely the constraints and affordances that are available in different cultural systems. Unfortunately, despite its important implications, this relationship has not been explored at all empirically. On the theoretical level, some proposals have been made by Van de Vliert (2013b) and Adamopoulos (2013a, 2013b). Figure 8.3 summarizes and combines these ideas, but it is important to note that the proposed relationships are highly tentative and speculative, and they are only presented as invitations to

Thermal Climate	Cold or Hot	Temperate		Cold or Hot
Climatic Demands	Demanding	Undemanding		Demanding
Monetary Resources	Poor	Poor	Rich	Rich
Habitat Appraisal	Threatening	Challenging	Comforting	Challenging
IND/COL Types				
Triandis (1995)	Vertical Collectivism	Vertical Individualism	Horizontal Collectivism	Horizontal Individualism
Adamopoulos (2012)	Relational and Referential Collectivism	Ego-protective and Acquisitive Individualism	Ideational and Altruistic Collectivism	Ego-sustaining and Egocentric Individualism

Figure 8.3 Some tentative connections between different habitats and types of individualism/collectivism (IND/COL).

Adapted from Van De Vliert (2013b) and Adamopoulos (2013a, 2013b).

further exploration rather than as well-established hypotheses. For example, local conditions could have a significant impact on the cultural patterns that emerge in two different communities, even if the overall habitat assessments are similar. Consider two habitats classified as "threatening." In one case, conditions may lead to cooperative behavior, coordinated activities, and the emergence of relational collectivism. If in the other habitat conditions are much worse, however, competition for scarce resources and the perception of life as a zero-sum game may lead to some forms of ego-sustaining individualism. In offering a framework for understanding and describing local conditions, social resource theory, as Foa (1993) insightfully suggested, can make a significant contribution to our understanding of the emergence of culture.

The Interpersonal Event Level

The theoretical strength and contribution of social resource theory is found primarily at the universal level of Figure 8.1, with additional but not necessarily systematic contributions at the cultural level. However, Foa and Foa (1974) recognized the need for describing the perception of individual social interactions or cognitive events in social exchange and framed it in the context of individual dynamics, development, and motivational states. During the past 40 years, a considerable amount of research established the utility of the formal model in describing the perceptual organization of resource exchanges and social relationships at the individual level, for specific groups of individuals, or for particular behavior domains (cf. Törnblom & Kazemi, 2012).

Social psychologists have generally been quite successful in applying and modifying formal, normative models of social relations at the individual level. For example, constructs such as Heider's structural balance have been examined as conceptual rules or organizing cognitive principles (e.g., Cottrell, 1975; Picek et al., 1975). Triandis et al. (1984) examined previously established universal interpersonal behavior structures as individual models of social behavior, whereas Adamopoulos and Stogiannidou (1996) used them in exploring the cognitive frames involved in the perception of social interaction.

Within this broad approach, in recent years researchers have examined the potential use of resource theory as an organizing principle in

284   PART II NEW THEORETICAL AND EMPIRICAL DEVELOPMENTS

conceptualizations of social relationships. Haslam (1994, 1995) explored the cognitive structure of resource classes—much like Foa and Foa (1974) had advocated in their original work. More important perhaps, Haslam and Fiske (1992) showed that resource exchange as conceptualized in the theory adequately predicts the implicit organization of relationships, although it is not necessarily superior to competing theories. The theory of elementary social relations (Fiske, 1992) also is successful in providing implicit prototypes for the encoding of relationships in different contexts (e.g., Gardikiotis & Tsingilis, 2019).

This research tradition reflects an effort to establish an isomorphism between a universal formal model as an abstraction and its application to individual cognitive activity (Adamopoulos, 2008)—a very worthwhile and essential part of the testing of social resource theory. However, this process does not capture all the possibilities that social resource theory offers at this level. I have proposed elsewhere (cf. Adamopoulos, 2012) that the theory can provide some of the most important constructs necessary to build models of interpersonal event cognition.

The Construal of Interpersonal Acts

Social resource theory may well capture the most basic assumption about all interpersonal interaction: It is a process that involves the exchange of resources and is subject to constraints identified in the early work of Foa and Foa (1974). Specifically, resources are (a) symbolic (abstract) or material (concrete), and (b) the relationship within which they are exchanged is either particularistic (target specific) or universalistic (target general). Additional constraints of all social behavior include (a) that it is intended to benefit either the self or another and (b) that it involves either giving or denying a resource. These notions, at least some of which come directly out of social resource theory, have formed the foundation for action construal theory (cf. Adamopoulos, 2012, 2013b).

Action construal theory (ACT) aims at the analysis of specific social behavior events, actions, or interaction episodes. Its goal is to develop a "grammar" of action in interpersonal settings or a set of tools to understand how different components of the social environment are put together to form socially meaningful behavior. This work takes a rule-theoretic approach to the construal of action in that interpersonal behavior is described as a configuration of components associated with social exchange that are integrated by certain rules. It proposes two sets of rules: (a) *componential* rules defining the most basic components or elements of action and (b) *syntactical* rules about the way in which components are combined to form meaningful action. Utilizing some of the constructs developed by Foa and Foa (1974), ACT rests on the fundamental principle that all interpersonal behavior is subject to basic constraints that characterize all social exchanges: In any particular interaction, a resource (a) must be given or denied (**transfer**), (b) must be aimed at benefiting the self or another (**intent**), (c) can be material or abstract/symbolic (**type**), and (d) can be oriented toward any person or a specific individual with regard to the actor (**relationship**). Different syntactical rules may be formulated to account for alternative ways in which these components of interaction are combined into unique cognitive configurations or conceptual units that are involved in the explanation of action.

Componential rules:
1. **Transfer** consists of *giving* a resource or *denying* a resource.
2. **Intent** can be to benefit *self* or the *other*.
3. **Type** of resource can be either *material* or *symbolic*.
4. **Relationship** can be either *target-specific* or *target-general*.

Syntactical rules: The problem of syntactical rules is a largely unexplored topic. The precise way in which the basic components of action are combined to form meaningful interaction events or episodes is unknown and, in fact, may be variable. I have proposed several different sets of syntactical rules that may result in reasonable models of the construal of action, which are summarized in Figures 8.4 and 8.5 (Adamopoulos, 2012, 2013a).

The base model described in Figure 8.4 involves a single syntactical rule and can be used as a baseline in comparisons with alternative formulations:

Action⟶ [transfer, intent, type, relationship]

In this model, it is the presence of the components of action, rather than any particular combination of them, that is critical in understanding what action is taking place. Thus, for example, helping a friend finish a job would involve

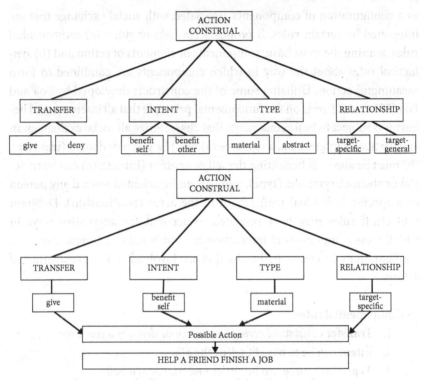

Figure 8.4 The construal of action: base model with example.

giving a material resource to a specific other with the intent to benefit that individual. A number of alternative plausible models may be generated by combinations of the four componential rules. Figure 8.5 presents two such models that have successfully predicted individuals' understanding of different actions (e.g., Adamopoulos, 2013a). The central idea in both cases is that the basic components may be combined to form more complex cognitive units that then contribute further to the understanding of action.

The first model in Figure 8.5 involves the following rules:

1. Action ⟶ [direction, resource]
2. Direction ⟶ [transfer, intent]
3. Resource ⟶ [type, relationship]

In this model, **direction** represents a meaningful social unit that provides context and reason for an act, and **resource** of course reflects well-documented

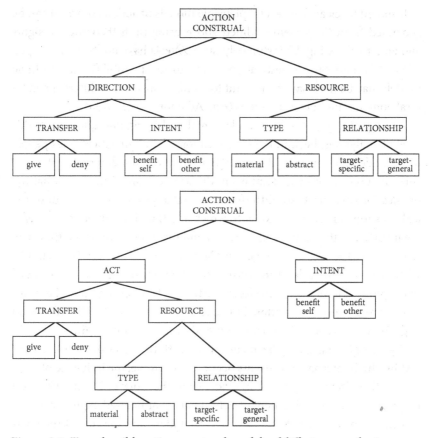

Figure 8.5 Two plausible action construal models of differing complexity.

research on the conceptual structure of resource classes in social resource theory (Foa & Foa, 2012; Foa et al., 1993).

The second model in Figure 8.5 involves a somewhat different set of rules:

1. Action ⟶ [act, intent]
2. Act ⟶ [transfer, resource]
3. Resource ⟶ [type, relationship]

In this model, the structure of the higher level component **Act** is analogous to a theme in a verb's argument in sentence parsing, which may have implications for encoding and recall and thus form a meaningful conceptual unit.

288 PART II NEW THEORETICAL AND EMPIRICAL DEVELOPMENTS

It should be clear that several plausible models of action construal can be generated from the system outlined above using both theoretical insights and empirical testing. Unfortunately, such criteria have not been developed adequately, and early investigations point to the possibility that multiple models may be necessary to account for action construal in different behavioral domains and social situations (e.g., Adamopoulos, 2013a).

As suggested previously, a fundamental and intriguing question at this level of analysis is, beyond the identification of the syntactical rules people use in understanding everyday social behavior, whether different syntactical rules are used in similar situations in different cultures and, if so, what the implications of that fact would be for social exchange processes. A second critical question concerns the extent to which additional cognitive components are involved in the perception of action and the manner in which they may interact with the social exchange constraints described by ACT. For example, what exactly is the role of the setting or situation in understanding social interactions? I have suggested elsewhere that, in fact, settings may play a significant role in event cognition, but such a role is not at all well understood (e.g., Adamopoulos, 1982; Adamopoulos & Stogiannidou, 1996).

Psychologists have long been concerned with the description of the context in which interpersonal events occur. For example, the influence of early Gestalt theorists is very much in evidence in the work of Lewin (1951) on life space and the development of field theory that focused explicitly on the context of social interaction. The quest to understand the role of the environment of social interaction is, naturally, found in the work of Lewin's student, Roger Barker, who elaborated the concept of "behavior setting" (e.g., Barker, 1965), and, of course, in the extensive amount of research produced in the quest to explicate the psychology of social situations (e.g., Furnham & Argyle, 1981). However, the ideas stemming from these research traditions have not yet been incorporated systematically into more recent theories of event cognition in social and cognitive psychology.

Social psychologists have been interested in the perception of behavior *units* since the pioneering research by Newtson in the 1970s (e.g., Newtson & Engquist, 1976). In recent years, cognitive psychologists have begun to identify some fundamental components involved in mental models of the perception of ongoing behavior or event cognition (e.g., Kurby & Zacks, 2008; Radvansky & Zacks, 2014). However, this work has not taken into consideration the complexity of social interaction, particularly as it involves the dynamics of resource exchange as captured in social resource theory and ACT.

The merging of all these theoretical traditions may result in the future in far greater insights into the perception of action and how human beings make sense of their social environment.

Conclusion

As discussed in the beginning of this chapter, there is little doubt that the original statement of social resource theory (Foa & Foa, 1974) was intended to cover a very wide range of phenomena, from the cognition of single "social events" (p. 56) to universal structures of interpersonal relations across cultures. Even the plan of the book attests to such intent: Part I dealt with the universal structure of social relations—and particularly resource exchange; Part II concerned, among other topics, the role of the individual actor in the exchange process; and Part III dealt with interpersonal cognition in different cultures, populations, and settings.

In this chapter, I have sought to refine and make this scheme more explicit by describing the hierarchical nature of the general theory. Furthermore, I have proposed a reconceptualization of the original structure to capture with greater precision the range of issues at the center of the original statement of social resource theory.

The core of social resource theory is the resource circumplex, whose structure has been supported empirically and is assumed to be universal, transcending cultural as well as individual boundaries (e.g., Foa & Foa, 1974, pp. 32ff, pp. 36ff, and Chapter 11). It is not surprising, therefore, that the major impact of the theory has been seen in the application of the circumplex to the exploration of a very wide set of topics concerning human social interaction (e.g., Törnblom & Kazemi, 2012).

In addition to the work on the universal structure of the resource circumplex, Foa and Foa (1974) attempted to explore the ways in which cultural mechanisms affect interpersonal exchange, as is evident in their statement, "Uniformity in categorizing social events is facilitated by a common culture. Culture thus constitute(s) a blueprint or template for the classification and organization of social events" (p. 5). However, the lack of adequate information and research at the time about culture-specific resource constraints and about the many ways in which different cultures distribute a variety of resources imposed limitations of such culture-level analyses. Foa and Foa (1974) acknowledged the importance of considering different types

290 PART II NEW THEORETICAL AND EMPIRICAL DEVELOPMENTS

of resources in social exchange (e.g., see pp. 381ff), yet there is little consideration in their theory of resources associated, for example, with climate and temperature, which may directly contribute to habitat conditions and quality of life—as discussed in the description of the cultural level in this chapter. The inclusion of an expanded view of the range of resources identified in more recent work (e.g., Van de Vliert, 2013a, 2013b) is likely to increase the range of phenomena to which social resource theory can be applied (happiness, aggression, interpersonal and international conflict, etc.).

Finally, the discussion of the "dynamics" of social interaction (e.g., Chapter 5, pp. 54ff) indicates very clearly a strong interest in event cognition. Foa and Foa (1974) considered several exogenous variables in their analysis of the perception of social events, including the "motivational style" of the exchange participants and the setting of the interaction. Such variables were considered "moderators" in an exchange, in the sense that they defined its appropriateness in the moment. However, a systematic analysis of the role of these variables in the construal of specific behavioral events was not attempted. ACT is an attempt to formalize the relationships among several variables involved in event cognition and thus, to a point, represents an extension of social resource theory.

The early statement of social resource theory by Foa and Foa (1974) was a remarkably far-reaching and ambitious framework, probably well ahead of its time. Since then, a number of research traditions have been inspired by this work and have embedded the analysis of interpersonal exchange processes in a wide variety of psychological domains. A central aim of this chapter was to outline, however inadequately, the breadth of this enterprise and to offer an overview of the exchange framework in a multilevel explanatory context. Such an approach highlights the strengths and potential of the theory as it expands into yet new areas of inquiry of the way human beings make meaning in their daily lives.

References

Adamopoulos, J. (1982). The perception of interpersonal behavior: Dimensionality and importance of the social environment. *Environment and Behavior, 14*(1), 29–44.
Adamopoulos, J. (1984). The differentiation of social behavior: Toward an explanation of universal interpersonal structures. *Journal of Cross-Cultural Psychology, 15*(4), 487–508.

RESOURCE THEORY AND LEVELS OF EXPLANATION   291

Adamopoulos, J. (1999). The emergence of cultural patterns of interpersonal behavior. In J. Adamopoulos & Y. Kashima (Eds.), *Social psychology and cultural context* (pp. 63–76). SAGE.

Adamopoulos, J. (2008). On the entanglement of culture and individual behavior. In F. J. R. van de Vijver, D. A. van Hemert, & Y. H. Poortinga (Eds.), *Multilevel analysis of individuals and cultures* (pp. 27–62). Taylor & Francis.

Adamopoulos, J. (2012). The emergence of social meaning: A theory of action construal. In K. Törnblom & A. Kazemi (Eds.), *Handbook of social resource theory: Theoretical extensions, empirical insights, and social applications* (pp. 255–272). Springer.

Adamopoulos, J. (2013a). [Sociocultural context and the emergence of social meaning: Toward a theory of action construal]. Keynote address at the biennial conference of the Hellenic Psychological Association, Alexandroupolis, Greece.

Adamopoulos, J. (2013b). Interpersonal exchange and freedom for resource acquisition: Comment on Van de Vliert. *Behavioral and Brain Sciences, 36*(5), 480–481.

Adamopoulos, J., & Lonner, W. J. (1994). Absolutism, relativism, and universalism in the study of human behavior. In W. J. Lonner & R. S. Malpass (Eds.), *Psychology and culture* (pp. 129–134). Allyn & Bacon.

Adamopoulos, J., & Lonner, W. J. (2001). Culture and psychology at a crossroad: Historical perspective and theoretical analysis. In D. Matsumoto (Ed.), *The handbook of culture and psychology* (pp. 11–34). Oxford University Press.

Adamopoulos, J., & Stogiannidou, A. (1996). The perception of interpersonal action: Culture-general and culture-specific components. In H. Grad, A. Blanco, & J. Georgas (Eds.), *Key issues in cross-cultural psychology* (pp. 263–275). Swets & Zeitlinger.

Ahl, V., & Allen, T. F. H. (1996). *Hierarchy theory: A vision, vocabulary, and epistemology.* Columbia University Press.

Barker, R. G. (1965). Explorations in ecological psychology. *American Psychologist, 20*(1), 1–14.

Caporael, L. R. (2007). Evolutionary theory for social and cultural psychology. In A. W. Kruglanski & E. T. Higgins (Eds.), *Social psychology: Handbook of basic principles* (2nd ed., pp. 3–18). Guilford.

Cottrell, N. B. (1975). Heider's structural balance principle as a conceptual rule. *Journal of Personality and Social Psychology, 31*(4), 713–720.

Fiske, A. P. (1991). *Structures of social life: The four elementary forms of human relations.* Free Press.

Fiske, A. P. (1992). The four elementary forms of sociality: Framework for a unified theory of social relations. *Psychological Review, 99*(4), 689–723.

Foa, E. B., & Foa, U. G. (2012). Resource theory of social exchange. In K. Törnblom & A. Kazemi (Eds.), *Handbook of social resource theory: Theoretical extensions, empirical insights, and social applications* (pp. 15–32). Springer.

Foa, U. G. (1961). Convergences in the analysis of the structure of interpersonal behavior. *Psychological Review, 68*(5), 341–353.

Foa, U. G. (1963). A facet approach to the prediction of communalities. *Behavioral Science, 8*(3), 220–226.

Foa, U. G. (1964). Cross-cultural similarity and difference in interpersonal behavior. *Journal of Abnormal and Social Psychology, 68*(5), 517–522.

Foa, U. G. (1965). New developments in facet design and analysis. *Psychological Review, 72*(4), 262–274.

Foa, U. G. (1993). Interpersonal and economic resources. In U. G. Foa, J. Converse, K. Y. Törnblom, & E. B. Foa (Eds.), *Resource theory: Explorations and applications* (pp. 13–30). Academic Press.

Foa, U. G., & Foa, E. B. (1974). *Societal structures of the mind*. Charles C Thomas.

Foa, U. G., Salcedo, L. N., Tornblom, K. Y., Garner, M., Ubman, H. G., & Teichman, M. (1987). Interrelation of social resources: Evidence of pancultural invariance. *Journal of Cross-Cultural Psychology, 18*(2), 221–233.

Foa, U. G., Tornblom, K. Y., Foa, E. B., & Converse, J. (1993). Introduction: Resource theory in social psychology. In U. G. Foa, J. Converse, Jr., K. Y. Törnblom, & E. B. Foa (Eds.), *Resource theory. Explorations and applications* (pp. 1–10). Academic Press.

Foa, U. G., Triandis, H. C., & Katz, E. W. (1966). Cross-cultural invariance in the differentiation and organization of family roles. *Journal of Personality and Social Psychology, 4*(3), 316–327.

Furnham, A., & Argyle, M. (Eds.). (1981). *The psychology of social situations: Selected readings*. Pergamon.

Gardikiotis, A., & Tsingilis, N. (2019, May). [The formation of relationship prototypes with friends in social media networks] [Paper presentation]. 17th Hellenic Congress of Psychological Research, Alexandroupolis, Greece.

Griffiths, T. L., Lieder, F., & Goodman, N. D. (2015). Rational use of cognitive resources: Levels of analysis between the computational and the algorithmic. *Topics in Cognitive Science, 7*(2), 217–229.

Haslam, N. (1994). Mental representation of social relationships: Dimensions, laws, or categories? *Journal of Personality and Social Psychology, 67*(4), 575–584.

Haslam, N. (1995). Factor structure of social relationships: An examination of relational models and resource exchange theories. *Journal of Social and Personal Relationships, 12*(2), 217–227.

Haslam, N., & Fiske, A. P. (1992). Implicit relationship prototypes: Investigating five theories of the cognitive organization of social relationships. *Journal of Experimental Social Psychology, 28*(5), 441–474.

Komorita, S. S. (1976). A model of the N-person dilemma-type game. *Journal of Experimental Social Psychology, 12*(4), 357–373.

Kurby, C. A., & Zacks, J. M. (2008). Segmentation in the perception and memory of events. *Trends in Cognitive Sciences, 12*(2), 72–79.

Lewin, K. (1951). *Field theory in social science*. Harper & Row.

Lieder, F., & Griffiths, T. L. (2020). Resource-rational analysis: Understanding human cognition as the optimal use of limited computational resources. *Behavioral and Brain Sciences, 43*, e1.

Lonner, W., & Adamopoulos, J. (1997). Culture as antecedent to behavior. In J. W. Berry, Y. H. Poortinga, & J. Pandey (Eds.), *Handbook of cross-cultural psychology: Theory and method* (Vol. 1, 2nd ed., pp. 43–83). Allyn & Bacon.

Markus, H. R., & Kitayama, S. (1991). Culture and the self: Implications for cognition, emotion, and motivation. *Psychological Review, 98*(2), 224–253.

Newtson, D., & Engquist, G. (1976). The perceptual organization of ongoing behavior. *Journal of Experimental Social Psychology, 12*(5), 436–450.

Picek, J. S., Sherman, S. J., & Shiffrin, R. M. (1975). Cognitive organization and coding of social structures. *Journal of Personality and Social Psychology, 31*(4), 758–768.

Radvansky, G. A., & Zacks, J. M. (2014). *Event cognition*. Oxford University Press.

Schwartz, S. H. (1992). Universals in the structure and content of values: Theoretical advances and empirical tests in 20 countries. *Advances in Experimental Social Psychology, 25,* 1–65.

Simon, H. A. (1973). The organization of complex systems. In H. H. Patee (Ed.), *Hierarchy theory: The challenge of complex systems* (pp. 1–27). Braziller.

Törnblom, K., & Kazemi, A. (Eds.). (2012). *Handbook of social resource theory: Theoretical extensions, empirical insights, and social applications.* Springer.

Triandis, H. C. (1977). *Interpersonal behavior.* Brooks/Cole.

Triandis, H. C. (1994). *Culture and social behavior.* McGraw-Hill.

Triandis, H. C. (1995). *Individualism & collectivism.* Westview.

Triandis, H. C. (2001). Individualism and collectivism: Past, present, and future. In D. Matsumoto (Ed.), *The handbook of culture and psychology* (pp. 35–50). Oxford University Press.

Triandis, H. C., Hui, C. H., Albert, R. D., Leung, S.-M., Lisansky, J., Diaz-Loving, R., Plascencia, L., Marin, G., Betancourt, H., & Loyola-Cintron, L. (1984). Individual models of social behavior. *Journal of Personality and Social Psychology, 46*(6), 1389–1404.

Van de Vliert, E. (2013a). Climato-economic habitats support patterns of human needs, stresses, and freedoms. *Behavioral and Brain Sciences, 36*(5), 465–480.

Van de Vliert, E. (2013b). White, gray, and black domains of cultural adaptations to climato-economic conditions: Van de Vliert's response. *Behavioral and Brain Sciences, 36*(5), 503–521.

Voelklein, C., & Howarth, C. (2005). A review of controversies about social representations theory: A British debate. *Culture & Psychology, 11*(4), 431–454.

Wright, J., & Drinkwater, M. (1997). Rationality vs. accuracy of social judgment. *Social Cognition, 15*(4), 245–273.

9

Resources and Social Justice in Meso- and Macro-Level Environmental Conflict

Susan Opotow

Uriel and Edna Foa's 1974 book, *Societal Structures of the Mind*, now out of print, is an important resource for psychologists and kindred scholars. Its contributions to resource theory are elegant and have been influential. The Foas' work resonates with Gestalt psychology's attention to the organization of elements in relation to one another, the subjective meaning of these elements in everyday life, and people's lived experiences in the constantly changing dynamics of everyday life (Ash, 1998; Koffka, 1936; Köhler, 1959; Sarris, 2020). In addition, their work resonates with Lewin's (1939) field theory and its emphasis on social behavior as a function of both people and context (Deutsch, 1968). Bringing the Foas' book back into print in conversation with new developments within psychology is therefore an exciting and valuable initiative.

In their comprehensive investigations of resources and their role in human relationships, Uriel and Foa (1974) closely examine resource exchanges in social relations, grounded in their conviction that "contact with people is of primary importance" (p. 3). Their analyses center on an empirically derived typology of six resource classes, offering researchers a framework for studying human interaction in a ubiquitous and prosaic activity: resource exchange. Their framework offers scholars theoretical tools that can analyze social interactions with systematicity and depth.

I write this chapter in appreciation of their work. It has offered me useful analytic tools to study the construct, *scope of justice*, the boundary within which moral values, rules, and considerations of fairness apply (Opotow, 1990). My studies of inclusionary and exclusionary change in society examine how the scope of justice shrinks and expands over time (Opotow, 1993, 1994). They are attentive to social issues that include environmental conservation, degradation, and conflict (e.g., Opotow, 2012, 2018).

Social Behavior as Resource Exchange. Kjell Yngve Törnblom and Ali Kazemi, Oxford University Press.
© Oxford University Press 2023. DOI: 10.1093/oso/9780190066994.003.0011

This chapter focuses on a specific and influential contribution of the Foas' work: the framework they developed that identifies six basic resource classes in social exchange—love, services, goods, money, information, and status. The Foas represent these six resource classes in an elegant circular figure (Foa & Foa, 1974, p. 82) framed by two dimensions, *particularism* and *concreteness*. Their investigations largely focus on interpersonal interactions, but in this chapter, I investigate the relevance of their framework to larger levels of analysis (cf., Pettigrew, 1997; Rubin & Levinger, 1995) and to a specific kind of social issue—environmental resource conflicts.

Like other scholars, I view the Foas' work as having societal-issues relevance at meso and macro levels as well as for individuals (e.g., Törnblom & Kazemi, 2012). Focusing on resource exchange at larger levels of analysis is timely because environmental issues are intensifying throughout the world, posing urgent challenges at all levels of analysis—for individuals (micro level); institutions, communities, and regions (meso level); as well as nations and the planet (macro level). Current environmental issues are challenging human and planetary well-being (Fountain, 2021; Intergovernmental Panel on Climate Change, 2021). These challenges include the rise of temperature throughout the world, the increasing threat to biodiversity, and pervasive environmental degradation that threatens the resources that humans have relied on to sustain life for millennia (United Nations, 2021).

In this chapter, I first define three key constructs—*resource, conflict,* and *justice*—and identify contested resources in five studies of environmental conflict. Then, utilizing these studies, I engage with three questions: (a) Are the Foas' six resource classes applicable to meso- and macro-level environmental contexts? (b) Are the two dimensions—particularism and concreteness—identified by Foa and Foa (1974) as germane in interpersonal exchange relationships also relevant in meso- and macro-level environmental resource conflicts? (c) What does the adaptation of resource exchange theory to meso and macro environmental issues tell us about the connection between resources and social justice?

Resources, Conflicts, and Justice
in Environmental Contexts

Resources, conflicts, and justice are closely linked in most conflicts, but this is especially evident in environmental issues. Drawing on my scholarship

296 PART II NEW THEORETICAL AND EMPIRICAL DEVELOPMENTS

examining the scope of justice in a range of environmental contexts (e.g., Opotow, 1994, 2012), I connect the Foas' six fundamental resources classes—love, services, goods, money, information, and status—with meso- and macro-level environmental resource conflicts that can negatively impact people, places, and nonhuman aspects of the natural world (cf., Leopold, 1949; Searles, 1960; Stone, 1974).

Because the constructs *resource, conflict,* and *justice* can be unclear, I discuss them by drawing on my theoretical and empirical work on inclusionary and exclusionary change (e.g., Opotow, 1990, 2018). With these constructs in mind, I present a synopsis of five studies of environmental conflicts in order to assess the relevance of the Foas' work to environmental issues.

Resources

Because of their ubiquity, complexity, and centrality, *resources* as a construct and *resource exchange* as an activity offer a useful lens for investigations of social justice. Törnblom and Kazemi (2012), experts on the Foas' scholarship, have comprehensively studied the construct, *resource,* and its role in theories of resource exchange. They observe that *resource* is an everyday word as well as a construct at the core of psychological research because of its centrality in human relations. As they observe, the Foas (1974) defined resource as "any commodity—material or symbolic—which is transmitted through interpersonal behavior" (p. 36).

Other definitions of resource offer additional insight into this construct. For example, the *Oxford English Dictionary* (2021) defines resource as a "means of supplying a deficiency or need; something that is a source of help, information, strength, etc." In its plural form, *resources* are defined as "stocks or reserves of money, materials, people, or some other asset, which can be drawn on when necessary." They are also "collective means possessed by a country or region for its own support, enrichment, or defense." The *Oxford English Dictionary* (2021) also defines the compound construct *natural resources*—the kinds of resources at issue in this study of environmental contexts and conflicts—as "those materials or substances of a place which can be used to sustain life or for economic exploitation."

Collectively, these definitions affirm: (a) that resources cannot be understood in the abstract as they emerge within the particulars of context and (b) that resources can produce harm as well as well-being (cf., Törnblom.

1988). This observation is especially evident in the environmental sphere, where the availability or unavailability of resources can be a matter of life and death. Both scarcity and excess can be catastrophic. For example, water is a vital resource that supports life on our planet but is implicated in both droughts and floods.

Delving into resources in environmental contexts, the *Environmental Encyclopedia* defines *environmental resources* as "any material, service, or information from the environment that is valuable to society" and includes "anything that people find useful in their environs" (Cunningham, 2011, p. 608), noting that environmental resources can have competing uses. A parcel of land, for example, could be

> a farm, a park, a parking lot, or a housing development. It could be mined or used as a garbage dump . . . [raising] the question, what do people find valuable in their environment, and how do people choose to use the resources that their environment provides?

As Cunningham (2011) observes, many environmental resources are being depleted by industrial and population growth, and although some environmental resources are renewable, others (e.g., oil and coal) cannot be reused after being extracted from the ground and burned.

Collectively, these definitions of environmental resources suggest that the six classes of resource the Foas proposed—love/caring, services, goods, money, information, and status—are different at meso and macro levels than they are at the micro/interpersonal level because they are more complex and more consequential at larger scales. In my work, I have translated Foa and Foa's resource, love, as *caring*. I do so because caring is apt at meso and macro levels. Although a person can love a country or a group of people, caring can be an important resource in human interactions at all levels beyond close, intimate, and romantic relationships.

Conflicts

Morton Deutsch (1973) and his students have emphasized that *conflicts* emerge from incompatibilities—when one party wants something that another resists doing or giving (Opotow & Deutsch, 1999; Rubin et al., 1994). Such incompatibilities motivate one party to prevent, obstruct, interfere,

298 PART II NEW THEORETICAL AND EMPIRICAL DEVELOPMENTS

injure, or in some other way make opposing parties' actions less likely to occur or be effective. Törnblom and Kazemi (2012) observe that actions can have different meanings between individuals, and this becomes especially salient in conflict. Similarly, when conflicts are between groups and about, for example, the use or abuse of environmental resources, they can be perceived differently by groups with divergent priorities and perceptions of justice (Clayton et al., 2016).

Although there are endless grounds for conflicts among friends, neighbors, colleagues, institutions, and nations, most conflicts can be characterized as conflicts of interests, conflicts of values, or conflicts over resources (Opotow, 2004). *Conflicts of interest* arise from the failure to understand another's perspective, which can lead to the failure to see possibilities for joint gain (Fisher et al., 1991).

Conflicts of values concern opposing worldviews and can arise in ethnic, religious, or political conflict. Although people and groups with different values and commitments can live together peacefully in societies that respect and value difference (cf., Deutsch, 2015), conflicts of values can fuel escalating dissension. Because conflicts of values can deepen the perceived stakes of a conflict, they can precipitate more extreme responses to conflict that trigger aggression and violence. As Coser (1956) has warned, "expect more violence to the extent that participants perceive the issues at stake in terms of abstract values transcending the specific case" (p. 112).

Conflicts over resources are common in most conflicts as parties in conflict seek to attain particular objects and objectives that may be incompatible with those of others. Any kind of resource conflict can precipitate squabbles in daily life, and resource conflicts can also precipitate intransigent, deadly conflicts throughout the world as groups or nations seek control of land, water, petroleum, minerals, and other valued resources (cf., Klare, 2001; Schellens & Diemer, 2020). Although compromises can resolve some resource conflicts, not all resources lend themselves to trade-offs or sharing because it is not always possible to simultaneously utilize, share, and conserve many kinds of environmental resources.

All environmental conflicts are complex because they involve (a) granting or withholding some tangible and valuable environmental good, such as clean water, land, and air; (b) distributing noxious environmental *bads*, such as the dumping of toxic effluent waste on land, in water, and in the air; (c) multiple natural systems; and (d) multiple stakeholder groups that can include individuals, the larger public, state and federal regulatory agencies, and citizen public and private organizations at local, regional, national, and international levels (Opotow & Weiss, 2000).

As a result, environmental conflicts can be difficult to resolve because they can involve scarce resources. They can therefore impinge on people's core ideological beliefs about what they want, believe they deserve, and their deeply held environmental identities (Clayton & Opotow, 2003; Thompson & Gonzalez, 1997). Finally, environmental conflicts can have uneven effects. In environmental conflicts, some communities fare better than others. Recipients of polluted air, water, and toxic waste (e.g., Bullard, 2019; Bullard et al., 2007; Pulido, 2000; Taylor, 2014) are largely poor communities and communities of color. This raises concerns about environmental injustice and its negative effects on individual, community, and societal health (Islam & Winkel, 2017; Opotow, 2012, 2018; World Health Organization, 2010).

Justice

The construct *justice* encompasses attitudes, morals, and values underlying people's beliefs about their own and others' deserving, rights, entitlement, responsibilities, and obligations (Deutsch, 1985; Opotow, 2009; Törnblom et al., 2007). Foa and Foa's (1974) book emerged at a time when the psychological literature on justice sought to spell out the "intuitive notion of fairness" (Foa & Foa, 1974, p. 244). It was a time when the influence of Equity Theory's economic logic with an emphasis on inputs versus outputs had been prominent in psychological studies of justice (e.g., Adams, 1965; Berscheid et al., 1968). Increasingly, equity theory was criticized by social psychologists who sought to extend justice research beyond economic contexts into other social relationships in other spheres of society that included families and other non-economic relationships in which norms other than equity were relevant (cf., M. Lerner, 1975; M. Lerner & Lerner, 1981; Montada, 2003; Montada & Lerner, 1996). This period gave rise to research on distributively just decisions (cf., Deutsch, 1975; Kazemi et al., 2015; Mikula, 1980) and procedurally just processes (Lind & Tyler, 1988; Thibaut & Walker, 1975)—lines of justice research that were inspired by emerging social issues and societal change.

These advances expanded the design of experiments, such as work that compared equity, equality, and need as distributive justice norms (Deutsch, 1975). Experimental studies, however, were designed so that regardless of their assignment to experimental condition, parties were approximately equal,

300 PART II NEW THEORETICAL AND EMPIRICAL DEVELOPMENTS

plausibly entitled to a share of a target resource (often tokens), and there was some potential for reciprocity. In everyday life, however, these conditions are not always met, particularly in contexts characterized by moral disregard and "normalized injustice" (McClelland & Opotow, 2011, p. 137). I proposed that in addition to the emerging emphasis on the *what* of distributive and the *how* of procedural justice, justice research should also be attentive to *who*—specifically who or *what* matters. This question is attentive to "who and what kinds of entities are inside or outside the scope of justice?" (Opotow, 1987, 1990).

The *Scope of Justice* is a construct acknowledging that there are human groups and environmental entities that we do and do not care about (Opotow, 1994, 1995). Those within our Scope of Justice matter to us. As a consequence, we may recognize a moral obligation to foster their well-being. But some people and environmental entities are perceived as outside the scope of justice. These can include people who are poor, young, old, members of disrespected classes, as well as disliked aspects of the natural world such as repugnant animals or habitats. These kinds of people and entities can be *morally excluded* and vulnerable to exploitation and harm that is then viewed as acceptable, normal, just, and as "the way things are" or ought to be (e.g., Opotow, 2008, 2009).

To conduct research on exclusionary and inclusionary dynamics, I designed empirical research yielding a Scope of Justice Scale consisting of three attitudes toward others: (a) believing that considerations of fairness apply to them, (b) willingness to allocate a share of community resources to them, and (c) being willing to make sacrifices to foster others' well-being (Opotow, 1987, 1990, 1993). This scale is attentive to the central role resources have in relationships. In inclusionary relationships, others' rights and needs are respected, and extending caring to others may entail giving up some of one's own resources so that others can thrive too. In contrast, in exclusionary relationships, considerations of fairness and caring do not extend to others, and such relationships are not characterized by a willingness to share resources with others. Instead, there is unwillingness to make sacrifices that could foster others' well-being and justify it on the basis of deeply rooted conventions of exclusion.

Environmental Resources and Justice Conflicts

Environmental injustice is the inequitable distribution of environmental resources and the lack of environmental protections and the representation of affected communities in decision-making bodies (Figueroa, 2005). It results from the "differential distribution of environmental hazards and susceptibility to hazards resulting in the differential achievement of health according to different groups in the population" (London et al., 2011, p. 441). As a construct, environmental injustice highlights the endangerment of individuals and communities because their exclusion from the scope of justice has negative effects on their health and well-being.

For example, common toxic waste disposal policies illustrate environmental injustice. No community wants to be a site for toxic waste disposal, and NIMBY (not-in-my-backyard) protests opposing hazardous waste facility siting near one's home and within or adjacent to one's community have been common for decades (Van der Horst, 2007). However, poor communities and communities of color (Bullard, 2019; Checker, 2019; Pulido, 2000), as well as developing nations (Clapp, 2010), shoulder toxic burdens within and between countries. Environmental injustice also occurs when environmental *goods* that people have relied on for their well-being, such as clean water, are appropriated by affluent urban centers, depleting freshwater at its source. This can increase hardship in rural areas as well as damage the ecology of affected regions (Garrick et al., 2019; Howe, 2021; U.S. National Academy of Sciences, et al., 1999).

The appropriation, exploitation, and competition for control of natural resources can precipitate violent conflict. The United Nations (2018) reports that "40 per cent of internal armed conflicts over the last 60 years have been linked to natural resources. With the increasing impacts of climate change evident in all regions, the risks are only going to grow." As populations grow, increasing consumption of environmental resources such as forests and other kinds of environmental degradation place significant and unsustainable pressure on such critical environmental resources as oil, gas, minerals, fresh water, and land. These environmental pressures exacerbate existing ethnic or religious divides within societies and across borders (United Nations, 2018). Therefore, environmental resource conflicts, already a major challenge, are worsening.

Environmental Resource Conflicts: Five Case Studies

To investigate the application of Foa and Foa's (1974) typology of key resource classes to environmental issues, I discuss five of my research studies

302 PART II NEW THEORETICAL AND EMPIRICAL DEVELOPMENTS

that investigated justice questions within environmental conflicts. Because these studies are attentive to resources that precipitate conflict, they provide an apt context to identify the various resources with implications for the well-being of communities, regions, and nations. These studies concern remediation of polluted sites (Bingham & Opotow, 2021), air pollution (Opotow & Weiss, 2000), environmentally burdened communities (Opotow, 2012), rangeland disputes (Opotow & Brook, 2003), and endangered species conservation (Chang & Opotow, 2009). Although these studies span two decades, each has contemporary relevance now throughout the world. I first present a synopsis of each study and in the section that follows discuss their connection to the Foas' typology of six key resource classes.

A Polluted Urban Canal

The first study (Bingham & Opotow, 2021) concerns the Gowanus Canal in Brooklyn, New York, a populous borough in New York City. Created in 1849, the canal became a repository for raw sewage from surrounding households and hazardous waste from industrial activity along its banks. Because industry on its banks was crucial for New York City's economy, polluting the canal and its surrounding land was allowed, placing the health of local workers and residents at risk (Bingham & Opotow, 2021; Gould & Lewis, 2017). Yet, despite the canal's pollution, in 2007, New York City Mayor Michael Bloomberg proposed rezoning the neighborhood to transform a historic, diverse, and largely industrial area into a luxury residential enclave. His proposal attracted investors, but it also catalyzed this working-class neighborhood, which included public housing residents, artists, industrial owners, and industrial workers, to demand that the government clean the canal first. Because they distrusted the mayor's plan, community members pursued a Superfund designation for the area. Although a Superfund designation would ordinarily be an unwanted encumbrance because it stigmatizes polluted communities, community activists sought this designation to save a neighborhood that had been struggling with significant environmental burdens for 150 years. They achieved Superfund designation, which set in motion a mandated process to remediate pollution collaboratively, a project that would take 20 years (cf., Zaveri, 2020). However, at its halfway point in 2021, over the protest of community groups, New York City Council approved then–New York City Mayor Bill de Blasio's plan to rezone the Gowanus neighborhood to allow upscale development (Hickman, 2021; Zaveri et al., 2021).

Interstate Transport of Air Pollution

Ozone at ground level is a main ingredient of smog, a harmful air pollutant with negative effects on people and the environment (U.S. Environmental Protection Agency, n.d.). This environmental harm is called a *disbenefit* in the air regulatory field. In the early 1990s, ozone was documented as traveling from upwind Midwestern states to downwind eastern United States.

Opotow and Weiss (2000) studied interstate ozone negotiations convened by the Ozone Transport Assessment Group (OTAG), which was convened for 2 years (1995–1997) and included 37 Midwestern and eastern states. OTAG was tasked with identifying control strategies that could reduce transported ozone (Weiss, 1996). OTAG's interstate deliberations concerned regulatory issues and differential outcomes experienced by various groups. Underlying this large-scale environmental problem was the political reality that stringent environmental standards mandated by law do not necessarily translate into stringent standards for compliance or enforcement. And during negotiations, several upwind states rebutted well-documented data on regional ozone transport to downwind eastern states. We noted that their arguments aligned with their interest in limiting emission controls and, in turn, triggered three kinds of denial we identified in our study of the negotiation process: (a) denying outcome severity, (b) denying concern for other stakeholders, and (c) denying their culpability (Opotow & Weiss, 2000). We also observed that these three kinds of denial supported the moral exclusion of stakeholders with different needs, positions, and concerns than their own (cf., Opotow, 1990). We therefore positioned denial as a driver of destructive conflict (cf., Deutsch, 1973) because it minimized the complexity and gravity of the issues at stake, distorted facts, and disregarded needs of affected parties.

We proposed that this kind of conflict can be managed more productively when diverse stakeholders are included in collective problem-solving. Doing so promotes perspective-taking that is attentive to the broad scope of harms that air pollution can inflict on diverse human stakeholders and on environmental entities, including harms that persist over time. We also proposed that positioning the environment itself as a stakeholder (Leopold, 1949; Stone, 1974; see also U.S. Supreme Court Justice W. O. Douglas's dissent in *Sierra Club v. Morton*, 1972). Doing so can offer a broader understanding of what well-being means for who or what, thereby enabling solutions that take a larger view for preventing or remediating macro-level environmental problems.

304 PART II NEW THEORETICAL AND EMPIRICAL DEVELOPMENTS

Pollution-Burdened Communities

The United States, like the rest of the world, struggles with environmental pollution. Whereas some kinds are widespread (e.g., smog), others are concentrated in or near such toxic sites as power plants, landfills, and brownfields (Bullard, 2019; Bullard et al., 2007). My research (Opotow, 2012, 2018) focuses on communities situated on or near toxic pollutants dubbed "sacrifice zones," "fence-line," and "throwaway" communities that are largely low-income and communities of color that live with contaminants in their water, air, and soil (S. Lerner, 2010). *The New York Times* columnist Bob Herbert (2006) described one such site, a tiny Black community, Eno Road, in Tennessee that abuts a landfill containing toxic chemicals that have polluted its water. Herbert writes that Eno Road is

> a quiet rustic area with an interesting history. Hundreds of acres of land along the road were acquired by blacks in the post-slavery period. Only recently freed, they were proud of being landowners. . . . Blacks make up just 4.5 percent of the Dickson County population, and they have always been clustered in the vicinity of Eno Road. This has been a great convenience for the whites, who have run the local governments. For six decades, the Eno Road community has been designated as the place for whites to dump their garbage. (p. 19)

Laura Pulido (2000) explains that environmental racism is "the product of relationships between distinct places, including industrial zones, affluent suburbs, working-class suburbs, and downtown areas, all of which are racialized" (p. 13). Studying "how did whites distance themselves from industrial pollution and nonwhites?" (p. 14), Pulido found that racism emerged not only from discriminatory attitudes and behavior but also—with larger and lasting effect—from social, political, economic, and cultural systems that offer White people environmental advantages that they come to expect and that are then protected by custom and law. Attentive to the spatiality of racism, she describes "distinct geographies of exposure" (p. 33) that have arisen when Whites have abandoned industrial zones abutting environmental hazards and these zones became increasingly occupied by racial and ethnic minorities. Therefore, she observes, environmental racism results not only from attitudes toward others but also from millions of choices made by individuals over time. In the aggregate, these choices constitute "a racial formation, and are a response to conditions deliberately created by the state and capital" (Pulido, 2000, p. 25).

Rangeland Conflict

Bitter, protracted rangeland conflicts in the southwestern United States concern the management of public and private land and the regulation of water allocations, grazing leases, and species preservation (Opotow & Brook, 2003). Some of these conflicts emerged from the 1973 Endangered Species Act (ESA) that some landowners found threatening because it contained potentially restrictive regulations. Since 1973, ESA regulations concerning grazing leases on public lands have generated countless conflicts within communities where ranchers, environmentalists, and federal land managers have struggled with different values, motives, needs, and cultures (Clayton & Brook, 2005). Although key protagonists are ranchers and environmentalists (both individuals and environmental groups), these are multiparty conflicts that include governmental regulatory bodies (e.g., U.S. Fish and Wildlife Service and the Bureau of Land Management), indigenous populations, local people who do not depend on the rangeland for their livelihood, the larger public, and the nonhuman animate and inanimate natural world.

In 2016, the Malheur National Wildlife Refuge in the northwestern United States was occupied by armed, anti-governmental militias whose members were affiliated with the sovereign citizen movement that is opposed to federal ownership and management of public lands. They sought to convey federally protected lands that are a birthright for all Americans to the states, claiming that their occupation was based on constitutional principles. This claim is viewed by constitutional scholars as meritless and inconsistent with U.S. Supreme Court interpretations of federal powers to manage federal public lands (e.g., Blumm & Jamin, 2016). However, the sovereign citizen movement's goal—federal divestiture of public lands—was adopted by the Republican Party as part of its 2016 platform for the national election that brought Donald Trump to power as U.S. President (Dare & Fletcher, 2019; K. Johnson, 2017).

Taking a world view of rangelands, the *Rangelands Atlas* published by the United Nations Environmental Programme (2021) defines rangelands as "vast tracts of land covered by grass, shrubs or sparse, hardy vegetation that support millions of pastoralists, hunter–gatherers, ranchers and large populations of wildlife—and store large amounts of carbon." Arguing the urgency of rangeland protection, the *Rangelands Atlas* observes that 54% of Earth's land surfaces are rangelands, including the steppes of Mongolia, the savannas of Africa, the pampas of South America, and the Great Plains in North America. Yet plans for alleviating climate change largely focus on the

306 PART II NEW THEORETICAL AND EMPIRICAL DEVELOPMENTS

role of forests, slighting the consequential role that rangelands can play in environmental planning. Therefore, policies developed to reduce poverty and threats to biodiversity as well as to protect freshwater and sustainable food systems should be attentive to rangelands' capacity to store carbon, provide wildlife habitat, and support the world's largest rivers and wetlands. Yet, currently, only 12% of the world's rangelands are protected.

Wildlife Conservation in the Kunene Region

This study examined people's values and beliefs about nature and environmental protection in Namibia's Kunene region, a remote area rich in wildlife and renowned for its charismatic megafauna (Chang & Opotow, 2009). In this region, the population of endangered black rhinoceros has been declining for decades due to environmental degradation, overexploitation, and poaching. At a biological research station, we conducted interviews of North Americans and Namibians to include nontraditional populations and geographic contexts in conservation psychology research. North Americans at the site were in the region for extended stays as environmental foundation employees, conservation field biologists, and researchers. Local people at the site were predominantly Damara and Herero people who worked in a range of occupations that included rhinoceros trackers, local conservancy employees, park rangers, police officers, livestock farmers, and wilderness safari guides. Many local people worked in the ecotourism industry, at the research station, and had other sources of employment, including subsistence farming and goat herding, to supplement their incomes.

Both Namibian and North American respondents described their deep love of nature and a desire to protect it. Respondents from both groups did not want to see animals' habitats destroyed nor animals become endangered or extinct. Both groups worried about ongoing environmental degradation and stated a need for collective action and education to protect nature. A key between-group finding of our research concerned the extrinsic valuing of nature. When asked about nature's value to people, North American respondents said little about its extrinsic value. In contrast to their more lengthy responses to other questions, their comments were strikingly brief and offered little detail. In response to the probe, "What do animals do for people?" a North American respondent said, "They pollinate the plants; they clean up our waste; they provide sustenance, shelter, and clothing." Another respondent described the utility of domesticated animals: "People produce animals in agriculture, and there is a history of using horses. Everyone loves their pets too" (Chang & Opotow, 2009, p. 83). North Americans' descriptions of nature's value were consistent with scholarly and popular writing on environmental conservation that emphasizes nature's intrinsic value.

Namibian respondents spoke at greater length and with nuanced detail about nature's extrinsic value. Asked "What do animals do for people?" they described the importance of goats, sheep, chickens, donkeys, and other animals' contributions to agriculture and human well-being (e.g., clothing and food). One respondent described the many ways animals benefit people and positioned both domestic and wild animals as part of nature (Chang & Opotow, 2009):

> Animals create game trails and can lead to water points for human beings in the field. Animals help fertilize grazing areas. [Animals] help some livestock. . . . Animals educate people about whether they're dangerous or angry or tame. They mean meat—food for human beings. (p. 83)

Domesticated animals have extrinsic value for Namibian respondents because they provide income, labor, meat, and status. They mentioned "game" often and noted the extrinsic value of wild animals for sport, meat, and income. Compared with the North American respondents, who offered universal and more abstract views of nature, Namibian respondents expressed a view of nature that is grounded in the specifics of the material and economic context of their lives. Of interest, they positioned the extrinsic valuing of nature as consistent with conservation concerns. Thus, contextual influences on environmental values need to be understood in light of the socioeconomic realities. They suggest the importance of including local people in deliberative decision-making to update and refine environmental rules and strategies to ensure that conservation policies are attentive to nature, people, and socioeconomic, cultural, and environmental contexts.

Summary of the Five Studies

The five studies suggest the varied resources underlying environmental issues and conflicts. They highlight the complexities of these conflicts and the diverse stakeholders affected (e.g., Opotow & Weiss, 2000). Both the Gowanus study (Bingham & Opotow, 2021) and the Kunene study in Namibia (Chang & Opotow, 2009) concern conservation of different kinds— community and wildlife, respectively. Both argue that ecologically sound planning requires involving local residents. The rangeland study (Opotow

308 PART II NEW THEORETICAL AND EMPIRICAL DEVELOPMENTS

& Brook, 2003) describes the challenges of achieving constructive resolution when parties embrace extreme and opposed political positions. Situating low-income communities and communities of color as sacrifice zones abutting toxic sites is a persistent and structural problem (Opotow, 2018). Together, the studies specify some of the many resources at issue in environmental conflicts. Drawing on these studies, I address the three questions I enunciated at the beginning of this chapter.

Connecting the Foas' Resource Classes with Environmental Contexts

In this section, I answer the three questions raised in this chapter's introduction.

Question 1: Are the Foas' six resource classes applicable to meso- and macro-level environmental contexts?

My approach to this question about the applicability of the Foas' resource classes to meso- and macro-level environmental contexts was empirical and systematic. I first identified key resources mentioned in the five studies. Working from these specifics, I created Table 9.1 (five studies × six resource classes), a compilation that placed resources at issue in these studies in relation to the six classes of resources proposed by Foa and Foa (1974) that were largely developed in their research on interpersonal relationships. Table 9.1 is meant to be suggestive rather than comprehensive in this listing of some of the many kinds of resources at issue in these environmental studies.

The 30 cells in Table 9.1 suggest, first, that there is a diverse array of resources in this small sample of meso- and macro-level environmental conflicts. Second, although contexts in these studies differ considerably from interpersonal relationships, the resources noted in this sample of studies have relevance to Foa and Foa's six resource classes. Third, and consistent with definitions of resources, natural resources, and environmental resources presented earlier (*Oxford English Dictionary*, 2021; *Environmental Encyclopedia* [Cunningham, 2011), the environmental resources in these studies include both positive *goods* (+) and negative *bads* (–) (cf., Törnblom, 1988). In short, the answer to the first question is "yes," the Foas' six resource classes are useful when applied to meso- and macro-level environmental

Table 9.1 Five Studies of Environment Conflict and Foa and Foa's (1974) Six Resource Classes[a]

Study	Foa and Foa's (1974) Six Resource Classes					
	Love/Caring	Services	Goods	Money	Information	Status
Pollution—canal (Bingham & Opotow, 2021)	(+) Community engagement	(+) Federally funded Superfund services	(−) Environmental degradation (−) Adverse zoning decisions	(+) Federal Superfund funding	(+) Community knowledge and participation	(+) Being part of a decision-making body
Air pollution (Opotow & Weiss, 2000)	(+) Public health concerns at all levels of analysis (−) Uncaring about effects of pollution	(−) Resistance to remediating downwind air pollution (smog)	(−) Ozone transport (smog) from the Midwest pollutes Eastern states	(−/+) Business interests and state coffers	(+) Scientific data (−) Denial and disinformation	(+) Having voice in interstate negotiations
Environmental degradation (Opotow, 2018)	(−) Uncaring policies (−) Burdening already burdened communities (+) Activist connection between groups	(+) Expert assistance provided by allies	(−) Environmental disbenefits and pollution	(+) Allies provide in-kind resources and funding (−) Outside interests dominate community issues	(−) Authorities are not forthcoming with information (+) Allies provide information on specifics and procedure	(−) Some interests are ignored (+) Collaboration with outside groups raises status and increases advocacy efficacy/skills

(*continued*)

Table 9.1 Continued

Study	Foa and Foa's (1974) Six Resource Classes					
	Love/Caring	Services	Goods	Money	Information	Status
Rangeland conflict (Opotow & Brook, 2003)	(−) Hostility between ranchers and environmentalists/ federal agencies	(+) Protective federal rules (−) Onerous federal rules	(+) Proceeds from rangeland farming (+) Water allocations (+) Grazing leases (+) Species preservation	(−) Economic effects of federal rules (+) Protection of valued rangeland for country at-large and for wildlife	(+) Stakeholders bring different perspectives to community deliberations (−) Stakeholders rely on different facts resulting in conflict	(+) Status differentials among stakeholders (e.g., government authorities, ranchers, environmentalists, locals)
Conservation— Namibia (Chang & Opotow, 2009)	(+) Concern about animal well-being and protecting habitat	(+) Scientific attention to wild animal habitat (+) Jobs for local people protect habitat	(+) Presence of wildlife generates tourism in area; sales of local goods	(+) Income from subsistence farming, crafts (+) Contributions to conservation projects	(+) Info exchange within and between groups	(−) Hierarchical structure of biological research station

[a]+, positive resources; −, negative resources.

contexts. However, adaptations are needed, as my answer to Question 2 will describe.

Question 2: Are the Foas' dimensions, *particularism* and *concreteness*, relevant in meso- and macro-level environmental conflicts?

Foa and Foa (1974) highlight the construct *resource* as fundamentally relational and as a vehicle for social exchange in relationships. They identify two dimensions underlying these six classes of resources: (a) particularism, which indicates "the extent to which the value of a given resources is influenced by the particular persons involved in exchanging it and by their relationship" (p. 80); and (b) concreteness, which ranges "from concrete to symbolic" (p. 81). Therefore, one answer to Question 2—Are these dimensions relevant in meso- and macro-level environmental conflicts?—is "yes" because environmental resources can vary on these dimensions. Environmental resources, however, are complex. They involve multiple issues and systems—natural, built, and human. And for each resource, there are multiple stakeholders. The distinctness of each of the Foas' six resource classes, therefore, cannot adequately encompass these complex resources. Thus, another answer to Question 2 is "no"—particularism and concreteness are not apt when applied to environmental resources.

However, Foa and Foa (1974) describe each resource in their typology as gradually merging "into its neighboring classes on both sides" (p. 82). This clarifies that resources that are adjacent to each other are not completely distinct. As the Foas describe, they are more similar to each other than to remote resources, an observation that was empirically confirmed by Dorsch et al. (2017). Taking this analytic suggestion and considering the broad range of environmental resources I noted in the five environmental studies, I observed that three pairs of the Foas' resources offer a good fit with meso- and macro-level environmental resources: (a) goods and services combine as *physical resources*, (b) information and money combine as *societal resources*, and (c) status and caring combine as *individual/psychological resources*.

Physical resources align with *goods* and *services*, which are adjacent resources in the Foas' typology. Physical resources encompass material environmental elements and can be small (e.g., a tree, a meadow, a freshwater spring, and an oasis) to vast in size (e.g., oceans, regions, and airsheds). Like physical environmental resources, goods and services have a materiality that

312   PART II NEW THEORETICAL AND EMPIRICAL DEVELOPMENTS

can be important because of their life-sustaining potential. They can foster well-being, or they can be damaging and cause harm.

Societal resources align with *information* and *money*, adjacent resources in the Foas' typology. Societal resources encompass environmental decision, policies, and priorities in communities of any size. They include local, regional, and national laws and policies; oversight by governmental agencies; and funding decisions affecting the management of environmental resources at local, national, or international levels. A focus on societal environmental resources is attentive to current and potential affordances of environmental resources for individuals, communities, regions, and nations; for nonhuman populations; and for ecological health (cf., Sommer, 2003; Törnblom, 1995). A societal focus also encompasses communication and coordination within and between various spheres of society and across levels of analysis to manage local environmental issues as well as issues that cross geopolitical borders.

Individual/psychological resources encompass *status* and *caring*. These adjacent resources in the Foas' typology include such within-person attributes as attitudes, beliefs, values, and identity. They also include people's justice beliefs and political positions such as lifestyle decisions about food and recycling as well as politically based support for or opposition to societal policies concerning environmental resources (cf., Opotow & Clayton, 1994; Clayton & Opotow, 2003).

These three environmental resource contexts—physical, societal, and individual/psychological—are consistent with Kurt Lewin's (1939) theorem that social behavior is a function of people and the environment: $B = f(P \times E)$. People are represented at two levels—individual and societal—and context concerns any element of the environment—tangible and intangible resources of any type within any locale. This conceptualization also resonates with *ecological psychology*, which is attentive to the personal well-being of individuals and the well-being of the planet (Sommer & Charles, 2012). Thus, these three resource contexts are both distinct and interrelated. Together, they offer a sturdy framework for studying meso- and macro-level environmental resource conflicts.

Question 3: What does the adaptation of resource exchange theory to meso- and macro-level environmental issues tell us about the connection between resources and social justice?

Environmental resources support well-being and, therefore, the loss or reduction of environmental *goods* and the increase of environmental *bads* increase environmental burdens and precarity (cf., Törnblom & Kazemi, 2012). Environmental conflicts can result in hardship when resources needed to sustain people and the ecosystem become scarce. Societal policies that support or ignore unequal procedural and distributive arrangements can result in social and environmental injustice, particularly when some people and places garner support while others do not.

Table 9.2 describes how three categories of environmental resources—physical, society, and individual/psychological—can support exclusionary or inclusionary policies, orientations, and actions.

As Table 9.2 describes, exclusionary policies diminish the well-being of people and nonhuman elements of the environment. Hardship and harm result from policies that do not protect environmental resources nor the people who depend on them to live healthy lives. As described previously, some communities suffer disproportionate exposure to toxins as a result of decisions that have disregarded their well-being and therefore are burdened by environmental disbenefits while others are not (Opotow, 2012, 2018). Similarly, some environmental resources are degraded by exclusionary, damaging, and exploitative policies. Policies that benefit some while harming others can be rationalized as a result of *denial*, a psychological process that can blunt concern for individuals, communities, and nonhuman entities that bear the brunt of environmentally harmful policies. They do so by minimizing such harms and by regarding those harmed as morally irrelevant because they are outside the scope of justice (Opotow & Weiss, 2000).

In contrast, inclusionary policies, orientations, and actions concerning environmental resources are cooperative endeavors recognizing that "everyone 'sinks or swims' together" (Deutsch, 1973, p. 20). An inclusionary orientation to people and contexts fosters a sense of community and engenders ecological health by attending to emerging problems and by prioritizing remedies that advance human and ecosystem well-being. A key element of inclusionary policies is being attentive to resource allocations that address the needs and interests of all parties. Although scarcity can test this commitment, resource sharing and generosity are key elements of inclusionary orientations and actions because they are efforts to contribute behaviorally, materially, and psychologically to human and ecological well-being (Opotow, 1990, 2021).

The Foas' typology of resource classes usefully differentiates among resource classes in interpersonal relationships. As Table 9.3 illustrates, it also

Table 9.2 Environmental Resources Conflicts

Environmental Resource Contexts	Foa and Foa's (1974) Resource Classes	Examples— Environmental Resources	Exclusionary Orientations/Actions	Inclusionary Orientations/Actions
Physical	Goods, services	Water, land, and clean air	Cause declining well-being for people, animals, and habitat Permit physical harms and hazards Despoil sites adjacent to minority communities Exploit environmental resources	Foster community and ecosystem health Value interdependence among diverse ecosystems elements Share scarce and valuable resources fairly among all stakeholders Safeguard environmental resources
Societal	Information, money	Environmental infrastructure, agencies, policies Laws, rights, and management decisions Scientific studies Funding	Normalize between-group disparities in well-being Support zoning rules with disparate impacts Marginalize poor and communities of color Promulgate mis- and disinformation Disregard protests from communities burdened with noxious resources Stifle recourse to political and legal remediation Reject evidence of declining population and environmental health Oppose environmental protection measures	Prioritize both human and ecological well-being Fund conservation and ecological health Base policies on science, knowledge, community concerns, and fairness Remain alert to and remedy emerging environmental challenges Fund ecosystem protection Oppose environmental degradation
Individual/ psychological	Status, caring	Values and beliefs Environmental identity Personal and collective histories	Unconcern for poor and minority communities and view them as morally irrelevant Value nature extrinsically Provoke conflict Generate self-serving rationales for harming the environment and people	Community engagement Concern for all parties' needs and interests Prioritize fairness and health Value nature intrinsically Encourage community engagement Be willing to make sacrifices to foster ecological and others' well-being

RESOURCES AND SOCIAL JUSTICE 315

Table 9.3 Foa and Foa's (1974) Resources in Inclusionary and Exclusionary Contexts

	Love	Service	Goods	Money	Information	Status
Inclusion	Caring	Helping	Sharing	Giving	Informing	Respecting
Exclusion	Uncaring	Harming	Withholding	Retaining	Misinforming	Disrespecting

aligns with inclusionary or exclusionary orientations and actions that can advance or obstruct social justice initiatives in meso and macro contexts.

This analysis places the Foas' framework in relation to attitudes and behaviors consistent with inclusionary and exclusionary action as delineated with the Scope of Justice Scale (Opotow, 1987, 1993). It describes an inclusionary orientation as having considerations of fairness for others, being willing to allocate resources to foster others' well-being, and being willing to make sacrifices (i.e., of material goods, privileges, etc.) to foster others' well-being. The scope of justice is therefore a critical construct because it is attentive to people and contexts that need to be considered to achieve constructive, consequential, collective, and sustainable well-being.

Conclusion

Having focused on the Foas' work and its relevance to meso and macro levels of analysis, environmental resources, and social justice, I conclude with an example of an urgent social issue in which physical, societal, and individual/psychological environmental contexts converge. Throughout the world, inequality has been increasing (Piketty, 2021; World Inequality Database, 2021). And, as a result of the COVID-19 pandemic, global poverty has risen sharply, with 163 million people now living on less than $5.50 a day (Sánchez-Páramo et al., 2021). Of all the human needs affected by poverty—including health, income, and education—housing may be the most basic because it has the potential to support people's physical, social, and psychological well-being (cf., Maslow, 1943).

However, an estimated 1.2 billion people—one-third of urban dwellers worldwide—lack secure housing (King, 2017). They live in dilapidated, substandard housing in marginal areas vulnerable to environmental hazards, including vermin and contaminated soil and water (Landrigan

316   PART II NEW THEORETICAL AND EMPIRICAL DEVELOPMENTS

& Fuller, 2014), and where disaster risks such as flooding have been increasing (Bramley & Bailey, 2017; Davis, 2006; Ross, 2021; Thomas et al., 2019). A 2022 United Nations climate change report indicates that 3.3 billion people are now "highly vulnerable to climate change" and 15 times more likely than before to die from extreme weather (Intergovernmental Panel on Climate Change, 2022). Increasing weather extremes will displace large numbers of people, with the world's poor most at risk. They will not only be hardest hit and experience severe emotional stress but also face barriers to receiving disaster aid, which is itself a stressor that can worsen physical and mental health (Substance Abuse and Mental Health Services Administration, 2017; Thomas et al., 2019; World Health Organization, 2010).

Between-group differences in human vulnerability to environmental hazards result from social, economic, historical, and political factors that operate at micro, meso, and macro scales, leaving some communities and groups disproportionately exposed to environmental threats. However, Islam and Winkel (2017) observe that although vulnerability is a multidimensional process, it need not be an unchanging state. Well-informed and comprehensive civic planning that allocates needed resources to vulnerable groups can mitigate harm, reduce danger, and foster resilience and recovery. They emphasize that the allocation of societal resources to vulnerable populations facing intensifying environmental challenges has proven preventative and ameliorative value.

To conclude, Foa and Foa (1974) have observed that our needs for tangible and intangible resources that promote well-being cannot be satisfied in isolation. People are interdependent with each other as well as with local, regional, and worldwide systems and environments that support their lives. When this interdependence is acknowledged and approached with inclusionary values and processes, it has the potential to support individual, societal, and planetary well-being.

References

Adams, J. S. (1965). Inequity in social exchange. Advances in *Experimental Social Psychology*, 2, 267–299.

Ash, M. G. (1998). *Gestalt psychology in German culture, 1890–1967: Holism and the quest for objectivity*. Cambridge University Press.

Berscheid, E., Boye, D., & Walster, E. (1968). Retaliation as a means of restoring equity. *Journal of Personality and Social Psychology, 10*(4), 370–376. https://doi.org/10.1037/h0026817

Bingham, B., & Opotow, S. (2021). Gowanus Canal and public policy. In C. Clauss-Ehlers (Ed.), *Cambridge handbook of community psychology: Interdisciplinary and contextual perspectives* (pp. 331–343). Cambridge University Press. doi:10.1017/9781108678971.020

Blumm, M. C., & Jamin, O. (2016). The property clause and its discontents: Lessons from the Malheur Occupation. *Ecology Law Quarterly, 43*(4), 781–826. http://www.jstor.org/stable/44202456

Bramley, G., & Bailey, N. (Eds.). (2017). *Poverty and social exclusion in the UK: Vol. 2. The dimensions of disadvantage.* Policy Press.

Bullard, R. D. (2019). *Dumping in Dixie: Race, class, and environmental quality* (3rd ed.). Routledge.

Bullard, R. D., Mohai, P., Saha, R., & Wright, B. (2007). *Toxic wastes and race at twenty: 1997–2007.* United Church of Christ.

Chang, V., & Opotow, S. (2009). Conservation values, environmental identity, and moral inclusion in the Kunene Region, Namibia: A comparative study. *Beliefs and Values, 1*(1), 79–89.

Checker, M. (2019). Environmental gentrification: Sustainability and the just city. In S. Low (Ed.), *Routledge handbook of anthropology and the city* (pp. 199–213). Routledge. https://doi.org/10.4324/9781315647098-14

Clapp, J. (2010). *Toxic exports: The transfer of hazardous wastes from rich to poor countries.* Cornell University Press. https://doi.org/10.7591/9781501735936

Clayton, S., & Brook, A. (2005). Can psychology help save the world? A model for conservation psychology. *Analyses of Social Issues and Public Policy, 5*(1), 87–102.

Clayton, S., Kals, E., & Feygina, I. (2016). Justice and environmental sustainability. In C. Sabbagh & M. Schmitt (Eds.), *Handbook of social justice theory and research* (pp. 369–386). Springer.

Clayton, S., & Opotow, S. (Eds.). (2003). *Identity and the natural environment: The psychological significance of nature.* MIT Press.

Cunningham, J. (2011). Environmental resources. In *Environmental Encyclopedia* (pp. 608–610). Gale/Thomson-Gale. https://www.encyclopedia.com/environment/encyclopedias-almanacs-transcripts-and-maps/environmental-resources

Coser, L. A. (1956). *The functions of social conflict.* Free Press.

Dare, A. M., & Fletcher, C. V. (2019). A bird's eye view of the Malheur Wildlife Refuge Occupation: Nonhuman agency and entangled species. *Environmental Communication, 13*(3), 412–423. doi:10.1080/17524032.2017.1412998

Deutsch, M. (1968). Field theory in social psychology. In G. Lindsey & E. Aronson (Eds.), *Handbook of social psychology* (pp. 412–487). Addison-Wesley.

Deutsch, M. (1973). *The resolution of conflict.* Yale University Press.

Deutsch, M. (1975). Equity, equality, and need: What determines which value will be used as the basis of distributive justice? *Journal of Social Issues, 31*(3), 137–149.

Deutsch, M. (1985). *Distributive justice: A social–psychological perspective.* Yale University Press.

Deutsch, M. (2015). Educating for a peaceful world. In P. T. Coleman, & M. Deutsch (Eds.), *Morton Deutsch: Major texts on peace psychology* (pp. 89–103). Springer.

318 PART II NEW THEORETICAL AND EMPIRICAL DEVELOPMENTS

Dorsch, M. J., Törnblom, K. Y., & Kazemi, A. (2017). A review of resource theories and their implications for understanding consumer behavior. *Journal of the Association for Consumer Research, 2*(1), 5–25.

Figueroa, R. M. (2005). Environmental justice. In C. Mitcham (Ed.), *Encyclopedia of science, technology, and ethics* (Vol. 2, pp. 665–670). Macmillan.

Fisher, R., Ury, W., & Patton, B. (1991). *Getting to yes: Negotiating agreement without giving in* (2nd ed.). Penguin.

Foa, U. G., & Foa, E. B. (1974). *Societal structures of the mind.* Charles C Thomas.

Fountain, H. (2021, October 26). 5 takeaways from the major new U.N. climate report. *The New York Times.* https://www.nytimes.com/2021/08/09/climate/un-climate-rep ort-takeaways.html

Garrick, D., De Stefano, L., Yu, W., Jorgensen, I., O'Donnell, E., Turley, L., Aguilar-Barajas, I., Dai, X., de Souza Leao, R., Punjabi, B., Schreiner, B., Svensson, J., & Wright, C. (2019, April 11). Rural water for thirsty cities: A systematic review of water reallocation from rural to urban regions. *Environmental Research Letters, 14*(4): 1–14. https://iopscience. iop.org/article/10.1088/1748-9326/ab0db7/meta

Gould, K., & Lewis, T. L. (2017). *Green gentrification: Urban sustainability and the struggle for environmental justice.* Routledge

Herbert, B. (2006, October 2). Poisoned on Eno Road. *The New York Times*, p. A19. https:// www.nytimes.com/2006/10/02/opinion/02herbert.html

Hickman, M. (2021, November 24). Contentious rezoning along Brooklyn's Gowanus Canal passes the NYC City Council. *The Architect's Newspaper.* https://www.archpaper. com/2021/11/contentious-gowanus-rezoning-passes-nyc-city-council

Howe, B. R. (2021, January 3). Wall Street eyes billions in the Colorado's water. *The New York Times.* https://www.nytimes.com/2021/01/03/business/colorado-river-water-rights.html

Intergovernmental Panel on Climate Change. (2021, August 9). *Climate change widespread, rapid, and intensifying—IPCC.* https://www.ipcc.ch/2021/08/09/ar6-wg1-20210809-pr

Intergovernmental Panel on Climate Change. (2022, February 27). *IPCC: Sixth Assessment Report—Climate change 2022: Impacts, adaptation and vulnerability.* https://www.ipcc. ch/report/ar6/wg2

Islam, S. N., & Winkel, J. (2017, October). *Climate change and social inequality.* United Nations Department of Economic and Social Affairs Working Papers No. 152. https:// doi.org/10.18356/2c62335d-en

Johnson, K. (2017, April 12). Siege has ended, but battle over public lands rages on. *The New York Times.* https://www.nytimes.com/2017/04/14/us/public-lands-bundy-malh eur-national-wildlife-refuge.html

Kazemi, A., Törnblom, K., & Mikula, G. (2015). Justice: Social psychological perspectives. In J. D. Wright (Ed.), *International encyclopedia of the social and behavioral sciences* (pp. 949–955). Elsevier. doi:10.1016/B978-0-08-097086-8.24019-1

King, R. (2017, October 2). *The crisis in affordable housing is a problem for cities everywhere.* World Resource Institute. https://www.wri.org/insights/crisis-affordable-hous ing-problem-cities-everywhere

Klare, M. T. (2001). *Resource wars: The new landscape of global conflict.* Macmillan.

Koffka, K. (1936). *Principles of Gestalt psychology.* Kegan, Paul, Trench, Trübner.

RESOURCES AND SOCIAL JUSTICE 319

Köhler, W. (1959). Gestalt psychology today. *American Psychologist, 14*(12), 727–734. https://doi.org/10.1037/h0042492

Landrigan, P. J., & Fuller, R. (2014). Environmental pollution: An enormous and invisible burden on health systems in low- and middle-income counties. *World Hospitals and Health Services, 50*(4), 35–40.

Leopold, A. (1949). *A Sand County almanac.* Oxford University Press.

Lerner, M. J. (1975). The justice motive in social behavior: Introduction. *Journal of Social Issues, 31*(3), 1–19.

Lerner, M. J., &. Lerner, S. C. (Eds.). (1981). *The justice motive in social behavior: Adapting to times of scarcity and change.* Plenum.

Lerner, S. (2010). *Sacrifice zones: The front lines of toxic chemical exposure in the United States.* MIT Press.

Lewin, K. (1939). Field theory and experiment in social psychology: Concepts and methods. *American Journal of Sociology, 44*(6), 868–896.

Lind, E. A., & Tyler, T. R. (1988). *The social psychology of procedural justice.* Springer.

London, T. K., Joshi, E., Cairncross, E., & Claudio, L. (2011). Environmental justice: An international perspective. In J. O. Nriagu (Ed.), *Encyclopedia of environmental health* (Vol. 2, pp. 441–448). Elsevier.

Maslow, A. H. (1943). A theory of human motivation. *Psychological Review, 50*(4), 370–396. https://doi.org/10.1037/h0054346

McClelland, S. I., & Opotow, S. (2011). Studying injustice in the macro and micro spheres: Four generations of social psychological research. In P. T. Coleman (Ed.), *Conflict, interdependence and justice: The intellectual legacy of Morton Deutsch* (pp. 119–145). Springer.

Mikula, G. (1980). *Justice and social interaction: Experimental and theoretical contributions from psychological research.* Springer-Verlag.

Montada, L. (2003). Justice, equity, and fairness in human relations. In T. Millon & M. J. Lerner (Eds.), *Handbook of psychology: Personality and social psychology* (Vol. 5, pp. 532–568). Wiley. https://doi.org/10.1002/0471264385.wei0522

Montada, L. & Lerner, M. J. (Eds.). (1996). *Current societal concerns about justice.* Plenum.

Opotow, S. (1987). Limits of fairness: An experimental examination of antecedents of the scope of justice [Doctoral dissertation]. Columbia University.

Opotow, S. (1990). Moral exclusion and injustice: An overview. *Journal of Social Issues, 46*(1), 1–20.

Opotow, S. (1993). Animals and the scope of justice. *Journal of Social Issues, 49*(1), 71–85. doi:10.1111/j.1540-4560.1993.tb00909.x

Opotow, S. (1994). Predicting protection: Scope of justice and the natural world. *Journal of Social Issues, 50*(3), 49–63. doi:10.1111/j.1540-4560.1994.tb02419.x

Opotow, S. (1995). Drawing the line: Social categorization, moral exclusion, and the scope of justice. In B. B. Bunker & J. Z. Rubin (Eds.), *Conflict, cooperation, and justice: Essays inspired by the work of Morton Deutsch* (pp. 347–369). Jossey-Bass.

Opotow, S. (2004). Conflict and morals. In T. A. Thorkildsen & H. J. Walberg (Eds.), *Nurturing morality* (pp. 99–115). Kluwer.

Opotow, S. (2008). "Not so much as place to lay our head . . .": Moral inclusion and exclusion in the American Civil War Reconstruction. *Social Justice Research, 21*(1), 26–49. doi:10.1007/s11211-007-0061-9

320 PART II NEW THEORETICAL AND EMPIRICAL DEVELOPMENTS

Opotow, S. (2009). Social injustice and moral exclusion. In *The Oxford international encyclopedia of peace* (pp. 51–55). Oxford University Press.

Opotow, S. (2012) Environmental injustice, collaborative action, and the inclusionary shift. In S. Clayton (Ed.), *The Oxford handbook of environmental and conservation psychology* (pp. 414–427). Oxford University Press.

Opotow, S. (2018). Social justice theory and practice: Fostering inclusion in exclusionary contexts. In P. L. Hammack (Ed.), *The Oxford handbook of social psychology and social justice* (pp. 41–56). Oxford University Press.

Opotow S. (2021). Promoting peace via inclusionary justice. In K. Standish, H. Devere, A. Suazo, & R. Rafferty (Eds.), *The Palgrave handbook of positive peace* (pp. 441–453). Palgrave Macmillan. https://doi.org/10.1007/978-981-15-3877-3_22-1

Opotow, S., & Brook, A. (2003). Identity and exclusion in rangeland conflict. In S. Clayton & S. Opotow (Eds.), *Identity and the natural environment: The psychological significance of nature* (pp. 249–272). MIT Press.

Opotow, S., & Clayton, S. (1994). Green justice: Conceptions of fairness and the natural world. *Journal of Social Issues, 50*(3), 1–11. doi:10.1111/j.1540-4560.1994.tb02416.x

Opotow, S., & Deutsch, M. (1999). Learning to cope with conflict and violence: How schools can help youth. In E. Frydenberg (Ed.), *Learning to cope: Developing as a person in complex societies* (pp. 198–224). Oxford University Press.

Opotow, S., & Weiss, L. (2000). Denial and exclusion in environmental conflict. *Journal of Social Issues, 56*(3), 475–490. doi:10.1111/0022-4537.00179

Oxford English Dictionary. (2021, December). Resource, n. Oxford University Press. https://www.oed.com/view/Entry/163768?rskey=UPUCVr&result=1&isAdvanced=false

Pettigrew, T. F. (1997). Personality and social structure: Social psychological contributions. In R. Hogan, J. Johnson, & S. Briggs (Eds.), *Handbook of personality psychology* (pp. 417–438). Academic Press.

Piketty, T. (2021). *Time for socialism: Dispatches from a world on fire, 2016–2021* (K. Couper, Trans.). Yale University Press.

Pulido, L. (2000). Rethinking environmental racism: White privilege and urban development in Southern California. *Annals of the Association of American Geographers, 90* (1), 12–40.

Ross, A. (2021). *Sunbelt blues: The failure of American housing.* Macmillan.

Rubin, J. Z., & Levinger, G. (1995). Levels of analysis: In search of generalizable knowledge. In B. B. Bunker & J. Z. Rubin (Eds.), *Conflict, cooperation, and justice: Essays inspired by the work of Morton Deutsch* (pp. 13–38). Jossey-Bass.

Rubin, J. Z., Pruitt, D. G., & Kim, S. H. (1994). *Social conflict: Escalation, stalemate, and settlement* (2nd ed.). McGraw-Hill.

Sánchez-Páramo, C., Hill, R., Gerszon Mahler, D., Narayan, A., & Yonzan, N. (2021, October 7). *COVID-19 leaves a legacy of rising poverty and widening inequality.* World Bank Blogs. https://blogs.worldbank.org/developmenttalk/covid-19-leaves-legacy-rising-poverty-and-widening-inequality

Sarris, V. (2020). *Max Wertheimer: Productive thinking.* Springer.

Schellens, M. K., & Diemer, A. (2020). *Natural resource conflicts: Definition and three frameworks to aid analysis.* Springer. https://doi.org/10.1007/978-3-319-71067-9_81-2

Searles, H. F. (1960). *The nonhuman environment in normal development and in schizophrenia.* International Universities Press.

Sierra Club v. Morton, 405 U.S. 727, 741–43 (USSC 1972).

Sommer, R. (2003). Trees and human identity. In S. Clayton & S. Opotow (Eds.), *Identity and the natural environment: The psychological significance of nature* (pp. 179–203). MIT Press.

Sommer, R., & Charles, E. (2012). Ecological psychology. In V. S. Ramachandran (Ed.), *Encyclopedia of human behavior* (2nd ed., Vol. 2, pp. 7–12). Academic Press.

Stone, C. D. (1974). *Should trees have standing? Toward legal rights for natural objects.* Kaufmann.

Substance Abuse and Mental Health Services Administration. (2017, July). *Greater impact: How disasters affect people of low socioeconomic status.* Disaster Technical Assistance Center Supplemental Research Bulletin. https://www.samhsa.gov/sites/defa ult/files/dtac/srb-low-ses_2.pdf

Taylor, D. (2014). *Toxic communities: Environmental racism, industrial pollution, and residential mobility.* New York University Press.

Thibaut, J., & Walker, L. (1975). *Procedural justice: A psychological analysis.* Erlbaum.

Thomas, K., Hardy, R. D., Lazrus, H., Mendez, M., Orlove, B., Rivera-Collazo, I., Roberts, J. T., Rockman, M., Warner, B. P., & Winthrop, R. (2019). Explaining differential vulnerability to climate change: A social science review. *Wiley Interdisciplinary Reviews: Climate Change, 10*(2), e565. https://doi.org/10.1002/wcc.565

Thompson, L. L., & Gonzales, R. (1997). Environmental disputes. In M. H. Bazerman, A. E. Tenbrunsel, & D. M. Messick (Eds.), *Environment, ethics, and behavior* (pp. 75–104). New Lexington Press.

Törnblom, K. (1988). Positive and negative allocations: A typology and a model for conflicting justice principles. In E. Lawler & B. Markovsky (Eds.), *Advances in group processes* (Vol. 5, pp. 141–168). JAI Press.

Törnblom, K. (1995). Individual and collective justice and injustice: Implications for intergroup conflict. *Social Justice Research, 8*(1), 91–101.

Törnblom, K., Jasso, G., & Vermunt, R. (2007). Theoretical integration and unification: A focus on justice. *Social Justice Research, 20*(3), 263–269.

Törnblom, K., & Kazemi, A. (2012). Some conceptual and theoretical issues in resource theory of social exchange. In K. Törnblom & A. Kazemi (Eds.), *Handbook of social resource theory: Theoretical extensions, empirical insights, and social applications* (pp. 33–64). Springer. https://doi.org/10.1007/978-1-4614-4175-5_3

United Nations. (2018, October 16). Meetings coverage and press releases: Sharing benefits of natural resources helps conflict prevention, sustainable development, Secretary-General tells Security Council. https://www.un.org/press/en/2018/sgsm19 303.doc.htm

United Nations. (2021, October 25). *Updated NDC synthesis report: Worrying trends confirmed* [Press release]. https://unfccc.int/news/updated-ndc-synthesis-report-worry ing-trends-confirmed

United Nations Environmental Programme. (2021, May 26). *New atlas reveals rangelands cover half the world's land surface, yet often ignored despite threats* [Press release]. https://www.unep.org/news-and-stories/press-release/new-atlas-reveals-rangelands-cover-half-worlds-land-surface-yet

U.S. Environmental Protection Agency. (n.d.). *Ground-level ozone basics.* https://www. epa.gov/ground-level-ozone-pollution/ground-level-ozone-basics

U.S. National Academy of Sciences, Israel Academy of Sciences and Humanities, Palestine Academy for Science and Technology, & Royal Scientific Society, Jordan

322 PART II NEW THEORETICAL AND EMPIRICAL DEVELOPMENTS

(1999). *Water for the future: The West Bank and Gaza Strip, Israel, and Jordan.* National Academies Press. https://www.nap.edu/catalog/6031/water-for-the-fut ure-the-west-bank-and-gaza-strip

Van der Horst, D. (2007). NIMBY or not? Exploring the relevance of location and the politics of voiced opinions in renewable energy siting controversies. *Energy Policy, 35*(5), 2705–2714.

Weiss, L. (1996). Justice issues and the negotiations of the Ozone Transport Assessment Group (OTAG) [Unpublished manuscript]. University of Massachusetts Boston.

World Health Organization. (2010). *Environment and health risks: A review of the influence and effects of social inequalities.* https://www.euro.who.int/__data/assets/pdf_file/0003/78069/E93670.pdf

World Inequality Database. (2021, December 7). *World inequality report 2022.* https://wid.world/news-article/world-inequality-report-2022

Zaveri, M. (2020, November 19, updated 2021, April 9, 2021). Getting "black mayonnaise" out of one of America's dirtiest waterways. *The New York Times.* https://www.nytimes.com/2020/11/19/nyregion/gowanus-canal-dredging-redevelopment.html

Zaveri, M., Hamilton, B., & Corona, J. (2021, April 9). Toxic canal zone is a litmus test for N.Y.C. development. *The New York Times.* https://www.nytimes.com/2021/04/09/nyregion/gowanus-canal-brooklyn-development.html

10

Extending Social Resource Exchange to Events of Abundance and Sufficiency

Jonas Bååth and Adel Daoud

Introduction

This chapter identifies how scarcity, abundance, and sufficiency influence exchange behavior. Analyzing the mechanisms governing people's exchange of resources constitutes the foundation of several social science perspectives (e.g., Baumgärtner et al., 2006; Daoud, 2018a, 2018b; Mullainathan & Shafir, 2013; Panayotakis, 2011; Turner & Rojek, 2001; Xenos, 2017). Neoclassical economics provides one of the most well-known perspectives of how rational individuals allocate and exchange resources. Using rational choice theory (RCT), neoclassical economics assumes that exchange between two individuals will occur when resources are scarce and that these individuals interact rationally to satisfy their requirements (i.e., preferences). Scarcity is a state in which available resources are insufficient to satisfy a set of requirements. This experience of insufficiency is arguably one primary motivator for why an individual engages in exchange. Although RCT is useful to characterize interaction in closed and stylized systems, it proves insufficient to capture social and psychological reality where culture, emotions, and habits play an integral part in resource exchange (Archer & Tritter, 2000; Bååth, 2022b; Boudon, 2003; Hedström & Stern, 2008; Kahneman, 2011). Another deficiency of neoclassical economics is that needs, wants, and requirements are taken as a given. As scarcity is postulated, neoclassical economics cannot explain how scarcity may arise and justify how abundance and sufficiency are not possible motivators of human exchange.

Social resource theory (SRT) improves on RCT in several respects by making the *social nature of resources* the object of study (U. Foa & Foa, 1974). SRT shows how human interaction is driven by an array of psychological mechanisms—from emotions to heuristics. Thus, SRT provides a

Social Behavior as Resource Exchange. Kjell Yngve Törnblom and Ali Kazemi, Oxford University Press.
© Oxford University Press 2023. DOI: 10.1093/oso/9780190066994.003.0012

more realistic foundation for analyzing and explaining social exchange than the stylized instrumental rationality of RCT. SRT does not shy away from unpacking the inherently psychological and sociological concept of preferences by showing how and why scarcity motivates human action. However, whereas scarcity is undoubtedly a key motivator, SRT has no clear place for events of abundance and sufficiency as additional motivations to exchange resources. For example, as the scarcity of food or love may motivate individuals to overcome their predicament, an abundance of weapons or money may motivate individuals in a different way (Bååth, 2018; Daoud, 2018a; Dugger & Peach, 2009). Or, an abundance of food or books may have unintended consequences leading to starvation amid obesity (Daoud, 2007) or paralysis due to information overload (Abbott, 2014). Likewise, sufficiency—neither too much nor too little—is the desired state of being for individuals attaining voluntary simplicity (Daoud, 2011b; Osikominu & Bocken, 2020). Consequently, if sufficiency and abundance affect human behavior besides scarcity, then how should scholars identify the dynamics among the three states that resources can attain: scarcity, abundance, and sufficiency.

The aim of this chapter is to synthesize and formalize a foundation for SRT using not only scarcity but also abundance and sufficiency. We achieve this using mainly the theory of scarcity, abundance, and sufficiency (SAS) (Daoud, 2011a, 2018b). This theory focuses on explaining SAS rather than assuming them. Our SRT–SAS synthesis provides a general theory that enables formulating new predictions, hypotheses, and explanations about the dynamics among all three SAS events. Unlike neoclassical economics that mathematically and conceptually requires scarcity to function, our SRT–SAS synthesis explains human actions under not only scarcity but also abundance and sufficiency.

Background

The assumption of scarcity is omnipresent in the social sciences. The most well-known example is neoclassical economics—the central tradition of economics—which assumes scarcity as the cause of all significant economic problems (Bronfenbrenner, 1962; Menger, 2007; Robbins, 2007; Zinam, 1982). For instance, Milton Friedman (2009) framed an economic problem in the following way: "An economic problem exists whenever scarce means are used to satisfy alternative ends. If the means are not scarce, there is no problem at all; there is Nirvana" (p. 6). Following Friedman's argument, there would be no reason for markets to exist in a world of resource abundance. Neoclassical economics generalizes these sorts of economic problems to any human behavior by postulating that scarcity is both natural and universal (Becker, 1965)—it exists and perpetuates all behavior (Daoud, 2011a). RCT is the vehicle through which this sort of economic problem is generalized to any domain (Elster, 2015).

Although SRT improves several aspects of how RCT depicts human behavior, SRT still assumes scarcity as the leading cause of human exchange. SRT is a theory about the configuration of societal structures and how their cognitive representations affect the dynamics of social resource exchange. SRT's definition of resources is inherently social—that is, a resource is a thing of value that is "transmitted through interpersonal behavior"(U. Foa & Foa, 1974, p. 36). By emphasizing the social nature of resources, SRT defines six resource classes: love, status, information, money, goods, and service. According to their relative position on two axes, these resource classes are positioned in a cognitive space: the degree of concreteness and particularism. Love is the most particularistic resource class because it is of great importance from whom one receives love. Money is the least particularistic resource because compared to the other resource classes, its value is less dependent on who gives and receives it. The remaining four resource classes are positioned in-between money and love on the degree of particularism axis. Goods and services are the most concrete resource classes because they are the most tangible ones. Information and status are the least concrete ones due to their intangible and symbolic nature. Money and love occupy the middle ground on the degree of concreteness axis due to their double nature as both tangible and intangible (U. Foa & Foa, 1974).

A resource's position on the degree of particularism and concreteness axes defines the rules of exchange for the resource's class. We limit our argument to two such rules (for a comprehensive outline, see E. Foa & Foa, 2012; see also Törnblom & Kazemi, 2012). First, as a rule, the more particularistic the resource class, the higher the frequency of interclass exchange. This exchange pertains to the flow of goods within the same resource class. For example, love is often exchanged for love, whereas money is never exchanged for money. Second, as a rule, the less concrete (i.e., more abstract) and more particularistic a resource is, the more one gains from giving of one's such resources to others. To some extent, one always loses when giving money, goods, or

326 PART II NEW THEORETICAL AND EMPIRICAL DEVELOPMENTS

services, and one gains when giving status and love, whereas information is neutral (E. Foa & Foa, 2012, pp. 20–22). SRT mobilizes social–psychological explanations for how and why individuals exchange these resource classes and what kinds of distributional outcomes this exchange leads to (U. Foa & Foa, 1974, pp. 178–180). The following section discusses the characteristics of SRT.

SRT and the Assumption of Scarcity

Social resource theory offers a sophisticated theory of how and why individuals exchange resources. We argue that its primary strength is that it emphasizes the social character of resources as exchange objects with a limited set of discrete qualities. This strength makes SRT a more realistic approach to exchange than neoclassical economics (which reduces all values to prices, losing out on the specific characteristics of different resources). However, we argue that SRT would benefit from developed theorizing in two regards: (a) how abundance and sufficiency affect the exchange; and (b) the relation between different levels of social reality, primarily between the individual and the (societal) system levels. Developing these two areas, we show how the theory of SAS offers useful concepts for developing SRT.

The implicit assumption of scarcity in SRT is best shown by considering how U. Foa and Foa (1974) define the concept need as "a state of deficiency in a given resource" for the individual (p. 130). To need a resource is to possess less than optimal amounts of that resource. That is scarcity. The opposite of needs is power, implying that the individual possesses more resources than they need and can use some resources for alternative ends than satisfying their needs (U. Foa & Foa, 1974, pp. 128–135). Power includes sufficiency and nonproblematic forms of abundance. This distinction might seem like a simple binary of need and non-need. However, resource optimum is defined as a range, implying that exceeding said range would be suboptimal. For example, it would be suboptimal to have more food than one wants to eat because it would lead to either the food spoiling or one suffering from overeating. In that event, the number of resources would amount to a negative abundance, causing the individual to experience some deficit or needs for welfare as a consequence (U. Foa & Foa, 1974, pp. 128–129).

Jerald Greenberg (1981) develops the concept of needs by suggesting a distinction between objective and felt needs. Objective needs imply actual dearth. Conversely, felt needs imply the impression of needs an individual might experience despite objectively possessing enough resources. Needs thus encompass all kinds of meaningful requirements for resources that an individual can experience. Although Greenberg's definition implies that needs arise from scarce resources, it begs the question of how needs affect an individual's motivations to engage in exchange (motivations, in short).

The concept of optimal range defines the relationship between needs and motivations. This concept means that when an individual possesses an amount of a resource that falls within a specific range's limits, the person experiences no needs. This limit varies between individuals and also between resources (U. Foa & Foa, 1974, pp. 125–129). This concept assumes that when an individual's available resources fall below this limit, scarcity arises and causes "motivational arousal" (p. 129). This arousal will result in two types of motivations: to maintain resource optimum or to maintain cognitive structures (p. 126). This chapter focuses on the former motivation.

The motivation to maintain resource optimum follows from the assumption that the individual experiences scarce resources as needs. Needs motivate individuals to engage in exchange to achieve resource optimum. Alternatively, the individual might fear future scarcity or, as Greenberg (1981) suggests, feel that they need more of a resource despite objectively possessing sufficient or abundant amounts. In the end, the experience of needs becomes the motivation to exchange. Consequently, scarcity is essential for exchange behavior in SRT. However, an assumption of scarcity also implies that sufficiency and abundance would be comparably less developed.

Whereas needs are important for explaining human action in general, SRT is diffuse about the motivations of actors who lack needs—those experiencing sufficiency or abundance. Although resource optimum equals power, it remains unclear how power motivates individuals to engage in further exchange. One explanation is that individuals experiencing resource optimum are motivated to maintain their cognitive structures, meaning to avoid experiences that dissonate with the individuals' imagined structures of social life. However, this explanation would demand that all individuals who exercise power do so to avoid cognitive dissonance. Such an argument is problematic because it excludes the possibility that resource states might motivate individuals out of need (cf. U. Foa & Foa, 1974, pp. 140–141). For example, power could motivate the individual to accumulate more power or to reduce the relative power of the individual's competitors.

328 PART II NEW THEORETICAL AND EMPIRICAL DEVELOPMENTS

Resource optimum implies a range defined by an upper and lower limit for a given resource class (U. Foa & Foa, 1974, p. 128). An individual experiencing more than optimal resources would experience an emergence of a new need—a need for welfare due to the discomfort and suffering caused by "oversatiation" (U. Foa & Foa, 1974, pp. 127–128, 138). An abundance of resources would—just like scarcity—arouse the motivation to maintain resource optimum. This consideration implies a definition of abundance that rests on the emergence of new scarcities. However, such an interpretation of abundance limits it to negative forms of abundance, meaning the events in which abundance results in different negative consequences. Any positive forms of abundance are left undefined.

By considering the relation between SRT's needs and motivations, our argument identifies that scarcity is intimately tied to how resource states affect exchange behavior. Nonetheless, SRT assumes this form of scarcity because it elevates scarcity to a more critical state than sufficiency or abundance. This elevation is evident in SRT's conception of sufficiency and abundance. The former is roughly the absence of need, and the latter is when new scarcities emerge due to super-optimal amounts of resources.

SRT's definition of scarcity and needs produces further conceptual tensions. SRT presupposes the assumption that all needs are fundamental and require satisfaction. Needs draw a normative boundary between the requirements that might be considered needs and others that might be considered—for example, wants and demands. This normative grounding is explicated in Greenberg's (1981) distinction between actual and felt needs, suggesting that the latter are less urgent or real. Such felt needs imply that individuals experiencing them would not objectively be in need. Although Greenberg's argument opens up for the possibility of motivations among actors out of objective need, it still assumes that the motivation must be tied to resource deficiency. Beyond affirming the conclusion that SRT rests on an assumption of scarcity, the concept "need" further limits that assumption to a normative conception of how scarcity is experienced, because any other—felt or otherwise—experience of scarcity would not be a legitimate requirement.

The scarcity assumption creates at least two problems for SRT's ambition to explain social resource exchange. The first problem is that the assumption of scarcity obscures how states of sufficiency and abundance might influence exchange in empirical work. Beyond being a normative concept, needs are difficult to observe empirically because they demand a method that can distinguish needs from non-needs (Springborg, 1981). This is especially the case

EXTENDING SOCIAL RESOURCE EXCHANGE 329

in measuring needs consistently, especially across different societies, cultures, and points in time. Törnblom and Nilsson (2008) engaged with this issue, seeking to nuance the conception of needs by qualifying different needs according to their importance. In another study, Törnblom and colleagues (2008) explored if a resource's source might affect its satisfactory effect toward a need. However, these studies still raise questions regarding to what extent satisfaction differs between needs and other kinds of requirements, and how the relative importance of needs interacts with other kinds of requirements.

The second problem pertains to defining need as "a state of deficiency in a given resource." This definition raises questions about the context in which that deficiency occurs. Generally, SRT studies limit their scope to the individuals involved in the exchange. Greenberg (1981) addresses this issue from a methodological angle, suggesting that SRT-based experiments on resource exchange do not account for the research subject's cultural context. However, U. Foa and Foa (1974) explicitly frame exchanges in institutions that define the "proper" (i.e., legitimate) settings and relations between resources in exchange (pp. 150–152). Although we agree that the institutional setting is essential for analyzing resource exchange, Foa and Foa's definition leaves out what resources and exchange offers are available for exchange beyond direct interaction.

In summary, SRT lacks operationalization and theoretical clarification of how structural or systemic forces, such as institutions, constrain and enable resource exchange. This issue stems from the assumption of scarcity. Because SAS events are experienced by individuals and groups embedded in social systems, a full-fledged SRT theory has to account for SAS dynamics. Although this focus on scarcity is purposeful, it allows SRT scholars to engage with some scientific issues; it leaves another set of relevant scientific problems unexplored. In contrast to neoclassical economics, SRT scope of analysis does not necessarily preclude the two other SAS events; however, to allow scholars to use these two concepts in tandem with scarcity, we need to redefine a set of concepts.

On the Dynamics of SAS

The SAS theory is a socioeconomic approach starting from the assumption that scarcity, abundance, and sufficiency are important resource states (or events) for human interaction (Daoud, 2018b). As individuals orient

330   PART II NEW THEORETICAL AND EMPIRICAL DEVELOPMENTS

themselves to these three states simultaneously, their perception and interaction create dynamics in resource exchange. While assuming one event's
existence over the other two is occasionally warranted, SAS theory begins
by acknowledging that these states are events to be explained. These events
emerge in the relationship between *sets* of human requirements (denoted
as a set, R) and available resources (denoted as a set, A). When empirically
observed, both R and A are sets tied to a specific actor or group of actors.
Consequently, in any given concrete situation or example, the sets R and A
are explicitly indexed for the individual by i in a group with 1, 2, . . ., to n
individuals, to define who possesses a specific requirement set R_i and who is
controlling a specific resource set A_i.

Set A implies a given resource that has the capacity to satisfy human
requirements. Although the SAS theory definition of resource set A is ago-
nistic to its content, SRT's resource classes can be used to populate A. The
six resource classes—love, service, goods, money, information, and status—
differentiate a superset of A containing these six classes (U. G. Foa & Foa,
1974, pp. 140–143):

$$A_{SRT} = \{A_{love}, A_{service}, A_{goods}, A_{money}, A_{information}, A_{status}\}$$

Although A can be any set, for simplicity, we let $A = A_{SRT}$, and henceforth use
A to signify A_{SRT}.

To evaluate if A is scarce, sufficient, or abundant, scholars must compare it to a set of *requirements* R. R can contain any defined requirement,
including but not limited to needs and wants. By definition, SAS theory
is agnostic about the content of R (Daoud, 2011a, 2018b). By *agnostic*, we
mean that SAS theory does not assign any scientific or normative priority
among the three SAS events. For example, scarcity of a resource may or may
not be scientifically or normatively prioritized over abundance. Whereas
scarcity of food may lead to the normatively undesired state of starvation,
scarcity of weapons may lead to the normatively desired state of the lack of
firearm deaths. The set R captures an observable, empirical manifestation
of underlying biological and social–psychological mechanisms. The manifestation might be any valid configuration of a requirement—anything a
human utters, prefers, indicates, or selects. The nature of R is thus an empirical question. In some cases, R might be defined as a range because R's
exact value would be imprecise to define categorically (e.g., the amount of

EXTENDING SOCIAL RESOURCE EXCHANGE   331

water required to sustain life or the amount of time required to complete a task).

Contrasting with SRT, "needs" is the concept functioning most similar to R. Yet the difference between them implies more than a choice of words. SAS theory relies on a layered ontology, differentiating the empirical (what is observed) from the transempirical (what is unobserved) (see Daoud, 2007). At the empirical level, researchers can only observe the manifestations of biological requirements that are mixed with cultural and psychological mechanisms. These observations manifest as (subjective) needs, wants, demands, and desires, crystallized as R. To be clear, such observations might include biomedical ones regarding biological requirements. At the transempirical level, however, SAS theory allows for different conceptions of human nature and thus definitions of human qualities, such as a (normative) categorization of requirements as needs and wants. This separation between empirical and transempirical helps avoid any normative conceptions that would prescribe any normative distinction of valid from invalid R (e.g., "false needs") in empirical work (Stillman, 1983). This layered ontology allows SAS theory to conduct agnostic analyses of empirical data and, after that, transgress the empirical level by introducing theories of non-observable qualities that might explain—or challenge—the empirical findings. Nonetheless, if we defer evaluating R's nature in terms of needs or non-needs, we can define the following SRT-compatible requirement set (U. Foa & Foa, 1974, pp. 140–143):

$$R_{SRT} = \{R_{love}, R_{service}, R_{goods}, R_{money}, R_{information}, R_{status}\}$$

Although R can take any elements, for simplicity, we let $R = R_{SRT}$ and henceforth in this chapter, we use R to signify R_{SRT}.

All actors have requirements despite being satisfied or not, in contrast to "needs," which, at least in SRT, imply that they are only held by individuals lacking resource optimum. Thus, actors holding resource optimum have no needs. Alternatively, following Greenberg (1981), individuals experiencing sufficiency or abundance might have "felt needs," which are qualitatively different from (actual or objective) needs. Consequently, although the choice of words describing the empirical observation it denotes might include the word need, R is observed by asking people what they require or identifying indirect indications of requirements. A is measured by asking people what is available to them to satisfy their R.

An individual possesses a set of resources, A, that might or might not match their requirements, R. The sets R and A are the two main concepts needed to distinguish SAS from each other. R's and A's cardinality determines these events—that is, their relative sizes implied by the pipes $| \, |$. For example, the set $A = \{a \text{ house, a car}\}$ has the cardinality $|A| = 2$ because this set has two objects. Here, we are assuming that the elements in R can appear in the exact shape and form of the elements appearing in A, allowing them to be matched—for other cases, this assumption can be relaxed. If the cardinality $|R|$ is larger than the cardinality $|A|$, it implies scarcity. This scarcity is implied by the relationship sign ">": $|R| > |A|$. When $|R|$ is smaller than $|A|$ implies abundance "<"; when $|R|$ is equal to $|A|$ implies sufficiency captured by the relationship sign "=":

Scarcity $|R| > |A|$: The cardinality of the requirement set is strictly larger than the resources set.

Abundance $|R| < |A|$: The cardinality of the requirement set is strictly smaller than the resources set.

Sufficiency $|R| = |A|$: The cardinality of the requirement set is equal to the resources set. This approximation can be defined either exactly or as a range.

An undefined relation is denoted with $\sim$ and can be used like the following: $R \sim A$. Such undefined relationships are useful when either the elements' cardinalities or qualities are yet to be evaluated. $R \sim A$ implies undefined SAS. Following SRT, we define the set of all relationships in the following way:

$$R \sim A = \left\{ \begin{array}{l} R_{love} \sim A_{love}, R_{service} \sim A_{service}, R_{goods} \sim A_{goods}, R_{money} \\ \sim A_{money}, R_{information} \sim A_{information}, R_{status} \sim A_{status} \end{array} \right\}$$

In $R \sim A$, we assume the exchange ability of elements in the sets according to their usefulness. For example, for transportation, a "black horse" is as usable as a "white horse" or perhaps a "donkey" or a "camel." However, the quality of these creatures in a different context might differ significantly. For example, using a white horse for a wedding gift signifies a different quality of that resource to that of a donkey. The social context of $R \sim A$ conditions the degree

EXTENDING SOCIAL RESOURCE EXCHANGE   333

of exchangeability between resources in the same resources class or across classes of resources (see also Törnblom & Kazemi, 2012).

How an individual dynamically shifts between SAS can be exemplified with a play from Shakespeare. His *Richard III* line, "A horse, a horse, my kingdom for a horse!" implies that King Richard III required a horse, $R = \{horse\}$, and was willing to exchange his kingship for getting one, $A = \{kingship\}$. To satisfy his requirements, King Richard III offers his kingship in exchange for an (available) horse. In the case of King Richard III, we can picture the two requirements: one for his means of transportation (i.e., the SRT resource class *goods*) and one for his requirement of kingship (i.e., the SRT resource class *status*), denoted by $R_{goods} = \{horse\}$ and $R_{status} = \{\varnothing\}$.

We can then formalize all the SAS relationships as follows:

$$\text{Scarcity} \quad \left|R_{goods} = \{horse\}\right| > \left|A_{goods} = \{\varnothing\}\right|$$
$$\text{Abundance} \quad \left|R_{status} = \{\varnothing\}\right| < \left|A_{status} = \{kingship\}\right|$$

If the proposed exchange is made (in the theater play, it is not), Richard would have a horse but no longer be a king, making both the relations $R_{goods} \sim A_{goods}$ and $R_{status} \sim A_{status}$ sufficient:

$$\text{Sufficiency} \quad \left|R_{goods} = \{horse\}\right| = \left|A_{goods} = \{horse\}\right|$$
$$\left|R_{status} = \{\varnothing\}\right| = \left|A_{status} = \{\varnothing\}\right|$$

A fundamental property of SAS theory is that it is agnostic about the $R \sim A$ relation. This agnosticism differs from, most distinctly, neoclassical economics, which assumes the normative position of limiting scientifically and socially relevant problems to those caused by scarcity, $|R| > |A|$ (e.g., Friedman, 2009; Zinam, 1982). This assumption forces any occurrence of abundance, $|R| < |A|$, to be explained as a symptom of some underlying scarcity (Zinam, 1982). Most conspicuously, John Maynard Keynes (2008) argued that an abundant supply is the consequence of scarce demand—a suggestion that might not always be true (e.g., Bååth, 2018; Daoud, 2007). As we have argued previously in this chapter, a normative prioritization of any SAS as especially problematic (or preferable) is unwarranted because they may all exist and have consequences. Moreover, there are cases in which scarcity is the desired state over abundance. For example, creating scarce availability of—or even

334 PART II NEW THEORETICAL AND EMPIRICAL DEVELOPMENTS

banishing—weapons of mass destruction is considered by many a noble ambition and desired goal. In other cases, people have been found to limit their requirements to achieve sufficiency rather than increase available resources (Daoud, 2011b; Osikominu & Bocken, 2020).

Having laid out SAS and how they relate to each other, we turn to how SAS affects motivations for action. Assuming that SAS might influence human motivations to act, we suggest that there are several strategies that would be available to individuals experiencing a defined SAS event (Table 10.1).

The strategies laid out in Table 10.1 suggest that individuals might act differently under a given resource state, generally adopting a coping strategy that includes one of four ambitions: to avoid, reduce, embrace, or inflate the resource state in question. These strategies contrast the motivations for exchange in SRT (U. Foa & Foa, 1974, p. 126). Rather than starting from intrinsic psychological motives, grounded in a transempirical conception of human nature, the strategies are derived from observable human action and thus agnostic of human nature. The agnosticism implies that SAS theory does not demand a definition of human nature to be employed at an empirical level. Although it is beyond the scope of this chapter to identify all possible human action motivations, we henceforth focus on motivations provoked by SAS. To do that, we incorporate a layered definition of SAS encompassing how an individual relates to another and how an individual relates to a social system.

Table 10.1 A Sketch of Some Individual and Social Strategies to Cope with SAS

	Scarcity	Abundance	Sufficiency
Defensive (avoid it)	(1) Borrow, indenture	(2) Market efficiency	(3) Greed, gluttony
Reactive (reduce it)	(4) Simplicity, austerity	(5) Homophily, stereotypes	(6) Opulence, self-destructiveness
Adaptive (embrace it)	(7) Innovation, martyrdom	(8) Serialism, multiculturalism	(9) Modesty, frugality
Creative (inflate it)	(10) Sadism, speculation	(11) Lavishness, feasting	(12) Generosity, charity

Notes: The strategies are adopted from Abbott (2014) and augmented to cases of scarcity and sufficiency. The concepts provided are indicatory and not exhaustive.

SAS, scarcity, abundance, and sufficiency.

Adapted from Daoud (2018b).

On the Layered Systems of SAS

The different strategies fostered by SAS events must be understood in the light of how the sets R and A are related, which they can be in two manners. Being grounded in critical realism, SAS theory stresses the importance of distinguishing what level of reality an analysis regards (Daoud, 2011a; Sayer, 2000). All reality levels are open systems, which might be influenced by other layers, with one exception.[1] That exception is if the highest level of reality is defined as a closed system, implying that it suffers no extrinsic influence. We limit the argument to the distinction between two levels: individual and systemic.

The distinction between the individual and the systemic level might be conceived as SAS theory's "cultural psychology." The individual, indexed by i, is the level of experience where R_i and A_i operate. Methodologically, this means observing the sociopsychological accounts of individuals. Generally, SRT studies tend to operate on this level, which we will have reasons to come back to. The system level, in contrast, is the aggregate of individual-level experiences within an analytically closed system. Such a system might differ in size and complexity, ranging from small groups to the world's total population. Thus, the system includes SRT's institutions that define legitimate forms of exchange (U. Foa & Foa, 1974, pp. 150–152) but is not limited to these exact structural features. In this case, we define the system level as a closed system encompassing all individuals, including collective social phenomena such as institutions.

The system level, indexed by s, is formalized by aggregating individual R and A, generating systemically available resources A_s and requirements R_s. These two sets aggregate resources and requirements in the system in the following way: $A_s = \cup_i^n A_i$ denotes the union of all available resources in the system with n individuals, and $R_s \cup_{i=1}^n A_i$ denotes the union of all requirements in the system.[2] R_s thus indicates aggregate observations of conceptions regarding material needs, social conventions, religious dogmas, biological conditions, political ideologies, norms, etc. that inform requirements for a given resource in a defined system. In effect, the distinction of and relation between $R_i \sim A_i$ and $R_s \sim A_s$ is the primary concern for

---

[1] See Koumakhov and Daoud (2017, 2021) for how critical realism and social psychology overlap.
[2] Mathematically, a regular set is defined by containing at maximum one element of the same type. We use a *multiset* (bags) definition that, unlike a regular set, accommodates several (multiple) instances for each element.

336 PART II NEW THEORETICAL AND EMPIRICAL DEVELOPMENTS

SAS theory, which, at a later stage, offers explanations of different observed strategies for coping with SAS (cf. Table 10.1).

So far, we have considered the direct relation of R and A (i.e., $R \sim A$), where no exchange is occurring. By differentiating individual and system level, it becomes possible to relate how elements in sets for the individual i, $R_i \sim A_i$, are exchanged with the elements in sets for another individual j, $R_j \sim A_j$, including their exchange with $R_s \sim A_s$ of the system s. We achieve this exchange via the concept entitlements (Daoud, 2010, 2018a; Reddy & Daoud, 2021).

Entitlements, denoted E, are relationships between individuals, or individuals and systems, defining the conditions for how they exchange resources they currently possess for resources they yet do not possess. This concept relates to U. Foa and Foa's (1974) concept of institutions: "mechanisms for facilitating the meeting of individuals having reciprocal needs and powers" (p. 150). Here, power refers to the amount of resources that an individual might give away (p. 135)—that is, whatever amount that exceeds resource optimum. Institutions thus produce various empirical effects of the acceptable conditions for exchange. Defined by culture and society, entitlements similarly rest on rules or conventions of legitimacy.

Entitlements are nested recursive relationships between individuals and systems. For example, I own a car. Why is this ownership accepted? This ownership is accepted because I exchange money to buy this car. Why is my ownership of money accepted? Because I got this money by exchanging my house for a profit. Why is my house ownership accepted? Because I inherited it from my mother. Why was her ownership accepted? And so on and so forth. Based on legitimacy, the chain of exchange recursively continues. Each link in this chain of entitlements rests on socially accepted rules for the exchange of resources.

We build on Amartya Sen's (1983) definition of entitlements:

> A person's ability to command food—indeed, to command any commodity he wishes to acquire or retain—depends on the entitlement relations that govern possession and use in that society. It depends on what he *owns*, what *exchange possibilities* are offered to him, what is *given to him free*, and what is *taken away* from him. (pp. 155–156, emphasis added)

In this quote, Sen defines entitlements as access to four types of relations that enable an individual to acquire resources: ownership, trade, gifts, and

EXTENDING SOCIAL RESOURCE EXCHANGE 337

extraction. Entitlements are thus culturally or politically defined relations of fair exchange according to any one of these four types. The four types of entitlements compare to U. Foa and Foa's (1974) five paradigms of interaction in SRT: giving, taking, restitution, "turning the other cheek," and "ingratitude" (pp. 178–180). Moreover, although individuals might have different entitlements, an entitlement exists on a systemic level. That is the case because for anything to be socially legitimate, its legitimacy has to be generally accepted or at least tolerated. For example, citizenship in a welfare state grants entitlements legitimizing the exchange of various resources for the status of citizenship. In effect, entitlements might be restricted to specific individuals or groups in a certain society. The most prominent case would be a feudal society, in which the estate of an individual would determine that person's entitlements, and the entitlements differ vastly between different estates.

Mathematically, the exchange of resources is then defined by the entitlements function $E_{ij}\left(A_i, A_j\right)$ that maps an exchange of resources between individual i and another actor (either the system or an individual). For clarity, we define the other actor as the individual j. An individual does not exchange with themself; we assume $j \neq i$. We define $E_{ij}\left(A_i = a_{ik}, A_j = a_{jz}\right)$ as the entitlement function that transforms two individuals' resource sets. The transformation described by this function is defined by whatever exchange conditions individual i and j agreed to be legitimate. E_{ij} defines a relation between two sets of available resources A_j and A_i, possessed by j and i. For example, j might be employed by i. By working for i, j gives her labor and thus is entitled to some of i's available resources. E_{ij} then functions similar to an exchange rate, defining how much or what of A_i that is legitimately transferred to A_j due to the employment relation.

Expanding our formalizations of SAS, we add entitlements to the relation denoted as $R \sim E(A)$. To describe an individual's perspective exchanging with a system, we use the notation $R_i \sim E_{is}\left(A_i, A_s\right)$. This notation is useful when an individual exchanges with "all other individuals' A" in some generalized system, such as the stock market or a welfare state. An entitlement denoting the relation between two individuals would work in the same way. On the system level, the relation would still be $R_s \sim A_s$ because the system itself does not have entitlements. The system cannot be entitled to anything that is not already available within the system, because nothing exists outside the system. Entitlements at the system level would only be relevant if

338 PART II NEW THEORETICAL AND EMPIRICAL DEVELOPMENTS

two systems are exchanging with each other—for example, two countries engaged in international trade.

On the individual level, we might then evaluate which of SAS the individual experiences. Suppose that an individual i requires all six resource classes, the cardinal definition of $|R_i|$. To what extent these requirements are fulfilled is then defined by the sets of resources the entitlement function $E_{is}(A_i, A_s)$ makes available for the individual. Failure or success on the entitlement function determines which SAS event the individual experiences. The outcome depends on the entitlement's ability to fulfill the individual's requirements. To evaluate SAS, we remain agnostic about why the entitlement has succeeded or failed. To explain SAS, we evaluate the nature of E. An entitlement might fail both because its institutional design is flawed, thus failing to meet the individual's requirements while working as intended, and because one of the involved individuals breaks the rules, disavowing the entitlement's legitimacy. In the end, what the failure consists of would be an empirical question. We denote success as E^+ and failure as E^-. On the individual level, the difference between SAS would be as follows:

$$
\begin{array}{ll}
\text{Scarcity} & |R_i| > |E_{is}^-(A_i, A_s)| \\
\text{Abundance} & |R_i| < |E_{is}^+(A_i, A_s)| \\
\text{Sufficiency} & |R_i| = |E_{is}^+(A_i, A_s)|
\end{array}
$$

By introducing entitlements, we have a function for what resources are available to an individual through an exchange. To be clear, the pipes imply the cardinality of the result of the entitlement function because the entitlement function cannot operate on a cardinal set. Effectively, if entitlements would change, the available resources for an individual would change. These are some of the new SRT questions scholars can embark on to investigate. Having defined SAS on an individual level, we now show how they produce new types of SAS.

Quasi-SAS

Individuals' experience of SAS varies depending on the system's aggregate resource state. Here, we relate individual sets of $R_i \sim E_{is}(A_i, A_s)$ to the $R_s \sim A_s$

set of the system in which the individual exists. To enable such comparisons is a core rationale of SAS theory and the advantage of distinguishing reality layers. By evaluating individual SAS in relation to the systemic SAS, we distinguish between if an individual experiences an absolute or quasi-SAS. Although absolute and quasi-sufficiency is possible, we focus on events of absolute and quasi-scarcity and abundance.

We distinguish absolute scarcity from quasi-scarcity as follows: *Absolute scarcity* is when scarcity on the individual level coexists with scarcity on the systemic level. The individual's entitlement fails to make the required resources available, simply because there are not enough to go around. Individual always starts with |Ri|, System always starts with |Rs|

$$\text{Absolute scarcity}: \quad \overset{\text{Individual}}{|R_i| > |E_{is}^-(A_i, A_s)|} \quad \overset{\text{System}}{|R_s| > |A_s|}$$

However, individuals might also experience scarcity even though the required resource is not scarce on a systemic level, but sufficient or abundant. Consequently, the individual's entitlement function fails to make the required resource available, but the failure is caused by something different than absolute scarcity. This state is what we call quasi-scarcity.

$$\text{Quasi-scarcity}: \quad \overset{\text{Individual}}{|R_i| > |E_{is}^-(A_i, A_s)|} \quad \overset{\text{System}}{|R_s| \le |A_s|}$$

For abundance, the relation between individual and system is the mirror image of scarcity. Absolute abundance is when the individual experiences an abundance of a required resource, which is also abundant on the systemic level. In this case, the entitlement function makes more resources available than requires.

$$\text{Absolute abundance}: \quad \overset{\text{Individual}}{|R_i| < |E_{is}^+(A_i, A_s)|} \quad \overset{\text{System}}{|R_s| < |A_s|}$$

Quasi-abundance is then when the individual's entitlement function enables more resources than required, while the relevant resource is scarce or sufficient on a systemic level.

340   PART II NEW THEORETICAL AND EMPIRICAL DEVELOPMENTS

$$\text{Quasi-abundance:} \quad \overset{\text{Individual}}{|R_i| < |E_{is}^+(A_i, A_s)|} \quad \overset{\text{System}}{|R_s| \geq |A_s|}$$

The ability to distinguish between absolute and quasi-states of SAS is useful because they warrant different descriptions on the empirical level and different explanations on the transempirical level. On the empirical level, the "quasi" prefix implies that the satisfaction of R_i deviates from the satisfaction of R_s. In effect, an individual experiencing a quasi-version of a certain SAS state might be motivated to act quite differently from one experiencing an absolute version of the same SAS state. That is the case because quasi-states imply inequality, in its most descriptive sense.

Enabled by the definition of the entitlement function, these distinctions between absolute and quasi-SAS tie in with the core ambition of SRT: to identify how mechanisms of resource exchange are characterized among social groups and their normative implications. The concept entitlement enables explanations of how the social group (here, system) influences the individual's possibility to, and motivations for, exchange. U. Foa and Foa (1974) define five paradigms of interaction that might occur in exchange. These paradigms are different combinations of two actors exchanging, where the first proactively gives or takes, and the second reacts by giving or taking (p. 179). By distinguishing the individual from the systemic level, and defining the entitlement function that governs exchange, SAS theory offers an explanation for how a combination of individual and systemic SAS states might cause a given exchange of resources. Moreover, SAS theory identifies what kinds of entitlements affect the resource exchange. Entitlements link individual and systemic levels, and thus provide SRT with a theoretically more developed explanation of the conditions and constraints of resource exchange, both in general and for specific resource classes.[3] Entitlements might thus affect SRT's rules of exchange (E. Foa & Foa, 2012), which we return to later.

The distinction between absolute and quasi-SAS has implications for how resource states influence motivations for exchange. For example, an individual experiencing quasi-SAS might be morally engaged because they do not have enough resources, even though the system has abundant resources. Those

---

[3] Sen (1983, Appendix A) offers a different formalization of exchange entitlements based on social welfare theory.

experiencing quasi-abundance might resist any change to the entitlement system that jeopardizes the current unequal distribution of resources. In contrast, an individual experiencing an absolute abundance might be content with the situation, if the resource is of general value (e.g., food). From an explanatory perspective, quasi-SAS might have arisen from inequality, kleptocracy, clientelism, and similar—that is, events that historically have fostered social transformations ranging from violent revolts to the institutionalization of black markets.

Having laid out the dynamics of SAS, it is worth considering if these dynamics have any consequences for SRT's definition of exchange rules. Previously, we explicated two such rules: (a) that the more particularistic the resource class, the higher the frequency of interclass exchange; and (b) the less concrete and more particularistic a resource is, the more one gains from giving of one's resources to others. Generally, SRT's exchange rules "concern variables or properties with regard to which resource classes differ systematically, such that some resources will be more similar to each other than to others" (Törnblom & Kazemi, 2012, p. 44). These rules modify the *qualities* of resource classes. These qualities are the degrees of particularity and concreteness of one, in relation to each other under exchange. SAS theory, however, concerns relative *quantities* of resources—that is, the relation between required and available resources. Our argument is thus that the relative quantities of resources, individual and systemic SAS, influence SRT's exchange rules but do not foster any novel rules. In the following applications, we consider the consequences that SAS theory's agnostic approach has for the aforementioned rules.

Given our SAS–SRT synthesis, we propose the following modified definition of an exchange rule: An exchange rule describes how variables or properties differ (a) systematically between resource classes, such that some resources will be more similar to each other than to others, and (b) in relation to their SAS event. Because there are several exchange rules, we propose that any exchange rule has to incorporate a definition about the resource classes' qualities (their substantive content) and their quantities (their SAS event). The next section discusses how our reformulated definition influences SRT analysis in two concrete applications.

How SRT Benefits from SAS Theory: Two Applications

Our analytical distinction between absolute and quasi-SAS allows SRT to benefit in at least two ways: (a) an agnostic approach to motivations

342 PART II NEW THEORETICAL AND EMPIRICAL DEVELOPMENTS

for exchange and (b) a social systems approach to SAS. The agnostic approach enables SRT to extend its analysis of exchange to events of abundance and sufficiency, accounting for the effects of such events on the exchange of different resource classes (Daoud, 2018b). The social systems approach to SAS benefits SRT by including institutional conditions for exchange, such as the availability of different resource classes and the effects of entitlements, in a systematic manner (Daoud, 2010). Thus, by conceptualizing SRT through SAS theory, expressed in our new definition of exchange rules (p. 15), we bring abundance and sufficiency into SRT. We demonstrate these benefits by applying SAS theory to two examples: Max Weber's Protestant's ethic-turn-capitalist spirit and global hunger in a world of food abundance.

Application 1: The Protestant Ethic and Abundance-Based Motivations

One of the most distinct consequences of the assumption of scarcity in SRT is that it limits the possible motivations for an actor who holds an abundance of resources. An actor experiencing abundance, we argue, might use one of four different strategies: defensive (avoid it), reactive (reduce it), adaptive (embrace it), or creative (inflate it) (see Table 10.1). U. Foa and Foa (1974) suggest two sources of abundance-based motivation: "pain and discomfort" and "satiation" (pp. 128, 138). These two motivations would warrant the actor to use a reactive strategy, or possibly a defensive one. In addition, Greenberg (1981) suggests that actors may experience "felt needs," despite not actually possessing scarce resources, which would motivate certain actors to use creative or adaptive strategies. However, SAS theory uses requirements that include any felt needs, wants, or preferences. From our SRT–SAS synthesis, requirements are the empirical manifestations of human needs mixed with psychological and cultural expressions.

People who knowingly possess an abundance of resources still tend to use creative and adaptive strategies. Weber's (2005) study of frugal Protestants turning capitalists offers an informative example. The Protestant's emphasis on saving and investing excess capital, rather than spending or destroying it, can be interpreted as a strategy for reducing abundance to sufficiency or scarcity. By locking any non-necessary capital in savings accounts and investments, the Protestants relieve themselves from the temptation to spend in an excessive or frivolous manner. Because U. Foa and Foa (1974) suggest that money might have an infinite optimal range (pp. 125–128), we simplify our example by focusing on capital as the resource class "goods." The Protestant, indexed by p, has the requirement R_p and the available resources A_p, the cardinalities of which stand in the following relation:

$$\left|R_{P_{goods}} = \{\text{porcelain, copper}\}\right| < \left|A_{P_{goods}} = \{\text{porcelain, copper, silk}\}\right|$$

The Protestant thus possesses an abundance of goods. However, by striking a deal with a merchant, indexed as m, the Protestant is entitled to investing some of his silk in the merchant's training company for a promise of a future return of a greater quantity of silk when the merchant has increased his shares of the silk market. The entitlement is denoted E_{pm}. Assuming that the entitlement exchange is successful between the Protestant and merchant, the relation now looks as follows:

$$\left|R_{P_{goods}} = \{\text{porcelain, copper}\}\right|$$
$$= \left| \begin{matrix} E_{pm}^+ (A_{P_{goods}} = \{\text{porcelain, copper}\}, \\ A_{P_{service}} = \{\text{a promise of future silk}\}, A_{m_{goods}} = \{\text{silk}\}) \end{matrix} \right|$$

By investing the silk, the merchant has achieved sufficiency. Although he has been given a promise in exchange, the promise is not classified as a good but, rather, as a service which might later provide goods, so far that the promise is honored. Although the Protestant is awarded something in exchange for his silk, that something is not a good. For the resource class goods, the relation between requirements and available resources is that of sufficiency. However, this exchange was motivated by neither a felt need for silk (as silk is abundant) nor pain and discomfort from satiation, as the Protestant could then have destroyed or given the silk away freely. However, by relating the Protestant's requirements and resources to the system level, we find justifications for assuming specific motivations. We evaluate first system abundance and then system scarcity of silk.

If silk is *abundant* on the system level, it means that the aggregate requirement R_s for silk overshoots the silk available within the system A_s:

$$\left|R_{s_{goods}} = \{\text{silk}\}\right| < \left|A_{s_{goods}} = \{\text{silk}\}\right|$$

344 PART II NEW THEORETICAL AND EMPIRICAL DEVELOPMENTS

In this case, the Protestant possesses an absolute abundance of silk. Ridding himself of the abundant silk, even if it is only exchanged for the promise of a future greater quantity of silk, would motivate the Protestant by the pain and discomfort of risking that the silk would never be utilized for any meaningful end, such as profits or beautiful clothing. U. Foa and Foa's (1974) suggestion that super optimum would self-regulate to optimum because of the troubles caused by the abundance may be true. However, the Protestant might as well be motivated by the experience of abundance to employ a reductive strategy, including but not limited to reduce pain and discomfort. Any reason for attaining sufficiency would motivate such a strategy, not only negative stimuli but also generosity. Whereas the SRT definition of motivations limits the possible motivations to one, the SAS theory's agnostic approach enables the inclusion of motivations stemming from other types of requirements.

If silk is *scarce* on the system level, it means that the aggregate requirement for silk overshoots the silk available within the system:

$$\left| R_{s_{goods}} = \{\text{silk}\} \right| > \left| A_{s_{goods}} = \{\text{silk}\} \right|$$

In this case, the Protestant possesses a quasi-abundance of silk. Although silk is required in the system, the Protestant himself does not require silk. The motivation for investing the quasi-abundant silk for a promise of a future greater abundance of silk cannot be rooted in pain or discomfort as in the previous case. Nor does the exchange fulfill any alternative need. Consequently, the Protestant's motivation is unexplainable in terms of scarcity or needs. However, the Protestant's motivation is explainable if we consider the investment of a creative strategy for dealing with abundance. In other words, the Protestant does not require the silk now, but he might require a greater quantity in the future. Such a strategy might be motivated by possessing quasi-abundance, because the aggregate demand means that it would be a good opportunity to invest the silk to (it is hoped) acquire a greater quantity of silk in a future of unknown SAS. In this case, the Protestant's strategy relates to SRT's concept "power"— that is, the amount of a resource that is available for giving (U. Foa & Foa, 1974, pp. 134–135). The Protestant might give the abundant silk away out of charity or, as in this case, invest it for (possible) future profits.

According to E. Foa and Foa's (2012) rules of exchange, resources classified as goods are primarily exchanged for resources from other classes, but occasionally for other kinds of goods (p. 21). Comparing the Protestant's motivations and strategies (see Table 10.1) under systemic scarcity and abundance, goods might still be primarily exchanged for other resource classes in general. However, using a reductive strategy to cope with absolute abundance implies that the Protestant follows a specific version of this rule of exchange for goods: to exchange for goods or other resources in a manner that reduces the abundance (rather than, e.g., inflating it). In contrast, using a creative strategy under quasi-abundance makes the Protestant follow the same rule, but a version of it in which the exchange enables the future acquirement of an even greater quantity of silk. Thus, although the creative strategy temporarily means a loss of goods, it might, in the long term, mean a gain of goods. This strategy thus challenges the validity of a rule of exchange stating that one generally loses goods when giving them away (cf. E. Foa & Foa, 2012, p. 20). We return to this problem later.

Application 2: Famine in an Abundant Global Food System

As previously mentioned, the global food supply is absolutely abundant and has so been since the United Nations (UN) started to measure it in the 1960s. Currently, the global food supply overshoots the basic human caloric need by approximately 60% (Food and Agriculture Organization et al., 2001, 2015). Despite this abundance, 10% of the global population suffers from famine. This is a case of quasi-scarcity.

In this case, we thus define R_i as the human caloric requirement, labeled "food." Mathematically, the following is true for approximately 1 billion poor individuals who are starving every day:

Individual

$$\left| R_{i_{-goods}} = \{\text{food}\} \right| > \left| A_{i_{-goods}} = \{\varnothing\} \right|$$

System

$$\left| R_{s_{-goods}} = \{\text{food}\} \right| > \left| A_{s_{-goods}} = \{\text{food}\} \right|$$

346 PART II NEW THEORETICAL AND EMPIRICAL DEVELOPMENTS

On the individual level, these 1 billion individuals experience food scarcity despite the fact that on the level of the (global food) system there is food abundance; these individuals thus experience quasi-scarcity. This state of food quasi-scarcity begs the question: Are all people entitled to food? According to Article 25 of the UN's (1948) Universal Declaration of Human Rights, "Everyone has the right to a standard of living adequate for the health and well-being of himself and of his family, including food." This article states that every individual, indexed by i, is entitled to sufficient food to avoid starvation and humanity's degradation. The entitlement charges the system, indexed by s, with providing the food. The exact mechanism through which the food is supplied may vary significantly between individuals and does not have to be defined. Article 25 states that everybody is entitled to some functional means of acquiring food, might that be buying it on a capitalist market or hunting and gathering. However, this entitlement function fails to make enough food available through any available mechanism for all starving people:

Individual

$$\left| R_{i_{-goods}} = \{food\} \right| > \left| E_{is}^{-} \left(A_{i_{goods}} = \{\varnothing\}, A_{s_{goods}} = \{food\} \right) \right|$$

System

$$\left| R_{s_{goods}} = \{food\} \right| < \left| A_{s_{goods}} = \{food\} \right|$$

In the equation, the individual requires food, $\left| R_{i_{-goods}} = \{food\} \right|$. However, due to the failure of the individual's entitlement, E_{is}^{-}, the set of available food for the individual turns out empty, $A_{i_{goods}} = \{\varnothing\}$—that is, less than, ">," the person's set of requirements. The individual thus experiences scarcity, despite the fact that there is food available on the systemic level, $A_{s_{goods}} = \{food\}$, indexed by s. Moreover, on the systemic level, the requirements for food, $\left| R_{s_{goods}} = \{food\} \right|$, are less than, "<," the food available, $\left| A_{s_{goods}} = \{food\} \right|$. Thus, although being entitled to food by the UN's declaration of human rights, that entitlement fails to secure the required amount of food for the individual. Consequently, the individual still experiences quasi-scarcity. This failure does not tell us what distribution mechanisms the individual hypothetically could have used to succeed. Any kind of mechanism, from capitalist markets to foraging, fails in this scenario (Sen, 1983, pp. 155–156).

For an individual who does not starve, and the entitlement succeeds to supply food, the following is true:

Individual

$$\left|R_{i_{goods}} = \{\text{food}\}\right| \leq \left|E_{is}^+ \left(A_{i_{goods}} = \{\text{food}\}, A_{s_{goods}} = \{\text{food}\}\right)\right|$$

System

$$\left|R_{s_{goods}} = \{\text{food}\}\right| < \left|A_{s_{goods}} = \{\text{food}\}\right|$$

The important difference to the previous example is the entitlement function, E_{is}^+, which succeeds, signified by the plus sign "+." Because of that success, the individual has enough food available, $A_{i_{goods}} = \{\text{food}\}$. As follows on Article 25, all humans have a right not to starve, but the mechanism which provides the food for that might differ as long as non-starvation is the outcome. In this case, the individual experiences sufficiency or abundance, begging the question of what entitlement succeeds in providing required amounts of food when the right to food does not seem to be a reliable option.

The International Monetary Fund is one of the most influential institutions in the trade of improving global economic conditions. Reviewing its demands on food supply for lender states, the International Monetary Fund generally demands liberalized markets as a means of improving the (economic) efficiency of food supply (Daoud et al., 2019). As shown in Table 10.1, market liberalization is one commonly suggested defensive strategy for coping with abundance. Economists often assume that liberalized markets maximize efficient resource allocation while simultaneously minimizing the risks of unrequired abundance and scarcity through the mechanism of supply and demand (Friedman, 2009; Hayek, 1945). However, in practice, liberalized markets under capitalism do not seem to have that effect. Instead, they oversupply the already wealthy (Bååth, 2018; Daoud, 2007) and reproduce existing social structures (Bååth, 2022b; cf. Bååth, 2022a). An increasing number of studies find that the huge trade surpluses of the world's wealthiest nations obstruct poorer nations' development of local systems of provisioning, foremost enriching the already entitled while not redeeming famine among the poor (see McGoey, 2018). In the United States, for example, the poorest neighborhoods have the least food outlets while also being subject to the steepest food prices due to the absence of competition and large-scale supermarkets (Walker et al., 2010). To conclude, although liberalized markets might be an efficient strategy for reducing the risk of food scarcity on a system level, this strategy does not seem to deliver equally well on an individual level. That is the case, it seems, because liberalized markets make wealthy consumers end up with an abundance of food, before feeding the poor consumers. Instead of minimizing scarcity on the individual level, it inflates or at least adapts the abundance of a subset of wealthy individuals. In summary, wealth—not human rights— entitles non-starving individuals to food.

Considering wealth as an entitlement E, rather than a resource, enables us to describe this case of quasi-scarcity better, establishing the exchange rate of food between the individual, indexed by i, and the global food system, indexed by g. By defining wealth as an entitlement, we argue not only that wealthy individuals possess more money to buy food but also that they are entitled to more and better offers for buying food. For example, poor people in the United States surely have less money to spend on food, but living in a poor neighborhood also means that the prices for food are comparably higher and the variety of foods offered is more limited than in a wealthy neighborhood (Bowen, Brenton, and Elliott, 2020).[4] In effect, it is of less importance what precisely the individual has to exchange for food. Whatever the individual has, their failing wealth entitlement means any available offers of food would not supply the person with sufficient amounts of food in return, despite the fact that the global food system supplies an abundance of food.

Individual

$$\left| R_{i_{goods}} = \{\text{food}\} \right| > \left| E_{ig}^{-} \left(A_{i_{goods}} = \{\varnothing\}, A_{g_{goods}} = \{\text{food}\} \right) \right|$$

System

$$\left| R_{s_{goods}} = \{\text{food}\} \right| < \left| A_{g_{goods}} = \{\text{food}\} \right|$$

[4] Wealth as an entitlement implies cumulative advantage; by being wealthy, one not only possesses more money but also is presented with more possibilities to adopt creative or adaptive strategies that inflate or embrace that wealth (cf. Table 10.1, adaptive and creative strategies of sufficiency).

EXTENDING SOCIAL RESOURCE EXCHANGE   349

In this equation, the entitlement's failure that is signified by the negative sign "–" implies that the individual's lack of wealth means that enough food to cover the human caloric requirement is not made available by any means. On the individual level, the term $\left| R_{i_{goods}} = \{\text{food}\} \right|$ means that individual i requires "food" for nourishment, which is of the resources class "goods." For poor individuals who lack sufficient nourishment, the requirements exceed what their entitlements allow them to acquire. This means that the set R is larger, ">," than the one E supplies. The term $\left| E_{ig}^{-} \left(A_{i_{goods}} = \{\varnothing\}, A_{g_{goods}} = \{\text{food}\} \right) \right|$ encodes entitlement failure, E_{ig}^{-}, which means that i's wealth is insufficient as to make the food available, A, to satisfy R. The individual thus suffers scarcity.

On the system level, however, $\left| R_{s_{goods}} = \{\text{food}\} \right|$ means all individual combined requirements for nourishment are less than, "<," the food available under the global food system, encoded $\left| A_{g_{goods}} = \{\text{food}\} \right|$. In summary, there is systemic abundance. Taken together, individual scarcity under systemic abundance means that i experiences quasi-scarcity of food. This quasi-scarcity might be due to a shortage of cash, but equally well the absence of food vendors. In addition, it might imply the financial inability to stave off land-grabbers, losing land access for sustenance farming or hunting and gathering. In the end, all these scenarios have the same outcome: starvation due to a lack of wealth. However, the wealth function of the individual who does not starve does deliver sufficient or abundant quantities of food.

Individual

$$\left| R_{i_{goods}} = \{\text{food}\} \right| \leq \left| E_{ig}^{+} \left(A_{i_{goods}} = \{\text{food}\}, A_{g_{goods}} = \{\text{food}\} \right) \right|$$

System

$$\left| R_{g_{goods}} = \{\text{food}\} \right| < \left| A_{g_{goods}} = \{\text{food}\} \right|$$

These relations indicate that the entitlement of wealth is dramatically unevenly distributed among the world's population. Following the entitlement

350   PART II NEW THEORETICAL AND EMPIRICAL DEVELOPMENTS

function, the global food system, supplying food through liberalized markets, is an efficient strategy for exchanging food (goods) for money. However, some individuals hold significantly more wealth than others, which entitles them to more and better offers to exchange food for money. As a result, the current global food system's orientation toward wealth entitles the wealthiest more food than they require before meeting all individual requirements (see also Sen, 1983, pp. 154–157). Moreover, an actor in a state of quasi-scarcity of food would be much more prone to revolts or riots. Food riots under quasi-scarcity have the possible outcome of feeding the rioting hungry, reducing famine, whereas food riots under absolute scarcity may either be futile or possibly redistribute some quasi-sufficiency or abundance, while not reducing famine.

Moreover, the experience of quasi-scarcity implies that another individual's abundance might very well serve as a provocation that motivates riots or other kinds of social upheaval and legitimizes violence as an entitlement. To avoid such upheaval, policymakers implement social policies such as minimum income or food coupons to give temporary entitlements for the poor (Conklin et al., 2019; Nandy et al., 2016). In the opposite case, foods have been systemically destroyed to mitigate abundance, effectively protecting wealth as an entitlement (Prasad, 2012). If the individual experiences quasi-scarcity or absolute scarcity, it thus affects their adoption of interaction paradigms (cf. U. Foa & Foa, 1974, pp. 178–180). Whereas there might be little to do about absolute scarcity, quasi-scarcity may provoke taking and ingratitude toward those who have sufficient or abundant amounts of food. This argument problematizes the second rule of exchange, which states that giving goods generally means a loss for the giver. Although it is true that loss would be the immediate effect of feeding the hungry, it might be considered a gain when compared to the losses from social unrest— that is, the consequences of taking and ingratitude. In short, we suggest that rules of exchange must be not only considered on the interpersonal level but also contextualized within a system, in order to understand the systematic production of gains and losses from exchange.

Discussion and Conclusion

This chapter synthesized SRT and SAS, enabling SRT to analyze abundance and sufficiency in tandem with scarcity for analyzing resource exchange.

First, we discussed how SRT rests on an assumption of scarcity as the primary resource state causing exchange motivations and the problems caused by that assumption. Second, we used SAS theory to formalize SAS in an agnostic manner, tying them to different behavioral strategies that individuals use when engaging with a specific resource state. Third, we formalized the relation between individual- and systemic-level SAS. This relation is influenced by entitlement functions, allowing the distinction between an individual's experiencing of absolute and quasi-SAS. This difference is essential because quasi-SAS implies different exchange motivations and strategies than absolute SAS. Last, based on our formalization, we offered a modified definition of exchange rules. This modification states that any exchange rule must define both the quality (the substantive content of a resource class) and quantity (what happens to their qualities in different SAS states) of a resources class. We exemplified our SAS–SRT approach through two applications showing how abundance-based motivations function and how quasi-scarcity requires different explanations than absolute scarcity.

The rationale of this chapter rested on the undertheorizing of two aspects of SRT. The first one regards how abundance and sufficiency affect exchange. By formalizing SAS's relations, SRT has a precise language to identify how sets of resources and requirements change through an exchange. By doing so, SRT achieves an agnostic outset for analyzing resource exchange and its underlying motivations, while still acknowledging existing findings regarding the effects of needs in exchange. We thus propose that SRT explicate the mechanisms and rules of exchange on all relevant levels of social reality to account for the context of exchange behavior.

An important consequence of our proposition to explicate mechanisms is that it enables SRT to redefine how abundance relates to resource exchange. While SRT defines negative abundances, which fosters the arousal of new needs (U. Foa & Foa, 1974, pp. 128, 138; Greenberg, 1981), the agnostic approach enables SRT to define also events of positive abundance. Such positive abundance might problematize, or at least nuance, SRT's exchange rules. As we showed in Application 1, investing in goods reduces the amount of goods possessed, as one of SRT's exchange rules predicts (see E. Foa & Foa, 2012, p. 21), but might in the long term increase that amount. The hope of such future gains is an important part of justifying investments (see Olofsson, 2020). We thus argue that giving has different consequences and allows for different strategies (see Table 10.1) in the event of scarcity than in the event of abundance.

352 PART II NEW THEORETICAL AND EMPIRICAL DEVELOPMENTS

Employing the SAS theory's agnosticism allows for SRT to nuance the relationship between giving and taking, and the gains and losses from giving to others, depending on if the resource exchanged is scarce, abundant, or sufficient. Thus, any of the 12 cells of Table 10.1 might warrant the formulation of a much more specific set of exchange rules that hold true for that specific coping strategy. Consequently, it is also reasonable to hypothesize that an individual's "resource optimum" might be affected by SAS events, including how narrow or wide that range is (see also Törnblom & Kazemi, 2012, p. 47).

The second aspect regards the undertheorizing of the relation between different social reality levels, primarily between the individual and the (societal) system levels. In general, SRT focuses on the individual level, which tends to leave out macro-scale social, political, and cultural processes that will affect an individual's exchange behavior. Distinguishing the individual level from the systemic level further nuances the exchange rules of SRT. First, it is the systemic level's SAS event that defines if the individual experiences absolute or quasi-SAS. Following on our previous argument, nuanced rules of exchange in relation to SAS events, we contend that it is necessary to define the SAS event on both the systemic and the individual level to attain an agnostic approach to SAS. Then, first, it is possible to contextualize any relevant exchanges and rules thereof. Second, distinguishing levels of social reality allows for SRT to account for different individuals' entitlements and how they influence each individual's resource state and exchange behavior. Any rule of exchange might be affected by an entitlement because entitlements affect the individual's access to exchanges. This proposition does not affect any rules of exchange directly. However, the proposition states that rules of exchange cannot be assumed in a social vacuum, but that existing entitlements must be taken into account to analyze exchange behavior or risk misinterpreting their effects as natural behavior. By including entitlements, SRT is enabled to identify and analyze the effects of both absolute and quasi-SAS. Such identification and analyses provide more in-depth knowledge of an individual's motivations to engage in exchange in a particular manner. Future studies in SRT may thus benefit from exploring the consequences of entitlements for rules of exchange.

Our proposal relates to Greenberg (1981), suggesting that "macro processes" influence requirements' formation, including the formation of needs. Greenberg's critique primarily regards that participants in exchange experiments might be affected by their everyday experience and understanding of need. However, it is equally applicable to scientific studies and theories of exchange in general. Our argument shows that SRT mechanisms exist on different levels of reality and that they might offer better explanations of exchange situations by explicating how those mechanisms function on these levels.

In a more general sense, although time is not the focus of this chapter, it is worth noting that the coping strategies (see Table 10.1) suggest that coping with SAS events takes time. For example, speculation demands a form of exchange that takes time, despite what resource class one uses to speculate, because the return comes in the future. Speculation thus fosters intraclass exchange also for goods and money. This is but one example, but it questions E. Foa and Foa's (2012) rule that individuals exchange comparably concrete and non-particularistic resource classes more swiftly than others (p. 23). Swiftly exchanged resource classes are those that individuals rarely exchange for the same class (E. Foa & Foa, 2012, p. 21). Thus, Foa and Foa's conception of time seems to ignore the prevalence of intraclass exchange of goods and money over a longer time (e.g., investment), while allowing such long-term exchange for other resource classes. In line with Törnblom and Kazemi (2012), we thus suggest that SRT might benefit from reassessing the role of time in exchange behavior.

Finally, throughout this chapter, we have stressed the agnosticism of SAS theory, emphasizing its descriptive and analytical usefulness in resource exchange studies. However, this agnosticism does not mean that normativity does not have a place in SRT. Although SAS theory's main ambition is to offer useful descriptions, the results can still be interpreted in a normative framework. For example, SRT is an essential theory in studies of distributive justice. By the variants of quasi-SAS and absolute SAS, our synthesis enables distributive justice studies to explicate the relation between systemic conditions for just exchanges and the individual's engagement in such exchanges.

References

Abbott, A. (2014). The problem of excess. *Sociological Theory, 32*(1), 1–26. https://doi.org/10.1177/0735275114523419

Archer, M. S., & Tritter, J. Q. (2000). *Rational choice theory: Resisting colonization.* Psychology Press.

Bååth, J. (2018). Production in a State of Abundance: Valuation and Practice in the Swedish Meat Supply Chain [Doctoral thesis]. Department of Sociology, Uppsala University.

354 PART II NEW THEORETICAL AND EMPIRICAL DEVELOPMENTS

Bååth, J. (2022a). How alternative foods become affordable: The co-construction of economic value on a direct-to-customer market. *Journal of Rural Studies*, 94: 63–72. https://doi.org/10.1016/j.jrurstud.2022.05.017

Bååth, J. (2022b). Towards a unified theory of market prices: Turning to pricing in practice. *Socio-Economic Review*, Online first. https://doi.org/10.1093/ser/mwac010

Baumgärtner, S., Becker, C., Faber, M., & Manstetten, R. (2006). Relative and absolute scarcity of nature: Assessing the roles of economics and ecology for biodiversity conservation. *Ecological Economics*, *59*(4), 487–498. https://doi.org/10.1016/j.ecolecon.2005.11.012

Becker, G. S. (1965). A theory of the allocation of time. *Economic Journal*, *75*(299), 493–517. https://doi.org/10.2307/2228949

Boudon, R. (2003). Beyond rational choice theory. *Annual Review of Sociology*, *29*(1), 1–21. https://doi.org/10.1146/annurev.soc.29.010202.100213

Bowen, S., Brenton, J., & Elliott, S. (2020). *Pressure cooker: Why home cooking won't solve our problems and what we can do about it.* Oxford University Press.

Conklin, A. I., Daoud, A., Shimkhada, R., & Ponce, N. A. (2019). The impact of rising food prices on obesity in women: A longitudinal analysis of 31 low-income and middle-income countries from 2000 to 2014. *International Journal of Obesity*, *43*(4), 774–781. https://doi.org/10.1038/s41366-018-0178-y

Daoud, A. (2007). (Quasi)scarcity and global hunger. *Journal of Critical Realism*, *6*(2), 199–225. https://doi.org/10.1558/jocr.v6i2.199

Daoud, A. (2010). Robbins and Malthus on scarcity, abundance, and sufficiency. *American Journal of Economics and Sociology*, *69*(4), 1206–1229. https://doi.org/10.1111/j.1536-7150.2010.00741.x

Daoud, A. (2011a). Scarcity, abundance and sufficiency: Contributions to social and economic theory [Doctoral thesis]. Gothenburg University.

Daoud, A. (2011b). The modus vivendi of material simplicity: Counteracting scarcity via the deflation of wants. *Review of Social Economy*, *69*(3), 275–305. https://doi.org/10.1080/00346764.2010.502832

Daoud, A. (2018a). Synthesizing the Malthusian and Senian approaches on scarcity: A realist account. *Cambridge Journal of Economics*, *42*(2), 453–476. https://doi.org/10.1093/cje/bew071

Daoud, A. (2018b). Unifying studies of scarcity, abundance, and sufficiency. *Ecological Economics*, *147*, 208–217. https://doi.org/10.1016/j.ecolecon.2018.01.019

Daoud, A., Reinsberg, B., Kentikelenis, A. E., Stubbs, T. H., & King, L. P. (2019). The International Monetary Fund's interventions in food and agriculture: An analysis of loans and conditions. *Food Policy*, *83*, 204–218. https://doi.org/10.1016/j.foodpol.2019.01.005

Dugger, W. M., & Peach, J. T. (2009). *Economic abundance: An introduction.* Routledge.

Elster, J. (2015). Explaining social behavior: More nuts and bolts for the social sciences (2nd ed.). Cambridge University Press. https://doi.org/10.1017/CBO9781107763111

Foa, E. B., & Foa, U. G. (2012). Resource theory of social exchange. In K. Y. Törnblom & A. Kazemi (Eds.), *Handbook of social resource theory: Theoretical extensions, empirical insights, and social applications* (pp. 15–32). Springer.

Foa, U. G., & Foa, E. B. (1974). *Societal structures of the mind.* Charles C Thomas.

Food and Agriculture Organization, International Fund for Agricultural Development, & World Food Programme. (2015). *The state of food insecurity in the world 2015.*

EXTENDING SOCIAL RESOURCE EXCHANGE 355

Meeting the 2015 international hunger targets: Taking stock of uneven progress. Food and Agriculture Organization of the United Nations.

Food and Agriculture Organization, World Health Organization, & United Nations University. (2001). *Human energy requirements* (No. 1: Food and Nutrition Technical Reports). Food and Agriculture Organization of the United Nations. http://www.fao.org/docrep/007/y5686e/y5686e04.htm

Friedman, M. (2009). *Price theory. The richest man in Babylon.*

Greenberg, J. (1981). The justice of distributing scarce and abundant resources. In M. J. Lerner & S. C. Lerner (Eds.), *The justice motive in social behavior: Adapting to times of scarcity and change* (pp. 289–316). Springer. https://doi.org/10.1007/978-1-4899-0429-4_13

Hayek, F. A. (1945). The use of knowledge in society. *American Economic Review, 35*(4), 519–530.

Hedström, P., & Stern, L. (2008). Rational choice and sociology. In S. N. Durlauf & L. E. Blume (Eds.), *The new Palgrave dictionary of economics* (2nd ed., pp. 872–877). Palgrave Macmillan.

Kahneman, D. (2011). *Thinking, fast and slow.* Farrar, Straus & Giroux.

Keynes, J. M. (2008). Economic possibilities for our grandchildren (1930). In L. Pecchi & G. Piga (Eds.), *Revisiting Keynes* (pp. 17–26). MIT Press. https://doi.org/10.7551/mitpress/9780262162494.003.0002

Koumakhov, R., & Daoud, A. (2017). Routine and reflexivity: Simonian cognitivism vs practice approach. *Industrial and Corporate Change, 26*(4), 727–743. https://doi.org/10.1093/icc/dtw048

Koumakhov, R., & Daoud, A. (2021). Decisions and structures: A dialogue between Herbert Simon and critical realists. *British Journal of Management, 32*(4), 1404–1420. https://doi.org/10.1111/1467-8551.12439

McGoey, L. (2018). Bataille and the sociology of abundance: Reassessing gifts, debt and economic excess. *Theory, Culture & Society, 35*(4–5), 69–91. https://doi.org/10.1177/0263276416637905

Menger, C. (2007). *Principles of economics.* Ludwig von Mises Institute.

Mullainathan, S., & Shafir, E. (2013). *Scarcity: Why having too little means so much.* Macmillan.

Nandy, S., Daoud, A., & Gordon, D. (2016). Examining the changing profile of undernutrition in the context of food price rises and greater inequality. *Social Science & Medicine, 149,* 153–163. https://doi.org/10.1016/j.socscimed.2015.11.036

Olofsson, T. (2020). Imagined futures in mineral exploration. *Journal of Cultural Economy, 13*(3), 265–277. https://doi.org/10.1080/17530350.2019.1604399

Osikominu, J., & Bocken, N. (2020). A voluntary simplicity lifestyle: Values, adoption, practices and effects. *Sustainability, 12*(5), 1903. https://doi.org/10.3390/su12051903

Panayotakis, C. (2011). *Remaking scarcity: From capitalist inefficiency to economic democracy.* Pluto Press.

Prasad, M. (2012). *The land of too much: American abundance and the paradox of poverty.* Harvard University Press.

Reddy, S. G., & Daoud, A. (2021). Entitlements and capabilities. In E. Chiappero-Martinetti, S. Osmani, & M. Qizilbash (Eds.), *The Cambridge handbook of the capability approach* (pp. 677–684). Cambridge University Press.

Robbins, L. (2007). *An essay on the nature and significance of economic science.* Ludwig von Mises Institute.

356 PART II NEW THEORETICAL AND EMPIRICAL DEVELOPMENTS

Sayer, A. (2000). Key features of critical realism in practice: A brief outline. In A. Sayer (Ed.), *Realism and social science* (pp. 10–28). SAGE.

Sen, A. (1983). *Poverty and famines*. Oxford University Press.

Springborg, P. (1981). *The problem of human needs and the critique of civilisation*. George Allen & Unwin.

Stillman, P. G. (1983). Scarcity, sufficiency, and abundance: Hegel and Marx on material needs and satisfactions. *International Political Science Review, 4*(3), 295–310.

Törnblom, K., & Kazemi, A. (2012). Some conceptual and theoretical issues in resource theory of social exchange. In K. Törnblom & A. Kazemi (Eds.), *Handbook of social resource theory* (pp. 33–64). Springer.

Törnblom, K. Y., & Nilsson, B. O. (2008). Effect of matching resources to source on their perceived importance and sufficiency. In U. G. Foa, J. Converse, K. Y. Törnblom, & E. B. Foa (Eds.), *Resource theory: Explorations and applications* (pp. 81–96). Emerald.

Törnblom, K. Y., Stern, P., Pirak, K., Pudas, A., & Törnlund, E. (2008). Type of resource and choice of comparison target. In U. G. Foa, J. Converse, K. Y. Törnblom, & E. B. Foa (Eds.), *Resource theory: Explorations and applications* (pp. 81–96). Emerald.

Turner, B. S., & Rojek, C. (2001). *Society and culture: Scarcity and solidarity*. SAGE.

United Nations. (1948). *Universal declaration of human rights*. http://www.ohchr.org/EN/UDHR/Documents/UDHR_Translations/eng.pdf

Weber, M. (2005). *The Protestant ethic and the spirit of capitalism*. Routledge.

Xenos, N. (2017). *Scarcity and modernity*. Routledge.

Zinam, O. (1982). The myth of absolute abundance: Economic development as a shift in relative scarcities. *American Journal of Economics and Sociology, 41*(1), 61–76. https://doi.org/10.1111/j.1536-7150.1982.tb01668.x

11

When Your Heart Goes Bumpity Bump: Neurological Characteristics of Love

Elaine Hatfield, Richard L. Rapson, and Stephanie Cacioppo

Foa and Foa's Classic Theory

Foa and Foa (Foa, 1971; Foa & Foa, 1974) attempted to develop a "unified theory" of social exchange. Defining resources as "anything that can be transmitted from one person to another," they proposed the existence of six major resource classes involved in such exchanges: love, services, goods, money, information, and status. These resources differ in particularism and concreteness (Figure 11.1). Love is said to be the most particular of resources (because passionate love can be directed to only one intimate) and can be expressed either symbolically (as in declarations of love) or concretely (with kisses, hugs, and the like). Since the Foas' original formulation, scholars have used this paradigm as an armature on which to drape various theories as to the scientific definition of the six resources and how similar these resources are to one another. They focused on the people who engage in various types of exchanges, the rules for the exchange of these resources, and the like. Törnblom and Kazemi (2012) provided a voluminous review of the way this theory has been articulated and expanded in the more than 40 years since it was first proposed.

In a chapter in Törnblom and Kazemi's (2012) *Handbook*, we attempted to provide an in-depth review of what was then known about the antecedents and characteristics of *one* of Foa and Foa's commodities—love (specifically passionate love).

Since the publication of that groundbreaking *Handbook*, a great deal of research has been conducted to increase our knowledge of the neurophysiological substrate of the various resources (Lieberman, 2007). In this chapter,

Social Behavior as Resource Exchange. Kjell Yngve Törnblom and Ali Kazemi, Oxford University Press.
© Oxford University Press 2023. DOI: 10.1093/oso/9780190066994.003.0013

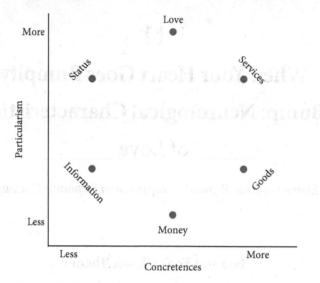

Figure 11.1 Foa and Foa's schematic representation of the circular structure of the six social resources.
Reproduced from Foa and Foa (1974).

we once again emphasize the same resource we discussed previously—passionate love. In other chapters and in other research, neuroscientists have focused on other kinds of love: companionate love (Avecedo et al., 2012), maternal love (Bartels & Zeki, 2004), friendship (Parkinson et al., 2018), and more. For a sampling of neuroscience research concerning other resource classes, see the following: services (Whitten, 2012), goods (Motoki et al., 2019), money (Motoki et al., 2019), information (D'Esposito et al., 1999), and status (Chiao et al., 2008; Ly et al., 2011).

Passionate Love

From a lay point of view, passionate love can be defined in many ways. However, it is typically defined by scientists as a complex emotional state involving cognitive, emotional, and goal-directed behavioral components. Specifically,

> Passionate love is a powerful emotional state. It has been defined as: A state of intense longing for union with another. Passionate love is a complex functional whole including appraisals or appreciations, subjective feelings,

expressions, patterned physiological processes, action tendencies, and instrumental behaviors. Reciprocated love (union with the other) is associated with fulfillment and ecstasy. Unrequited love (separation) is associated with feelings of emptiness, anxiety, and despair. (Hatfield et al., 2020, p. 2)

The Passionate Love Scale (PLS) is designed to tap the cognitive, emotional, and behavioral indicants of such longings (Hatfield & Sprecher, 1986). The scale states,

> Please think of the person whom you love most passionately *right now*. If you are not in love, please think of the last person you loved. If you have never been in love, think of the person you came closest to caring for in that way.

Then follow 15 statements designed to assess the types of appraisals, feelings, and expressions that constitute passionate love. Typical statements include the following: "Sometimes I feel I can't control my thoughts; they are obsessively on _____," "I would feel deep despair if _____ left me," and "I sense my body responding when _____ touches me."

Other popular definitions and measures of passionate love include Robert Sternberg's triangular theory of love (Sternberg & Barnes, 1988), Clyde and Susan Hendrick's (1987) love styles, and Phillip Shaver and Cindy Hazan's (1987) attachment styles.

Neuropsychological Explorations of Passionate Love

In recent years, neuroscientists have made great strides in understanding the nature of passionate love (Cacioppo & Cacioppo, 2015; Hatfield & Rapson, 2009; Lieberman, 2007; Matusall et al., 2011).

Andreas Bartels and Semir Zeki
In 2000, two London neuroscientists, Andreas Bartels and Semir Zeki, attempted to identify the brain regions associated with passionate love and sexual desire. They tacked up posters around London, seeking men and women who were "truly, deeply, and madly in love." They also recruited participants via the internet. Seventy young men and women from 11 countries and several ethnic groups responded. Respondents were asked to write about their feelings of love and to complete the PLS. Seventeen men and women, ranging in age

from 21 to 37 years, were selected for the study. They were then placed in a functional magnetic resonance imaging (fMRI) scanner, which constructs an image of the brain, in which changes in blood flow (induced by brain activity) are represented as color-coded pixels. Bartels and Zeki (2000) gave each participant a color photograph of their beloved to gaze at. They then alternated the picture of the beloved with pictures of a trio of casual friends. Finally, they digitally compared the scans taken while the participants viewed their beloved's picture with those taken while they viewed a friend's picture, creating images that represented the brain regions that became more (or less) active in both conditions. These images, the researchers contended, showed the brain regions involved when a person experiences passionate love (Figure 11.2).

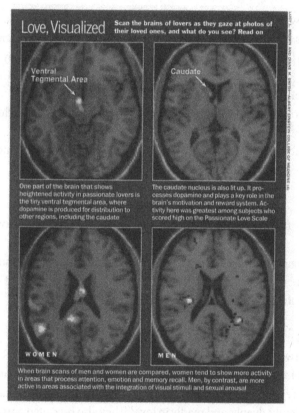

Figure 11.2 Functional magnetic resonance imaging of "the brain in love." Permission Granted. Cambridge University Press. Reprinted in Hatfield, E., Rapson, R. L. & Purvis, J. (2020). *What's next in love and sex: psychological and cultural perspectives* (p. 92). Oxford University Press.

Bartels and Zeki (2000) discovered that passion sparked increased activity in the brain areas associated with euphoria and reward, and decreased activity in the areas associated with sadness, anxiety, and fear. Activity seemed to be restricted to foci in the medial insula and the anterior cingulated cortex and, subcortically, in the caudate nucleus and the putamen, all bilaterally. Most of the regions that were activated during the experience of romantic love were those that are active when people are under the influence of euphoria-inducing drugs such as opiates or cocaine. Apparently, both passionate love and those drugs activate a "blissed-out" circuit in the brain. The anterior cingulated cortex has also been shown to be active when people view sexually arousing material. This makes sense because passionate love and sexual desire are generally assumed to be tightly linked constructs.

Among the regions where activity *decreased* during the experience of love were those previously implicated in the areas of the brain that control critical thought (the sort of mental activity involved when people are asked to make social judgments or to "mentalize"—that is, to assess other people's intentions and emotions). Such brain areas are also activated when people experience painful emotions such as sadness, anger, and fear. Bartels and Zeki argued that once we fall in love with someone, we feel less need to assess critically their character and personality. (In that sense, love may indeed be "blind.") Deactivations were also observed in the posterior cingulated gyrus and in the amygdala and were right-lateralized in the prefrontal, parietal, and middle temporal cortices. The authors also found passionate love and sexual arousal to be tightly linked. Not surprisingly, the research by Bartels and Zeki (2000, 2004) sparked a cascade of fMRI research.

Helen Fisher, Arthur Aron, and Lucy Brown

In *Why We Love*, Helen Fisher (2004a) wrote that individuals possess a trio of primary brain systems designed to deal with close, intimate relationships. These are attraction (passionate love), lust (sexual desire), and attachment (companionate love). Presumably, this trio of systems developed during humankind's long evolutionary history. Each, she said, is designed to play a critical role in courtship, mating, and parenting, respectively. In theory, *attraction* evolved to persuade our ancestors to focus attention on a single favored courtship partner. *Sexual desire* evolved to motivate young people to seek a wide range of sexual partners. *Attachment* evolved to ensure that

362   PART II NEW THEORETICAL AND EMPIRICAL DEVELOPMENTS

devoted parents would remain together during the crucial first 4 years of a child's life.

Fisher (2004a) went on to contend that attraction (passionate love) is characterized by a yearning to win a preferred mating partner. She speculated that three chemicals—dopamine, norepinephrine, and serotonin—play crucial roles in romantic passion. Sexual desire (lust), on the other hand, is characterized by a general craving for sexual gratification and can be directed toward many potential partners. In men and women, she observed, the androgens, particularly testosterone, are central to sparking sexual desire. Attachment (companionate love) is composed of feelings of calm, social comfort, emotional union, and the security felt in the presence of a long-term mate. It sparks affiliative behaviors, the maintenance of close proximity, separation anxiety when that closeness erodes, and a willingness to participate in shared parental chores. Animal studies suggest that this brain system is primarily associated with oxytocin and vasopressin in the nucleus accumbens and ventral pallidum.

The Joys of Love
In focusing on passionate love, Fisher (2004b) observed,

> I speculated that the feelings of euphoria, sleeplessness and loss of appetite as well as the lover's intense energy, focused attention and increased passion in the face of adversity might all be caused in part by heightened levels of dopamine or norepinephrine in the brain. Similarly, I believed that the lover's obsessive thinking about the beloved might be due to decreased brain activity of some type of serotonin. I also knew these three compounds were much more prevalent in some brain regions than in others. If I could establish which regions of the brain become active while one is feeling romantic rapture, that might confirm which primary chemicals are involved. (p. 77)

To test these notions, Fisher and colleagues Arthur Aron and Lucy Brown (along with graduate students Deborah Mashek and Greg Strong) conducted a series of fMRI studies. "Have you just fallen madly in love?" asked the announcement posted on a bulletin board on the State University of New York (SUNY) Stony Brook campus. Fisher received a flood of replies. On the basis of interviews, she selected 17 young lovers. All of these men and women had high scores on the PLS.

WHEN YOUR HEART GOES BUMPITY BUMP   363

Fisher followed the prototype described by Bartels and Zeki (2000). She asked lovesick men and women to view pictures of their beloved and "a boring acquaintance" while an fMRI imager recorded the activity (blood flow) in their brains.

Fisher (2004b) found that when lovesick men and women gazed at their beloved, activity was sparked in many brain areas. (This should come as no surprise because as Acevedo et al. [2012] and Carlson and Hatfield [1992], noted, passionate love is associated with a wider array of related feelings and emotions [guilt, sadness, anger, jealousy, sexual desire, etc.] than any other basic emotion.) Two areas were found to be critically important: the caudate nucleus (a large, C-shaped region deep in the center of the brain) and the ventral tegmental area (VTA), a group of neurons at the very center of the brain. "I was astonished," Fisher (2004b) said. The caudate is "a key part of the brain's 'reward system,' the mind's network for general arousal, sensations of pleasure and the motivation to acquire rewards" (p. 79). The VTA is a central part of the reward circuitry of the brain.

Fisher (2004b) observed,

> I had hypothesized that romantic love is associated with elevated levels of dopamine or norepinephrine. The VTA is a mother lode for dopamine-making cells. With their tentacle-like axons, these nerve cells distribute dopamine to many brain regions, including the caudate nucleus. And as this sprinkler system sends dopamine to various parts of the brain, it produces focused attention as well as fierce energy, concentrated motivation to attain a reward, and feelings of elation—even mania—the core feelings of romantic love.
>
> No wonder lovers talk all night or walk till dawn, write extravagant poetry and self-revealing e-mails, cross continents or oceans to hug for just a weekend, change jobs or lifestyles, even die for one another. Drenched in chemicals that bestow focus, stamina and vigor, and driven by the motivating engine of the brain, lovers succumb to a Herculean courting urge. (p. 79)

Lucy Brown added, "That's the area that's also active when a cocaine addict gets an IV injection of cocaine. It's not a craving. It's a high" (quoted in Blink, 2007, p. 3).

Blink (2007) observes,

> You see someone, you click, and you're euphoric. And in response, your ventral tegmental area uses chemical messengers such as dopamine, serotonin,

364 PART II NEW THEORETICAL AND EMPIRICAL DEVELOPMENTS

and oxytocin to send signals racing to a part of the brain called the nucleus accumbens with the good news, telling it to start craving. [Certain regions] are deactivated—areas as within the amygdala, associated with fear. (p. 3)

Fisher (2004a) concluded by observing that the chemistry of romantic attraction may also elevate sexual motivation—even though the two derive from different brain systems. She notes that all the brain areas are connected with one another. (For more detailed descriptions of this research, see Aron et al. [2005] and Fisher et al. [2005].)

Alas, other neuroscientists (such as Bartels and Zeki [2000], who studied the fMRI responses of joyous lovers) have secured slightly different results than those described by Fisher and colleagues (2002). Bartels and Zeki, for example, considered passion to be an emotion and found a close connection between passionate love and sexual desire.

Fisher speculates that such differences may be due to the fact that whereas she and her colleagues studied young people who are in the first throes of love, her critics focused on men and women who fell in love some time ago. (Fisher's participants had been in love for an average of 7 months; Bartels and Zeki's participants had been in love for 2.3 years.) In addition, Fisher studied a homogeneous group of SUNY students, whereas Bartels and Zeki studied people from different cultural backgrounds and of a variety of ages. Whether or not these facts adequately account for these differing results is yet unknown.

The Dark Side of Love: Anger, Sadness, and Misery

Joyous passionate love is only one-half of the equation, of course. Love is often unrequited. What kind of brain activity occurs when passionate lovers are rejected?

In a second study, Fisher and colleagues (2005) studied 15 men and women who had just been jilted by their beloved. Fisher et al. hung a flyer on the SUNY Stony Brook bulletin board that read, "Have you just been rejected in love. But can't let go?" Rejected sweethearts were quick to respond. In initial interviews, Fisher found that heartbroken men and women were caught up in a swirl of conflicting emotions. They were still wildly in love, yet feeling abandoned, depressed, angry, and in despair.

But what was going on in their brains? To find out, Fisher and colleagues (2005) followed the same protocol they had utilized in testing happily-in-love men and women—that is, they asked participants alternately to view a photograph of their one-time beloved and a photograph of a familiar but emotionally neutral individual. The authors found that when rejected lovers contemplated their beloved, they displayed greater activity in the right nucleus accumbens/ventral putamen/pallidum, lateral orbitofrontal cortex, and anterior insular/operculum cortex than they did when contemplating neutral images.

In short, the brains of jilted lovers "lit up" in the areas associated with anxiety, pain, and attempts at controlling anger. Also, areas correlated with addiction, risk-taking, and obsessive–compulsive behaviors were activated. Jilted lovers did, indeed, appear to experience a storm of passion—passionate love and sexual desire, in addition to anguish, rejection, rage, emptiness, and despair.

Other neuroscientists who have studied the fMRI responses of lovers actively grieving over a recent romantic breakup have secured slightly different results than those obtained by Fisher and colleagues (see Najib et al., 2004). Fisher (2004a) speculates that her critics may have focused on men and women who broke up some time ago and have presumably adapted to their losses. Instead of being at the grief stage, they may have been at a subsequent stage in the grieving process—experiencing resignation and despair. This assumes, of course, that the "stages of grief" model is valid—an assumption not universally accepted.

Meta-Analyses

Neuroscientists have contributed greatly to a better understanding of the complexity of love by demonstrating that (a) each subtype of love has specific neural correlates that extend beyond those typically recruited by rewarded resources such as money, goods, and services (Ortigue et al., 2010) and (b) passionate love has different neural correlates than lust (Cacioppo et al., 2012a, 2012b; Cacioppo & Cacioppo, 2013). Because the low statistical power characteristic of contemporary neuroimaging studies not only reduces the chance of detecting true effect but also reduces the likelihood that a statistically significant result reflects a true effect (Cacioppo et al., 2012), Cacioppo and colleagues performed quantitative meta-analyses (Cacioppo et al., 2012; see also Ortigue et al., 2010) to obtain a better indication of the brain regions activated by love than those provided in any single empirical investigation.

Overall, Cacioppo's fMRI meta-analyses revealed that passionate love sparks increased activity in the subcortical brain areas sustaining basic emotions, euphoria, reward, and motivation, and in cortical brain areas involved in more complex emotional and cognitive processing (e.g., embodied cognition, body image, and attention). By demonstrating such a specific subcortico-cortical network, these results provide further evidence that love is a complex emotion rather than a basic emotion only.

Interestingly, when comparing passionate love with lust, Cacioppo et al.'s (2012a, 2012b) results revealed not only an overlapping brain network within subcortical emotion-related areas and the higher order cortical areas but also neural differences in the two. For instance, the anterior insula was significantly more activated by feelings of passionate love (than lust), whereas the posterior insula was significantly more activated by feelings of lust (than passionate love). This result was reinforced by a case study of a patient with a lesion in the anterior insula who showed a selective decision-making deficit for love but not for lust (Cacioppo et al., 2012). This is in line with the view that love might be perceived as a holistic construct with integrated bodily experiences. This specific pattern of activation suggests that love builds upon a neural circuit for emotions and pleasure, adding regions associated with reward expectancy and habit formation.

Love, termed pair bonding in nonhuman mammalian species, has an evolutionary base, a distinctive neurobiological substrate, and in humans manifests as a combination of physical bodily and mental sensations that occur in response to certain stimuli or events. However, whether or not it can be concluded from this research that love is a basic emotion depends on one's definition of a basic emotion. See Hatfield and Rapson (1993) for a discussion of this distinction.

Social Exchange in Love Relationships

In all societies, people are concerned with social justice. "What's fair is fair!" "She deserves better." "It's just not right." "He can't get away with *that*!" "It's illegal." "It's unethical!" "It's immoral." These are all fairly common laments. In the 11th century, St. Anselm of Canterbury argued that the will possesses two competing affinities: (a) an affection for that which is to a person's own selfish advantage and (b) an affection for justice. The first inclination is surely stronger, but the second also matters. Equity theory, too, posits that in personal, social, and societal relationships, two concerns stand out: How much reward does a person reap from a given social relationship? and How fair, rewarding, and equitable is that relationship? Equity theory contends that the same rules apply in exchanges of *all* of the Foa (1971) resources.

Equity Theory

Equity theory is a straightforward theory. It consists of four propositions:

Proposition I: Men and women are "hardwired" to try to maximize pleasure and minimize pain.

Proposition II: Society has a vested interest in persuading people to behave fairly and equitably. Groups will generally reward members who treat others equitably and punish those who treat others inequitably.

Proposition III: Given societal pressures, people are most comfortable when they perceive that they are getting roughly what they deserve from life in terms of love, status, money, and other resources. If people feel overbenefited, they may experience guilt and shame; if the feel underbenefited, they may experience anger, sadness, and resentment.

Proposition IV: People in inequitable relationships will attempt to reduce their distress through a variety of techniques—by restoring psychological equity, actual equity, or leaving the relationship.

Assessing Equity

Technically, equity is defined by a complex formula (Traupmann et al., 1981; Walster, 1975). In practice, however, a relationship's fairness, benefits, and equity can be reliably and validly assessed with the use of a simple measure. Specifically, research participants are asked, "Considering what you put into your dating relationship or marriage, compared to what you get out of it . . . and what your partner puts in compared to what (s)he gets out of it, how does your dating relationship or marriage 'stack up'?" Respondents are given the following response options:

+3: I am getting a much better deal than my partner.
+2: I am getting a somewhat better deal.

368 PART II NEW THEORETICAL AND EMPIRICAL DEVELOPMENTS

+1: I am getting a slightly better deal.
 0: We are both getting an equally good, or bad, deal.
-1: My partner is getting a slightly better deal.
-2: My partner is getting a somewhat better deal.
-3: My partner is getting a much better deal than I am.

On the basis of their answers, persons can be classified as overbenefited (receiving more than they deserve), equitably treated, or underbenefited (receiving less than they deserve). (For a comprehensive list of the rewards and costs found to be important in dating relationships or marriages, see Young and Hatfield, 2009.)

We argue that notions of social justice came to be writ in the mind's "architecture" because a concern with social justice possessed survival value (see Tooby & Cosmides, 1996). A concern with social justice, in all its forms, is extant today (in all cultures and all social structures) because fairness in love, work, or other domains of one's social life often remains a wise and profitable strategy. (For a further discussion of these points, see Hatfield et al., 1978; Jost & Major, 2001).

Although equity has been found to be important in a wide variety of relationships—social, romantic, and familial relationships, as well as helping, exploitative, and work relationships—here, we again focus on romantic and marital relationships (for a summary of this voluminous research, see Hatfield et al., 2008,).

Equity in Love Relationships: Classic Research

There is considerable evidence that in love relationships, equity matters (Figure 11.3).

Currently, some of the most interesting research on the nature of social justice emanates from scholars from three different intellectual traditions: (a) primatologists and evolutionary psychologists, who argue that a concern for justice arose early in humankind's evolutionary history and who speculate about how this ancient "wiring" affects visions of social justice of contemporary men and women; (b) cultural researchers interested in changing societal definitions as to what is fair and equitable; and (c) social psychologists, who have explored people's definitions of fairness and justice and have studied the impact of perceived fairness and equity on couple's thoughts, feelings, and

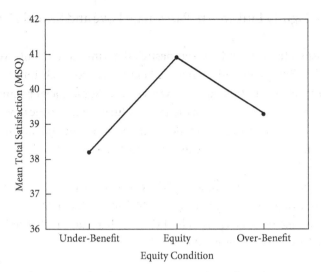

Figure 11.3 The relationship between equity and satisfaction.

behaviors. In addition to the above four propositions, researchers specifically find the following:

1. Couples will attempt to restore psychological equity to reduce distress in the relationship.
2. The more socially desirable people are (the more attractive, personable, famous, intelligent, rich, or considerate they are), the more socially desirable they will expect a mate to be.
3. Dating couples will be more likely to fall in love if they perceive their relationships to be equitable.
4. Couples are likely to end up with someone fairly close to themselves in social desirability. They are also likely to be matched on the basis of self-esteem, looks, intelligence, education, and mental and physical health (or disability).
5. Couples who perceive their relationships to be equitable are more likely to become sexually involved.
6. Equitable relationships are satisfying and comfortable; inequity is associated with distress, guilt, anger, and anxiety.
7. Those in equitable relationships are less likely to risk extramarital affairs than are their peers.
8. Equitable relationships possess more stability than do inequitable relationships.

370 PART II NEW THEORETICAL AND EMPIRICAL DEVELOPMENTS

How Tightly Linked Are Passionate Love and Sexual Desire?

Are "passionate love" and "sexual desire" the same thing? Fifty years ago, when Ellen Berscheid and Elaine Hatfield began research into the nature of love, the answer to this question was certain. Some social commentators insisted that the two were one. In the 18th century French erotic novel *Histoire de Dom Bougre*, for example, a cynical nun disclosed the true meaning of the expression, "to be in love." It meant, she said, to be "in lust":

> When one says, the Gentleman . . . is in love with the Lady . . . it is the same thing as saying, the Gentleman . . . saw the Lady . . . the sight of her excited his desire, and he is dying to put his Prick into her Cunt. That's truly what it means. (as quoted in Ellrich, 1985, p. 222)

Others insisted that the two were very different. In the 18th century, the Marquis de Sade (1797/1968) violently opposed the equation of love and pleasure:

> I do not want a woman to imagine that I owe her anything because I soil myself on top of her. . . . I have never believed that from the junction of two bodies could arise the junction of two hearts: I can see great reasons for scorn and disgust in this physical junction, but not a single reason for love. (p. 148)

In the Victorian era, romantic love was considered to be a delicate, spiritual feeling—the antithesis of crude, animal lust. Freudians, of course, mocked such claims. They irritated romantics by insisting that chaste love was simply a sublimated form of carnal love, which lay bubbling just below the surface.

What about today? In the West, most individuals make a sharp distinction between "being in love" (which embodies feelings of love and sexual feelings) and "loving" someone (which is not necessarily associated with sexual desire). In a study of college students, Meyers and Berscheid (1997) found that while most assumed that you could "love" someone platonically, you could only be "in love" with someone you were sexually attracted to and desired sexually. They concluded, "Thus, our findings suggest that although sexuality may not be a central feature of love, it is most definitely a central feature of the state of being in love" (p. 24). In a national survey, Andrew Greeley (1991) interviewed newly married couples who said they were still in the "falling in love" stage of marriage. He found that passionate love is a highly sexual state. He described the falling in love stage of marriage as follows:

> When one is in love, one is absorbed, preoccupied, tense and intense, and filled with a sexual longing which permeates the rest of existence, making it both glorious and exhausting.... Those who are falling in love seem truly to be by love possessed. (pp. 122–124)

In the end, both Ellen Berscheid and Elaine Hatfield concluded that passionate love and sexual desire were "kissing cousins." Passionate love was defined as "a longing for union," whereas sexual desire was defined as "a longing for *sexual* union" (Hatfield & Rapson, 1996/2005). Of course, this linkage gained strength only after contraceptive technology, particularly the pill, became commonly available to women. Before then, and for most historical time, sexuality was connected at least as much to pregnancy as it was to love. Thus the importance of cultural forces in most matters related to love.

Today, this debate seems settled. As Susan and Clyde Hendrick (1987) note,

> It is apparent to us that trying to separate love from sexuality is like trying to separate fraternal twins: They are certainly not identical, but, nevertheless, they are strongly bonded.... Love and sexuality are strongly linked to each other and to both the physical and spiritual aspects of the human condition. For romantic personal relationships, sexual love and loving sexuality may well represent intimacy at its best. (pp. 282 and 293)

There is abundant social psychological evidence in support of the contention that in most people's minds, love and sex today are tightly related—in fact, most people find it difficult to imagine passionate love absent sexual desire (Hatfield & Rapson, 2005; Regan, 2004; Regan & Berscheid, 1999; Regan & Dreyer, 1999; Ridge & Berscheid, 1989). (Naturally, men and women can easily imagine the converse—sexual desire without passionate love.) As Pamela Regan (2004) observes,

> Theoretical discourse from a number of disciplines suggests that sexual desire is a distinguishing feature of the passionate love experience.... Empirical research substantiates this hypothesis. People believe that sexual desire is part and parcel of the state of being in love, assume that couples who desire

372 PART II NEW THEORETICAL AND EMPIRICAL DEVELOPMENTS

each other sexually are also passionately in love, and report a similar association when reflecting on their own dating relationships. (p. 115)

Of course, again, culture surely has a powerful impact on how likely young
couples are to link passionate love, sexual desire, and sexual *expression*
(Hatfield & Rapson, 2005). Many men, for example, are taught to separate
sex and love, whereas many women are taught to connect the two. The different meanings attributed to sexual activity have been known to cause lovers
much distress (Hatfield & Rapson, 2006).

Neuroscientists and evolutionary psychologists, however, are still in
sharp disagreement as to whether love and lust are very different systems
(Diamond, 2003, 2004; Gonzaga et al., 2006) or are tightly linked (Bartels &
Zeki, 2000). Neuroscientists do agree, however, that all of the brain systems
for passionate love, sexual desire, and attachment do in fact communicate
and coordinate with one another.

When the dust settles, we suspect neuropsychologists will come to ac-
knowledge that although love and lust may possess a few distinct features,
they are tightly linked, especially now that sexual activity can be disengaged
from procreation. It is difficult to imagine that two phenomena so linked in
the public mind could be such disparate entities. Thus, the contention that
love and sexual desire are "kissing cousins" seems to be an appropriate one.

In summary, although we are learning a great deal about the brain and
love, it would not be correct to assume that the "lit" parts of the brain *cause*
the emotions of passion and love. Just as sex and passionate love have become
"kissing cousins" due to advances in reproductive technology, so are the cultural, cognitive, neurophysiological, and behavioral aspects of love. Great
discussions lie ahead about their interactions

References

Acevedo, B. P., Aron, A., Fisher, H. E., & Brown, L. (2012). Neural correlates of long-term
intense romantic love. *Social Cognition Affect Neuroscience, 7*, 145–159.
Aron, A., Fisher, H. E., Mashek, D. J., Strong, G., Li, H., & Brown, L. L. (2005). Reward,
motivation, and emotion systems associated with early-stage intense romantic love.
Journal Neurophysiology, 94, 327–337.
Bartels, A., & Zeki, S. (2000, November 27). The neural basis of romantic love. *Neuroreport,
11*, 3829–3834.
Bartels, A., & Zeki, S. (2004). The neural correlates of maternal and romantic love.
Neuroimage, 21, 1155–1166.

Blink, S. (2007, July 30). This is your brain on love. *Los Angeles Times*. http://www.latimes. com/features/health/la-he-attraction30jul30.1.68965446.story?coll=la-headlines-hea lth&ctrack=1&cset

Cacioppo, S., Bianchi-Demicheli, F., Frum, C., Pfaus, J., & Lewis, J. W. (2012a). The common neural bases between sexual desire and love: A multilevel kernel density fMRI analysis. *Journal of Sexual Medicine, 9*, 1048–1054.

Cacioppo, S., Bianchi-Demicheli, F., Hatfield, E., & Rapson, R. L. (2012b). Social neuro-science of love. *Clinical Neuropsychiatry, 9*, 3–13.

Cacioppo, S., & Cacioppo, J. T. (2013). Lust for life. *Scientific American Mind, 24*, 56–63.

Cacioppo, S., & Cacioppo, J. T. (2015). Comment: Demystifying the neuroscience of love. *Emotion Review, 8*, 108–114. doi:10.1177/1754073915594432

Carlson, J. G., & Hatfield, E. (1992). *Psychology of emotion*. Harcourt, Brace, Jovanovich.

Chiao, J. Y., Adams, R. B., Jr., Tse, P. U., Lowenthal, L., Richardson, J. A., & Ambady, N. (2008). Knowing who's boss: fMRI and ERP investigations of social dominance percep-tion. *Group Process Intergroup Relations, 11*, 201–214.

D'Esposito, M. D., Postle, B. R., Ballard, D., & Lease, J. (1999). Maintenance versus manip-ulation of information held in working memory: An event-related fMRI study. *Brain and Cognition, 41*, 66–86.

Diamond, L. M. (2003). What does sexual orientation orient? A biobehavioral model dis-tinguishing romantic love and sexual desire. *Psychological Review, 110*, 173–192.

Diamond, L. M. (2004). Emerging perspectives on distinctions between romantic love and sexual desire. *Current Directions in Psychological Science, 13*, 116–119.

Ellrich, R. J. (1985, May). Modes of discourse and the language of sexual reference in eighteenth-century French fiction. Eighteenth-Century Life [special issue]. Tri-Annually By the College of William & Mary..

Fisher, H. (2004a). Why we love: The nature and chemistry of romantic love. Holt.

Fisher, H. (2004b, January 19). Your brain in love. *TIME*.

Fisher, H., Aron, A., & Brown, L. L. (2005). Romantic love: An fMRI study of a neural mechanism for mate choice. *Journal of Comparative Neurology, 493*, 58–62.

Fisher, H. E., Aron, A., Mashek, D., Li, H., & Brown, L. L. (2002). Defining the brain systems of lust, romantic attraction, and attachment *Archives of Sexual Behavior, 31*, 413–419.

Foa, U. G. (1971). Interpersonal and economic resources. *Science, 171*, 345–351.

Foa, U. G., & Foa, E. B. (1974). *Societal structures of the mind*. Charles C Thomas.

Foa, E. B. & Foa, U. G. (1976). Resource theory of social exchange. In J. W. Thibaut, J. T. Spence & R. C. Carson (Eds.), Contemporary topics in social psychology (pp. 99–131). General Learning Press.

Gonzaga, G. C., Turner, R. A., Keltner, D., Campos, B., & Altemus, M. (2006). Romantic love and sexual desire in close relationships. *Emotion, 6*, 163–179.

Greeley, A. (1991). *Faithful attraction: Discovering intimacy, love, and fidelity in American marriage*. St. Martin's Press.

Hatfield, E., & Rapson, R. L. (1993). Historical and cross-cultural perspectives on pas-sionate love and sexual desire. *Annual Review of Sex Research, 4*, 67–98.

Hatfield, E., & Rapson, R. (2005). *Love and sex: Cross-cultural perspectives*. Allyn & Bacon. (Original work published 1996)

Hatfield, E., & Rapson, R. L. (2006). Love and passion. In I. Goldstein, C. M. Meston, S. R. Davis, & A. M. Traish (Eds.), *Women's sexual function and dysfunction: Study, diagnosis and treatment* (pp. 93–97). Taylor & Francis.

374 PART II NEW THEORETICAL AND EMPIRICAL DEVELOPMENTS

Hatfield, E., & Rapson, R. L. (2009). The neuropsychology of passionate love and sexual desire. In E. Cuyler & M. Ackhart (Eds.), *Psychology of social relationships* (pp. 519–543). Nova Science.

Hatfield, E., Rapson, R. L., & Aumer-Ryan, K. (2008). Social justice in love relationships: Recent developments. *Social Justice Research, 21*, 413–431.

Hatfield, E., Rapson, R. L., & Purvis, J. (2020). *What's next in love and sex: Psychological and cultural perspectives.* Oxford University Press.

Hatfield, E., & Sprecher, S. (1986). Measuring passionate love in intimate relations. *Journal of Adolescence, 9*, 383–410.

Hatfield, E., Walster, G. W., & Berscheid, E. (1978). *Equity: Theory and research.* Allyn & Bacon.

Hazan, C., & Shaver, P. (1987). Romantic love conceptualized as an attachment process. *Journal of Personality and Social Psychology, 52*, 511–524.

Hendrick, S. S., & Hendrick, C. (1987). Love and sex attitudes: A close relationship. Advances in *Personal Relationships, 1*, 141–169.

Jost, J. T., & Major, B. (2001). *The psychology of legitimacy: Emerging perspectives on ideology, justice, and intergroup relations.* Cambridge University Press.

Lieberman, M. D. (2007). Social cognitive neuroscience: A review of core processes. *Annual. Review of Psychology, 58*, 259–289.

Ly, M., Ryan-Haynes, M., Barter, J. W., Weinberger, D. R., & Zink, C. F. (2011). Subjective socioeconomic status predicts human ventral striatal responses to social status information. *Current Biology, 21*, 794–797.

Marquis de Sade. (1968). *Justine* (P. Casavini, Trans.). Oxford University Press. (Original work published 1797)

Matusall, S., Kaufmann, I. M., & Christen, M. (2011). The emergence of social neuroscience as an academic discipline. In J. Deacy & J. Cacioppo (Eds.), *The Oxford handbook of social neuroscience* (pp. 9–27). Oxford University Press.

Meyers, S., & Berscheid, E. (1997). The language of love: The difference a preposition makes. *Personality and Social Psychology Bulletin, 23*, 347–362.

Motoki, K., Sugiura, M., & Kawashim, R. (2019). Common neural value representations of hedonic and utilitarian products in the ventral stratum: An fMRI study. *Scientific Repots, 9*, Article 15630. https://doi.org/10.1038/s41598-019-52159-9

Najib, A., Lorberbaum, J. P., Kose, S., Bohning, D. E., & George, M. S. (2004). Regional brain activity in women grieving a romantic relationship breakup. *American Journal of Psychiatry, 161*(12), 2245–2256.

Ortigue, S., Bianchi-Demicheli, F., Patel, N., Frum, C., & Lewis, J. (2010). Neuroimaging of love: fMRI meta-analysis evidence towards new perspectives in sexual medicine. *Journal of Sexual Medicine, 7*, 3541–3552.

Parkinson, C., Kleinbaum, A. M., & Wheatley, T. (2018). Similar neural responses predict friendship. *Nature Communications, 9*, Article 332.

Regan, P. C. (2004). Sex and the attraction process: Lessons from science (and Shakespeare) on lust, love, chastity, and fidelity. In J. H. Harvey, A. Wenzel, & S. Sprecher (Eds.), *The handbook of sexuality in close relationships* (pp. 115–133). Erlbaum.

Regan, P. C., & Berscheid, E. (1999). *Lust: What we know about human sexual desire.* SAGE.

Regan, P. C., & Dreyer, C. S. (1999). Lust? Love? Status? Young adults' motives for engaging in casual sex. *Journal of Psychology & Human Sexuality, 11*(1), 1–24.

Ridge, R. D., & Berscheid, E. (1989, May). On loving and being in love: A necessary distinction [Paper presentation]. Annual convention of the Midwestern Psychological Association, Chicago.

Sternberg, R. J., & Barnes, M. L. (1988). *The psychology of love*. Yale University Press.

Tooby, J., & Cosmides, L. (1996). Friendship and the banker's paradox: Other pathways to the evolution of adaptations for altruism. *Proceedings of the British Academy, 88*, 119–143.

Törnblom, K. Y., & Kazemi, A. (Eds.). (2012). *Handbook of social resource theory: Theoretical extensions, empirical insights, and social applications*. Springer.

Traupmann, J., Peterson, R., Utne, M., & Hatfield, E. (1981). Measuring equity in intimate relations. *Applied Psychological Measurement, 5*, 467–480.

Walster, G. W. (1975). The Walster et al. (1973) equity formula: A correction. *Representative Research in Social Psychology, 6*, 65–67.

Whitten, L. A. (2012). *Functional magnetic resonance imaging (fMRI): An invaluable tool in translational neuroscience*. RTI Press Occasional Papers. RTI Press.

Young, D., & Hatfield, E. (2009). Measuring equity in close sexual relationships. In T. D. Fisher, C. M. Davis, W. L. Yaber, & S. L. Davis (Eds.), *Handbook of sexuality-related measures: A compendium* (3rd ed., pp. 469–472). Taylor & Francis.

12

Evaluating Foa and Foa's Social Resource Theory: A Data-Analytic Perspective

Clara Sabbagh and Manfred Schmitt

Introduction

Uriel G. Foa was closely acquainted with Louis Guttman's idea of facet theory (Guttman, 1982, 1991; Levy, 1994, 2005) and participated in the early stages of its development (Foa, 1961, 1963, 1965). Foa's social resource theory (SRT) borrows notions from facet theory (for earlier ideas and their later elaboration, see Foa, 1961; Sabbagh et al., 1994), although it does not further develop facet theory within its general framework (Borg & Shye, 1995; Levy, 1985, 2005). As described and illustrated below, the method of smallest space analysis, a sort of multidimensional dimensional scaling, was developed in the framework of facet theory.[1]

As discussed in more detail in other chapters of this volume, the point of departure of SRT is that interpersonal relations can be understood in terms of a mutual exchange (giving and receiving) involving a social resource. Nevertheless, scholars have differed as to the nature and dynamics of such a transaction. Foa and Foa's (1974) SRT is premised on the assumption that the rules and behavioral implications of social exchange are not determined solely by economic (self-interested) considerations (as posited by other social sciences paradigms) but also by the *quality* of the resource being exchanged (Donnenwerth & Foa, 1974; Teichman & Foa, 1975). The theory specifies six types of resources that become the object of exchange among individuals: love (e.g., warmth), status (esteem), information (instruction), money (currency), goods (tangible products), and services (labor

---

[1] The data used in this chapter are part of a comprehensive survey conducted in Israel by Nura Resh and Clara Sabbagh, which focused on the role of the sense of injustice in shaping democratic attitudes and civic behaviors among middle school students. The data are available upon request. The Israeli Science Foundation funded the survey (Grant No. 568/09).

Social Behavior as Resource Exchange. Kjell Yngve Törnblom and Ali Kazemi, Oxford University Press.
© Oxford University Press 2023. DOI: 10.1093/oso/9780190066994.003.0014

for another). SRT classifies these resources according to two properties or dimensions: concreteness (less–more) and particularism (less–more). The latter signifies the degree to which the resource value is determined by the provider's and recipient's identity and relationship (Foa & Foa, 2012). For instance, goods and services involve a tangible activity or product, and hence these are concrete resources. Also, love and status are largely particularistic resources because their value is context- and person-bound. This typology generates a circular structure or circumplex (Figure 12.1), which reflects not only the similarities and differences between resources but also the degree of their exchangeability (Foa & Foa, 1974). Resources that are adjacent in the structure are expected to be exchanged more frequently. For instance, love and services are adjacent and therefore easily exchangeable. By contrast, money and love have no shared properties and are therefore not easily exchangeable.

In this chapter, we provide an overview of the traditional research methods (e.g., design and types of data analyses) that have been applied to examine and validate SRT, since it was first developed until the present day. We also provide a comparative perspective of the strengths and shortcomings of two main traditional methods that have been used to examine and validate SRT.

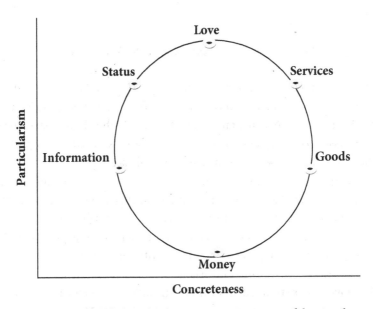

Figure 12.1 Foa and Foa's (1974) schematic representation of the circular structure of social resources.

378 PART II NEW THEORETICAL AND EMPIRICAL DEVELOPMENTS

Specifically, we compare smallest space analysis (SSA), the original multidimensional scaling method from which SRT stemmed, and factor analyses (FAs) used to validate SRT. In this regard, we use an existing database to illustrate the commonalities and unique features of these two traditional methods empirically. Finally, we discuss the potential use of other multivariate (untraditional) methods for exploring new research questions and hypotheses derived from SRT, hence expanding its scope and providing further possible validation to the theory.

First, we review the main traditional methods that have been applied to examine and validate SRT. Then, we provide a conceptual methods framework for comparing SSA and FA, which is illustrated empirically with a database that examines SRT in the context of the classroom. Finally, we discuss the underuse of multivariate methods, which may be applied for examining SRT and hypotheses deriving from it.

Traditional Methods Used in SRT: Selected Studies

Appendix 12.1 summarizes the SRT selected studies reviewed in this section according to the applied traditional method.

Analysis of Variance: Experimental Designs

A large part of related research conducted by Uriel Foa, Edna Foa, and their colleagues (e.g., Donnenwerth & Foa, 1974; Teichman & Foa, 1975; Turner et al., 1971) used experimental designs to validate the circular structure of the six classes of resources. This body of research showed the importance of the resource types when considering a social exchange. That is, it showed that resource types proximal in the circular order (e.g., love and services) appear more related and more likely to be exchanged with each other than with resources from distal classes (e.g., love and money) (Turner et al., 1971). Although the preference for receiving a resource is contingent upon the resource given and perhaps also upon the institutional context, both of these factors seem to leave the order invariant.

Moreover, these studies demonstrated the influence of resource properties on the intensity of retaliation (Donnenwerth & Foa, 1974), satisfaction with a relationship (Teichman & Foa, 1975), and frequency of social interaction

(Turner et al., 1971). That is, the attitudinal and behavioral outcomes resulting from an exchange, such as being either satisfied or hostile and ready to retaliate, were assumed to be more similar for resources that are proximate in the circular ordering than for those that are distant (Donnenwerth & Foa, 1974; Teichman & Foa, 1975). In the case of frequency of social interaction, Turner et al. (1971) predicted that given a resource type, the frequency of the resources desired in exchange would correspond to the circular structure of resources. For instance, when the given resource is love, this resource is also the most chosen in exchange. Moving around the circular ordering of resources, the frequency of choice decreases for status, still further for information, and reaches the lowest point for money. Then it increases again for goods and more so for services (Turner et al., 1971, p. 173).

Correlation Analysis

Foa and colleagues (1987) added to the above studies a further cross-cultural test of the generalizability of resources' circumplex structure. It tested whether the structure replicates across different types of instruments and samples, which differed substantially in terms of country of origin (Israel, Sweden, Mexican American, and Philippines), age, language, religion, and background of subjects (see also Foa, 1961, 1964). Applying simple correlation analyses resulting from subjects' evaluations of the six classes of SRT resources, the authors provided evidence across different sample properties that empirically supported the distinctions among social resources, properties, and exchange rules.

Another study using correlation analysis to validate SRT was performed by Johnson and Long (2019). Specifically, the authors provide further empirical support to Berg and Wiebe's (1993) resource exchange scale, derived from SRT, by examining its reliability and validity among line workers in a manufacturing facility. Berg and Wiebe assumed that even though workers exchange their labor (i.e., services and time) with receiving an income, exchanging other types of resources in the working set is at play. Accordingly, in their survey, Johnson and Long included questions concerning the likelihood of exchanging paired resources and satisfaction with these exchanges. For instance, respondents were asked to evaluate how often they have "given loyalty and devotion to the company [i.e., a status resource] when the company has given them good working conditions [i.e., a service resource]."

380 PART II NEW THEORETICAL AND EMPIRICAL DEVELOPMENTS

Another question asked, "In all aspects of the workplace have you given a good day's work [i.e., a service resource] when the company has told you more about what is going on [i.e., an information resource]?" Findings revealed that the correlations among the above paired resource questions fit the resource's predicted location on the SRT circular structure. These findings were further validated when the likelihood of exchange scores was examined separately or in combination with their satisfaction scores.

Multidimensional Scaling and Smallest Space Analysis

Multidimensional scaling and smallest space analysis (also lately labeled as similarity structure analysis) are often used in the social sciences to graphically represent a configuration of multivariate correlations, such as the SRT circular ordering of resources. Smallest space analysis is a multidimensional method that targets nonmetric content regions in the space of variables rather than metric solutions specifying coordinate systems (Borg & Lingoes, 1987; Guttman, 1968; Lingoes, 1968). It is a data analysis technique for examining a similarity coefficient matrix (e.g., Pearson correlations). Specifically, each variable is represented as a point in a multidimensional space. The intercorrelations are mapped into distances in Euclidean space: The higher the correlation between two items, the closer the points representing those items. The smallest possible number of dimensions is chosen to simplify interpretation. Optimally, each two-dimensional smallest space analysis projection is represented by the predicted structure of a content facet, such as the circumplex structure of social resources (Borg & Shye, 1995; Levy, 1985).

To the best of our knowledge, Bringberg and Castell's (1982) study was pioneering in its attempt to validate SRT applying the multidimensional scaling method. They provided additional evidence for validating both the circumplex structure of resources and the "functional" relations among them; that is, "resources perceived as similar are more likely to be exchanged than dissimilar resources" (p. 262) in the context of interpersonal interactions. Specifically, subjects were first given a particular resource, represented by two stimuli (a total of $6 \times 2 = 12$) reporting interaction behaviors. Respondents were asked to rate the similarity/dissimilarity among all possible combinations of stimuli pairs—for example, giving a hug versus fixing a car or earning money for versus telling about a book. Then, respondents chose a pair of stimuli and rated to what extent their relations were "functional"—that is, they are likely to be exchanged (giving a hug exchanged with talking about a book). Based on SRT, the authors predicted that "the greater the perceived similarity in the resource categories, the more likely a person would be to exchange a resource in those categories" (p. 263). Applying multidimensional scaling to the different ratings supported SRT, although regarding the particularism dimension, the stimuli concerning love and money were perceived as proximal in the circular structure rather than opposite, as predicted in SRT. Rather than interpreting this deviation from the SRT to the resource classification of the behavior, the authors suggested that it can be explained by the possible inconsistent "meanings" assigned to the resource stimuli. Specifically, the study participants, for instance, are likely to spend money on a present or a café for receiving a hug. Thus, they concluded that it is important to consider the meanings attributed to the resources and the resource classification.

Based on Parsons' (1967) social systems theory relating to means of exchange, Sabbagh and colleagues (Sabbagh, 2005; Sabbagh et al., 1994) suggested that resource exchange can be further regulated by a cybernetic hierarchy of control that orders resources according to their capacity for convertibility. In other words, they proposed an alternative dimension for understanding the structural exchange relations among resources. Specifically, the authors claimed that the resources could be ordered from the easily converted resources, such as money, to the least convertible resources, such as love. Hence, as Sabbagh and colleagues noted, one could expect a concentric radex structure whereby the less convertible and central resources (affective resources) are located in the concentric circle's inner bands. In contrast, the more convertible resources (instrumental resources) are located in the more peripheral bands. Thus, SRT is expanded from a circle (circumplex) to a two-dimensional concentric (radex) structure (Guttman, 1954).

To validate the predicted concentric (radex) alternative ordering of resources, Sabbagh et al. (1994) surveyed a national sample of 9,140 Israeli middle school students' distribution preferences when distributing social resources in the broader society—that is, subjects' evaluations of the importance that should be assigned to six distribution rules (arithmetic equality and equality of opportunities, need, effort, performance, and talent) when distributing four types of resources—prestige, power, learning opportunities, and money—that are distributed in the broader society. Based on the items' correlations matrix representing the distribution items, the authors applied smallest space analysis. Findings revealed that a two-dimensional projection

382 PART II NEW THEORETICAL AND EMPIRICAL DEVELOPMENTS

of the smallest space analysis solution could be partitioned into four concentric resource regions representing the predicted structure of resources, organized by the convertibility dimension. A later study by Sabbagh (2005) replicated these findings in a national sample including 3,331 high school students in the state of Lower Saxony in 1992, after Germany's reunification.

Factor Analysis

In addition to multidimensional scaling, factor analysis (FA) is another major method employed in the social sciences for structural analyses of variables (e.g., Cooper-Thomas et al., 2018; Haslam, 1995; Lemmon et al., 2016; Seers et al., 2006). Like multidimensional scaling, FA aims at reducing the multidimensional space of several variables (items, parcels of items, and scales) to a smaller and more parsimonious factor space. Exploratory FA (EFA) is used when no a priori assumptions on the size of the factor space and the relations between the factors and the variables exist. Confirmatory FA (CFA) is appropriate whenever theoretical assumptions about the number of factors and their relations with the variables exist. Every factor model can be formalized mathematically as a set of structural equations with variables as dependent and factors as independent variables. Variables are defined as weighted linear combinations of factors in these equations (see for example Equation 12.1). Applied to SRT, the six resources are the variables of the model, and the two dimensions of concreteness and particularism are the factors of the model. Each resource is a linear combination of these two factors. In other words, each resource is loaded by the two factors. The weights of the factors are called factor loadings.

Foa and Foa's (1974) SRT, and the circumplex structure derived from it, was evaluated in a couple of studies that used FA. For instance, Haslam (1995, p. 218) examined the extent to which SRT can be integrated into the typology of social relationships proposed by Fiske (1991). Fiske identified the distribution rules underlying social exchange, which are embedded in four basic forms of sociality. These forms included communal sharing (equivalent treatment of all members belonging to a category); authority ranking (people are positioned along with a hierarchical category), equality matching (keeping track of imbalances among individuals), and market pricing (orientation to ratio values). Applying FA, Haslam examined whether these two understandings of social exchange elicit shared empirical factor configurations. He included several items for measuring both SRT resources and the above types of relationships in this regard. The FA concerning these items elicited a two-factor solution that was interpreted in terms of social relations. One factor labeled "communality" included the love and services items, whereas the second factor, labeled "equality–inequality," included the money and goods items. Thus, Haslam concluded that the SRT typology can be integrated into Fiske's typology of relationships. However, the location of the different SRT resources on the FA space did not correspond to their dimensions (i.e., particularism and concreteness) and circular order.

Another illustration of using FA in the context of SRT appeared in a study by Seers et al. (2006). The authors developed a measure of SRT's resources that could fit different kinds of exchange relations (i.e., reciprocation of behaviors) in the workplace, "such as between supervisors and subordinates or between employees and [team] work-group peers" (p. 508). For this purpose, they defined a pool of item pairs that reflected giving and receiving different resources in hierarchical and team relations. In a pilot study, university students were asked to inspect five times a list of items and each time rate the extent to which each item reflects a given resource (e.g., respect, information, or liking). An exploratory FA elicited factors that corresponded to the types of resources (e.g., a factor of contributed respect). On the basis of these findings, the authors deleted items or worded them differently to increase reliability (Cronbach's alpha). The reviewed instrument was then distributed among 260 employees in diverse organizations, varying in tenure, job title, and sex. The FA applied in this condition elicited a four-factorial solution that corresponded to the SRT resources.

Smallest Space Analysis and Factor Analysis: A Methods Framework and Its Empirical Examination

As shown above, SSA and FA have been traditionally used to examine SRT. Of these two methods, SSA has been applied more frequently than FA. Moreover, factor analytical studies did not directly address the assumed circular structure of the resources in their two-dimensional space. Therefore, it seems worth taking a closer factor analytic look at SRT and discussing its implications on the pattern of factor loadings and correlations among the resources. The resources model depicted in Figure 12.1 can be interpreted as a factor model with the dimensions of concreteness and particularism as factors (denoted as $\eta_j, j = 1 \ldots k$) and the six resources as variables (denoted

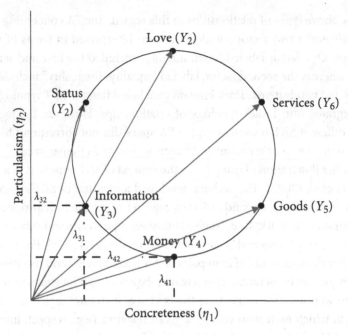

Figure 12.2 Two-dimensional factor model for the six Foa and Foa (1974) social resources.

as $Y_i, i = 1 \ldots m$). The location of resources in the two-dimensional resources space is determined by the factor loadings (denoted as λ_{ij}).

The model in Figure 12.2 is an idealized version of SRT, as depicted in Figure 12.1. It is an ideal version of this model for two reasons. First, equal differences (segments of the circle) between the resources were assumed. Second, the circle on which the resources are located is equally distanced to both dimensions. These restrictions are not part of the theory. They were chosen here to simplify the illustration of FA. Figure 12.2 depicts the factor loadings of the resources information (Y_3) and money (Y_4).

Each resource can be formulated as a structural equation defining its regression on the two factors. For example, the structural equation for love (Y_1) reads as follows:

$$Y_1 = \lambda_{11} \eta_1 + \lambda_{12} \eta_2 \qquad (12.1)$$

Note that the equation does not contain a residual (error) variable because the factor space is exactly two-dimensional in our idealized example,

EVALUATING FOA AND FOA'S SRT 385

Table 12.1 Factor Loadings of the Factor Model in Figure 12.2

	Concreteness (η_1)	Particularism (η_2)
Love (Y_1)	0.5	0.85
Status (Y_2)	0.2	0.67
Information (Y_3)	0.2	0.33
Money (Y_4)	0.5	0.15
Goods (Y_5)	0.8	0.33
Services (Y_6)	0.8	0.67

implying that the two factors fully determine each variable without losing information. Accordingly, each resource can be decomposed into the two factors of concreteness and particularism, with the weights of these factors being the factor loadings. Table 12.1 contains the factor loadings of the resources if the factors are standardized: $\mathrm{Var}(\eta_1) = \mathrm{Var}(\eta_2) = 1$

In addition to the location of the six resources on a circle in the two-dimensional space of concreteness and particularism, Figure 12.2 contains six arrows. These arrows are called variable vectors. Their length corresponds to the variances of the resources. The angle between any two vectors corresponds to the correlation of the variables they represent.

The variances of the resources can be computed as follows, with love taken as an example:

$$\mathrm{Var}\left(Y_1\right) = \lambda_{11}^2 \, \mathrm{Var}(\eta_1) + \lambda_{12}^2 \, \mathrm{Var}(\eta_2) + 2\lambda_{11}\lambda_{12}\mathrm{Cov}(\eta_1, \eta_2) \quad (12.2)$$

Because the two factors η_1 and η_2 are orthogonal (uncorrelated, $\mathrm{Cov}(\eta_1, \eta_2) = 0$)), Equation 12.2 can be simplified as follows:

$$\mathrm{Var}\left(Y_1\right) = \lambda_{11}^2 \, \mathrm{Var}(\eta_1) + \lambda_{12}^2 \, \mathrm{Var}(\eta_2) \quad (12.3)$$

If the factors are standardized ($\mathrm{Var}(\eta_1) = \mathrm{Var}(\eta_2) = 1$), Equation 12.3 can be simplified as follows:

$$\mathrm{Var}\left(Y_1\right) = \lambda_{11}^2 + \lambda_{12}^2 \quad (12.4)$$

386 PART II NEW THEORETICAL AND EMPIRICAL DEVELOPMENTS

Equation 12.5 defines the covariance between two resources, with love (Y_1) and status (Y_2) taken as examples:

$$\begin{aligned}
\text{Cov}\left(Y_1,Y_2\right) &= \text{Cov}((\lambda_{11}\eta_1+\lambda_{12}\eta_2),\ (\lambda_{21}\eta_1+\lambda_{22}\eta_2)) \\
&= \lambda_{11}\lambda_{21}\text{Var}(\eta_1)+\lambda_{11}\lambda_{22}\text{Cov}(\eta_1,\eta_2)+\lambda_{12}\lambda_{21}\text{Cov}(\eta_1,\eta_2) \quad (12.5) \\
&\quad +\lambda_{12}\lambda_{22}\text{Var}(\eta_2)
\end{aligned}$$

Because the two factors η_1 and η_2 are orthogonal, Equation 12.5 can be simplified as follows:

$$\text{Cov}\left(Y_1,Y_2\right)=\lambda_{11}\lambda_{21}\text{Var}(\eta_1)+\lambda_{12}\lambda_{22}\text{Var}(\eta_2) \qquad (12.6)$$

If the factors are standardized, Equation 12.6 can be simplified as follows:

$$\text{Cov}\left(Y_1,Y_2\right)=\lambda_{11}\lambda_{21}+\lambda_{12}\lambda_{22} \qquad (12.7)$$

Finally, the correlations among the resources can be computed as follows from their covariances and variances, with love and status serving as an example:

$$\text{Cor}\left(Y_1,Y_2\right)=\frac{\text{Cov}\left(Y_1,Y_2\right)}{\sqrt{\text{Var}\left(Y_1\right)}\sqrt{\text{Var}\left(Y_2\right)}} \qquad (12.8)$$

Equations 12.4, 12.7, and 12.8 show that the variances, standard deviations (square roots of the variances), covariances, and correlations of the variables can be calculated solely from the factor loadings if the factors are orthogonal and standardized. Table 12.2 presents the results of these calculations.

It is important to realize that the coefficients in Table 12.2 are implications of the model in Figure 12.2 and the idealized assumptions that define it. Different variances, covariances, and correlations would be implied by the model if the resources were not equally spaced on a circle, if the circle was located closer to one dimension than to the other, if the circle was located closer to or further away from both dimensions, or if the diameter of the circle was different. In each of these alternative cases, the loadings would differ from those in Table 12.1. Consequently, the variances, covariances, and correlations of the

Table 12.2 Covariances (Cov), Variances (Var), Standard Deviations (SD), and Correlations (Cor) Implied by the Factor Model in Figure 12.2 with the Factor Loadings in Table 12.1

	Cov					Var	SD	Cor				
	Y_1	Y_2	Y_3	Y_4	Y_5			Y_1	Y_2	Y_3	Y_4	Y_5
Love (Y_1)						0.97	0.99					
Respect (Y_2)	0.67					0.49	0.70	0.9709				
Information (Y_3)	0.38	0.26				0.15	0.39	0.9999	0.9677			
Money (Y_4)	0.38	0.20	0.15			0.27	0.52	0.7333	0.5493	0.7422		
Goods (Y_5)	0.68	0.38	0.27	0.45		0.75	0.87	0.7974	0.6298	0.8053	0.9950	
Services (Y_6)	0.97	0.61	0.38	0.50	0.86	1.09	1.04	0.9421	0.8345	0.9464	0.9188	0.9536

388 PART II NEW THEORETICAL AND EMPIRICAL DEVELOPMENTS

resources would also differ from those in Table 12.2. However, the idealized model we fabricated for illustrative purposes seems a reasonable representation of the conceptual model in Figure 12.1. Therefore, the coefficients in Table 12.2 are instructive and noteworthy.

First, these coefficients show that the variances differ substantially between the resources. This result reflects that the resources contain their components of concreteness and particularism to different degrees. Second, all correlations are positive. Third, the correlations differ in size. Fourth, some correlations are very high, with love (Y_1) and information having a correlation close to unity. The correlation between love and information is close to unity because the ratio of their factor loadings ($\lambda_{12}/\lambda_{11}$; $\lambda_{32}/\lambda_{31}$) is almost identical (1,7; 1,65). Fifth, the pattern of correlations does not correspond to the pattern of distances between the resources on the circle. Sixth, the pattern of correlations does not correspond to the characteristic pattern of a circumplex (correlations first dropping across the subdiagonals of the correlation matrix and then rising again). However, seventh, the structure of the factor loadings as defined by their relative sizes is consistent with a circumplex (Nagy et al., 2019). This pattern is given in Tables 12.3 and 12.4.

The model we have discussed so far defines the factors as monopolar. A resource can be more or less concrete, which means that it is less or more symbolic. Accordingly, a resource can be more or less particularistic, which means that it is less or more universal. In psychology, circumplex models are usually applied to bipolar constructs. In personality models, this means, for example, that extraversion and introversion are considered opposite poles

Table 12.3 Relative Size of Factor Loadings Across Variables Within Factors

	Concreteness (η_1)	Particularism (η_2)
Love (Y_1)	$\lambda_{11}: < \lambda_{61}, \lambda_{51}; > \lambda_{21}, \lambda_{31}$	$\lambda_{12}: > \lambda_{22}, \lambda_{32}, \lambda_{42}, \lambda_{52}, \lambda_{62}$
Status (Y_2)	$\lambda_{21}: < \lambda_{11}, \lambda_{41}, \lambda_{51}, \lambda_{61}$	$\lambda_{22}: < \lambda_{12}; > \lambda_{32}, \lambda_{42}, \lambda_{52}$
Information (Y_3)	$\lambda_{31}: < \lambda_{11}, \lambda_{41}, \lambda_{51}, \lambda_{61}$	$\lambda_{32}: < \lambda_{12}, \lambda_{22}, \lambda_{62}; > \lambda_{42}$
Money (Y_4)	$\lambda_{41}: < \lambda_{51}, \lambda_{61}; > \lambda_{21}, \lambda_{31}$	$\lambda_{42}: < \lambda_{12}, \lambda_{22}, \lambda_{32}, \lambda_{52}, \lambda_{62}$
Goods (Y_5)	$\lambda_{51}: > \lambda_{11}, \lambda_{21}, \lambda_{31}, \lambda_{41}$	$\lambda_{52}: < \lambda_{12}, \lambda_{22}, \lambda_{62}; > \lambda_{42}$
Services (Y_6)	$\lambda_{61}: > \lambda_{11}, \lambda_{21}, \lambda_{31}, \lambda_{41}$	$\lambda_{62}: < \lambda_{12}; > \lambda_{32}, \lambda_{42}, \lambda_{52}$

Table 12.4 Relative Size of Factor Loadings Across Factors Within Variables

	Concreteness (η_1)		Particularism (η_2)
Love (Y_1)	λ_{11}	<	λ_{12}
Status (Y_2)	λ_{21}	<	λ_{22}
Information (Y_3)	λ_{31}	<	λ_{32}
Money (Y_4)	λ_{41}	>	λ_{42}
Goods (Y_5)	λ_{51}	>	λ_{52}
Services (Y_6)	λ_{61}	>	λ_{62}

of one dimension (Hofstee et al., 1992). A bipolar version of the SRT would consider concreteness versus symbolism as opposite poles of the first dimension and particularism versus universalism as opposite poles of the second dimension. Figure 12.3 depicts this type of model.

Consistent with the monopolar model in Figure 12.2, the bipolar version of the model in Figure 12.3 locates the six resources in a two-dimensional space and assumes equal distances between adjacent resources on a circle. Different from the monopolar version of the model, the variable vectors are equal in length in the bipolar model. Setting the

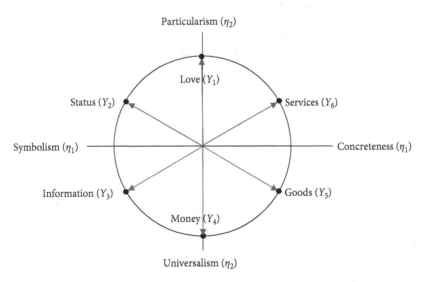

Figure 12.3 Bipolar version of Foa and Foa's (1974) model.

390 PART II NEW THEORETICAL AND EMPIRICAL DEVELOPMENTS

Table 12.5 Factor Loadings of the Factor Model in Figure 12.3

	Concreteness (η_1)	Particularism (η_2)
Love (Y_1)	0	1
Status (Y_2)	−0.866	0.5
Information (Y_3)	−0.866	−0.5
Money (Y_4)	0	−1
Goods (Y_5)	0.866	−0.5
Services (Y_6)	0.866	0.5

radius of the circle to 1 (unity circle) implies the factor loadings given in Table 12.5.

These loadings were used to compute the variances, covariances, and correlations of the resources given in Table 12.6. They differ remarkably from those in Table 12.2. First, the variances of all resources are equal. Second, only resources adjacent to each other on the circle have positive correlations. Third, the correlation matrix has a systematic pattern of positive and negative correlations that are equal in size for resources with equal distances on the circle. In other words, the pattern of correlations corresponds perfectly to the pattern of distances between the resources on the circle. Fourth, this pattern is fully consistent with a circumplex (Nagy et al., 2019). Fifth, the pattern of loadings is consistent with the circumplex criteria given in Tables 12.3 and 12.4.

Table 12.6 Covariances (Cov), Variances (Var), Standard Deviations (SD), and Correlations (Cor) Implied by the Factor Model in Figure 12.3 with the Factor Loadings in Table 12.5

	Cov					Var	SD	Cor				
	Y_1	Y_2	Y_3	Y_4	Y_5			Y_1	Y_2	Y_3	Y_4	Y_5
Love (Y_1)						1	1					
Respect (Y_2)	0.5					1	1	0.5				
Information (Y_3)	−0.5	0.5				1	1	−0.5	0.5			
Money (Y_4)	−1	−0.5	0.5			1	1	−1	−0.5	0.5		
Goods (Y_5)	−0.5	−1	−0.5	0.5		1	1	−0.5	−1	−0.5	0.5	
Services (Y_6)	0.5	−0.5	−1	−0.5	0.5	1	1	0.5	−0.5	−1	−0.5	0.5

What conclusions can be drawn from our comparative analysis? First, although the monopolar model in Figure 12.2 is consistent with a pattern of loadings (Tables 12.3 and 12.4) that generate a circular arrangement of resources in the two-dimensional factor space according the SRT (Figure 12.1), the pattern of correlations it implies does not correspond to the pattern of distances between the resources. It also does not correspond to the characteristic pattern of a circumplex. Second, by contrast, the bipolar model in Figure 12.3 meets the loading criteria and implies a pattern of correlations that is fully consistent with the pattern of distances between the resources in the two-dimensional space. Moreover, the pattern of correlations corresponds to the characteristic pattern of a circumplex. However, this model implies the existence of negative correlations. Moreover, it implies that opposite resources can be mapped on a single bipolar resource dimension (love versus money, status versus goods, and information versus services). Third, both models cannot generate a pattern of correlations that is consistent with SRT (Figure 12.1). The unipolar model (Figure 12.2) generates positive correlations among the resources, but these correlations do not have the characteristic structure of a circumplex. The bipolar model (Figure 12.3) can generate such a characteristic pattern of correlations but implies negative correlations among resources, which are not allowed in SRT (see Sabbagh & Levy, 2012).

As it turns out, there is a factor model that can generate correlations that are both exclusively positive and have the characteristic structure of a circumplex. This model is depicted in Figure 12.4. Unlike the two-factor models we have discussed so far, the model in Figure 12.4 is a three-factor model. Its three dimensions are monopolar and mutually orthogonal. If the variables have identical variances, their vectors create an oblique cone. The origins of the vectors and the three dimensions define the cone's vertex, and the endpoints of the vectors define the cone's circular base. If the variables are located in the three-dimensional factor space according to the loadings in Table 12.7, the implied variances, covariances, standard deviations, and correlations in Table 12.8 result.

Table 12.8 shows that now, the correlations between the variables correspond to the characteristic circumplex pattern. Moreover, all correlations are positive. If they are submitted to SSA, the resulting two-dimensional plot of resources (Figure 12.5) fits perfectly with SRT (Figure 12.1).

Table 12.7 Factor Loadings of the Factor Model in Figure 12.4

	η_1	η_2	η_3
Love (Y_1)	0.33	0.8	0.5
Status (Y_2)	0.33	0.5	0.8
Information (Y_3)	0.5	0.33	0.8
Money (Y_4)	0.8	0.33	0.5
Goods (Y_5)	0.8	0.5	0.33
Services (Y_6)	0.5	0.8	0.33

Table 12.8 Covariances (Cov), Variances (Var), Standard Deviations (SD), and Correlations (Cor) Implied by the Factor Model in Figure 12.4 with the Factor Loadings in Table 12.7

	Cov Y_1 Y_2 Y_3 Y_4 Y_5	Var	SD	Cor Y_1 Y_2 Y_3 Y_4 Y_5
Love (Y_1)		1	1	
Respect (Y_2)	0.91	1	1	0.91
Information (Y_3)	0.83 0.97	1	1	0.83 0.97
Money (Y_4)	0.78 0.83 0.91	1	1	0.78 0.83 0.91
Goods (Y_5)	0.83 0.78 0.83 0.97	1	1	0.83 0.78 0.83 0.97
Services (Y_6)	0.97 0.83 0.78 0.83 0.91	1	1	0.97 0.83 0.78 0.83 0.91

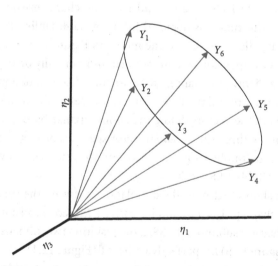

Figure 12.4 Unipolar three-factor model generating a circumplex of exclusively positive correlations among the variables.

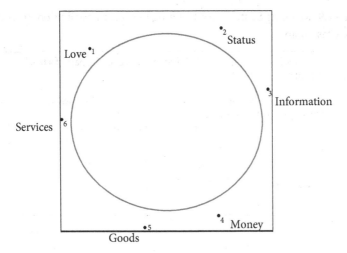

Figure 12.5 SSA elicited by the three-dimensional factor model for the six Foa and Foa (1974) resources (from the correlations in Table 12.8; SSA dimensionality 2, axes 1 and 2).

Empirical Examination of Two SRT Methods (SSA and FA) in a Classroom Setting

We focus on SRT in a classroom setting as an applied illustration in which we can formally test and validate SRT using SSA and FA. In educational settings, in addition to grades, teachers distribute to their students a wide range of resources as needed, such as attention and help. These resource distribution practices (RDPs) are important because they affect students' learning motivation and behavior, potentially creating a positive or negative learning climate (Ehrhardt-Madapathi et al., 2018; Peter & Dalbert, 2010; Wubbels & Brekelmans, 2005).

We identified four main types of resources that teachers distribute to students in the classroom. These resources correspond to four of the six categories defined by Foa and Foa 1974: (a) affection (love), (b) respect (status), (c) knowledge (information), and (d) learning assistance (money). The two remaining resources in the typology—that is, goods and services—did not apply to the classroom setting and were not investigated in the current study. These resources are not inherent to teaching, namely teachers do not distribute tangible resources. Moreover, teaching itself is a kind of labor (service) that is not evaluated by students. We predicted that these RDPs

Table 12.9 Mapping Sentence for Defining Resource Distribution Practices in the Classroom

A student (recipient) X evaluates a distribution practice on the part of a teacher (provider) (Y) of a

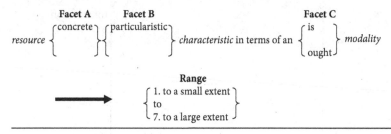

would be organized in correspondence with SRT—that is, according to facets (or dimensions) concreteness (facet A) and particularism (facet B). The study also included an additional third facet, C, which gauges the modality of the evaluation, whether it targets an *actual* or *desired* state of affairs—that is, how the students believe a resource distribution "is" or "should" be (Sabbagh & Levy, 2012). The three facets and their respective elements are formally represented in the mapping sentence in Table 12.9, a conceptual definitional framework for a universe of interpersonal resource exchange contents in the school classroom setting (Guttman, 1982; Levy, 1985).

Sample and Instrument

The database, which we used for the comparison of the two methods SSA and FA, was collected during the 2010–2011 school year in the framework of a comprehensive study. Participants were 5,084 eighth and ninth graders from a national sample of 48 Israeli middle schools. Schools were sampled countrywide to represent the schools' socioeconomic standing.

The instrument included a total of 20 items (V1–V20) that were used to measure the deserved (should) and received (is) exchange of resources (Appendix 12.2). The wording of these items is provided in Appendix 12.2. Responses ranged on a 7-point Likert scale from 1 = to a small extent to 7 = to a large extent.

Results

Smallest Space Analysis

The 20 items were subjected to SSA in order to determine their dimensionality and interrelationship structure (Pearson coefficients). As shown in Table 12.10, in most cases, the correlations between RDP variables emerged as positive (ranging from .024 to .525). Three dimensions were required to adequately represent the correlations among the variables and obtain a close correspondence between the facet design and the space diagram regions. The value of Guttman's (1968) coefficient of alienation was .115. This coefficient measures the goodness of fit between the derived configuration and the correlation matrix of social justice judgments. The low value obtained here attests to a very good fit. Findings indicate that the three facets in the mapping sentence hold two orthogonal projections (Figures 12.6 and 12.7). The resource facets (A and B) are represented in a two-dimensional projection spanned by axes 2 and 3 (Figure 12.6) of the SSA configuration. This projection is orthogonal to the modality facet (C), which is represented in a two-dimensional projection spanned by axes 1 and 2 (Figure 12.7).

The circular arrangement in Figure 12.6, which displays the correlation matrix's geometric configuration, corresponds to the contents of facets A and B. These facets' arrangement plays a *polarizing* (circular) role in that they partition the space into wedge-like regions sharing a common origin. In the two-dimensional SSA projection, the four resource regions within the approximate circle pertain to affection, respect, knowledge, and instrumental help, respectively. All variables relating to a given resource are found in the region it covers, except for V8, located in the neighboring learning assistance region rather than in that of knowledge. Technically, within a correlation matrix, this space partition is expressed through the larger coefficients next to the main diagonal; the coefficients become gradually smaller with distance from the latter but then increase again.

This structure (Figure 12.6) aligns with the two facets of concreteness and particularism suggested by Foa and Foa (2012). The large empty region on the right side of the circular structure between affection and instrumental help (besides two equivocal items V11 and V12 that could not be properly classified) would pertain to "goods" and "services" in SRT. However, as stated previously, these resource types are less relevant to the educational domain and were thus not operationalized in the current study. Note, however, that

Table 12.10 Pearson Correlations Among Resource Distribution Practices Variables

	V1	V2	V3	V4	V5	V6	V7	V8	V9	V10	V11	V12	V13	V14	V15	V16	V17	V18	V19	V20
V1 Learning help–is	1	.212	.464	.121	.413	.102	.409	.157	.455	.127	.245	.121	.424	.143	.398	.168	.409	.156	.439	.182
V2 Learning help–ought	.212	1	.143	.323	.142	.345	.223	.326	.152	.313	.066	.116	.125	.321	.188	.314	.108	.259	.158	.295
V3 Affection 1–is	.464	.143	1	.284	.457	.089	.398	.092	.471	.132	.306	.137	.403	.117	.390	.148	.477	.200	.421	.182
V4 Affection 1–ought	.121	.323	.284	1	.174	.310	.178	.253	.160	.286	.122	.230	.145	.301	.176	.255	.204	.354	.161	.325
V5 Respect 1–is	.413	.142	.457	.174	1	.180	.428	.159	.525	.097	.298	.150	.403	.125	.396	.163	.459	.158	.457	.180
V6 Respect 1–ought	.102	.345	.089	.310	.180	1	.165	.348	.098	.391	.068	.141	.109	.342	.142	.343	.069	.271	.124	.347
V7 Knowledge 1–is	.409	.223	.398	.178	.428	.165	1	.318	.473	.189	.232	.132	.340	.180	.518	.292	.366	.172	.411	.221
V8 Knowledge 1–ought	.157	.326	.092	.253	.159	.348	.318	1	.159	.336	.096	.165	.163	.321	.224	.416	.058	.189	.178	.287
V9 Respect 2–is	.455	.152	.471	.160	.525	.098	.473	.159	1	.187	.275	.104	.382	.104	.459	.185	.531	.195	.492	.215
V10 Respect 2–ought	.127	.313	.132	.286	.097	.391	.189	.336	.187	1	.023	.099	.072	.291	.147	.357	.087	.314	.113	.376
V11 Personal life–is	.245	.066	.306	.122	.298	.068	.232	.096	.275	.023	1	.393	.371	.128	.234	.048	.306	.103	.322	.138
V12 Personal life–ought	.121	.116	.137	.230	.150	.141	.132	.165	.104	.099	.393	1	.247	.260	.148	.105	.163	.188	.188	.212

V13 Learning problems–is	.424	.125	.403	.145	.403	.109	.340	.163	.382	.072	.371	.247	1	.313	.389	.141	.386	.127	.443	.187
V14 Learning problems–ought	.143	.321	.117	.301	.125	.342	.180	.321	.104	.291	.128	.260	.313	1	.185	.367	.110	.302	.174	.382
V15 Knowledge 2–is	.398	.188	.390	.176	.396	.142	.518	.224	.459	.147	.234	.148	.389	.185	1	.327	.439	.205	.447	.194
V16 Knowledge 2–ought	.168	.314	.148	.255	.163	.343	.292	.416	.185	.357	.048	.105	.141	.367	.327	1	.153	.340	.211	.389
V17 Affection 2–is	.409	.108	.477	.204	.459	.069	.366	.058	.531	.087	.306	.163	.386	.110	.439	.153	1	.433	.537	.237
V18 Affection 2–ought	.156	.259	.200	.354	.158	.271	.172	.189	.195	.314	.103	.188	.127	.302	.205	.340	.433	1	.232	.470
V19 Affection 3–is	.439	.158	.421	.161	.457	.124	.411	.178	.492	.113	.322	.188	.443	.174	.447	.211	.537	.232	1	.366
V20 Affection 3–ought	.182	.295	.182	.325	.180	.347	.221	.287	.215	.376	.138	.212	.187	.382	.194	.389	.237	.470	.366	1

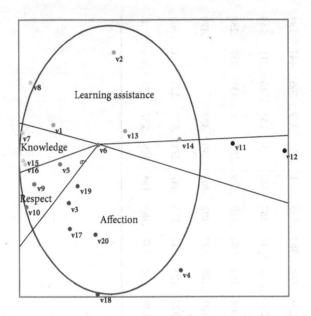

Figure 12.6 SSA circular representation of the resource distribution practices correlations—a two-dimensional SSA projection (dimensions 2 and 3) of facet A (particularism) and facet B (concreteness).

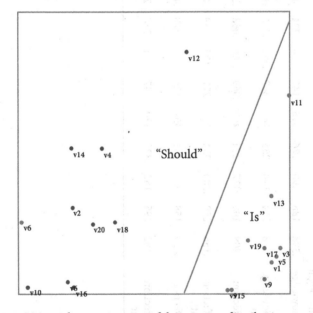

Figure 12.7 SSA axial representation of the resource distribution practices correlations—two-dimensional SSA projection (dimensions 1 and 2) of facet C (modality facet).

Table 12.11 Pearson Correlations ($p < .01$) Among the Resource Distribution Practices Scales

	1	2	3	4
1. Affection	1			
2. Respect	.623	1		
3. Knowledge	.536	.587	1	
4. Learning help	.575	.552	.550	1

the empirical pattern of correlations in Table 12.11, which displays RDP items on the level of scales, does not entirely fit the circumplex's conditions.

Figure 12.7 represents the modality facet (C) in a projection that is orthogonal. Findings indicate that this facet has an axial role. The SSA space can be partitioned by a line creating two parallel regions of points, thus separating the "is" and "should" modalities of distribution practices.

Factor Analysis

Our previous factor analytic perspective on the Foa and Foa model was exclusively formal. We now use our data to explore whether or not they fit with the three factor analytic models we have discussed (Figures 12.2–12.4). Knowing whether data fit with models can be investigated via CFA. In our case, Browne's (1992) circular stochastic process model for the circumplex could be used and tested with his CIRCUM program (Browne & du Toit, 1995). An appropriate specification of the CFA model would require inequality constraints imposed on the loadings according to Tables 12.3 and 12.4. In addition, the latent factors' variances would have to be set to 1 and their correlation to 0.

However, CFA makes sense only if the empirical pattern of correlations comes reasonably close to the pattern of correlations implied by a model. Table 12.11 can indicate whether or not this is the case in our study. It reports the correlations of the four resources in our data set on the level of scales. The numbers in Table 12.11 show, first, that all empirical correlations are positive. This pattern is inconsistent with the bipolar two-factor model (Figure 12.3) but consistent with the monopolar two-factor model (Figure 12.2). However, the pattern of correlations is not consistent with this model. Although the empirical pattern of correlations in Table 12.11 comes closer to the pattern of correlations implied by the three-factor model (Figure 12.4), the similarity of the model implied correlations in Table 12.8 with the empirical correlations in Table 12.11 is limited. Specifically, according to SRT, the correlation of money (learning help) with status (respect) should be lower than the correlation of money (learning help) with information (knowledge). These two correlations are virtually identical in our data set, however, amounting to $r = .552$ and $r = .550$, respectively (Table 12.11).

What happens if the correlations in Table 12.11 are submitted to SSA? Figure 12.8 reports the two-dimensional SSA plot of the four resources. Their order and location correspond well with SRT (Figure 12.1). Notwithstanding this correspondence, the empirical pattern of correlations in Table 12.11 deviates from the pattern of correlations implied by the factor models we have considered (Tables 12.2, 12.6, and 12.8). Thus, there is no point in testing these models via CFA.

Despite this conclusion, we considered it worthwhile to explore the resources factor structure by running a series of EFAs on the item level. What results can be expected? If resources were the main source of common variance, four factors would emerge. If the mode of exchange (*is* versus *should*) were the main common variance source, two common factors would show

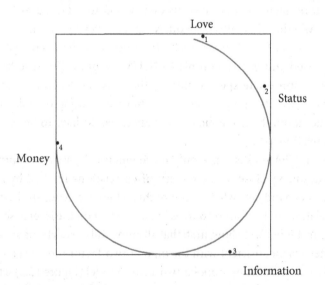

Figure 12.8 SSA elicited by the empirical correlations among variables in the data set for the four Foa and Foa (1974) resources (dimension 2 and axes 1 and 2) (Table 12.11).

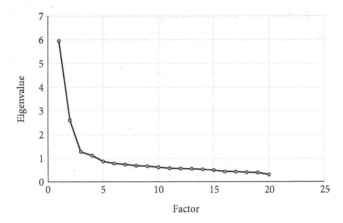

Figure 12.9 Eigenvalues of exploratory factor analysis 1.

up. If resource and mode were equally strong and independent sources of common variance, eight factors were to be expected.

The first EFA included all 20 items. The eigenvalues of this analysis are presented in Figure 12.9. According to the scree criterion, the common variance of the items was generated by two factors. According to the Kaiser criterion (eigenvalue > 1), the items have four factors in common. Both solutions were rotated to a simple structure. Note that the loadings of the theoretical models necessarily deviate from a simple structure. However, because the data did not fit with these models, rotation to a simple structure seemed reasonable for understanding the factors' substantive meaning. In the four-factor model, oblique (oblimin) and orthogonal (varimax) rotations revealed highly similar solutions. Therefore, we report only the varimax solution of the four-factor model. In the two-factor model, a better simple structure was obtained with oblique rotation of the factors. Therefore, we report only the oblimin solution of the two-factor model.

Table 12.12 contains the four (varimax) loadings and the two-factor (oblimin) solutions. In the four-factor solution, all items have positive loadings on the first factor, and most of these loadings are substantial. The second factor contrasts *is* items and *should* items. The former has negative and the latter positive loadings on this factor. The third factor loads the two personal life items (V11 and V12). Note that these two items were outliers in the SSA (Figure 12.6). The fourth factor loads the two affection items (V17 and V18). In the SSA, these two items were not outliers. In the two-factor solution, *is* items have positive and substantial loadings on the first factor,

402 PART II NEW THEORETICAL AND EMPIRICAL DEVELOPMENTS

Table 12.12 Factor Loadings of the Rotated Four- and Two-Factors Solution

	Four-Factors Solution (Varimax)				Two-Factors Solution (Oblimin)	
	1	2	3	4	1	2
V1 Learning help–is	.576	−.271	−.125	.061	.650	−.027
V2 Learning help–ought	.383	.369	−.091	.053	−.014	.541
V3 Affection 1–is	.599	−.283	−.015	−.058	.680	−.032
V4 Affection 1–ought	.423	.315	.108	−.076	.061	.500
V5 Respect 1–is	.601	−.281	−.080	.032	.679	−.028
V6 Respect 1–ought	.363	.462	−.043	.055	−.106	.631
V7 Knowledge 1–is	.617	−.127	−.255	.139	.554	.137
V8 Knowledge 1–ought	.398	.389	.155	.245	−.010	.549
V9 Respect 2–is	.642	−.319	−.150	−.071	.735	−.047
V10 Respect 2–ought	.364	.439	−.112	−.050	−.084	.603
V11 Personal life–is	.435	−.217	.383	.222	.471	−.019
V12 Personal life–ought	.343	.084	.484	.226	.182	.214
V13 Learning problems–is	.576	−.237	.122	.209	.612	.011
V14 Learning problems–ought	.439	.411	.124	.147	−.003	.600
V15 Knowledge 2–is	.620	−.174	−.173	.063	.601	.090
V16 Knowledge 2–ought	.463	.405	−.192	.018	.021	.604
V17 Affection 2–is	.663	−.326	.109	−.361	.725	−.033
V18 Affection 2–ought	.487	.315	.194	−.459	.123	.476
V19 Affection 3–is	.662	−.249	.018	−.033	.700	.030
V20 Affection 3–ought	.523	.368	.096	−.134	.095	.592

whereas *should* items have positive and substantial loadings on the second factor. Accordingly, factor 1 can be interpreted as an *is* factor and factor 2 as a *should* factor. A correlation of $r = .41$ was estimated between both factors.

Three important conclusions can be drawn from these results. First, individual differences in considering a resource as deserved (*should*) are generalized across resources. In other words, the sense of deserving is not resource-specific. Second, individual differences in perceiving the actual receipt (*is*) of a resource are also generalized across resources. Third, the *is* and *should* items of a resource overlap moderately. Fourth, the emergence of two main common factors reflecting the exchange mode is fully consistent with its SSA representation (Figure 12.7).

In the second set of EFAs, the *is* items and the *should* items (Appendix 12.2) were analyzed separately. The first three eigenvalues of the *is* items amounted to 4.77/0.88/0.71. Thus, the items share only one common factor according to both the scree criterion and the Kaiser criterion. The first three eigenvalues of the *should* items amounted to 3.70/1/0.89. Again, one factor seems sufficient to explain common item variance. A straightforward conclusion can be drawn from these results: The four resources did not generate common variance in our students' sample. Rather, individual differences between the students are the main source of common variance, and these differences are generalized strongly across resources within modes (*is* and *should*) and to a much smaller degree across modes.

SSA and FA Results: A Comparative Perspective

The results from the two types of structural analyses, SSA and FA, we reported converge in some respects but differ in others. With regard to convergence, both analyses identified an exchange mode (deserving versus receiving a resource) as an important facet. In the SSA, this facet is represented by the SSA solution's first dimension (Figure 12.7). In the FA, a common *should* factor and a common *is* factor could be extracted. Although these factors correlate, they are distinct. Regarding differences, in the SSA solution, the four resources could be differentiated in a two-dimensional projection of the items (Figure 12.6) using conventional graphic principles. In the FA, the resources could not be discriminated. The location of the items in the space defined by dimension 2 and dimension 3 of the SSA (Figure 12.6) helps one understand this result. Whereas in SSA the plane regions can be identified by visual inspection and graphically using straight lines, curved lines, and circles, FA applies much more rigid criteria for the extraction of common factors. Specifically, four resource factors within modes would be obtained if the items representing the same resource were located proximal to each other and items representing different resources distant from each other. Our EFA did not detect such distinct sets of items within sets being homogeneous (relatively high correlations among items) and items from different sets being heterogeneous (relatively low correlations among items). The degree of convergence and divergence among the 20 items of our study was not pronounced enough for extracting four common resource factors.

404 PART II NEW THEORETICAL AND EMPIRICAL DEVELOPMENTS

Underused Multivariate Statistical Methods to Validate SRT

As discussed above, earlier SRT studies applied traditional statistical methods to assess and validate explicitly the different SRT elements, namely the dimensions for organizing the resources (i.e., particularism and concreteness), its circumplex structure, and predicted outcomes concerning the exchange of the different resources. Based on a literature search of later SRT studies, mostly since the 2000s, we noted that SRT had been used in a wide range of domains (Törnblom & Kazemi, 2012), such as support groups and environment (Brown et al., 2014; Margetts & Kashima, 2017), though mainly in organizational and marketing research (Arnould, 2008; Chen & Lin, 2019; Cooper-Thomas et al., 2018; Dorsch et al., 2017; Farshid et al., 2021; Flynn, 2003; Huang & Knight, 2017; Lemmon et al., 2016; Martin & Harder, 1994; Mitchell et al., 2012; Omilion-Hodges & Baker, 2017; Rodrigues et al., 2019; Wilson et al., 2010; for a general reference to these selected studies, see Appendix 12.1).

However, this body of research does not adopt the entire SRT framework as the basis for derivation and testing of hypotheses. Instead, with a couple of exceptions, the studies mention or apply SRT mainly regarding the resource types, often classified as economic versus social resources. In other words, in most of the papers, there is no explicit reference to the SRT's dimensions of particularism and concreteness, and the use of the circumplex structure is rare. Moreover, the theoretical papers do not mention implications for discussing or comparing different methods associated with SRT.

Against this background, in the following, we discuss multivariate statistical methods that can be used but have been used less often, if at all, in developing and expanding and validating SRT.

We begin by describing conjoint measurement. This method can be used to assess resource preferences indirectly instead of via direct ratings of resources. Next, we describe cluster analysis, which can be performed with either direct or indirect resource preference scores. Cluster analysis and related methods, such as latent class analysis, allow for the discrimination of groups based on their distinct variable profiles (Collins & Lanza, 2009; Kaufman & Rousseeuw, 2009). In the case of SRT, these variables are evaluations of resources. Importantly, the groups that can be distinguished based on their resource evaluations are unknown prior to analyses. Discriminant analysis is similar to cluster analysis and latent class analysis in its purpose of discriminating groups based on a set of variables (Lachenbruch, 1975). Unlike cluster analysis and latent class analysis, discriminant analysis is used when groups are known. Finally, we introduce structural equation modeling and hierarchical modeling/multilevel modeling as methods that allow linking resource preferences to third variables. We illustrate all methods with real or hypothetical examples from SRT research.

Conjoint Measurement

Conjoint measurement is a method that allows the decomposition of the total value or utility of an object into the contributions of its attributes (Green & Srinivasan, 1990; Luce & Tukey, 1964). Because the potential contributions of attributes to the overall utility of an object can vary between individuals, they are determined for each individual separately. The measurement design and the object variants to be compared depend on the number of attributes and their levels. For an object that can be mapped on six attributes with two levels each (e.g., high versus low), $2^6 = 64$ distinct attribute profiles are possible. In other words, 64 variants of the object can be distinguished and compared. To estimate how much each attribute contributes to the overall utility of the object, participants are presented with all 64 object variants and asked to rank them from 1 (most valuable) to 64 (least valuable). The (inverted) rank of an object version reflects its utility. The contributions of the attributes to the object's utility are estimated via multiple regression, with the rank serving as the dependent variable and the attributes as its predictors. The regression weights of the attributes are called part-worth estimates. In a fully crossed design, the attributes are orthogonal to each other. In this case, the standardized regression weights are identical to the bivariate correlations between the attributes and the rank. Realizing a fully crossed design becomes practically challenging as the number of attributes and their levels can get extremely large. In the case of 12 attributes with 4 levels each, the number of distinct object variants amounts to 16,777,216. To avoid such an unreasonable number of objects to be compared, fractional designs can be utilized or participants can be randomly assigned a subset of object variants. In the latter case, attributes will be confounded, and part-worth estimates are no longer identical to bivariate correlations between the attributes and the rank.

406 PART II NEW THEORETICAL AND EMPIRICAL DEVELOPMENTS

In addition to the part-worth estimates, the proportion of variance of each attribute's rank uniquely can be determined. This coefficient is called importance estimate. Because part-worth estimates and importance estimates are computed for each individual, they can be related to third variables such as demographic variables, attitudes, values, personality traits, ability, and behavioral choices.

Dorsch and Brooks (2012) applied conjoint measurement to SRT. Their study investigated how likely customers of traditional and online retailers would be to revisit a store after a first business transaction. Retailors differed in the profile of resources they invested in customers in order to promote their loyalty to the store. Two levels (present and absent) of each resource (love, status, information, money, goods, and services) were operationalized and combined into 64 vignettes describing retail encounters. Employing a fractional design, each participant was assigned a set of 25 vignettes. Participants were instructed to rank the vignettes according to the likelihood that they would return to the store. Individual part-worth and importance estimates were submitted to cluster analysis to identify customer segments whose loyalty to the store was differentially affected by the retailer's resource investments. The results of this analysis are described next.

Cluster Analysis

Participants in the Dorsch and Brooks (2012) study who were presented traditional (brick-and-mortar) retailor vignettes could be discriminated into three clusters. The first cluster contained service-oriented shoppers. For participants belonging to this customer segment, retailer services had the strongest influence on their willingness to revisit the store. Specifically, 32% of these customers considered services the most important resource retailers could invest in, whereas love was the least important. The second segment consisted of affection-oriented shoppers: 49% of participants belonging to this segment prioritized love as the most important resource a retailer could invest in to boost their loyalty to the store. Information and goods were the least important for these customers. The third segment included respect-oriented shoppers: 50% of participants belonging to this group placed the highest importance on status. Information and goods were the least important. The results of Dorsch and Brook's (2012) study demonstrate that resource preferences can be assessed indirectly via conjoint measurement and that customer segments can be meaningfully discriminated based on these preferences.

Discriminant Analysis

Discriminant analysis is a method for the optimal distinction of known groups with a set of manifest variables. The manifest variables are condensed into linear combinations such that the variance of these hybrid variables is as large as possible between groups and as small as possible within groups. If k denotes the number of groups, $k - 1$ linear combinations are needed to discriminate the groups. Applied to SRT, directly or indirectly assessed resource preferences could be used for the optimal distinction between known groups—for example, gender groups, political parties, or religious groups. To the best of our knowledge, discriminant analysis has not yet been used in SRT research.

Structural Equation Modeling

Structural equation modeling is a summary term for many specific model variants based on the general linear model (GLM; Rencher & Schaalje, 2008). Although many multivariate models such as multiple regression and factor analysis are based on the GLM and are therefore structural equation models, the term is mostly used in a narrower sense for denoting models that include manifest (observed and measured) and latent (unobserved) variables. The structural equations that specify associations (correlations and regression effects) among the latent variables define the structural model, whereas the structural equations that connect the latent variables with the manifest variables define the measurement model. Applied to SRT, structural equation models could be used for estimating links between latent resource preferences and third latent variables such as the ones mentioned previously (antecedents, correlates, and consequences). The latent resource preferences could be assessed with direct indicators, such as ratings of resources according to their value, and with indirect

408 PART II NEW THEORETICAL AND EMPIRICAL DEVELOPMENTS

indicators, such as part-worth and importance estimates. Importantly, at least two indicators are necessary for the assessment of each latent variable. However, more indicators per latent variable are statistically advantageous. To the best of our knowledge, structural equation modeling has not yet been employed in SRT research.

Hierarchical or Multilevel Modeling

Hierarchical or multilevel models are needed whenever data have a nested structure (Snijders & Bosker, 2011). For example, in a longitudinal study with students from different classes and schools, time points (level 1) would be nested in students (level 2), students would be nested in classes (level 3), and classes would be nested in schools (level 4). The same or different variables can be measured on different levels. Applied to SRT, directly or indirectly assessed resource preferences could be measured repeatedly (level 1) for all students (level 2). Classes could be described, for example, in terms of average student achievement. Finally, the percentage of parents holding a university degree could be used for describing schools (level 4). If resource preferences and associated third variables would not only vary on level 1 (changes within students across time) and level 2 (differences between students) but also on level 3 (differences between classes) and level 4 (differences between schools), unbiased estimates of parameters (e.g., correlations and regression weights) and their standard errors on levels 1 and 2 would require taking into account the variances and covariances of the variables on levels 3 and 4. In addition to controlling bias, hierarchical models allow for estimating cross-level effects and cross-level interactions. In our hypothetical example, level 3 (average achievement) and level 4 (parental education) could be used to predict individual resource preferences on level 2. A cross-level interaction would exist in our example if the effect of resource preference on behavioral choices on level 1 or level 2 were moderated by the average academic achievement of the students' class (level 3) or by average parental education (level 4). These effect patterns demonstrate the great potential of multilevel models for investigating complex research questions. To the best of our knowledge, this potential has not yet been utilized in SRT research.

Conclusion

This chapter has shown that SRT has remained vivid since its appearance in the 1960s. Until the 2000s, the theory was mostly validated and used as a basis for testing structural hypotheses related to different behavioral outcomes. This body of knowledge tested these hypotheses using experimental and survey designs applying traditional statistical methods (analysis of variance, correlation analysis, multidimensional scaling, SSA, and FA). However, since the early 2000s, the theoretical and empirically based developments of SRT seem to have stagnated. Relatively recent studies (see Appendix 12.1) refer to the six resources specified in SRT (often collapsed into two types of economic versus interpersonal resources) (Berg & Wiebe, 1993; Cropanzano & Mitchell, 2005; Flynn, 2003). However, to the best of our knowledge, most of these reviewed studies do not refer to the typology's dimensions of particularism and concreteness. Also, there is no mention of the functional exchange relations implied in the resources' circular structure and possible outcomes.

Against this background, this chapter first elaborated a conceptual methods model for comparing SSA and FA and how these two methods correspond. On this basis, and using an existent database for illustration, we conducted an empirical analysis to compare the findings elicited by the SSA and FA methods. The FA findings distinguished between items along the mode dimension (*is* versus *should*). However, the substantive meaning of a three-dimensional factors' solution could not be equated with the particularism/concreteness SRT dimensions. Thus, only the SSA analysis elicited a spatial representation of the resource types and their respective dimensions. Second, we mapped more recent statistical methods and explored possible ways for developing SRT.

In summary, SRT has aided the understanding of social exchange dynamics and their favorable and harmful outcomes in both economic and more general social settings. This chapter suggests that further elaborations and validations of SRT require the development of measurements and methods appropriate for representing the spatial configuration of resources' circumplex and dynamics.

Acknowledgment

Authors are listed in alphabetical order.

Appendix 12.1 Annotated SRT Studies According to Traditional Methods and Applications (Selected)

Reference	Design	Subjects	Independent Variable	Dependent Variable	Statistical Method
Traditional Methods Applied in SRT					
Donnenwerth & Foa (1974)	Experimental			Retaliation	Analysis of variance Trend analysis (i.e., quadratic and U-shape relationship between the variables)
Teichman & Foa (1975)	Experimental		Manipulation of a kind of resource given and a kind of resource received (reciprocated)	Satisfaction (satisfaction, attraction for the partner and fairness)	Mean satisfaction of subjects following exchange Coxe–Stewart Trend test
Turner et al. (1971)	Experimental	37 university students in the United State	Study 1, for instance, manipulated 18 statement cards representing 3×6 resources. Two groups of participants received a card and were asked to return the most similar/ dissimilar card to the one they received.	Distribution of resources returned for each resource received according to the circular structure	Friedman two-way analysis of variance
			Study 3, Validation of resource exchange (giving and receiving paired resources)		Correlation analysis
Foa et al. (1987)	Survey	220 Israeli adolescents 47 Swedish university students 32 Mexican American Spanish-speaking families 16 Filipino female university students and their parents			Correlation analysis

Appendix 12.1 Continued

Reference	Design	Subjects	Independent Variable	Dependent Variable	Statistical Method
Johnson & Long (2019)	Survey	Line workers in a manufacturing facility	Validation of Berg & Wiebe's (1993) Resource Exchange Scale, which is designed to evaluate the exchange of paired resources at the workplace and the satisfaction with these exchanges		Correlation analysis
Brinberg & Castell (1982)	Experimental	60 university students	Similarity/dissimilarity ratings and likelihood to exchange among 12 stimuli (behaviors) representing the six types of resources		Multi-dimensional scaling
Sabbagh et al. (1994)	Survey	9,140 Israeli middle school students	Similarity/dissimilarity of 16 resource-specific distribution preferences		Smallest space analysis
Sabbagh (2005)	Survey	3,331 East German high school students	Similarity/dissimilarity of 16 resource-specific distribution preferences		Smallest space analysis
Haslam (1995)	Survey	50 university students in the United States	Integrates Fiske's relational classification and SRT. SRT is supported partially.		Factor analysis
Seers et al. (2006)		260 employees in different organizations	Uses the SRT resources to measure social exchange		Factor analysis

Recent SRT-Related Research Organizations and Marketing (Selected)

Arnould (2008)	SRT is of interest to marketers because of its effort to systematize consumer resources but has fallen out of favor, perhaps because of doubts about the robustness of the resource constructs and their underlying dimensions (i.e., concreteness and particularism). However, there was no elaboration on this point.
Chen et al. (2019)	Mentions SRT by referring to the reciprocal exchange of economic and interpersonal resources in organizations. However, their model and empirical examination do not refer to derived SRT.
Cooper-Thomas et al. (2018)	Uses the SRT typology of resources to predict engagement at work. However, there is no mention or use of the SRT dimensions of concreteness and particularism or their circular structure.
Dorsch et al. (2017)	Is theoretical in kind. SRT is one of multiple approaches to understand the role of economic versus interpersonal resources. However, there is no mention of methodologies through which SRT and its effects can be examined.
Farshid (2021)	The paper mentions SRT, but it focuses on a different mapping of resources. That is, SRT resources and their dimensions and circular structure are not mentioned. Also, there is no mention of the methodological implications of SRT.
Flynn (2003)	Briefly mentions SRT's resource types but the focus is social exchange theory. There is no mention or use of the SRT dimensions and circular structure for understanding social exchange.
Huang & Knight (2017)	The paper includes a theoretical elaboration of social exchange theory in the domain of entrepreneurship. It refers to the SRT's circumplex and how it helps to distinguish between economic and social resources. However, it does not specify possible methods for its examination.

(continued)

Appendix 12.1 Continued

Reference	Design	Subjects	Independent Variable	Dependent Variable	Statistical Method
Lemmon et al. (2016)		Develops a measure of resources and tests its factorial structure. However, there is no explicit reference to SRT's dimensions and its circular structure.			
Martin & Harder (1994)		It is a theoretical paper that discusses SRT in the organizational setting. But it only distinguishes between economic and interpersonal resources. The SRT dimensions are mentioned briefly.			
Mitchell et al. (2012)		It mentions SRT in the framework of social exchange theory, but it does not elaborate its methodological implications.			
Omilion-Hodges & Baker (2017)		It mentions the SRT's resources in the context of leadership. However, it does not refer to SRT's dimensions or circular structure.			
Rodrigues et al. (2019)		Discusses the SRT's circumplex, but it does not discuss its implication for deriving and testing hypotheses.			
Wilson et al. (2010)		This is a theoretical paper that uses the SRT dimension of particularism in the context of leadership. However, there is no mention of methodological implications of its framework.			

Recent SRT Related Research in Other Fields (Selected)

Reference	Design	Subjects	Independent Variable	Dependent Variable	Statistical Method
Margetts & Kashima (2017) Environment		Mentions SRT in the framework of environmental spillover. However, it only distinguishes between economic and interpersonal resources.			
Brown et al. (2014) Support groups		Refers to SRT by specifying four resources in its typology in the context of support groups. The aim was to develop a measurement of these resources, adapting them to the support groups setting. Using factor analysis and structural equation modeling findings revealed no distinction among resources. However, there is no mention of SRT dimensions and their circular structure.			

Appendix 12.2 Items Gauging Resource Distribution Practices in the Classroom by Facet

No.	Item	Resource	Modality
V1	When I need learning help, teachers grant it to me	Learning assistance	Actual
V2	When I need learning help, teachers *should* grant it to me	Learning assistance	Should
V3	My teachers are attentive to me within and outside class	Affection	Actual
V4	My teachers *should* be attentive to me within and outside class	Affection	Should
V5	My teachers treat me with respect when I present my views, even if they are critical	Respect	Actual
V6	My teachers *should* treat me with respect when I present my views, even if they are critical	Respect	Should
V7	I feel that my teachers impart knowledge	Knowledge	Actual
V8	I *expect* from my teachers to impart knowledge	Knowledge	Should
V9	I feel that teachers respect me as a person	Respect	Actual
V10	I think that teachers *should* respect me as a person	Respect	Should
V11	I feel that my teachers are interested in my personal life	Outlier	Actual
V12	I think my teachers *should* be interested in my personal life	Outlier	Should
V13	I feel that my teachers spend time with me in order to help me with learning problems	Learning assistance	Actual
V14	I think teachers *should* spend time with me in order to help me with learning problems	Learning assistance	Should
V15	The knowledge imparted to me at school is of high quality	Knowledge	Actual
V16	I think that the knowledge imparted to me at school *should* be of high quality	Knowledge	Should
V17	I feel that teachers treat me with sympathy	Affection	Actual
V18	I feel that teachers *should* treat me with sympathy	Affection	Should
V19	When I need advice, my teachers are available and willing to hear me	Affection	Actual
V20	When I need advice, my teachers *should* be available and willing to hear me	Affection	Should

References

Arnould, E. J. (2008). Service-dominant logic and resource theory. *Journal of the Academy of Marketing Science, 36*(1), 21–24.

Berg, J. H., & Wiebe, F. A. (1993). Resource exchange in the workplace: Exchange of economic and interpersonal resources. In U. G. Foa, K. Y. Törnblom, E. B. Foa, & J. Converse, Jr. (Eds.), *Resource theory: Explorations and applications* (pp. 97–122). Academic Press.

Borg, I., & Lingoes, J. C. (1987). *Multidimensional similarity structure analysis.* Springer.

Borg, I., & Shye, S. (1995). *Facet theory: Form and content.* Springer.

Brinberg, D., & Castell, P. (1982). A resource exchange theory approach to interpersonal interactions: A test of Foa's theory. *Journal of Personality and Social Psychology, 43*(2), 260–269.

Brown, L. D, Tang, X., & Hollman, R. L. (2014). The structure of social exchange in self-help support groups: Development of a measure. *American Journal of Community Psychology, 53*(1–2), 83–95.

Browne, M. W. (1992). Correlation matrices for circumplex models. *Psychometrika, 57,* 469–497.

Browne, M. W., & du Toit, S. (1995). *Circum: Notes on usage.* Browne.

Chen, A., & Lin, Y.-C. (2019). Speak to your heart: The joint moderating effects of language proficiencies on cultural intelligence and expatriates' work performance. *Corporate Management Review, 39*(1), 119–154.

Collins, L. M., & Lanza, S. T. (2009). *Latent class and latent transition analysis: With applications in the social, behavioral, and health sciences.* Wiley.

Cooper-Thomas, H. D, Xu, J., & Saks, A. M. (2018). The differential value of resources in predicting employee engagement. *Journal of Managerial Psychology, 33*(4–5), 326–344.

Cropanzano, R., & Mitchell, M. S. (2005). Social exchange theory: An interdisciplinary review. *Journal of Management, 31*(6), 874–900.

Donnenwerth, G. V., & Foa, U. G. (1974). Effect of resource class on retaliation to injustice in interpersonal exchange. *Journal of Personality and Social Psychology, 29*(6), 785–793.

Dorsch, M. J., & Brooks, C. L. (2012). Initiating customer loyalty to a retailer: A resource theory perspective. In K. Y. Törnblom, A. Kazemi (Eds.), *Handbook of social exchange theory* (pp. 311–331). Springer.

Dorsch, M. J., Törnblom, K. Y., & Kazemi, A. (2017). A review of resource theories and their implications for understanding consumer behavior. *Journal of the Association for Consumer Research, 2*(1), 5–25.

Ehrhardt-Madapathi, N., Pretsch, J., & Schmitt, M. (2018). Effects of injustice in primary schools on students' behavior and joy of learning. *Social Psychology of Education, 21*(2), 337–369.

Farshid, M., Lord Ferguson, S., Pitt, L., & Plangger, K. (2021). People as products: Exploring replication and corroboration in the dimensions of theory, method and context. *Journal of Business Research, 126,* 533–541.

Fiske, A. P.. (1991). *Structures of social life: The four elementary forms of human relations.* Free Press.

Flynn, F. J. (2003). How much should I give and how often? The effects of generosity and frequency of favor exchange on social status and productivity. *Academy of Management Journal, 46*(5), 539–553.

Foa, E. B., & Foa, U. G. (2012). Resource theory of social exchange. In K. Y. Törnblom & A. Kazemi (Eds.), *Handbook of social resource theory* (pp. 15–32). Springer.

Foa, U. G. (1961). Convergences in the analysis of the structure of interpersonal behavior. *Psychological Review, 68*(5), 341–353.

Foa, U. G. (1963). A facet approach to the prediction of communalities. *Behavioral Science, 8*(3), 220–226.

Foa, U. G. (1964). Cross-cultural similarity and difference in interpersonal behavior. *Journal of Abnormal and Social Psychology, 68*(5), 517–522.

Foa, U. G. (1965). New developments in facet design and analysis. *Psychological Review, 72*(4), 262–274.

Foa, U. G., & Foa, E. B. (1974). *Societal structures of the mind.* Charles C Thomas.

Foa, U. G., Salcedo, L. N., Tornblom, K. Y., Garner, M., Ubman, H. G., & Teichman, M. (1987). Interrelation of social resources: Evidence of pancultural invariance. *Journal of Cross-Cultural Psychology, 18*(2), 221–233.

Green, P. E., & Srinivasan, V. (1990). Conjoint analysis in marketing: New developments with implications for research and practice. *Journal of Marketing, 54*(4), 3–19.

Guttman, L. (1954). A new approach to factor analysis: The radex. In P. F. Lazarsfeld (Ed.), *Mathematical thinking in the social sciences* (pp. 258–348). Free Press.

Guttman, L. (1968). A general non-metric technique for finding the smallest coordinate space for a configuration of points. *Psychometrika, 33*, 469–506.

Guttman, L. (1982). What is not what in theory construction. In R. M. Hauser, D. Mechanic, & A. Haller (Eds.), *Social structure and behavior* (pp. 331–348). Academic Press.

Guttman, L. (1991). The language of science. In L. Guttman (Ed.), In memoriam: Chapters from an unfinished textbook on facet theory. Israel Academy of Sciences and Humanities and the Hebrew University of Jerusalem.

Haslam, N. (1995). Factor structure of social relationships: An examination of relational models and resource exchange theories. *Journal of Social and Personal Relationships, 12*(2), 217–227.

Hofstee, W. K., de Raad, B., & Goldberg, L. R. (1992). Integration of the Big Five and circumplex approaches to trait structure. *Journal of Personality and Social Psychology, 63*(1), 146–163.

Huang, L., & Knight, A. P. (2017). Resources and relationships in entrepreneurship: An exchange theory of the development and effects of the entrepreneur–investor relationship. *Academy of Management Review, 42*(1), 80–102.

Johnson, C., & Long, J.. (2019). The Berg/Wiebe Resource Exchange Scale: A reliability and validity study. *American Journal of Management, 19*(4), 65–82.

Kaufman, L., & Rousseeuw, P. J. (2009). *Finding groups in data: An introduction to cluster analysis.* Wiley.

Lachenbruch, P. A. (1975). *Discriminant analysis.* Hafner.

Lemmon, G., Glibkowski, B. C., Wayne, S. J., Chaudhry, A., & Marinova, S. (2016). Supervisor-provided resources: Development and validation of a measure of employee resources. *Journal of Leadership & Organizational Studies, 23*(3), 288–308.

Levy, S. (1985). Lawful roles of facets in social theories. In D. Canter (Ed.), *Facet theory: Approaches to social research* (pp. 59–96). Springer.

Levy, S. (Ed.). (1994). *Louis Guttman on theory and methodology: Selected writings.* Dartmouth Publishing.

Levy, S. (2005). Guttman, Louis. In *Encyclopedia of social measurement* (Vol. 2, pp. 175–188). Elsevier.

Lingoes, J. C. (1968). The multivariate analysis of qualitative data. *Multivariate Behavioral Research, 3*, 61–94.

416 PART II NEW THEORETICAL AND EMPIRICAL DEVELOPMENTS

Luce, R. D., & Tukey, J. W. (1964). Simultaneous conjoint measurement: A new type of fundamental measurement. *Journal of Mathematical Psychology, 1*(1), 1–27.

Margetts, E. A., & Kashima, Y. (2017). Spillover between pro-environmental behaviours: The role of resources and perceived similarity. *Journal of Environmental Psychology, 49,* 30–42.

Martin, J., & Harder, J. W. (1994). Bread and roses: Justice and the distribution of financial and socioemotional rewards in organizations. *Social Justice Research, 7*(3), 241–264.

Mitchell, M. S., Cropanzano, R. S., & Quisenberry, D. M. (2012). Social exchange theory, exchange resources, and interpersonal relationships: A modest resolution of theoretical difficulties. In K. Y. Törnblom & A. Kazemi (Eds.), *Handbook of social resource theory* (pp. 99–118). Springer.

Nagy, G., Etzel, J. M., & Lüdtke, O. (2019). Integrating covariates into circumplex structures: An extension procedure for Browne's circular stochastic process model. *Multivariate Behavioral Research, 54*(3), 404–428.

Omilion-Hodges, L. M., & Baker, C. R. (2017). Communicating leader–member relationship quality: The development of leader communication exchange scales to measure relationship building and maintenance through the exchange of communication-based goods. *International Journal of Business Communication, 54*(2), 115–145.

Parsons, T. (1967). *Sociological theory and the modern society.* Free Press.

Peter, F., & Dalbert, C. (2010). Do my teachers treat me justly? Implications of students' justice experience for class climate experience. *Contemporary Educational Psychology, 35,* 291–305.

Rencher, A. C., & Schaalje, G. B. (2008). *Linear models in statistics.* Wiley.

Rodrigues, M. D., de Oliveira Inácio, R., Botelho, D., & Shimabukuro Sandes, F. (2019). Interactive value formation: Types of crowdfunding and exchanged resources' characteristics. *Revista Administração em Diálogo, 21*(3), 74–86.

Sabbagh, C. (2005). Toward a multifaceted model of the structure of social justice judgments: Initial explorations in Israel and Germany. *Journal of Cross-Cultural Psychology, 35*(1), 74–95.

Sabbagh, C., Dar, Y., & Resh, N. (1994). The structure of social justice judgments: A facet approach. *Social Psychology Quarterly, 57*(3), 244–261.

Sabbagh, C., & Levy, S. (2012). Toward an expansion of resource exchange theory. In K. Y. Törnblom & A. Kazemi (Eds.), *Handbook of social resource theory* (pp. 67–80). Springer.

Seers, A., Wilkerson, J. M., & Grubb, W. L., III. (2006). Toward measurement of social exchange resources: Reciprocal contributions and receipts. *Psychological Reports, 98*(2), 508–510.

Snijders, T. A. B., & Bosker, R. J. (2011). *Multilevel analysis: An introduction to basic and advanced multilevel modeling.* SAGE.

Teichman, M., & Foa, U. G. (1975). Effect of resources similarity on satisfaction with exchange. *Social Behavior and Personality, 3*(2), 213–224.

Törnblom, K. Y., & Kazemi, A. (Eds.). (2012). *Handbook of social resource theory.* Springer.

Turner, J. L., Foa, E. B., & Foa, U. G. (1971). Interpersonal reinforcers: Classification, inter-relationship and some differential properties. *Journal of Personality and Social Psychology, 19,* 168–180.

Wilson, K. S., Sin, H.-P., & Conlon, D. E. (2010). What about the leader in leader–member exchange? The impact of resource exchanges and substitutability on the leader. *Academy of Management Review, 35*(3), 358–372.

Wubbels, T., & Brekelmans, M. (2005). Two decades of research on teachers–students relationships in class. *International Journal of Educational Research, 43,* 6–24.

PART III
HISTORICAL NOTES

How and Why This Volume Came Into Existence

The primary purpose of this book is threefold: (a) to present an abbreviated version of the original presentation of social resource theory (SRT) by Foa and Foa as published in the 1974 monograph *Societal Structures of the Mind*, (b) to present new theoretical developments of SRT, and (c) to provide an overview of some contemporary empirical research based on SRT.

Although Foa and Foa's original 1974 monograph has been out of print for a long time, SRT has remained a significant and relevant theoretical framework that has become increasingly influential and is currently experiencing something of a resurgence. The ideas in SRT have contributed to a wide variety of disciplines and have inspired and generated both basic and applied research in general psychology, social psychology, organizational psychology, sociology, consumer behavior, and other disciplines. The number of fields and subfields enriched and illuminated by resource theory is likely to grow.

A quote from Morton Deutsch (one of the most influential pioneers of social psychology) testifies to the value of making resource theory more visible to today's researchers. His statements were made in our *Handbook of Social Resource Theory* (Törnblom & Kazemi, 2012), which contains vivid evidence of the ways today's researchers are adopting, amplifying, and integrating ideas from SRT into their own work. He stated,

> I was enormously impressed when I first read Foa and Foa's *Resource Theory of Social Exchange* in 1980. It seemed to me that it opened up an area in social psychology which had largely been ignored. It shed new light on an important aspect of social interaction—the resources being exchanged— and it formulated many interesting, testable hypotheses. . . . I now realize it was an important complement to some of the theoretical ideas I had developed. (p. v)

Social Behavior as Resource Exchange. Kjell Yngve Törnblom and Ali Kazemi, Oxford University Press.
© Oxford University Press 2023. DOI: 10.1093/oso/9780190066994.003.0015

420 PART III HISTORICAL NOTES

The origin of the 1974 Foa and Foa monograph was actually Uriel Foa's ideas as presented in his influential brief article (seven pages) published 1971 in *Science*. In that article, he effectively addressed the surprising oversight by most theoretical and empirical social science research (e.g., and notably, by exchange theory in the behavioral sciences) to ask systematic questions about the nature of the transacted resources. Most discussions were based on economic foundations where monetary and related resources were more or less automatically assumed to be the primary and significant objects that were exchanged and amenable to objective measurements. Uriel Foa proposed that the social resource should be a primary unit of analysis and include not only economic but also symbolic resources. Resource was now defined as "any commodity—material or symbolic—which is transmitted through interpersonal behavior" (Foa & Foa, 1974, p. 36) or as "any item *concrete* or *symbolic*, which can become the object of exchange among people" (Foa & Foa, 1980, p. 78).

The limited accessibility of the 1974 monograph to younger generations of researchers prompted us to put together this revised version containing the most essential ideas from the original edition, supplemented with an update of SRT's theoretical and empirical status today. Subsequent to the publication of the Foas' 1974 monograph, two edited books focusing on SRT were published, but neither contained original materials from their book: *Resource Theory: Explorations and Applications* (U. Foa et al., 1993) and *Handbook of Social Resource Theory: Theoretical Extensions, Empirical Insights, and Social Applications* (Törnblom & Kazemi, 2012). The Foa and Foa SRT has inspired a significant number of theoretical developments and applications in various areas of inquiry as well as several attempts at integrating and combining SRT with other theories as clearly shown in Part II of this book.

We started discussing the benefits and possibilities regarding a re-publication of Foas' 1974 monograph approximately 5 years ago. At that point in time, we had, jointly as well as separately, already conducted theoretical and empirical research based on Foas' theory. Most of this work has been published as edited books, chapters, and journal articles. Other scholars in the social and behavioral sciences had also incorporated insights from SRT in their research. Unfortunately, because the Foa and Foa monograph has for many years been out of print and difficult to access, students and researchers often had to consult relatively brief and incomplete overviews of specific topics of the book in the form of scattered chapters or articles. We have long

HOW AND WHY THIS VOLUME CAME INTO EXISTENCE   421

believed that new generations of social scientists should be able to access and benefit from the many valuable insights in the Foas' 1974 monograph as they are increasingly central to many disciplines and a growing number of subfields, such as consumer behavior, organizational behavior, and management. In addition, and much due to currently growing social inequalities in different contexts at both micro and macro levels, we are likely to see an increase in thinking about how inequality and injustice operate across different types of resources.

Subsequently, we prepared a proposal to Oxford University Press for an edited book in which one part would consist of an abbreviated version of *Societal Structures of the Mind* and a second part would include five invited chapters featuring current developments of SRT. Our proposed project was enabled by Edna Foa, who transferred the rights to her and Uriel's book to Kjell. Uriel was one of his professors during his doctoral studies at the University of Missouri–Columbia, and Uriel's wife Edna was a doctoral student in clinical psychology and personality there as well. In addition to her full-time studies, she managed to find extra time and energy to collaborate with Uriel discussing the theory, rewriting and clarifying sections, suggesting elaborations, etc. Subsequent to the publication of the book, Edna focused completely on clinical psychology and did not pursue further research on SRT.

Uriel and Kjell started research collaboration when both had left Columbia, visiting each other in the United States and Sweden. Uriel was an early bird, going for a jog before Kjell awakened, fit for fight and creative thinking. Kjell's mind was not cleared from fog until after lunch, but then ready to go until well past midnight. As Uriel's alertness started to fade early evenings, their shared windows of productivity were limited to about 5 hours in the afternoons. Work during weekends was a no-no for Uriel.

After several years of university appointments in the United States and Canada, Kjell accepted an invitation from University of Skövde in Sweden where, in 1998, he met Ali Kazemi, an undergraduate social psychology student. Ali often visited Kjell's office to discuss theory and inspired him to put down several of his ideas on paper, which, coupled with Ali's own theorizing, resulted in a fruitful long-term collaboration with a focus on the combination between resources and social justice. Ali, a full professor since 2016, co-directed several of our projects involving resource theory (including our 2012 *Handbook of Social Resource Theory*) in addition to

422 PART III HISTORICAL NOTES

our 13-year-long task as co-editors-in-chief for the journal *Social Justice Research*.

Our proposal for this book to Oxford University Press went through a rigorous evaluation process involving four anonymous scholars, all of whom enthusiastically recommended acceptance. To quote one of the evaluators,

> The influence of SRT faded after Uriel Foa died in 1990 but never vanished completely. To the contrary, a recent revival of SRT can be witnessed in the literature. This revival is probably due, at least in part, to the fabulous *Handbook of Social Resource Theory: Theoretical Extensions, Empirical Insights, and Social Applications* (2012) edited by Törnblom & Kazemi—the authors of the present proposal. The new edition of *Societal Structures of the Mind* as proposed by Törnblom and Kazemi will most likely make an important contribution to the field.

The production of this book has not been a dance on roses. It required much more time and effort than we originally had anticipated. Apart from various unforeseen circumstances and technical problems, personal challenges intervened, and the pandemic resulted in frustrating delays. However, Oxford University Press has been very patient and understanding, granting us a couple of deadline extensions.

The presently selected and abbreviated chapters by Foa and Foa that are reprinted in this volume are followed by our presentation of recent developments of SRT as well as five invited chapters that present various applications and extensions of SRT. We hope that this book will spark interest in researchers but also graduate and undergraduate students in psychology, sociology, social psychology, education/pedagogy, social work, and management, studying and trying to understand social behavior in a broad sense. We also hope that this book prompts textbook writers, primarily at the undergraduate levels, to include the original formulation and further refinements and elaborations of SRT in their books to help SRT become more widely known and used than it has been to date.

The editors have contributed equally to this book.

Ali Kazemi and Kjell Y. Törnblom
Sweden, June 14, 2022

References

Foa, U. G. (1971). Interpersonal and economic resources. *Science, 171*(3969), 345–351.

Foa, U. G., Converse, J., Törnblom, K. Y., & Foa, E. G. (1993). Resource theory: Explorations and applications. Emerald Group.

Foa, U. G., & Foa, E. B. (1974). Societal structures of the mind. Charles C Thomas.

Törnblom, K., & Kazemi, A. (Eds.). (2012). *Handbook of social resource theory:* Theoretical extensions, empirical insights, and social applications. Springer.

Foa, E. B., & Foa, U. G. (1980). Resource theory: Interpersonal behavior as exchange. In K. J. Gergen, M. S. Greenberg, & R. H. Willis (Eds.), *Social exchange: Advances in theory and research* (pp. 77–94). Plenum Press.

What Is Included and Omitted from the Original Foa and Foa Monograph?

The original text contained 11 chapters and five appendixes. We have, except for some minor details and parts that have been removed, kept the full contents of four of those chapters (1, 2, 7, and 11), as well as Appendixes A–E. The list of references in the 1974 monograph has not been adjusted according to the omitted text materials, except for a few references whose accuracy we were unable to confirm. We have excluded the following parts from Chapter 3: pages 57–61 (the subsection titled Some Other Models of Developmental Sequence), pages 72–80 (the section titled The Perceptual Structure), and pages 83–89 (the section titled Empirical Testing of the Order Among Resources). The following part was omitted from Chapter 5: pages 150–160 (the section titled The Institutional Setting). Misspellings have been corrected. To avoid confusion, we have renumbered the chapters, tables, and figures we have retained from the original monograph.

We have also excluded five full chapters (4, 6, and 8–10). Each of those was omitted for different reasons. The main reason (in common for all five) is that their contents seem, besides being outdated in parts, to have had less impact on subsequent scholarly interest and theoretical or empirical developments compared to the ideas in the retained chapters. Chapter 4 focuses on family roles, Chapter 6 focuses on aftermath of exchange, Chapter 8 discusses cognitive matching and mismatching in communication, Chapter 9 analyzes interpersonal cross-cultural structures in different societies, and Chapter 10 attends to the interpersonal cognition of deviant individuals.

Social Behavior as Resource Exchange. Kjell Yngve Törnblom and Ali Kazemi, Oxford University Press.
© Oxford University Press 2023. DOI: 10.1093/oso/9780190066994.003.0016

Index

For the benefit of digital users, indexed terms that span two pages (e.g., 5–53) may, on occasion, appear on only one of those pages.

Tables, figures, and boxes are indicated by *t*, *f*, and *b* following the page number. Numbers preceded by n. indicate footnotes.

absolute abundance, 339
absolute scarcity, 339
abstract attraction, 143
abstract resources, 245–46
abundance
  absolute, 339
  dynamics of, 329–41
  formula for, 332
  global food system, 345–50
  layered systems of, 335–38
  motivations based on, 342–45
  quasi-abundance, 339–40
  quasi-SAS, 338–41
  social resource exchange in, 323–56
  strategies for coping with, 334, 334*t*
  theory of scarcity, abundance and
    sufficiency (SAS), 263–64, 324,
    329–38, 341–53
acceptance, 36–37. *See also* love
  definition of, 3, 54
  schematic representation of, 39*f*, 39
  self-acceptance, 64
accommodation, 30–31
acquisition
  vs. production, 256–58
  of resources, 258–60
acquisitive individualism, 278*f*, 279
action construal theory (ACT), 284–85,
  288–89, 290
  base model, 285–87, 286*f*
  componental rules, 284–85
  models of differing complexity,
    287*f*, 287–88
  syntactical rules, 284, 285
actor(s): generalization of, 136–38

actual behavior, 47, 55
actual needs, 86–88
actual power, 90–91
Adamopoulos, John, 227–28
Adler, A., 171
adualism, 37
adult structure, 57–78
advising, 33
affect: messages exchanged between adults
  that deal with, 41
affection. *See also* love
  exchange possibilities, 4
affiliation, need for, 84–85, 87
aggression, 127–28
  definition of, 127, 166
  displacement of, 134
  as exchange of taking, 122–40
  fantasy, 135
  frustration–aggression sequence, 5,
    122–40, 165–66
  frustration–aggression studies, 123–24
  object and actor in, 130–36
  self-aggression, 134–35
  vicarious, 136–38, 166
air, clean, 244
air pollution: interstate transport of, 303,
  308–15, 309*t*
algorithms, 275n.1
alienation, 116, 121
allocentrism, 271–72
altruism, 279–80
altruistic collectivism, 278*f*, 279
ambivalence, 64–65, 106–7, 250
American blacks, 164, 168–69, 178.
    See also Blacks

426 INDEX

analysis
  cluster, 404–5, 406–7
  correlation, 379–80
  discriminant, 404–5, 407
  factor (*see* factor analysis [FA])
  latent class, 404–5
  similarity structure, 380
  smallest space (*see* smallest space
    analysis [SSA])
  of variance, 378–79
anger, 364–65
Anselm of Canterbury, St., 366–67
anthropology, 15
appropriateness, 168
approval, need for, 84–85, 84*t*, 87
Aron, Arthur, 361–65
arousal, motivational, 327
assimilation
  generalizing, 30–31
  recognitory, 30–31
association, status by, 244–45
assumed similarity, 49
attachment, 361–62
attachment styles, 359
attraction, 361–62
  abstract, 143
  definition of, 167
  interpersonal, 5, 142–46
  social attractiveness, 43–44
attractiveness, 143, 167
attribution theory, 12
available resources (*A*), 329–31
avoidance, 17–18
awareness, 13–14

Bååth, Jonas, 229
Barker, Roger, 288
Bartels, Andreas, 229–30, 359–61
basic social concepts: development
  of, 29–56
behavior(s)
  actual, 47, 55
  advising, 33
  and brain functioning, 19–20
  classification of, 47
  construal of, 271–93
  descriptive models, 273
  of giving, 186

giving information, 33
giving love, 33
giving services, 33
ideal, 47, 55
imitative, 40
intercorrelations among love and status
    behaviors, 69–71, 70*t*
intercorrelations in different roles and
    cultures, 65–66, 66*t*
interpersonal, 24–27, 30–31, 33–34,
    165, 284–89
licit but roundabout patterns, 164–65
manipulative techniques, 155–65
meaning of, 20–21
motivations for, 80–104
negative (*see* taking away)
negativistic, 53–55
normative models, 273
semantic features, 33–34
social, 80–104
statements describing, 186
and structuring, 24–27
techniques for controlling, 93–94
undifferentiated, 30–31
behavioral classes
  differentiation sequence, 58–60, 60*f*,
    62–63, 63*t*, 77
  vs. norms and viewpoints, 47
behavioral structure, 63–74. *See also*
    structure(s)
behavior setting, 288
behavior units, 288–89
belonging, sense of, 112
Berscheid, Ellen, 370, 371
bipolar model, 388–91, 389*f*
  covariances (Cov), variances
    (Var), standard deviations
    (SD), and correlations (Cor),
    390, 390*t*
  factor loadings, 389–90, 390*t*
blackmail, 156, 163
black markets, 340–41
Blacks
  American blacks, 164, 168–69, 178
  Eno Road, Tennessee, 304
  pollution-burdened communities, 304
black studies, 164
Bloomberg, Michael, 302

boundaries, 34–36
cognitive, 35
development of, 50–54
brain function
behavior and, 19–20
in passionate love, 359–61, 360*f*, 363–64, 365–66
Brown, Lucy, 361–65

Cacioppo, Stephanie, 229–30
capital
cultural, 260
human, 260
social, 260
capital resources, 260. *See also* resource(s)
capital theory, 260
caring. *See also* love
in environmental conflicts, 312, 313, 314*t*
case studies, 301–8
categorization, 20
caudate nucleus, 363
causal attribution, 15
CFA (confirmatory factor analysis), 382, 399–400
change vs. stability, 172–73
charity, 168–69
child development, 15, 29, 54–56
children, negativistic, 53–55
circular response, 38
classification systems, 240
classroom settings
empirical examination of SRT in, 393–403
resource distribution practices in, 393–94, 394*t*, 395–99, 396*t*, 398*f*, 399*t*, 400–1, 400*f*, 401*f*, 413*t*
types of resources that teachers distribute to students in, 393–94
clean air, 244
clean water, 244
clientelism, 340–41
climate change, 315–16
cluster analysis, 404–5, 406–7
coercive power, 88–89
cognition, 9–14
awareness and, 13–14
congruence between event and, 11–13

definition of, 3
descriptive models, 273
inducing dissonance by cognitive change, 100–1
normative models, 273
and perceived events, 12
processing input, 110
of social events, 3, 54
study of, 20–21
cognitive boundaries, 35
cognitive complexity, 16–17
cognitive development, 24, 30–36
resource properties and, 113–14
summary, 54–56
cognitive growth, 54
definition of, 3
differentiation and, 32–34
dissonance and, 104
cognitive psychology, 288–89
cognitive structure(s), 170–75. *See also* structure(s)
abstract, 11–12
perceived, 11–12
preservation from dissonant events, 94–104
of resource classes, 74–77, 76*f*
societal, xiii–xvii
collectivism, 271–72, 278*f*
altruistic, 278*f*, 279
associations with resources, 277–79
connections with different habitats, 281–83, 282*f*
horizontal, 277–79, 278*f*
ideational, 278*f*, 279
referential, 278*f*, 279
relational, 278*f*, 279
vertical, 277–79, 278*f*
commitment: effects of, 99–100
communality, 382–83
communication
interpersonal, 24–27
messages exchanged between adults, 41
verbalization of need, 108, 250
community development, pollution-burdened, 304, 308–15, 309*t*
companionate love, 362
competence, 43–44
composite resources, 245

428 INDEX

computation, 275n.1
concreteness
  empirical/concrete instances, 236–37
  in environmental conflicts, 295, 311–12
  of interpersonal resources, 3–4, 74–77,
    76f, 78, 239–40, 245
condition resources, 235–36, 235b
confidence plots, 163
confirmatory factor analysis (CFA), 382,
    399–400
conflicts, 297–99
  case studies, 301–8
  environmental, 295–308, 313, 314t
  of interest, 298
  justice, 300–8
  rangeland, 305–6
  resource, 298
  of values, 298
conformity, 5, 157–60, 168–69
conjoint measurement, 404–6
conservation
  community, 302, 307–8
  wildlife, 306–15, 309t
Conservation of Resources (COR)
    Theory, 261
construct validity, 16–17
contact resources, 235–36, 235b
content resources, 235–36, 235b
contiguity, 71
coordinates, 14–15
COR (Conservation of Resources)
    Theory, 261
correlation analysis, 379–80
costs
  of economic development, 176–77
  of non-economic poverty, 175–76
COVID-19 pandemic, 315
crime, 115–16, 121
criticism, self-, 39–40, 39f
cultural capital, 260
cultural psychology, 335
culture, 272–73, 289–90
  blueprint for meaning, 25
  collectivist, 277–79, 278f
  environmental constraints
    and, 280–83
  individual deviance from, 26–27
  individualistic, 277, 278f

integrating resource theory with types
    of, 276–80
intercorrelations among types of
    behavior, 65–66, 66t
level of explanation, 273–75,
    274f, 276–83
patterns of resource exchange, 277–80,
    278f
reinforcement contingencies
    and, 25–26

Damara people, 306
Daoud, Adel, 229
delay of reinforcement, 123
delay of reward, 110–11, 254
delivering, 255
denial, 255, 313
dependence, need for, 84–85
deprivation, 125–26
derogation, 124
descriptive models, 273
desire
  vs. norms and viewpoints, 47–48
  sexual, 361–62, 364, 370–72
Deutsch, Morton, 297–98, 419
development
  of basic social concepts, 29–56
  of boundaries, 50–54
  child, 15, 29, 54–56
  cognitive, 24, 30–36, 54–56
  community, 304, 308–15, 309t
  differentiation sequences, 58–63
  economic, 176–77
  psychological, 24
  urban, 302
differentiation(s), 23–24, 275–76
  behavioral sequence, 58–60, 60f, 62–63,
    63t, 77
  and cognitive growth, 32–34
  developmental sequences, 58–63
  of direction, 37, 39, 39f
  facets of, 35
  and generalization, 31–32
  between goods and money, 42–43,
    43f, 55
  between goods and services, 42, 43f, 55
  between information and status, 42–43,
    43f, 44, 55

INDEX 429

between love and esteem or status, 41–
42, 43–45, 43f, 55, 59, 60f
of mode, 37, 39, 39f
by object, 50, 59
perceptual sequence, 60–63, 62f,
63t, 77–78
by power, 133–34
of resource classes, 41–45, 43f
self–other, 37–40, 39f, 54–55
of social events, 58–63, 63t
and social growth, 36
by viewpoint, 48–50, 61–62
diffusion, 34
dimensional learning, 29
dimensions, 14–15
direct retaliation, 166–67
disbenefits, 303
discriminant analysis, 404–5, 407
displaced retaliation, 166–67
displacement, 132–34, 166
of aggression, 134
definition of, 136
symbolic, 135–36
towards a third individual, 132–34
dissonance, 94, 103–4
and cognitive growth, 104
definition of, 95–98
induction by cognitive change, 100–1
preservation of structure from
dissonant events, 94–104
and psychopathology, 101–3
vs. reinforcement, 98–100
schematic representation of, 96–97, 97f
and visual illusions, 104
ways to resolve, 95
dissonance theory, 95
distribution
of resources, 258, 259–60
of wealth, 349–50
distributive justice, 122, 147–49, 168, 262
DNA, 18–19
drive for meaning, 94
drive for understanding, 94
drugs, 117, 121
dynamics, 23–24

ecological psychology, 312
economic development, 176–77

economic exchange
costs of non-economic poverty, 175–76
laws of, 114
economic resources, 171. *See also*
resource(s)
designation, 235–36, 235b
economics, neoclassical, 324–25
EFA. *See* exploratory factor analysis
egocentric individualism, 278f, 279
ego-protective individualism, 278f, 279
ego-sustaining individualism, 278f, 279
ego threat, 124
Einstein, Albert, 14–15, 172–73
empirical/concrete instances, 236–37
empirical examination
in classroom settings, 393–403
new developments, 225–322
Endangered Species Act (ESA), 305
energy resource(s). *See also* resource(s)
designations, 233, 235–36, 235b
types of, 244
Eno Road, Tennessee, 304
entitlements *(E),* 336–38
definition of, 336–37
types of, 336–37
wealth, 348–50
environmental conditions, 80, 295–300
constraints, 280–83
and culture, 280–83
current issues, 295
and development of boundaries, 50–54
Foas' resource classes in, 308–15, 309t
and individualism/collectivism, 281–
83, 282f
resource properties, 110–13, 121
social behavior as function of people
and, 312
urban environment, 115–17, 121
environmental injustice, 300–1
environmental racism, 304
environmental resources, 297
conflicts over, 298–99, 300–15,
309t, 314t
rangeland, 305–6
and social justice, 312–15
wildlife, 306–7
equality–inequality, 382–83
equitable relationships, 368–69

430 INDEX

equity, 5, 149, 168, 262
  assessing, 367–68
  definition of, 367
  in love relationships, 368–69, 369*f*
  resources and, 152–55
  and satisfaction, 368, 369*f*
  tendency toward, 150–52
equity theory, 366–67
ESA (Endangered Species Act), 305
esteem. *See also* status
  differentiation from love, 42
  self-esteem, 55–56
exchange(s). *See also* resource exchange(s);
    social resource exchange
  economic, 114, 175–76
  fairness in, 146–55
  interpersonal relationship and, 253–54
  laws of, 114
  physical proximity and, 252–53
  range of, 251
  rules of, 249–54, 325–26, 341
  theoretical formulations of, 147–50
exchangeability, 250–51
exchange partners, 140–42
exchange theory, xiii–xiv
exclusionary contexts, 313–15, 315*t*
exhaustiveness, 242
experimental designs, 378–79
expert power, 88–89
exploratory factor analysis
    (EFA), 382
  of classroom resource distribution
    practices, 400–1, 401*f*, 403
  illustration of use, 383

facet(s), 35
facet elements, 35
facet theory, 376
factor analysis (FA), 22–23, 230, 377–78,
    382–91, 409
  bipolar model, 388–91, 389*f*, 390*t*
  of classroom resource distribution
    practices, 399–403, 401*f*, 402*t*
  confirmatory, 382, 399–400
  exploratory, 382–83, 400–1, 401*f*, 403
  illustrations of use, 382–83
  three-dimensional factor model,
    391, 393*f*

two-dimensional factor model, 383–88,
    384*f*, 385*t*, 387*t*, 388*t*, 389*t*, 391
  unipolar three-factor model, 391, 392*f*,
    392*t*
fairness
  in exchange, 146–55
  intuitive notion of, 299
familial resources, 235–36
family size, 112
famine, 345–50
fantasy aggression, 135
father figures, 59, 133
father–mother generalization, 31–32
Female Resource Theory, 261
field theory, 294
Fisher, Helen, 229–30, 361–65
Foa, Edna, 421
Foa, Uriel, 376, 420, 421, 422
Foa, Uriel and Edna, xiii. See also *Societal*
    Structures of the Mind
food system, global, 345–50
foreign aid, 148–49
Freud, Sigmund, 15, 37, 171
Friedman, Milton, 324–25
friendship, 33
frustration, 123–26
  definition of, 123
  and delay of reinforcement, 52–54
frustration–aggression sequence, 5,
    140, 165–66
  as exchange of taking, 122–40
  object and actor in, 130–36
frustration–aggression studies, 123–24
function, structure and, 23–24
functional magnetic resonance imaging
    (fMRI), 359–61, 360*f*, 362–63, 364,
    365, 366

general linear modeling (GLM), 407–8
generalization, 15–16, 54
  of actor, 136–38
  differentiation and, 31–32
  father–mother, 31–32
  response, 34
generalizing assimilation, 30–31
generosity, 85–86
Gestalt school, 17, 294
Gestalt theory, 288

INDEX 431

giving, 45–46, 50–51, 64–65, 254–56
  correlations between love and status behaviors, 69–71, 70*t*
  correlations between taking away and, 68, 69*t*
  definition of, 45, 54, 254–55
  schematic representation of, 39, 39*f*
  to self and other, 66–67, 66*t*, 249
  social interaction inventory for, 187–92
  statements describing behaviors of, 186
  and taking away, 250
giving goods, 45
giving information, 33
giving love, 33, 45
giving money, 45
giving services, 33, 45
giving status, 45
global food system, 345–50
goods, 325, 376–77
  differentiation from money, 42–43, 43*f*, 55
  differentiation from services, 42, 43*f*, 55
  in environmental conflicts, 311–12, 313, 314*t*
  example instances, 236–37
  exchange between adults, 41
  giving, 45
  needs that refer to, 84–85, 84*t*
  resource classification, xiv, 41
  statements describing behaviors of giving, 186
  taking away, 45
Gowanus Canal (Brooklyn, New York), 302, 307–15, 309*t*
Greeley, Andrew, 370–71
Greenberg, Jerald, 326–27
grief, 365
group encounters, 121
group interaction inventory, 193–200
groups
  larger, 112
  optimum size, 111–13, 254
growth
  cognitive, 32–34, 104
  dissonance and, 104
  social, 36
Guttman, Louis, 376

handwriting, 19–20
Hatfield, Elaine, 229–30, 370, 371
Hazan, Cindy, 359
Hendrick, Clyde and Susan, 359, 371
Herbert, Bob, 304
Herero people, 306
hierarchical modeling, 404–5, 408
Histoire de Dom Bougre, 370
homeostasis, 81
housing, 315–16
human capital, 260
human nature, 171
hypotheses, testable, 241

Id, 15
ideal behavior, 47, 55
ideational collectivism, 278*f*, 279
idiocentrism, 271–72
IET (Interpersonal Evaluation Theory), 263
illusions, visual, 104
imitation, 40, 52
  basis for, 40
  classification of, 40
  types of, 40
impostors, 163
inclusionary contexts, 313–15, 315*t*
incongruity, 94
independence, need for, 84–85
individual differences
  deviance from culture, 26–27
  in optimal range, 83
  in preferences for resources, 262
individual/psychological resources, 311, 312. *See also* resource(s)
individualism, 271–72, 277
  acquisitive, 278*f*, 279
  connections with different habitats, 281–83, 282*f*
  ego-protective, 278*f*, 279
  ego-sustaining, 278*f*, 279
  egocentric, 278*f*, 279
  horizontal, 277–79, 278*f*
  vertical, 277–79, 278*f*
inequality, 340–41, 382–83
inequity, 349–50
infant–father interactions, 59
infant–mother interactions, 59

432 INDEX

influenceability, 158–59
information, 376–77
  correlations between giving and taking
    away of, 68, 69t
  differentiation from status, 42–43,
    43f, 44, 55
  in environmental conflicts, 312,
    313, 314t
  giving, 33
  messages exchanged between adults
    that deal with, 41
  needs that refer to, 84–85, 84t
  resource classification, xiv, 41
  statements describing behaviors of
    giving, 186
  taking away, 45
information processing, 171
informational power, 88–89
ingratiation, 5, 155–57, 168–69
injustice
  environmental, 300–1
  normalized, 299–300
input processing time, 110
institutional settings, 273–75
institutions, 336
insult-failure technique, 124
integrated psychological
    theory, 27–28
integrated resource models, 261
integration, 23–24
intelligence, 22
interaction. See social interaction
International Monetary Fund
    (IMF), 347–48
interpersonal attraction, 5, 142–46
interpersonal behavior, 165
  cognitive structures in, 4
  construal of acts, 284–89
  event level, 273–75, 274f, 283–89
  licit but roundabout patterns, 164–65
  manipulative techniques, 155–65
  semantic features, 33–34
  undifferentiated, 30–31
interpersonal communication, 24–27
Interpersonal Evaluation Theory
    (IET), 263
interpersonal relationships, 253–54,
    376–77

interpersonal resources, 40–45, 74–77. See
    also resource(s)
  classification of, 3–4, 55
  definition of, 3
  designation, 235–36, 235b
  particularism of, 3–4, 74–77, 76f,
    78, 239–40
irradiation, 34
Israel
  foreign aid, 148–49
  intercorrelations among love and
    status behaviors, 65–66, 66t, 67,
    69–71, 70t

Jerusalem, Israel: intercorrelations among
    love and status behaviors, 65–66, 66t,
    69–71, 70t
justice, 257–58, 299–300, 366–67
  distributive, 122, 147–49, 168, 262
  in environmental contexts, 295–300
  environmental injustice, 300–1
  normalized injustice, 299–300
  procedural, 262
  scope of, 294, 300
  social, 262, 312–16, 366–67, 368
justice conflicts, 300–8

Kazemi, Ali, 419–23
Kelly, G. A., 15
Key resource theories, 261
Keynes, John Maynard, 333–34
kleptocracy, 340–41
Kunene (Namibia): wildlife conservation,
    306–15, 309t

language, xv
latent class analysis, 404–5
laws of exchange, 114
learning
  dimensional, 29
  imitation model, 52
  reinforcement model, 52
Levi-Strauss, C. L., 15
Lewin, Kurt, 14–15, 312
licit but roundabout patterns, 164–65
life span resource models, 261
linguistics, 15
losing, 254–55

love, 113–14, 171, 229–30, 376–77. *See also* acceptance
  behaviors of, 69–71, 70*t*
  companionate, 362
  correlations between giving and taking away of, 68, 69*t*
  correlations with status, 69–71, 70*t*, 386
  covariance with status, 386
  dark side of, 364–65
  differentiation from esteem or status, 42, 43–45, 43*f*, 55, 59, 60*f*
  differentiation from services, 41–42, 43–44, 43*f*, 55
  equity in love relationships, 368–69, 369*f*
  exchange possibilities, 4
  giving, 33, 45
  joys of, 362–64
  laws of exchange, 114
  maternal, 230
  messages exchanged between adults that deal with, 41
  needs of exchange partners, 141
  needs that refer to, 84–85, 84*t*
  neuropsychological explorations of, 359–65
  optimal range, 82–83
  passionate, 358–65, 360*f*, 366, 370–72
  paternal, 230
  poverty of, 174
  resource classification, xiv, 41
  romantic, 244, 370
  and sexual desire, 370–72
  simultaneous transmission with another resource, 252
  social exchange in love relationships, 366–72
  statements describing behaviors of giving, 186
  and status, 60*f*, 66*t*, 67–69
  structural equation for, 384–85
  triangular theory of, 359
  types of, 248
  types of behavior in different roles and cultures, 65–66, 66*t*
  variances, 385
love styles, 359
lovers' quarrels, 80

LSD (lysergic acid diethylamide), 117
lust, 362, 366

Machiavellianism, 5, 155, 160–64, 168–69
macro processes, 352–53
magnetic resonance imaging, functional (fMRI), 359–61, 360*f*, 362–63, 364, 365, 366
Malheur National Wildlife Refuge, 305
manipulative techniques, 155–65, 168–69
marihuana, 117
marketing, 410*t*
Marx, Karl, 171
Mashek, Deborah, 362
mastery, 235–36
material resources, 235–36, 235*b*. *See also* resource(s)
maternal love
  differentiation of, 230
  father–mother generalization, 31–32
  infant–mother interactions, 59
meaning, 244–45
  cultural blueprint for, 25
  drive for, 94
  study of, 20–21
mentalization, 361
metatheoretical considerations, 71–74
methodological problems, 177–78
misery, 364–65
modern society, 173–75
money, 325, 376–77
  differentiation from goods, 42–43, 43*f*, 55
  in environmental conflicts, 312, 313, 314*t*
  exchange between adults, 41
  exchange possibilities, 4
  giving, 45
  laws of exchange, 114
  needs of exchange partners, 141
  needs that refer to, 84–85, 84*t*
  resource classification, xiv, 41
  statements describing behaviors of giving, 186
  taking away, 45
mothers, 59
motivation, 80–104, 171
  abundance-based, 342–45
  resource properties that affect, 106–10

434 INDEX

motivational arousal, 327
motivational style, 290
multidimensional scaling, 380–82
multilevel modeling, 404–5, 408
multiple-component resource
    theories, 261
multivariate statistics, 404–8
mutual exclusiveness, 241

Namibia: Kunene region wildlife
    conservation, 306–15, 309*t*
narcissism, primary, 37
natural resources, 244, 301
  conflicts over, 298–99, 300–8
  definition of, 296
  rangeland, 305–6
  wildlife, 306–7
nature, human, 171
need (term), 85–86
need(s), 83–88, 119–20, 125–26
  actual and potential, 86–88
  definition of, 79, 81, 83, 326–27, 329
  examples, 84–85, 84*t*
  of exchange partners, 140–42
  objective vs felt, 326–27
  vs. requirements, 330–31
  verbalization of, 108, 250
negative behavior. *See* taking away
negativistic behavior, 53–55
neoclassical economics, 324–25
network resources, 260. *See also*
    resource(s)
  designation, 235–36, 235*b*
neuropsychology, 359–65
new social forms, 178–79
new theoretical and empirical
    developments, 225–322
New York: Gowanus Canal (Brooklyn),
    302, 308–15, 309*t*
NIMBY (not-in-my-backyard)
    protests, 301
normalized injustice, 299–300
normative models, 273
norms, 46–50
not-self, 37

object(s)
  differentiation by, 50
  variety of, 262–63

object resources, 235–36, 235*b*. *See also*
    resource(s)
observer(s), 61–62
Opotow, Susan, 228–29
optimal conditions, 79
optimal range, 79, 81–83, 327
optimum, resource, 327–28, 352
optimum group size, 111–13, 254
order, 73–74
other
  displacement towards a third
    individual, 132–34
  giving and taking away from, 66–67,
    66*t*, 69–71, 70*t*
  giving resources to, 249
  relationship between self and, 106
  self and/or other, 3, 54–55, 59, 64
  self–other differentiations, 37–40,
    39*f*, 54–55
  techniques for controlling, 93–94
  viewpoint of, 48, 49–50
other (term), 49–50
oversatiation, 328
Ozone Transport Assessment Group
    (OTAG), 303

pair bonding, 366. *See also* love
parsimony, 240–41
part (term), 17–18
particularism
  in environmental conflicts,
    295, 311–12
  of interpersonal resources, 3–4, 74–77,
    76*f*, 78, 239–40
passionate love, 358–65
  brain regions involved in, 359–61,
    360*f*, 366
  dark side, 364–65
  definition of, 371
  neuropsychological explorations
    of, 359–65
  vs. sexual desire, 370–72
Passionate Love Scale (PLS), 359
paternal love
  differentiation of, 230
  father figures, 59, 133
  father–mother generalization, 31–32
pay-off matrix, 149–50, 168
perceived cognitive structures, 11–12

perceived events, 12
perceptual classes, 60–63, 62*f*, 63*t*, 77–78
personal resources, 235–36, 235*b*. *See also* resource(s)
personality traits, 262
physical proximity, 252–53
physical resources, 311–12. *See also* resource(s)
Piaget, Jean, 15, 30–31, 33, 38, 53–54
pollution
    case studies, 302–4, 308–15, 309*t*
    communities burdened by, 304, 308–15, 309*t*
    Gowanus Canal (Brooklyn, New York), 302
    interstate transport of, 303, 308–15, 309*t*
    remediation of, 302
    urban, 302
positive psychology, xvi
positive organizational scholarship, xvi
potential needs, 86–88
potential power, 90–91
poverty
    global, 315
    love, 174
    non-economic, 175–76
power, 88–93, 326, 344
    accumulation of, 92–93
    actual and potential, 90–91
    classes of, 4, 89
    coercive, 88–89
    definition of, 4, 79, 88–89, 244n.5
    differentiation by, 133–34
    expert, 88–89
    informational, 88–89
    legitimate, 88–89
    of the powerless, 93–94
    referent, 88–89
    social influence, 244
    symmetry of, 90–91
    transitivity of, 92
    types of, 88–89
powerless people, 93–94
proaction–reaction sequence, 40
procedural justice, 262
procedure, 258
process resources, 235–36, 235*b*. *See also* resource(s)

process rewards, 243–44
production
    vs. acquisition, 256–58
    of resources, 258–60
profit, 149
Protestant ethic, 342–45
psychological development, 24
psychological dimension, 14–15
psychological resources. *See also* resource(s)
    classification of, 311, 312
    designation, 235–36, 235*b*
psychology, 15
    cultural, 335
    ecological, 312
    integrated psychological theory, 27–28
psychopathology, 101–3
psychosocial resources, 235–36, 235*b*. *See also* resource(s)
public goods, 257

quality, resource, 376–77
quality of life, 176–77
    resources for, 235–36, 235*b*, 237–38, 242
    social indicators, 175–78
quasi-abundance, 339–40
quasi-SAS, 338–41
quasi-scarcity, 339, 345

racism, environmental, 304
rangelands, 305–6, 307–15, 309*t*
Rapson, Richard L., 229–30
rational choice theory (RCT), 323–25
rational process models, 275n.1
RBT (Resource-Based Theory of the Firm), 261
RCT (rational choice theory), 323–25
RDPs. *See* resource distribution practices
reaction, 125–26
receiving, 254–55
reciprocity, 129–30, 147
recognitory assimilation, 30–31
referent power, 88–89
referential collectivism, 278*f*, 279
Regan, Pamela, 371
reinforcement, 52
    delay of, 52–54, 123
    vs. dissonance, 98–100

436 INDEX

reinforcement theory, 95
rejection, 36–37, 59, 364–65
  definition of, 3, 54
  schematic representation of, 39, 39f
  self-rejection, 39–40, 39f
relational collectivism, 278f, 279
relationships
  equitable, 368–69
  equity in, 368–69, 369f
  interpersonal, 253–54, 376–77
  love, 366–72, 369f
  between self and other, 106
  social exchange in, 366–72
  wife–husband, 181–84, 185t
research
  classic, 368–69
  classroom empirical examination of
    SRT, 393–403
  on equity in love relationships, 368–69
  evaluative studies of SRT, 376–416, 410t
  evidence for the tendency toward
    equity, 150–52
  experimental designs, 378–79
  frustration–aggression studies, 123–24
  neuropsychological explorations of
    passionate love, 359–65
  new developments, 225–322
  new empirical developments, 225–322
  recent, 410t
  selected studies, 378–83
  socio-psychological, 122–69
resource(s), xiii. See also social resource(s);
    specific resources
  abstract, 245–46
  acquisition of, 256–60
  allocations of, 257–58
  associations with individualism/
    collectivism, 277–79
  available, 329–31
  capacity for convertibility, 246–47
  capital, 260
  classification of, 236–37, 261, 376–77
  collectively owned, 257
  composite, 245
  configurations, 237–38
  conflicts over, 298
  Conservation of Resources (COR)
    Theory, 261

contexts, 228–29
deficits, 5
definition of, 40–41, 235, 237b, 296,
  325, 357, 420
designations, 233–37, 235b, 261, 264
differences, 80
distribution of, 258, 259–60
economic, 171
energy, 244
environmental, 297, 300–8, 312–15
in environmental contexts, 280–
  83, 295–97
and equity, 152–55
exchangeability, 250–51
in exclusionary contexts, 313–15,
  315t
Female Resource Theory, 261
in frustration–aggression
  studies, 123–24
higher-order, 244–45
in inclusionary contexts, 313–15, 315t
individual preferences for, 262
individual/psychological, 311, 312
intangible, 246
inter-class differences, 248
interpersonal, 3–4, 40–45, 55, 74–77,
  76f, 78, 239–40, 245
intra-class differences, 248
key resource and multiple component
  resource theories, 261
manipulative techniques to
  get, 155–65
natural, 244, 296, 301
network, 235b, 235–36, 260
optimal range, 79, 81–83, 327
origin of, 257
other related theories, 260–61
physical, 311–12
production of, 256–60
properties, 104–19
quality of, xiii, 376–77
quantities of, xiii
seeking, 171–72
and social justice, 312–16
social nature of, 323–24
societal, 311–12
sources, 248–49
subtypes, 236–37

symbolic, 245–46
tangible, 246
types that become objects of exchange among individuals, 376–77
types that teachers distribute to classroom students, 393–94
typology of, xiv
verbalization of need for, 250
resource amount, 252
Resource-Based Theory of the Firm (RBT), 261
resource classes, 295, 325. *See also* social resource class(es)
in environmental contexts, 308–15, 309*t*, 314*t*
qualities of, 341
rules of exchange for, 325–26
subclasses, 236–37, 247–49
resource distribution practices (RDPs)
in classroom settings, 393–94, 394*t*, 395–403, 396*t*, 398*f*, 399*t*, 400*f*, 401*f*, 402*t*, 413*t*
factor analysis (FA) of, 399–403, 401*f*, 402*t*
smallest space analysis (SSA) of, 395–99, 396*t*, 398*f*, 399*t*, 400*f*, 400, 403
resource exchange(s), 296. *See also* giving; taking away
cultural level explanation for, 273–75, 274*f*, 276–83
cultural patterns, 277–80, 278*f*
environmental conditions for, 80
fairness in, 146–55
Foas' new rules for, 249–54
interclass, 325–26
interpersonal, 253–54, 273–75, 274*f*, 283–89
laws of, 114
levels of explanation for, 271–93, 274*f*
licit but roundabout patterns, 164–65
manipulative techniques, 155–65, 168–69
moderators, 290
modes of, 254–56, 265
needs of exchange partners, 140–42
optimal condition for, 79
physical proximity and, 252–53
prelude to, 79–121

simultaneous transmission with love, 252
social behavior as, xiii–xvii
theoretical formulations of, 147–50
universal level explanation for, 273–76, 274*f*
Resource Exchange Theories, 261
resource models, 261
resource optimum, 327–28, 352
resource profile, 248–49
resource reciprocity, 129–30
resource theory, 261. *See also* social resource theory (SRT)
resource transformations, 259
resource valence, 255, 257
response generalization, 34
restitution, 138–40
restoration, 138–40, 166–67
restructuring, 23–24
retaliation
direct, 131–32, 166–67
displaced, 166–67
vicarious, 166–67
reward, delay of, 110–11, 254
reward power, 88–89
Richard III (Shakespeare), 333
role behavior test, 181–84, 185*t*
role differences, 65–66, 66*t*
romantic love, 244, 370
roundabout patterns, 164–65
rules of exchange, 249–54, 325–26, 341

sacrifice zones, 304, 307–8
Sade, Marquis de, 370
sadness, 364–65
SAS (scarcity, abundance and sufficiency) theory, 263–64, 324, 350–53
applications to SRT, 341–50
assumption of scarcity, 326–29
dynamics of, 329–41
layered systems of, 335–38
quasi-SAS, 338–41
scaling, multidimensional, 380–82
scarcity, 229, 326
absolute, 339
assumption of, 324–25, 326–29
dynamics of, 329–41
formula for, 332

438 INDEX

scarcity (*cont.*)
  layered systems of, 335–38
  quasi-scarcity, 339, 345
  strategies for coping with, 334, 334*t*
Scope of Justice Scale, 300
security, need for, 84–85
Selective Optimization with
    Compensation (SOC), 261
self (term), 49–50
self-acceptance, 64
self-aggression, 134–35
self and/or other, 54–55, 59, 64
  definition of, 3
  differentiation of viewpoint, 48, 49–50
  giving and taking away from, 66–67,
    66*t*, 69–71, 70*t*
  giving resources to, 249
  relationship between self and other, 106
  self–other differentiations, 37–40,
    39*f*, 54–55
self-consistency, 161–62
self-construal, 277
self-criticism, 39*f*, 39–40
self-effacement, 155–56
self-enhancement, 155–56
self-esteem, 55–56, 64, 100–1, 102
  and attractiveness, 144, 145
  and conformity, 158–60
  and influenceability, 158–59
self-hatred, 64
self-made man, 89
self-rejection, 39*f*, 39–40
selfishness, 366–67
semantic features, 33–34
semantic principle, 71–73
Sen, Amartya, 336
service(s), 249–50, 325, 376–77
  differentiation from goods, 42, 43*f*, 55
  differentiation from love, 41–42, 43*f*,
    43–44, 55
  in environmental conflicts, 311–12,
    313, 314*t*
  exchange between adults, 41
  giving, 33, 45
  needs that refer to, 84–85, 84*t*
  resource classification, xiv, 41
  statements describing behaviors of
    giving, 186

taking away, 45
sex, 133–34, 244
sexual desire, 361–62, 364
  definition of, 371
  vs. passionate love, 370–72
Shakespeare, William, 333
Shaver, Phillip, 359
similarity, assumed, 49
similarity structure analysis, 380
smallest space analysis (SSA), 230, 377–78,
    380–82, 383–91, 409
  of classroom resource distribution
    practices, 395–99, 396*t*, 398*f*, 399*t*,
    400*f*, 400, 403
  of three-dimensional factor model,
    391, 393*f*
smog, 303
social attractiveness, 43–44
social behavior, 294
  cognitive development of, 29–56
  as function of people and
    environment, 312
  motivations for, 80–104
  as resource exchange, xiii–xvii
social capital theory, 260
social comparison theory, 262–63
social concepts: basic development
    of, 29–56
social direction, 19–20
social events, 289
  classes of, 39*f*, 39–40
  cognition of, 3, 54
  differentiation sequences, 58–63, 63*t*
  dissonant, 94–104
  preservation of structure from, 94–104
social exchange
  in love relationships, 366–72
  unified theory of (*see* social resource
    theory [SRT])
social experiences, 4
social forms, new, 178–79
social growth, 36
social indicators, 175–78
social influence, 244
social instinct, 84–85
social interaction
  development of, 54–56
  dimensions of, 36–50

dynamics of, 290
foundation of, 36–37
paradigms of, 336–37, 340
social interaction inventory
for exchanges of giving, 187–92
for exchanges of taking, 193–98
group interaction inventory, 193–200
social justice, 312–16, 366–67, 368
Social Justice Research, 421–22
social justice theory, 262
social network theories, 260
social psychology, 288–89
social resource(s). *See also* resource(s)
bipolar model, 388–91, 389*f*, 390*t*
circular structure of, 357, 358*f*, 376–77, 377*f*
configurations, 237–38
correlations among, 386
covariance between, 386
definition of, 232–33
designations, 235*b*, 235–37
Foa and Foa's typology of, xiv, 239–54
three-dimensional factor model, 391, 393*f*
two-dimensional factor model, 383–88, 384*f*, 385*t*, 387*t*, 388*t*, 389*t*, 391
unipolar three-factor model, 391, 392*f*, 392*t*
variances, 385
social resource class(es), 41
cognitive structure of, 74–77, 76*f*
definition of, 232–33
differentiation of, 41–45, 43*f*, 55, 77–78
social resource exchange. *See also* resource exchange(s)
in abundance and sufficiency, 323–56
extension, 350–53
paradigms of interaction, 336–37, 340
requirements *(R)*, 329–32
social resource theory (SRT), 323–24. See also *Societal Structures of the Mind* (Foa and Foa)
analysis of variance examination of, 378–79
assumption of interpersonal interaction, 284
assumption of scarcity, 324–29

benefits from SAS theory, 341–50
bipolar version, 388–91, 389*f*, 390*t*
central principle, xiii–xiv
classroom empirical examination of, 393–403
cluster analysis of, 406–7
conjoint measurement study of, 405
definition of need, 79, 81, 83, 326–27, 329
definition of resources, 40–41, 232–35, 296, 325
discriminant analysis of, 407
evaluative studies, 376–416, 410*t*
experimental designs, 378–79
factor analysis examination of, 382–91, 409
hierarchical modeling of, 408
integration with cultural types, 276–80
integration with other frameworks, 261–64
levels of explanation, 272–75, 274*f*
multidimensional scaling of, 380–82
smallest space analysis examination of, 380–82, 383–91, 409
structural equation modeling of, 407–8
summary, xiv
synthesis with SAS (quasi-SAS), 338–41
theoretical foundations, 3, 7–28
three-dimensional factor model of, 391, 393*f*
traditional methods used in, 378–83
two-dimensional factor model of, 383–88, 384*f*, 385*t*, 387*t*, 388*t*, 389*t*, 391
unipolar three-factor model of, 391, 392*f*, 392*t*
validation of, 404–8
social support, 233–36
societal resources, 311–12. *See also* resource(s)
societal structures. *See* structure(s)
Societal Structures of the Mind (Foa and Foa), 294, 323–24, 357
abridged version, xiv, 1–179, 424
appendixes A–E, 181
areas of socio-psychological research, 122–69
culture-level analyses, 289–90

440 INDEX

Societal Structures of the Mind
(Foa and Foa) (*cont.*)
  data-analytic perspective
    on, 376–416
  definitions, 237*b*, 296, 357
  development of adult structure, 57–78
  development of basic social
    concepts, 29–56
  epilogue, 170–79
  evaluation of, 376–416
  historical notes, 419–21
  introduction, xiii–xiv, 7–28
  issues, 254–60
  original text, 424
  précis of chapters included, 3–5
  prelude to resource exchange, 79–121
  resource classes, 308–15
  theoretical formulations, 147–50
  typology of resources, xiv, 239–54
society, 170–79
socio-psychological research, 122–69
source, 248–49
SRT. *See* social resource theory
SSA. *See* smallest space analysis
stability vs. change, 172–73
statistics: underused multivariate
  methods, 404–8
status, 376–77
  by association, 244–45
  correlations between giving and taking
    away of, 68, 69*t*
  correlations between love and status
    behaviors, 69–71, 70*t*
  correlations with love, 386
  covariance between love and, 386
  definition of, 233
  differentiation from information, 42–43,
    43*f*, 44, 55
  differentiation from love, 42, 43*f*, 43–45,
    55, 59, 60*f*
  in environmental conflicts, 312,
    313, 314*t*
  giving, 45
  love and, 60*f*, 66*t*, 67–69
  messages exchanged between
    adults of, 41
  needs of exchange partners, 141–42
  needs that refer to, 84–85, 84*t*

  statements describing behaviors of
    giving, 186
  types of, 248
  types of behavior in different roles and
    cultures, 65–66, 66*t*
status resources
  classification, xiv, 41
  designation, 235*b*, 235–36
Sternberg, Robert, 359
storage, 253
stress coping resources, 261
Strong, Greg, 362
structural equation modeling, 404–5, 407–8
structural resources, 235*b*, 235–36
structural theory of intelligence, 22
structuralism, 10
structure(s), 9, 14–24
  adult, 68, 77–78
  behavioral, 63–74
  cognitive, xiii–xvii, 11–12, 74–77, 76*f*
    (*see also* cognitive structure[s])
  definition of, 3, 14–15, 57
  development of, 57–78
  and function, 23–24
  identification of, 22–23
  and interpersonal
    communication, 24–27
  preservation from dissonant
    events, 94–104
  reasons for studying, 17–20
  of resource classes, 74–77, 76*f*
  restructuring, 23–24
  in science of man, 15–17
  types of changes in, 23–24
sufficiency
  dynamics of, 329–41
  formula for, 332
  layered systems of, 335–38
  quasi-SAS, 338–41
  social resource exchange in, 323–56
  strategies for coping with, 334, 334*t*
  theory of scarcity, abundance and
    sufficiency (SAS), 263–64, 324, 329–
    38, 341–53
Superfund sites, 302, 309*t*
symbolic displacement, 135–36
symbolic resources, 245–46
symbolism, 245

INDEX 441

taking away, 45–46, 50–51, 64–65, 254–56
  correlations between giving and, 68, 69*t*
  correlations between love and status
    behaviors, 69–71, 70*t*
  definition of, 45, 54, 254–55
  frustration–aggression as, 122–40
  giving and, 250
  intercorrelations among love and status
    behaviors, 69–71, 70*t*
  schematic representation of, 39*f*, 39
  from self and other, 66–67, 66*t*
  social interaction inventory for
    exchanges of, 193–98
taking away goods, 45
taking away information, 45
taking away money, 45
taking away services, 45
taxonomy, 240
teachers, 393–94
Teichman, Meir, 68, 110
terminology, 232–37, 235*b*, 237*b*, 245–46
testable hypotheses, 241
theory
  action construal theory (ACT), 284–89,
    286*f*, 287*f*, 290
  Conservation of Resources (COR)
    Theory, 261
  dissonance, 95
  evaluation criteria, 240
  facet, 376
  formulations, 147–50
  Gestalt school, 288
  integrated psychological, 27–28
  integration attempts, 261–64
  Interpersonal Evaluation Theory
    (IET), 263
  key resource theories, 261
  levels of explanation, 272–75, 274*f*
  of love, 359
  multiple-component resource
    theories, 261
  new developments, 225–322
  other resource-related theories, 260–61
  quasi-SAS, 338–41
  recent advances, 232–70
  reinforcement theory, 95
  Resource-Based Theory of the Firm
    (RBT), 261

Resource Exchange Theories, 261
resource theory, 271–93
  of scarcity, abundance and sufficiency
    (SAS), 263–64, 324, 329–53
  of Selective Optimization with
    Compensation (SOC), 261
  social comparison theory, 262–63
  social resource theory (SRT), xiii–xiv, 3,
    7–28, 227–29, 232–70, 284, 288–89,
    290, 376–416
  structural theory of intelligence, 22
threat, 91–92
  ego, 124
three-dimensional factor model, 391, 393*f*
time, 353
  for processing input, 110, 254
  as resource, 242–43
time budget, 243
time sequence, 243
tolerance limits, 81–82
Törnblom, Kjell Y., 419–23
toxic waste
  communities burdened by, 304
  disposal of, 301
traditional society, 173–75
triangular theory of love, 359
Trump, Donald, 305
trust, 163
two-dimensional factor model, 383–84,
    384*f*, 391
  covariances (Cov), variances (Var),
    standard deviations (SD), and
    correlations (Cor), 385–88, 387*t*
  factor loadings, 384–85, 385*t*, 388,
    388*t*, 389*t*
typology, 240

understanding, drive for, 94
unipolar three-factor model, 391, 392*f*
  covariances (Cov), variances (Var),
    standard deviations (SD), and
    correlations (Cor), 391, 392*t*
  factor loadings, 391, 392*t*
United Nations (UN), 346
United Nations Environmental
    Programme, 305–6
Universal Declaration of Human
    Rights, 346

442 INDEX

universal level, 273–76, 274f
universal structure, 271–93
University of Missouri, 68
urban development, 302
urban environment, 121
  effects of, 115–17
  polluted (case study), 302
U.S. Peace Corps, 148–49
U.S. Supreme Court, 305

values
  conflicts of, 298
  symbolic, 245
  valued resources, 235b, 235–36
variance, analysis of, 378–79
variety of objects, 262–63
ventral tegmental area (VTA), 363–64
verbalization of need, 108, 250
vicarious aggression, 136–38, 166
vicarious retaliation, 166–67

Victorian era, 370
viewpoint, 3, 46–50, 53–54, 55
  differentiation by, 48–50, 61–62
  of the other, 48, 49–50
visual illusions, 104

water, clean, 244
wealth
  distribution of, 349–50
  as entitlement, 348–50
whole (term), 17–18
wife–husband relationship, 181–84, 185t
wildlife conservation, 306–15, 309t
will, 366–67
wish, 47–48
withdrawing, 255
withholding, 255, 265
work ethic, Protestant, 342–45

Zeki, Semir, 229–30, 359–61